NOVELS
for Students

Advisors

Jayne M. Burton is a teacher of secondary English and an adjunct professor for Northwest Vista College in San Antonio, TX.

Klaudia Janek is the school librarian at the International Academy in Bloomfield Hills, Michigan. She holds an MLIS degree from Wayne State University, a teaching degree from Rio Salado College, and a bachelor of arts degree in international relations from Saint Joseph's College. She is the IB Extended Essay Coordinator and NCA AdvancEd co-chair at her school. She is an IB workshop leader for International Baccalaureate North America, leading teacher training for IB school librarians and extended essay coordinators. She has been happy to serve the Michigan Association for Media in Education as a board member and past president at the regional level, advocating for libraries in Michigan schools.

Greg Bartley is an English teacher in Virginia. He holds an M.A.Ed. in English Education from Wake Forest University and a B.S. in Integrated Language Arts Education from Miami University.

Sarah Clancy teaches IB English at the International Academy in Bloomfield Hills, Michigan. She is a member of the National Council of Teachers of English and Michigan Speech Coaches, Inc. Sarah earned her undergraduate degree from Kalamazoo College and her Master's of Education from Florida Southern College. She coaches the high-ranking forensics team and is the staff adviser of the school newspaper, Overachiever.

Karen Dobson is a teen/adult librarian at Plymouth District Library in Plymouth, Michigan. She holds a Bachelor of Science degree from Oakland University and an MLIS from Wayne State University and has served on many committees through the Michigan Library Association.

Tom Shilts is the youth librarian at the Okemos branch of Capital Area District Library in Okemos, Michigan. He holds an MSLS degree from Clarion University of Pennsylvania and an MA in U.S. History from the University of North Dakota.

NOVELS
for Students

**Presenting Analysis, Context, and Criticism
on Commonly Studied Novels**

VOLUME 54

Kristin B. Mallegg, Project Editor

Foreword by Anne Devereaux Jordan

GALE
CENGAGE Learning·

Farmington Hills, Mich • San Francisco • New York • Waterville, Maine
Meriden, Conn • Mason, Ohio • Chicago

Novels for Students, Volume 54

Project Editor: Kristin B. Mallegg

Rights Acquisition and Management:
 Ashley Maynard

Composition: Evi Abou-El-Seoud

Manufacturing: Rita Wimberley

Imaging: John Watkins

For product information and technology assistance, contact us at
Gale Customer Support, 1-800-877-4253.
For permission to use material from this text or product,
submit all requests online at **www.cengage.com/permissions.**
Further permissions questions can be emailed to
permissionrequest@cengage.com

Gale
27500 Drake Rd.
Farmington Hills, MI, 48331-3535

ISBN-13: 978-1-4103-2837-3
ISSN 1094-3552

This title is also available as an e-book.
ISBN-13: 978-1-4103-2842-7
Contact your Gale, a part of Cengage Learning sales representative for ordering information.

Printed in Mexico
1 2 3 4 5 6 7 20 19 18 17

Table of Contents

ADVISORS ii

THE INFORMED DIALOGUE: INTERACTING WITH LITERATURE
(by Anne Devereaux Jordan) ix

INTRODUCTION xi

LITERARY CHRONOLOGY xv

ACKNOWLEDGEMENTS xvii

CONTRIBUTORS xix

AMERICANAH
(by Chimamanda Ngozi Adichie) 1
   Author Biography 1
   Plot Summary 2
   Characters 10
   Themes 14
   Style 17
   Historical Context 18
   Critical Overview 19
   Criticism 20
   Sources 27
   Further Reading 27
   Suggested Search Terms 28

THE BUDDHA IN THE ATTIC
(by Julie Otsuka) 29
   Author Biography 29
   Plot Summary 30
   Characters 33

Themes 34
Style 36
Historical Context 36
Critical Overview. 37
Criticism. 38
Sources 45
Further Reading 46
Suggested Search Terms 46

A GARDEN OF EARTHLY DELIGHT

(by Joyce Carol Oates) 47
Author Biography 47
Plot Summary. 49
Characters 52
Themes 55
Style 58
Historical Context 59
Critical Overview. 61
Criticism. 62
Sources 70
Further Reading 71
Suggested Search Terms 71

HOPE WAS HERE

(by Joan Bauer) 72
Author Biography 73
Plot Summary. 74
Characters 79
Themes 82
Style 84
Historical Context 85
Critical Overview. 88
Criticism. 89
Sources 97
Further Reading 97
Suggested Search Terms 98

INDIAN KILLER

(by Sherman Alexie) 99
Author Biography 100
Plot Summary. 101
Characters 105
Themes 108
Style 111
Historical Context 111
Critical Overview. 114
Criticism. 115
Sources 127
Further Reading 127
Suggested Search Terms 128

JANE EYRE

Plot Summary. 130
Characters 134

Themes 137
Style 139
Cultural Context 140
Critical Overview. 142
Criticism. 142
Sources 152
Further Reading 152
Suggested Search Terms 152

LIBRA

(by Don DeLillo) 153
Author Biography 154
Plot Summary. 154
Characters 159
Themes 162
Style 164
Historical Context 165
Critical Overview. 167
Criticism. 167
Sources 175
Further Reading 176
Suggested Search Terms 176

THE LOVELY BONES

(by Alice Sebold) 177
Author Biography 177
Plot Summary. 179
Characters 182
Themes 185
Style 187
Historical Context 188
Critical Overview. 189
Criticism. 190
Sources 198
Further Reading 199
Suggested Search Terms 199

THE NARROW ROAD TO THE DEEP NORTH

(by Richard Flanagan) 200
Author Biography 200
Plot Summary. 201
Characters 205
Themes 207
Style 209
Historical Context 210
Critical Overview. 211
Criticism. 211
Sources 222
Further Reading 222
Suggested Search Terms 222

SNOW IN AUGUST

(by Pete Hamill) 223
Author Biography 224
Plot Summary. 225

Characters 229
Themes 233
Style 235
Historical Context 236
Critical Overview. 239
Criticism. 239
Sources 245
Further Reading 245
Suggested Search Terms 246

THE TEMPLE OF MY FAMILIAR
(by Alice Walker). 247
Author Biography 247
Plot Summary. 248
Characters 251
Themes 253
Style 255
Historical Context 257
Critical Overview. 259
Criticism. 260
Sources 264
Further Reading 265
Suggested Search Terms 265

THEIR EYES WERE WATCHING GOD
Plot Summary. 267
Characters 270
Themes 273
Style 276
Cultural Context 276
Critical Overview. 277
Criticism. 277
Sources 282
Further Reading 282
Suggested Search Terms 283

THE TREE BRIDE
(by Bharati Mukherjee) 284
Author Biography 284
Plot Summary. 285
Characters 289
Themes 292
Style 294
Historical Context 294
Critical Overview. 296
Criticism. 297
Sources 305
Further Reading 306
Suggested Search Terms 306

THE WOMAN IN WHITE
(by Wilkie Collins) 307
Author Biography 308
Plot Summary. 309
Characters 314
Themes 315
Style 318
Historical Context 318
Critical Overview. 320
Criticism. 322
Sources 330
Further Reading 331
Suggested Search Terms 332

GLOSSARY OF LITERARY TERMS. . . . 333

CUMULATIVE AUTHOR/TITLE INDEX . . 345

**CUMULATIVE NATIONALITY/
ETHNICITY INDEX** 359

SUBJECT/THEME INDEX 371

The Informed Dialogue:
Interacting with Literature

When we pick up a book, we usually do so with the anticipation of pleasure. We hope that by entering the time and place of the novel and sharing the thoughts and actions of the characters, we will find enjoyment. Unfortunately, this is often not the case; we are disappointed. But we should ask, has the author failed us, or have we failed the author?

We establish a dialogue with the author, the book, and with ourselves when we read. Consciously and unconsciously, we ask questions: "Why did the author write this book?" "Why did the author choose that time, place, or character?" "How did the author achieve that effect?" "Why did the character act that way?" "Would I act in the same way?" The answers we receive depend upon how much information about literature in general and about that book specifically we ourselves bring to our reading.

Young children have limited life and literary experiences. Being young, children frequently do not know how to go about exploring a book, nor sometimes, even know the questions to ask of a book. The books they read help them answer questions, the author often coming right out and *telling* young readers the things they are learning or are expected to learn. The perennial classic, *The Little Engine That Could, tells* its readers that, among other things, it is good to help others and brings happiness:

"Hurray, hurray," cried the funny little clown and all the dolls and toys. "The good little boys and girls in the city will be happy because you helped us, kind, Little Blue Engine."

In picture books, messages are often blatant and simple, the dialogue between the author and reader one-sided. Young children are concerned with the end result of a book—the enjoyment gained, the lesson learned—rather than with how that result was obtained. As we grow older and read further, however, we question more. We come to expect that the world within the book will closely mirror the concerns of our world, and that the author will *show* these through the events, descriptions, and conversations within the story, rather than *telling* of them. We are now expected to do the interpreting, carry on our share of the dialogue with the book and author, and glean not only the author's message, but comprehend how that message and the overall affect of the book were achieved. Sometimes, however, we need help to do these things. *Novels for Students* provides that help.

A novel is made up of many parts interacting to create a coherent whole. In reading a novel, the more obvious features can be easily spotted—theme, characters, plot—but we may overlook the more subtle elements that greatly influence how the novel is perceived by the reader: viewpoint, mood and tone, symbolism, or the use of humor. By focusing on both the obvious and more subtle literary elements within a novel,

Novels for Students aids readers in both analyzing for message and in determining how and why that message is communicated. In the discussion on Harper Lee's *To Kill a Mockingbird* (Vol. 2), for example, the mockingbird as a symbol of innocence is dealt with, among other things, as is the importance of Lee's use of humor which "enlivens a serious plot, adds depth to the characterization, and creates a sense of familiarity and universality." The reader comes to understand the internal elements of each novel discussed—as well as the external influences that help shape it.

"The desire to write greatly," Harold Bloom of Yale University says, "is the desire to be elsewhere, in a time and place of one's own, in an originality that must compound with inheritance, with an anxiety of influence." A writer seeks to create a unique world within a story, but although it is unique, it is not disconnected from our own world. It speaks to us *because* of what the writer brings to the writing from our world: how he or she was raised and educated; his or her likes and dislikes; the events occurring in the real world at the time of the writing, and while the author was growing up. When we know what an author has brought to his or her work, we gain a greater insight into both the "originality" (the world of the book), and the things that "compound" it. This insight enables us to question that created world and find answers more readily. By informing ourselves, we are able to establish a more effective dialogue with both book and author.

Novels for Students, in addition to providing a plot summary and descriptive list of characters—to remind readers of what they have read—also explores the external influences that shaped each book. Each entry includes a discussion of the author's background, and the historical context in which the novel was written. It is vital to know, for instance, that when Ray Bradbury was writing *Fahrenheit 451* (Vol. 1), the threat of Nazi domination had recently ended in Europe, and the McCarthy hearings were taking place in Washington, D.C. This information goes far in answering the question, "Why did he write a story of oppressive government control and book burning?" Similarly, it is important to know that Harper Lee, author of *To Kill a Mockingbird,* was born and raised in Monroeville, Alabama, and that her father was a lawyer. Readers can now see why she chose the south as a setting for her novel—it is the place with which she was most familiar—and start to comprehend her characters and their actions.

Novels for Students helps readers find the answers they seek when they establish a dialogue with a particular novel. It also aids in the posing of questions by providing the opinions and interpretations of various critics and reviewers, broadening that dialogue. Some reviewers of *To Kill A Mockingbird,* for example, "faulted the novel's climax as melodramatic." This statement leads readers to ask, "Is it, indeed, melodramatic?" "If not, why did some reviewers see it as such?" "If it is, why did Lee choose to make it melodramatic?" "Is melodrama ever justified?" By being spurred to ask these questions, readers not only learn more about the book and its writer, but about the nature of writing itself.

The literature included for discussion in *Novels for Students* has been chosen because it has something vital to say to us. *Of Mice and Men, Catch-22, The Joy Luck Club, My Antonia, A Separate Peace* and the other novels here speak of life and modern sensibility. In addition to their individual, specific messages of prejudice, power, love or hate, living and dying, however, they and all great literature also share a common intent. They force us to *think*—about life, literature, and about others, not just about ourselves. They pry us from the narrow confines of our minds and thrust us outward to confront the world of books and the larger, real world we all share. *Novels for Students* helps us in this confrontation by providing the means of enriching our conversation with literature and the world, by creating an *informed* dialogue, one that brings true pleasure to the personal act of reading.

Sources

Harold Bloom, *The Western Canon, The Books and School of the Ages,* Riverhead Books, 1994.

Watty Piper, *The Little Engine That Could,* Platt & Munk, 1930.

Anne Devereaux Jordan
Senior Editor, TALL (Teaching and Learning Literature)

Introduction

Purpose of the Book

The purpose of *Novels for Students* (*NfS*) is to provide readers with a guide to understanding, enjoying, and studying novels by giving them easy access to information about the work. Part of Gale's "For Students" Literature line, *NfS* is specifically designed to meet the curricular needs of high school and undergraduate college students and their teachers, as well as the interests of general readers and researchers considering specific novels. While each volume contains entries on "classic" novels frequently studied in classrooms, there are also entries containing hard-to-find information on contemporary novels, including works by multicultural, international, and women novelists. Entries profiling film versions of novels not only diversify the study of novels but support alternate learning styles, media literacy, and film studies curricula as well.

The information covered in each entry includes an introduction to the novel and the novel's author; a plot summary, to help readers unravel and understand the events in a novel; descriptions of important characters, including explanation of a given character's role in the novel as well as discussion about that character's relationship to other characters in the novel; analysis of important themes in the novel; and an explanation of important literary techniques and movements as they are demonstrated in the novel.

In addition to this material, which helps the readers analyze the novel itself, students are also provided with important information on the literary and historical background informing each work. This includes a historical context essay, a box comparing the time or place the novel was written to modern Western culture, a critical essay, and excerpts from critical essays on the novel. A unique feature of *NfS* is a specially commissioned critical essay on each novel, targeted toward the student reader.

The "literature to film" entries on novels vary slightly in form, providing background on film technique and comparison to the original, literary version of the work. These entries open with an introduction to the film, which leads directly into the plot summary. The summary highlights plot changes from the novel, key cinematic moments, and/or examples of key film techniques. As in standard entries, there are character profiles (noting omissions or additions, and identifying the actors), analysis of themes and how they are illustrated in the film, and an explanation of the cinematic style and structure of the film. A cultural context section notes any time period or setting differences from that of the original work, as well as cultural differences between the time in which the original work was written and the time in which the film adaptation was made. A film entry concludes with a critical overview and critical essays on the film.

To further help today's student in studying and enjoying each novel or film, information on media adaptations is provided (if available), as well as suggestions for works of fiction, nonfiction, or film on similar themes and topics. Classroom aids include ideas for research papers and lists of critical and reference sources that provide additional material on the novel. Film entries also highlight signature film techniques demonstrated, and suggest media literacy activities and prompts to use during or after viewing a film.

Selection Criteria

The titles for each volume of *NfS* are selected by surveying numerous sources on notable literary works and analyzing course curricula for various schools, school districts, and states. Some of the sources surveyed include: high school and undergraduate literature anthologies and textbooks; lists of award-winners, and recommended titles, including the Young Adult Library Services Association (YALSA) list of best books for young adults. Films are selected both for the literary importance of the original work and the merits of the adaptation (including official awards and widespread public recognition).

Input solicited from our expert advisory board—consisting of educators and librarians— guides us to maintain a mix of "classic" and contemporary literary works, a mix of challenging and engaging works (including genre titles that are commonly studied) appropriate for different age levels, and a mix of international, multicultural and women authors. These advisors also consult on each volume's entry list, advising on which titles are most studied, most appropriate, and meet the broadest interests across secondary (grades 7–12) curricula and undergraduate literature studies.

How Each Entry Is Organized

Each entry, or chapter, in *NfS* focuses on one novel. Each entry heading lists the full name of the novel, the author's name, and the date of the novel's publication. The following elements are contained in each entry:

Introduction: a brief overview of the novel which provides information about its first appearance, its literary standing, any controversies surrounding the work, and major conflicts or themes within the work. Film entries identify the original novel and provide understanding of the film's reception and reputation, along with that of the director.

Author Biography: in novel entries, this section includes basic facts about the author's life, and focuses on events and times in the author's life that inspired the novel in question.

Plot Summary: a factual description of the major events in the novel. Lengthy summaries are broken down with subheads. Plot summaries of films are used to uncover plot differences from the original novel, and to note the use of certain film angles or other techniques.

Characters: an alphabetical listing of major characters in the novel. Each character name is followed by a brief to an extensive description of the character's role in the novel, as well as discussion of the character's actions, relationships, and possible motivation. In film entries, omissions or changes to the cast of characters of the film adaptation are mentioned here, and the actors' names— and any awards they may have received— are also included.

Characters are listed alphabetically by last name. If a character is unnamed—for instance, the narrator in *Invisible Man*—the character is listed as "The Narrator" and alphabetized as "Narrator." If a character's first name is the only one given, the name will appear alphabetically by that name.

Variant names are also included for each character. Thus, the full name "Jean Louise Finch" would head the listing for the narrator of *To Kill a Mockingbird*, but listed in a separate cross-reference would be the nickname "Scout Finch."

Themes: a thorough overview of how the major topics, themes, and issues are addressed within the novel. Each theme discussed appears in a separate subhead. While the key themes often remain the same or similar when a novel is adapted into a film, film entries demonstrate how the themes are conveyed cinematically, along with any changes in the portrayal of the themes.

Style: this section addresses important style elements of the novel, such as setting, point of view, and narration; important literary devices used, such as imagery, foreshadowing, symbolism; and, if applicable, genres to which the work might have belonged, such as Gothicism or Romanticism. Literary terms are explained within the entry but can also be found in the Glossary. Film entries cover how the director conveyed the meaning, message, and mood of the work using film in comparison to the author's use of language, literary device, etc., in the original work.

Historical Context: in novel entries, this section outlines the social, political, and cultural climate in which the author lived and the novel was created. This section may include descriptions of related historical events, pertinent aspects of daily life in the culture, and the artistic and literary sensibilities of the time in which the work was written. If the novel is a historical work, information regarding the time in which the novel is set is also included. Each section is broken down with helpful subheads. Film entries contain a similar Cultural Context section because the film adaptation might explore an entirely different time period or culture than the original work, and may also be influenced by the traditions and views of a time period much different than that of the original author.

Critical Overview: this section provides background on the critical reputation of the novel or film, including bannings or any other public controversies surrounding the work. For older works, this section includes a history of how the novel or film was first received and how perceptions of it may have changed over the years; for more recent novels, direct quotes from early reviews may also be included.

Criticism: an essay commissioned by *NfS* which specifically deals with the novel or film and is written specifically for the student audience, as well as excerpts from previously published criticism on the work (if available).

Sources: an alphabetical list of critical material used in compiling the entry, with full bibliographical information.

Further Reading: an alphabetical list of other critical sources which may prove useful for the student. It includes full bibliographical information and a brief annotation.

Suggested Search Terms: a list of search terms and phrases to jumpstart students' further information seeking. Terms include not just titles and author names but also terms and topics related to the historical and literary context of the works.

In addition, each novel entry contains the following highlighted sections, set apart from the main text as sidebars:

Media Adaptations: if available, a list of audiobooks and important film and television adaptations of the novel, including source information. The list also includes stage adaptations, musical adaptations, etc.

Topics for Further Study: a list of potential study questions or research topics dealing with the novel. This section includes questions related to other disciplines the student may be studying, such as American history, world history, science, math, government, business, geography, economics, psychology, etc.

Compare and Contrast: an "at-a-glance" comparison of the cultural and historical differences between the author's time and culture and late twentieth century or early twenty-first century Western culture. This box includes pertinent parallels between the major scientific, political, and cultural movements of the time or place the novel was written, the time or place the novel was set (if a historical work), and modern Western culture. Works written after the mid-1970s may not have this box.

What Do I Read Next?: a list of works that might give a reader points of entry into a classic work (e.g., YA or multicultural titles) and/ or complement the featured novel or serve as a contrast to it. This includes works by the same author and others, works from various genres, YA works, and works from various cultures and eras.

The film entries provide sidebars more targeted to the study of film, including:

Film Technique: a listing and explanation of four to six key techniques used in the film, including shot styles, use of transitions, lighting, sound or music, etc.

Read, Watch, Write: media literacy prompts and/or suggestions for viewing log prompts.

What Do I See Next?: a list of films based on the same or similar works or of films similar in directing style, technique, etc.

Other Features

NfS includes "The Informed Dialogue: Interacting with Literature," a foreword by Anne Devereaux Jordan, Senior Editor for *Teaching and Learning Literature* (*TALL*), and a founder of the Children's Literature Association. This essay provides an enlightening look at how readers interact with literature and how *Novels for Students* can help teachers show students how to enrich their own reading experiences.

A Cumulative Author/Title Index lists the authors and titles covered in each volume of the *NfS* series.

A Cumulative Nationality/Ethnicity Index breaks down the authors and titles covered in each volume of the *NfS* series by nationality and ethnicity.

A Subject/Theme Index, specific to each volume, provides easy reference for users who may be studying a particular subject or theme rather than a single work. Significant subjects, from events to broad themes, are included.

Each entry may include illustrations, including photo of the author, stills from film adaptations, maps, and/or photos of key historical events, if available.

Citing Novels for Students

When writing papers, students who quote directly from any volume of *NfS* may use the following general forms. These examples are based on MLA style; teachers may request that students adhere to a different style, so the following examples may be adapted as needed.

When citing text from *NfS* that is not attributed to a particular author (i.e., the Themes, Style, Historical Context sections, etc.), the following format should be used in the bibliography section:

> "*The Monkey Wrench Gang.*" *Novels for Students.* Ed. Sara Constantakis. Vol. 43. Detroit: Gale, Cengage Learning, 2013. 157–193. Print.

When quoting the specially commissioned essay from *NfS* (usually the first piece under the "Criticism" subhead), the following format should be used:

> Holmes, Michael Allen. Critical Essay on "*The Monkey Wrench Gang.*" *Novels for Students.* Ed. Sara Constantakis. Vol. 43. Detroit: Gale, Cengage Learning, 2013. 173–78. Print.

When quoting a journal or newspaper essay that is reprinted in a volume of *NfS,* the following form may be used:

> Bryant, Paul T. "Edward Abbey and Environmental Quixoticism." *Western American Literature* 24.1 (1989): 37–43. Rpt. in *Novels for Students.* Vol. 43. Ed. Sara Constantakis. Detroit: Gale, Cengage Learning, 2013. 189–92. Print.

When quoting material reprinted from a book that appears in a volume of *NfS,* the following form may be used:

> Norwick, Steve. "Nietzschean Themes in the Works of Edward Abbey." *Coyote in the Maze: Tracking Edward Abbey in a World of Words.* Ed. Peter Quigley. Salt Lake City; University of Utah Press, 1998. 184–205. Rpt. in *Novels for Students.* Vol. 43. Ed. Sara Constantakis. Detroit: Gale, Cengage Learning, 2013. 183–85. Print.

We Welcome Your Suggestions

The editorial staff of *Novels for Students* welcomes your comments and ideas. Readers who wish to suggest novels to appear in future volumes, or who have other suggestions, are cordially invited to contact the editor. You may contact the editor via e-mail at: **ForStudentsEditors@cengage.com.** Or write to the editor at:

Editor, *Novels for Students*

Gale

27500 Drake Road

Farmington Hills, MI 48331-3535

Literary Chronology

1816: Charlotte Brontë is born on April 21, in Thornton, West Yorkshire, England.

1824: Wilkie Collins is born on January 8 in London, England.

1847: Charlotte Brontë's *Jane Eyre* is published.

1855: Charlotte Brontë dies of complications from pregnancy on March 31 in Haworth, West Yorkshire, England.

1859–1860: Wilkie Collins's *The Woman in White* is published.

1889: Wilkie Collins dies of a stroke on September 23 in London, England.

1891: Zora Neale Hurston is born on January 7 in Notasulga, Alabama.

1925: Pete Hamill is born on June 24 in Brooklyn, New York.

1936: Don DeLillo is born on November 20 in New York, New York.

1937: Zora Neale Hurston's *Their Eyes Were Watching God* is published.

1938: Joyce Carol Oates is born on June 16 in Lockport, New York.

1940: Bharati Mukherjee is born on July 27 in Calcutta, India.

1944: Alice Walker is born on February 9 in Putnam County, Georgia.

1951: Joan Bauer is born on July 12 in River Forest, Illinois.

1960: Zora Neale Hurston dies of heart disease on January 28 in Fort Pierce, Florida.

1961: Richard Flanagan is born in Longford, Tasmania.

1962: Julie Otsuka is born on May 15 in Palo Alto, California.

1963: Alice Sebold is born on September 6 in Madison, Wisconsin.

1966: Sherman Alexie is born on October 7 in Wellpinit, Washington.

1967: Joyce Carol Oates's *A Garden of Earthly Delight* is published.

1969: Joyce Carol Oates is awarded the National Book Award for *them*.

1977: Chimamanda Ngozi Adichie is born on September 15 in Enugu, Nigeria.

1983: Alice Walker is awarded the Pulitzer Prize for Fiction for *The Color Purple*.

1988: Don DeLillo's *Libra* is published.

1988: Don DeLillo is awarded the National Book Award for *White Noise*.

1989: Alice Walker's *The Temple of My Familiar* is published.

1996: Sherman Alexie's *Indian Killer* is published.

1997: Pete Hamill's *Snow in August* is published.

2000: Joan Bauer's *Hope Was Here* is published.

2002: Alice Sebold's *The Lovely Bones* is published.

2004: Bharati Mukherjee's *The Tree Bride* is published.

2005: The film *Their Eyes Were Watching God* is released.

2011: Julie Otsuka's *The Buddha in the Attic* is published.

2011: The film *Jane Eyre* is released.

2013: Chimamanda Ngozi Adichie's *Americanah* is published.

2013: Richard Flanagan's *The Narrow Road to the Deep North* is published.

2014: Richard Flanagan is awarded the Man Booker Prize for *The Narrow Road to the Deep North*.

Acknowledgements

The editors wish to thank the copyright holders of the excerpted criticism included in this volume and the permissions managers of many book and magazine publishing companies for assisting us in securing reproduction rights. We are also grateful to the staffs of the Detroit Public Library, the Library of Congress, the University of Detroit Mercy Library, Wayne State University Purdy/Kresge Library Complex, and the University of Michigan Libraries for making their resources available to us. Following is a list of the copyright holders who have granted us permission to reproduce material in this volume of *NfS*. Every effort has been made to trace copyright, but if omissions have been made, please let us know.

COPYRIGHTED EXCERPTS IN NfS, VOLUME 54, WERE REPRODUCED FROM THE FOLLOWING PERIODICALS:

Bookpage, July 19, 2002. Copyright © 2002 Bookpage.—*Bookpage*, April, 2015. Copyright © 2015 Bookpage.—*Christian Science Monitor*, July 25, 2002. Copyright © 2002 Ron Charles. All rights reserved. Reproduced with permission.—*Commonweal*, Vol 124, No 14, August 15, 1997. Copyright © 1997 Commonweal. All rights reserved. Reproduced with permission.—*Daily Mail*, September 8, 2011. Copyright © 2011 Solo Syndication. All rights reserved. Reproduced with permission.—*Entertainment Weekly*, March 2, 2005. Copyright © 2005 Entertainment Weekly.—*Granta*, October 13, 2011. Copyright © 2011 Granta Books. Originally published in Granta magazine. All rights reserved. Reproduced with permission.—*Horn Book*, Vol 76, No 5, September 2000. Copyright ©2000 Horn Book Incorporated.—*Independent*, October 25, 2007. Copyright © 2007 Independent Print Ltd. All rights reserved. Reproduced with permission.—*Kirkus Review*, May 7, 1997. Copyright © 1997 Kirkus Media. All rights reserved. Reproduced with permission.—*London Review of Books*, Vol 36, No 24, December 18, 2014. Copyright © 2014 London Review of Books. All rights reserved. Reproduced with permission.—*New Yorker*, October 15, 2014. Copyright © 2014 Code Nast Publications. All rights reserved. Reproduced with permission.—*PMLA* (1939):128-135. Reprinted by permission of copyright owner, the Modern Language Association of America.—*Poets & Writers*, Vol 39, No 5, September-October, 2011. Copyright © 2011 Poets & Writers Magazine. All rights reserved. Reproduced with permission.—*Publishers Weekly*, Vol 244, No 11, March 17, 1997. Copyright © 1997 PWXYZ, LLC.—*Publishers Weekly*, Vol 247, No 36, September 4, 2000. Copyright © 2000 PWXYZ, LLC.—*Publishers Weekly*, July 3, 2002. Copyright © 2002 PWXYZ, LLC—*Teenreads*, September 11, 2000. Copyright © 2000 Teenreads.com—*Women's Review of Books*, Vol 29, No 1, January-February, 2012. Copyright © 2012 Old City Publishing. All rights reserved. Reproduced with permission.

COPYRIGHTED EXCERPTS IN NfS, VOLUME 54, WERE REPRODUCED FROM THE FOLLOWING BOOKS:

Alam, Fakrul. From *Bharati Mukherjee*. Twayne Publishers 1996 © 1996 Gale, a part of Cengage Learning, Inc.—Bauer, Joan. From *United in Diversity: Using Multicultural Young Adult Literature in the Classroom*. National Council of Teachers of English, 1998. Copyright © 1998 National Council of Teachers of English. All rights reserved. Reproduced with permission.—Civello, Paul. From *American Literary Naturalism and Its Twentieth-Century Transformations: Frank Norris, Ernest Hemingway, Don DeLillo*. University of Georgia Press, 1994. Copyright © 1994 University of Georgia Press. All rights reserved. Reproduced with permission.—CodebŒ, Marco. From *Narrating from the Archive: Novels, Records, and Bureaucrats in the Modern Age*. Fairleigh Dickinson University Press, 2010. Copyright © 2010 Fairleigh Dicksinson University. All rights reserved. Reproduced with permission.—Elam, Angela. From *Conversations with Bharati Mukherjee*. University Press of Mississippi, 2009. Copyright © 2009 University Press of Mississippi. All rights reserved. Reproduced with permission.—Fraser, Joelle. From *Conversations with Sherman Alexie*. University Press of Mississippi, 2009. Copyright © 2009 University Press of Mississippi. All rights reserved. Reproduced with permission.—Friedman, Ellen G. From *Joyce Carol Oates*. Frederick Ungar Publishing, 1980. Copyright © 1980 Bloomsbury Publishing. All rights reserved. Reproduced with permission.—Grassian, Daniel. From *Understanding Sherman Alexie*. University of South Carolina Press, 2005. Copyright © 2005 University of South Carolina Press. All rights reserved. Reproduced with permission.—Heather Hewett s Rewriting Human Rights: Gender, Violence, and Freedom in the Fiction of Chimamanda Ngozi Adichie, pages 166-173 in The *Critical Imagination in African Literature: Essays in Honor of Michael J.C. Echeruo*, (Syracuse University Press, Syracuse, NY 2015). All rights reserved. Reproduced with permission.—James, Meredith. From *Sherman Alexie: A Collection of Critical Essays*. University of Utah Press, 2010. © 2010 University of Utah Press. All rights reserved. Reproduced with permission.—Johnson, Greg. From *Understanding Joyce Carol Oates*. University of South Carolina Press, 1987. Copyright © 1987 University of South Carolina Press. All rights reserved. Reproduced with permission.—Lupack, Barbara. *NINETEENTH-CENTURY WOMEN AT THE MOVIES*. © 1999 by the Board of Regents of the University of Wisconsin System. Reprinted by permission of The University of Wisconsin Press.—Nayder, Lillian. From *Wilkie Collins*. Twayne Publishers, 1997. Copyright © 1997 The Gale Group.—Richardson, Michael. From *Newtown Review of Books*, 2013. Copyright © 2013 Newtown Review of Books. All rights reserved. Reproduced with permission.

Contributors

Susan K. Andersen: Andersen is a writer and teacher with a PhD in English literature. Entry on *Hope Was Here*. Original essay on *Hope Was Here*.

Bryan Aubrey: Aubrey holds a PhD in English. Entry on *The Narrow Road to the Deep North*. Original essay on *The Narrow Road to the Deep North*.

Rita M. Brown: Brown is an English professor. Entry on *The Temple of My Familiar*. Original essay on *The Temple of My Familiar*.

Kristen Sarlin Greenberg: Greenberg is a freelance writer and editor with a background in literature and philosophy. Entry on *Indian Killer*. Original essay on *Indian Killer*.

David Kelly: Kelly is an instructor of creative writing and literature. Entry on *Snow in August*. Original essay on *Snow in August*.

Amy L. Miller: Miller is a graduate of the University of Cincinnati, and she currently resides in New Orleans, Louisiana. Entries on *The Buddha in the Attic*, *The Lovely Bones*, and *Their Eyes Were Watching God*. Original essays on *The Buddha in the Attic*, *The Lovely Bones*, and *Their Eyes Were Watching God*.

Michael J. O'Neal: O'Neal holds a PhD in English. Entry on *The Woman in White*. Original essay on *The Woman in White*.

Jeffrey Eugene Palmer: Palmer is a scholar, freelance writer, and teacher of high school English. Entry on *Americanah*. Original essay on *Americanah*.

April Paris: Paris is a freelance writer with a background in academic writing. Entry on *The Tree Bride*. Original essay on *The Tree Bride*.

Laura B. Pryor: Pryor has a master's degree in English and over thirty years of experience as a professional writer. Entry on *Jane Eyre*. Original essay on *Jane Eyre*.

William Rosencrans: Rosencrans is a writer and copy editor. Entry on *Libra*. Original essay on *Libra*.

Bradley A. Skeen: Skeen is a classicist. Entry on *A Garden of Earthly Delights*. Original essay on *A Garden of Earthly Delights*.

Americanah

**CHIMAMANDA NGOZI
ADICHIE**

2013

Americanah is an acclaimed, best-selling novel by Nigerian-born author Chimamanda Ngozi Adichie. Adichie's third full-length novel, published in 2013, *Americanah* paints a stunning modern portrait of two estranged lovers, Ifemelu and Obinze, who attempt to assimilate into two alien cultures before returning to their homeland of Nigeria to rekindle their romance and start life anew. The novel is at once simple in plot and majestic in scope, touching briefly upon the intertwined lives of roughly two hundred characters over the course of several decades. Without becoming distracted from the main story line, Adichie's narrative also manages to encompass and explore such dynamic topics as racial hierarchy, socioeconomic disparity, cultural antagonisms, and the nature of love itself.

In addition to its tremendous commercial success, *Americanah* was the recipient of numerous honors and awards, including the 2013 National Book Critics Circle Award, and won recognition by the *New York Times Book Review* as one of the ten best novels of 2013. The novel was widely reviewed as the most ambitious and daring of Adichie's novels to date, an uncompromising classic of modern world literature.

AUTHOR BIOGRAPHY

On September 15, 1977, Adichie was born into the Igbo tribe as the fifth child of Grace and

Chimamanda Ngozi Adichie (© *Jeff Morgan 01 / Alamy*)

James Adichie. Although she was born in the small hamlet of Enugu, Nigeria, Adichie spent much of her childhood in Nsukka, closer to the University of Nigeria, where both of her parents worked. She grew up steeped in the literary lore of the nearby institution, even coming of age in the house owned by famed Nigerian novelist Chinua Achebe, and studied medicine for a time at the University of Nigeria while editing one of the school's esteemed literary publications. Adichie's formal education in Nigeria proved short-lived, however, and in 1997 she traveled to the United States to complete her undergraduate degree at Eastern Connecticut State University, majoring in communication and political science. Adichie would later go on to earn a master's degree in creative writing at Johns Hopkins and to study African history at Yale.

It was during her graduate school years that Adichie released her first novel, *Purple Hibiscus*, to overwhelming acclaim in 2003. In 2006, only three years after the success of this literary debut, Adichie received recognition for *Half of a Yellow*

Sun, a haunting account set in Nigeria at the height of the Biafran War. With the funds provided by a prestigious fellowship awarded by Harvard's Radcliffe Institute for Advanced Study, Adichie was able to finish her most recent novel, *Americanah*, in 2013. In keeping with her past successes, the much-anticipated novel was honored with numerous accolades and critical praise. It was selected for the National Book Critics Circle Award for the year of its publication and reviewed as a modern masterpiece by several major newspapers.

Now a married woman, Adichie and her husband divide their time between the United States and Nigeria. When not writing, she fills her time by traveling on book tours, delivering university lectures, and hosting creative writing workshops in her native Nigeria.

PLOT SUMMARY

Part One

CHAPTER ONE

The novel opens on a station platform where Nigerian-born Ifemelu is waiting to take a train to nearby Trenton to have her hair braided. Ifemelu reflects on the tremendous success of her recently concluded blog on race in America. She dwells also on her failing relationship with her boyfriend, Blaine, and her gradual surrender to fat since first moving to America.

After her train ride and catching a taxi from the station to the braiding parlor, Ifemelu is careful to keep to herself and avoid any unnecessary conversation. Immediately upon entering the ramshackle establishment, she is overcharged and assigned to a petite, Senegalese woman who gossips at great length, braids too tightly, and annoys Ifemelu by making generalizations about Africa and the Nigerian Igbo tribe. Ifemelu messages her Americanized cousin, Dike, to distract herself and then, somewhat on a whim, sends an e-mail to her first love in Nigeria, a wealthy married man named Obinze. Ifemelu informs Obinze that she is planning to leave the United States and return home.

CHAPTER TWO

The narrative shifts to Nigeria, where Obinze is considering his complicated marriage to the beautiful but uninspiring Kosi and the seedy origin of his newfound wealth. He recalls his initial introduction to the local "big man," Chief, who

MEDIA ADAPTATIONS

- In 2013, Recorded Books released an audiobook of *Americanah*. The recording is narrated by Adjoa Andoh and runs approximately seventeen and a half hours.

brought Obinze into his inner circle and transformed him into one of Nigeria's elite almost overnight. Despite his humble origins, Obinze now works as a fraudulent land speculator making millions. His palatial residence, obedient trophy wife, and young daughter, Buchi, cannot distract him from a sense of growing discontent and a yearning for Ifemelu.

Part Two

CHAPTER THREE

Ifemelu's thoughts wander to her own mother's hair and how it was the envy of her town in Nigeria until she cut it off. She recalls her mother's corresponding conversion from Catholicism to increasingly unforgiving and evangelical Christian congregations, collection fronts for local warlords. Because of her mother's fanaticism, Ifemelu looked to her Aunty Uju for guidance growing up. Ifemelu's father is a comparatively quiet man, made insecure by his lack of higher education and beleaguered by a succession of unpleasant jobs. Trying to find a middle way between the opposing personalities of her parents, Ifemelu early demonstrates a tendency towards headstrong rebellion. She is severely reprimanded for disrespecting Sister Ibanabo, a charismatic leader at her mother's newest church, and takes pride in being able to think and act for herself.

CHAPTER FOUR

Ifemelu and Obinze first meet at a party at their exclusive Nigerian school. They feel an instant attraction and distance themselves from the party to be alone with each other. Ginika, Ifemelu's best friend, who is also interested in Obinze, bears her disappointment with grace. Ifemelu is drawn in by Obinze's air of authenticity

and confidence. After the party, they begin to date in earnest, and Ifemelu becomes intoxicated by the glow of first love.

CHAPTER FIVE

Ginika's family moves to America, which eases Ifemelu's guilt over her budding romance with Obinze. Much to Ifemelu's surprise and anxiety, Obinze's mother insists on meeting her over an intimate lunch. She soon wins Ifemelu over with her warmth and candor, speaking freely of the proper relations between young men and women.

Although Ifemelu is not yet wise in the ways of the world, she comes to understand that her Aunty Uju is the mistress of a married man known as "the General." When Ifemelu's father loses his job and falls behind on the family's rent, he grudgingly accepts the General's money from his sister. Ifemelu feels deeply ambivalent because the General is at once kind and a mark of shame for her family.

CHAPTER SIX

Aunty Uju learns she is pregnant. The General forbids an abortion and preens over the prospect of an illegitimate child. About the time that Ifemelu's cousin, Dike, is born, the current government erupts into turmoil, and the General's position is threatened by a military coup. A week later, a plane crash ends the life of the General and several prominent members of the Nigerian administration. Aunty Uju is left to bear her shame and support her child in poverty, eventually leaving for America in search of a better life.

CHAPTER SEVEN

As they prepare to graduate from secondary school, Ifemelu and Obinze entertain dreams of pursuing higher education at the University of Ibadan, the romanticized center of progressive Nigerian thought, but settle instead upon Nsukka. Civil unrest and university budget cuts interrupt their studies and prompts the couple to participate in widespread student activism.

While engaged with student unions, Ifemelu meets an attractive, understated young man named Odein and entertains romantic fantasies about him. She admits her feelings to Obinze, and the tenor of their relationship begins to change. Perhaps to restore their previous intimacy, Ifemelu participates in unprotected sex with Obinze and soon after experiences intense pains in her side. She fears she is pregnant, but a doctor diagnoses appendicitis.

CHAPTER EIGHT

The strikes at the university worsen. Many students leave Nigeria to study abroad. When Aunty Uju extends Ifemelu an invitation for temporary lodging, Obinze encourages her to go and accept a scholarship at an American university. He assures her that he will join her once his own studies in Nigeria are concluded and promises never to fall out of touch. Obinze's mother bids Ifemelu her own heartfelt farewell.

CHAPTER NINE

The sweltering heat at the Trenton salon reminds Ifemelu of her first summer in America. She was shocked by the defeated and easily angered Aunty Uju and how much she changed. Dike, a young boy beginning school now, redeems his mother with his already irresistible charm, quick wit, and cheerful manner. Ifemelu soon learns that poverty and unhappiness exist even in a country like America. She also becomes aware of the disturbing racial hierarchy and for the first time comes to think of herself as "black."

CHAPTER TEN

Ifemelu's sense of estrangement grows. She is appalled when one of Aunty Uju's suitors, a man named Marlon, makes a half-hearted attempt at seducing her. Ifemelu feel sullied, and she begins searching for an apartment of her own. Meanwhile, she forms an increasingly dim view of American schooling and takes Dike's education into her own hands.

CHAPTER ELEVEN

Aunty Uju latches on to a new boyfriend, a Nigerian named Bartholomew, whom Ifemelu likes even less than Marlon. Bartholomew is self-important and misogynistic, dispensing expert advice where none is wanted and lording his imagined authority over the household. He takes to blogging, which inspires Ifemelu to do the same to counteract his posts. In spite of her home situation, Aunty Uju is overjoyed when she passes her medical licensing exam. Ifemelu decides to move from Brooklyn to Philadelphia to start school in the fall.

CHAPTER TWELVE

Ifemelu meets with Ginika, who also lives in Philadelphia, and is struck by the changes America has wrought in her old friend. Although Ginika extends a kind offer of free lodging, Ifemelu declines to live closer to campus. Ifemelu's awareness of race continues to grow in proportion to her sense of alienation, and she finds the easy affluence of Americans disquieting. Ifemelu leases a room with a handful of unfamiliar roommates and is plagued by financial worries.

CHAPTER THIRTEEN

Ifemelu interviews for a number of unpleasant jobs and is rejected from all of them. She begins to fall behind in her rent, and her school records are frozen until further tuition is paid.

CHAPTER FOURTEEN

Ifemelu is unintentionally belittled by a university employee and decides the secret to her success is to become completely Americanized. Although she starts off subdued in her classes and is ashamed to have to borrow textbooks from her classmates, Ifemelu eventually comes to enjoy the American emphasis on class participation. Her newfound confidence allows her to excel at her studies. After taking part in a class discussion involving racial slurs, Ifemelu is approached by a fellow African student and asked to join the university African Students Association.

CHAPTER FIFTEEN

In her desperation for money, Ifemelu considers taking illegitimate work when she is contacted by Ginika, who recommends her for a babysitting position within an affluent household. At the interview, Ifemelu makes the acquaintance of bubbly Kimberly and her less friendly sister, Laura. She becomes uncomfortable with the unspoken antagonism between the sisters and does not get the job.

In desperation, Ifemelu accepts the proposition of a muscle-bound tennis coach: money in exchange for sexual services. Guilt-stricken, Ifemelu succumbs to a deep depression and ignores all contact from concerned friends and family. Obinze's entreaties become fewer and fewer and eventually cease altogether. At long last, Ginika breaks through by telling Ifemelu she landed the nanny job with the family who initially rejected her. Ifemelu is overcome with relief and gratitude but decides not to contact Obinze, feeling she betrayed him.

CHAPTER SIXTEEN

Ifemelu is treated with kindness and condescension by her employer and picks up on the social dynamics of the new household. She forms a friendship with the mother, the beautiful but insecure Kimberly, and comes to suspect her suave husband, Don, of infidelity. She feels protective of Taylor, a sweet-natured boy, and is charmed by the fiery conviction of his sister, the strong-willed Morgan. Kimberly invites Ifemelu to live with the family, an offer that she accepts and that incurs the jealousy of Kimberly's sister, Laura.

When a carpet cleaner arrives at the house and treats Ifemelu as a servant, she becomes aware of the stigma that accompanies the color of her skin in America. Meanwhile, Aunty Uju worries over Dike's schooling and the overwhelming whiteness of their present neighborhood, causing Ifemelu further worry and homesickness.

CHAPTER SEVENTEEN

The narrative jumps forward to Ifemelu's purchase of a studio apartment in what is hailed as an especially dangerous neighborhood. With her sense of newfound freedom, Ifemelu resolves to drop her American pretensions and more fully embrace her Nigerian accent and identity. This corresponds with her first meeting with Blaine on a train ride to visit Aunty Uju and Dike, who have moved to the small hamlet of Warrington. Ifemelu is instantly attracted to Blaine, a tall, graceful Yale professor, and is overjoyed by his willingness to talk about the political realities of Africa and racial prejudices in America. Ifemelu gives Blaine her phone number before getting off the train but soon realizes he has no intention of contacting her.

Ifemelu is overjoyed to spend time with Dike, who has grown into a handsome and personable adolescent, but is hurt by what she perceives as his sense of alienation from his predominantly white neighborhood and school. She is moved to write a blog about the hierarchical structure of America, likening it to the tribal system in Africa.

CHAPTER EIGHTEEN

Ifemelu is once again at the hair-braiding salon, listening with increasing annoyance to what she deems the uneducated judgments of Nigeria from the Senegalese woman serving her. She watches with a mix of amusement and disdain while a petite blonde woman, Kelsey, has her hair braided in the African fashion and balks at the necessary use of extensions. Kelsey evokes the memory of Ifemelu's former boyfriend, Curt, Kimberly's handsome and wealthy brother, who made her wish she was someone

else. Ifemelu found Curt's childlike optimism and inherent graciousness endearing. As his girlfriend, Ifemelu slipped by degrees into the complacency afforded by her honorary inclusion in America's leisured class.

CHAPTER NINETEEN

Ifemelu is introduced to Curt and Kimberly's mother, who regards her son's new Nigerian girlfriend with wariness and disdain. Nevertheless, Curt and Ifemelu continue to grow closer and talk of marriage and a future together. Her connection to Curt gives her security she could not achieve on her own, such as a green card and a privileged position within a major firm. When Ifemelu's hair begins to fall out under the duress of constant chemical straighteners, Curt encourages her to embrace her natural appearance and forsake harsh beauty treatments. Ifemelu composes a blog entry about the aspirations of WASPs in America to help organize and express her conflicted feelings about belonging to Curt's exclusive circle.

CHAPTER TWENTY

Aided by Curt's money and connections, Ifemelu is able to secure an upscale apartment in Baltimore, a city she comes to love for its air of faded grandeur and offbeat charm. Meanwhile, she continues her uneasy relationship with her natural hair and shaves it all off in a fit of despair. Horrified at her altered appearance, Ifemelu seeks out Curt for consolation and, while she is at his apartment, discovers suggestive e-mails he exchanged with a woman he claims to have met at a conference.

Later, when Curt comes to apologize, Ifemelu grudgingly accepts his assurances, and the incident fades from memory. Through the help of online forums dedicated to the beauty of natural African hair, Ifemelu begins the slow process of self-acceptance, weaning herself from her reliance on Curt's approval and the opinions of coworkers. This personal change prompts Ifemelu to write a blog praising the beauty of America's first lady, Michelle Obama.

CHAPTER TWENTY-ONE

Aunty Uju comes to Ifemelu hysterical over what she views as the cultural perversion of Dike. Ifemelu intercedes and helps to negotiate a middle ground between mother and son. She brings Curt to visit her relatives and is gratified by how he charms them. Perhaps inspired by

Ifemelu's new relationship, Aunty Uju dumps the tyrant Bartholomew and moves with her son to the town of Willow, hoping for a clean start. The chapter concludes with another of Ifemelu's blog entries detailing the dissolution of African tribal identity by American racial stigma.

CHAPTER TWENTY-TWO

While out shopping, Ifemelu runs into an old friend from Nigeria, Kayode Dasilva. Although it is initially enthusiastic, the conversation is dampened when Kayode mentions Obinze and his tremendous concern for Ifemelu in the intervening years of her silence. Later, in the comfort of her apartment, she sends an e-mail to her long-lost boyfriend, hinting at the reason for her coldness and entreating his forgiveness. Obinze does not respond. Curt senses intuitively that Ifemelu's heart is divided and responds by lavishing more money and affection on her.

Part Three

CHAPTER TWENTY-THREE

The narrative shifts to Obinze's experience abroad in London, a city he soon comes to equate with misery and desperation, and his meeting with two criminals known only as the Angolans. The Angolans are arranging a marriage to a British citizen for Obinze, which would allow him to work. He meets the proposed match, a young woman of mixed Portuguese and Angolan parentage named Cleotilde, and is surprised by the level of real intimacy that begins to grow between them. Obinze reflects on the turmoil of the years leading up to this day, the growing unrest in Nigeria, and his continued inability to be granted a passport to visit America and study, a dream he has harbored since childhood. Moved by her son's desperation, Obinze's mother sought a legally dubious arrangement to secure him a temporary passport to leave Nigeria and seek success in England.

CHAPTER TWENTY-FOUR

Obinze goes to England and lives with his cousin, Nicholas, and his wife, Ojiugo, and finds a job cleaning restrooms to help earn his keep. The job is bearable until someone intentionally fouls the bathroom. Revulsion and shame prompt Obinze to quit. He struggles to find new job. When confronted with Ifemelu's e-mail, Obinze allows his anger and frustration at her long silence to prevail over his other confused

emotions. He deletes the message and resolves to forever excise Ifemelu from his life.

CHAPTER TWENTY-FIVE

The chapter introduces Emenike, a former classmate of Obinze back in Nigeria who is ashamed of his impoverished and provincial roots. Despite his humble beginnings, Emenike finds great success abroad and goes to great lengths to ingratiate himself into English high society. Obinze turns to Emenike in his desperation and is greeted warmly but offered no immediate assistance. He contacts other friends now residing in England, among them a man named Iloba, who brokers a meeting with a small-time criminal named Vincent Obi, who transfers his identity to Obinze in exchange for a substantial cut of his future salary.

CHAPTER TWENTY-SIX

Armed with his false identity, Obinze lands a string of jobs as a laborer and eventually finds himself at a London warehouse under the management of the kind Roy Snell. For the first time since he arrived in England, Obinze begins to feel he is secure and among friends. He forms a special bond with his coworker Nigel, who initiates him into many of the secrets of English life, helping him adapt to his new environment.

CHAPTER TWENTY-SEVEN

Obinze often visits a local bookstore after work, fueling his hunger for all things American by reading gossip magazines and scanning the local papers for further employment. The headlines reflect a growing climate of xenophobia and mistrust of immigrants, and Obinze realizes his days in England are numbered. He feels profoundly alienated and lonely.

CHAPTER TWENTY-EIGHT

The real Vincent phones and demands a substantial raise from an already overtaxed Obinze, who has no choice but to refuse. The next day, Roy Snell summons Obinze to his office and apologetically questions his identity on the basis of an anonymous phone tip. Obinze promises to return the next day with the necessary documents but never shows his face at the warehouse again. The narrative jumps forward many years to Obinze, now a Nigerian Big Man, phoning his old friend Nigel with the offer of a job opportunity abroad.

CHAPTER TWENTY-NINE

The Angolans claim that the cost of the sham marriage between Obinze and Cleotilde has gone up because of unforeseen complications. Obinze is forced to crawl to Emenike for a loan, who takes pride in providing twice the requested amount and refusing to accept repayment. To further showcase his wealth, Emenike insists that Obinze visit his estate for dinner and meet his pretty, competent English wife.

CHAPTER THIRTY

Obinze is at the Civic Center preparing for his marriage to Cleotilde when he is approached by an immigration officer with a police escort. Because of his expired visa, Obinze is arrested, briefly imprisoned, and deported. Upon arriving in Nigeria, he is greeted by his mother, which heightens his sense of failure and shame.

Part Four

CHAPTER THIRTY-ONE

Ifemelu sleeps with an unnamed neighbor in her apartment building and afterward attempts to justify her decision to be unfaithful to Curt. The squalid, almost arbitrary details of her affair are recounted, as well as Curt's refusal to forgive or even acknowledge Ifemelu after her confession. After some feeble attempts to renew the relationship, she accepts that her idyllic time with Curt is at an end. The chapter ends with a blog entry dedicated to Michelle Obama and her treatment of her natural African hair as a metaphor for irreconcilable racial difference.

CHAPTER THIRTY-TWO

Ifemelu struggles to redefine her identity without Curt. When her parents come to America for a three-week visit, she sinks to new depths of despondency and resigns from the job Curt helped her secure. A short, somewhat grim blog entry questions the legitimacy of race on the basis of concrete physical differences between blacks and whites and their susceptibility to various diseases.

CHAPTER THIRTY-THREE

Readership and financial support of Ifemelu's blog increases. In addition to writing, Ifemelu hosts numerous talks and begins to travel to speak at far-flung universities and diversity conferences. She especially enjoys the depth and breadth of commentary from her readers and is equally gratified by their praise and criticism of her views.

CHAPTER THIRTY-FOUR

Ifemelu is reunited with Blaine while attending a conference in Washington, DC, and the two immediately hit it off. Blaine attributes his earlier silence to a failed relationship. After a brief courtship, they move in together in New Haven, where Blaine works as a professor. Ifemelu writes a blog entry about the changing language surrounding the persistent reality of racism in America.

CHAPTER THIRTY-FIVE

Ifemelu becomes increasingly curious about Shan, Blaine's sister, whom he seems to at once idolize and consider dangerous and emotionally unstable. When Ifemelu finally meets Shan, she begins to understand his conflicted feelings. Shan intrigues Ifemelu with her complexity, charm, and brilliance but wounds her with harsh, uncompromising judgments. Ifemelu begins to feel out of her depth with Blaine. In her next blog, Ifemelu writes on the controversial speech made by Obama's pastor, the Reverend Wright, and marvels at the stereotypical perfection of the president himself.

CHAPTER THIRTY-SIX

Ifemelu attends a surprise party for one of Blaine's intellectual friends and gains an intimate glimpse into his social circle. The subject of race and opinionated blogging enters the conversation, and Ifemelu suddenly feels uncomfortable and under hostile scrutiny. The chapter ends with a blog entry detailing the anomalies inherent to being a black traveler.

CHAPTER THIRTY-SEVEN

The narrative returns to a discussion of teenage Dike, whose now impressive height and physique is paired with a careless charisma and affability. Ifemelu reflects on how fortunate Dike must feel to have grown into so fine a specimen of a young man.

Ifemelu attends a party hosted by Shan and is struck once again by the woman's mesmerizing charm and her casual cruelty. Shan mounts a public assault on Ifemelu's blog, and she feels her complex feelings towards Blaine's sister harden into dislike. Ifemelu composes an entry on the racial controversy surrounding Obama and his mixed African and American heritage.

CHAPTER THIRTY-EIGHT

Ifemelu is charmed by one of Blaine's fellow professors, Boubacar, a Francophone African with a considerable ego, whom her boyfriend actively dislikes. Boubacar refers Ifemelu to a humanities fellowship at Princeton University, a prospect she initially tucks away but returns to as her relationship with Blaine becomes strained. Rather than attend a protest organized by her boyfriend in defense of the school's African American librarian, Mr. White, Ifemelu chooses to attend a luncheon hosted by Boubacar. Blaine is incensed by her decision, causing a rift in their relationship. Ifemelu crafts a blog entry on issues of race and class from the perspective of American academics like Blaine.

CHAPTER THIRTY-NINE

Ifemelu spends more time with Aunty Uju and Dike to limit her exposure to Blaine. Aunty Uju relates an incident in which her son is falsely accused by his school's administration of hacking into their computer network. Ifemelu is incensed by what she views as racial discrimination, but Dike laughs off the incident as one of many ways he is singled out for the color of his skin.

After a period of weeks of estrangement from Blaine, Ifemelu attempts reconciliation, with little success. She begins to tire of New Haven and reflects that her life in America no longer seems exciting or novel. The chapter ends with a blog entry about the discomfort most Americans experience in discussing issues of race and the ill-defined, often hypocritical commitment they demonstrate to diversity.

CHAPTER FORTY

Ifemelu and Blaine's relationship is increasingly without passion or a sense of connection. Ifemelu is deeply moved after reading Obama's memoir *Dreams from My Father* and falls in love with the presidential candidate and the racial triumph he represents. She receives a research fellowship from Princeton University, and Blaine travels with her to New Jersey to help select an apartment for the upcoming term. Their fractured relationship rises and falls with the success of Obama's presidential campaign. When he is finally elected, Ifemelu feels a renewed sense of hope for the future of the nation. She writes a blog entry about friendship between members of different races.

CHAPTER FORTY-ONE

The narrative returns to the hair-braiding salon, where Ifemelu has promised to meet Chijioke, the Nigerian suitor of her stylist, Aisha. They exchange stories of their childhood in Africa and their struggles to assimilate in America. On her way home to Princeton, Ifemelu receives a call from an inconsolable Aunty Uju relating how she discovered Dike lying on the downstairs couch after what appears to be an intentional overdose of pills. Dike is alive but in critical condition at the local hospital.

Part Five

CHAPTER FORTY-TWO

In Nigeria, Obinze begins to dwell increasingly on thoughts of Ifemelu, following her blog and creating social media profiles to keep track of her life. Obinze composes a long email about the recent death of his mother and his sense of loss, which seems to worsen rather than diminish with time. Ifemelu's outpouring of grief at receiving the news both comforts and emboldens Obinze, and he allows himself to feel a renewed sense of romantic connection. He tries to articulate his feelings in another e-mail, but Ifemelu does not respond for several days. The silence causes Obinze to regret his forwardness.

When Ifemelu does finally respond, she tells Obinze of Dike's suicide attempt and her growing terror of leaving her cousin alone. Obinze walks around in a daze for several days, and his wife, Kosi, remarks on his distracted state.

Part Six

CHAPTER FORTY-THREE

In the weeks following Dike's attempted suicide, Ifemelu remains in a state of denial and nearly suffocates him with concern. She resents what she views as Aunty Uju's failed parenting and its contribution to Dike's crippling depression. It is many weeks before Ifemelu begins to trust in her cousin's recovery and whisks him away to Miami to celebrate his newfound emotional stability. While there, Dike urges Ifemelu to return to Nigeria and secure her own happiness.

Part Seven

CHAPTER FORTY-FOUR

Ifemelu returns to Lagos, Nigeria, and feels disoriented. She is shocked by the changes in her childhood home. An old friend, Ranyinudo, provides Ifemelu with temporary lodging and support while she readjusts, teasing her about her Americanized ways. They exchange memories of a shared past, kindling in Ifemelu a sense of longing and long-denied contentment.

CHAPTER FORTY-FIVE

Ifemelu attends an interview for a job as a writer for the well-known Nigerian gossip and fashion magazine *Zoe*. Its owner, a scandalous socialite known as Aunty Onenu, courts Ifemelu for the American mystique she has acquired in her years abroad. As Ifemelu seeks an apartment of her own in Lagos, she begins to imagine sightings of Obinze, which fill her with tremendous excitement and anxiety.

CHAPTER FORTY-SIX

Ifemelu spends much of her free time with her family and childhood friends and feels uncomfortable whenever they raise the topic of marriage. She is advised to ignore the dictates of passion and settle down with the man who can best provide for her.

CHAPTER FORTY-SEVEN

Ifemelu makes acquaintances at work and realizes how poorly the magazine is being run. In particular, she finds herself caught between her two antagonistic coworkers, a fellow Americanah named Doris and the provincial beauty Zemaye.

CHAPTER FORTY-EIGHT

Initially, Ifemelu throws in her lot with Doris, who invites her to attend the Nigerpolitan Club, a community of worldly Nigerians who meet to network and discuss the problems confronting the country. Ifemelu comes to feel at home there.

CHAPTER FORTY-NINE

Ifemelu settles back into the familiar routine of life in Nigeria even as her discontent at work grows. Her employer sends her to cover an endless array of identical and insincere parties hosted by Nigeria's elite, and Ifemelu feels increasingly unfulfilled. Ifemelu's editorials begin to reflect her growing disdain for high society, prompting Doris to criticize her writing. Ifemelu refuses to back down even when confronted by the magazine's owner, and the issue is left unresolved.

Ifemelu becomes concerned with dubious medication prescribed to the firm's receptionist, a guileless woman named Esther, and seeks to write an article about rampant medical abuses in Nigeria. Doris opposes the magazine's taking on an edge of political activism and explains that the Nigerian elite pay Aunty Onenu to publish inane articles showcasing their wealth. Ifemelu is

appalled at this prospect, and she and Doris have a falling out. Ifemelu uses the incident as an excuse to quit and begin a new blog dedicated to uncovering Nigeria's dirty secrets.

CHAPTER FIFTY

Dike continues the process of emotional mending. He visits Ifemelu in Nigeria and falls in love with the country. He no longer feels like a dark-skinned pariah, as he does in America. Ifemelu's new blog, *The Small Redemption of Lagos*, takes off and includes contributions from some of her friends and her former coworker Zemaye. Ifemelu is especially proud of her own piece dissecting the Nigerpolitan club.

Ifemelu has an emotional talk with Dike concerning the true nature of the relationship between his father and mother, and he seems relieved to finally know the truth. She secretly wishes her cousin will stay in Nigeria rather than return to America. Dike boards the plane to go home, leaving Ifemelu feeling lonely.

CHAPTER FIFTY-ONE

One day, while depositing money in a local bank, Ifemelu once again mistakes a stranger for Obinze. Fired by a new resolve to clear her head of these persistent phantasms, Ifemelu musters the courage to call Obinze and arrange a meeting. Upon being reunited with Obinze, Ifemelu is pleasantly surprised by his confident but unassuming manner, which puts her at ease. Obinze is unchanged despite being a man of such immense wealth and prestige. He addresses Ifemelu with utter honesty regarding his dubious profession and lackluster marriage.

The following morning, Obinze arrives at Ifemelu's newly decorated apartment and broaches the topic of Ifemelu's blog. At first, she is pleased by his high praise but becomes offended when he offers to fund the endeavor. After this initial stumbling block, their conversation resumes its earlier intimacy, and Ifemelu discloses the secret shame that initially prompted her to cut off contact with Obinze in America. His calm and understanding response is a great comfort to her. She realizes the true depth of the feelings she still harbors for Obinze.

CHAPTER FIFTY-TWO

Obinze and Ifemelu begin to see each other with increasing frequency, ignoring the sexual tension that has blossomed between them. After many more meetings and moments charged with desire, Ifemelu broaches the topic and wears down Obinze's resolve to remain loyal to his wife. Their affair takes on a sexual dimension.

CHAPTER FIFTY-THREE

Ifemelu feels invigorated by her love of Obinze. She considers herself blessed to have so attentive and considerate a lover and begins to introduce him openly to her friends and colleagues. Eventually, she succumbs to jealousy and feels a growing disdain for Obinze's wife. Obinze affirms his love for Ifemelu over Kosi but suggests a temporary break in their illicit relations to better consider the future of the affair. Ifemelu is enraged at this suggestion and delivers an ultimatum.

CHAPTER FIFTY-FOUR

Lost in his thoughts of Ifemelu, Obinze travels on business to Abuja, a city charged with the suggestion of vice, opulence, and limitless opportunity. He agrees to a hard bargain with a land speculator named Edusco and then tries to contact Ifemelu and mend their relationship. Instead, Obinze's wife calls to remind him of a social obligation, prompting waves of guilt and self-loathing.

Unable to stand the secrecy any longer, Obinze wakes the following morning and informs his wife of the affair in clear, uncompromising language. To his mingled surprise and dismay, Kosi already knows of her husband's infidelity but refuses to dissolve the marriage and forfeit any aspect of her opulent lifestyle. Her mercenary view of their relationship sickens Obinze and strengthens his resolve to pursue Ifemelu.

Kosi ignores her husband's confession and insists on attending a high-profile social function scheduled for the following morning. Obinze feels duty-bound to accompany her and talks with friends and business associates at the party. In the middle of a heated debate regarding financial transactions and corrupt government officials, Obinze announces his intent to leave his wife for another woman and incites the scorn of his fellow Big Men. He is forced to leave the party early after his young daughter, Buchi, falls.

CHAPTER FIFTY-FIVE

Ifemelu throws herself into the distraction of her blog but is plagued by a persistent sadness over her estrangement from Obinze. To fill the void, she begins halfheartedly to date and renews contact with many of her old friends and lovers from America in an attempt to make peace with her past. Just as she has achieved some measure of her old contentment, Ifemelu opens the door to an unexpected visit from Obinze. He tells her of the dissolution of his marriage and his intention to chase Ifemelu until she accepts him back into her life. Ifemelu fights with her conflicted feelings for many moments before inviting Obinze to cross the threshold and enter her home.

CHARACTERS

Mr. Agbo
Mr. Agbo is an especially memorable English teacher from Ifemelu's school in Nigeria.

Aisha
Ifemelu moves past her initial dislike of Aisha, a Senegalese hairdresser who makes judgmental comments about Nigeria, and comes to feel protective of the emotionally damaged woman as she relates her struggles to find love and happiness in America.

Angolans
The two unnamed Angolans Obinze encounters in Britain facilitate his sham marriage to Cleotilde in an ultimately unsuccessful attempt to secure him British citizenship.

Lawrence Anini
Lawrence Anini is a famous Nigerian criminal. His televised execution is Ifemelu's first exposure to the reality of death and murder.

Araminta
Araminta is Blaine's best friend.

Athena
Athena is the neglected and sickly looking daughter of Laura.

Bartholomew
Bartholomew is Aunt Uju's abrasive boyfriend.

Blaine
Handsome, well-spoken, and unwavering in his moral convictions, Ifemelu's longtime boyfriend, Blaine, teaches at Yale and actively champions racial causes. Although she shares

many of his convictions, Ifemelu feels herself unworthy of a man as inherently good and selfless as Blaine. This insecurity later contributes to the dissolution of their relationship.

Boubacar

A man of great brilliance and correspondingly great ego, Boubacar is a Yale professor of Francophone African stock who unintentionally causes strife between Ifemelu and Blaine.

Brown

Brown furnishes Obinze with false papers to undergo his marriage to Cleotilde.

Buchi

Obinze's young daughter by the beautiful Kosi, Buchi greatly complicates her father's desire for a divorce.

Carpet Cleaner

The unnamed carpet cleaner who comes to clean Kimberly's house treats Ifemelu as hired help because of the color of her skin.

Chief

Nigerian Big Man Chief provides Obinze with the necessary introductions into the country's corrupt elite. Obinze grows immensely wealthy and influential under Chief's employ.

Chijioke

Aisha proclaims her love for Chijioke, who refuses marriage on the basis of his Igbo tribal identity.

Claire

Curt's liberated aunt living in Vermont, Claire annoys Ifemelu by too frequently and emphatically proclaiming her love of all races.

Cleotilde

Of Angolan and Portugese parentage, the beleaguered Cleotilde seeks a sham marriage with Obinze to earn money for her aging and neglected mother. Over the course of their association, a romantic attraction begins to grow between Cleotilde and Obinze despite the mercenary nature of their arrangement.

Coach

Described as muscle-bound and balding, the unnamed tennis coach sexually propositions the impoverished Ifemelu in exchange for

money. Her acceptance of his offer is a source of enduring shame over the course of the novel.

Curt

Ifemelu's classically handsome, immensely wealthy, and stereotypically American boyfriend, Curt, embodies innocence and optimism. Through his spotless reputation and displays of easy money, the Potomac millionaire opens up the doors of American opportunity for his Nigerian girlfriend. Ifemelu ends her relationship with Curt through an act of infidelity, a decision she comes to regret deeply.

Curt's Mother

Immaculately preserved despite her advanced age, Curt's mother regards Ifemelu with amused condescension as one girl in the long line of her son's exotic dalliances.

Kayode Dasilva

One of Obinze's closest friends growing up, Kayode epitomizes the privileged and charismatic stereotype of a Nigerian playboy.

Dike

Dike is the illegitimate son of Aunty Uju and the Nigerian state official known only as the General. Knowing little of his past and parentage, Dike comes of age in a predominantly white American society in which he feels victimized and alone. His good looks, cheerful demeanor, and charisma belie the crippling depression that contributes to his teenage suicide attempt.

Don

Ifemelu suspects Don, a self-styled womanizer, of being unfaithful to his wife, Kimberly. Ifemelu struggles with the decision to share these suspicions with her employer.

Doris

Although Doris feels kinship with Ifemelu as a fellow Americanah and introduces her to the Nigerpolitan Club, the two coworkers grow estranged after a vicious disagreement regarding the future of the magazine.

Edusco

Obinze respects the humble origins and unshakable confidence of his business associate Edusco.

Emenike

Teased during his childhood in Nigeria for being the son of a provincial farmer, Emenike harnesses his insecurity to become a wealthy and well-connected man abroad. He wines and dines Obinze and gifts him with money to emphasize his newfound success in the eyes of his old friends.

Esther

Ifemelu feels protective of the too-trusting Esther, who hands over most of her income to her congregation and falls prey to the lies of unscrupulous doctors.

Fred

Harvard-educated and dripping with confidence, Fred belongs to the Nigerpolitan club and expresses interest in pursuing a romantic relationship with Ifemelu.

General

A complex and morally ambiguous character, the General is a high-ranking member of the famously corrupt political regime in Nigeria. He takes Aunty Uju as a favored mistress and provides for her lavish lifestyle. She and the General have a son together: Dike. When the General dies in a freak plane accident, however, Aunty Uju and Dike are forced to flee to America to escape the vengeance of the deceased's political rivals.

Georgina

Georgina is Emenike's English wife and an emblem of his newfound wealth and social class.

Ginika

When Obinze chooses Ifemelu over her best friend, Ginika, the relationship becomes strained. Ifemelu is secretly relieved when her girlhood companion moves to America.

Sister Ibanabo

The iron-willed and unsmiling Sister Ibanabo acts as the grim enforcer of a Christian congregation that doubles as a collection agency for certain corrupt officials. Ifemelu's mother is horrified when her daughter openly flaunts the authority of Sister Ibanabo and demands a public act of contrition.

Ifemelu

The central character of Adichie's novel, Ifemelu is a complex character who adheres to her own moral compass and takes pride in always expressing her opinion. The story of Ifemelu's epic tale of self-discovery while balancing two distinct cultures is punctuated with entries from her blogs

Ifemelu's Father

Described as a downtrodden civil servant who laments his lack of higher education, Ifemelu's father compensates for his perceived inadequacy with his affectations of speech and manner.

Ifemelu's Mother

When Ifemelu's mother forsakes her native Catholicism for increasingly severe sects of evangelical Christianity, she becomes estranged from her husband and young daughter. She becomes obsessed with exchanging sacrifice for salvation and is rewarded with frequent visions, which take precedence over her home life.

Iloba

An old friend of Obinze and his family, Iloba indoctrinates Obinze into many of the harsh secrets of surviving abroad and introduces him to the unscrupulous Vincent.

Kelsey

A petite, blonde woman, Kelsey arouses the amusement of the Senegalese hairdressers when she asks to have her too-fine hair braided in African fashion. Kelsey reminds Ifemelu of her time with Curt and her own intermittent desire to be somebody else.

Kimberly

An affluent, well-intentioned woman of faded prettiness, Kimberly acts as both benefactor and friend to Ifemelu, whom she employs as the caretaker of her two children. For her part, Ifemelu feels increasingly protective towards Kimberly, whom she believes to be the victim of her husband's infidelity.

Kosi

Known in her youth as a great beauty of even greater virtue, Kosi is an adept homemaker and attends to the every need of her husband, Obinze. Despite this, Obinze becomes increasingly dissatisfied with his wife, whom he married not for love but as an emblem of his new status as a Nigerian Big Man. Although she is aware of her husband's unfaithfulness, Kosi clings to the illusion of a seamless home life and seeks to preserve the façade of her marriage.

Landlord

The landlord who rents to Ifemelu's family is uncompromising in his demands for punctual payment, forcing the head of the household to turn to the General for financial support rather than be evicted.

Laura

Kimberly's severe and embittered sister, Laura, takes an instant dislike to Ifemelu, which she nurses over the course of their professional relationship.

Marlon

Marlon, Aunty Uju's first boyfriend in America, attempts to seduce Ifemelu right under her aunt's nose.

Morgan

Despite her extreme youth, Kimberly's red-headed daughter displays a jaded steeliness and the uncanny wisdom of a full-grown woman. Morgan resists opening up to Ifemelu until the babysitter becomes involved with her beloved uncle, Curt.

Nicholas

Obinze seeks lodging and advice from his cousin Nicholas upon first traveling to England. Obinze is shocked by the dramatic change in his kinsman from careless and wild youth to worry-worn and reserved adult.

Nigel

Of all his coworkers at the warehouse, Obinze becomes the closest to Nigel, who treats him as an equal and as a friend in a time of great need. When Obinze returns to Nigeria and becomes one of the country's elite, he remembers Nigel's kindness and offers the lowly English laborer a chance at attaining incredible wealth and prestige within corrupt government circles.

Vincent Obi

Vincent Obi sells his identity to Obinze, which allows him to live and work in England until the illegal identity is revealed and he is deported.

Obinze

Obinze is Ifemelu's enduring love interest throughout the novel and one of its most central characters. Although less openly judgmental than Ifemelu, Obinze is a man of high principles who struggles with his decision to join Nigeria's corrupt elite and destroy his loveless marriage for the sake of personal passion. Ifemelu is attracted to Obinze for his quiet attentiveness and confidence.

Obinze's Mother

A celebrated academic at a Nigerian university, Obinze's mother is a learned and opinionated woman accustomed to speaking her mind. Attracted to her frankness and genuine regard for her own well-being, Ifemelu grows close to Obinze's mother. Both Obinze and Ifemelu are devastated by her passing in the final pages of the novel.

Odein

Ifemelu entertains an emotional affair with the soft-featured Odein, who organizes student protests at her university. Although nothing comes of it, Ifemelu reveals this attraction to Obinze and causes the first major rift in their relationship.

Ojiugo

Ojiugo is the wife of Obinze's cousin Nicholas. Obinze prefers Ojiugo to her husband for her undiminished spirit and persistent sense of humor in the face of adversity.

Mrs. Ojo

Mrs. Ojo ministers to Ifemelu's mother and inspires her conversion to increasingly radical sects of Christianity.

Okwudiba

One of Obinze's fellow Big Men, Okwudiba counsels his friend against dissolving his otherwise idyllic family for love of a mistress.

Chief Omenka

Tithes collected by the congregation attended by Ifemelu's mother line the pockets of local scamlord Chief Omenka.

Aunty Onenu

A scandalous socialite, Aunty Onenu founds *Zoe* magazine as a direct affront to a romantic rival, who manages the better-known *Glass* publication. She employs Ifemelu as a gossip columnist for her social prestige as an Americanah.

Ranyinudo

Ifemelu's childhood friend Ranyinudo provides much-needed shelter and support to the Americanah upon her return to Nigeria. When Ifemelu writes a blog entry at Ranyinudo's expense, the two engage in a heart-to-heart discussion that steels Ifemelu's resolve to seek out Obinze and secure her own happiness.

Shan

Described as effortlessly beautiful, brilliant, and self-absorbed, Shan destroys every relationship she touches and causes considerable anxiety for her brother, Blaine. Try as she might to dislike Shan on principle, Ifemelu, too, falls under her spell.

Roy Snell

Described as a ruddy and cheerful English stereotype, Roy Snell shows himself to be a kind employer to Obinze, who works under an assumed identity. When Snell is tipped off to this illegal activity in his firm, he chooses to give Obinze the benefit of the doubt rather than subject the matter to police scrutiny.

Taylor

Taylor is Kimberly's son and Morgan's younger brother. He is affectionate, excitable, and brimming with childish optimism.

Tile Man

Ifemelu upbraids the Nigerian tiling contractor for the poor quality of his craftsmanship, proving herself capable of incredible powers of command and intimidation.

Aunty Uju

Ifemelu's favorite aunt and role model growing up, Aunty Uju is changed after her affair with the General and her years of struggle trying to maintain an income and raise Dike in America.

Mr. White

The elderly African American charged with checking out books at the Yale library, Mr. White is arrested under suspicion of dealing drugs when he engages in an innocent conversation with his friend. This egregious breech of justice fires Blaine to organize a campaign against racial prejudice on campus. Ifemelu's pointed lack of involvement in her boyfriend's cause spells the beginning of the end for their relationship.

Zemaye

The soft-spoken, provincial coworker of Doris and Ifemelu, Zemaye reveals herself to be more genuine and principled than either of her Americanah counterparts. Ifemelu respects Zemaye for these qualities and later welcomes her contributions to *The Small Redemption of Lagos*.

THEMES

Alienation

The title of Adichie's novel, *Americanah*, hints at its central theme of alienation and refers to an Americanized Nigerian. The enduring legacy of colonialism in Nigeria lives on in both Obinze and Ifemelu, manifesting itself in their childhood yearning to seek assimilation and acceptance in cultures far from their own. From an early age, both are encouraged to elevate Western ideals and standards of education above their Nigerian cultural roots and seek more fulfilling lives abroad. The reality of self-imposed exile, both Obinze and Ifemelu come to understand, is far from idyllic.

Throughout the narrative of Ifemelu's life in America, she struggles with conflicting desires to at once nourish and destroy her African identity. The changes wrought in her childhood friend, Ginika, and second mother, Aunty Uju, serve to dismay Ifemelu and shatter many of her illusions surrounding this fabled land of opportunity. Her otherness in the eyes of her American counterparts make her feel painfully singled out and inadequate, and yet, upon returning to the land of her birth, Ifemelu clings to her foreign pretensions and begins to feel equally estranged from her countrymen.

For his part, Obinze fares even worse in England where he works illegally under an assumed identity. Confronted at every turn by anti-immigrant sentiment and paranoia, the young man learns what it is to be a detested segment of society always under suspicion. He begins to measure his success not by personal achievement but by the outward trappings of affluence and superiority flaunted by his Anglicized friends. This acquired mentality follows Obinze back to Nigeria and comes to shape his unsavory and unfulfilled future as a henchman for Chief.

TOPICS FOR FURTHER STUDY

- The narrative of Adichie's novel is arranged around Ifemelu's blog entries, which contain ideas and opinions central to the plot. With a partner, decide upon a single entry that you feel to be especially compelling and worthy of further exploration. Independently respond to the same entry in your journal and then, to simulate the ongoing exchange inherent to an online forum, swap your responses and craft a rejoinder to your partner's entry. Drawing upon your own examples, discuss the role of perspective in *Americanah* and the suitability of the blog form to the story.

- *Americanah* opens with Ifemelu's beautifully rendered impressions of the many cities she has come to love during her years spent in America. Later, upon returning to Nigeria, she turns these same powers of description upon the much-changed communities where she spent her childhood. In this same spirit, reflect upon some of the places you've lived and bring to mind the sights, sounds, and smells of one in particular. Compose a poem containing as many of these intimate details as possible to attempt to do justice to the place you've selected. Share your poetic creation with your classmates and elicit their feedback.

- Though it is masterfully woven together into a dazzling, complex narrative, the intricate chronology of *Americanah* may stump many readers upon their first read. In a small group, select one distinct story line from the novel to render visually for your classmates in a linear story board form. To make your presentation especially eye-catching and memorable, construct it online with the free animation program PowToon,

balancing text and visual elements to best show off and elucidate your thread of the story.

- Adichie has often been compared to her fellow Nigerian writer Chinua Achebe, who is acknowledged as the father of the modern African novel. One of Achebe's best-loved works of young-adult fiction, *Chike and the River*, deals with many of the same themes of alienation and assimilation faced by Ifemelu and Obinze in their lives abroad. Read *Americanah* and *Chike and the River* side by side, constructing a Venn diagram of the similarities and differences in the obstacles confronting these characters as they strive to adapt to their new, often hostile environments.

- The tremendous success of Ifemelu's blog in *Americanah* is due in large part to her tireless observation of the personalities she encounters in her daily life and her gift for extracting lessons from their example. Armed only with a journal and a writing implement, take time to sit in a café, public park, or well-trafficked mall and take discreet notes on some of the most interesting personalities and interactions you observe. Seize upon one of these examples to expand into your own entry, articulating a philosophy or generalized attitude on the basis of their behavior.

- Notions of social hierarchy—racial, national, and socioeconomic—dominate Adichie's novel and fuel many of its central revelations. What hierarchies exist within the context of your life, and what are some of the factors that determine status? Formulate your own theory of social standing and use a flow chart to provide a visual representation of your proposed model.

Corruption

Adichie is unflinchingly honest in her portrayal of widespread corruption across three continents. From the institutionalized system of

patronage and bribery that plagues Nigeria to the sham marriages and false credentials facilitated by the Angolans in Britain, Obinze is the most obvious victim of these societal abuses in

Ifemelu and Obinze meet as teenagers in school in Lagos, Nigeria (©Bill Kret / Shutterstock.com)

the novel. Ironically, he transforms from a victim of corruption during his stay abroad to one of its agents upon returning to Nigeria. Aware that he is making a deal with the devil, Obinze compromises many of his most essential beliefs to broker fraudulent land speculations on behalf of Chief and share in his enormous wealth and influence. The emotional strain of participating in a business he feels to be dishonorable takes its toll on Obinze, however, and manifests itself in his fraying marriage and business relationships.

Ifemelu, too, comes to terms with the ambiguity of inherent corruption and social bias. Growing up in Nigeria, she is appalled by the charismatic congregations that demand constant tithes from her mother and keep her constrained by devotion. Similarly, Ifemelu's father struggles under constant administrative changes at the university and loses his job to more unquestioning and less qualified candidates. Ifemelu faces a similar struggle in America and is propositioned by numerous seedy employers in her struggle to make a livable wage from respectable work. Upon returning to Nigeria, however, Ifemelu benefits from the preferential treatment afforded

"Americanahs" and demonstrates her willingness to lord her newfound authority over others.

Race Relations

While they were unknown to Ifemelu during her childhood in Nigeria, differences of race and the hierarchy these differences promote strike the adult protagonist as inescapable realities of American life. Through dozens of subtle exchanges with store clerks, university representatives, and prospective employers, she is shocked and frequently amused by how issues of skin color permeate every social interaction in her new life. These observations form the foundation for what becomes Ifemelu's tremendously successful blog and allow her an outsider's perspective tempered by direct experience.

The views put forth by Ifemelu on race are frequently challenged by the evolving narrative. In addition to several online opponents, she experiences criticism closer to home and from those she holds dear. Ifemelu's boyfriend Blaine, a Princeton professor and tireless advocate of African American rights, is dismayed and often angered by what he views as her detached and dispassionate judgments. What is for him an issue of deep significance is for Ifemelu a mere hobby and an endless source of fascination. Additionally, Ifemelu's haughty, condescending treatment of her fellow Africans at the hair salon raises the suggestion of hypocrisy and complicates the construction of social hierarchy along purely racial lines. Most poignantly, Dike's childhood inferiority complex involving the color of his skin and culminating in his suicide attempt as a young adult shakes Ifemelu's racial convictions to their core. This grim incident undermines the flippant observations contained in many of the blog entries sprinkled throughout the text.

Romantic Love

Although it is perhaps an overly simplistic analysis, many of Adichie's critics contend that *Americanah* is, on its most basic level, a classic love story. The narrative's unifying story line, the enduring if evolving romance between Obinze and Ifemelu, is punctuated by rich anecdotes of relationships ranging from incidental attraction to deep connection, tackling head on the difficult topics of heartbreak and betrayal. While Adichie refuses to pull her punches in portraying all that is most good, bad, and ugly about romance, the stark honesty of her account is also largely free from judgment. Ifemelu is herself sexually liberated and participates in numerous infidelities, many of them shocking and unexpected, over the course of the novel. Although she suffers from personal feelings of guilt and shame, the protagonist feels little need to explain or justify her actions to the reader.

While the turbulent love lives of Obinze and Ifemelu dominate the novel, *Americanah* is liberally sprinkled with alternate models of romance demonstrated by minor and major characters alike. The trajectory of Aunty Uju from pampered paramour to virtual property, the marital despair of the Senegalese hairdresser, Kurt's lengthy list of exotic girlfriends, and Shan's self-destructive whirlwinds of passion all contribute to the novel's evolving portrayal of what it takes to find true love. Despite all its compelling plot turns and sweeping historical and social anecdotes, the narrative ends with a romance renewed.

STYLE

Antihero

Ifemelu, and to a lesser extent Obinze, are both examples of antiheros, central characters who lack certain traditional virtues and admirable qualities. Although readers come to respect and even empathize with Ifemelu, she is open and unabashed in expressing many of her shortcomings, including an imperious and judgmental nature, a lack of empathy, and romantic infidelity. Rather than detract from her complex character, these attributes render Ifemelu thoroughly believable and temper the unforgiving opinions expressed in the text with an understanding of imperfect humanity.

By contrast, Obinze is initially depicted as stalwart, reasonable, and dedicated, but these virtues become increasingly at odds with the choices he makes. He betrays himself by throwing in his lot with Chief and participating in what he knows to be an unworkable and ultimately loveless marriage. By the time Obinze experiences misgivings and attempts to extricate himself from this new life, he is able to do so only by cruelly compromising the happiness of his wife and young daughter.

Conflict

Americanah is relentless in its portrayal of conflict, the existence of opposition in the plot, that propels the narrative forward at a dizzying pace. From the novel's opening pages to its last, Ifemelu and Obinze struggle in their respective environments to attain personal fulfillment and success in the eyes of their family and peers. In the process, both sacrifice a great deal and struggle against crushing social realities like institutionalized prejudice, corruption, and scarce, abusive jobs. More intimate conflicts punctuate the narrative as well, as evidenced by angry exchanges that strain romantic and family relations and inflict lasting psychological trauma on the novel's main characters. The conclusion of *Americanah*, while optimistic in tone, brings no resolution to these conflicts and denies readers the satisfaction of a completely happy ending.

Didacticism

Mediated through Ifemelu's personal convictions, the novel is marked by frequent and unapologetic didacticism, a style of writing that aims to instruct or pass judgment. Compelling, sometimes inflammatory entries from Ifemelu's blog punctuate the narrative and suggest an overlay of opinion to the events and characters described. In this way, readers of *Americanah* are strongly encouraged to adopt Ifemelu's views and her impressions of America, Nigeria, and the social customs that govern each. The almost limitless wealth of characters depicted in the novel are the most obvious targets of the protagonist's scrutiny and sentencing. These judgments are translated into sweeping generalizations and lessons that Ifemelu dispenses to her online followers through her blog and, by extension, through the novel itself.

Despite constituting a virtual survival guide for illegal immigrants, Obinze's struggles in England are rendered in language less instructive and openly opinionated. His understated, quiet suffering and desire to fit in soften the didactic edge of the many lessons he learns abroad. Readers are swayed by the poignancy of his experience rather than commanded by the force of his conviction. Adichie switches between these two forms of didacticism with ease, immersing readers in two distinct and brilliantly illuminated personalities within the same novel.

Flashback

The narrative of *Americanah* is alinear and jumps freely between musings in the present and recollections of the past. The novel's reliance on depictions of events that have already transpired, referred to as flashbacks, qualify the ongoing story and provide context for each of its developments. Further contributing to the complexity of the novel, these manipulations of time occur across the three continents of North America, Europe, and Africa and are divided between the viewpoints of Obinze and Ifemelu. Many of the tangled memories and experiences are unique to these two characters, while others are held in common. In this way, Adichie's masterful use of flashbacks serves to strengthen the impression of lives shares, lives severed, and lives reunited.

HISTORICAL CONTEXT

Beginning at the turn of the twentieth century, Nigeria was claimed by the British Empire as an overseas colony and carved up into distinct regions somewhat arbitrarily and without regard to preexisting boundaries or tribal relations. Lagos, a city described extensively in *Americanah*, was designated as the seat of colonial power and grew considerably in importance during the years of World War I and the joint English and French invasion of nearby Cameroon. By the end of World War II and into the 1950s, the European colonial powers moved toward gradually

relinquishing their overseas empires. In Nigeria, Britain attempted to reconcile antagonistic tribes and lay the groundwork for workable self-government, a process greatly complicated by their former missteps in administration. Nevertheless, 1960 saw the full independence of the country under the democratically elected Prime Minister Abubakar Tafawa Belawa.

The years leading up to Ifemelu's birth and extending into her early childhood were marked equally by national expansion and the outbreak of tribal tensions and territorial disputes. The Igbo tribe to which Ifemelu belongs rose up in 1966 and murdered Belawa and many prominent members of his cabinet, resulting in bloody retaliation by other unified tribes. Taking advantage of the bloodshed and confusion, army officer Yakubu Gowon seized control of the nation and once again carved up tribal lands in an attempt to discourage further conflict. Displeased with this arrangement, Igbo tribal leaders seceded from Nigeria to form the independent state of Biafra. The Biafran War became an international cause célèbre, with the French supporting Biafra and England and America backing the Nigerian Federal Government. The secessionist movement collapsed in 1970 after mass bloodshed and starvation.

The discovery of vast reserves of petroleum over the next decade resulted in widespread corruption and political discontent among aspiring leaders. The most infamous of these, mentioned by Ifemelu's parents and many of her older neighbors, was a military despot named Ibrahim Babangida, whose widespread abuses led to a national push for true democratic elections in the 1990s. Equally controversial, Olusegon Obasanjo was elected by popular vote, and his leadership saw little decline in either corruption or conflict. Obasanjo's emphasis on enforcing Christian ideals in Nigeria—of the type so zealously adopted by Ifemelu's mother—led to tensions with Muslim tribes in the north and an increase in bloodshed into the new millennium.

The University of Ibadan, which both Ifemelu and Obinze dream of attending, was established as a haven for freethinking and forward-thinking Nigerian intellectuals in the final years of British colonial rule. The incredible optimism and romanticism embodied by the institution was somewhat devalued by the establishment of numerous and vastly inferior institutions under money-hungry warlords in the years

Ifemelu achieves success in America with her blog about race *(©Milles Studio | Shutterstock.com)*

following the Biafran War. The high degree of governmental control in the new Nigerian educational system, coupled with poor management and misappropriated funds, caused widespread discontent, intellectual stagnation, and striking by thousands of students and staff. Many Nigerians, like Ifemelu, were forced to seek educational opportunities abroad rather than suffer constant interruptions to their studies.

CRITICAL OVERVIEW

As her third full-length novel, Adichie's *Americanah* is measured largely against the example set by her prior literary successes, *Half of a Yellow Sun* and *Purple Hibiscus*. In her 2013 article, Kathryn Schulz praises *Americanah* for its uncompromising insight into the inner workings of American society and recognizes the novel as the most ambitious of Adichie's works to date. Schulz comments especially upon the unprecedented chronological and geographical scope of the novel, as well as the rare ability of the

narrative to blend traditionally exclusive genres and encompass such a wealth of human interaction and social quirks. "With this new book, Adichie has scaled up," praises Schulz. She goes on to comment:

> *Americanah* traverses three genres (romance, comedy of manners, novel of ideas) three nations (Nigeria, Great Britain, the United States) and, within each, a swath of the social spectrum as broad—and as difficult to nail—as the hand spans in a Rachmaninoff concerto. It is a book about identity, nationality, race, difference, loneliness, aspiration, and love, not as distinct entities but in the complex combinatorial relations they possess in real life.

This same virtue of dynamism, however, also contributes to what Schulz condemns as a narrative unwieldiness and an attempt by the author to tag the elements of human experience that defy such simple categorization. Additionally, Schulz claims that the excess of voice and opinion detract from concrete characterization. As a result, Ifemelu in particular is obscured by her blog and loses something of her humanity and relatability. Schulz's most central criticism, however, revolves not around stylistic flaws in the novel but around a perceived lack of passion. She bolsters this criticism with the comparison of *Americanah* to *Half of a Yellow Sun*, Adichie's harrowing novel of the Biafran War:

> *Half of a Yellow Sun*, a book about atrocities, overflows with love; its characters are inclined by kindness, and forced by war, to transcend both the narrow fissures of private difference and the broad fissures of nationality and class. By contrast, this new book, about lesser atrocities, is cool and withholding.

In her *New York Times* book review, "Braiding Hair and Issues about Race," Janet Maslin acknowledges Adichie's incredible talent and promise as a writer but states that in *Americanah*, these gifts are sorely misappropriated. Maslin's review is as much an attack on the author as it is on the novel itself and references Adichie and her literary invention Ifemelu almost interchangeably. "Ifemelu, like Ms. Adichie, bristles at facile generalizations," Maslin asserts, "And she knows as much about splitting hair as she does about styling it." While acknowledging *Americanah* as a technical masterpiece and a font of social insight and piercing wit, Maslin, like Schulz, describes the novel's central deficiency against the backdrop of its literary predecessor. It is not passion the novel is missing, Maslin asserts, but direction and emotional import:

> *Half of a Yellow Sun* was just as fine-tuned. But it played out against the backdrop of the Biafran War, with a stark clarity that automatically gave it gravitas. *Americanah* is less authoritative, because its stakes are lower and because Ifemelu's sharp opinions are not accompanied by a strong, aggressive personality.

Maslin further criticizes the way Adichie "drifts passively through a long, winding story. And *Americanah* comes dangerously close to the 'exaggerated histrionics' and 'improbable plots' that she ascribes to Nigerian, or Nollywood, films."

Although *Americanah* is a comparatively recent publication and book reviews still eclipse critical scholarship, the novel is beginning to be examined in light of its contributions to the field of postcolonial studies and the growing canon of African literature. In his 2014 article "Negotiating Africa Now," scholar Madhu Krishnan sees Adichie's literary trajectory from *Half of a Yellow Sun* to *Americanah* as an evolution of the success of the modern African novel from one of localized to global significance. *Americanah*, he claims, demystifies Africa for the international reader and makes it as accessible, dynamic, and

relevant a locale as any in the Western world. Krishnan writes in his essay,

> In the author's 2013 *Americanah*, Africa takes its roots in Nigeria and extends across the globe, taking hold in America and enlivening the continuities of transnational blackness. . . . Africa, unmoored from its determinants, is a place of darkness and light, compassion and violence, rife with complexities and nuance like any other place, and connected to the rest of the world in a dense network of intellectual and cultural exchange.

CRITICISM

Jeffrey Eugene Palmer

Palmer is a scholar, freelance writer, and teacher of high school English. In the following essay, he examines political representations in Adichie's Americanah.

Although the novel is lauded largely in terms of its piercing insight into the complexity of human relationships and dynamics of race and social standing, Adichie's *Americanah* provides an equally compelling dissection of political influence in the modern world. Adichie does not limit her observations to one continent but infuses the adventures of Obinze and Ifemelu abroad—from a nationalistic dispute in a hair salon, to the election of African American President Barack Obama, to an immigrant crisis in England—with deep political relevance. The rampant corruption experienced by the estranged lovers both at home and in their respective travel destinations suggests the universality of this unscrupulous mode of being. More specifically, however, the author explores through her characters the easy seduction and very real danger inherent to the system of patronage that dominates political, personal, and spiritual realities over the course of the novel.

In her examination of the trajectory of Adichie's political outspokenness across *Purple Hibiscus* and *Half of a Yellow Sun*, scholar Susan Z. Andrade remarks on the growing confidence of the author in addressing power dynamics directly rather than allegorically. Although Andrade's "Adichie's Genealogies: National and Feminine Novels" predates *Americanah* by two years, it establishes a pattern of representation both substantiated and complicated by the later novel:

WHAT DO I READ NEXT?

- Joseph Conrad's famed 1899 classic, *Heart of Darkness*, is set against the majesty of the Congo River and explores many of the grim, unsettling realities of colonialism, greed, and the barbarism inherent to all men regardless of the color of their skin.

- Zadie Smith's acclaimed 2012 novel *NW* paints a gritty, detailed portrait of the very London immigrant neighborhoods experienced by Obinze during his time abroad.

- Published in 2003, Adichie's acclaimed literary debut, *Purple Hibiscus*, provides an intimate perspective on domestic abuse, social upheaval, and survival in war-torn Nigeria.

- *Nigeria Revisited: My Life and Loves Abroad* is a 2014 travel memoir of Peace Corps member Catherine Onyemelukwe's time spent in the modern Nigeria experienced by Ifemelu upon her homecoming.

- *Out of Africa* (1937) is the well-loved memoir of a Danish baroness, writing under the nom de plume Isak Dinesen, who travels to Kenya to manage a coffee plantation. It is a majestic, dynamic tale of love, loss, cultural discovery, and the timeless allure of the Dark Continent in the eyes of the West.

- Chinua Achebe's most widely read novel, *Things Fall Apart* (1958), bears witness to the early years of colonialism and English subjugation in Nigeria.

- *No Longer at Ease* (1960), published only two years after Achebe's international debut, provides an equally compelling portrait of the aftermath of imperialism and its enduring legacy for the future of Nigeria.

- Barbara Kingsolver's acclaimed 2008 epic, *The Poisonwood Bible*, is a sweeping, multi-generational tale of family, fortune, and evangelical Christianity in a divided postcolonial Africa.

- The 2015 best seller *Between the World and Me* is a memoir by educator and journalist Ta-Nehisi Coates that provides an extensive exploration of the enduring question of race in America.

- Straddling mature and young-adult fiction, Meja Mwangi's *The Mzungu Boy* (2005) is the inspiring tale of an unlikely friendship between a Kenyan villager and a boy from England

---

Her two novels illustrate the strength and coherence of my argument that earlier female writers' representations of national politics become most sharply visible through allegorical readings of familial structures and institutions and, more important, that over time, female writers have changed their writing style and now represent the national imaginary more directly.

Famed for her fearless observations and, at times, shameless didacticism, Adichie demonstrates her ability to approach even the most controversial of issues from two sides at once. *Americanah* is not solely representative of Adichie's overcoming the timidity of her literary predecessors but incorporating their strengths of allusion and subtlety into her own, contrastingly bold style. This has the benefit of doing comprehensive justice to the complexity of political machinations and their repercussions across all segments of society, from the most affluent businessman to the most provincial Nigerian villager. Three dominant currents in *Americanah* work to demonstrate Adichie's syncretic approach to voicing difficult but necessary political truths through the medium of her fiction. The first of these, organized religion, blends seamlessly into ancillary issues of domestic authority. One of Ifemelu's earliest memories of charismatic, controlling leadership, and her subsequent disdain for this form of power, occurs when her mother

> **BY HER LOVE OF BOTH BLUNT STATEMENT AND SUBTLE EXAMPLE, ADICHIE REPRESENTS A FULFILLMENT RATHER THAN A DEPARTURE FROM THE MODE OF POLITICAL CRITICISM FAVORED BY HER LITERARY PREDECESSORS."**

converts from her native Catholicism to increasingly severe sects of Christianity. Even at a young age, Ifemelu is struck by the demands placed upon her previously lively parent and begins to resent the steady stream of money leaving the household to line the pockets of evangelists. Ifemelu's tongue-in-cheek description of this shift in her mother's attitude—attributing its specific dictates to a higher power—implies that she understands, on some level, the entanglement of faith with the larger potential for political corruption and the propagation of unquestioning authority.

> After that afternoon, her God changed. He became exacting. Relaxed hair offended Him. Dancing offended Him. She bartered with Him, offering starvation in exchange for poverty, for a job promotion, for good health.

In particular, Ifemelu becomes suspicious of the intentions of the congregation's central organizer, the grim Sister Ibanabo, who comes to embody the oppressive potential of her mother's unquestioning fanaticism and devotion. Ifemelu's open defiance to the ironclad will of Sister Ibanabo is a small but symbolic act of resistance undertaken not only for herself but also for her mother. The placement of Ifemelu's introduction to organized religion during the uncertain period of childhood, as well as its couching within the context of family rather than larger Nigerian politics, somewhat softens the outspoken views of the author expressed in various interviews and lectures, quoted here by scholar Cheryl Stobie in her "Dethroning the Infallible Father: Religion, Patriarchy and Politics in Chimamanda Ngozi Adichie's Purple Hibiscus":

> I am fascinated by the power of religion.... Religion is such a huge force, so easily corruptible and yet so capable of doing incredible good. The streak of intolerance I see masquerading itself as faith and the way we create an image of God that suits us, are things I am interested in questioning.

A comparably subtle and yet pervasive strain of societal dissection occurs in Ifemelu's observation of, and participation in, relationships that couple romance and patronage. She is critical and yet deeply ambivalent regarding her favorite aunt's relationship with a Nigerian mover and shaker known simply as "the General," a relationship her relatives and neighbors seem to either unconditionally condemn or tactfully ignore. To Ifemelu's mind, the shame of Aunty Uju's position as paramour is balanced by the obvious affection and regard shown to her by the General and his casual use of massive sums of money to ensure her comfort. Ifemelu's eyes are opened to the dangers inherent in such an arrangement; however, when the General dies unexpectedly, leading his assets to be seized and his known associates to be bullied by his political rivals, Aunty Uju is forced to flee to America to ensure a fresh start for her son, the infant Dike, and is left penniless and entirely unaccustomed to self-reliance. Consequently, Ifemelu's childhood idol becomes the victim of dependency and falls prey to increasingly abusive and lowbrow suitors. Despite Ifemelu's dim view of her aunt's willingness to subject herself to the will of unworthy men, she too allows herself to become the beneficiary of a romantic patron. Handsome, wholesomely blond, and to the manor born, Curt is the American blue-blood equivalent of a Nigerian "Big Man." Throwing herself headlong into Curt's world of moneyed ease and boundless possibility, the young woman begins to adopt an imperious manner and reaches new heights of success solely on the basis of her boyfriend's reputation and family name. Although the termination of her relationship with Curt is largely amicable and nowhere near as dramatic as the forced parting between Aunty Uju and the General, the allure and false sense of security inherent to this form of borrowed power is made clear in both instances. The final chapters of the novel return to Nigeria and bring startling clarity to these earlier political truths couched in romantic relationships and organized religion. The third major current that highlights grim political truths is illustrated by Obinze's narrative, which concerns the national power structure and details how his loyalty towards Chief, and not his decades of hard work and study, catapulted him to immense wealth and success almost overnight. The ugly reality of the present state of affairs in Nigeria from which men like Obinze seek to profit is expressed with a shocking starkness pointedly

Obinze and Ifemelu both leave Nigeria's military dictatorship legally but Obinze illegally *(©punghi /*
Shutterstock.com)

free from allegory. Obinze finds it easy to rationalize his dishonesty:

> Look, it's very hard to be a clean public official in this country. Everything is set up for you to steal. And the worst part is, people want you to steal. Your relatives want you to steal, your friends want you to steal.

The gnawing shame of his participation in corruption and cronyism, however, begins to make Obinze dissatisfied with his opulent existence and seek a return to the freedom and self-reliance of his earlier years. His newfound privilege and prestige in the eyes of his countrymen, and even his beautiful and unquestioningly obedient wife, serve only to reinforce his growing discontent and feelings of unworthiness in belonging to so exclusive and corrupt a club. Ifemelu's return to Nigeria, therefore, corresponds with this change of heart and provides the catalyst for Obinze's liberation from the fetters of political patronage. His fellow "Big Men" are shocked when he announces his intention to divorce his wife and openly forsake the pristine façade of his new life. For the first time in a novel

of considerable breadth and complexity, the importance of appearance over reality so central to politics is addressed in terms both simple and direct:

> Okwudiba took a deep breath and exhaled, as though to brush aside the alcohol. "Look, The Zed, many of us didn't marry the woman we truly loved. We married the woman that was around when we were ready to marry. So forget this thing. You can keep seeing her, but no need for this kind of white-people behavior. If your wife has a child for somebody else or if you beat her, that is a reason for divorce. But to get up and say you have no problem with your wife but you are leaving her for another woman. *Haba*. We don't behave like that, please."

By her love of both blunt statement and subtle example, Adichie represents a fulfillment rather than a departure from the mode of political criticism favored by her literary predecessors. Her novel is greatly enriched by anecdotes of relationships, religion, and cultural peculiarities, all of which serve to augment, and not obscure, her boldly expressed opinions. Through this masterful fusion of the often exclusive modes of showing and telling, Adichie expands the implications of the politics of power in her novel to encompass the myriad facets of everyday existence. *Americanah*'s complementary strains of didacticism and storytelling represent a landmark approach to addressing the hard truths of the modern age in a style that submits to universal empathy while holding firm to individual opinion.

Source: Jeffrey Eugene Palmer, Critical Essay on *Americanah*, in *Novels for Students*, Gale, Cengage Learning, 2017.

Heather Hewett

In the following excerpt, Hewett examines how Adichie uses her work to critique human rights issues in Africa.

Human rights activists and scholars have frequently voiced disappointment in the failure of the human rights community to prevent, address, and redress violations on the African continent. Others have raised questions about the validity of human rights ideals as they are currently defined and deployed by international governmental and nongovernmental organizations. For example, scholars such as Makau Mutua fault human rights frameworks for limitations ranging from an "unrelenting focus on individualism" to their failure to "address economic powerlessness and the scandalous international order," arguing that their Eurocentric origins and ideological alliance with a "free market vision of political democracy" have prevented human rights from being useful to postcolonial African states (2008, 34, 35, 31). In response, other scholars point out that many African states have participated in the human rights legislative process, authoring human rights declarations and conventions such as the African Charter on Human and Peoples' Rights. As the scholar Fareda Banda observes, the founding documents of organizations such as the African Union suggest that a human rights ideology "appears to have been voluntarily embraced by African states" (2005, 3).

The topic of human rights becomes even more complex when we consider the images and stories about Africa disseminated globally by the news media, particularly in the United States and Europe. While Africa has experienced more than its fair share of human rights violations, it has also witnessed more than its fair share of news stories focusing on human rights atrocities and humanitarian crises, often to the exclusion of any other news. The writer

> WHILE ADICHIE'S CRITIQUE SUGGESTS THE PARALLELS BETWEEN DOMESTIC VIOLENCE AND STATE-SPONSORED VIOLENCE, IT SIMULTANEOUSLY REVEALS HOW THE HUMAN RIGHTS MOVEMENT HAS NOT ALWAYS VIEWED THE VICTIMS OF DOMESTIC VIOLENCE, OR VIOLENCE AGAINST WOMEN AND GIRLS, AS PART OF ITS AGENDA."

Binyavanga Wainaina shows the irony of these stories and their accompanying stereotypes in his article "How to Write about Africa":

> Among your characters you must always include The Starving African, who wanders the refugee camp nearly naked, and waits for the benevolence of the West. Her children have flies on their eyelids and pot bellies, and her breasts are flat and empty. She must look utterly helpless. She can have no past, no history; such diversions ruin the dramatic moment. Moans are good. She must never say anything about herself in the dialogue except to speak of her (unspeakable) suffering. (2005, 93)

Wainaina's description suggests how images of passive and suffering Africans are frequently gendered: The Starving African is a mother, a homeless and historyless refugee who is unable to care for her children without outside help. Centuries-old narratives about "saving" Africa inform this particular image, which, in turn, performs the cultural work of "proving" the need for such missionary impulses and the need for benevolent Westerners—thus constructing the binary of voiceless victim and the humanitarian savior. This binary informs many narratives about Africa, including, Mutua argues, human rights. Indeed, Mutua indicts human rights discourse itself for its dependence on Western missionary ideologies, arguing that the "grand narrative of human rights" is marked by the "damning metaphor" of the "savages-victims-saviors" triad: although the human rights movement originated in response to the atrocities of the Holocaust, its "theoretical underpinnings" can be traced back to Western colonial attitudes that viewed Africans as either savages or victims, and in need of saving by Western saviors (2001, 202, 213).

The Nigerian-born writer Chimamanda Ngozi Adichie has written directly about these Western stereotypes of Africa, pointing out that early twenty-first-century stereotypes of Africa as "sex[y] and hip" presents a "new afro-fashion... based in part on the stereotype of the poor starving African in need of salvation by the West" (2008, 44). Adichie argues that fiction provides a way to combat "simple stories" about Africa and to present, instead, a complex picture that moves beyond stereotypes (45). As she puts it, "literature is one of the best ways to come closer to the idea of a common humanity, to see that we may be kind and unkind in different ways, but that we are all capable of kindness and unkindness" (46). As a result of giving voice to multiple stories, Adichie's fiction delves deeply into many of the issues and debates surrounding human rights in Nigeria. In stories such as "The American Embassy" and novels such as *Purple Hibiscus* and *Half of a Yellow Sun*, the author critiques the "grand narratives of human rights" by complicating our preconceived notions about who is a savior, a victim, or a perpetrator. These texts simultaneously claim and question human rights ideals as they have been defined and practiced in the twentieth century, performing a kind of ideological human rights work in the realm of the imaginary and the fictional. The resulting critique resonates with the political work of many African feminists, womanists, and women's rights advocates who have sought to redefine and expand human rights ideals and practices to include and address the needs and concerns of all Africans, including women and girls.

MAKING VISIBLE THE INVISIBLE: GENDER, THE PRIVATE SPHERE, AND HUMAN RIGHTS REGIMES

Adichie's critique of human rights begins in her first novel, *Purple Hibiscus* (2003), a young girl's coming-of-age story. Fifteen-year-old Kambili Achike suffers under the domination of her father, Eugene, a successful and dogmatic newspaper publisher who fights against political tyranny and corruption in Nigeria. State-sponsored violence and intimidation provide the backdrop to Kambili's story, as an unnamed Abacha-like dictator seizes power in a military coup and serves as the target for the prodemocracy editorials and reportage of the *Standard*, Eugene's newspaper. Early in the narrative, we learn that Eugene has received a human rights award from *Amnesty World*, and his editor publicly thanks him for being "a man of integrity, the bravest man I know" (Adichie 2003). Yet the novel charts the distance between his public and private persona, revealing this brave man to be domineering and physically abusive at home. Despite the high walls that protect Kambili's home, these walls do not keep her safe: she is physically abused by her father and suffers from an inability to speak (Hewett 2005, 85–86). Juxtaposing the violence outside and inside her home, the novel exposes the parallels between military rule and Eugene's abusive authoritarianism, rooted in the abuse of the colonial missionaries who educated him. Furthermore, his domestic despotism produces effects similar to that of Nigeria's ruler. Just as the father abuses and silences his daughter, the government terrorizes and finally kills the newspaper editor, Ade Coker.

While Adichie's critique suggests the parallels between domestic violence and state-sponsored violence, it simultaneously reveals how the human rights movement has not always viewed the victims of domestic violence, or violence against women and girls, as part of its agenda. Part of the problem emerges from the fact that human rights instruments and institutions did not originally define or practice "human rights" in a way that considered the "larger socioeconomic web that entraps women" (Bunch 1990, 488). As Charlotte Bunch points out, "The narrow definition of human rights, recognized by many in the West as solely a matter of state violation of civil and political liberties, impedes consideration of women's rights" (488). Rather than jettisoning the system of human rights altogether, many feminists and women's rights activists have claimed human rights ideals for women at the same time that they have critiqued the human rights regime for its inattention to gender as well as other intersectional components of identity. Thus many feminists around the world have worked to expand definitions of human rights to consider not only a much broader and interconnected range of economic, cultural, and social rights but also to make visible the range of ways in which women's rights can be denied or violated. As Banda argues in her examination of women and human rights in Africa, "the lives of women are lived out largely in the private sphere, where violations against women are more likely than not to be committed by nonstate actors," often in the name of custom or tradition (2005, 43). Indeed, one such domestic violation—violence against women and girls—only became an international agenda item in the

1980s; as Margaret Keck and Kathryn Sikkink document, for much of the twentieth century, violence against women was "on the agenda of neither the women's movement nor international human rights groups" and did not become a priority for these groups until the mid-1990s (1998, 166). In many African states, women's organizations and networks "have spearheaded initiatives to build support for [human rights] treaties and protocols" (Tripp 2009, 7) and have brought global attention to violence against women as an important issue (Banda 2005, 159–206). In a narrative strategy that parallels that of many transnational and African feminists, *Purple Hibiscus* makes visible the invisibility of domestic violence by revealing how a human rights discourse focused solely on the state's abrogation of civil and political rights cannot see or address the full extent and range of violence that entire families can suffer at the hand of an all-powerful patriarch.

Adichie extends her critique of the limitations of human rights discourse in her short story "The American Embassy," first published in *Prism International* in 2002 and subsequently included in the collection *The Thing around Your Neck* (2009d). "The American Embassy" locates a story of personal trauma within a society suffering from the military violence of the Abacha regime: we are introduced to the unnamed protagonist, a woman waiting in a long line outside the embassy for a US visa, while a soldier flogs a man across the street. The story makes clear both the everyday nature of such shocking violence as well as the powerlessness of Nigerian citizens through its description of the casual commentary of the other visa applicants: "'Our people have become too used to pleading with soldiers,'" observes the man standing behind the protagonist.

The woman's personal tragedy provides a feminist critique of human rights activism that makes visible the unseen victims of state terrorism, allowing the story to pose questions about the price of prodemocracy work when women and children become the targets of retaliation and revenge. The woman's husband is a prodemocracy journalist at *The New Nigeria*, lauded for his bravery in a manner reminiscent of the praise surrounding Eugene Achike. The day after her husband writes one of his articles for the paper, the "BBC carried the story on the news and interviewed an exiled Nigerian professor of politics who said her husband deserved a Human Rights

Award. *He fights repression with the pen, he gives a voice to the voiceless, he makes the world know.*" But his wife knows how he allowed his work as a journalist to feed his ego; she understands that his motives are neither selfless nor altruistic. In a flashback, she remembers his behavior after he returns from being interrogated:

> She remembered her husband's expression, that look of the excited messiah, as he talked about the soldier who had given him a cigarette after beating him, all the while stammering in the way he did when he was in high spirits. She had found that stammer endearing years ago; she no longer did.

The phrase "excited messiah" captures his inflated view of himself as a redeemer, thus obliterating any idealized image of a victim of human rights abuse. The protagonist also knows that "fear" and self-preservation led him to flee the country, leaving both her and their child, Ugonna, behind—the child for whom she gave up her own career as a journalist, and who subsequently becomes a victim when soldiers come looking for her husband. When the man standing behind her wishes for more newspaper editors "with that kind of courage," she thinks: "It was not courage, it was simply an exaggerated selfishness."

By narrating these events from the wife's perspective, the story powerfully and unflinchingly examines the unseen victims of human rights activism: a child made vulnerable because of his father's surfeit of self-involvement and lack of foresight; a woman left alone and bereft, traumatized by her own "fail[ure]" to protect her son. It pierces the rhetoric of public human rights talk, particularly the valorization of courage and self-sacrifice that can mask and obscure male privilege. Just as soldiers whip civilians with impunity—indeed, just as soldiers kill children, betraying the pleasure of their own power with their "glower" and "swagger"—so too human rights activists can fight against tyranny without full consideration of the consequences and reverberations of their struggles. Those within the private space of domesticity are not protected by international human rights regimes but are, instead, rendered vulnerable to state-sponsored violence and its psychological effects. Ugonna's story will never appear in the newspaper; the depth of his mother's own trauma will never be recognized; and more likely than not, neither will be connected with the activism of her husband. Their lives contain unspoken truths and agonizing realities beyond the orbit of official human rights discourse: "She had the urge to ask the visa interviewer if the stories in *The New Nigeria* were worth the life of a child. But she didn't."

In refusing to speak about these matters to the visa interviewer, Ugonna's mother chooses to keep her own story private, outside of the official diplomatic discourse governing amnesty applications. This official discourse requires applicants to perform a particular identity for diplomats, translated to her by the other applicants in line as well as her friends who have been helping her: "Make Ugonna real. Cry, but don't cry too much." She refuses to perform her own mourning for a stranger or to tell the story that is expected of her; but unlike the narrator in *Purple Hibiscus*, her silence signals resistance and agency, not powerlessness. With this silence, the story indicts the mechanisms of an international system set up to help victims of human rights violations—victims who must provide "evidence" of their suitability for political asylum to diplomats seemingly unaware that military violence regularly takes place across the street from their own embassy. Ultimately Ugonna's mother rejects this system entirely by refusing to "hawk" her son's story in exchange for her own safety. If she has somehow failed him as a mother, she refuses to leave Nigeria as her husband did.

Taken together, both *Purple Hibiscus* and "The American Embassy" expose the failings of human rights ideals when they participate in, and reproduce, larger systems of gendered inequity. They reveal that the focus of human rights regimes—the abuse of civil and political rights—does not address all forms of violence. Put another way, these stories explore how human rights discourse can participate in the illusion that the private space of domesticity provides a safe haven from the violence of a patriarchal and militaristic state; on the contrary, the brutal acts that can take place behind closed doors not only terrorize but also destroy....

Source: Heather Hewett, "Rewriting Human Rights: Gender, Violence, and Freedom in the Fiction of Chimamanda Ngozi Adichie," in *The Critical Imagination in African Literature*, edited by Maik Nwosu and Obiwu, Syracuse University Press, 2015, pp. 166–73.

SOURCES

Andrade, Susan Z., "Adichie's Genealogies: National and Feminine Novels," in *Research in African Literatures*, Vol. 42, No. 2, 2011, pp. 91–101.

"Biography," Chimamanda Ngozi Adichie website, http://www.l3.ulg.ac.be/adichie/ (accessed May 1, 2016).

Chude-Sokei, Louis, "The Newly Black Americans," in *Transition*, No. 113, 2014, pp. 52–71.

"History of Nigeria," in *History World*, http://www.historyworld.net/wrldhis/PlainTextHistories.asp?historyid = ad41 (accessed May 1, 2016).

"History of UI," University of Ibadan website, http://www.ui.edu.ng/uihistory (accessed May 1, 2016).

Krishnan, Madhu, "Negotiating Africa Now," in *Transition*, No. 113, 2014, pp. 11–24.

Luebering, J.E., "Chimamanda Ngozi Adichie," in *Encyclopædia Britannica Online*, http://www.britannica.com/biography/Chimamanda-Ngozi-Adichie (accessed May 1, 2016).

Maslin, Janet, "Braiding Hair and Issues about Race: *Americanah* by Chimamanda Ngozi Adichie," in *New York Times*, May 19, 2013, http://www.nytimes.com/2013/05/20/books/americanha-by-chimamanda-ngozi-adichie.html?_r = 0 (accessed May 1, 2016).

Saint, William, Teresa A. Hartnett, and Erich Strassner. "Higher Education in Nigeria: A Status Report," World Education News and Reviews website, September 1, 2004, http://www.wes.org/ewenr/04sept/Feature.htm (accessed May 1, 2016).

Schulz, Kathryn, "Schulz on *Americanah* by Chimamanda Ngozi Adichie," in *Vulture*, May 26, 2013, http://www.vulture.com/2013/05/schulz-on-americanah-by-chimamanda-ngozi-adichie.html (accessed May 1, 2016).

Stobie, C., "Dethroning the Infallible Father: Religion, Patriarchy and Politics in Chimamanda Ngozi Adichie's *Purple Hibiscus*," in *Literature and Theology*, Vol. 24, No. 4, December 2010, pp. 421–35.

FURTHER READING

Achebe, Chinua, *There Was a Country: A Personal History of Biafra*, Penguin Press, 2012.

Made available to the public in 2012, *There Was a Country* is the posthumously published memoir of famed Nigerian author Achebe, providing a counterpart to Adichie's fictionalized account of the horrors of the Biafran War.

Adichie, Chimamanda Ngozi, *Half of a Yellow Sun*, Alfred A. Knopf, 2006.

Adichie's 2006 *Half of a Yellow Sun* is set amidst the horrors of the Biafran War that ravaged Nigeria in the decade before Adichie's birth. The book provides context for the more modern political realities depicted in *Americanah*.

——, *We Should All Be Feminists*, Harper Collins, 2014.

Published in 2014 partly as a response to the success of *Americanah*, Adichie's essay *We Should All Be Feminists* is a composite of her views regarding sexual and racial politics originally expressed through various interviews and televised lectures.

Laumann, Dennis, *Colonial Africa: 1884–1994*, Oxford University Press, 2012.

Laumann provides a historical, political, and social backdrop for the carving up and colonial administration of Africa by European political powers, as well as the response of numerous native tribes to this century of subjugation.

Quayson, Ato, *The Cambridge Companion to the Postcolonial Novel*, Cambridge University Press, 2016.

For this volume, Quayson gathered pieces to serve as a beginner's guide to the complexity and wealth of postcolonial scholarship surrounding modern fiction like *Americanah*.

SUGGESTED SEARCH TERMS

Chimamanda Ngozi Adichie

Adichie AND Americanah

Adichie AND Ted Talk

Adichie AND Biafran War

Adichie AND Achebe

Nigerian authors

postcolonial African literature

We Should All Be Feminists

The Buddha in the Attic

In Julie Otsuka's 2011 novel, *The Buddha in the Attic*, a chorus of Japanese women narrates the journey across the Pacific Ocean to the United States. Once they arrive, these "picture brides" will start a new life in a foreign land with husbands they have never met. The women, who speak from the first-person-plural point of view as "we," must first face disappointments, loss, struggle, and pain before they begin at last to adjust to life in the United States. With time they find their independence, have children, start businesses, build homes, and grow into a strong community. Then, as the cloud of war settles over their lives, they find themselves suddenly stripped of everything they have striven for and forced to leave their homes with only what they can carry to board trains for the internment camps of World War II. Otsuka tells their tale with masterfully concise prose in which the smallest details pierce the heart.

JULIE OTSUKA

2011

AUTHOR BIOGRAPHY

Otsuka was born on May 15, 1962, in Palo Alto, California. One of three children, Otsuka is the daughter of Japanese Americans: her father was an Issei, meaning an immigrant born in Japan, while her mother was a Nisei, or a Japanese American born in America to Issei parents. She earned her bachelor of arts from Yale University in 1984 and began a career in painting. At the age

Julie Otsuka (© epa european pressphoto agency b.v. | Alamy)

of thirty, however, she decided to return to school—this time to pursue her interest in writing fiction. She earned her MFA from Columbia University in 1999. Her first novel, *When the Emperor Was Divine*, was published in 2002 to great critical acclaim. The novel, which takes as its subject the internment of innocent Japanese Americans during World War II, has been translated into over eleven languages and was chosen as a *New York Times* Notable Book as well as a *San Francisco Chronicle* Best Book of the Year. In addition, it was added to the National Endowment for the Arts' "The Big Read" Library and named a Barnes & Noble Discover Great New Writers finalist.

Her second novel, *The Buddha in the Attic*, was published in 2011. The novel won the prestigious PEN/Faulkner Award, the Langum Prize for American Historical Fiction, and the Prix Femina Étranger and was named a National Book Award finalist. Otsuka has received the Asian American Literary Award, a Guggenheim Fellowship, the *Los Angeles Times* Book Prize, the International IMPAC Dublin Literary Award, and an Arts and Letters Award in Literature from the American Academy of Arts and Letters. Her work has appeared in *The Best American Short Stories* anthologies as well as *The Best American Nonrequired Reading of 2012*. She lives in New York City.

PLOT SUMMARY

Come, Japanese!

The Buddha in the Attic begins with a description of a diverse group of Japanese picture brides on the boat that will take them to the United States to meet their new husbands for the first time. They come from all walks of life—the city, the country, the mountains, and the coast. They compare their photographs of their husbands, who will be waiting for them at the dock in San Francisco. The photographs show handsome, well-dressed men standing in front of neat houses or Ford Model T cars. The brides sleep in steerage, dreaming of their new lives and of the lives they are leaving behind in Japan. Their mothers taught them to serve tea, arrange flowers, help with household chores, speak softly, and walk with small steps.

They are curious about the strange people and foreign customs in the United States but confident their lives will be better across the ocean than in the villages of their birth. They range in age from twelve to thirty-seven and come from Yamanashi, Tokyo, Kagoshima, Hiroshima, Nagoya, and Niigata. They carry trunks filled with kimonos, calligraphy brushes and ink, statues of the Buddha and the fox god, and their childhood dolls. They carry letters from their husbands promising a beautiful new life.

On the boat with the brides are Sikhs, Chinese laborers, Russians fleeing revolution, German tourists, a Spanish priest, a king, and an Englishman named Charles who speaks perfect Japanese and has been to America many times before. The women ask him questions about their new home throughout the journey that he happily and patiently answers. Some of the women fall in love with the Japanese deckhands, some fall in love with other passengers, and some fall in love with each other, but all must decide whether to stay true to their new husbands or make a leap of faith in a new direction entirely.

Though they spend hours dreaming, hoping, wishing, and agonizing over what waits for them

MEDIA ADAPTATIONS

- *The Buddha in the Attic* is available as an audiobook, narrated by Samantha Quan and Carrington MacDuffie and published by Random House Audio in 2011. The run time is three hours and fifty-five minutes.

on the other side of the ocean, they have no way of knowing the truth: that the pictures of their husbands are outdated—some by twenty years—and that the stories their husbands told of their success were lies. Some turn their heads and cry for home when they arrive at the dock and see the crowd of shabby men waiting to receive them, but they walk calmly toward their fate: "*This is America*, we would say to ourselves, *there is no need to worry.* And we would be wrong."

First Night

The new husbands and wives consummate their marriages in rented rooms throughout San Francisco, from the lowliest inn to the finest hotel in the city that will allow Japanese patrons. The experience of the brides' first night in America ranges from violent to gentle, but whether or not they found comfort in their new husband's arms during the night, by morning they are bound together.

Whites

Alongside their husbands, the women work as fruit pickers and field hands for white farmers, moving on after the harvest is done. The first word of English they learn is "water," so that they will not faint or die from heatstroke. They live in poor conditions, sleeping in bunks, on piles of hay, on flea-infested mattresses, or on the floor. At first they are curious about the whites. Their husbands advise caution when dealing with them. The husbands are more familiar with their customs, as well as their language, and can speak to them with more ease than their wives. Sometimes the whites surprise them with their kindness, though in many towns the Japanese are not

welcomed at all. The farmers are particularly impressed by the women—their stamina, speed, and docility as workers makes them preferred over all other migrant workers. The women dream at night of home and write letters to their mothers about their new lives.

Some of the couples become successful sharecroppers. Some of them become successful farmers themselves. The farming industry begins to change as Japanese farms have a monopoly in strawberries, spinach, and beans. Sometimes their farms are attacked, their crops destroyed, and their animals driven off, but the women's response is to throw themselves even harder into their work, until they stop being women at all but become efficient, silent farm equipment.

Rather than work on farms, some of the picture brides work as servants in suburban houses. They learn American culture from the white women, who teach them to shake hands, light a stove, operate a faucet, and curl their hair. The white women give them new, Americanized names and confess their secrets to the picture brides in moments of loneliness and vulnerability. When they have the house to themselves, the brides pretend the house is theirs, and revel in the feeling of contentment and peace. Others work as laundresses or in the restaurants, pool halls, brothels, or groceries in J-town—Japantown—where they rarely encounter whites. No matter where they work, the brides dream of one day returning home to their mothers: "But until then we would stay in America just a little bit longer and work for them, for without us, what would they do?"

Babies

The women give birth: sometimes successfully and sometimes not. They give birth alone, without the help of a midwife or their husbands. They give birth with the help of doctors, friends, or strangers. They have many babies or struggle to have even one. Some die in childbirth, while some give birth to children who have died in the womb. Some babies are wanted, and others are not. Some are born healthy, and others are born deformed or too sick to make it through their first night. The women name the ones who live and strap the babies to their backs when they return to the field.

The Children

The children are left lying in the shade as the women work the fields. Some are patient, and others so rambunctious they have to be tied to chairs. They worry about their mothers, refusing to let their mothers carry them after a long day of work. They are a comfort compared with the inattentive and uninterested husbands, who do not help with child care. The mothers act as messengers between their children and their fathers. The children are too afraid to speak to the grim men, and the fathers see the children as strangers. As soon as they are old enough, the children work alongside their parents in the fields. They have vivid imaginations and endless energy, and they trade rumors about the white children they have heard of but never seen. Their parents teach them everything they know, and they have rituals and good luck charms of their own invention as well. They die young from accidents as well as disease.

In J-town they help their parents with simple tasks, for example, stacking crates or separating laundry by color. At school they sit in the back of the classroom, too shy to participate. Though at first they beg their parents not to send them back, they soon become comfortable with the English language. They surpass their parents' understanding of English, speaking it effortlessly and forgetting Japanese in the process. They rename themselves to reflect their American identity. They grow bigger than their parents, eating bacon and eggs for breakfast instead of bean-paste soup. The children find their parents' enduring devotion to Japanese culture embarrassing. They do not attend festivals or go to the temple. Instead, they learn how to survive in the white world—calling ahead to restaurants to ask if they allow Japanese people inside, knowing by heart what days they can swim at the YMCA, walking in groups during the daytime, and standing up for themselves if cornered at night. They fantasize of college, of owning a drum set, of starting a vineyard of their own, of playing piano, of becoming a doctor, or of having a paper route. The parents let them continue to dream even as they sense danger on the horizon.

Traitors

On the second day of World War II, rumors of Japanese men being arrested spread through the community. Families keep their shades drawn over their windows and their children home from school. No one comes for them yet. They gather together at night to trade rumors of towns raided, houses searched, men taken away on trains, a list of names of suspected enemy collaborators. They receive threatening anonymous letters. Their white neighbors, bosses, and customers begin to treat them warily, with fear. Much of the whites' fear is caused by sensationalist newspaper articles about Japanese Americans in Hawaii helping the attack on Pearl Harbor and those stateside celebrating the Japanese victory. They begin to burn their mementos from home, fearful of being seen as sympathetic. More men are arrested all the time.

In January they are made to register their names with the government and hand over anything that could used as a weapon or to signal the enemy: guns, bombs, long knives, flares, and flashlights. They are put under travel restrictions and a curfew. They hear talk of a potential mass removal to camps as their men continue to be arrested without explanation. By spring, some communities have no men left. Evacuation orders are finally posted on telephone poles. The women prepare to leave, buying suitcases and sleeping bags for their children. Their older children return home after quitting their jobs and dropping out of school. They help bring in the last harvest. Their neighbors offer to buy their farm equipment, household items, even their pets. Some of the customers of their laundries, fruit stands, and groceries stay loyal to the end. Then the end comes: "We shuttered our groceries. We swept our floors. We packed our bags. We gathered up our children and from every town in every valley and every city up and down the coast, we left." Looters begin to rob their homes as soon as they are gone, erasing the evidence of the lives they had built.

Last Day

Some leave crying, others laughing, others silent, and others asking endless questions about what their new lives will be like. Some are in their best clothes, and others wear their only clothes. They leave their homes and businesses neat and orderly or else trashed in the last-minute rush to pack. Some are heartbroken, but others are happy to escape their situation. Some leave their homes confused and others clear-eyed: "Futaye, who had the best vocabulary of us all, left speechless." Some feel as if they are in a dream and want to wake up, others as if they are being punished for a sin committed in a previous life. Men, women, and children of all classes and all walks of life leave their lives behind, taking only what they can carry, while onlookers on the sidewalks watch the exodus of the Japanese.

A Disappearance

Those left behind wonder after their vanished Japanese neighbors. Their houses are empty, lawns overgrown, mailboxes overflowing, cars abandoned in their driveways. Their businesses have reopened under new management. Harada Grocery is empty, but everyone remembers fondly how Mr. Harada would rush from behind the counter in his green apron. They mayor claims the Japanese are safe, but he cannot say where they were taken. The citizens do not understand what place could be safer than their own town. They worry about the missing families. Some cannot sleep. The faded notices of evacuation still hang from the telephone poles. Those left behind admit they never took notice. More than anyone, the children suffer. They misbehave, fearful and anxious over the fate of their classmates and friends. They worry that the missing children are lost or dead.

Some are glad the Japanese are gone. They rest easier knowing the threat to their safety has been neutralized. But most cannot imagine the Japanese people they knew as secret spies or enemy sympathizers. The pets they left behind are adopted. Their gardens grow wild. The notices of evacuation are one day gone, and it is as if the Japanese were never there. A handful of Japanese people are left behind in hospitals, prisons, and asylums. Japanese art and home goods begin to appear in pawnshops and then in people's homes.

They wait for their return for weeks, in vain. They blame themselves for their complacency in their disappearance. Letters arrive from the Japanese to their friends with stories of their journey to the camps. The towns demand answers from the government. The mayor urges patience but gives no definite information. Summer comes, and the war continues. Families stay inside, gas is rationed, victory gardens are planted, and rubber is collected. New faces move into the abandoned houses, causing their neighbors to miss the Japanese. Rumors spread of the trains, packed with Japanese people of all ages, headed into the desert. Autumn comes, and they have not returned. By winter their names are beginning to fade from memory, though they appear sometimes, vividly, in dreams: "All we know is that the Japanese are out there somewhere, in one place or another, and we shall probably not meet them again in this world."

CHARACTERS

Charles

Charles is an Englishman on the same boat as the picture brides. He speaks Japanese, has a Japanese wife, and teaches foreign languages at the university in Osaka. He has been to America many times and answers the brides' questions about the country's customs and people with patience and humor.

Children

The children of the picture brides are Japanese Americans, born in the United States. In school they are shy at first but soon have a firm command of the English language. They quickly surpass their parents in their knowledge of American culture, but they forget Japanese culture as a result. They are embarrassed of their parents' devotion to the ways of their home country and refuse to attend Japanese festivals with their families. They move away to attend universities or find work but return when the Japanese are ordered to evacuate their homes in order to help their families prepare.

Chizuko

Chizuko is a picture bride who runs the kitchen at the Kearney Ranch. When Japanese men begin to disappear after the attack on Pearl Harbor, she packs a suitcase for her husband in case he is taken. Inside are a variety of items he may need—a change of clothes, a bar of chocolate, soap, a toothbrush, a shaving kit—and she leaves it by the front door. She worries constantly that she has left something out of the suitcase that will make all of the difference. Her husband is taken in the middle of the night, without warning. He forgets the suitcase. When Chizuko realizes he is gone, she opens the suitcase and eats the chocolate bar she packed inside.

Chizuko's Husband

Chizuko's husband is arrested and taken away without explanation. He forgets to take the suitcase his wife packed him.

Futaye

Futaye has the biggest vocabulary of the picture brides, but when it is time to leave her home for the trains, she is left speechless.

Dr. Giordano

Dr. Giordano is a successful thoracic surgeon in Alameda, California. He has Japanese groundskeepers and maids.

Lucia Giordano

Lucia is Dr. Giordano's elderly mother, who follows the Japanese maids from room to room. She is very lonely, extremely talkative, and adored by the maids. Long after her death, they cherish the memory of her ecstatic descriptions of Italy as if they had been there themselves.

Rose Giordano
Rose is Dr. Giordano's wife, a kind woman with wavy brown hair who insists the maids call her by her first name.

Mr. Harada
Mr. Harada is the owner of Harada Grocery. He leaves a sign behind in the empty window of his store: "*God be with you until we meet again.*" Those who pass remember how Mr. Harada would come rushing from behind the counter in a faded green apron to offer his customers a taste of fresh strawberry, stalk of asparagus, or sprig of mint.

Haruko
Haruko is a picture bride who left behind a tiny brass statue of the laughing Buddha in the corner of the attic of her house when she left for the internment camp, where it remains to this day.

Husbands
The husbands are initially a disappointment to the picture brides. They are neither as attractive nor as wealthy as the brides were led to believe. They work as laborers on farms, groundskeepers for big houses in the suburbs, or in restaurants, laundries, and groceries in J-town. They help their wives understand American culture and teach them the English language. Some are inattentive, and others are caring. They have children, raise families, and carve out their own spaces in the world as they become more successful. After the attack on Pearl Harbor, they are arrested at all hours of the day and night and taken away from their families without explanation. Those still walking free when the evacuation orders are posted must leave their homes and businesses behind to board trains for the internment camps along with their wives and children.

Mayor
The mayor answers to the people of his town after the Japanese have left. He emphasizes that the Japanese are safe but that he cannot reveal their location. He reassures the people that the Japanese are in good spirits and that their resettlement is going as planned. He reminds them that they are a country at war and sacrifices have to be made.

Picture Brides
The picture brides are a large group of women from Japan who travel by boat to the United States to meet their husbands. They are put to work in fields as laborers, in suburban homes as maids, and in J-town as laundresses, cooks, waitresses, and more. They have children, grow more established as a community, and, in some cases, prosper. They make friends with each other and those outside their culture. When World War II breaks out, they are seen as potential spies for the enemy. They burn their mementos from home so that they are not seen as traitors. Their husbands are arrested without cause or explanation. They are ordered to evacuate their homes and leave everything they have worked for behind.

Whites
The whites interact with the Japanese as bosses, neighbors, customers, friends, and sometimes lovers. Some whites are prejudiced against the Japanese and fear for their safety around them. Japanese children attend school alongside white children and make easy friendships. When the Japanese disappear from towns all across the West Coast, the whites in their community are left wondering where they went, if they are safe, and how much they themselves are to blame for the Japanese people's absence.

Yoshiko
Yoshiko is a picture bride who was raised in a luxurious estate in Kobe by wet nurses. She has never worked in her life and dies of heatstroke in her sleep after her first day of weeding.

THEMES

Domesticity
The picture brides arrive in the United States prepared for lives as obedient housewives, taught by their mothers all the right manners of a respectable married woman: how to walk with small steps; speak in girlish, high voices; arrange flowers; and compose haiku. They expect to live in large American houses and have successful, attentive husbands who will handle the finances while they handle the upkeep of the home. Most of all, they expect to be comfortable and safe in the United States. But like most American Dreams, the dreams of the picture brides are too good to be true.

TOPICS FOR FURTHER STUDY

- Read Matt Faulkner's young-adult graphic novel *Gaijin: American Prisoner of War* (2014). What similarities can you find between Gaijin's life and the lives of the picture brides in *The Buddha in the Attic* in the days leading up to their internment? What are the major differences between Gaijin and the picture brides? Organize your thoughts into an essay.

- Rewrite the text of Executive Order 9066 in your own words. What is stated explicitly in the document? What is left unsaid? Research online to discover why the government believed such an order was necessary. Write an essay in answer to this question to turn in along with your interpretation of the order. Be sure to cite any sources you use.

- Create a time line of Japanese American internment, beginning with the attack on Pearl Harbor. You should include at least ten important events, with dates, locations, and a short description of the event itself and its repercussions. Be sure to cite your sources. Free infographics are available at easel.ly.

- Write a scene or short story in which you use the first-person-plural point of view. Along with your creative writing sample, include a paragraph in which you describe the unique challenges this style of writing poses as well as any benefits you found to using it for your story or scene.

Domesticity becomes a distant, unreachable goal in the fields, the sheds where they sleep on the dirt, and the crowded bunks of J-town. The brides work in the suburban homes as maids, not mistresses, and feel the peace of ownership only when they are all completely alone in the house. Their husbands are rarely the men they were led to believe they would find waiting across the ocean, and there is little use for elegant poems or soft, meaningless speech in the harsh conditions they endure, without a place to call their own.

After years in the United States, some women work beside their children in the fields, but others have managed through sheer luck, hard work, or business savvy to rise in the world enough to own their homes. They start in dusty huts as sharecroppers, but they soon own houses with porches, pets, cars, and gardens. They have a place to raise their Americanized children, money for new clothes and groceries, and shrines to their ancestors. They have white neighbors, some of whom welcome them as friends and others who find their success in the country threatening. It is their children's turn to dream, this time of becoming doctors, dancers, musicians, engineers, and entrepreneurs.

However, these dreams are, like their mothers' dreams before them, dashed in an instant. The paranoid atmosphere of World War II brings about the demise of a hundred thousand Japanese American households. The domesticity the brides dreamed of, lost, and found again is stripped away in the night. They are ordered to give up their belongings, from the largest estate to the smallest statue of Buddha, in order to be safely locked away for the remainder of the war.

Immigrant Life

The Buddha in the Attic portrays immigrant life as a shared but varied experience. On the boat, the picture brides come from all classes but are united by their anticipation of a new life in the United States. None of the women have reason to suspect that their husbands were not honest in their application for a bride, and none could guess the kind of life waiting for them when they arrive. The first disappointment of their lives as immigrants is seeing their husbands for the first time, gathered on the dock in their tattered coats. The picture brides disperse then, to begin lives so drastically different from one another as to be unrecognizably from the same group. The field workers are migrant, destitute laborers; the maids and groundskeepers have sleeping quarters of their own but are at the mercy of their bosses' whims; while those in J-town rarely interact with whites but live in overcrowded conditions and work exceptionally long hours. All struggle to learn English as well as American customs, which to them are nonsensical to the extreme: for example, the opposite of white in the United

The women come from Japan, leaving everything familiar behind, to husbands in America of whom they know nothing (© Captblack76 | Shutterstock.com)

States is black instead of red, as they were taught in Japan. As immigrants, they are subject to mistreatment, harassment, and prejudice. Their children find their parents' devotion to Japanese culture embarrassing. They are, from the moment they step off the boat, at war. This personal war is waged for their dignity and peace of mind. They fight hard, with nothing to lose after coming to the United States on false promises. Those who succeed make a place for themselves in their new country and rise from the fields to the farmhouse, from maid to homeowner, or from waiter to businessman. Those who fail to maintain their pride in the face of the harsh trials of immigrant life fall to their vices: gambling and drinking, hiding from their families in pool halls. Yet, in the end, all meet the same fate as they are sent en masse to the desert in a heinous violation of their civil rights. An immigrant's life is lived at the mercy of the new home. Just when they found themselves comfortable, the Japanese immigrants were betrayed.

STYLE

First Person Plural

Otsuka utilizes the first-person-plural point of view in order to capture the collective experience of Japanese American women in *The Buddha in the Attic*. The first-person-plural point of view is narration that uses "we" as a narrator instead of the much more common "I" narrator of the first-person point of view. First person plural is rarely used as a point of view, but Otsuka employs it to great effect, combining the myriad voices of a large and diverse group of immigrants into one epic narrative of their journey across the Pacific to begin their new lives in the United States and the various and wildly unpredictable ways in which they become part of the American landscape. The third-person-plural narrative is lifted briefly as they leave for the internment camps in the chapter "Last Day," as the women are named one by one as they make their exits from the novel. The narration returns to first person plural in the novel's final chapter, but the "we" becomes their neighbors, friends, and community members who are left behind wondering at the disappearance of the Japanese.

Minimalism

Minimalism is a style of art, music, and literature characterized by efficiency of composition. For example, a minimalist text would feature simple, short sentences with few descriptive adjectives and adverbs. Otsuka's minimalism in *The Buddha in the Attic* is enhanced by her use of the third person plural. Instead of hearing the details of an individual character's life in America—how they arrived, whether or not they were successful, and how they reacted to Executive Order 9066—the reader is given the briefest glimpse of their situation in only a sentence or two before the narration moves on. Minimalism is an important traditional aspect of Japanese culture, making Otsuka's use of it as a literary style especially poignant in her portrayal of the life of picture brides.

HISTORICAL CONTEXT

Picture Brides

Between 1908 and 1924, over twenty thousand women emigrated from Japan to the United States as picture brides. These brides—known as *shashin hanayome* in Japan—were women whose families had arranged their marriages to men living abroad through a go-between, or matchmaker, who facilitated the exchange of photographs and information about the families of the two prospective spouses. In the early 1900s, Japanese men living in California and other West Coast states were forbidden to marry outside their race owing to miscegenation laws. In addition, they could not freely travel between the United States and Japan owing to the Gentleman's Agreement of 1908, which restricted immigration in an attempt to ease tension between the two countries. Instead, the men sent word home of their interest in a bride, often exaggerating their success in America and providing photographs that rarely reflected reality. When a match was made, the wedding ceremony took place in Japan without the groom present, before the bride boarded a boat bound for the United States and a new life with her husband.

The brides themselves were, as illustrated by Otsuka in *The Buddha in the Attic*, often unpleasantly surprised to find their circumstances far more challenging than they were led to believe and their husbands frequently a decade older than the photograph they had been given. Yet they persevered through intensive labor, unimaginable culture shock, and hostile treatment, to establish homes, families, careers, and communities. Today, it is believed that most Japanese Americans have a picture bride ancestor.

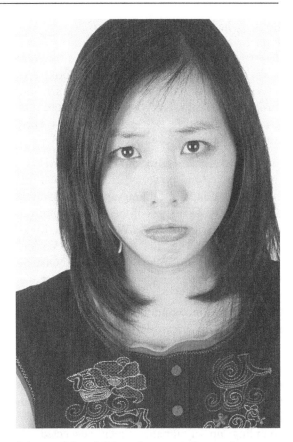

Many of the children face prejudice and are ashamed of their immigrant parents (© qingqing / *Shutterstock.com*)

Executive Order 9066

Executive Order 9066 ordered the removal of all persons of Japanese descent from the West Coast of the United States to internment camps during World War II. President Franklin D. Roosevelt signed the order on February 19, 1942, as a protective measure against domestic sabotage following the December 7, 1941, Japanese attack on Pearl Harbor. Though the order was nominally attributed to military necessity, the true motivation behind the internment was a rash of xenophobic and racist sentiment toward those of Japanese ancestry following the strike on Pearl Harbor. As a result, over 110,000 innocent Japanese immigrants and Japanese Americans were forced to leave their homes, taking only what they could carry, to be relocated into desert camps until the end of the war.

Despite the fact that the large majority of those interned were citizens of the United States who had not been officially accused of or tried for a specific crime, the Supreme Court upheld the order in *Korematsu v. United States* in 1944. It would later be revealed that evidence was withheld by the government that would have called into doubt the severity of the danger the Japanese Americans allegedly posed to American society. In 1988, President Ronald Regan signed the Civil Liberties Act, officially apologizing to those interned during World War II and authorizing restitution payments to the survivors. The internment of loyal Japanese American citizens and immigrants without trial remains a dark mark in the history of the United States and a reminder of the dangers of racism and hatred inspired by the insecurities and fears of wartime.

CRITICAL OVERVIEW

The Buddha in the Attic won the PEN/Faulkner Award, the Langum Prize for American Historical Fiction, the Prix Femina Étranger, and Best

Book of the Year from the *Boston Globe* and *San Francisco Chronicle*. Both *Vogue* and *Library Journal* named it a Top Ten Book, and the *New York Times* selected it as a Notable Book. The novel was a National Book Award Finalist, and a *New York Times*, *Los Angeles Times*, and *San Francisco Chronicle* best seller and has been translated into over twenty-two languages.

Critics immediately embraced the novel for the poignancy and power of its depiction of the experience of Japanese immigrants to the United States and the unjustness of their forced removal to internment camps during World War II. Meganne Fabrega writes in "A Chorus of Voices, Mostly Unheard," for the *Star Tribune*: "Otsuka masterfully creates a chorus of unforgettable voices that echo throughout the chambers of this slim but commanding novel, speaking of a time that no American should ever forget."

In her review for *SF Gate*, Jane Ciabattari writes with specific admiration for the scenes of slow-building paranoia and fear following the attack on Pearl Harbor: "With suspense and heart-wrenching detail, Otsuka describes the rounding up of Japanese men suspected of being traitors, and the ways in which communities turned against the Japanese."

Elizabeth Day writes in her review of the novel for the *Guardian* in praise of the novel's originality in its use of the first-person-plural point of view: "Although there are no dominant characters, Otsuka's brilliance is that she is able to make us care about the crowd precisely because we can glimpse individual stories through the delicate layering of collective experience."

Many critics praised the minimalist style of the novel, especially the paradoxically powerful force of Otsuka's simple sentences. B. J. Fischer writes in his review of the novel for *ARDOR* that *The Buddha in the Attic* "is a compelling and impactful book that tells a horrifying story in an understated way, the perfect formula for delivering an emotional punch to readers."

For her review in the *Chicago Tribune*, Elizabeth Taylor summarizes the hypnotic effect of the novel on its readers: "Read the book in a single sitting, and this chorus of narrators speaks in a poetry that is both spare and passionate, sure to haunt even the most coldhearted among us."

FROM A SINGLE STARTING POINT—THE BOAT— THE WOMEN EMBARK ON INNUMERABLE PATHS, UNTIL THE 'WE' OF THE NARRATION COVERS A GROUP OF WOMEN SO DIVERSE THAT THE ONLY COMMON FACTOR IS THEIR HERITAGE. YET IT IS THAT HERITAGE ALONE THAT SPELLS THE END OF THEIR DREAMS."

CRITICISM

Amy L. Miller

Miller is a graduate of the University of Cincinnati, and she currently resides in New Orleans, Louisiana. In the following essay, she studies the effectiveness of the first-person-plural point of view in Otsuka's The Buddha in the Attic.

Using the first-person-plural point of view, Otsuka's *The Buddha in the Attic* expresses the collective experience of Japanese picture brides immigrating to the United States. This rare stylistic choice plays on the mismatch between Japanese and American culture. The Japanese women, raised to honor their ancestors, obey their family, and remain respectable in the eyes of their community, are thrust into a society in which they are unknown, unaccounted for, and often invisible. The steps they take to flourish in the United States are their steps alone. Their families are simply too far away for their judgment to be felt. If their husbands are disagreeable, the picture brides are free to leave them without fear of the scorn of their village. They are mobile, untied to any specific place or job. They can become wealthy in America, and some do, while some remain for decades in the fields. From a single starting point—the boat—the women embark on innumerable paths, until the "we" of the narration covers a group of women so diverse that the only common factor is their heritage. Yet it is that heritage alone that spells the end of their dreams. They are gathered once more into a group, but this time the plural narration cannot contain them in all their diversity. Their names ring out as they walk away from their lives and begin a new journey into the unknown.

WHAT DO I READ NEXT?

- In Otsuka's *When the Emperor Was Divine* (2002), a family's internment during World War II is told with startling force and melancholy beauty. Not long after her husband is arrested and taken away without explanation, a woman sees notices posted in her neighborhood explaining that Japanese Americans must prepare to leave their homes for relocation. She, along with her daughter and son, spends three years in an internment camp before the family is released and reunited, only to find her home stripped of all valuables when she returns. The rebuilding process begins, but nothing can ever be the same.

- Carlos Bulosan's *America Is in the Heart: A Personal History* (1943) is the touchstone text of the Filipino experience in the United States, describing Bulosan's childhood in and journey from the Philippines and his life as a laborer in the harsh conditions of the American West.

- *Nisei Daughter*, by Monica Sone (1953), recounts Sone's childhood in Seattle and the growing anti-Japanese sentiment following the attack on Pearl Harbor that culminated in her family's imprisonment in an internment camp.

- Kevin C. Pyle's young-adult graphic novel *Take What You Can Carry* (2012) follows the lives of two teenagers: Kyle, a Chicago delinquent roaming the city streets in the late 1970s, and Ken, a Japanese American incarcerated along with his family in the Manzanar internment camp in the 1940s. Though they are separated by time and space, the two boys' stories intersect as they learn to harness their anger and feelings of helplessness into compassion and emotional maturity.

- Jeanne Wakatsuke Houston's *Farewell to Manzanar* (1983) is the true story of Jeanne's childhood spent inside a Japanese internment camp. After being relocated with her family at the age of seven to the Manzanar internment camp, Jeanne recounts the bizarre juxtapositions of her wartime imprisonment, including barbed wire fences, armed guards, school dances, and cheer squad.

- *A Tale for the Time Being*, by Ruth Ozeki (2013), tells the story of a Japanese girl named Nao who records the history of her grandmother's life as a Buddhist nun in a diary in order to escape the daily torture of her classmates' bullying. Across the ocean, an American novelist named Ruth finds a Hello Kitty lunchbox full of Nao's belongings washed up on the shore following the 2011 tsunami and becomes fascinated by the life and ultimate fate of the strange girl.

- In John Okada's *No-No Boy* (1956), considered the first Japanese American novel, Ichiro Yamada, whose family was imprisoned in an internment camp during World War II, answers no twice on a required government form: once to say he will not enlist in the military and once to say he does not swear loyalty to the United States. His choice leads to devastating personal and social consequences, but he will not forgive or forget the government's crime against him so easily.

- Joy Kogawa's *Obasan* (1981) was the first published novel to address the unjust internment of Japanese Canadians during World War II, based on the Kogawas' experiences in an internment camp in Slocan, British Columbia.

The women on the boat believe that they are prepared for marriage:

> Most of us on the boat were accomplished, and were sure we would make good wives. We knew how to cook and sew. We knew how to serve tea and arrange flowers and sit quietly.

The traditional skills of a Japanese housewife that the women have mastered will prove

---

useless, as they will be expected from their first day in America to work long hours in difficult conditions. On the boat, they compare photographs of their husbands: "They were handsome young men with dark eyes and full heads of hair and skin that was smooth and unblemished. Their chins were strong. Their posture, good. Their noses were straight and high." The photographs, too, prove false. Their husbands are much older than their photographs, impoverished, and often miserable. But there is no going back to Japan for the picture brides, who must not only learn a new language, new culture, and new set of skills but do so alongside a strange man with whom their fate is tied. The women, so similar on the boat in their hopes and fears, begin their individualization immediately. Though they all looked forward to meeting the man in their precious photograph, some picture brides find their husbands agreeable, while others do not. Some take advantage of their new freedom to flee their marriage, while others remain unhappily wedded all their lives.

They work for years in thankless jobs such as weeding, picking crops, washing clothes, and cleaning houses. Then they begin to climb from their initial posts into positions of power, represented in an accumulation of material goods. The apex of their American success is reached when their children—schooled in the English language and in American culture—begin to express great dreams of their own, unwittingly mirroring the brides' hopes for a bright future as they whispered together at night on the boat. This is the last bright moment of the novel, from which point their lives unravel. Fischer writes:

> Otsuka employs her unsparing detail on the agonizing and slow descent of the story—a tragedy made more poignant by the fact that the reader knows the end of the story but the victims don't.

No one of Japanese descent on the West Coast will be spared the internment camps, no matter how young or old, rich or poor. The brides will be reunited, but not in celebration of their achievements.

Fabrega writes: "For every step forward there are two steps back for these women, who did their best to build a life and a home in a country that was largely unsympathetic to their isolation." The plural narrative voice serves to separate the "we" of the picture brides from the "they" of their husbands, their children, and the whites. However, as the "we" becomes increasingly separated—first

divided up among their husbands, then taken to fields, suburban homes, and J-town, then further removed as they prosper or fail—the novel's motif of isolation begins to strengthen. The women are invisible to their bosses, who seem to see straight through them. Their inner turmoil goes unnoticed by their distracted, disinterested husbands. Their children, a comfort to them when young, grow up to be Americans and dissociate themselves from their mothers' Japanese ways. Once war is declared, curfews and travel restrictions are passed, and husbands are mysteriously arrested, reinforcing the women's isolation through paranoia. The thick atmosphere of fear becomes such a burden that the brides are relieved when the evacuation order is at last posted, as the tension is finally dispelled into a reality for which they can distract themselves from their isolation by making preparations.

Throughout the novel, the plural narration pauses to pluck an individual from the crowd, but never for more than a brief sketch of their lives or a few short sentences. Alida Becker writes in "Coming to America, Lured by a Photograph" for the *New York Times*: "While it appears to hold the characters at a formal distance, [the novel's] reticence infuses their stories with powerful emotion." For example, the story of Chizuko, the bride who is terrified of leaving an item out of the suitcase she packed for her husband to take if he is arrested, emphasizes the lack of control the women have over their own lives toward the novel's end. Chizuko attempts to plan for the arrest as if her husband were going on a business trip, but the arrests are at random and cannot be predicted. After he has been taken, leaving the briefcase behind, she is shown eating the chocolate bar she packed inside in a gesture of helpless submission to the chaos of her life: she has given up.

These brief glimpses into the individual brides' lives prepare the reader for the parade of names and faces that pass the day of the evacuation. Fischer writes:

> The variety and richness of the detail allow us to truly understand that what was done to the Japanese was done not ... to a class of people but to a large number of diverse individuals.

The Japanese walk down the street in every imaginable emotional state, from frantic to devastated to content. They wear furs or rags, they speak perfect English or strict Japanese, and they are surrounded by family members or utterly alone. The women on the boat have multiplied and brought forth a new generation. "We" can no longer describe the group, who become instead the intelligent Futaye, the forgetful Haruko, and a thousand others with individual stories to tell. But at this moment of clarity, in which each face is recognized as different and special to the reader, the government has declared them all the same. They are potential traitors, spies, and enemies stationed in the midst of the whites. Though they have done no harm in the novel, they are guilty of being Japanese. Their struggles as Americans are dismissed. Their American children are sentenced to serve with them. They are grouped together as a unit and sent away until the end of the war.

The voice that replaces the brides is that of the whites, who are left scratching their heads. Portrayed as bighearted but complacent, this new "we" was too busy in their own world to read the signs posted on telephone poles throughout town: "Many of us admit that although we passed by the notices every day on our way into town, it never occurred to us to stop and read one. 'They weren't for us,' we say." This attitude leads them, now that the Japanese are gone, to spring to action. Suddenly they want answers from the mayor as to where their fellow citizens were taken, but the mayor pleads wartime secrecy, and soon their anger is forgotten as war efforts drive them to take special measures themselves. Ciabattari writes: "*The Buddha in the Attic* is an understated masterpiece about our treatment of the 'other,' the distillation of a national tragedy that unfolds with great emotional power." Most heartbreaking is the reaction of the schoolchildren to the disappearance of their classmates, proof that racism and xenophobia are not innate traits but learned. The children left behind are frightened, and the adults should be too. In a country where an entire ethnicity can be quietly swept aside, there is little hope for the safety of the citizens, no matter their heritage.

The Buddha in the Attic uses the first-person-plural point of view to illustrate the many paths that led from a boat docking in San Francisco to a train leaving for the desert. With her light touch, Otsuka fills the years between the brides' arrival in the United States and departure for the internment camps with a thousand narratives of failure and success, sadness and joy, until the voices blend together to create the image of the picture bride: an isolated and unsung American heroine.

After the attack on Pearl Harbor, everyone worries as many Japanese American men are taken away for questioning (©elwynn | Shutterstock.com)

Source: Amy L. Miller, Critical Essay on *The Buddha in the Attic*, in *Novels for Students*, Gale, Cengage Learning, 2017.

Mako Yoshikawa

In the following review, Yoshikawa praises the way Otsuka tells a familiar story in a surprising way.

In Julie Otsuka's compelling new novel, *The Buddha in the Attic*, a group of Japanese picture brides—women who have been married to men they know only through photos—voyage across the ocean; meet and sleep with their Japanese immigrant husbands for the first time; work as field hands, cooks, maids, or prostitutes; struggle with English; try to understand the ways of white Americans; and give birth and raise children who grow up ashamed of their mothers' thick accents. After Pearl Harbor, the women endure the suspicion of their white neighbors and employers; eventually they are rounded up and shipped off to internment camps. Their story is dramatic and moving. It is also familiar, known to us from history books although not from many novels or films—yet the way that Otsuka tells it is anything but.

The Buddha in the Attic employs a collective narrator, and there's no protagonist or even identifiable characters; while names such as Urako and Chiyoko abound, and lines of dialogue from individual women are scattered in italics throughout the book, because we hear only one detail about their lives they are essentially uncredited. Their identities are lost among all the others in the narrative. In this sense, the novel is like "The Things They Carried," the iconic Tim O'Brien story about a platoon of soldiers in Vietnam. But with "we" substituted for "they," Otsuka's characters never emerge as distinct entities out of the pack, and her narrative is stretched to the length of a novel, albeit a slim one. Moreover, Otsuka's storyline has no sustained conflict to give it structure. These elements make her work daring as well as formally unique. That she can sustain our interest for 131 pages without the storytelling pillars of character and overarching conflict—and there's no question that she can—testifies to the power of her prose, which is spare, precise, and often pitch perfect. Otsuka's first novel, *When the Emperor Was Divine* (2003), was justly celebrated for its writing; this one tops it.

The Buddha in the Attic begins deceptively simply: "On the boat we were mostly virgins. We had long black hair and flat wide feet and we were not very tall." The second line suggests that the group is uniform, but the teasing phrase "mostly virgins" cues us that these women resist easy categorization, and in the lines that follow, the "we" becomes increasingly diverse. "Some of us had eaten nothing but rice gruel as young girls and had slightly bowed legs, and some of us were only fourteen years old and were still young girls ourselves," Otsuka writes. "Some of us came from the city, and wore stylish dry clothes, but many more of us came from the country and on the boat we wore the same old kimonos we'd been wearing for years." The diversity is regional as well as economic and generational.

At the end of the first paragraph there's a turn: "Perhaps we had lost a brother or father to the sea, or a fiance, or perhaps someone we loved had jumped into the water one unhappy morning and simply swum away, and now it was time

for us, too, to move on." The line is noteworthy, and not only because it speaks to the losses that have already shadowed these women's lives. The word "too" in the last phrase, which equates the women's journey to America with a death or suicide at sea, hints at how ghostly and insubstantial these characters are, foreshadowing how their voices will blur together in the narrative as well as how they will eventually vanish into the camps. After all, even though we do hear the words of individual women here and there, their full stories remain untold. Otsuka achieves a rare and paradoxical double feat: she gives these oppressed and silenced women voice and at the same time illuminates how their voices have been lost to history.

And these are voices we want to keep. Snappy, down to earth, wry, and often very funny, they provide a sharp and effective contrast to the poetic, elegiac narration. They demonstrate how little historical and cultural differences matter: we feel as if we know these women. Here's a picture bride from a region without many eligible men speaking of the husband she has yet to meet: "I took one look at his photograph and told the matchmaker, 'He'll do.'" Another, who lost one husband to flu and a second to a younger woman, says of her third: "He's healthy, he doesn't drink, he doesn't gamble, that's all I needed to know." Discussing how laboring in the fields has made her forego make-up, one woman complains, "Whenever I powder my nose it just looks like frost on a mountain," and we hear the following about Tommy Takayama's mother, who is known as a whore: "She has six different children by five different men. And two of them are twins."

Otsuka renders these vivid characters' disappearance into the camps beautifully. "Iyo left with an alarm clock ringing from somewhere deep inside her suitcase but did not stop to turn it off. Kimiko left her purse behind on the kitchen table but would not remember until it was too late. Haruko left a tiny laughing brass Buddha up high, in a corner of the attic, where he is still laughing to this day." The presence of these objects stands in stark and poignant contrast to the absence of their owners.

Yet it is the absence of their voices that we feel most acutely. So captivating are they that when they are gone and a new chorus, this one from the white community they left behind, takes up their story, we miss them, and that's

Otsuka's point. By the end of the novel, the Japanese are ghostly figures who are spoken of rarely, with wistfulness or something like hope. "[W]ord from the other side of the mountains continues to reach us from time to time," the second collective narrator tells us; "entire cities of Japanese have sprung up in the deserts of Nevada and Utah, Japanese in Idaho have been put to work picking beets in the fields, and in Wyoming a group of Japanese children were seen emerging, shivering and hungry, from a forest at dusk." But finally, the white community must acknowledge that this is only hearsay: "All we know is that the Japanese are out there somewhere, in one place or another, and we shall probably not meet them again in this world." The Japanese women's voices—each of them so precious and alive—are gone, and all that we who are left behind can do is mourn.

Source: Mako Yoshikawa, "The Things They Left Behind," in *Women's Review of Books*, Vol. 29, No. 1, January–February 2012, p. 18.

Renee H. Shea

In the following excerpt, Shea calls the novel's ending "risky."

. . . In both of her novels, Otsuka excavates and explores her personal Japanese heritage within a larger historical context. Her family has only distant relatives in Japan, in the mountains outside of Tokyo, and they have little contact even today. The summer after her freshman year at Yale, she went to Japan after studying the language in intensive workshops. She has not been back. Acknowledging that she and her mother experienced the "usual mother-daughter conflicts," she describes her first book as a way of trying to figure out what happened to her mother during the war and how that experience formed her: "There was so much silence in my family about what happened during World War II, and a lot of repressed anger and sadness, too, so writing the novel helped me to understand what that silence was all about." Researching and writing the second novel has, she says, given her a deeper understanding of the reticence and reluctance to stand out that is a hallmark of Japanese culture, an understanding that has brought her and her father, who still lives in California, closer. (Her mother suffers from Alzheimer's disease.)

A fascination with the related notion of fate—of accepting the cards you've been dealt and making the best of it—is part of what drew Otsuka to the picture brides. In her new, slim novel, Otsuka focuses each chapter on the women's common experience in the "invisible world," as she describes their existence in America. She says that she floundered for about a year after *When the Emperor Was Divine* came out, knowing she wanted to write about the picture brides, but remaining uncertain of the form. She knew the book would start on a boat, and she eventually focused each chapter on the picture brides' shared experiences and the public history that enfolds the lives of the issei, or first generation Japanese immigrants.

Initially she didn't think her second novel would extend to World War II and the camps, but, she says, the process took her there again: "It seemed there was a story left over, unfinished business from the first book—the disappearance. I always wondered what the white townspeople thought after their neighbors were gone. When I was traveling and talking about the first book, I often met people who were alive during World War II on the West Coast, and someone would say, 'There was a Japanese girl who sat next to me in class, and then she was gone.' What did the parents or teachers of the white children tell them? How did people process the disappearance of their neighbors?" Otsuka remembers her mother saying that when she returned to Berkeley from the camp, no one from her school asked where she'd been for three and a half years.

Otsuka wrote the last chapter long before the novel was finished, but continued to believe it would be "the perfect ending, a kind of twist." It's a different choral voice—that of the white townspeople who wonder where the Japanese have gone. The mayor tells them, "The Japanese are in a safe place," and assures them that they "have left us willingly . . . without rancor; per the President's request." Ultimately, their absence is forgotten: "With each passing day the notices on the telephone poles grow increasingly faint. And then, one morning, there is not a single notice to be found, and for a moment the town feels oddly naked, and it is almost as if the Japanese were never here at all."

It's a risky ending, but it's a risk that in some ways Otsuka has taken before. The ending of *When the Emperor Was Divine* was a "twist" also, as the father of the family indicts with bitter sarcasm the racism and xenophobia that destroyed so many lives. Otsuka says that her agent and editor warned her that if the book would be criticized, it would be for the final chapter, and they were right. Kakutani, for one, called this final chapter a "shrill diatribe" that lacked the "subtle, emotional power" of the rest of the novel. But even now, nine years later, Otsuka stands firm: It is the right ending.

The Buddha in the Attic ends with a similar, though perhaps more understated indictment of that same chapter of American history. Filled with speculations, haunting images of Japanese culture, litanies of names of places and people, and vague recollections, the final chapter offers no forgiveness for those whose silence made them complicit: "And after a while we notice ourselves speaking of [the Japanese] more and more in the past tense. Some days we forget they were ever with us, although late at night they often surface, unexpectedly, in our dreams." Otsuka says she believes that "nobody really wanted to know" what happened, but in her first novel and now in *The Buddha in the Attic*, she insists on the urgency of that knowing, however belatedly.

So while most are thinking of Japan in terms of the recent earthquake, tsunami, and nuclear meltdown, perhaps listening admiringly to reports that there was no looting, no lamenting of the unfairness of the triple disaster, but instead a communal resolve to accept the situation and move forward, Otsuka offers a parallel narrative from another time that is both a tribute to this same community and a reminder of where prejudice and fear can lead. She won't let us forget this chapter in the history books, this episode of America's polyglot culture, this Buddha in the attic.

Source: Renee H. Shea, "The Urgency of Knowing: In Her Second Novel, Julie Otsuka Returns to the Chapter in Japanese American History That Captured the Attention of So Many Fans of Her Debut: The Relocation Camps of World War II," in *Poets & Writers*, Vol. 39, No. 5, September–October 2011.

Patrick Ryan and Julie Otsuka

In the following interview, Otsuka talks about her choice of a first-person plural narrative in The Buddha in the Attic.

PR: Would you say that The Buddha in the Attic *has no central main character, or that it has many central main characters?*

JO: I'd say it has one central main character, which is everyone: the collective "we." No one "I" is more important than any other.

What do you think was the benefit of writing in the "we" voice, the first-person plural, as you got into the world of these mail-order brides? It's a stylistic technique novelists rarely employ.

Using the "we" voice allowed me to tell a much larger story than I would have been able to tell otherwise. At first I tried telling the story from the point of view of a single picture bride, but this approach felt too narrow and confining. In my research, I had run across so many fascinating stories, and I wanted to tell them all. Using the "we" voice allowed me to weave them all in. It's a very capacious and infinitely expandable voice. Each sentence gives you a brief window into somebody's life—it's like catching a glimpse of someone's house from a train—and then we move on.

Also, since Japan is a very group-oriented culture (my father, who immigrated from Japan after World War II, once said to me, "Japan is the opposite of America"—meaning, I think, that here in America, the emphasis is on the individual), it made sense to speak of the picture brides as a collective entity.

Given that you resist settling into the head of any one of these women for very long, did you find that one collective personality emerged as you were writing?

At the beginning of the novel, when the women arrive in America, they conform more to the "typical" Japanese personality—quiet, stoic, uncomplaining, obedient, respectful of authority (i.e. the perfect wife or maid). But the longer they stay in America, the more they are able to individuate. And while many of them remained "typically" Japanese till the end of their lives, there were variations on the typical, as well as a few outliers—women who were loud and outspoken, women who left their husbands shortly after arriving in America, women who kept secret bank accounts, women who defied their parents' wishes by coming to America, etc.

An image that stays in my mind: Japanese women smashing their valuable, much cherished tea sets to the ground rather than selling them to their white neighbours for pennies at the "evacuation sales" that took place before the Japanese left for the camps. Showing your anger in front of someone outside the family: this is not typical Japanese behaviour. In Japan, where much is made of saving face, such behaviour would be considered shameful.

Also, the women who sailed to America tended to be braver, more adventurous souls to start with. So already, just by wanting to leave, they're a bit atypical.

Can you talk a little about the hope these women start off with, and the deceit they encounter, and how that shapes the course of their lives?

Most started out with very high hopes—they expected to marry handsome, wealthy young men (as "advertised" by their future spouses in their photographs and letters) and live a life of leisure. Or, if they expected to work, then they thought that after several years they'd be able to save up enough money to sail back home to Japan and live out the rest of their days "with a cat in their lap and a fan in their hand."

But life in America was not what they expected. It was one deceit after another. Some of them were deceived by their husbands, who had lied about their age and financial status. Within days of their arrival, many of the women found themselves picking strawberries in the fields, living in migrant labour camps or working as maids for white women in the city.

(On the other hand, a few of the women had deceived their husbands as well. They had "pasts" in Japan—perhaps they'd had an affair, or given birth to an illegitimate child, or maybe they were just widows who stood no chance of remarrying if they remained in their village. Remember, the first line of the book is "On the boat we were mostly virgins.")

And then they were betrayed by America, or the promise of America—they were despised because of their race, suspected of being disloyal and sent away to the camps.

I think that quite early on, these women—most of whom had no idea of the prejudice they would encounter in America—realized that they would only be allowed to accomplish so much in their own lives, and so they put all their hopes onto the lives of their children. Which is a huge burden, if you're one of the children.

In this and your previous novel, and in some of your shorter pieces, you often write clusters of sentences that begin in a similar, repeated fashion and then go where they need to go. The result of reading your work—for me, and I suspect for many other readers—is a kind of hypnosis or meditation; it's impossible not to be drawn in, submerged, seduced. Are you conscious of strategically using repetitive sentence structures? Or

is it maybe that you're drawn into the rhythm of the words you're putting down? Or is it something that just . . . happens?

A kind of hypnosis or meditation, I love that. Someone suggested that if there were a soundtrack to my novel, it would be something by Steve Reich, and I immediately thought, yes, *Music for 18 Musicians* . . . that hypnotic beat that just puts you into a trance.

I was obsessed with the rhythm of the language while writing this novel. I was constantly reading my sentences out loud so I could hear where the accents fell. I could often hear the rhythmic pattern of the next sentence I wanted to write before I knew the exact words to drop into that pattern. And at times I found myself doing things like searching for the right three-syllable town in California where they had Japanese migrant laborers working in the peach orchards . . . A two-syllable town with orange groves just would not do.

Most of my writing is very intuitive and falls under the "just happens" category. I think the best way to put it is this: it's like there's this underground aural grid that's secretly holding everything together.

There's an obvious bridge between this book and your first novel, When The Emperor Was Divine. The Buddha in the Attic *serves as a prequel. Do you have any plans to explore a third book about the lives of these people?*

Not in the immediate future. I think my next book will be about dementia and . . . swimming. That's all I can say about it right now. People have asked me, however, if I'm going to write a book about the post-war experience of the Japanese Americans—their lives after they came back from the camps (and this, in my opinion, is where the *real* hardship began). Maybe that'll be book four?

Source: Patrick Ryan, "Interview: Julie Otsuka," in *Granta*, October 13, 2011.

SOURCES

"About Julie Otsuka," Julie Otsuka website, http://www.julieotsuka.com/about/ (accessed March 24, 2016).

Becker, Alida, "Coming to America, Lured by a Photo," in *New York Times*, August 26, 2011, http://www.nytimes.com/2011/08/28/books/review/the-buddha-in-the-attic-by-julie-otsuka-book-review.html?_r=0 (accessed March 24, 2016).

"Books Pick: Wives' Tale," in *New Yorker*, October 18, 2011, http://www.newyorker.com/culture/goings-on/books-pick-wives-tale (accessed March 24, 2016).

Charles, Ron, Review of *The Buddha in the Attic*, in *Washington Post*, November 16, 2011, https://www.washington post.com/entertainment/books/julie-otsukas-the-buddha-in-the-attic-reviewed-by-ron-charles/2011/11/08/gIQAH xqhPN_story.html (accessed March 24, 2016).

Ciabattari, Jane, Review of *The Buddha in the Attic*, in *SF Gate*, August 28, 2011, http://www.sfgate.com/books/article/The-Buddha-in-the-Attic-by-Julie-Otsuka-2332818.php (accessed March 24, 2016).

Danley, Sharon Yamato, "Japanese Picture Brides Recall Hardships of American Life," in *Los Angeles Times*, May 11, 1995, http://articles.latimes.com/1995-05-11/news/cb-64865_1_picture-bride (accessed March 25, 2016).

Day, Elizabeth, Review of *The Buddha in the Attic*, in *Guardian*, April 7, 2012, http://www.theguardian.com/books/2012/apr/08/buddha-in-attic-julie-otsuka-review (accessed March 24, 2016).

Fabrega, Meganne, "A Chorus of Voices, Mostly Unheard," in *Star Tribune*, August 28, 2011, http://www.startribune.com/fiction-a-chorus-of-voices-mostly-unheard/128387353/?adxnnl=1&adxnnlx=1311785799-xkTdvUTN K07aUIy%20bIGiJg (accessed March 24, 2016).

Fischer, B. J., Review of *The Buddha in the Attic*, in *ARDOR*, March 28, 2014, http://www.ardorlitmag.com/blog/review-the-buddha-in-the-attic-by-julie-otsuka (accessed March 24, 2016).

Nakamura, Kelli, "Picture Brides," in *Densho Encyclopedia*, May 27, 2014, http://encyclopedia.densho.org/Picture %20brides/ (accessed March 25, 2016).

Niiya, Brian, "Executive Order 9066," in *Densho Encyclopedia*, August 25, 2015, http://encyclopedia.densho.org/Executive%20Order%209066/ (accessed March 25, 2016).

Otsuka, Julie, *The Buddha in the Attic*, Anchor Books, 2012.

Taylor, Elizabeth, Review of *The Buddha in the Attic*, in *Chicago Tribune*, September 30, 2011, http://www.chicago tribune.com/lifestyles/books/ct-books-1001-editors-choice-20110930-story.html (accessed March 24, 2016).

"Transcript of Executive Order 9066: Resulting in the Relocation of Japanese (1942)," Our Documents website, http://www.ourdocuments.gov/doc.php?flash=false&doc=74& page=transcript (accessed March 25, 2016).

FURTHER READING

Gruenewald, Mary Matsuda, *Looking like the Enemy: My Story of Imprisonment in Japanese American Internment Camps*, NewSage Press, 2005.
>Gruenewald's memoir recounts the indignities and strife of her imprisonment in an internment camp at the age of sixteen. Told with powerfully emotional prose and unflinching detail, *Looking like the Enemy* recreates the world inside the barbed wire where over 110,000 Japanese Americans spent the years of World War II.

Inada, Lawson Fusao, *Only What We Could Carry: The Japanese American Internment Experience*, Heyday, 2000.
>This anthology brings together a remarkable collection of art, prose, poetry, propaganda, articles, cartoons, government documents, personal letters, and biographies on the subject of the Japanese American experience of internment. From an autobiography of the actor and activist George Takei, to woodblock prints, to the text of Executive Order 9066, the portrait painted of the internment of innocent American citizens is as complete as it is heartbreaking.

Spickard, Paul, *Japanese Americans: The Formation and Transformation of an Ethnic Group*, Rutgers University Press, 2008.
>This compelling history of Japanese immigration to the United States begins with the arrival of the first Japanese to American shores in 1855 through the enormous wave of immigration that took place between 1890 and 1924. Spickard examines the changing motivations behind Japanese immigration, the lives they found in the United States, and the ways in which the Nisei and Issei generations adjusted differently to their home, as well as the forced internment of the vast majority of the Japanese American population during World War II.

Uchida, Yoshiko, *Picture Bride*, University of Washington Press, 1997.
>Uchida's historical fiction novel follows the journey of Hana Omiya from her arrival in the United States as a picture bride in 1917 through her imprisonment in the Japanese internment camps during World War II. In addition to Hana, the novel tells the tale of her husband, Taro, and the community of Japanese Americans to which they belong, all of whose lives are uprooted by Executive Order 9066.

SUGGESTED SEARCH TERMS

Julie Otsuka

The Buddha in the Attic

Otsuka AND The Buddha in the Attic

The Buddha in the Attic AND 2011

The Buddha in the Attic AND 1900s

The Buddha in the Attic AND Japanese Americans

Japanese Americans AND picture brides

Otsuka AND first person plural

California AND Japanese immigration AND 1900s

Japanese Americans and internment

A Garden of Earthly Delight

In *A Garden of Earthly Delights* (1967; rewritten 2003) Oates turns to her family's history, giving a vivid depiction of life during the Great Depression and World War II. At the same time, she has produced a powerful psychological novel. The characters seem tossed in a maelstrom of disconnected, savage, destructive emotions that they can neither understand nor control, and the success of Oates's art is to seduce the reader into feeling the same way. The result is unnerving but seems to accomplish Oates's purpose. Readers are left feeling they are about to be caught in a storm when it finally breaks. It is an achievement of literary art to control the reader's emotions in this way, but it is unsettling to experience it. Plato suggested that art should imitate the beautiful. It is as though Oates sought to prove him wrong, finding inspiration instead in anxiety and unease.

JOYCE CAROL OATES

1967

AUTHOR BIOGRAPHY

Oates was born on June 16, 1938, in Lockport, a suburb of Buffalo, New York. She was the first member of her working-class family to graduate from high school. Oates has written a good deal about her childhood, both fiction and nonfiction, and she recalls her early years as being remarkably stable and happy. She concedes, however, that to an outsider her childhood

Joyce Carol Oates *(©ZUMA Press, Inc. | Alamy)*

literary influence. She read classic literature such as the works of William Faulkner, Franz Kafka, and Feodor Dostoevsky voraciously while she was in high school and began writing novels, although she would throw away each book as soon as she finished it. Her first publication was a short story that won a writing contest in the popular magazine *Mademoiselle*. In 1963 she began publishing seriously, both short stories and novels but also poetry, drama, and essays, and she has written over forty books. Her best-known work is the short story "Where Are You Going, Where Have You Been?" from 1966, about a child murderer. Her work often deals with violence and conflict and particularly with the injustices in society related to class, wealth, and race, as in her novel *them* (1969), which won the National Book Award. *A Garden of Earthly Delights* (1967) was her second published novel. It was the first book in her Wonderland quartet, which continues with *Expensive People* (1968), *them* (1969), and *Wonderland* (1971). She published *Marya: A Life* in 1986. She has been nominated for the Pulitzer Prize many times but has never won it. She has, however, won numerous literary prizes, including the O. Henry Award in 1967 (for "In the Region of Ice") and 1973 (for "The Dead"), the Pushcart Prize (1976), the Prix Femina Étranger in 2005 (for "The Falls"), and the World Fantasy Award for Best Short Fiction in 2011 (for "Fossil-Figures"). She is often discussed as a likely candidate for the Nobel Prize in Literature. In the 1980s, Oates experimented with gothic themes and magic realism in novels such as *Bellefleur* (1980) and *A Bloodsmoor Romance* (1982). In the 1990s she began publishing mystery novels under the pen names Rosamond Smith and Lauren Kelly. Oates also writes extensively for popular magazines. In the late 1990s an assignment to interview her mother and write a piece about her family's influence in her writing resulted in the play *When I Was a Little Girl and My Mother Didn't Want Me* (1998).

Oates was devastated by the death of her husband, Smith, in 2008. In early 2009, she married Charles Gross, a professor of psychology at Princeton. Her writing pace has not slackened, and she has published one or two novels a year since then, including most recently *The Man without a Shadow* in 2016.

growing up on a farm with her family, impoverished by the Depression, might look different. Only as an adult did she find out that one of her grandfathers had committed suicide after abandoning his family and that the other had been murdered. Oates excelled in school and was able to attended Syracuse University on a scholarship, taking a degree in English and graduating as valedictorian in 1960. She received an MA in English from the University of Wisconsin and while she was there met her first husband, Raymond Smith. Both would become English professors. Oates taught for many years at the University of Windsor in Canada and moved to Princeton in 1978, from where she retired in 2014. She and Smith founded the literary journal *Ontario Review* and its associated press, which published many of her writings.

Oates received Lewis Carroll's *Alice's Adventures in Wonderland* as a gift from her grandmother while she was in grade school and counts this work as her most profound

PLOT SUMMARY

Carleton

A Garden of Earthly Delights is told by an impersonal narrator, but it is nevertheless told from the point of view of a main character, a different one in each section. In "Carleton" the narrator is naturally Carleton Walpole. The story begins during the Depression with a truckload of migrant workers traveling from Kentucky to Arkansas. They are at a halt during a rainstorm, because their truck has had an accident and is lying in the ditch. Carleton is among the workers. When Carleton's father died, his farm was liquidated for debt, and any remaining money was lost in a bank failure. Just as the tow truck comes to get their truck out of the ditch, Carleton's wife, Pearl, goes into labor in a makeshift tent set up on the roadside and gives birth to their daughter, Clara.

After five years, social workers have intervened and forced the Walpole children to attend school. Oates's usual technique with these chronological jumps is to slowly fill in the events of the interval. In this case Pearl became pregnant again, and the Walpole family is living in a shanty town in Florida, provided by the farmers whose crops they are picking. One evening, Carleton goes to a tavern with his friend Rafe for the express purpose of picking up a girl, since he is becoming increasingly disgusted with Pearl, who seems to be descending into some kind of dementia. At the bar, the two men wager a dollar (a larger sum than it seems, because in light of their poverty and the deflation of the Depression, neither man has more than a few dollars to his name) over arm wrestling, and Carleton wins. He considers it a point of honor to refuse to take the money, however. Rafe is just as concerned for his reputation and considers that Carleton has condescendingly insulted him. Rafe provokes a fight that has to be moved outside among a crowd of other drinkers eager to watch. As Rafe has the worst of it, he becomes more violent, and finally Carleton has to stab him with a switchblade to stop him.

After another five years, the Walpole family are in a new shanty town in South Carolina. Carleton, who is now about forty, has an eighteen-year-old girlfriend, Nancy. Pearl died in childbirth. Carleton was tried and acquitted for killing Rafe, on the ground of self-defense. The family moves again, this time to New Jersey.

Clara makes friends with a girl named Rosalie from another migrant family. Rosalie initiates her into shoplifting when they visit the local town. A few months later Rosalie delivers a stillborn child at the same moment that members of the Ku Klux Klan kidnap and murder her father. Nancy hopefully suggests that "they only punish people who need punishing."

Back in Florida a few years later, Clara is visited by church ladies from the local Methodists and agrees to attend a service, which she cannot relate to herself or her own experience. The son of one of the ladies drives Clara back home but stops at a roadhouse, intending to seduce her. Instead, she feels desire for the first time for a strange man, who turns out to be a bootlegger. He takes her to his rooming house, but when he realizes she is only thirteen years old, he returns her home in the middle of the night. Carleton is enraged at Clara and beats her. When he wakes up the next morning, badly hung over, Nancy informs him that Clara has run off. He sends Nancy and the other children to the fields but sets out to find Clara. He proceeds as if he is in a trance or possessed. On one hand, he takes effective and deliberate action (perhaps for the first time in his life), discovering that the man who went with Clara is a bootlegger based in Savannah, Georgia, and obtaining a car to go there. Once there, his imagination lures him to a church, because he recalls that Clara went to church the night before she left. Carleton's trance is soon transformed into a frenzy, and he begins attacking the stained glass windows and the statues in the church with a large candlestick. Finally, he goes outside and, incensed that other white people are looking down on him as a pathetic figure, he tears off part of his car and starts attacking passersby with it. When a police officer tries to stop him, Carleton attacks him too and is shot and killed.

Lowry

The narrative in this section begins to be told from Clara's viewpoint. The bootlegger who takes Clara in is named Lowry. He takes her to his hometown, Tintern, New York. Through contacts he has there, he gets her a job as a salesgirl in Woolworth. He sets her up in her own apartment, paying her rent. Lowry takes some pride in the fact that he does not take advantage of her, regarding her as if she were the little sister he never had, although Clara desperately wants to make love to him. He remains secretive about his life and his past, but Clara learns that his father, too, had lost his farm, like her grandfather, but he then killed himself. Lowry visits her occasionally, perhaps once or twice a month.

When she attends the wedding of one of her coworkers, Clara meets Curt Revere, the patriarch of the only wealthy family in the town; his family had bought Lowry's father's farm at auction. He drives her home and is obviously interested in her. After a few months (possibly more like a year and a half, because Clara seems to be about sixteen now), Lowry decides to make love to her and takes her away for a few days to the beach. She is hopelessly in love with him, but he cannot envision himself every marrying or devoting himself to Clara the way she desires. He promises to come and see her again two weeks later. By that time, she is beginning to suspect she is pregnant.

On that very day, when Lowry is expected in the evening, Clara attends a charity picnic and is again driven home by Revere. He tells her that his first wife died in childbirth along with the baby and he is distant from his present wife, who is ill, but by whom he has three children. Clara reminds him of the first girl he loved when he was a teenager. Lowry indeed visits but cannot stay; he has evidently taken a large sum of money that he believes is rightfully his from a higher-up in the bootlegging business and fears his fellow gangsters may be pursuing him. He is going to Mexico and tells Clara he will see her again, but not for a long time, and he will be a different and more substantial person by then.

She soon confirms that she is pregnant. Awakened by this circumstance, as she puts it, Clara takes action in a way her father never could have but in the calculating, deliberate way that Lowry would. She contrives to meet Revere again. He again offers to drive her home, but this time she says she would not mind if he drives around a bit first. So he takes her to an empty farmhouse he owns and makes love to her. After sufficient time, she tells him she is pregnant. Revere readily believes the child is his; he wants to believe it. He is deeply in love with her. He pays to have that same house repaired and renovated and gives it to Clara to live in. He seems to spend more time with her than he does with his legal wife and family, yet Clara spends all of her time thinking of how much she loves Lowry. Living in a small town,

everyone is soon aware of the relationship Clara has contracted with Revere; because they consider it shameful, she is ostracized.

When Clara's delivery date approaches, Revere takes her to a doctor in a large city. She is horrified, because in her experience seeing a doctor means that death is eminent, but she is in no position to overrule Revere. The doctor sees something he does not like, so the delivery takes place in a hospital, without incident. In fact, the reader is told almost nothing about these events, as if Clara does not want to think about them.

Not that it surprises her, but Clara feels the town's moral disapproval when Swan becomes ill and she has to drive to the drugstore to get medicine for him. A year later, when Clara attends the funeral of one of her old coworkers from Woolworth (who has been murdered in an act of domestic violence), it is not so bad.

Four years later, Lowry returns. He drives out to Clara's farmhouse, having asked about her in town. He had tried various businesses in Mexico, but they all failed. He had married a schoolteacher but divorced. Clara is at best dimly aware that a war is being fought in Europe, because it is not a matter that concerns her directly. Lowry fought in France, and, in fact, he has been discharged because he was wounded. Though it is not clear how (it has something to do with veteran status), he is about to be able to buy a large farm in Canada and wants Clara to go there with him, bringing Swan (although Clara tells him Revere is the boy's father). She feels powerless to resist him and makes no effort against his seduction, but ultimately she does refuse to go with him, preferring the security she has with Revere to the indulgence she could have with Lowry. He confesses that the story he had told about his father losing his farm was a lie; he came from a family of migrant workers no higher in social status than Clara's family. Lowry leaves, but he makes a point of saying goodbye to Swan. When he looks at the boy, Lowry says prophetically that he can tell that Swan killed something (which he denies), a snake or some other animal. Lowry can tell the boy will kill again, a great deal in fact.

Swan

The narrative in this section begins to be told from Swan's viewpoint. Revere's wife has died, and he is marrying Clara. She and Swan move into the house the day of the wedding, with considerable tension between Clara and Swan and Revere's sons, Clark, Jonathan, and Robert (respectively about seven, five, and two years older than Swan). The wedding is not described at all. Revere makes Clara start to call Swan "Steven" (as everyone else does), but she always forgets.

Two years later, when Swan is seven, the family attends the funeral of one of Revere's relatives in Hamilton, a city a few hours' drive away, where most of the extended Revere family lives. The Revere sons are still hostile to Swan outside Revere's or Clara's direct observation; Robert seems to like him but still sticks with his brothers when they are around. At the funeral, the dead man is never named, nor is his relationship to Revere made clear. The point is to show how detached Clara and Swan remain from the extended Revere family. The only connection Swan makes is with his cousin Deborah. She teaches him to do crossword puzzles.

Oates begins a new subsection (when Swan is ten years old) by telling the reader that it takes place a year after the funeral, on the day Clara will miscarry the baby she is carrying. There is some altercation at the breakfast table about guns. Hunting is one of Revere's chief pastimes, which he naturally expects his sons to share with him. Swan protests that he does not like the idea of killing animals or even firing a gun. It is agreed that that morning Swan (who has been to the shooting range a few times) will go out hunting with Robert. They do not kill anything, but when they return, they meet Jonathan, who is riding a horse. He viciously taunts Swan and threatens to ride him down but soon leaves. Swan asks Robert why everyone hates him, but Robert does not hate him and dismisses the question. They start to climb a barbed-wire fence to take a shortcut home across a pasture, and Swan hits Robert in the back just as he is at the top of the fence, causing him to fall. Robert's shotgun has its safety off, a fact Swan had carefully observed, and it discharges, shooting him in the neck. The narrative becomes a mere summary of events, with Robert bleeding to death in Clara's car as she drives him to the doctor and Clara herself miscarrying from the stress of events. Swan never mentions what he has done, and it is easy enough for others to understand the event as a simple accident. Nevertheless, Clara warns Swan to keep his mouth shut about what happened, as if she somehow

knows he played a role in Robert's death. Revere puts away all ideas that the boys will hunt or use guns and takes to reading the Bible to the family in the evening.

Clara takes Swan, whom even she calls Steven now, on a trip to Hamilton to visit his relatives, who seem over time to have grown less hostile toward her. One of the relatives offers to take Clara and Swan to visit the local museum and then shopping. Clara buys Swan an antique iron statue of a gazelle. Unexpectedly to the boy, they drop him off at the public library, where he has to wait for hours for his mother to return. It is not exactly spelled out, but she spent the afternoon in a hotel room with their guide. She has forgotten the gazelle, left behind in the back of a cab.

Revere realizes that his sons are going to have girlfriends from among their schoolmates, but he cautions them that he will never allow them to marry beneath their class. Jonathan in his teenage years falls into alcoholism, drops out of school, and takes up with low companions, the kind of men who frequent roadhouses (like Clara's father). He eventually drives off and is never seen by the family again. Clark defies his father by marrying one of his local girlfriends. Revere sets him up with an income as the director of a sawmill he owns, but it is made clear he will never inherit the Revere fortune.

Swan, too, has girlfriends, but he finds that he is in love with his cousin Deborah, from whom he has grown apart and whom he imagines despises him. College seems out of the question for Swan as he starts to take over running Revere's business interests. By the time he is in his mid-twenties, he is quite adept at it, expanding the fortune considerably and at least seeming to take pleasure in vanquishing business rivals (especially other Reveres). The narrative gives a keen description of his inner torment, made all the more effective by the reader's being at a loss to understand any rational basis for it. Revere declines badly with age, but Clara makes frequent trips to Hamilton, where she carries on affairs with various members of the Revere family there; she also sleeps once with Clark, just before his marriage. One night Swan meets Deborah in a hotel room in Hamilton. She has married another man, but she and Swan have been having an affair for some time. As they make love, they tell each other they are in love; according to the narrative voice of the novel, each does love the other, but something neither they nor the narrator can articulate keeps them from feeling being in love or loved. That night Swan drives back to the Revere farm, arriving about dawn. He confronts his mother and demands that Revere come down to talk with him. He produces a gun and intends to shoot Clara. She thinks that it must be revenge for the lost gazelle, but really she thinks that this was fated from the beginning. As Swan is standing quite close to her, Clara grabs his hand to defend herself, and Swan instead shoots Revere and then himself. Whether on the scene or a short time later, Clara has the first of a series of strokes and goes into a long decline in a nursing home in Hamilton, where Clark is her only visitor. On one visit, she tells Clark of how she envies her own mother, who died peacefully in a field while picking tomatoes.

CHARACTERS

Lowry

Lowry is a bootlegger. His work as a gangster takes place after Prohibition; even then many individual counties, especially in the South, still prohibited alcohol. Lowry is the man who saves Clara after she runs away from home when her father beats her. He is benevolent to her because he thinks he is atoning for ancestral and inheritable sin:

> A way a woman talks to me, says things to me I don't know and am astonished to hear and I'll know her as soon as I hear her. Or maybe I never will hear her, and that's all right, too. Because my father was poison to women, and damned if I will be, too. And some things, the worst things, run in your blood.

Notice he is waiting for fate to send the right woman to him, and he rejects Clara for so long because he does not see the appropriate signs in her; when he does see them in the woman he marries, it ends in failure. His return for Clara shows that he has grown away from such magical thinking and wants to make a rational choice, taking responsibility for the boy. Lowry stands, from various viewpoints, as an agent of fate, promoting the biblical ideas of sin and punishment running down through the generations of a family, as well as the idea of prophecy, since he is somehow able to divine Swan's murderous nature while he is still a small child. As Swan's true father, Lowry perhaps represents an alternative to the awful state of affairs at the novel's

conclusion. If Clara had decided to take Swan and go with Lowry after the war was over, things might have turned out very differently, allowing Swan to grow up in an environment from which he was not alienated. He is a third model of masculinity, seductive and violent but also resourceful and successful—not a failure like Carleton or hampered by social convention like Revere. The tragedy of the novel is that his is a path not taken.

Nancy

Nancy (whose surname is never mentioned) is an eighteen-year-old girl that Carleton takes in as his mistress after Pearl dies. Once she becomes pregnant, it dawns upon her that the Walpole household is no place for her to raise a baby. Like Clara, Nancy ran away from home because her father beat her. Rather than confront the injustice of the violence the Ku Klux Klan uses to enforce their will over the poor white community when Klansmen murder a migrant worker, she rationalizes their actions as punishment for some crime on his part the Klan had found out about.

Rafe

Rafe is one of Carleton's essentially interchangeable friends among his fellow migrant workers. Just as Carleton is obsessed with his own honor, when Carleton wins a bet from him and refuses to collect the money, because he considered the matter trivial compared with his friendship for him, Rafe becomes insulted and provokes a fight with Carleton, in which he is himself killed.

Clark Revere

Clark is the eldest of Revere's sons. His marriage to a lower-class girl disappoints his father and causes him to reject his son. His punishment is the mildest, being consigned to a middle-class life. Perhaps he breaks the cycle of embracing his family's privilege. His is the only life of all the characters in the novel that does not end in tragedy.

Curt Revere

Revere (even Clara after her marriage to him can think of him only by his more formal surname) is the second to save Clara. He is the richest and most powerful man in the county and part of a wealthy family with connections throughout the state. He falls in love Clara out of nostalgia, seeing in her a chance to realize his youthful

love for a poor farm girl, which could never
flourish because his family would never allow
him to marry beneath him. Yet when the time
comes, he cannot see any other way than to treat
his sons in the same way, estranging them as he
himself felt alienated. This, too, seems to be a
family curse. Clara uses the metaphor of playing
cards to characterize her two lovers, Revere and
Lowry (the jack in this case):

> If Curt Revere was a playing card, Clara
> thought, he was one of the kings. Heavy-
> jawed, inclined to brooding. Not fast and sexy-
> treacherous like the jacks. You were supposed
> to think that the king of spades was stronger
> than the jack of spades, but that wasn't so.
> Having so much, knowing so much wore out
> your soul, for you knew that you could lose it.

Although Revere is Clara's (and Swan's)
savior from a life of poverty and eventually Clara's husband and Swan's stepfather (or father, as
he thinks), he never means anything to his wife
or his stepson. Because the novel is told from
their viewpoint, his inner life is never explored,
except to the limited degree that it compels him
to seek out Clara. He reverence for tradition,
another kind of nostalgia, leads him to destroy
the lives of his sons. His third son Robert's death
is meant to echo or even foreshadow his proud
rejection of Jonathan and Clark.

Deborah Revere
Deborah is the daughter of Revere's brother and
so is the ostensible cousin of Swan. Like all of the
women in the Revere family, including Revere's
first two wives, she is prone to ill health and
melancholy. In the world of the novel, this is
perhaps a cosmic punishment for their aligning
with the Revere family, which is accursed
because of its wealth and privilege. (Notice that
Clara suffers a miscarriage and a stroke after she
becomes a Revere, whereas before she had been
remarkable for her good health.) She and Swan
were childhood playmates, and although she
accepts an arranged marriage with a *suitable*
husband, as an adult she has an affair with
Swan. She and Swan believe that they love each
other, but their inner alienation prevents them
from experiencing the feeling of love that might
have saved them.

Jonathan Revere
Jonathan is the middle child among Revere's
sons. For reasons that do not make sense in the
real world but do function within the fate-driven

fictive world of the novel, his adolescence is a
long decline into failure, dropping out of school
and taking up with low companions unsuitable
for a Revere. His father becomes so disaffected
from him that he does not even condemn him,
and the boy eventually drifts away from existence within the narrative.

Robert Revere
Robert is the youngest of Revere's sons. He is the
most sympathetic of the Revere brothers to
Swan. Perhaps for that reason, after Revere bullies Swan into going hunting (because that is
what men are expected to do) Swan kills him,
showing his true position as utterly on the outside of the family of which he is supposed to be a
member.

Steven (Swan) Revere
Swan is the illegitimate child of Clara and
Lowry, but Revere believes him to be his own
son, a belief that Clara fosters to bind herself to
him. The young Swan is raised knowing no one
but his mother, apart from occasional visits from
Revere, with whom he is able to make no connection. He is precociously intelligent. Because
Revere married Clara out of love (unlike his first
two wives), he is ready to favor him over his
older sons. After Robert's death, when Revere
turns to the consolation of religion, Swan, who
has absorbed his mother's indifference to religion, considers the Bible stories he is being
read, comparing them to adventure comic
books, and rejects religion altogether. He asks
Revere whether there were dinosaurs in the Garden of Eden, a question that cannot have a
rational answer, and quickly comes to consider
that the narratives of religion and science are
incompatible. The science book and articles
Swan is increasingly reading never mention
God, but they would have to take him into
account if God were intimately involved in the
operation of the natural world the way the Bible
describes. Paradoxically, then, Swan, more than
any other character, is driven by apparently
supernatural forces of fate that decree that his
life will be playing the role of a murderer, something his true father, Lowry, is able to divine
from looking into his five-year-old eyes. Swan
is unable to make connections with his new family, in part because the specter of his true father,
whom he can never mention, haunts him, but
also because fate has determined that he will
not. The forces of alienation that torment him

and drive him to murder, just as they deny him the ability to love, can be seen as a sort of modern equivalent to possession or a curse driving his tragic fate.

Rosalie

Rosalie, the daughter of a family of migrant workers, is a few years older than Clara. She becomes Clara's friend and initiates her into the white trash crimes of shoplifting and vandalism. The oppression of poverty weighing upon the migrant workers is symbolized by the two punishments she receives at the same moment a short time before Clara runs away from her father. Rosalie delivers a stillborn baby on the same night her father is kidnapped and murdered by the Ku Klux Klan.

Carleton Walpole

Carleton is the main character of the first section of the novel. His life story is based on an amalgamation of Oates's two grandfathers. Carleton is more than usually talented, though the prevailing poverty of his situation prevents him from making any accomplishment: "In a group of men Carleton would be the first to smile and the first to stop, because he was the smartest." Carleton is keenly aware of his failure, or perhaps one should say the impossibility of his success, and constantly thinks that he will someday change things for himself and his family even if he is never able to do so. Clara is the only thing that Carleton has ever loved. Interestingly, during his chase after her, he cannot distinguish clearly in his mind the image of Clara (his daughter) from the image of Pearl (his wife).

Carleton's life is dominated by the difference between his actual situation and the one he feels he ought to occupy. This awareness is why he is so ready to accept that some outsider groups—Jews or Mexicans—must be responsible for the disconnect, somehow causing the wealthy white farmers he works for to pay him less than the true value of his labor. When he destroys the only thing that matters to him—his relationship with his daughter—Carleton is shattered, and Oates finally uses surreal imagery to show the difference between the world and Carleton's perception of it, as when the narrative of the novel states: "Time was slowing down for him. Never before in his life had time slowed down so you could feel it, like melting tar." After that, Carleton is finally able to use his talents to take effective action, in chasing after

his daughter, but he ends his life with actions that must seem insane to the reader, desecrating a church and attacking a police officer (both symbols of the social hierarchy weighing down on him). Their meaning is that Carleton's life—his poverty—is an artificial construct brought about by economic forces over which he has no control and in which he can find no rational meaning.

Clara Walpole

Clara is the main character of *A Garden of Earthy Delight*. The first section of the novel concerns mainly her father, Carleton; the second focuses on her lover, Lowry, and her husband, Revere; and the third turns attention to her son, Swan. She is raised in the direst poverty and lack of education and so remains self-absorbed throughout her life, her only impulse to secure her son's future. Clara becomes a more prominent character as she grows up. At the crisis of her adulthood, she is taken to a church for the first time by Methodist missionaries but cannot find any meaning in their religious rituals. That same night, she mistakes the first stirrings of desire for the presence of the god the Methodists had taught her about. This is with reference to Lowry, the bootlegger with whom she seems destined to fall in love. When she finally returns home in the middle of the night, her father, Carleton, beats her, probably, as he thinks, as punishment for her having sex. She runs back to Lowry, who in contrast does nothing to abuse her and treats her with respect and kindness. For the middle years of her life, she is consumed by love for Lowry and, even after he abandons her, always thinks about him. At one point, when she is flirting with Revere, she realizes that a child raised by him would receive the best education, so she thinks, "Lowry would want his children to be educated."

The middle section of the novel is told from Clara's point of view. At first reading, the reader is meant to side with her, to believe that Clara is right to cherish Lowry. She is unable to think anything else because she is so smitten. From that perspective, it looks as if Revere is taking advantage of her: a married man old enough to be her father lecherously seducing a girl who is only sixteen or seventeen years old. It is clear, however, that Revere is completely honest with her and that his love for her is the most genuine and the most vulnerable exposure of his inner self: "They acted out two roles, not quite consciously:

Revere was the guilty one, because he believed he had made her pregnant, and Clara was the victimized one." Yet Clara never considers for a moment that she might have any reason to love Revere. Later she does come to call what she feels for Revere *love*, but it is never the same thing she felt for Lowry. Nevertheless, once she rejects Lowry out of what she considers is the best interest of their son and as she becomes more content with the wealth Revere provides her, Lowry disappears entirely from her consciousness. Because she still does not love Revere, she slips into a life of adultery, perhaps searching for something she might have had with Lowry or, just as likely, trying to pass the time.

Clara easily accepts the fate-driven world of the narrative she inhabits. When she is giving a highly fictive account of her life to Revere (covering up her family's extreme poverty), she suddenly realizes that "she hadn't run away from her family because Pa was hitting her but because it had been time." Clara's assessment of others' actions shows she has no concern for their motives:

> She remembered her father's anger that had never been directed toward anything that made sense and Lowry's insatiable yearning, a hunger that could take him all over the world and never give him rest; these impulses belonged to men and had nothing to do with her. She could not understand them.

For the same reasons, or the same lack of reasons, she rewrites her own history to suit her current needs. She hates and fears doctors (because the very poor see doctors only when they are dying) and especially resents Revere's insistence that she be seen by a doctor when she is pregnant and that the baby be born in a hospital. She tells herself that nothing bad can happen during childbirth, forgetting, or keeping herself from remembering, that she watched her mother bleed to death when her youngest brother was born. Similarly, when she wants to die peacefully at the end of the novel, she tells her stepson Clark that her mother died at peace working in the fields.

Pearl Walpole

Pearl is the wife of Carleton. Because of her family's poverty, she has one child after another until she dies in childbirth. Her apparent descent into schizophrenia at the same time is a symbolic conceptualization of the meaninglessness of the world imposed by poverty.

Sharleen Walpole

Sharleen is the daughter of Carleton and Pearl, Clara's older sister. Carleton drives her out of the family with his cruelty when she reaches maturity, reduced by his poverty to acting almost like the leader of a pack of animals driving off the mature offspring.

THEMES

Nostalgia

Nostalgia is the longing one feels for a time, and perhaps a place, out of one's past. Everyone feels it to one degree or another, but it is particularly strong in Oates, reflected in her longing even for a past she never knew through her well-known interest in genealogy. Her characters, not unexpectedly, share her feelings. Oddly, in Oates's work it is a particularly male feeling. Carleton, whose childhood must have seemed a paradise compared with his adult life, thinks, "Everything is harder if you compare *what is* with *what was*." Because *what is* always seems inferior to *what was*. *What was* is the memory of life being judged by the mind of a child, while *what is* is all too closely analyzed by an adult mind. Similarly, when Lowry and Clara arrive in Tintern, it is almost the only time he speaks to her about himself, "as if now, seeing this town, that was run-down and jumbled but somehow beautiful he was shaken in some way, and moved to speak." Reliving memories of the lost past is an intense emotional experience. Clara, in contrast, rarely thinks about her past; when she does, what she recalls is a confabulation that suits her present needs. The narrative voice of the novel, which must come terribly close to being Oates's own voice, feels nostalgia for her. In the afterword to the 2003 edition of *A Garden of Earthly Delight*, Oates explains the longing for a childhood as awful as she considers her own, when viewed objectively, or even for Clara's still worse childhood:

> Can one be nostalgic for a world in which, in fact, one would not wish to live, as for incidents one would not wish to relive? The stab of emotion I feel at recalling my one-room schoolhouse in Millersport, so very like the schoolhouse Clara Walpole briefly attends, is difficult to analyze. I would not wish any child I know to endure such experience, yet I could not imagine my life without them.

It is the lost childhood that one longs for, whatever its circumstances.

TOPICS FOR FURTHER STUDY

- *A Garden of Earthly Delights* has its genesis in Oates's family history, as does much of her work, and she is a keen enthusiast for genealogy. One way to explore your own family history is by interviewing your older family members. One venue for this is the Story Corps project, which allows interviews by one family member of another (typically a young person of a grandparent or other relative of a previous generation) to be recorded and posted online. Many of them are played on NPR programs. Go to the Story Corps website (http://storycorps.org), which provides helpful tips and suggestions, and set up an interview with one of your family members.

- *After the Wreck, I Picked Myself Up, Spread My Wings, and Flew Away* (2006) is one of Oates's numerous novels for young adults. It deals with the difficulties of a teenage girl who has to deal with her mother's death. Write a paper comparing this novel with *A Garden of Earthly Delights*, particularly comparing its protagonist with the presentation of the young Clara.

- *The Good Earth* (1931), by Pearl S. Buck, is a classic depiction of the life of a family of poor farmers in China in the 1920s. Write a paper contrasting their way of life with that of the Walpoles in the first section of *A Garden of Earthly Delights*.

- In *A Garden of Earthly Delights*, Carleton Walpole suggests that his accent means that he and another farmworker with a similar accent, named Pickering, had ancestors who came from Newcastle in England. (While Newcastle is a reasonable guess for Pickering, the name Walpole comes from East Anglia.) This probably reflects Oates's own well-known interest in genealogy. Today resources on the web make it possible to hear a wide range of English accents (British Library, Sound Map, Accents and Dialects, http://sounds.bl.uk/Sound-Maps/Accents-and-Dialects; Linguistics 201: The Dialects of American English, http://pandora.cii.wwu.edu/vajda/ling201/test3materials/americandialects.htm) and to quickly search for the local origin of surnames (http://named.publicprofiler.org/). Use the Internet to research the places of origin of your classmates' surnames or particular accents and show the results in a class poster.

- The title *A Garden of Earthly Delights* obviously refers to Hieronymus Bosch's fifteenth-century painting *The Garden of Earthly Delights*. Yet Oates never mentions the painting or explicitly refers to its fantastic themes in the text of the novel. The painting was an altarpiece, which means, in part, that it is composed of three panels and has a religious theme, ostensibly showing heaven in the first panel and hell in the third. A closer examination of the painting shows that much else is going on. As Adam and Eve worship Jesus in paradise in the first panel, a cat is shown carrying a dead rat in its mouth. This and much else in the painting are out of place, but reading it from left to right, the three panels are always utterly fantastic (and probably allegorical) and become more disturbing as the eye progresses across the image. Write a paper suggesting how the novel may reflect the painting.

Poverty

At the beginning of *A Garden of Earthly Delight*, the Walpole family, working as migrant laborers, are as poor as any Americans can be. They are in real danger of suffering starvation if day-to-day labor is not forthcoming. Pearl, the mother of the family, dies in childbirth, but as the doctor who was called once it was obvious she was bleeding to death points out, she was killed by poverty. The family cannot afford clean water and had no way for Pearl to give birth in even a clean, to say nothing of a sterile, environment. Pearl herself

Lowry sets Clara up in a small Southern town but then abandons her (©Kenneth Sponsler / Shutterstock.com)

was malnourished and afflicted by parasites. There was no question of having a doctor or even a midwife oversee the birth or going to a hospital. Where would that kind of money come from? The pregnancy was unplanned and far past any reasonable expectation that she would able to physically endure another birth, but the family's poverty and attendant ignorance made birth control impossible. Despite their dire circumstances, Carleton insists that he, his family, and his fellow migrant workers "were good people." But they are not good people.

Carleton, who is no different from anyone around him, is a racist, who loathes the "spics and niggers that you hated on principle." He consoles himself with the thought that "he had his dignity.... Always he would have his white skin, that was a fact." He has a primitive sense of honor that demands that he be constantly ready to meet insults with violence (leading him to kill his own friend in a knife fight). Carleton, moreover, looks down on even his fellow whites as trash, making a distinction between them and himself on the ground that at least his father had once owned his own farm (as he imagines

he himself will one day). When his daughter Sharleen announces that she is engaged, Carleton reacts by accusing her of having become pregnant out of wedlock, suggesting she is good for nothing else. She cannot recover from this blow to her dignity and never speaks to her own father again. He beats Clara when he believes she is going the same way.

Carleton is conscious that he is being crushed from above, that the structure of society has made him and his family desperately poor and oppressed and killed his wife, but he has no idea how to fight back against the forces that are oppressing him or even to see what they are. When Carleton actually meets an official from one of the New Deal programs meant to help the poor, he mistakes him for a Jew because the only dim idea he has of why he has do backbreaking physical labor that does not even pay enough to feed his family, the reason why he has heard that even millionaires were forced to kill themselves after the stock market crash, is that society is run by Jews for the purpose of oppressing non-Jews. Anti-Semitism is a story he can understand because he does not know any more realistic account of his circumstances. Because he is constantly afraid without even knowing why, he lashes out with hatred and violence against the only people he knows are weaker than he himself: blacks, Mexicans, poor white trash, and women. Even as he is oppressed, he has to build up his own identity by oppressing others. Oates is showing how poverty not only destroys the very bodies of the poor but also destroys their humanity, turning them into animals with no empathy left in the face of a primitive instinct for violence and hatred. (Carleton is convinced that the lawyers and jurors who tried him for the fight with Rafe considered him no different from a dog.) Carleton dies fighting reasonlessly, like a wounded, cornered dog. The same structure of society that keeps him poor directs his fears into hatred against other races, against women, and against those he can perceive as of a lower class than he is, suggesting why the oppression of these groups was tolerated for so long.

STYLE

Rewriting

In an almost unprecedented step, Oates decided to extensively rewrite *A Garden of Earthly Delights* when it was to be republished by Modern Library in 2003. By her own estimate she rewrote approximately three-quarters of the text. Nor is this the first example of Oates rewriting older work. She completely revised the ending of *Wonderland* when it was reissued in paperback in 1972. The scope of the rewriting goes more to style and less to theme and can be judged by the opening paragraphs of the two versions:

> Arkansas. On that day, many years ago, a truck carrying a number of migratory workers collided with a car on a country highway. It was May 19, the side of the road was soft with red clay, and in the light rain the people milled about with an air of festivity. (1967)

> *Arkansas*. On that day many years ago a rattling Ford truck carrying twenty-nine farmworkers and their children sideswiped a local truck carrying hogs to Little Rock on a rain-slick country highway. It was a shimmering-green day in late May, the Ford truck ended up on its side in a three-foot drainage ditch, and in the hazy rain everyone milled about in the road amid broken glass, a familiar stink of gasoline and a spillage of hog excrement. Yet among those who hadn't been hurt, the predominant mood was jocular. (2003)

The rewriting for the most part presents the same information as the original but seems to have been changed for the sake of style. There is new information inserted, for example Carleton's repeated fantasies of suicide (revolving around taking control of the bus transporting him and his fellow migrants and driving it over the side of a bridge), which help to build up more complex characterization. One wonders if Oates's impulse to rewrite the novel had to do with the lack of fixed reference points in her memory. While it would go too far to say that she did not remember the first version, the solid reality of the text had no greater, or even lesser, importance for her than her imaginative vision of the second.

Chronology

There are serious problems with the chronology of *A Garden of Earthly Delights*. Oates is purposefully vague about dates, frequently mentioning the month and the day but rarely the year. The reader quickly develops a sense that the first section of the novel is set during the Great Depression, the period between the stock market crash of 1929 and American entry into World War II in 1941. The earliest point mentioned in the novel is recalled as a past event by Carleton from before the beginning of the text. His father died, leaving his heavily mortgaged farm to be auctioned off to pay creditors. This would seem to be a typical event of the Depression era, but it is possible that an individual farmer could have failed before 1929; in any case, Carleton ascribes the failure to drought. However, even after that, Carleton inherited some money, but that was lost the following week in a bank failure.

The sequence of economic disaster certainly suggests the Depression. The loss of the farm took place an unknown number of years before the beginning of the novel. Only ten years after the beginning is a date mentioned, so the failure was more than ten years earlier. At that ten-year mark, the narrative voice of the novel recalls that Carleton's "family owned land and were farmers and he was about ready to go back there himself. The problem was that in 1933 everyone had it bad." So the time when everyone had it bad was 1933, but it is ambiguous if that time pinpoints the loss of the land or the current circumstances of the novel. It would make perfect sense that the farm had been lost in 1933, because that was one of the worst years of the Depression. That would make the date of the narrative 1943 or later, that is, in the middle of World War II. The war has never been mentioned up to that point, however,

COMPARE
&
CONTRAST

- **1930s:** In the United States, only about a third of babies are born in hospitals, which is correlated with family income and class.

  1960s: Great Society social programs begin to make medical care, including obstetrical care, more available to the poor.

  Today: Total out-of-hospitals births (of which only part are home births) amounted to 1.36 percent of the total births in 2012. Medicaid can often aid parents who are unable to pay the full cost of giving birth.

- **1930s:** Cars do not have seat belts, and government offices do not keep statistics related to injuries and fatalities in traffic accidents. Clara's practice of driving with a young baby lying loose on the front seat next to her would not seem particularly foolish to most people.

  1960s: Issues with auto safety come into public consciousness through the work of activists such as C. Hunter Shelden and Ralph Nader, and by the 1960s seat belts are optional equipment on most cars, and the shoulder restraint has been developed.

  Today: State laws require that infants and toddlers be placed in child safety seats in the rear seats of cars; small children may use

  booster seats. Depending on their age, height, and weight, older children may use an adult safety belt.

- **1930s:** Migrant workers in the agricultural industry are mostly Americans, as the industrial workforce shrinks during the Great Depression.

  1960s: After World War II diverted American manpower from the migrant workforce to industrial production and postwar prosperity made the return of Americans to such low-wage work unlikely, Mexican immigrants, either legal or illegal, are used in agricultural labor with government and popular support. After the war, particularly during economic downturns, the government has occasionally taken steps to stop or reverse immigration, and illegal immigration has become a concept. Activists like Caesar Chavez are beginning to work for the rights of immigrant farmworkers.

  Today: With downward pressure on American wages from a variety of factors (none of which are competition with illegal immigrants) over the past few years, immigrant farm labor is today a prominent political issue.

and it seems unlikely that Carleton himself and the hordes of young men among the migrant workers would be laboring in the fields when they could have earned a considerably higher wage by enlisting in the armed forces. (In fact, the war did trigger a shortage of agricultural labor, which occasioned the importing of large numbers of Mexicans as farmworkers.) If 1933 is that point in the narrative, then the farm was lost in 1923 or before, long before the Depression. Oates is certainly evoking the historical events of the Depression throughout this section of the novel, and she must simply consider the establishment of a precise chronology to be beside the point.

HISTORICAL CONTEXT

Clara, the main character of *A Garden of Earthly Delight*, is possessed of such ignorance and indifference to the larger world around her that the dramatic world events that form its background, the Great Depression and World War II, come into the story far less than one would expect in a novel with a historical setting. The point for Oates is that the novel is set during her own childhood; she is far more interested in *family* history than she is in world history or economic history or any other academic understanding of

Clara wants more than the migrant existence of her family, so she runs off with Lowry *(©Tyler Olson /*
Shutterstock.com)

history. Carleton and Clara experience the Great Depression firsthand and are aware of how it affects them. Even the meager wealth of Carleton's farmer father was lost because of a bank failure, and the family was forced to live literally hand to mouth doing the most menial and underpaid form of agricultural labor, all too common experiences for Americans at the time. Similarly, Lowry fought his way through France after the Normandy invasion in World War II, but Clara experiences it and understands it only to the degree that she realizes it affects her lover's character. Clara's rise from being the daughter of migrant farmer to being the wife of a millionaire might seem improbable and even contrived, but it is meant to echo the rising tide of economic growth that lifted the United States as a nation from poverty to prosperity, from the Depression to the economic boom of the war years.

The most striking intrusion of history into the novel comes from Oates's projection of her own interest in genealogy onto her characters. Oates casually mentions that Carleton

befriended one his fellow farmworkers based on their accents:

> The way they pronounced their *a*'s and *i*'s, the way their words slurred out into an extra syllable, turned out their father's families—Walpoles, Pickerings—were both from North England, the countryside around Newcastle—but a long time ago—neither could have said how long.

One may add that is it hard to see how either could have said their pronunciation was descended from the Newcastle accent, because neither would be likely to have gone beyond grade school (we know Carleton graduated from the sixth grade) if they were not, in fact, illiterate. More realistic is Carleton's pride in his white heritage, a manufactured identity that is one of the social structures used to control the poor, substituting bigotry for a real historical sense. Carleton's philological learning, however, clearly reflects Oates's own interests rather than the plausible concerns of her characters. Paradoxically, Oates reveals why academic historians generally regard genealogy as a pseudo-science, namely, the uncertainty of family descent due to the all-too-human practice of adultery. In *A Garden of Earthly Delight*, Swan is accepted as the heir of the Revere family and even becomes the final instrument and victim of the seeming curse on the family, but biologically he has no connection to the Reveres at all.

CRITICAL OVERVIEW

As a major work of a prominent novelist, Oates's novel *A Garden of Earthly Delights* has been extensively examined by scholars. Among original reviewers of the novel, Leonard Quirino wrote a rare scathing notice of the book, calling it out for Oates's failure in characterization. He says: "When one finishes the book, one remembers about as much of it as of a Barbara Stanwyck movie of the Thirties." He finds that the main characters have needs that cannot be fulfilled for reasons that cannot be understood and concludes: "Inscribed over the entrance to her garden of earthly delights might be the words, 'Nothing Satisfies.'" Richard Clark Sterne, characterized the work as being seen through reflections in the broken pieces of a mirror. Picking up on this idea in later studies, the novel's style is most often seen as a sort of broken naturalism where the pressures on the characters force them to move outside of all naturalistic expectations, as in Steven Barza's "Joyce Carol Oates: Naturalism and the Aberrant Response" (1979). Ellen G. Friedman, in her *Joyce Carol Oates* (1980), finds the main theme of the novel to be the control of fate over human life and the impossibility of free will. She notes that the character's fates are symbolized by their names, and when their names are abandoned (as when Clara pretends she cannot remember the name Walpole) or changed (as from Swan to Steven), the fate of the character also changes. Marilyn C. Wesley, in her *Refusal and Transgression in Joyce Carol Oates' Fiction* (1993), views the circumstances of Swan's paternity as related to myths in which a heroic figure has a divine as well as a human father (such as Romulus or Jesus). She observes that this indeterminacy is common across many of Oates's works and results in the violence of the true father being visited upon the ideological father. But she then switches to a discussion in which Lowry is not mentioned, and it is the anger of Carleton that Swan is channeling when he murders Revere.

Oates's biographer, Greg Johnson, in his *Invisible Writer* (1998), has thrown interesting light on the relationship between *A Garden of Earthly Delights* and Oates's own life and family. Johnson takes an interest in *When I Was a Little Girl and My Mother Didn't Want Me* because it is one of her most clearly autobiographical works. Johnson finds that Oates's play did not spring from some sudden revelation, as Oates herself insisted:

> As she grew older, however, Joyce's expressions of nostalgia for her family heritage appeared often in her private journal, and by the 1990s her parents' and her own recollections became the focus of several autobiographical essays.

Oates seemed to be exploring her family history systematically. "She had become particularly obsessed with the early lives of her parents," Johnson adds. The key event from Oates's background is that "Joyce's maternal grandfather, Stephen Bush, also met a violent end: he was murdered in a tavern brawl." Johnson remarks that "in 1986, when Joyce Carol Oates published *Marya: A Life*, she described the novel as a blending of her mother's early life and her own." In particular, Johnson observes: "In *Marya* the emotional matrix of Marya's childhood is virtually identical to Carolina's [Oates's mother]." Johnson points out the fact that the character of Marya's father had been killed in a bar fight and she was subsequently given away by her mother to other relatives to raise, mirroring the very circumstances of the childhood of Oates's mother Carolina. As Johnson notes, in her lecture "Beginnings," however, Oates had talked of discovering the parallel between Marya's and Carolina's childhoods only after she had completed the first draft of the novel. This seems inconsistent to Johnson with the fact that Oates had already used the same plot element in her 1967 novel *A Garden of Earthly Delights*. Oates supposedly discovered the same fact again when she interviewed Carolina, leading to the 1997 play *When I Was a Little Girl and My Mother Didn't Want Me*. Johnson excuses the contradiction in Freudian terms, suggesting that

> a note of surprised discovery has often characterized Joyce's reflections upon the details of her family history. Some of these recollections, previously denied or repressed, have struck her with the force of revelation.

The facts of Oates's life that contribute to the plot of *A Garden of Earthly Delights* seem already better known to Oates's biographer than they are to Oates herself.

IN *A GARDEN OF EARTHLY DELIGHTS* OATES PERFORMS A STRANGE DANCE OF HISTORY AND MEMORY."

CRITICISM

Bradley A. Skeen

Skeen is a classicist. In the following essay, he explores the role of memory and recollection in A Garden of Earthly Delights *and a group of closely related writings by Oates.*

In *A Garden of Earthly Delights* Oates performs a strange dance of history and memory. Events come in and out of focus with no relationship to chronology or to conventional plotting (scenes like weddings, funerals, and childbirth taking place entirely offstage). True to the maxim that the writer writes what she knows, Oates seems to be genuinely reflecting her own chaotic inner chronology. The novel takes place during the Great Depression and World War II, events that Oates refers to in the text. But she does not do so in a way that makes it possible to establish a definite chronology. Her characters are only vaguely aware of these great events, because they affect their lives very little (at least not in a way that they understand). Having been born in 1938, Oates knows these events firsthand only through the confused memories of early childhood and disjointed stories she may have heard from the older generation of her family. That seems to be the effect she is trying to capture. One can contrast the attitude shown in her contemporary Margaret Atwood's book *The Blind Assassin*, which takes place in the same period but for which Atwood hired a team of historical researchers to keep everything straight. Oates's tendency to get into chronological trouble without such help is illustrated in *A Garden of Earthly Delight* by a scene that can be dated surely no later than the late 1940s, of Swan's telling Revere that an asteroid impact was largely responsible for the extinction of the dinosaurs. This is a generally accepted hypothesis in the scientific community, which, while it was suggested as early as 1953, was not put on a firm evidentiary basis until the 1980s and did not become known to the general public (through newspaper articles and television science documentaries) until later than that. It seems to be one of many things that Oates knows and which she assumes her characters would know, without a moment's consideration of the chronological problems involved.

The failure of chronology is far from accidental. Oates positively portrays it as the natural intellectual state of her characters. In *A Garden of Earthly Delight*, the narrative voice mentions that "whenever there was an accident or motor trouble everyone was disgusted and angry and threatening to quit but a few hours later they forgot." As far as Oates is concerned, memory is a fleeting trace that is soon lost in the onrush of new events. She has to assume her characters think in the same way. A far more extreme example occurs when Clara's son, Swan, is about to be born. Clara is convinced that she does not need to go to a hospital for the birth, since she is confident nothing bad can happen during childbirth. She does not recall that a few years earlier she watched her mother die in childbirth and her friend Rosalie delivered a stillborn baby less than a year after that. She does not and cannot recall these events (though at other times and in other circumstances, she does). At the end of her own life, Clara remembers that her mother died peacefully in a farm field, because it is convenient for her to remember that. This is not simply denial, refusing to remember something too awful to remember, but a unique and selective operation of memory and fabulation. It extends to all Oates's characters, so it is something that Oates understands quite well:

> [Carleton] didn't try to add up how long he and Pearl had hired out for farmwork, how many seasons. It was like cards in a deck: shuffled together, in no order. There was no point in trying to remember because there was nothing to remember.

She does not seem to be able to understand any other relationship of memory to the past.

By examining Oates's whole career—her writings, her biography, her interviews and meta-discussions of her works—the reader can

WHAT DO I READ NEXT?

- *Joyce Carol Oates: Conversations, 1970–2006*, edited by Greg Johnson and published in 2006, is a collection of interviews with Oates, gathered from all periods of her career.

- Oates's 2001 novel *Blonde*, which was nominated for both the Pulitzer Prize and the National Book Award, examines the interior life of the American icon Marilyn Monroe.

- Oates was inspired to write her 2003 young-adult novel *Freaky Green Eyes* by the collision of media celebrity and domestic violence that came to the public's attention in the O. J. Simpson trial.

- Shilpi Somaya Gowda's 2010 novel, *Secret Daughter*, follows an Indian family from the slums of Bombay, where poverty forces them to give up their daughter for adoption, and, in alternating chapters, the life of the professional Indian American family that adopts the little girl. As she grows to adulthood, the novel contrasts the main character's past in poverty and her present in prosperity.

- *Dr. Magic: Six One Act Plays*, published in 2004, is the most recent collection of Oates's drama.

- *The Man without a Shadow* (2016) is Oates's most recent novel. Based partly on the neurophysiology of rare types of amnesia caused by brain injury, this novel is also a love story between a doctor and her patient, who is unable to form new memories.

---

gain a glimpse into Oates's detachment from the ordered, sequential world that others take for granted. Indeed, Oates's talent to write seems to arise from her unique detachment. A particularly striking example is *them*, another novel in Oates's Wonderland quartet. When it was published in 1969, she said that it was written nearly as a documentary, in the then-popular confessional style (represented by poets such as Sylvia Plath

or Robert Lowell). It had its origin, she claimed, in the book's foreword, in a correspondence she had with the matriarch of a working-class black family who had lived through the dislocations of the Detroit race riots in 1967. The letters were reproduced verbatim (with only the names changed) in the text of the novel. When the book was reissued by Modern Library in 2000, Oates stated in an afterword that the book was entirely fictitious and that she had written the letters herself, like any other fictional document. Oates molds or fabricates reality to fit her needs. If she needs a fact to be true, it is true; if she needs a memory to come to her for the first time as a startling revelation, that is what it does.

A Garden of Earthly Delights is an especially important work for understanding Oates's memory, since it is among her most autobiographical works. Yet the novel is less like remembering than it is dreaming, as Oates herself says in her afterword to the 2003 edition: "The novel opens before you like a dream, drawing you into it, yet it's a dream in which you are somehow participating, and not merely a passive observer." The autobiographical character of the book was clear to her in 2003, as it had not been in 1967. Contrasting the state of her memory in the two periods, Oates says,

> So swift and obsessive was the original composition of *A Garden of Earthly Delights* for the young writer in her mid-twenties that it didn't dawn upon me, preposterous as it must sound, that "Carleton Walpole" might have been partially modeled upon my paternal grandfather, Carlton Oates.

The circumstance she is referring to is that her "grandfather [was] . . . an apparently violent and often abusive alcoholic who had abandoned his young family to destitution in Lockport, New York, in the early 1920s." While she did not have her grandfather Carlton in her conscious mind while writing her character Carleton, perhaps, she thinks, her grandfather "acquired a mythic significance in my unconscious, if one believes in 'the unconscious' as a putative wellspring of creativity." Interestingly in regard to the connection between her family history and the plot of her novel, she says, "Only when I read biographical material about my family, in Greg Johnson's 1998 biography of my life titled *Invisible Writer*, did the connection seem obvious." This is far from the only thing Oates could have learned about her own biography and its relationship to her writing by reading Johnson's study.

Another salient fact about the character of Carleton Walpole is that he gets into a fight in a bar and kills a man. This is a motif that will be repeated in many of Oates's works throughout her career. It also derived from her biography. Johnson describes how Oates's maternal grandfather, Stephen Bush, was killed in a bar fight. In Carleton's case the action is reversed, and he kills in a bar fight (though one can almost imagine it as a symbolic struggle between the two halves of the family). Usually when Oates draws on autobiographical data, she sticks closer to the facts, showing the character's father or grandfather as the victim rather than the killer. It is also significant that after her own father's death, Oates's mother, Carolina, was given by her mother to other relatives to raise, since she could not maintain the family intact after the death of her husband.

The odd thing is that every time Oates has used this theme, she has commented about it in a lecture or an afterword, and the comments are not at all what one would expect. As we have seen, in the afterword to the 2003 edition of *A Garden of Earthly Delights*, she has said that she wrote without conscious memory of her family history and saw the parallels only from reading Johnson's biography of her, although she does not mention there the fight and death explicitly. Oates's 1986 novel *Marya: A Life* features a title character whose life was transformed when she was eight years old and her father was killed in a fight in a bar and she was subsequently sent away by her mother to other relatives to raise. The Hopwood Lecture is an annual talk given by a distinguished writer at the University of Michigan. In 1987 Oates was invited to give the lecture, and her composition is titled "Beginnings." She spoke about the process of literary creativity and gave specific examples from her then recently completed *Marya*. Oates talked about memory or, perhaps better, forgetfulness and how her family history had informed the creation of that novel:

> It wasn't until I finished a first draft of the novel that I learned, by chance, that the story I believed I had invented recapitulated an incident in my mother's early life. Not my father, of course, but her father had been murdered; not I, but my mother, had been "given away" after her father's death, to be brought up by relatives.

This goes quite a bit further than her comments about *A Garden of Earthly Delights* in the afterword to the rewritten edition. Here, Oates does not just fail to realize that her novel is rewriting her family history but positively asserts that somehow she had written in her text the same things that had happened to her mother and grandfather, without knowing it. She makes the point very clearly:

> Somehow, without knowing what I did, without knowing, in fact, that I was doing anything extraordinary at all, I had written my mother's story by way of a work of prose fiction I had "invented"....

The ellipsis is in the original. The lecture simply trails off rather than ends. It has to do so, since the implication is that some kind of force of prophecy or divination must have been at work inspiring Oates's writing against the weight of materialist science. The most generous interpretation of Oates's statement is that she consciously forgot or repressed what she had recalled and used unconsciously.

This is not the last instance. In 1998, Oates published a play, *When I Was a Little Girl and My Mother Didn't Want Me*. It is a dramatic monologue told by an actress playing the part of an old woman. She begins by simply stating what had happened to her:

> My Father was killed and I never knew why.
>
> Then, I was given away. By my mother.
>
> I was so little . . . six months.
>
> There were too many of us, nine of us,
>
> My mother gave me away.
>
> When I was old enough to know . . . I cried a lot.

The speaker goes on to fill in the tale of how this dramatic turn of events affected the course of her life. She specifies that her father died in a fight in a tavern when he was forty-four years old. So this play, too, tells the story, by now familiar. In an article Oates originally published in *O Magazine* and which she later reprinted in her own *Ontario Review*, she explains the genesis of the play. Oates had been commissioned to write a magazine story based on an interview with her mother, Carolina. One night in 1997, Oates telephoned her mother and started the interview. Their conversation did not go as Oates had imagined and at the very beginning, Carolina surprised her daughter by blurting out the statement: "Well, you know Joyce—my

Clara ends her life in a nursing home, spending her days watching television (©BrAt82 / Shutterstock.com)

mother didn't want me. When I was a baby. My mother gave me away. I used to cry a lot, I was so ashamed. My mother didn't want me." Oates says she was stunned by what she considered a revelation. As they continued to talk,

> the story emerged: my mother's father was killed at the age of 44 in a tavern fight and because there were nine children in the family, my mother, six months old, was "given away" by her desperate mother.

Oates makes it clear that this was something she was hearing for the first time, a startling revelation about her family she naturally turned into a literary work, the same thing she did each of the other times she remembered it, in *A Garden of Earthly Delights* and *Marya*. The same thing she had remembered or learned twice before. Seemingly, by 2003 when she wrote the afterword to *A Garden of Earthly Delights* she had forgotten it again, since she mentions only the parallel of her other grandfather's leaving his family, not the murder. How can Oates keep remembering the same story over and over?

An answer to this paradox can be found in Oates's journal, the first years of which were

published in 2007. In the entry for August 6, 1979, Oates writes,

> Having lived away from home for so many years now, "breaking away" at the age of eighteen, I have to nudge myself to remember, to recall, that I am a daughter as well as an individual.

In the entry for April 6, 1976, Oates writes, "I can't remember my childhood. It is lost." These statements seem prosaic enough. Written by another author, they might only mean that the life of the child seems alien to the adult, but Oates's imagination is not so simple. For Oates, memory does not function as it does for other people or as it does for other writers. It may be that Oates means that her own memories are not alive to her unless she is vividly experiencing them through recollection. Also in the April 6 entry, she says: "Memories come back spottily, disjointed, confused in time. I don't remember so much as see. Images, scenes without people, intensely-felt sights." This strengthens the hypothesis that Oates counts her memories as present only while she is remembering them. Just like most people, she does not constantly relive the events of her childhood, but when she does, they come alive to her and seem new in a way that is also unique to her, as if she is remembering for the first time.

In her journal entry for March 27, 1979, Oates writes: "The continual raking and reraking of the past doesn't interest me in itself but . . . but I halfway think it should . . . for I lose myself daily . . . hourly . . . it simply flows away . . ." Oates put the ellipses in the original text to suggest the disjointed character of her thought. It really seems as though when Oates is not actively remembering them, her memories do not exist for her. In her own perception, she can remember an old memory and feel that she is remembering it for the first time. A dormant memory means nothing to Oates until the process of creativity brings it to life to her.

Source: Bradley A. Skeen, Critical Essay on *A Garden of Earthly Delight*, in *Novels for Students*, Gale, Cengage Learning, 2017.

Greg Johnson

In the following excerpt, Johnson reads A Garden of Earthly Delights *as a critique of American greed for wealth and power.*

A Garden of Earthly Delights, Joyce Carol Oates's second novel, encompasses three generations of American life and may be considered her first major attempt to "get the whole world into a book." Opening in the early 1920s with the birth of its central character, Clara Walpole, and ending some forty years later with the tragic defeat of this vital, attractive woman, the novel is characteristically Oatesian in its sweeping inclusiveness, its attempt to dramatize a variety of social issues through the experiences of its protagonist, and its use of quasi-allegorical characters and settings. The novel considers the plight of migrant farm workers, the realities of the Depression and World War II and their relationship to American capitalism, the myth of America as a social and economic paradise, and perhaps above all the dilemma of a disenfranchised American like Clara, who is born with two strikes against her: she is a woman and she is poor.

Divided into three sections entitled "Carleton," "Lowry," and "Swan," the novel focuses on the important male figures in Clara's life: her father, lover, and son, respectively. In itself this structure suggests that *A Garden of Earthly Delights* may be read on one level as a feminist

> BUT THIS NOVEL IS RELENTLESS IN EXPOSING THE LARGER CONTEXT OF CLARA'S LIFE, A CONTEXT TO WHICH CLARA HERSELF IS LARGELY BLIND; HER SHORT-LIVED SENSE OF COMPLETION, ACHIEVED THROUGH HER VITALITY AND ABILITY TO DEAL WITH LIFE, MAKES HER LATER FALTERING AND DEFEAT SEEM ALL THE MORE DEVASTATING."

novel, the exposition of a woman's necessary relationships to men and how they affect her emotional and economic survival. Ultimately the novel depicts Clara as stronger and more vital than any of the men in her life, but as someone who is nonetheless defeated—as the men are, too—by cruel and deterministic social forces which they can scarcely perceive, much less comprehend or control.

Like much of Oates's early fiction, *A Garden of Earthly Delights* is set in the mythical Eden County, whose name—like the novel's title—represents an ironic comment on the hardscrabble and often desperate economic conditions of its inhabitants. Early in her career Oates seems to have wanted an allegorical setting not unlike Faulkner's Yoknapawtawpha County, a world of her own creation whose distinctive geography and culture might serve as a metaphor for certain universals of American life. Oates has said that Eden County is actually a portrait of Erie County in western New York, where she grew up: "I imagined the county named Eden with just certain similar elements. I don't know that it's paradise lost. It's not paradise at all. It's pretty bad as a matter of fact." Yet in Oates's rendering, especially in her first two novels, Eden County suggests the underside of the American dream, depicting America's rural dispossessed battling for survival in an economically barren, often violent world.

Her first novel, *With Shuddering Fall*, had told the story of Karen Herz's passage out of the "innocence" represented by her father's farm in Eden County and by his own strict, authoritarian control; developing a desperate infatuation with a race-car driver named Shar, who might be viewed as the snake in her father's garden, Karen bursts free of parental authority and environmental determinism only to become involved in a violent and destructive encounter with the chaotic world outside. Likewise, such notable early short stories as "In the Old World" and "The Census Taker" (from *By the North Gate*) and "Upon the Sweeping Flood" (from *Upon the Sweeping Flood*) are miniature allegorical dramas in which decent, bewildered people confront their own spiritual alienation, usually through epiphanies of emotional or physical violence. Virtually all the characters in these early works are poor and inarticulate; their stories, often beginning with the phrase "Some time ago in Eden County...," have an uncanny power as dark fables of disillusionment and defeat. Alfred Kazin has described Oates's genre in such works as "silent tragedy," a tragedy whose characters struggle vainly against the environment: "They touch us by frightening us, like disembodied souls calling to us from another world. They live through terrifying events but cannot understand them."

The opening sections of *A Garden of Earthly Delights* set the tone for a series of such terrifying events: a truck carrying migrant workers collides with a car on a country highway, causing Clara Walpole's premature birth and beginning a life story marked by external, uncontrollable forces. Oates focuses the early chapters on Clara's father, Carleton, a young man "who looked as if he had forgotten his age." Forced into migrant farm work by the loss of his own farm, Carleton has reached the breaking point after years of poverty, uncertainty, and the responsibilities of a wife and five children. Though he and his fellow workers dream of someday returning home and regaining economic stability, the long hours of numbing farm work have encouraged passivity and resignation: "They liked to stare out at the road and watch it move under them because this meant they were getting somewhere, but as for really seeing anything—no. They needed eyes only for getting around and picking fruit and taking care of themselves. They did not need to see anything or to be conscious of anything."

...In the final pages of the novel Swan has become a troubled, unpredictable young man who has abandoned intellectual pursuits: "He was safe forever from the great bulging shelves of libraries everywhere, all those books

demanding to be read, known, taken into account—that vast systematic garden of men's minds that seemed to him to have been toiled into its complex existence by a sinister and inhuman spirit." He has become a self-consciously ruthless businessman who is apparently following in Revere's footsteps, although the reader understands that his psychological turmoil has reached a dangerous intensity. Thus, like many of Oates's fictions, the novel ends in an eruption of violence that resembles the last act of a Renaissance tragedy: Swan brings home a gun and confronts his parents, threatening his mother first but turning the gun at last upon Revere and then upon himself. The brief concluding chapter shows Clara as a defeated, broken woman in her mid-forties, driven mad by her experiences and living in a private nursing home. She spends her time staring at the television, and the novel concludes: "She seemed to like best programs that showed men fighting, swinging from ropes, shooting guns and driving fast cars, killing the enemy again and again until the dying gasps of evil men were only a certain familiar rhythm away from the opening blasts of the commercials, which changed only gradually over the years."

The ultimately tragic action of *A Garden of Earthly Delights* may best be understood as a critique of the American dream and its relentless drive toward money, acquisition, and power. The three generations of the Walpole family—Carleton, Clara, Swan—present a microcosm of American society ranging from the economic outcast to the youthful heir; but even though the Walpoles advance themselves materially, they cannot escape the spiritual destruction ensured by their assuming the perverted and antihumanistic values of the surrounding culture. Like the sixteenth-century painting by Heironymous Bosch from which Oates has borrowed her title, the novel is finally allegorical. According to Rose Marie Burwell, who has studied the Bosch triptych in relation to Oates's novel, the painting shows "the creation of Eve in Eden, the debauchery of her descendants in the earthly garden of delights, and the punishment of mankind in hell." In the novel, however, "Eden" is a barren, ungiving world at the outset, and the "debauchery" of the characters is merely their frantic effort to survive. Their punishment, then, is unmerited, and the moral burden of the novel does not rest upon individual "sin" but upon the basic imperatives of American economic and social reality. The Walpoles cannot know themselves and each other because their individual struggles for survival lead them away from personal integrity and dignity into fragmentation, self-delusion, and an ultimate frustration that leads, in turn, to insanity and violence.

Because of the terrible burden placed upon the male in a society that emphasizes brute power and conquest, both Carleton and Swan become old men before their time, destroyed by a sense of personal inadequacy and failure. It is Clara who forms the bridge between these two very different but equally tragic figures, and in her early life Clara seems to represent the possibility of transcendence. As a child she is a delight and comfort to her father; as a teen-ager she gives her sincere, ardent love to Lowry; and finally she gives birth to a golden-haired son whom she calls "Swan." In her spontaneity, resilience, and sensual power the youthful Clara is emblematic of a garden spiritually untouched by the American machine. Despite her childhood poverty and separation from her family, Clara embodies a natural strength and potential for growth that Oates clearly respects. She once told an interviewer, "I have a great admiration for those females who I know from my own life, my background, my family—very strong female figures who do not have much imagination in an intellectual sense, but they're very capable of dealing with life." In this sense, of course, Clara's going after and "landing" Curt Revere may be seen as admirable rather than pernicious, as she is seeking her own and her son's survival. She is dealing with life in the only way open to her. After moving into the house owned by Revere, she enters for a time into the self-created transcendence of her own motherhood and a luxuriant isolation. Not surprisingly, the house has a garden in back:

> It was a large garden for just a woman to handle. . . . [It] was Clara's garden and no one else's, and when her eyes moved from plant to plant, pausing at each dusty familiar flower and occasional insects she'd flick off with an angry snap of her fingers, a feeling of accomplishment rose up in her. The garden was as much of the world as she wanted because it was all that she could handle, being just Clara, and it was beautiful. She did not want anything else.

But this novel is relentless in exposing the larger context of Clara's life, a context to which Clara herself is largely blind; her short-lived

sense of completion, achieved through her vitality and ability to deal with life, makes her later faltering and defeat seem all the more devastating. Inevitably she progresses from being Revere's mistress to being his wife, naturally seeing this rise in her status as a personal victory and as an opportunity for Swan, whom she has allowed Revere to think is his own son. Yet her rise toward economic security and power exacts a tragic spiritual cost, resulting in the breakdown and suicide of her son, and finally her own breakdown. Ironically, the reader's last glimpse shows Clara watching television programs depicting violent conflicts between men that are alternated with commercials, suggesting the symbiotic forces—masculine violence and American capitalism—that have destroyed Clara's innocence and, finally, her spirit . . . .

Source: Greg Johnson, "*A Garden of Earthly Delights*," in *Understanding Joyce Carol Oates*, University of South Carolina Press, 1987, pp. 28–32, 43–47.

Ellen G. Friedman

In the following excerpt, Friedman sums up a major lesson in A Garden of Earthly Delights: *the world cannot be defeated, and one cannot escape one's past.*

The idea of fate, the idea that one cannot transcend the conditions of one's existence, is central to Oates's vision. In *With Shuddering Fall*, it means that Karen cannot escape the fact that she is a Herz; to Oates man is an associated being, defined by the circumstances of his life and by the circumstances of his culture. She has said, "It's difficult for individuals to go beyond their culture, in terms of individuation, to break through to a higher, transpersonal set of ideals." In her novels this "difficulty" is repeatedly portrayed. Unlike romantic writers who value the attempt of their protagonists to defy or transcend their society, Oates sees meaning in the defeat of this attempt because it demonstrates what is for her a more compelling truth: that the world cannot be defeated. Fate is thus an instrument of history, whether personal or collective, or of culture, or of time; it is always an instrument of those implacable forces that limit the horizons of man's destiny. Oates's shift in the Romantics' emphasis on the heroic struggle to the inevitable defeat may be gleaned from a passage in her essay on *Troilus and Cressida*. "Man's goals are fated to be less than his ideals would

" WHEN THE ESTABLISHMENT OF SELF DEPENDS SOLELY ON THE ASSERTION OF WILL, SUCCESS IS DETERMINED BY ONE'S PREDATORY POWERS, BY ONE'S ABILITY TO BE VICTORIOUS IN A DARWINIAN STRUGGLE."

have them and when he realizes this truth he is 'enlightened' in the special sense in which tragedy enlightens men—a flash of bitter knowledge that immediately precedes death." For Oates enlightenment is a product of the defeat, rather than a product of the struggle. Her aim is not to sanctify the isolated hero, but, we remember, to sanctify the world.

Her next three novels—*A Garden of Earthly Delights* (1967), *Expensive People* (1968), and *them* (1969)—comprise a trilogy. These books, which deal explicitly and self-consciously with American culture, are set respectively in rural, suburban, and urban America. According to Oates, they concern "social and economic facts of life in America, combined with unusually sensitive—but hopefully representative young men and women, who confront the puzzle of American life in different ways and come to different ends." Despite the differences among them in style and subject matter, each of these novels describes the defeat of the romantic, over-reaching will that strives to overcome fate.

In Oates, the great symbol of American dis-location is the Depression. It is a palpable historical symbol of dislocation because it is still within memory. If it has not immediately affected our lives, it has affected the lives of our fathers. Indeed, Oates has spoken of the impact the Depression had on her father's life. In *A Garden of Earthly Delights* and *Wonderland*, and to a lesser extent in *them* and *Childwold*, it is the initial impetus for the disintegration of an associated life, rooted to family and place.

After the protagonists of *A Garden of Earthly Delights* and *Wonderland* are deprived of their pasts, of their family and home, by the Depression, the crucial question for them becomes the creation of a self that can be

projected into the future. Dislocated, they depend solely on the sufficiency of the self. In order to maintain that self, they begin to assert their will over their environment until the environment is subordinated to the isolated will, in a sense conquered by it.

The process by which the self becomes autonomous, by which the self is substituted for the world, repeatedly leads Oates's characters to a denial of their pasts. Oates often depicts this denial of the past through her characters' denial of the names with which they were born. Both Clara in *Garden of Earthly Delights* and Jesse in *Wonderland* disavow their surnames; this disavowal represents their refutation of their personal history and their attempt to create their own identity with nothing but their own volition. In fact, in a repudiation of her origins, Clara refuses to even remember her surname; and the underlying cause of her son's misery and his eventual suicide is this very repudiation of origins, which is a repudiation of his origins as well. Moreover, her son's Christian name is also changed—from Swan to Steven. In Oates, name is a metaphor for fate, and in attempting to change fate, which name changes imply, one risks an irrevocable alienation. The mother in *Expensive People*, for instance, changes her name from the prosaic "Nancy" to the exotic "Nada," but her new name betrays her accomplishment; she has exchanged "Nancy," signifying a person associated to the world in ordinary ways, for "Nada," signifying nothingness.

In *A Garden of Earthly Delights*, the dislocation that begins with the historical circumstance of the Depression is intensified by the assertion of the Faustian, overreaching will, which in conquering a world, begets megalomania, solipsism, and nihilism, stances of the homeless self. Unlike Karen (*With Shuddering Fall*), the protagonist does not find his way back home because he has no authentic "home" to which to return.

The book begins in the early 1920's and ends in the mid 1960's, and the great events that mark this period—the Depression, World War II, the postwar economic boom—serve not only to give the book a chronology that locates the action, but also to set the limits against which the individual strains.

The novel follows three generations of the Walpole family, from the land-and-family-oriented grandfather, Carleton, to the dispossessed and alienated grandson, Swan. The family's growth into dislocation is paralleled by the dislocation of the population of Tintern—where the novel's second and third sections are set—as well as America, by the Depression, war, and postwar industry. In Oates, the personal drama always reflects an historical or a cultural drama. Sons and fathers and husbands lose their share in the world during the Depression and have to work for others. Then they are torn from their families by war; everyone is set loose to encounter life on his own; the fine web of ties unknots, setting people adrift. And the increasing centralization of postwar industry and agriculture draws Tintern's population away until Tintern becomes a community of outsiders.

... It is this predatory landscape, Oates is suggesting, that is the legacy of the imperialistic will, Clara's legacy. When the establishment of self depends solely on the assertion of will, success is determined by one's predatory powers, by one's ability to be victorious in a Darwinian struggle. It is ironic that Clara, who is responsible for shaping the world into Boschean proportions for Swan, is the only character who even momentarily finds Wordsworthian harmony: she finds it in her garden, which she cultivates while waiting for Revere's wife to die. "The garden was as much of the world as she wanted because it was all that she could handle. . . . " In her garden, "she would stand transfixed, as if she were at the threshold of a magic world." It is ironic, too, that Lowry offers her this kind of world and that she rejects it.

For Clara, who, as suggested, is an embodiment of American imperialism, Wordsworthian harmony with nature is no longer a compelling idea. The hope for conquest, not harmony motivates her actions. Faust, not Wordsworth, is her true romantic ancestor; and it is finally Faust's legacy, Oates suggests, with which we must grapple.

The value of Clara's assertion of will is judged in the end by its results. In the climactic scene, Swan, now a young man whose violent ambivalence toward the Revere name and wealth builds to an intolerable level, confronts Clara and Revere with a gun. His intention is to kill Clara, but when she calls him "weak," because he does not have the strength of will to assume his usurped role, he shoots Revere and himself, resolving his ambivalence in nihilism.

In Oates's vision, the world that the will forces into existence is a world that leaves behind no legacy and which is finally not self-serving. Indeed, Oates ends the novel with an ironic image of Clara in middle age: She is subject to moments of paralysis; the entire Revere fortune is used to support her existence in a nursing home, where she spends her time watching television programs "that showed men fighting . . . killing the enemy again and again until the dying gasps of evil men were only a certain familiar rhythm away from the opening blasts of commercials, which changed only gradually over the years." In these television shows, she watches versions of the Darwinian drama of her life. Clara's megalomania has finally defeated her. The "home" she has won is a place where senescent, homeless strangers await death. Ironically, her efforts have succeeded in providing her with only enough money to sustain her homelessness in style.

Finally, however, we do not feel moral outrage at Clara's actions; we merely observe her and even admire, just a little, her audacity, her success. And though we admit that she deserves her end, we also admit that Swan does not. He is a type of modern man, struggling against his own dislocation and incoherence, his "world alienation," inheriting a conflict he cannot satisfactorily resolve. We sympathize with his view of existence as a grotesque Boschean landscape. Although the assumption which vitalizes the art of the religious painter Bosch—that life is a struggle between good and evil—is not Oates's, or ours, the image of existence that he creates is perhaps a valid representation of the fruits of a greedy and imperialistic assertion of will that not only intensifies the individual's isolation, but that makes of him a predator who stalks the world, and stalks it alone.

Source: Ellen G. Friedman, "World Alienation: *A Garden of Earthly Delights*," in *Joyce Carol Oates*, Frederick Ungar Publishing, 1980, pp. 35–38, 51–53.

SOURCES

Barza, Steven, "Joyce Carol Oates: Naturalism and the Aberrant Response," in *Studies in American Fiction*, Vol. 7, No. 2, 1979, pp. 141–51.

Centers for Disease Control and Prevention, Trends in Out-of-Hospital Births in the United States, 1990–2012, CDC website, http://www.cdc.gov/nchs/products/data briefs/db144.htm (accessed July 30, 2016).

Friedman, Ellen G., *Joyce Carol Oates*, Frederick Ungar, 1980, pp. 35–53.

Johnson, Greg, *Invisible Writer: A Biography of Joyce Carol Oates*, E. P. Dutton, 1998, pp. 1–11.

Oates, Joyce Carol, "Beginnings," Hopwood Lecture 1987, in *Michigan Quarterly Review*, http://prod.lsa.umich.edu/content/dam/hopwood-assets/documents/Hopwood%20Lectures/HopwoodLecture-1987%20Joyce%20Carol%20Oates.PDF (accessed April 1, 2016).

———, *A Garden of Earthly Delights*, Vanguard, 1967, pp. 38–39.

———, *A Garden of Earthly Delights*, Modern Library, 2003, p. 398.

———, "Interview with Carolina Oates," https://web.archive.org/web/20110817081335/http://www.planetbookgroupie.com/MemorybyPhilippeGrimbert.htm (accessed March 25, 2016).

———, *The Journal of Joyce Carol Oates, 1973–1982*, edited by Greg Johnson, HarperCollins, 2007, pp. 101, 310, 321.

———, *Marya: A Life*, E. P. Dutton, 1986, pp. 28–30.

———, *When I Was a Little Girl and My Mother Didn't Want Me*, in *New Plays*, Ontario Review Press, 1998, pp. 279–82.

Quirino, Leonard, Review of *A Garden of Earthly Delights*, in *Novel: A Forum on Fiction*, Vol. 2, No. 2, 1969, pp. 188–90.

Sterne, Richard Clark, "Versions of Rural America," in *Nation*, April 1, 1968, pp. 448–49.

Wesley, Marilyn C., *Refusal and Transgression in Joyce Carol Oates' Fiction*, Greenwood Press, 1993, pp. 75–79.

FURTHER READING

Oates, Joyce Carol, *Bellefleur*, E. P. Dutton, 1980.
    This novel deals with Oates's family origin in the Hungarian immigrant community of Buffalo but treats the material in a magic realist, or gothic, way.

———, *A Widow's Story: A Memoir*, Ecco, 2011.
    In this memoir Oates explores the impact on her life of the death of her first husband, Raymond Smith.

Steinbeck, John, *The Grapes of Wrath*, Viking, 1939.
    The Grapes of Wrath is the classical tale of the journey of a family of dispossessed farmers across the country to California in the hope of finding new opportunity in the midst of the Great Depression.

Wagner, Linda W., ed., *Critical Essays on Joyce Carol Oates*, G. K. Hall, 1979.
    This older collection of Oates scholarship illustrates the period of Oates's reception during which she was recognized as a major modern author, far earlier in her career than is usually the case.

SUGGESTED SEARCH TERMS

Joyce Carol Oates

Oates AND A Garden of Earthly Delights

The Garden of Earthly Delights AND Hieronymus Bosch

modernism

Great Depression AND novels

World War II AND novels

childhood memories

nostalgia AND childhood

genealogy

Hope Was Here

JOAN BAUER

2000

Joan Bauer's sixth young-adult novel, *Hope Was Here*, published in 2000, is her most popular and well known, and her own favorite. It epitomizes the philosophy in every one of her novels that adversity can make one stronger if one keeps hope. This Newbery Honor Book is often taught in schools and has the praise of teachers and librarians. Bauer was surprised when she went to Kazakhstan, Croatia, and Shanghai on cultural exchange visits to find that teens all over the world loved *Hope Was Here* and could understand it as relevant to their lives. The messages of making it through tough times with hope, faith, and community and fighting corruption resonate everywhere. The novel has been translated into German, Italian, Spanish, and Mandarin. In addition to having her book taught in schools, Bauer has been a guest speaker at community workshops on grief, where the book is used for group healing.

Central to the power of *Hope Was Here* are the quests of the sixteen-year-old waitress Hope Yancey for a place in life and for a father. Her finding a dad in G.T. Stoop as he is dying of cancer but also engaged in a mayoral campaign, in which he enlists Hope, is depicted in a touching and delicate way. G.T. shows Hope how to grow up in the world by not being afraid, by being honest, and by being herself. He rallies the teens to fight political corruption in their small town of Mulhoney, Wisconsin, thus bringing them through a rite of passage as his last act.

Joan Bauer (©ZUMA Press, Inc. | Alamy)

The novel is classified as a realistic quest. The ritual of G.T.'s accepting Hope as his daughter by grafting two tree branches together makes this novel almost mythic in places, yet the dirty small-town politics of Mulhoney sound real.

AUTHOR BIOGRAPHY

Bauer was born on July 12, 1951, in River Forest, Illinois, the eldest of four sisters. She was raised by her mother, a high school English teacher, and her grandmother. Her alcoholic father was seldom around and committed suicide when Bauer was in her twenties. Like Hope in the novel, Bauer was devastated by the loss of her father. Her grandmother was a professional storyteller and told stories to her granddaughters with humor, using various voices. As a child, Bauer kept a diary and wrote poems, stories, and folk songs. She loved humor and wanted to be a comedian or comedy writer.

Bauer had a troubled adolescence because of her relationship with her father. She dropped out of high school and left home at seventeen to work as a waitress, as Hope does in the novel. Bauer also worked as an assistant typing teacher and a freelance writer. She lucked into a writing career in advertising for the *Chicago Tribune*, McGraw-Hill, and *Parade* magazine but felt frustrated at the lack of creativity. She took college courses in writing and screenwriting and never stopped writing from childhood on, often winning poetry contests. She met and married her husband, Evan, a computer engineer, in 1981. Her daughter, Jean, was born in 1982. As of mid-2016, Bauer lives with her family in Brooklyn, New York, and is a cooking enthusiast.

Bauer decided to change direction after being injured in a severe car crash. During a long recovery after neurosurgery, she began to write young-adult fiction. Her first novel, *Squashed* (1992), is about an overweight teen who raises a champion three-hundred-pound pumpkin. The book won the Delacorte Prize for a first novel and marked the beginning of Bauer's successful career as a writer and speaker. *Thwonk* (1995) is about the pitfalls of teen romance. Another favorite, *Rules of the Road* (1998), about a young woman who learns the world of business, was named one of the top young-adult novels of the last quarter century by the American Library Association. *Hope Was Here* (2000) is Bauer's best-known work. *Stand Tall* (2002) has a male protagonist, a six-foot-three twelve-year-old boy named Tree. *Best Foot Forward* (2005), the sequel to *Rules of the Road*, is about the main character's promotion. *Peeled* (2008) is a about a teen reporter. *Close to Famous* (2011) tells the story of Foster McFee, who dreams of hosting her own show on the Food Network. *Almost Home* (2012) is the story of a homeless mother and daughter in Chicago. *Soar* (2015) is about a boy who undergoes a heart transplant.

Hope Was Here was a Newbery Honor Award Book. Bauer won the American Library Association Best Book for Young Adults Award for *Thwonk*, *Rules of the Road*, *Hope Was Here*, and *Close to Famous*; the ASTAL/Rhode Island College Award for Outstanding Contributions to Literature for Young People, 2007; two Christopher Awards; the *Chicago Tribune* Young Adult Literary Prize, 2011; a New England Booksellers Award; the Literary Light Award from the Boston Public Library; the *LA Times* Book Prize; and the Judy Lopez Memorial Award, among others.

PLOT SUMMARY

Chapter 1

The first-person narrator of *Hope Was Here*, Hope Yancey, is a teen-aged waitress recalling how she first got the job. She was a bus girl in the Rainbow Diner in Pensacola, Florida, when a waitress accidentally spilled soup on a customer and became hysterical. The manager fired her and turned to fourteen-year-old Hope, asking if she wanted the job, provided she was not the kind who fell apart when things got rough. That was Hope's clue that the restaurant business required courage, and she decided she could handle it. She makes good money as a teen waitress at three different restaurants, moving each time with her aunt, Addie, a short-order cook who is raising her.

Hope's favorite job is at the Blue Box in Brooklyn, New York. Addie is a cook and part owner with Gleason Beal, who absconds with their money and leaves Addie with the debts and bills. Addie has to close the diner and take a stab at an unknown position in Wisconsin, so at sixteen, Hope is moving again and bitter about it. Hope has a way of saying good-bye to a place. She writes *Hope was here* in some small place to show that she has been there. Addie and Hope fill Addie's old Buick and the trailer that it hauls. Hope is going to miss her best friends from high school, Miriam Lahey and Harrison Beckworth-McCoy.

Hope is upbeat even though she has had a rough life. She was born prematurely, weighing two pounds. Her mother, Deena, a waitress, did not want a child and left her with her older sister, Addie. Hope does not know who her father is, and she has seen her mother only three times. Her mother named her Tulip, but Addie let her change her name to Hope when she was twelve. Addie never gives up on Hope and has stood by her, so Hope sees her as her mother figure. Hope also accepts that she is in a nontraditional family.

Chapter 2

Hope looks at the cardboard boxes on the back seat of the Buick. They contain the remnants of her life—dictionary and thesaurus, globe, and

MEDIA ADAPTATIONS

- An unabridged audiobook of *Hope Was Here*, read by Jenna Lamia, was produced by Listening Library in 2003. The run time is four hours and thirty-one minutes.

eleven scrapbooks to show her biological father if he ever enters her life again. She has the feeling that this man is searching for her. Hope explains that her philosophy of life is not to expect roses. That way she can regroup more easily if things are hard.

On the trip, Hope nostalgically remembers the good times at her last school and wonders how she will make new friends in Wisconsin. She remembers how she threw a tantrum when she was ten and ran away when Addie said they had to move. She hides in a friend's attic but then becomes frightened and runs home, not wanting to be abandoned. Addie explains that she would not leave without Hope because she needs Hope as much as Hope needs a mother. Hope remembers all the new starts in Atlanta, Pensacola, Brooklyn, and now, Mulhoney, Wisconsin, outside Milwaukee. The new diner is called Welcome Stairways Diner for the double welcome stairways in the Quaker style in front of the two-story building. They will live in a free apartment upstairs, given them by the owner, G.T. Stoop, who has to have help because he has leukemia.

As they approach Mulhoney, Hope and Addie see a sign reading "Reelect our mayor, Eli Millstone." They sit in the car outside the restaurant and watch patrons come out. Addie decides from looking at their faces that the food is not that good. She is a take-charge cook and plans to start right away.

Chapter 3

Addie and Hope sit in the diner studying the decor, layout, and menu. Addie is critical. They meet the bus man, Yuri, and the floor manager and waitress, Flo. Some men come into the restaurant and demand that Flo place a sign for Eli Millstone in the window. She tells them G.T. is against that. The men sit down to eat and make fun of Yuri's accent and Russian origin. Addie tries to rescue Yuri by asking for coffee.

They move into their apartment, and Addie gives wise counsel to Hope not to let the incident with the con man, Gleason Beal, destroy her heart. He has taken their money but not their souls. Hope had been particularly hurt by the betrayal because Gleason played up to her as a possible father figure.

Chapter 4

Addie and Hope watch G.T. in his kitchen cooking short orders. He is cheerful and jokes with the customers and waitresses. He does not look as if he has cancer. He is thin and bald and wears glasses. Addie claims that she can improve his business with new dishes. G.T. is sympathetic with what the move means to a teenager like Hope, but she bravely claims she is adaptable. He tells her to be herself around him. He jokes about his cancer, saying he is not dead yet. A tall, young cook comes to work and is introduced as Braverman, the grill man, second in command. Hope gives him a 6.7 on the male cuteness scale.

The other waitress, Lou Ellen, is not happy about Hope's arrival and challenges her about her waitressing experience. Hope says she worked in New York when there were lines so long she could not go to the bathroom for five hours. She can carry five platters on her arm, and Lou Ellen can carry only three. Addie criticizes the coffee cake, but G.T. says it is based on his mother's recipe. Braverman and G.T. are both experts and throw their spatulas into the air and catch them to show off.

The next day Braverman takes Addie and Hope to the town parade, where there are election signs for Millstone. Braverman explains angrily that the bully Millstone has been the unchallenged mayor for eight years. Millstone is at the microphone when G.T. interrupts to announce his candidacy for mayor. He is fifty-four years old and has cancer, but in his remaining time he wants to clean up the town. City government favors Real Fresh Dairy, the big business that has come in and caused the local dairies to close. The town needs better roads and day care, a community center, and jobs for the young. G.T. says he has done research and found out that Real Fresh Dairy has not paid taxes for

five years. Braverman begins to clap. Millstone is angry, but G.T. gets the crowd on his side with jokes and common sense.

Chapter 5

After G.T.'s announcement, the diner is even busier, especially on Memorial Day. G.T. is answering questions from patrons about politics while Addie cooks in unfamiliar surroundings and Hope practices her serving skills to prove she is up to the mark, despite Lou Ellen's pessimism. Hope balances six coffee cups at once. Sheriff Greebs comes in to announce the diner is illegally over the occupancy limit and threatens to shut them down. He is Millstone's man and harassing G.T.

Hope describes the fierceness of food service and the rush she gets from being fast and competent. Cecelia Culpepper, the editor of the *Mulhoney Messenger*, interviews G.T. about why he is running for office and takes notes. G.T. says he has tried to talk to Millstone about the dairy's not paying its taxes but that the mayor will not meet with him. Flo introduces Hope to Brenda Babcock, the sheriff's deputy who has just transferred from Minneapolis. Hope manages to loosen up an uptight customer by recommending a new dish to him. He smiles in appreciation.

G.T. is trying to get people to sign a petition to put him on the ballot, and Sheriff Greebs is hanging around to intimidate the crowd. The people who have jobs at the Real Fresh Dairy are afraid to sign the petition for fear of losing their jobs. Pastor Al B. Hall comes in and brings support for his friend, G.T. Braverman gets one of Hope's orders wrong, but she has learned that the cook is always right and does not give him a hard time. Hope remembers the waitressing advice her mother has given her, but she is disappointed that her mother is not interested in her. Braverman asks Hope to join in with the other high school students to get signatures for G.T.'s petition. He is loyal to G.T. because G.T. gave him his job and training when his mother was out of work. Braverman is working to support his family instead of going to college. At the end of the trying first day in the Welcome Stairways Diner, Hope is close to tears, but G.T. finds her and tells her she is a fine waitress and knows how to connect with people. She is happy.

Chapter 6

Hope joins Braverman and four students from Mulhoney High School to get signatures for G.T.'s petition. One is Adam Pulver, the president of the political club. Adam tells his crew that if any information is wrong on the petition or the person is not a registered voter, the signature does not count. More teenagers arrive to help, all with stories about how G.T. has helped them and their families. Hope runs into stubborn people who do not want to sign because G.T. is dying or because they don't want to lose their jobs.

Braverman reminds people that G.T. gives food to people who are out of work, that he has helped establish the emergency medical center in town, and that he is always looking out for others. Hope sticks with G.T. as they go around town, but she misses New York. Braverman tells her that the Real Fresh Dairy backs Millstone and basically controls how its employees vote. He shows her the mayor's brand-new mansion. Millstone is best friends with Cranston Broom, the dairy owner. Hope thinks back to the crook Gleason Beal, who seemed to give favors while stabbing people in the back by taking their money. At the end of the day, Hope raises Braverman's score to a 7.4. Millstone hassles G.T. by hiring a funeral hearse to park in front of his diner. The students are angry, but G.T. tells them the bully tactics are designed to get a reaction.

Chapter 7

Hope has her room arranged and boxes unpacked but wonders when the feeling of belonging will come. She looks at her boxing gloves. A policeman friend taught her to box when she was eleven years old. She punched the bag until tears came down her face at being left by her mother. When she was exhausted, the anger was gone. In the back section of her scrapbook, she keeps pictures of men she thinks look like her father, mostly businessmen with smiles holding their children. She has a fantasy session talking to her father, asking his advice about how she will adapt to this small town. She goes to work early, at five in the morning. Addie has been there since four, baking bread. The doors open at six, and the diner is packed by seven o'clock.

Adam Pulver tells G.T. about his uncle Sid Vole, a spin doctor who can help with the campaign. Hope waits on the table that becomes a political conference with Sid, G.T., Adam, the students, and other locals, such as the barber and Pastor Hall. Sid tells G.T. to find the vision thing, a clear goal. He could make the cancer work for him. He should have the image of

Mr. Clean. They all laugh because G.T. is bald from chemotherapy. Sid tells the table that politics is war and that they must be united. He advises G.T. to do something to combat Cranston Broom about the hearse's being parked out front, which is harassment and a reminder that G.T. is dying. G.T. does not listen to this advice but instead goes out to shake the hearse driver's hand and invite him in for a free meal. Hope gets the point and gets the man a delicious meal of Addie's specialties. G.T. makes a speech using the hearse as an example, and people in the diner applaud.

Chapter 8

After Sid leaves, the people at the campaign table argue about whether they need a spin doctor. Finally, G.T. turns to Hope to ask her opinion. She is surprised. She makes a restaurant metaphor about how it is like working with a difficult cook to achieve magic. G.T. agrees with her. Town emotion is high, and discussions in the diner about politics become heated. In the kitchen, Addie lectures Braverman on cooking. On a break, G.T. shows Hope the trees he planted in the backyard: the oak when he married, the dogwood when his wife died, the maple when Al opened his church. Adam Pulver interrupts with the news that the election board has denied the petition. Sid advises a showdown with the board the next day.

Lou Ellen breaks down crying during work, explaining that her fourteen-month-old baby is sick. The child does not sit up or respond to stimuli. Braverman is angry and flares up at Hope. A crowd of men from the Elks Club come in, and the restaurant is swamped, but Lou Ellen has to go home. Hope turns into a warrior waitress. She thinks fast, trying to talk all of the customers into ordering the same thing. It works. Braverman and Hope make it through the rough night together as a team and congratulate each other.

Chapter 9

The next morning, G.T., Braverman, Adam, Sid, Pastor Hall, and the students, including Hope, show up at the election board. All fifty-five names on the petition have the wrong address, the clerk says. Braverman and Sid are angry and challenge the findings, but the case is closed. Just then, Pastor Hall speaks in his powerful preacher's voice, saying the Lord always gives a second chance. The clerk says she will give them until five o'clock that afternoon. The group spreads out to find more signatures, and Hope is attacked by a group of men who try to take the petition. Deputy Babcock races to respond to Hope's screams for help and is followed by Addie. Deputy Babcock takes the men in a squad car to the police station. These are the Carbinger boys, who live on the edge of town and are known as troublemakers. The students led by Adam get the required signatures by five o'clock, and G.T. is on the ballot. There is celebration in the diner that night. Cecelia Culpepper, the newspaper editor, is there to hear the statements of both candidates. G.T. offers to give Millstone a free dinner, and the photographer snaps pictures. Millstone becomes uncomfortable and leaves.

Chapter 10

Lou Ellen's baby, Anastasia, is allowed to remain with her while she works. The staff sets up a portable playpen in the diner office, now the campaign headquarters, run by Adam. The diner staff take turns watching the baby. G.T. is out giving campaign speeches. Sid tries to teach G.T. how to compose a proper speech, but G.T. refuses, saying that his Quaker roots have taught him to rely on God to give him the right words. G.T. tells the truth and does not hide that he is dying of cancer. Hope gets a long letter from her New York friends with postcards of New York and puts them around her room, remembering the poetry readings they used to attend. Braverman has ten-year-old twin sisters who try to get Anastasia to respond, but they cannot. Adam organizes Students for Stoop, and Hope becomes friends with Jillian. Jillian believes Adam is a genius and will be president someday. She has made a web page for G.T. Braverman is going to edit a newsletter. Jillian tells Hope she and Braverman would be a perfect couple. She says that Braverman was going to major in journalism, but his mother became ill, and his dad ran out on the family, so Braverman has to support them. She hints that Braverman likes Hope.

Chapter 11

Teens keep coming to support G.T., and Cecelia prints letters supporting his campaign. She has written an editorial demanding proof that the dairy has paid its taxes. G.T. is driving himself too hard, but Addie is becoming famous for her cooking. Still, things start to become complicated: four burglaries have occurred in town, one of them at Adam's house. Deputy Babcock says it is the work of the same person or people. The burglars have chosen houses of people who signed G.T.'s petition. Real Fresh Dairy also cancelled its advertising in Cecelia's newspaper. Hope becomes friends with Lou Ellen and tries to help with Anastasia, who has no dad, just like Hope. Cranston Broom, the president of Real Fresh Dairy, announces support for Millstone. Braverman is exhausting himself working for G.T. Brenda Babcock is sitting in the diner on her day off when a woman screams and reveals a dead mouse in a salad. Brenda whips out her deputy badge and asks the couple, who are from out of town, to sign a document. She then takes the mouse from them for evidence. They say they will not press charges and just want to go. Brenda announces to the customers that the visitors were trying to shut down the diner.

Chapter 12

G.T. asks Hope to come along with him for a day of campaigning. G.T. refuses to look at the list of those who contributed money to his campaign. He is running for everyone, he says. Hope sees that the people love G.T. He connects to each one personally. Hope is inspired and worries about how hard he is pushing himself. G.T. asks Hope about her mother, and Hope says she has had to deal with the fact that her mother does not want her. G.T. tells her that you can face down disappointments until they become strengths, as he has done with his cancer. They talk to a group of cancer survivors who have learned to live one day at a time. When G.T. looks bad, Hope persuades him to go home.

Chapter 13

Hope sees G.T. to his apartment and then goes to the kitchen, where she expects to find Braverman, but instead Addie is cooking his shift. Braverman has been beaten up and is in the hospital. It happened to be Brenda Babcock's day off. Hope calls Jillian and cries over the phone, showing that she cares for Braverman. She goes to his house and finds him wearing bandages over his broken ribs. Three guys have attacked him, and he is very angry.

When Jillian spreads the word online about the beating, many teens come to sign up for the campaign. G.T. goes to the mayor's office to demand an investigation into the beating. He says he does not believe Sheriff Greebs will tell the truth. Braverman writes an article for the paper describing the beating. He goes around speaking out for the election. The lab report shows there were no rodent hairs in the Welcome Stairways kitchen. The mouse had been dead for a week, and the couple had been arrested for passing bad checks. Braverman, however, is changing, consumed with the desire for revenge against Millstone. G.T.'s health is up and down, but Hope is getting close to him. They understand each other. Meanwhile, Sid Vole leaves town for another campaign.

Chapter 14

Hope has a customer, Mr. Woldenburg, who always orders the same thing, an American cheese sandwich, though she tries to get him to try new things. He also mentions he never votes. The campaign is receiving wider publicity, and reporters from outside the area come to interview G.T. Hope begins working with Anastasia, identifying with her because she also was a slow starter as a two-pound baby. The baby starts to respond as Hope teaches her to hold a bottle and feed herself. Lou Ellen starts crying; she and Hope have become friends. Addie tells Hope that her mother is coming to visit because she has read about the campaign. Hope is not happy about the news.

A reporter interviews Hope about why she is working for Stoop. She says that even if he dies, she will know there are honest adults who are working to change things, whom she can trust. He has inspired her to work for change and be involved. Braverman laughs when Hope tells him her mother is visiting and that her real name is Tulip. He tells her Hope is the perfect name for her.

Chapter 15

Hope has a hard time when her mother visits the diner. She is angry that Deena does not care about her and keeps calling her Tulip. Braverman helps Hope by giving her a red clown nose to wear. Though her heart is breaking, Hope wears the nose during the lunch rush because it has some power to make people laugh. She makes funny gestures, and the children in the diner are happy. She takes her mother's order to the table and pretends to be a fancy waiter. Deena is proud and tells the other customers that Hope is her daughter. Deena watches Hope's waitress performance and the children following

her. G.T. comes into the diner and starts laughing. The nose has turned everything to hope. Hope writes her mother's waitressing tips on the back of her pad.

Chapter 16

Addie and G.T. are getting along now that he stays out of the kitchen and lets her have her way. He asks her out to dinner. Flo says it is about time, because they are made for each other. Hope worries because Addie has had a bad marriage. Braverman takes the opportunity to ask Hope out too. She stalls but finally says yes. He cooks them dinner at the diner after closing time. They talk till midnight, and then he kisses her.

Chapter 17

It is time to go back to school. Hope is a junior and ahead in some subjects, behind in others. She and Braverman still work together part-time at the diner. Anastasia is holding her own bottle, and G.T.'s cancer is in remission. Brenda arrests the thieves who broke into Adam's house, the Carbingers, who had been paid by the dairy to harass people like Braverman. The sheriff had been paid off. G.T. is ahead in the polls. He asks Addie to marry him. Hope realizes she will have a dad. Hope and Braverman hear a negative radio advertisement about G.T. that claims he has brain cancer. It is a lie, but people begin to believe it. The students go door to door to tell the truth, but G.T. loses the election.

Chapter 18

G.T. does not feel bad about losing because he has awakened people's consciences. Adam does not believe the results are fair, but no signs of vote tampering have been found. Hope says her hope is dead. Her political science teacher shows the students a copy of the vote statistics, and Hope is surprised to see that Mr. Woldenburg has voted, for he was the cranky customer who said he would not. Hope sees him in the store and congratulates him on voting after all. He claims he did not vote. The election board starts another investigation and finds fraud. The students protest outside city hall and call for the mayor to resign. He does, and G.T. becomes mayor.

Chapter 19

G.T. appoints Brenda Babcock as the new sheriff. Greebs is indicted for corruption, and G.T. fines Real Fresh Dairy for not paying taxes. G.T.

and Addie marry, with Pastor Hall officiating and Addie cooking the dinner for one hundred guests. G.T. asks Hope if he can adopt her as his daughter, and she is in heaven, showing him her scrapbooks. She proclaims G.T. to be her real father. The days are special now for no one knows how long G.T. will be around. G.T. starts real reform in Mulhoney.

Chapter 20

The year Hope graduates G.T. becomes ill again. Hope is accepted to Michigan State University. Braverman is going to the University of Wisconsin on a scholarship G.T. has set up. For four weeks they take turns tending to G.T. in bed. Hope reads G.T. the letter she wrote but did not send to Gleason Beal, the crook. She tells Gleason that he can take their money but cannot take her hope. She will get it back again. G.T. tells her that if Beal had not cheated them, then Addie and Hope never would have come to him, so it has turned out all right. He dies the next day.

Chapter 21

Addie and Hope are grief stricken and close the diner for the funeral. Mounds of flowers arrive from people G.T. has touched and helped. They turn the diner into a memorial with flowers and candles everywhere. Pastor Hall preaches the sermon. Brenda Babcock is appointed acting mayor. Hope realizes that she has been the perfect daughter for G.T. She understands that life is hard, but she also knows how to be strong, as G.T. was. She writes *Hope was here* on the counter and leaves for college.

CHARACTERS

Aunt Addie

Addie is Hope's aunt, Deena's older sister, who willingly takes Deena's abandoned child as her own, because she cannot have children. Addie's no-good husband has deserted her, and Addie stands by the hospital incubator, talking the two-pound baby Hope (Tulip) into living after the doctors give up on her. Addie is the one constant in Hope's life, and Hope knows her aunt is honest and trustworthy and keeps her promises. Addie never lies to Hope. She explains that the move to Wisconsin is going to be difficult but is what they have to do. Addie is full of common sense and the wisdom of life. She is a

voluntary single mother and a talented cook who has to move around to restaurants in different cities to make her living. Hope follows Addie and Deena, her waitress mother, into food service. Addie is a brusque woman, jealous of the kitchen as her territory. She does not like interference with her work. Hope has learned how to stay out of her way, and soon, G.T. and Braverman learn the same. Addie is good and kind but a fanatic cook set in her ways. She marries G.T. as he is on his deathbed and remains his wife for his last two years.

Anastasia

Anastasia is the infant daughter of the waitress Lou Ellen. Her mother brings her to the restaurant and keeps her in a playpen while she works. The employees keep an eye on the child. Hope was a two-pound baby who almost died, so she has sympathy for Anastasia, who is developmentally delayed. Lou Ellen fears autism, but Hope works with the baby and gets her to respond.

Brenda Babcock

Brenda Babcock is the African American deputy of Sheriff Greebs. She has been a police detective in Minneapolis but moves to Mulhoney to care for her mother. She solves the mysteries of the dead mouse in the diner and the robberies at Adam Pulver's house. She becomes sheriff after Greebs is indicted and becomes acting mayor after G.T. dies.

Gleason Beal

Gleason Beal is the sleazy man who becomes partners with Addie at the Blue Box Diner in Brooklyn and then absconds with their funds, so that Addie has to close the diner and move to Wisconsin. Hope is very angry with Beal and is devastated by his betrayal, because she thought he might be a father figure. She calls him the king of falsehood and writes a letter to him that she never sends, sharing it only with G.T. as he is dying. G.T. helps Hope to forgive Beal, for without him, she never would have moved to Mulhoney and become his daughter.

Harrison Beckworth-McCoy

Harrison Beckworth-McCoy is Hope's high school friend from Brooklyn. She likes him because he is sensitive. They wrote and shared poems together. He gives her a good-bye present of a prism, telling her a move is a chance to see things in a new light.

Eddie Braverman

Eddie Braverman, usually called Braverman, is the teen short-order cook at the Welcome Stairways Diner. He has been trained by G.T. and is his right-hand man at the diner. Braverman is conscientious and grateful to G.T. for helping his desperate family. Braverman's father has deserted them, and when his mother falls sick, he becomes the head of the family, supporting her and his two sisters instead of going to college. He becomes G.T.'s champion during the political campaign, rallying the local teens to help. He meets Hope at the diner, and while working together there and on the campaign, he becomes her friend and then her boyfriend. He is very tall. Hope thinks he is good-looking and sensitive. Braverman becomes a martyr during the campaign when the Carbinger boys are hired to beat him up. Eventually, he is able to attend college and major in journalism through a scholarship that G.T. sets up.

Cranston Broom

Cranston Broom is the president of Real Fresh Dairy, the agribusiness that has moved to town, shut down local dairies, and employed many of the locals in a sort of political blackmail. He supports Mayor Millstone, and his employees have to vote Broom's way or lose their jobs. Broom has not paid the dairy's taxes for five years, and Millstone looks the other way.

Carbinger Boys

The five Carbinger boys are no-good teens who live on the edge of town. Cranston Broom hires them to harass Hope in the street, beat up Braverman, and burglarize Adam Pulver's house to discourage them from helping G.T. in his campaign.

Cecilia Culpepper

Cecilia Culpepper is the editor of the *Mulhoney Messenger* and runs articles and editorials supporting G.T. for mayor, even when Broom reduces the paper's circulation.

Deena

Deena is the empty-headed waitress who is Hope's birth mother. She is described as having a different hair color and boyfriend every time Hope sees her, which is only three times before the start of the story. Hope is angry that Deena is not interested in her, but she keeps a book of her waitressing tips. Hope hates the name

Deena has given her, Tulip. When Deena visits her in Wisconsin, she finally acknowledges pride in her daughter and calls her by her chosen name, Hope.

Flo

Flo is the African American floor manager of G.T.'s diner. She is capable and competent, like her name, controlling the flow of the food from cooks to waitresses to tables. Hope thinks Flo is beautiful. Flo knows everything that is going on, even predicting the marriage of G.T. and Addie.

Sheriff Greebs

Sheriff Greebs is the plump, red-faced sheriff of Mulhoney, depicted as a corrupt good old boy working for Cranston and Millstone. He is exposed as having hired the couple who plant a dead mouse in food to get the diner shut down. After Greebs is removed from office, his deputy, Brenda Babcock, takes over.

Al B. Hall

Al B. Hall is the pastor of the largely African American church in Mulhoney, the Gospel of Grace Evangelical Center, also known as GOG. He is a close friend of G.T.'s and always arrives with the right wisdom or help in any situation. He rallies his church members behind G.T., officiates at his wedding, and presides over his funeral.

Jillian

Jillian is Hope's new friend in Mulhoney, one of the high school students who help on G.T.'s campaign. She makes a web page for students to sign up to help.

Miriam Lahey

Miriam Lahey is Hope's friend in Brooklyn whom Hope remembers fondly when she is lonely in Mulhoney. Hope writes to Miriam about her new life.

Lou Ellen

Lou Ellen is a single mother, one of the waitresses at the Welcome Stairways Diner. She is hostile to Hope at first, thinking she is an amateur and rival. She mends her opinion when she sees that Hope is competent and helps her with her baby.

Eli Millstone

Eli Millstone is the fat bully who has been mayor for eight years but is being challenged by G.T. He is Cranston Broom's man and is using town revenues to build a mansion. He does not take care of the people of Mulhoney, and social services and roads are in disrepair. He knows that the dairy has not paid its taxes and covers up for Broom. Millstone tries to harass G.T. by hiring a hearse to park outside the diner to remind people G.T. is dying. Broom uses illegal means to rig the election but is found out, so Millstone loses and G.T. wins.

Adam Pulver

Adam Pulver is the community organizer who goes to the high school and decides to run G.T.'s campaign with student help. He calls in his uncle, Sid Vole, a political spin doctor, to help. Adam is a talented worker and strategist and predicted by his classmates to be president someday.

G.T. Stoop

G.T. (Gabriel Thomas) Stoop is the owner of the Welcome Stairways Diner in Mulhoney, Wisconsin. He has leukemia and has had to hire Addie to cover for him as a cook. G.T. is the wise man in the story. His mother has raised him as a Quaker, and he has a vast store of old sayings from her about living an ethical life with kindness and faith. He is a pacifist and refuses to fight Millstone in the election. He believes he will win by telling the truth and trying to help others. Most of the people in Mulhoney have received G.T.'s help in hard times. He has a special spot in his heart for young people and tries to inspire them to community action. G.T. is a community builder, and his campaign for mayor, even though he is dying, defeats the town's corrupt politics. G.T. plants trees to memorialize events, like his marriage, his wife's death, and the establishment of Pastor Hall's church. After he marries Addie, he grafts together two tree branches to symbolize his adoption of Hope. G.T. initiates reform in the town with social services for old and young. His legacy to the town survives him.

Sid Vole

Sid Vole is Adam's uncle and a political spin doctor who manages the campaigns of candidates for office. Adam calls him in to help G.T., but though he helps get G.T. on the ballot, G.T. rejects his tactics because he does not want to use dishonest or evasive methods to be elected. A vole is a rodent that is considered a pest. Perhaps the name symbolizes that Vole's tactics are small and short-sighted.

Mr. Woldenburg

Mr. Woldenburg is the cranky customer who says he will not vote and does not, yet his name appears on the list of people who vote for Millstone. This is the clue Hope finds as evidence of election fraud.

Hope Yancey

Hope Yancey is the sixteen-year-old first-person narrator who relates memories of her life as an abandoned child raised by her aunt Addie. She changes over the three-year period represented in the book, from a girl looking for roots and security to a fully blossomed young adult ready to go to college. What makes the difference is finding her adoptive father, G.T. Stoop, the restaurant owner in Mulhoney whom her aunt marries. He adopts Hope and fulfills her dreams of a father, home, and community. Hope changes her name from Tulip, the name given by her flaky mother, taking seriously the meaning of hope and vowing to live up to it.

Hope has been a waitress since age fourteen and is outstanding in her work. This job is her main source of self-esteem and she prides herself on passing on cheer and hope to others through food service. Hope has had to move often, leaving her signature *Hope was here* at each place, but always brings her scrapbooks to show her father if he should ever enter her life again. She is angry at her waitress mother, Deena, for leaving her but makes peace by making a book called *Best of Mom*, which contains Deena's waitressing tips.

Hope is good at making friends but mourns every time she moves and she has to leave them. Hope and G.T. take to each other immediately, and he passes on his wisdom to her before he dies, giving her a moral legacy as well as a family. Hope finds the grill cook, Braverman, a kindred spirit and becomes his girlfriend until they part to go to college. Hope joins Braverman's group of teens who support G.T. in his mayoral race.

Yuri

Yuri is the Russian immigrant and bus man at the Welcome Stairways Diner in Mulhoney. He is a nice man, good at his job, and eager to become an American citizen. He is exposed to the rudeness of diners who make fun of his accent and foreign ways.

THEMES

Challenges

Hope Yancey is a teen with challenges. She was born underweight, was abandoned by her mother, and does not know her father. She has been raised by an aunt who has had her own challenges with a no-good husband who leaves her. Aunt Addie is a short-order cook raising her niece as a single mother and moving around the country wherever the jobs are. By age fourteen, Hope has been to six different schools in five states. In Brooklyn, Aunt Addie goes into business with Gleason Beal, who steals her money and leaves her with bills. She has to uproot Hope, who is happy with her life in Brooklyn, and take a chance on an obscure job in Wisconsin to help a man with leukemia.

Everyone Hope comes in contact with has a challenge, it seems. Her boyfriend, Braverman, the grill man, cannot go to college because he has to support his family. Lou Ellen, the waitress, is a single mother whose baby has developmental delays. G.T. Stoop, the restaurant owner, has leukemia and knows his days are limited. Yuri, the bus man, is a Russian immigrant and is hassled by local bigots. All these people in Hope's life put her own challenges in perspective, as she watches them handle their life burdens. She learns how to deal with the challenges of life, especially by watching Aunt Addie and G.T. They are wise adults who show her one does not have to give up. Even her mother has taught her how to deal with life by teaching her how to be a good waitress. When Hope is deep in the weeds, a term for being swamped, she turns into warrior waitress, remembering her mother's tips about how to make customers happy.

Hope

When Hope changes her name from Tulip to Hope at age twelve, she chooses carefully, for hope is what she stands for and practices every day to get through. Addie tells her the name is a lot to live up to. Hope understands this, but it is her chosen identity, and when she leaves a place, she always stamps her presence on the place: Hope was here. It seems to be true, for she makes friends everywhere she goes, and people enjoy being with her. She uses her dictionary to find her direction sometimes, especially copying out different definitions of Hope on three-by-five-inch cards. One meaning is the expectation of fulfillment of desires. Hope has many desires,

especially for family and a father, that are fulfilled by the end of the story though not in an expected way. She brings hope to others too, as to G.T., Addie, Braverman, and Lou Ellen. Hope knows her name stands for faith and trust, something she has to rebuild after the hurt from the crook Gleason Beal, who steals her hope as well as her money. G.T. is the one who helps her find her hope again and her belief in herself.

Family

Hope feels abandoned by her real parents, and even though Addie is a perfect surrogate mother, Hope is bitter about her mother's, Deena's, lack of interest in her. Hope feels the want of roots and stability in her life and once even runs away when Addie tells her they have to move again. Hope begins to come to terms with her odd family life when Addie confesses to the ten-year-old Hope that she understands Hope's feelings of abandonment but that she, Addie, is not going to leave her, because she needs Hope as much as Hope needs her. Addie has always wanted to be a mother and considers Hope her daughter. Hope is not the only one in an unconventional family situation. She reflects that many of her friends have similar families of one parent or remarried parents or do not know their fathers. Her favorite book as a child is one in which animal babies are raised by a mother of another species. Hope's biggest desire is for a father, and for that, she keeps the scrapbooks that she hopes to share with him someday when he finds her. She ends up sharing the scrapbooks with G.T., her adoptive father, but though she has him for only two years before he dies of cancer, it is enough. She decides Webster's definition of a father is too narrow, because G.T. is more than a biological father. He is the sturdy tree in her life that she has longed for.

Community

The community theme is held together through G.T.'s election campaign. Even though he is dying of leukemia, G.T. decides to use his last strength to better his community by running for mayor. His friends consider it a crazy or quixotic gesture, but they soon see that G.T. has the power to awaken the consciences of others and make them demand more from the town. Mulhoney has not been a community because the townspeople live in fear of the bully Eli Millstone and his henchmen, the mill owner Cranston Broom

TOPICS FOR FURTHER STUDY

- Bauer admires the humor of Garrison Keillor. Read *Lake Wobegon Days* (1985), in which Keillor creates a fictitious small town in Minnesota. Write a critical paper on how Bauer similarly creates the small town of Mulhoney, Wisconsin, with a variety of characters. How does each author use metaphor and humor to create characters and situations? Give examples from both books.

- Bauer drew on her teen waitress experience for Hope's character. Collect accounts of how famous people used the experience of teen jobs in their later careers and make a presentation to a group using a program such as PowerPoint and slides. Draw conclusions about whether there is a connection between the type of teen job and the later career or whether it is general work experience itself that is helpful.

- Create a wiki on teens in politics. Show examples of teens in the United States or in other countries and cultures who have made a difference in a political situation or for a social cause. You can also look back in history for examples. If there are any filmmakers or photographers in the group, add films and photos of teens contributing to the public good, as Mulhoney's teens did.

- As an individual or in a group write a short story about a teen on a quest. Decide whether it will be a realistic quest like Hope's or a mythical quest like Bilbo Baggins's in *The*

Hobbit, by J. R. R Tolkien. Outline the goal and stages of this quest. Make a list of characters, including the main character, filling in their descriptions and personalities. Work from this preparation and use a platform that allows group collaboration and multiple versions. Record spoken versions and share and evaluate in a group after the project is finished.

- Using your own scrapbooks or those of a friend or relative, write your memoir or a biography of the other person, such as the history of her significant moments that Hope shows to G.T. The memoir or biography can be written or oral. Make a web page of your work that includes the photos and mementos and text or voice commentary..

- *Esperanza Rising* (2000), by Pam Muñoz Ryan, is a lyrical young-adult novel about a Mexican family's struggle to survive as they flee to the United States. Esperanza was once a girl in a wealthy family but must become a laborer in California during the Great Depression to help the family after her father is killed. The name Esperanza means "hope." Read the novel and in a group discuss how Esperanza and Hope compare and contrast in character, work, and family experience. Afterward, write a short summary comparing and contrasting the main characters, using examples from the books.

and Sheriff Greebs. Everyone is afraid to speak out for fear of losing a job or being hassled.

G.T. is not afraid and uses the tactics of love and respect to win and build a new community. G.T. has the power to rally others because he has stood by many in their time of need, giving free food to those without jobs or in trouble. Braverman fights loyally for him because G.T. came to

the rescue of his family and gave him his job. On the other hand, Millstone and his cronies think only of themselves. Millstone uses town money to build himself a mansion, and the big dairy does not pay taxes. G.T., on the other hand, gets the dairy to pay back taxes to finance health care and day care and to improve roads and services. The center of this new community is

Some of the novel's plot revolves around the election for the town's mayor (©Joe Belanger | Shutterstock.com)

G.T.'s Welcome Stairways Diner, where he treats all with joy and fairness. G.T. gives Hope not only the father she wants but also the community she wants to be part of. All the teens rally to work for G.T., thus showing there is no need for a generation gap. G.T. likes to help teens find themselves through jobs and his wisdom and humor. He inspires them to be leaders and build community.

STYLE

Young-Adult Novel

Bauer is well known for writing specifically for teens. These young-adult novels deal generally with coming-of-age themes, the transition from childhood to adulthood. On the whole, this genre is optimistic, showing young people that determination and ethical behavior lead to success, even though there may be challenges. The young characters make worthy accomplishments as they learn how to be adults, emulating a mentor. Modern young-adult fiction came of age with S. E. Hinton's *The Outsiders* (1967) and

works by such renowned authors as Judy Blume, Madeleine L'Engle, Anne McCaffrey, Ursula K. LeGuin, Jaqueline Woodson, Orson Scott Card, and Terry Pratchett. Traditional young-adult fiction includes such classics as Louisa May Alcott's *Little Women* (1868), Robert Louis Stevenson's *Treasure Island* (1883), Kate Douglas Wiggin's *Rebecca of Sunnybrook Farm* (1903), and Lucy Maud Montgomery's *Anne of Green Gables* (1908). Today young-adult fiction is so popular that it is a separate industry and has a separate section in bookstores.

Bauer is known for her strong female protagonists and her sense of humor. She uses humor to sweeten the message and to build bridges to universal truths. Having studied film writing, she also creates visual scenes, viewing them as film scenes as she writes. Her love of words and inventive metaphor is evident in this novel. Bauer often uses the sound of names as metaphors for characters, such as Mayor Millstone, Eddie Braverman, Sheriff Greebs, and, of course, Hope Yancey. Hope herself always carries a dictionary and thesaurus, consulting these books as she would an oracle.

Realistic Quest

Young-adult fiction is so large a category that it is subdivided into different genres. Bauer has written several journey personal quest stories in which the protagonist takes physical and moral journeys at the same time, seeking something. Mythic quests in the genre of fantasy, as in Tolkien's *Lord of the Rings* (1954), are popular with teens, but there are also realistic quests, which portray life in the everyday world. Hope Yancey is forced by circumstances to move often with her aunt in search of restaurant work, but her emotional quest is to journey toward her unknown father and roots. She wants a place, to be loved, and to have a family.

A quest implies something more than a goal like a career or a mate. A quest has greater spiritual or emotional significance. The hero seeks a lost part of the self or a boon for a whole group. Hope has carried on through all difficulty but feels a father will complete her. She makes scrapbooks to show him her life, to gain his love and validation. G.T. becomes both mentor and father as he shows her how to be heroic, fighting with his last breath for the welfare of others. When G.T. fills the need for an honorable and loving father, Hope moves on to adulthood, feeling accepted and inspired. Other young-adult realistic quests include John Green's *An Abundance of Katherines* (2006) and Rachel Cohn's *Gingerbread* (2002).

Cooking Novel

One of the organizing structures of *Hope Was Here* is food service. The diner is the setting of the action. Hope is naturally shown in her life as a waitress and her aunt as a short-order cook. They travel and work together. Hope takes her waitressing quite seriously, and it becomes the controlling metaphor for the life lessons she is learning. Hope uses food service language for the challenges she faces, such as being in the weeds when a place is too busy. She learns to handle the rush, however, because she is an expert warrior waitress. She shares with the reader her mother's waitressing tips and details of her aunt's cooking and special dishes that have made her a popular cook.

The novel is like a growing body of cooking and food novels with a focus on the preparation and serving of food. Examples are *Chocolat* (1999), by Joanna Harris, about a chocolate shop in France; *The Flounder* (1977), by Günter Grass, about women, war, and food; *Mangoes and Quince* (2001), by Carol Field (2010), the story of a mother-daughter restaurant in Amsterdam; *Blue Plate Special: A Novel of Love, Loss, and Food* (2005), by Frances Norris, about a food stylist trying to find her place; and *Crescent* (2003), by Diana Abu-Jaber, about an Iraqi American cook trying to find love. Bauer, a cooking enthusiast herself, treats the subject again in her novel *Close to Famous*, in which Foster McFee dreams of hosting a show on the Food Network. Important human traits and desires are revealed in the making and serving and eating of food, as these authors have found. Food service provides the background and metaphorical framework for the hopes, challenges, and triumphs of daily life. Food in its physical and symbolic value keeps humans alive. A restaurant is the meeting place for all kinds of interactions, and it is where Hope finds her hope and her family.

HISTORICAL CONTEXT

Wisconsin

Hope Yancey is upset at moving from Brooklyn, New York, to a small town in Wisconsin that seems like exile from the excitement of life. Though she is has worked from an early age, she has also managed to enjoy culture in New York, such as poetry readings. She is a reader and writer. Wisconsin seems mostly rural, though it does have large cities, such as Milwaukee and Madison, the capital. The fictional town of Mulhoney has five thousand people and is located between Madison and Milwaukee. Hope groans at the small-town amusements and entertainments, such as the Memorial Day Parade, which includes the mediocre high school band, Miss Pittypat's Tap Dancing Darlings, veterans, antique cars, and farmers. The town's main industry is a dairy.

Wisconsin is a beautiful state of green rolling hills, bounded by Lake Superior, Lake Michigan, and the Mississippi River. It is known for its many dairies and production of cheese. The name of the state comes from the Wisconsin River with its red sandstone banks. The Algonquin, Iowa, Ho-Chunk, Menominee, Sauk, Fox, Kickapoo, Pottawattamie, and Ojibwa Indians lived there before Europeans. Jean Nicolet, Jacques Marquette, and Louis Jolliet were the first

COMPARE
&
CONTRAST

- **2000:** In national politics, the presidential campaign shows the country polarized and equally divided between the liberal candidate Al Gore and the conservative George W. Bush. The election result is determined by Supreme Court decision.

  Today: The election of an African American president, Barack Obama, in 2008, opens up the possibility of diverse choices in the 2016 election. During primary voting, the candidates include a Jewish democratic socialist (Bernie Sanders), a woman (Hillary Clinton), two Cuban Americans (Ted Cruz and Marco Rubio), and a television personality and businessman who has never held public office (Donald Trump).

- **2000:** There are false beliefs that autism is caused by the emotional coldness of the mother or by childhood vaccinations.

  Today: Autism is known to be a genetic disorder, but earlier diagnosis with whole-genome sequencing leads to earlier intervention and, in some cases, recovery.

- **2000:** Treatment of leukemia with stem cell transplants and certain drugs leads to longer remissions of the disease and to cures.

  Today: Leukemia is understood to be many diseases, and treatment is more targeted, including immunotherapy, in which antibodies are attached to drugs for those who have relapses. Treatments are targeted for individual patient molecular combinations.

- **2000:** Restaurants are regularly inspected for compliance with sanitation rules. Word of mouth is important for establishing customer trust.

  Today: The Food Safety Modernization Act of 2011 focuses on preventing food contamination rather than responding to reports of violations. Regional workshops are conducted for implementation. Cities such as New York offer online sanitation ratings of restaurants.

Western explorers to arrive, in the 1600s, bringing French fur traders. The British took over Wisconsin during the French and Indian War of the 1700s. The state earned its nickname, the Badger State, from the mineral miners who came in the 1800s and, like badgers, dug holes for shelter.

Wisconsin became a US territory in 1836, when farmers from New England settled there. It became a state in 1848. Nelson Dewey, the first governor of Wisconsin, was an abolitionist and opposed the spread of slavery into the territories. This set the tone for Wisconsin's liberal politics, represented by G. T. Stoop in the novel. Wisconsin was a center for northern abolitionism. In 1854, a mob of abolitionists helped Joshua Glover, a runaway slave from Missouri, escape from prison in Racine. The Republican Party was founded in Wisconsin on an antislavery platform. In the 1860s, Wisconsin was a primary producer

of wheat in the southern part of the state and a timber producer in the north. By the end of the nineteenth century, ecological damage to the state was extensive owing to deforestation and soil depletion. By the 1890s, a majority of farmers had switched from wheat to dairy to make better use of the land. Many immigrants brought their cheese-making talents from Scandinavia and Europe. The dairy farmers who moved from New York, the leading dairy state before Wisconsin, also contributed to the success of dairying.

In the twentieth century, Aldo Leopold, a professor at the University of Wisconsin, became a leading conservationist, one of the founders of American environmentalism, helping to reintroduce sustainable forestry. Robert M. La Follette championed the progressive politics in Wisconsin that led to the nation's first statewide primary election system. Wisconsin instituted tax proportional to earnings and worker compensation and unemployment insurance. The University of Wisconsin established branch extensions throughout the state for more accessible education. G.T.'s pacifism is a reminder that the Madison campus became a center for radical antiwar protests in the 1960s and 1970s.

At the end of the twentieth century, the economy of Wisconsin changed toward agribusiness, as the novel highlights with the Real Fresh Dairy as the villainous agribusiness that supplants local family dairy farms. Though Wisconsin gave birth to the Republican Party and Joseph McCarthy's anticommunism campaign, it has been thought of mostly in terms of progressive politics and has voted Democratic in national elections. Madison was in the national news again in 2011 with demonstrations against a bill to strip collective bargaining rights from state employees. It was a rallying point for unions, which have lost power in recent decades.

Quakerism

G.T.'s ethical approach to politics and campaigning in the novel is attributed to his mother's Quakerism. The Quakers, or the Religious Society of Friends, derived from a seventeenth-century movement started in England by George Fox in dissent against the Church of England. It is a democratic movement that believes in the priesthood of all believers. Meetings of Friends include sitting in silence until God speaks through the conscience of one of the participants, who then speaks out to the group. G.T. refers to this when he refuses to have a spin doctor craft his speeches. He says he will let God speak out spontaneously from him. Quakers emphasize a personal and direct relationship with Christ and God. They believe in ethical and loving behavior to all. Quakers have been known historically for their pacifism, abstention from alcohol, opposition to swearing of oaths, practice of nonviolence, abolitionism, plain dress, and self-correction of mistakes and weaknesses.

G.T. recalls Benjamin Franklin (1706–1790), who while he was not a Quaker still adhered to Quaker teachings in many respects. Franklin was a self-educated and self-made man of practical wisdom who excelled in politics, science, and arts and letters. He was morally engaged and an abolitionist, inventor, publisher, statesman, and diplomat to France, where he was widely admired. As he mentions in his *Autobiography*, Franklin kept his account books not only for business but also for his own moral behavior, so he could mend his faults. His popular *Poor Richard's Almanack*, published from 1732 to 1758, extols the virtues of thrift, hard work, and honesty. G.T. improves his community not only by action but also by his example, showing others that honesty and caring for others pay off. Almost everyone in town has received his help and support in bad times, and this is how he builds consensus and community harmony.

Teens and Work

In all her novels, Bauer upholds the value of teen work. Before the twentieth century, a person assumed adult workloads on entry into the teen years. Most people grew up in extended families of several generations, all cooperating to support the family. Young men became soldiers, laborers, apprentices, and clerks. Women became wives and mothers, domestic servants, nurses, and even teachers by the age of eighteen. Children of both sexes worked in family businesses or on family farms. There was no prolonged adolescence. Benjamin Franklin began his printing and journalism career as a teen. Those attending universities were the privileged few, the rich, or professionals destined for careers in education, medicine, law, or the church.

After World War II and the baby boom, American culture changed. The United States enjoyed a prosperous middle class; nuclear families lived in urban and suburban centers. The family and family need no longer defined the life of a child. Society was child oriented, and consumerism arose with the baby boomer generation because parents were affluent and spent money on children. When baby boomers became teens, they related to peers rather than elders, forming the first generation of adolescents who were independent of family, having their own money, cars, and freedom to travel by themselves. Age twelve to twenty-one was a new category of life in which an individual came of age, testing the waters, choosing work or college or travel, trying to find a direction for the future through personal experience rather than family traditions. Many did not have to work, receiving money from parents, or they took summer and part-time jobs, as Hope does in the novel. In general, however, the money was used for discretionary teen spending on clothes and cars. Bauer brings up Braverman as an example of the poorer classes, whose children still loyally worked to support the family.

The baby boomer generation marked greater self-confidence on the part of the young, who dabbled in business, travel, or service in the Peace Corps or became the new educational elite of the country at universities. They were rebellious and wanted to learn for themselves rather than take accepted wisdom from elders. Social engagement to help others through protest and liberal politics became a hallmark of this generation, who involved themselves in the civil rights movement and protests against the war in Vietnam. Bauer has this background in mind because she is a boomer. The Welcome Stairways Diner represents many of the rights that the boomers won politically for Americans, such as racial equality with Flo, the black floor manager, and Brenda, the black police officer who becomes mayor after G.T. dies. The novel shows that it is not acceptable to harass a woman or member of an ethnic minority, as when Hope is attacked on the street and Yuri is ridiculed for his accent. Political corruption is overcome through community solidarity, and the reinstitution of social services to children, parents, old, poor, and sick by G.T. after his election.

Bauer has described herself as a rebellious punk when she was a teen, but she learned her values through work. She takes especial pains to show teens in the political process and the workforce. Braverman is a protégé of G.T.'s and learns from him how to be a top cook and a good and ethical young man. He leads the teens in a powerful movement to elect G.T. Adam Pulver is the student predicted to be a future president because he is a community organizer. Jillian helps with her computer skills by creating web pages. The high school students go door to door to register voters and inspire and inform. The tide turns because of them, especially when Hope discovers the voting fraud.

Hope has been waitressing for several years before she arrives in Wisconsin. At sixteen, she is confident and professional, able to outperform the veteran Lou Ellen, not only because she can carry five platters but also because she takes joy in her competence and ability to make others happy. She is earning good money and, more important, learning life skills to become a balanced adult. She uses incidents from waitressing to demonstrate her growth. In public speaking and interviews, Bauer mentions the importance of teens' having jobs to build character. In the twenty-first century, there has been a decline in teens' working while in school. One factor is the economic recession, but beyond that, fewer teens

Hope works at a diner with Addie (©Phovoir / Shutterstock.com)

are interested in summer jobs and part-time work because they have money from parents or are engaged in extracurricular activities. This decline in job experience leads to loss of soft skills among the young, including humility, respect, responsibility, teamwork, a positive attitude, getting along with others, and solving problems in the workplace, to say nothing of the confidence that comes with earning one's own money. Bauer presents teens who work and have these important skills.

CRITICAL OVERVIEW

Hope Was Here is Bauer's sixth novel. She was already an award-winning young-adult author, but this novel has been especially popular with readers and was a Newbery Honor Book. Frances Bradburn in *Booklist* mentions that *Hope Was Here* provides a microcosm of society in its characters, who represent "the best and the worst of a teenager's support system." Bauer's humor is cited as making the humanitarian themes work. A reviewer in *Publishers Weekly* praises the book as having Bauer's hallmarks: "a strong female protagonist on the road to self-discovery, quirky characters, dysfunctional families, a swiftly moving story, moments of bright humor." The review also mentioned Bauer's rich use of metaphor. Roger Sutton in *Horn Book* noted that the book illustrates one of Bauer's consistent themes: the value of work for teens. He also, however, considered the novel somewhat larger than life and to have stereotypical characters, such as the evil mayor Millstone. The strong character of Hope and the humor carry the story. A review in *Journal of Adolescent and Adult Literacy* praised the novel for its humor and interesting characters.

In a review of the audiobook of *Hope Was Here*, read by Jenna Lania for Listening Library (2003), Laurie Hartshorn in *Booklist* praised the oral version, calling it sassy and tender. She likes the interpretation of Hope as "innocence with brass tacks." In a review of the same audiobook for *School Library Journal*, Phyllis Levy Mandell and Francisca Goldsmith called the production an enhancement of the delightful book. They note: "Like Bauer's other heroines, Hope is both strong and a bit uncertain, her story tinted with good humor and touched by pathos." The young-adult literature scholar Alleen Pace Nilsen and her coauthors of the ninth edition of *Literature for Today's Young Adults* placed *Hope Was Here* on an honor list of the best of the best of 1980–2011. Bauer continues to uphold her track record for sensitive and relevant young-adult themes. In a review of her latest and twelfth novel, *Soar* (2015), for *Booklist*, Michael Cart states "Bauer's latest feel-good novel is distinguished by a largehearted warmth, its able characterizations, a page-turning plot, and winning humor." The author proves that despite the current emphasis on dark topics in young-adult novels, feel-good stories never go out of date.

CRITICISM

Susan K. Andersen

Andersen is a writer and teacher with a PhD in English literature. In the following essay, she considers the ethical emphasis of Bauer's young-adult novel Hope Was Here.

> **IT IS A REFRESHING SIGN THAT BAUER'S NOVELS ARE POPULAR WITH BOTH TEENS AND ADULTS, BECAUSE THEY SELL GOODNESS AND HOPE AS THE IMPORTANT INGREDIENTS OF THE HUMAN CONDITION."**

Bauer's *Hope Was Here* is the heir of a long legacy of young-adult fiction, but it also has its own philosophy of hope for the young. Young adults in the early nineteenth century were encouraged to read religious works like the Bible and John Bunyan's *The Pilgrim's Progress* (1678) to learn proper behavior and religious principles. The idea was that children were born into original sin and had to be corrected or disciplined to grow up into good adults. The romantic movement in literature (1750–1850) was based on the opposite assumption that children were born innately good and were then corrupted by civilization. The growing body of children's literature in the nineteenth and early twentieth centuries, read by both children and adults, portrayed childhood as lost innocence, as in *Peter Pan and Wendy* (1911), by J. M. Barrie. In children's fiction in the early twentieth century, ethical principles were still emphasized, as were happy or hopeful resolutions, for it was thought that children should grow up feeling they lived in a safe and moral world where crime was punished and virtue rewarded.

The 1960s changed the direction of young-adult literature because the young were participating in the serious social conflicts of the day, such as the Vietnam War and civil rights protests. Harper Lee's *To Kill a Mockingbird* (1960) approaches racism from a child's point of view and was one of Bauer's favorites as a teen. In the 1960s it was deemed necessary to prepare children for the adult world of conflict with novels about sexuality, war, drugs, abuse, racism, and poverty. These problem novels addressed specific issues, emphasizing social realism. By the 1980s and 1990s, almost every hitherto forbidden topic, such as homosexuality, pregnancy, abortion, family abuse, incest, prostitution, crime, and mental illness, had been treated in young-adult fiction and recommended for teens by experts.

WHAT DO I READ NEXT?

- *Defining Dulcie* (2006,) by Paul Acampora, is a young-adult novel that tells of a realistic quest by Dulcie, whose father dies in Connecticut. Her mother moves her to California, but Dulcie takes the truck and drives back home to spend the summer with her grandfather, thus learning about her own competence.

- *Me and Earl and the Dying Girl* (2012), by Jesse Andrews, is a young-adult novel about teen death. Rachel is dying of leukemia, and Greg and Earl make a movie for her. The novel has been made into a popular film.

- *Hope Was Here* should ring a bell for anyone who has waitressed. In *The Waiter and Waitress and Waitstaff Training Handbook* (2005), Laura Arduser and Douglas Robert Brown describe the performance of each job in a restaurant and provide instructions for proper hosting, seating, taking orders, handling problems, and tips. Hope has written down what she has learned from her mother, demonstrating that waitressing is a serious profession.

- Bauer's *Rules of the Road* (1998) is a hero quest about sixteen-year-old Jenna Boller, who sells shoes and drives her boss from Chicago to Texas to uncover a mystery about the decline of the shoe business.

- *Teen Power Politics*, by Sara Jane Boyer, (2000) is a book for teens who cannot yet vote but who can be inspired to play a role in politics to bring social change, the way the teens of Mulhoney do in *Hope Was Here*.

- Madeleine L'Engle's *A Ring of Endless Light* (1980) concerns Vicky Austin's fear of death as the teen cares for a grandfather, who has leukemia.

- Lou Ellen in *Hope Was Here* fears her child may be autistic. In *A Corner of the Universe* (2002), by Ann Martin, a young-adult novel that was a Newbery Honor Book, Hattie befriends her uncle Adam, who has been placed in an institution because he has autism.

- Richard Peck's *A Long Way from Chicago* (1998) was a Newbery Honor Book. It is a young-adult book consisting of a short-story cycle about the two Dowdel children, who spend summers with their grandmother in rural Illinois.

- *Buried Onions* (1997), by the Mexican American author Gary Soto, is a sad young-adult story about a nineteen-year-old Chicano teen, Eddie, who cannot win in his tough life in Fresno, California. The novel offers a contrast to uplifting stories in its realistic account of street life in the city.

- *Little House in the Big Woods* (1932) is the first of the Little House series of novels for children and young adults by Laura Ingalls Wilder about her childhood in a pioneer family. The big woods are in Wisconsin, where Wilder was born in 1867. The novel tells of the homesteading and survival skills pioneer children had to learn.

- *Kitchen* (1988, translated into English by Megan Backus in 1993), a best-selling novel by the Japanese author Banana Yoshimoto is a coming-of-age story about a young Japanese woman who learns about life through food preparation. The novel has beautiful descriptions of contemporary Japan and its food.

Perhaps as an antidote to so much reality, fantasy also became popular with J. R. R. Tolkien's *The Lord of the Rings* (1954), but this fantasy concerned the darkness of evil that the author thought he had to address after two world wars. Though Tolkien was himself religious and shows darkness overcome, the industry of dark fantasy spawned from his success has not been particularly based on the positive, with its abundance of vampires, demons, and cruelty. Dark fantasy has become one of the more lucrative directions of young-adult literature. It is a refreshing sign that Bauer's novels are popular with both teens and adults, because they sell goodness and hope as the important ingredients of the human condition. Bauer has managed to combine realistic issues with the quest for moral integrity. In *Hope Was Here*, G. T. Stoop becomes the father figure Hope is looking for, but he is also her moral mentor.

Bauer claims that fiction helped her to make sense of the world as she was growing up in the 1960s during great social change. She liked the novels of Joseph Conrad, Ernest Hemingway, F. Scott Fitzgerald, C. S. Lewis, Jack London, and Harper Lee. She loved Robert Frost and Bob Dylan, also trying her hand at poetry and songwriting. Bauer read many plays, including those of Edward Albee and Thornton Wilder, and studied screenwriting. She had studied the comedy writing of *The Dick Van Dyke Show*, *The Bill Cosby Show*, and the Smothers Brothers, wanting to be a comedy writer. Bauer uses this wealth of knowledge about humor and dialogue in her novels. She gives many of her own characteristics as a teen to Hope Yancey, although from her own accounts, Bauer was more depressed and rebellious than Hope is, dropping out of high school and leaving home at the age of seventeen. Hope Yancey represents what Bauer learned from life, looking back at adolescence and passing on the wisdom to teens, as she expresses in Alleen Pace Nilsen's *Joan Bauer*: "Don't give up—*never* give up. There are so many ways to learn, so many people out there who can help you."

Bauer's main conflict as a teen was the one she gives to Hope—the lack of a father in the home. Bauer's father was unstable and not present, was married several times, was alcoholic, and committed suicide. Hope has a problem with both of her parents. She has been abandoned by her mother, Deena, a waitress, who goes from boyfriend to boyfriend and does not want to be burdened with a child. The reader immediately loves the character of Hope because while she may be in a tough situation, she never wallows in self-pity. Instead, she has trained herself, with her gutsy aunt's help, to climb out of dark holes by the strength of her hope.

Though Hope has daunting problems, she also has positive qualities that she has learned to value: a quirky and loving aunt as a role model, her ability to make friends wherever she goes, her humor, her waitress work, and her writing and reading skills. If Hope had not already learned to make the best of her life before she came to Mulhoney, Wisconsin, she would not have been able to win the affection of Braverman, her boyfriend, also a survivor, and G. T. Stoop, who becomes her father.

Hope has always wanted her unknown biological father to find her, and she is not idle. She prepares to meet him by becoming a worthy young woman. When the novel opens, she is sixteen years old and has gone as far as she can by herself and needs the help of an adult to make the transition to adulthood. She understands this and has already surrendered to Aunt Addie, the passionate cook obsessed with perfection and order. She has made her peace with Addie and portrays her with affection, detailing her authoritative ways in the kitchen and her confrontations with G.T. and Braverman. Aunt Addie is her real mother as G.T. is her real father in this nontraditional family. Addie fought for Hope's life when she was a two-pound baby and the doctors gave up on her. Hope describes Addie humorously as a missionary of food, for she believes in the emotional power of food to save the soul. Addie becomes prickly when anyone tries to tell her how to cook, but she keeps her promises, and she has street wisdom from living a nomadic life.

Hope is bitter about Gleason Beal, the man who steals from Addie and her. He tricks Hope by implying he wants to be her dad, and she finds ways to deal with her anger. She writes a letter to Gleason that she never sends but that expresses her feelings. Addie buys her boxing gloves so she can punch away her anger toward her mother. Finding something positive about her mother, Hope keeps a book she calls *The Best of Mom*, which contains Deena's professional waitressing tips. Hope's eleven scrapbooks document who she is so that she can show her life's events to her father some day. She has faith that he will show up somehow and want to know about her.

Another sustaining influence in Hope's life is the friends she grieves over every time she moves. Hope is not shy. In Pensacola she shouts out in the gym on her arrival: "Look, does anyone here want to be my friend?" Two kids come

When they move to a small town in Wisconsin, Hope and Addie again find work in a diner (© *Petar Djordjevic /*
Shutterstock.com)

forward. She shares poetry readings with her
sensitive male friend in Brooklyn, Harrison
Beckworth-McCoy, but believes she will have
no real buddies in Mulhoney. She is wrong; she
is immediately immersed in the group of teens
working for G.T.'s election. The Brooklyn
friends come through school, but the Wisconsin
friends come through work and social action.
Braverman is the cook she meets, and the two
begin to admire each other during a rush in the
restaurant when they are alone and have to work
as a perfect team to make it through. Hope
comes to admire the boy who gives up college
to support his mother and sisters. Braverman
has become sensitive not by reading poetry but
by dealing with hardship and mustering his
courage.

As a survivor like Braverman, Hope has had
to build her identity on her own from the scraps
she has been able to put together, symbolized by
her scrapbooks, her *Best of Mom* tips, her dictionary and thesaurus, and by naming herself.
She looks up the important words in *Webster's*,
especially *hope*. She looks it up every time she is

running low on optimism. She decides consciously to build her identity and life around
hope and to pass it on, thus her sign *Hope was
here* when she leaves a place. One definition of
hope that Hope finds is "to cherish a desire with
expectation of fulfillment." Other meanings are
faith, trust, and confidence. Hope diligently
works on these virtues in her life, using her waitress job as a testing ground. Instead of becoming
angry or frustrated with customers, she takes the
high road, bustling around with cheer and coffee, putting on a red clown nose to make people
laugh, and learning her craft with the joy of
being competent.

G. T. Stoop notices Hope as special right
away. He is a fatherly type and seems to enjoy
helping teens get started; he has given Braverman his break so that he can support his family.
He takes in Hope, consulting her about his campaign and restaurant business. She immediately
responds and is surprised at her own intelligent
suggestions. In return, she looks up to him as he
fights cancer and conducts his political campaign, becoming a father figure she can admire

and emulate. G.T. elaborates his Quaker faith and philosophy on his menu, symbolized by the two sets of stairs, which welcome guests from all directions: "we must greet whatever changes and difficulties life may bring with firm faith in God." G.T. shows Hope an oil painting by his mother that shows a ship on the sea trying to get to shore. His mother once told him, "You don't become a real sailor until you sail in a storm."

G.T. lives his faith and philosophy, and his last gift to the town is to summon them all to community through his run for mayor. He refuses to use tactics of revenge or violence as Millstone's followers do. G.T. constantly quotes his Quaker mother, telling the teens working on his campaign: "She said you've got to love yourself with all your shortcomings, and you've got to love the world, no matter how bad it gets." Adam Pulver tells G.T. that if they do not fight as in a war, they will not win the election. G.T. replies that it is not worth winning then. His victory by honest means shows Hope how to live her life. He tells her that facing down disappointment, as he is doing with cancer, is the way to find one's strength.

Instead of being angry when Millstone harasses him by hiring a hearse to park outside his door, G.T. welcomes it: "Nobody knows how long they've got on this earth. And we all need to live our lives just a little bit like the hearse is outside ready to cart us away." When a reporter asks her why vote for a dying person, Hope replies, "When you listen to G.T. Stoop, you understand the importance of being an honorable person, you get charged to fight for the truth." G.T. teaches the indifferent citizens of Mulhoney that "one person can make a difference, two can lift a burden, and more than that can start a revolution." Hope learns that "when hope is released in a place, all kinds of things are possible."

In the interview in Nilsen's book, Bauer quotes one of her own favorite characters from *Rules of the Road*, Harry Bender, who says, "If you set your mind and heart toward a healthy way of living and thinking, you'll find a way to climb out of the biggest pit life throws your way." Bauer comments, "I believe that with all my heart because I've done it—not alone, but with God's astonishing grace."

Source: Susan K. Andersen, Critical Essay on *Hope Was Here*, in *Novels for Students*, Gale, Cengage Learning, 2017.

Audrey Marie Danielson

In the following review, Danielson sums up Hope Was Here *as "satisfying."*

When Tulip changes her name to Hope, she figures that it would make everything okay in her life. She soon discovers that a name, no matter how positive it is, doesn't always ensure a perfect life. Nevertheless, she keeps hoping that her life will change as she tries to be the best waitress in the world—that is Hope's challenge, and turns out to be one of her best assets in Joan Bauer's new book, *Hope Was Here*.

Ever since Hope's mother abandoned her as a baby, Hope has followed her Aunt Addie around the country, longing for a permanent home and always looking for the father she doesn't know. However, she and her aunt, who is an extraordinary cook, go where the jobs and the money are. This last move is to Mulhoney, Wisconsin. Leaving the greatest diner in Brooklyn—after Aunt Addie's partner, Gleason Beal, cleaned out the business bank account—is the hardest challenge Hope has had to face. Hope says good-bye to New York by leaving her usual calling card, "Hope Was Here" written in half-inch tall letters on one of the boards.

Hope does find a lot of hope in Mulhoney, though. She falls in love with Braverman the cook, and she helps G. T. Stoop with his election campaign. But even hope can't always assure success. G. T. loses the election, and crooked politician Eli Millstone is reelected as Mayor of Mulhoney. However, everything looks brighter when G. T. finds out that his leukemia is in remission.

Will Hope find her father? Will Aunt Addie and Hope find happiness and permanence with G. T. Stoop and the Welcome Stairways Diner? Hope struggles with these questions as she tries to grow up and remember that, although she has a lot to overcome, she also has a lot for which to be thankful.

Hope Was Here is a deliciously funny look at Mulhoney's corrupt small-town politics and Hope and Aunt Addie's struggles to be successful in the food service industry. It is sometimes sad and always poignant as the characters try to work out their problems. G. T. Stoop fights to overcome his leukemia. There's a mouse in the salad, and a hearse following G. T. around town, parking outside the diner. Braverman is beaten for standing up for what he believes is right, and Hope keeps fighting her past and looking for her future. Once again, Joan Bauer delivers a fast-paced and satisfying young adult novel.

Source: Audrey Marie Danielson, Review of *Hope Was Here*, in *Teenreads*, September 11, 2000.

R.S.

In the following review, the reviewer praises Bauer's use of humor.

"You think all teenagers care about are musicians and movie stars?" Then have a listen to Hope, the latest of Joan Bauer's strong, kind, and funny heroines. The value of work has always been one of Bauer's consistent themes, and Hope takes great pride in her job: she's a short-order waitress who has come from Brooklyn with her aunt Addie to run a small-town diner in Wisconsin, its proprietor sidelined by leukemia. Hope, now sixteen, has lived with Addie since being left by her mother, who, in addition to having more of a gift for waitressing than she did for motherhood, had the dubious taste to name her daughter Tulip, which Hope changed as soon as she hit twelve. Addie and Hope, long peripatetic, find a new life in Wisconsin as well as a cause: G.T., the owner of the diner, has decided to take on the corrupt Eli Millstone, challenging his long incumbency as mayor. The nasty mayor is something of a stereotype (think of Mr. Potter in *It's a Wonderful Life*) as are some of the other characters, but because the whole book seems larger than life, broad strokes on a broad canvas, its personalities are necessarily outsized. Too, there's quite a bit of preaching, but most of it comes from Hope herself, building her character as much as our own. Not that she always takes her own advice. After telling another waitress her mother's Number One Cardinal Rule of Waitress Survival—"DO NOT, UNDER ANY CIRCUMSTANCES, DATE THE COOK"—Hope does anyway, and her tentative romance with Braverman is sweet indeed. Hope is a strong girl in a strong story, its humor warm and real.

Source: R. S., Review of *Hope Was Here*, in *Horn Book*, Vol. 76, No. 5, September 2000, p. 563.

Publishers Weekly

In the following review, the anonymous reviewer compares Hope Was Here *to "comfort food."*

Bauer (*Rules of the Road*; *Squashed*) serves up agreeable fare in this tale of a teenage waitress's search for a sense of belonging. Sixteen-year-old Hope has grown used to the nomadic life she has built with her aunt Addie, a talented diner cook. She doesn't mind the hard work it takes to make a diner hum; she seems to have inherited a knack for waiting tables from the free-spirit mom (Addie's younger sister) who abandoned her years ago. But Hope would gladly give up always having to say good-bye to friends and places she loves. When Addie accepts a new job that takes the pair from Brooklyn to the Welcome Stairways Diner in Mulhoney, Wis., Hope never could have imagined the big changes ahead of her. She and Addie shine in the small-town milieu and gladly offer to help diner owner G.T. Stoop, who is battling leukemia, run for mayor. Along the way, Addie and Hope both find love, and Hope discovers the father figure she has so desperately wanted. Readers will recognize many of Bauer's hallmarks here—a strong female protagonist on the road to self-discovery, quirky characters, dysfunctional families, a swiftly moving story, moments of bright humor. Her vivid prose, often rich in metaphor (e.g., Hope's description of the Brooklyn diner: "The big, oval counter . . . sat in the middle of the place like the center ring in a circus"), brings Hope's surroundings and her emotions to life. The author resolves a few of her plot points a bit too tidily, but her fans won't mind. They're likely to gobble this up like so much comfort food.

(Review of Hope Was Here, *in* Publishers Weekly, *Vol. 247, No. 36, September 4, 2000, p. 109.)*

Joan Bauer

In the following essay, Bauer explains the usefulness of humor to tackle difficult subject matter in fiction.

I have a six-inch-long rock in my office that my husband gave me for Christmas. No, he is not a boor or a cheapskate; he is a wise, instinctive man. For carved into the rock is a word: LAUGH. And the laugh rock, as it has come to be called, sits on my desk as a reminder of a truth about life that, for me, is carved in stone: Laughter is imminently, undeniably crucial.

E. B. White said, "A life without humor is like a life without legs." But why? What is it about humor and laughter that provides such support?

I believe, firstly, that humor intersects life and our humanness. There has yet to be a culture discovered where humor is not evident. Babies laugh the world over. Funny stories are shared in all countries and religions. The clown who fails miserably at some task and the adolescent storming off after a row with her impossible mother are reminders to us all that we are imperfect, fallible human beings. We learn about life through laughter. It is one of the great gifts we've been given as thinking souls. Humor puts life in perspective. It builds bridges between people, brings connections, and can take us from pain to redemption. But it does not stand separate from serious issues. Laughter and tears are connected. How many of us have laughed so hard that we've cried or, depending on our physiologies, wet ourselves?

The sheer magic of humor is present all around us. In a classroom setting it can provide an uproarious "welcome to the club." Humor, by its very nature, is uniting and multicultural. The task for educators, then, is to uncover the humor in multicultural settings that is already there.

As a children's and young adult novelist, I am constantly looking for passageways between life's difficulties and humor. When I speak at schools, I encourage students to "perform" stories. I find this can often best illustrate where conflict, character development, and resolutions intersect. On one occasion, in a seventh-grade classroom, I tried an experiment. I asked two male students to come forward, one white, one black, and told them to talk about how they felt about school, but that they must exchange races when they did it.

"You be the white kid," I instructed the young black man who grimaced. "You be the black," I said to the white student.

They and the class looked at me like I'd just grown a third eye. This is not for the fainthearted. After some resistance, they agreed to try.

We went through several false starts when the black student finally said, "I don't know how to act white."

The white student shifted nervously in agreement and smoothed back his hair. The black student watched him, then grinned broadly, and did the same thing.

The white student flopped deeper in the folding chair. The black student copied him perfectly.

The white student, catching on, crossed his legs and raised his hands to the ceiling as the two began a back-and-forth mimic of great complexity and good-natured laughter. Finally, the black student, in the ultimate tour de force, jumped up and spun around in a spectacular twirl; the white student attempted to follow, but knocked over a chair, ending the exercise. They returned to their seats to riotous applause—distinct, yet together.

"I'll teach you the spin," the black student said to the white student. And he did, at recess.

Sometimes multicultural influences can be mighty plot thickeners and the key to fostering understanding.

At another school I visited, the class and I were brainstorming about a story that I hoped would illustrate the role of conflict and motivation in fiction writing. The class (mostly boys) had come up with an idea about a middle school boy who wanted more than anything to play football.

"What's keeping him from doing it?" I asked.

Viable answers came. He's got a broken leg. His mother doesn't want him to get hurt. He can't afford the equipment.

But I saw the light go on in the eyes of a Japanese student who raised his hand and announced, laughingly, "Because he lives in Japan."

"So what?" asked several students, less than charitably.

"Because," the Japanese student replied, "in Japan there is no football."

"Now *that's* story conflict," I shouted.

And we proceeded to roar into a wonderfully comic, twisting plot about a boy living in Japan who dreamed of becoming a professional football player, and all the crazy things he did to get his parents to move to the United States so he could play the game. There was great laughter and discovery shared that day, and the students learned two lessons about humor writing:

1. Conflict breeds laughter.

2. Always push the envelope as far as it will creatively go.

Also, happily, throughout the exercise, the Japanese student starred—patiently, proudly instructing his American classmates about life and sports in his country.

FINDING THE VOICES

As a novelist, I'm intrigued by how a simple exchange between characters can be layered to have deeper meaning. In my third novel, *Sticks*, which is the story of a ten-year-old boy and his math genius sidekick who learn about life, determination, math, and science in a pool hall, I've attempted to describe a multicultural setting in the first-person narrative of Mickey Vernon, age ten, without him ever describing another character as black, white, or Hispanic. In fact, I wanted Mickey to be color-blind in that sense—to distinguish and celebrate people for their accomplishments while respecting their cultural milieus. Here, Mickey is sitting in art class trying to gain courage about facing his thirteen-year-old nemesis, Buck Pender, in the local pool tournament:

> I'm working on my African warrior mask, painting the papier-mâché cheeks bright gold and purple. I stick feathers at the top and make the mouth look angry and I picture this huge warrior with a spear doing a death dance around Buck Pender. T. R. Dobbs is working on his mask next to me. He's descended from African Zulu warriors and he says a Zulu never retreats in the face of the enemy. I'm descended mostly from potato farmers, which isn't a lot to hold on to when you need to be tough. I lift the mask to my face and shout the Zulu war cry T. R. taught me.
> "Zuuuuluuuu Zuuuuluuuu!"
> Mr. Pez, the art teacher, looks up. I look down and keep painting. Nobody turns me in.
> It's easy to be brave when the enemy isn't around.

Blasting stereotypes gives me soul satisfaction. And blasting them in a classroom setting bridges the way to common ground as students are brought into a larger place of acceptance of others.

Certainly the joy of finding universal experiences draws people together wonderfully. I spoke during an assembly at a New Jersey high school and announced to the assembled masses: "I promise you this will be the easiest test any of you have taken all year. True or false: Teenagers repeatedly have conflicts with their parents."

A pulsating, thundering "True!" rang out.

I continued: "True or false: These conflicts can be a royal pain, particularly when the parents are being thick-headed and unfair, particularly when they're not paying attention to anything the poor kid says."

The "True!" was a hundred times louder.

Of course, I knew how they would respond, and they knew that I knew. But their affirmation was the connection—black, white, Asian, Hispanic, old, young, rich, poor—united by adolescent angst.

"Anybody ever been in love with somebody who didn't know you were alive?" I asked.

Knowing nods.

So I read to them from *Thwonk*, my second YA novel, about a seventeen-year-old lovelorn photographer who learns about love, self-esteem, and forgiving her father from the hands of an exasperated cupid. Here, pre-cupid, she explains her lot.

> The whole thing with Peter Terris started five months ago, and I'd like to say from the outset that I wasn't looking for trouble. I was walking through the Student Center, speed-reading *Beowulf*, when I tripped over Peter's flawless foot and crashed at his feet like a complete spaz. I would have written the whole thing off to consummately bleak timing had I not gazed into his ice-green eyes, observed that they were positively riveting, and frozen in time.

HUMOR AT OUR VERY ROOTS

The power of humor to lift, heal, and define in all facets of life and culture is well documented, from author Norman Cousins's bold remission from cancer that he chronicled in *Anatomy of an Illness* to every joke told by every comic down through the ages trying to make sense of their cultural heritage. Here's one of my favorites, written by Milt Josefsberg for Jack Benny:

> A rabbi receives a phone call from an IRS investigator. "Rabbi, do you know a man named Hyman Shapiro?"
> "I do."
> "Does he belong to your congregation?"
> "He does."
> "Did he make a $10,000 donation to your temple?"
> "He will."

Why do we laugh at that joke? Because in some ways, we've all been there. Because with a few short lines it tells us all we need to know about the rabbi and Hyman Shapiro. Does that make it a universal teaching tool?

Yes!

Humor is appreciating the ludicrous and comic absurdity of life. Humor works when it allows us to laugh *with*, not *at*, another person or different culture. Humor teaches when it springs from life's experiences, especially if those experiences are painful, because laughter can help put painful experiences and feelings in perspective and allow us to move toward healing.

Children, however, will not all laugh at the same thing. But neither will they cry, be moved, or respond to anything uniformly. I believe, though, that they must be taught the difference between humor that uplifts and regenerates and humor that is thoughtless and cruel. In that, humor can be a bridge to the wider world view we seek for ourselves and our future.

As literature removes boundaries and explores universal themes, as the heart of cultures are examined and differences celebrated, we make another step toward unity and understanding. I believe that the simple, profound gift of shared laughter can help to show us the way. Garrison Keillor said it all: "Humor isn't tricks, it isn't jokes. Humor is like grace and falls on everyone."

Source: Joan Bauer, "Helping to Improve Multicultural Understanding through Humor," in *United in Diversity: Using Multicultural Young Adult Literature in the Classroom*, edited by Jean E. Brown and Elaine C. Stephens, National Council of Teachers of English, 1998, pp. 27–31.

SOURCES

Bauer, Joan, *Hope Was Here*, G. P. Putnam's Sons, 2000.

———, "Transcript from an Interview with Joan Bauer," in *Adolescent Literacy*, www.adlit.org/transcript_display/ 18955 (accessed May 11, 2016).

Bradburn, Frances, Review of *Hope Was Here*, in *Booklist*, Vol. 97, No. 2, September 15, 2000, p. 231.

Cart, Michael, Review of *Soar*, in *Booklist*, Vol. 112, No. 8, December 15, 2015, pp. 55–56.

Hartshorn, Laurie, Review of *Hope Was Here*, in *Booklist*, Vol. 100, Nos. 9–10, p. 894.

Jones, Landon Y., *Great Expectations: America & the Baby Boom Generation*, Coward, McCann & Geoghegan, 1980, pp. 1–13, 38–84.

Lesesne, Teri, "A Passion for Humor: An Interview with Joan Bauer," in *Teacher Librarian*, Vol. 27, No. 3, February 2000, p. 60.

———, "Words, Words, Words," in *Teacher Librarian*, Vol. 28, No. 2, December 2000, p. 54.

Mandell, Phyllis Levy, and Francisca Goldsmith, Review of *Hope Was Here*, in *School Library Journal*, Vol. 49, No. 12, December 2003, p. 77.

Nilsen, Alleen Pace, *Joan Bauer*, Greenwood Press, 2007, pp. 5–6, 10, 143.

———, James Blasingame, Kenneth L. Donnelson, and Don L. F. Nilsen, *Literature for Today's Young Adults*, 9th ed., Pearson, 2013, pp. 1–64, 103–42.

Review of *Hope Was Here*, in *Journal of Adolescent and Adult Literacy*, Vol. 46, No. 3, November 2002, p. 215.

Review of *Hope Was Here*, in *Publishers Weekly*, September 4, 2000, p. 109.

Sutton, Roger, Review of *Hope Was Here*, in *Horn Book*, Vol. 76, No. 5, September 2000, p. 563.

FURTHER READING

Bauer, Joan, "Bearers of Light: The Caring Community of Young Adult Literature," in *ALAN Review*, Vol. 33, No. 2, 2006, pp. 29–33.

Bauer shows how young-adult literature fills a mentoring and emotional need for young adults facing multiple challenges.

———, "Children of War," in *911: The Book of Help*, edited by Michael Cart with Marc Aronson and Marianne Carus, Crickett Books, 2002, pp. 39–47.

Bauer is one of the young-adult authors who wrote short stories to console after 9/11. A teen who witnesses the tragedy loses faith in life and takes a while to decide to go to college to be a teacher.

Hubler, Angela E., "Faith and Hope in the Feminist Political Novel for Children: A Materialist Feminist Analysis," in *Lion and Unicorn*, Vol. 34, No. 1, January 2010, pp. 57–75.

Hubler analyzes several children's novels, such as *The Midwife's Apprentice* (1991), by Karen Cushman; *Uncommon Faith* (2003), by Trudy Krisher; and *Hope Was Here* (2000), for the feminist political angle.

Leopold, Aldo, *A Sand County Almanac*, Ballantine Books, 1986.

G.T. Stoop in *Hope Was Here* is a tree planter. Leopold was a forester at the University of Wisconsin who formulated the important land ethic, which became a cornerstone of

American environmentalism. This book originally appeared in 1949.

Nilsen, Alleen Pace, and Don L. F. Nilsen, "Humor That Works in YA Fiction," in *Arizona English Bulletin*, Vol. 48, No. 1, 2006, pp. 11–16.
The Nilsens consider Bauer one of the important young-adult authors and point out how she uses humor to carry her message and develop characters.

West, Jessamyn, *The Friendly Persuasion*, Harcourt, 1945.
This novel about a pacifist Quaker farm family in Indiana during the Civil War was made into a film in 1956 with Gary Cooper and Dorothy McGuire.

SUGGESTED SEARCH TERMS

Joan Bauer

Hope Was Here AND Bauer

young-adult fiction

Quakerism

Wisconsin AND politics

teen work

leukemia

quest literature

Aldo Leopold

Wisconsin AND dairy

Indian Killer

SHERMAN ALEXIE

1996

Sherman Alexie's *Indian Killer* (1996) provokes hugely varying reactions among readers and critics. The novel portrays various characters living in Seattle while a serial murderer terrorizes the city. The killer is believed to be Native American because he scalps his victims and leaves behind two owl feathers, which are symbolic of death in tribal lore. The murders are interpreted as acts of revenge for the American genocide of Indians, and, indeed, scenes from the killer's point of view confirm that he acts through anger and vengeance.

Some readers appreciate Alexie's gift for characterization and his trademark wit, which shines through in spite of the grim story. Others believe the novel is too steeped in anger, glorifying violence and justifying racism. Alexie had mixed feelings about the novel. He explained to the *Guardian*'s Maya Jaggi that he came to see the book as the product of youthful rage. He changed after the terrorist attacks of September 11, 2001, which made him see the "end game of tribalism—when you become so identified with only one thing, one tribe, that other people are just metaphors to you." Moreover, in an interview with Sarah T. Williams in the *Star Tribune*, Alexie dismisses *Indian Killer* as "very much a tribal and fundamentalist book." He says he has "worked hard since then to shed the negative parts of tribal thinking" and disowned the novel. In spite of Alexie's condemnation of his work and his rejection of tribalistic thinking,

Sherman Alexie *(©Ulf Andersen / Getty Images)*

Indian Killer is fascinating as a study of the deep-seated bitterness and anger felt by many Native Americans after a long history of mistreatment of their people at the hands of the US government. Because of the violence of the murders, *Indian Killer* is more appropriate for older students.

AUTHOR BIOGRAPHY

Alexie was born on October 7, 1966, on the Wellpinit Spokane reservation near Spokane, Washington. When he was six months old, he underwent surgery to correct congenital hydrocephalus. His parents were told that he might not survive the procedure and that if he did he might have brain damage. Though Alexie experienced seizures throughout his childhood, there were no other lasting effects. He was very bright, learning to read at age three and becoming an avid reader.

Neither of Alexie's parents finished high school. His mother, a social worker and quilt maker, was Spokane. His father, who was Coeur d'Alene, worked various blue-collar jobs and suffered from depression and alcohol addiction. Though he was never violent, he would occasionally disappear on drinking binges.

Although Alexie was always a good student, many on the reservation did not value education and intellectual curiosity. To get a better education, he decided to enroll at an all-white school twenty miles away from the reservation. He excelled at his studies and became class president. His success in high school earned him a scholarship to Gonzaga University. He later transferred to Washington State University, graduating in 1991. When he started college, Alexie thought he would become a doctor, but then he took a creative writing class. His professor shared an anthology of poems by Native American writers that Alexie credits with changing his life, sparking his literary career.

Another major change occurred in Alexie's life around this time. While at college, he began drinking heavily. In 1992, however, he published both *I Would Steal Horses*, a poetry collection, and *The Business of Fancydancing*, a unique mixture of poetry and prose. His literary successes earned him a National Endowment for the Arts fellowship for poetry (a twenty-thousand-dollar award), so he was able to put aside other career ideas and concentrate on his writing. He has remained sober ever since.

Since 1992, Alexie has published a poetry collection every few years. In addition to his poetry, he has written several collections of short stories and four novels: *Reservation Blues* (1995), *Indian Killer* (1996), *The Absolutely True Diary of a Part-Time Indian* (2007), and *Flight* (2007). He also produced and wrote the screenplay for the film *Smoke Signals* (1998), which is based on his short story "This Is What It Means to Say Phoenix, Arizona" (1993), and wrote and directed the film adaptation of his book *The Business of Fancydancing* (2002).

Alexie has received numerous awards, including a PEN/Hemingway Award, a PEN/Malamud Award, a PEN/Faulkner Award, a lifetime achievement award from the Native Writers' Circle of the Americas, a Mason Award, a Stranger Genius Award, a Pushcart Prize, and a National Book Award for Young People's Literature. As of 2016, Alexie was still writing and lived with his wife and two sons in Seattle.

PLOT SUMMARY

Section 1: Owl Dancing

CHAPTER 1: MYTHOLOGY

As *Indian Killer* begins, John Smith is taken from his fourteen-year-old Native American mother at the reservation hospital where she gives birth. He is flown in a helicopter to his adoptive family, a white couple living near Seattle, Washington.

CHAPTER 2: THE LAST SKYSCRAPER IN SEATTLE

Olivia and Daniel Smith, unable to conceive a child, decide to adopt. They are white but decide to adopt a minority child to avoid the long wait for a white baby. Olivia tries to educate John about his Indian heritage, though in a haphazard and general way. Daniel tries to connect through playing sports with his son. John feels out of place as the only Native American student in his school, but his relationship with Father Duncan, a Spokane Jesuit priest, helps ground the boy until he is seven years old, when Father Duncan disappears. As an adult, John gets a job working construction straight out of high school because he has learned about the Mohawk Indian steelworkers. John has a mental illness and hears voices in his head.

CHAPTER 3: OWL DANCING AT THE BEGINNING OF THE END OF THE WORLD

John resolves to kill a white man because he believes white men are responsible for everything that goes wrong. Uncertain how to go about it, he wanders the city and meets Marie Polatkin. They dance at an event on the University of Washington campus.

CHAPTER 4: HOW HE IMAGINES HIS LIFE ON THE RESERVATION

John imagines what his life would have been like if his birth mother had not given him up for adoption. Although his imagined family is poor, there is a lot of love and laughter in their home.

CHAPTER 5: HOW IT HAPPENED

The unnamed killer selects Justin Summers, an arrogant white businessman, as his first victim.

CHAPTER 6: TRUCK SCHULTZ

The radio talk show host Truck Schultz leaks the news of the murder on the air, revealing that the victim was scalped.

MEDIA ADAPTATIONS

- A CD recording of *Indian Killer* was produced by Recording for the Blind & Dyslexic in 2009. A cassette recording was produced by Audio Literature in 1996.

CHAPTER 7: INTRODUCTION TO NATIVE AMERICAN LITERATURE

Marie attends the first session of her Native American literature class and identifies her teacher, Dr. Clarence Mather, as a wannabe Indian. Another student, David Rogers, is fascinated by Marie and tries to engage her in conversation, but she quickly dismisses him. David remembers a night when he was a boy when his father, Buck, encouraged him and his brother, Aaron, to shoot at a Native American family digging for camas root on the Rogers farm.

CHAPTER 8: TESTIMONY

The police question Mr. Russell, who sees the killer carrying Justin Summers on the night of his death.

CHAPTER 9: BUILDING

Olivia and Daniel come to John's apartment concerned about him, but he will not speak to them. He remembers being teased at school because he was different and the anger he felt.

CHAPTER 10: CONFESSIONS

Marie confronts Dr. Mather, and he closes his office door in her face. David once again tries to connect with Marie, and she brushes him off.

CHAPTER 11: COUSINS

Marie's cousin Reggie visits. He used to be a student like her but now is aimless, asking for money. She cannot lend him anything but feeds him and lets him stay the night. A flashback shows the abuse Reggie has suffered from his white father, Bird Lawrence.

CHAPTER 12: SEATTLE'S BEST DONUTS

John remembers how when he was twenty years old, he thought he was pregnant. He visits Seattle's Best Donuts. Paul, the server, and Paul Too, a regular customer, recognize John and are kind to him. They tell him about the murder of Justin Summers, and John becomes upset, crying and laughing.

CHAPTER 13: INDIAN GAMBLING

David visits a reservation casino and wins two thousand dollars. When he goes out to his pickup truck to drive home, he is hit on the head and loses consciousness.

CHAPTER 14: TESTIMONY

The police question Mrs. Johnson, who sees David at the casino.

CHAPTER 15: VARIATIONS

Olivia and Daniel try again to speak to John.

CHAPTER 16: GREEK CHORUS

On his radio show, Truck discusses David's disappearance, blaming Native Americans.

CHAPTER 17: ALL THE INDIANS IN THE WORLD

Buck and Aaron drive to the casino from which David has disappeared. They learn nothing, but Buck is angry seeing the local Native American residents going about their lives. Aaron posts missing person signs.

CHAPTER 18: IN SEARCH OF

Sweet Lu, a Native American guide, takes John into the woods to look for Bigfoot.

CHAPTER 19: NATIVE AMERICAN STUDIES

A flashback explains the argument between Reggie and Dr. Mather that has caused Reggie to leave school. Mather has been compiling recordings of traditional Spokane stories, and Reggie objects, believing the stories belong only to the people who tell them. Mather hides the tapes and lies about it. Reggie confronts him and punches him, and for this he is expelled from the university.

CHAPTER 20: THE SANDWICH LADY

Marie does volunteer work serving sandwiches to the homeless. She sees John briefly.

CHAPTER 21: KILLING THE DRAGON

The killer singles out six-year-old Mark Jones on the playground because he seems to be a leader. Later, the killer sneaks into the Jones house and kidnaps the boy.

Section 2: Hunting Weather

CHAPTER 1: THE ARISTOTLE LITTLE HAWK FAN CLUB

Jack Wilson was a beat cop and a detective before retiring and taking up writing. He has written two popular novels about a Native American private detective. Wilson goes to his former precinct and learns about the Indian killer.

CHAPTER 2: TESTIMONY

The police question Mark's mother about the boy's disappearance.

CHAPTER 3: THE LEARNING CURVE

John watches Marie and Dr. Mather leave the university campus.

CHAPTER 4: CHEMISTRY

Arthur Two Leaf, a Native American chemistry student walking on the Burke-Gilman trail, is assaulted by three white men in masks.

CHAPTER 5: BIG HEART'S SODA AND JUICE BAR

Wilson goes to Big Heart's, a popular hangout for Seattle's Native American community, to ask people about the killer. He talks to Reggie and his friends Ty Williams and Harley Tate.

CHAPTER 6: TESTIMONY

Arthur Two Leaf tells the police about being beaten up.

CHAPTER 7: MARK JONES

Mark wakes up in a dark place. The killer gives him a drink, and Mark cries himself to sleep.

CHAPTER 8: THE MESSENGER

Truck receives a package containing a piece of the pajamas Mark is wearing when he was abducted and two owl feathers—the killer's calling card.

CHAPTER 9: JOHN SMITH

While John is walking, he is stopped by three young men in a pickup truck. John loses control, screaming until they leave him alone. John remembers the death of one of his classmates in high school, a popular bully. Distraught, John goes into a church and speaks to the priest.

CHAPTER 10: FINDING THE BODY

An unnamed Spokane couple finds David's body in the woods.

CHAPTER 11: FIRE STARTER

Truck learns about the discovery of David's body and goes on the air to deliver a rant, blaming and belittling Native Americans.

CHAPTER 12: THE BATTLE OF QUEEN ANNE

After hearing that his brother's body has been found, Aaron persuades his roommates, Sean Ward and Barry Church, to get what he sees as revenge for David's death. They don masks and beat up a homeless Indian couple.

CHAPTER 13: NIGHT TERRORS

Daniel goes downtown looking for John. He speaks to a homeless man but learns nothing useful. Late that night, Olivia wakes, certain that John has been in the house.

CHAPTER 14: BLANK PAGES

Wilson is edgy. He is trying to write a book about the killer but is experiencing writer's block. He walks to a downtown park, where Marie recognizes him from his book jacket photos. Marie talks with King, a homeless man, and gives him a sandwich.

CHAPTER 15: MARK JONES

The killer continues to hold Mark in the dark place.

CHAPTER 16: THE LAST PRECINCT

Wilson goes to a bar where cops gather to try to learn more about the killer.

CHAPTER 17: DECONSTRUCTION

Mather speculates about the killer in class, and Marie challenges him.

CHAPTER 18: COUSINS

John prevents three white men from hurting an old homeless woman.

CHAPTER 19: THE AURORA AVENUE MASSACRE

Reggie, Ty, and Harley attack a white hitchhiker camping in a football field.

CHAPTER 20: THE ELLIOTT BAY BOOK COMPANY

Wilson performs a reading at Elliott Bay Book Company. A group of Native Americans, including Marie, stand outside to protest. After the reading, Wilson flees in a taxi. John finds Marie at the protest, and in her sandwich van they follow Wilson's taxi. There is a confrontation, but no one is hurt.

CHAPTER 21: TESTIMONY

Robert Harris, who has been attacked by Reggie and his friends, gives a statement to the police.

CHAPTER 22: SLOW DANCING WITH THE MOST BEAUTIFUL INDIAN WOMAN ON EARTH

John goes to Big Heart's to feel safe among those who look like him. He dances with a beautiful woman named Fawn. Reggie picks a fight with John, but Ty and Harley do not join in.

CHAPTER 23: A CONVERSATION

Aaron and Buck talk on the phone about the time they shot at the Native American family trespassing on their land.

CHAPTER 24: MARK JONES

The killer watches Mark sleeping and then picks him up and carries him out of the dark place.

CHAPTER 25: HOW HE IMAGINES HIS LIFE ON THE RESERVATION

In another idealized daydream, John imagines what it would have been like to leave his birth mother on the reservation and go to college.

CHAPTER 26: HUNTING WEATHER

Remembering a hunting trip with his father when he was young, Truck feels hunted himself in the dark alley near the radio station. He convinces himself that the killer is stalking him.

Section 3: Last Call

CHAPTER 1: MARK JONES

The killer returns Mark to his sleeping mother's arms. She wakes screaming—first in joy to find Mark safe, then in fear knowing the killer has entered her home again.

CHAPTER 2: TESTIMONY

Truck tells the police about his scare in the alley, but the officer is skeptical that anyone was even there, much less the killer.

CHAPTER 3: SEATTLE'S BEST DONUTS

John visits the doughnut shop and alarms Paul and Paul Too with his erratic behavior.

CHAPTER 4: HIGHER EDUCATION

Mather files a formal complaint about Marie's disruptive behavior in his classroom, but she is not cowed.

CHAPTER 5: OLIVIA AND DANIEL

Olivia and Daniel seem to drift apart as they worry about John.

CHAPTER 6: THE SEARCHERS

Reggie, Harley, and Ty watch a movie on television and discuss the racist themes in the film. Ty and Harley are nervous about Reggie's anger and the assault on the hitchhiker.

CHAPTER 7: TESTIMONY

The police ask Mark about his abduction. The boy insists the kidnapper has feathers and wings.

CHAPTER 8: HOW IT HAPPENED

The killer watches Edward Letterman, a traveling business man, visit a pornography shop and follows him to his rental car. Though Letterman shows the killer pictures of his family and begs for his life, the killer brutally stabs him.

CHAPTER 9: MARIE

Marie makes sandwiches at the shelter with Boo, a homeless man, and they speculate about the identity of the killer.

CHAPTER 10: TRUCK

On his radio show, Truck gives the news of Letterman's murder.

CHAPTER 11: WILSON

Wilson still struggles with writer's block. He goes to his former precinct hoping to learn something useful and meets John's foreman from the construction site, who hands over a photo of John. Wilson recognizes John from the confrontation the other night after the bookstore reading.

CHAPTER 12: TRUCK

Truck delivers another racist diatribe on his show.

CHAPTER 13: ANGER

Aaron, Sean, and Barry beat up more homeless Indians. Sean finally stands up to Aaron and, once Aaron and Barry drive off, goes to the police.

CHAPTER 14: A CONVERSATION

Reggie talks to his mother on the phone.

CHAPTER 15: MOTHER

After learning John's address from the foreman, Wilson goes to his apartment. He meets Olivia and asks about John.

CHAPTER 16: MARIE

Marie and Boo are delivering sandwiches when they come across King, who has been beaten up by two white men.

CHAPTER 17: CATHOLICISM

John is praying, kneeling in the street. A police officer approaches, and John runs away.

CHAPTER 18: LAST CALL AT BIG HEART'S

Wilson returns to Big Heart's. He speaks to Reggie, Fawn, and Ty but hears laughter as he leaves.

CHAPTER 19: RUNNING

When John stops running, Aaron and Barry find him and attack him. Marie finds him curled up to protect himself, and she and a small band of homeless people chase off Barry and Aaron. Everyone is kind to John, wanting to help, but he walks away from the sandwich van.

CHAPTER 20: RADIO SILENCE

Truck is banned from doing his program. The city is in chaos—many of the disturbances caused by racial issues—and the police fear Truck's rants will add fuel to the fire

CHAPTER 21: HOW IT HAPPENED

A flashback offers the true story of David Rogers's death. Rather than falling victim to the Indian killer, David was killed by two young white men who wanted to steal his casino winnings.

CHAPTER 22: TESTIMONY

In the hope of preventing further attacks, Sean confesses to the police about the crimes he commits with Aaron and Barry.

CHAPTER 23: DREAMING

Wilson parks near his apartment and is knocked unconscious. His attacker pushes him out of the driver's seat, climbs in, and drives away.

CHAPTER 24: TESTIMONY

Mather tells the police that Marie has threatened him. He also shares his suspicions about Reggie's violent tendencies.

CHAPTER 25: THE LAST SKYSCRAPER IN SEATTLE

Wilson regains consciousness at the construction site where John works. John has tied him up and threatens him with a gun. Wilson tries to reason with him.

CHAPTER 26: TESTIMONY

The police question Ty about the attack on the hitchhiker and about Reggie.

CHAPTER 27: DECISIONS

As Wilson talks and weeps, John tries to figure out what to do next.

CHAPTER 28: LEAVING

Reggie hitches a ride out of town.

CHAPTER 29: FLYING

John cuts Wilson's face with a knife. Then he calmly jumps off the building. The fall kills him, but his spirit rises and walks away.

CHAPTER 30: TESTIMONY

Marie is questioned by the police. They ask about Reggie, John, and David Rogers. She answers belligerently.

CHAPTER 31: A CREATION STORY

The killer dances in an Indian cemetery, suggesting the traditional Ghost Dance to raise the dead.

CHARACTERS

Beautiful Mary

Beautiful Mary is a homeless Indian woman whom Jack Wilson meets while he is a beat cop. When he finds her body and the detective assigned to the case considers it a low priority, Wilson conducts the investigation. His work on the case helps him make detective.

Boo

Boo is a homeless man who helps Marie make the sandwiches one day.

Sidney Bush

Sidney is John's classmate who was bullied by Scott O'Brien. After hearing of Scott's death, Sidney hides his face so that no one will see that he is laughing instead of mourning.

Barry Church

Barry is friends with Aaron and David Rogers and one of their roommates. After David's disappearance, Barry and Sean Ward accompany Aaron when he goes out to take his revenge on homeless Native Americans downtown. Although Barry wants to stop hurting people almost as much as Sean does, he is too afraid of Aaron to object.

Cornelius

Cornelius and his companion, Zera, both homeless, are attacked by Aaron Rogers and his friends.

Darla

Darla is Truck Schultz's assistant at the radio station.

Father Duncan

Father Duncan is the Jesuit priest who baptizes John. He is a Spokane Indian. He acts as a kind of mentor until he disappears when John is seven years old. Father Duncan never quite disappears in John's mind, however. For years after Father Duncan leaves, John imagines him walking in the desert.

Estelle

Estelle is the wife of John's foreman, who confides in her that he is worried about John.

Fawn

Fawn is a beautiful woman who dances with John at Big Heart's. Reggie uses this as an excuse to pick a fight with John.

Foreman

John's foreman is a middle-aged white man who respects that John is a hard worker. He grows concerned when John's mental illness becomes more evident.

Robert Harris

Robert Harris is the white hitchhiker who testifies to the police about being attacked by Reggie Polatkin and his friends.

Mrs. Johnson

Mrs. Johnson speaks to the police about seeing David Rogers at the casino.

Erin Jones

Erin is Mark Jones's mother. She is distraught and angry over his disappearance and frustrated by the questions and lack of progress from the police.

Mark Jones

Mark is the six-year-old blond boy kidnapped by the killer. He is taken from his bedroom in the middle of the night and returned to his home days later. The killer picks Mark after visiting the playground and seeing in the way Mark leads his playmates that he will grow into a powerful man.

The Killer

Although the killer is never named, several chapters are presented from the killer's point of view. The text in these sections is matter of fact—almost simple—as if to reflect his black-and-white view of the world, which allows him to take human life in the firm conviction that what he is doing is right.

King

King is a homeless Indian. Marie gives him a peanut butter and jelly sandwich and later helps him after he is beaten up by Aaron Rogers.

Bird Lawrence

Bird is Reggie Polatkin's father. He is white and works for the Bureau of Indian Affairs. He is a racist, dividing the Native American population into those he considers good Indians, who are docile and go along with what the government wants, and hostile Indians, who stand up for themselves and their people. Bird is verbally and physically abusive to Reggie and forces him to use his mother's Indian surname until he can prove himself worthy of sharing Bird's surname.

Martha Polatkin Lawrence

Martha is Reggie Polatkin's mother. She marries Bird Lawrence because she knows he can give her material comfort but seems to do nothing to protect Reggie from Bird's physical and verbal abuse.

Edward Letterman

Edward Letterman is one of the Indian killer's victims. He is a business traveler. Though he visits a pornography shop, he seems a harmless, decent enough man, thinking only of his wife and sons when he fears he will die.

Lyle

Lyle is one of the two white men who jump David Rogers and steal his money.

Dr. Clarence Mather

Mather is the professor of Marie's Native American literature course. She thinks of him as a wannabe Indian, a white person so enamored of traditional native culture that he pretends to be Native American himself. Marie's challenges anger Mather, who years ago had a conflict with

Marie's cousin Reggie, regarding white appropriation of Indian culture. The altercation results in Reggie's having to leave the university.

Michael

In a flashback to John's days at school, Michael makes inappropriate remarks about the attractiveness of John's mother.

Mick

Mick is the bartender at Big Heart's Soda and Juice Bar, where Jack Wilson goes to socialize with Native Americans, wanting to feel as if he belongs.

Scott O'Brien

In a flashback, Scott is a boy who dies during John's senior year of high school. Scott is popular but a bully. John does not like him, and he notices the laughter of Sidney Bush, a frequent victim of Scott's bullying.

Paul

Paul is a young African American man who works at the doughnut shop that John frequents. Paul is an art major at the University of Washington during the day, so he works the graveyard shift. Paul helps Olivia and Daniel keep tabs on John when he falls out of touch with them.

Paul Too

Paul Too is an older African American man who hangs out at Seattle's Best Donuts. Both Pauls are kind to John, knowing that he has a mental illness. Paul Too tastes John's coffee and doughnut to reassure him that they are not poisoned.

Father Phil

Father Phil is kind to John Smith when he arrives, confused, at his church. Because John admits that he is angry and calls himself the devil, Father Phil worries that he is the Indian killer.

Marie Polatkin

Marie is a student at the University of Washington. She is a Spokane Indian and active in politics. She takes part in a protest on the campus and in one at a bookstore where Jack Wilson is doing a reading. Marie is outspoken against Professor Mather, a wannabe Indian who has no Native American blood but appreciates the culture. She does not approve of whites appropriating native traditions as their own. Although

Marie is angry at the treatment of her people, she is also kind. She serves sandwiches to Seattle's homeless population.

Reggie Polatkin

Reggie is Marie's cousin. When he was younger, he had great promise: "the mysterious urban Indian, the college student, the ambitious half-breed, the star basketball player, the Indian who would make a difference." Reggie is particularly determined to succeed after being abused by his white father, who tries to make him hate the Indian part of himself. After his disagreement with Mather, Reggie must leave the university. He ends up aimless and bitter, and when the Indian killer threatens the city, Reggie vents his own anger and frustration by beating up a white hiker.

Aaron Rogers

Aaron is Buck's son and David's older brother. Unlike David, Aaron shares their father's anger and aggression toward the Native Americans who forage on the Rogers family farm. After David disappears, Aaron vents his grief and anger by beating up homeless Indians.

Buck Rogers

Buck is David and Aaron's father. He does not understand David's gentle nature and assumes that he is gay. In a flashback, Buck encourages the boys to shoot at an Indian family foraging on the Rogers farm. He justifies this aggression by bragging that the land has been in his family for over a hundred years. Buck's point is ironic in that while Buck is complaining about the Native Americans' stealing camas root, the white settlers have stolen the land, where the local tribes had lived for thousands of years.

David Rogers

David is a white college student who meets Marie in Mather's Native American literature class. Although David's father, Buck, and his brother, Aaron, are prejudiced against Native Americans, even resorting to shooting at an Indian family who comes to dig for camas root, a traditional food for their tribe, on the Rogers farm, David himself is interested in and sympathetic to Indian issues. However, he is not one of the fake Indians whom Marie scorns. When David goes missing, his friends and family fear he has fallen victim to the Indian killer, but he

dies after leaving a tribal casino, killed by two white men stealing his winnings.

Rupert

Rupert is Jack Wilson's agent. He is able to get Wilson a deal on a book he has not yet written because, as Rupert puts it, "Indians are big right now."

Mr. Russell

Mr. Russell sees the killer carrying Justin Summers along the hiking trail.

Sarah

Sarah is Mark Jones's nanny. She is with Mark at the park when the killer sees the boy and follows him home.

Truck Schultz

Truck Schultz is a conservative local radio talk show host. He calls himself the voice of reason, but his diatribes promote fear and hate rather than reason. He uses the controversy surrounding the Indian killer to increase his ratings and comes to fear that he himself will become a victim.

Daniel Smith

Daniel is John's adoptive father and Olivia's husband. Like Olivia, he is a devoted parent. He tries to connect with John over a love of sports, coaching him in basketball for endless hours, but John never improves.

John Smith

John is one of the central characters of the novel. He is given up or taken from his Indian mother immediately after his birth and adopted by Daniel and Olivia Smith, a white couple living in the suburbs of Seattle. John feels cut off from his past, struggles to form his own identity, and believes himself to be an outsider everywhere. He does not fit in with the mostly white community where he lives, but he feels he can never be a real Indian. As an adult, John has a mental illness that further confuses him. His anger and confusion about his own identity drive him to fear that he may be the serial killer and not remember what he has done. He kidnaps Jack Wilson and after slashing Wilson's face with a knife jumps off a skyscraper to his death.

John Smith's Birth Mother

John's birth mother appears only briefly in the novel. She is fourteen years old and gives birth in an ill-equipped reservation hospital. Though John never knows her, he imagines what his life would have been like if he had grown up living with her on a reservation.

Olivia Smith

Olivia is John's adoptive mother and Daniel's wife. From the time John is put in her arms until his death, Olivia does everything she can to help him. She learns about Native American culture herself and makes every effort to educate John about his heritage, but her knowledge is limited and generalized and does not give him any true connection to his past. When John is an adult with a mental illness, Olivia and Daniel still try to help him, going to his apartment to check on him and make sure he takes his medicine.

Spud

Spud is one of the two white men who jump David Rogers and steal his money. Spud kills David with a revolver.

Stink

Stink is the homeless white man Wilson arrests for killing Beautiful Mary. Although Stink confesses, he never goes to trial because he hangs himself during his first night in jail.

Justin Summers

Justin is walking home on the Burke-Gilman Trail when the killer confronts him and stabs him in the stomach. The killer picks Justin as a victim not only because he is white but also because of his arrogance as he "strolled down the middle of the sidewalk, forcing others to walk around him."

Sweet Lu

Sweet Lu is the Native American guide who takes John to look for Bigfoot.

Harley Tate

Harley is one of Reggie Polatkin's friends. Harley is deaf and communicates through sign language. When Reggie attacks Robert Harris, the white camper, Harley and Ty Williams are also there.

Arthur Two Leaf

Arthur Two Leaf is a chemistry student attacked by three white men (presumably Aaron Rogers, Sean Ward, and Barry Church) while walking home from the university.

Sean Ward

Sean is friends with Aaron and David Rogers and one of their roommates. After David's disappearance, Sean and Barry Church accompany Aaron when he goes out to take his revenge on the innocent homeless Native Americans downtown. Sean finally speaks up and tells Aaron he will not take part in the violence.

Ty Williams

Ty is one of Reggie Polatkin's friends. He and Harley Tate are with Reggie when he attacks Robert Harris, the white camper.

Jack Wilson

Wilson is a retired policeman and writer who is convinced he has Native American blood. His books feature a private detective, the very last Shilshomish Indian, a tall, handsome man named Aristotle Little Hawk. Experiencing writer's block, Wilson heads to his former precinct and learns about the Indian killer. He starts a novel on the subject and becomes obsessed. Near the end of the novel, John Smith kidnaps Wilson and slashes at him with a knife, leaving him screaming when John jumps to his death.

Zera

Zera and her companion, Cornelius, a homeless couple, are cruelly beaten by Aaron Rogers and his friends.

THEMES

Anger

Anger is a central theme in *Indian Killer*. Readers may assume at the start that the killer is driven by anger, but in the section of the novel from the killer's point of view, he seems oddly detached and unemotional. Almost all of the other characters, however, experience intense anger in different forms. Marie, for example, feels intense anger when she has a confrontation with Professor Mather and he closes the door in her face. She "felt a sudden urge to smash the glass, break down the door, pull down the building. She wanted to tear apart the world." Her anger here results from being powerless against Mather and from the unfairness of his treatment of her. She is certain that "Mather would have never treated a white student that badly, nor would he have shut the door in the face of a man." Her rage against

TOPICS FOR FURTHER STUDY

- The protagonist of Chris Crutcher's young-adult novel *Whale Talk* (2001) is T. J. Jones, a teenager of mixed heritage who has been adopted by a white family living outside Spokane, Washington. T.J. is the only person of color in his high school. Read *Whale Talk* and compare T.J. with John Smith in *Indian Killer* as a teenager. How is T.J.'s experience in school like John's, and how is it different? Discuss whether you think the differences result from the differences between T.J. and John as people—the latter's mental illness, for example—or from other variables, such as their families, schools, and communities. Write an essay to explain your thoughts; use examples from both texts.

- Alexie portrays the traditional Ghost Dance at the close of *Indian Killer* and uses the imagery and theme of dancing in many of his novels, poems, and stories. Using print and online sources, research the importance of dance in Native American culture. Share your findings with your classmates in a presentation.

- Using a free online service such as Wix or Weebly, create a website to share information about Alexie with other students. Include a brief biography, a list of his works, and links to readily available interviews, literary criticism, reviews, and recordings of public appearances.

- Since colonial times, the treatment of Native Americans by European settlers and the US government has forced native peoples out of their homelands, robbed them of their culture, separated families, and led to countless deaths. Create a time line that shows major events in history that both injured and attempted to help Native Americans. Share your time line with your class.

Mather expands. First she wants her professor to disappear. Then her anger spreads, and she wants "every white man to disappear. She wanted to burn them all down to ash and feast on their smoke."

Later, when Marie meets up with King, one of the homeless Indians beaten up by Aaron and his friends, Marie feels what she describes as a beautiful kind of anger. The feeling becomes beautiful to her likely because she has a target for her anger in this situation. She and some of the homeless people attack Aaron and Barry and stop them from their unprovoked assault on John. During the confrontation, Marie is nearly blind with rage. She wants "to tear out their blue eyes and blind them," though later she is shocked at the violence of her emotions.

Aaron's crimes come from a different kind of anger: roommates notice that he has had a short fuse since David's disappearance. Because David is missing, his family has no body to bury and therefore has no funeral. Aaron feels the lack of "some kind of ceremony in which to express his grief, but he was without ceremony. Without the ability to mourn properly, Aaron could only steep in his anger." It is ironic that though Aaron directs his anger at Indians, his lack of ceremony reflects the situation of Native Americans, who have had so many of their traditions and ceremonies taken away from them when they are not allowed to practice their religion freely.

Reggie's anger shares elements with both Marie's and Aaron's. Like his cousin Marie, Reggie struggles with the long history of mistreatment of his people and with day-to-day prejudice and feelings of powerlessness. But like Aaron, Reggie acts out with Ty and Harley just as Aaron acts out with Sean and Barry, attacking innocent victims who are bewildered at being treated with such anger.

Most important in the novel is John's anger, because of what he represents. The way John is separated from his culture—taken from his mother and his people and their traditions—reflects the destruction of Native American population and their culture by US colonialism. His anger is an individual version of their collective anger at a long history of genocide, even more so than that of Marie and Reggie. When Wilson sees a photograph of John at the construction site, it reminds him of "all those old-time warrior Indians who were forced to sit still for Army photographers." John stares angrily into the camera just as those warriors do: "Those defeated warriors always had smooth faces and flat expressions, but their eyes were dark and filled with a feral, kinetic hate." All his life, John has been forced to swallow his anger and push it into a small place. Sometimes his anger frightens him, as when he stands over Wilson and the cab driver with the golf club: "He stood over those two white men and wanted to kill them both. He wanted to smash their faces, break their bones, and crush their blue eyes." As Marie points out to the police when questioned about John, Native Americans have a long history of wrongs that make them justifiably angry: "If some Indian is killing white guys, then it's a credit to us that it took over five hundred years for it to happen."

Mystery

As readers make their way through *Indian Killer*, one question is constant in their minds: Who is the killer? There are details in every character's actions and thoughts that can be seen as hints that they could be the killer. Because anger is a central theme in the novel, all of the major characters have moments in which their rage threatens to take over. Anger drives both Reggie and Aaron to hurt others, but that they act out in this way—impulsively, if not stupidly—makes it hard to believe that they would undertake the cold, calculated murders described from the killer's point of view.

Though she is intelligent and articulate, Marie has anger constantly simmering under her controlled exterior, and at times the feeling threatens to turn into physical violence. It bursts out of her at inappropriate times, such as when she yells at one of the homeless men helping her make sandwiches. He tries to joke with her: "You sound like that Indian Killer or something," which makes Marie want "to scream at him. She felt the anger in her belly and hands." She does get her anger under control in this situation and several others, but it never quite goes away. It seems unlikely, however, that Marie is the Indian killer. After helping King and stopping Aaron from hurting another victim, Marie is shocked by her anger. She feels anger, but she does not like to let it control her. Rather, she uses her anger to fuel her actions. She works to help her community and acts with kindness, as in her work as the sandwich lady.

Even Jack Wilson's attempt to write a novel about the Indian killer seems suspect. He imagines himself as the killer in order to write the

Marie resents her professor, a "Wannabe Indian," for appropriating Native American culture (©arek_malang | Shutterstock.com)

book convincingly, but it goes a bit further than that: he "saw himself with that knife. Wilson saw himself pushing the knife into one white body, then another, and another, until there were multitudes. Isn't that how it happened?" His obsession with becoming Native American makes him want to identify even with Indian anger.

Perhaps the most obvious possibility as the killer is John Smith. Like the other characters, he carries a lot of anger, and he is desperate to define himself as a real Indian. When he sneaks into his parents' house, he hovers in their bedroom much as the killer hovers in Mark and his mother's. John kidnaps Wilson and slashes him with the knife. In addition, because of his mental illness, it is possible that John could be the killer and not understand what he has done or remember it. That John kills himself rather than Wilson argues against his being the killer, but after his death, he is shown walking away, like Father

Duncan disappearing into the desert. This adds a mystical element to the novel, especially in relation to Alexie's references to the Ghost Dance.

The one witness who sees the killer and survives is Mark Jones, the six-year-old kidnapped boy. He is certainly frightened and not thinking clearly, but after he returns home and is questioned by the police, he cannot describe the killer at all. He says he saw lots of feathers and insists that it was a bird. This fits with the killer's owl feather calling card and thematically reinforces the image of the owl as a traditional Native American symbol of death. It also adds yet another layer of mystery—and mysticism—to the puzzle regarding the killer's identity.

The mystery is central to the book, though it does not fit precisely into the genre of the mystery novel because Alexie does not offer the reader the solution. However, the lack of resolution reinforces Alexie's theme of anger. Many of the characters have reason to be angry and could lash out in unexpected ways. Without a fixed solution, the killer can be anyone.

STYLE

Third-Person Alternating Narration

With the huge cast of characters in *Indian Killer*, it would be extremely challenging to give insight into each of them if the narrative stayed with one character's point of view. By using third-person narration that alternates many characters' perspectives, Alexie gives readers a glimpse into those characters' minds, opening windows into their thoughts and emotions. This narrative form is especially illuminating in relation to characters like John and the killer, whose minds work differently from most people's and would be difficult to understand from an outsider's point of view.

Chapter Titles

A novel's chapter titles are often more descriptive than significant. Many books have only numbers to differentiate the chapters. In *Indian Killer*, however, Alexie uses some chapter titles to clue in readers to larger themes of the story. For example, in the chapter titled "The Searchers," Reggie, Ty, and Harley are watching a movie by that name on television. By using the movie's title as the name of the chapter, Alexie draws extra attention to it. The film is significant

because of its depiction of race. The Comanche in the movie are completely ruthless, and though John Wayne's character is ostensibly searching for his kidnapped niece to save her, it is clear, as Alexie explains that "he planned on killing her if he ever found her, because she'd been soiled by the Indians."

Alexie also makes a sly reference to history with the title of the chapter in which Reggie and his friend attack the white camper: "The Aurora Avenue Massacre." Reggie is angry about injustice to his people, both historically and in everyday modern life. The chapter title echoes some of the worst of these injustices, such as the Wounded Knee and Sand Creek massacres.

Some of the chapter titles repeat in significant ways. For example, the two chapters called "The Last Skyscraper in Seattle" appear at the beginning and the end of the novel, acting as bookends to John's story. The two chapters titled "Seattle's Best Donuts" also show the progress of John's story. In the first, John is seen through the eyes of Paul and Paul Too, people who know him, though not as well as his parents do. The second shows how John's mental illness has worsened. Paul Too says, "He's worse than I ever seen him." Several other chapter titles are also repeated, including "Testimony" and "How It Happened." These chapters serve as status reports about what is going with the overall story arc, as minor characters testify to the police, and to what is going on with the killer.

HISTORICAL CONTEXT

Native American References

Throughout *Indian Killer*, Alexie refers to historical events and people. Some—like Pocahontas, Sitting Bull, Crazy Horse, Geronimo, Chief Joseph, George Armstrong Custer, and the Battle of Little Bighorn—are well known. Others are less well known but are relevant to Alexie's themes and message.

Sand Creek, Colorado

Westward expansion was a key issue in the Civil War. The argument centered on whether new states would join the union as slave states or free states, but another obstacle to white settlement of the West was the Plains Indians. Some Native Americans accepted white settlers peacefully,

COMPARE
&
CONTRAST

- **1990s:** In *Indian Killer*, the radio talk show host Truck Schultz claims there are more Indians today than when Columbus stepped onto American shores, but he is grossly mistaken. Though there is no way to know the precise number, historians estimate that seven to ten million people lived in North America north of the Rio Grande when Columbus arrived. The 1990 US census totals the American Indian and Alaskan Native population at approximately two million.

  Today: The number of American Indians and Alaskan Natives in the United States totals over five million. The huge increase in the last twenty years is not due to true population growth. Rather, more people are choosing to identify themselves as Native American. Only about half of this number indicate in the census that their heritage is solely American Indian or Alaskan Native; the other half are of mixed heritage.

- **1990s:** The 1990 US census is the first attempt to count the number of homeless people in the country. Federal and local officials visit shelters and comb the streets of major cities and count 228,621 homeless people. However, this number is a very low estimate considering the difficulties faced. The homeless hide to survive and move often to find temporary shelter, and many are afraid to speak to official personnel or to admit they are homeless. Changes in counting methods for the 2000 census improve accuracy somewhat, but the total number

(280,527 people) is still believed to be a gross underestimation of the homeless population in the United States.

  Today: The homeless population is estimated to be well over five hundred thousand. Approximately 15 percent of these people are considered chronically homeless rather than temporarily without a place to live. Although Native Americans make up approximately 2 percent of the total US population, they make up almost 3 percent of the homeless population.

- **1990s:** A political push in the 1970s and 1980s to remove mentally ill patients from institutions and integrate them into their communities leads to inadequate care for many people in the 1990s because sufficient outpatient services do not yet exist. Trends in psychiatric care favor treatment by medication, but the high costs of medicines and the difficulty of ensuring that patients take the proper doses reduce the number of people truly helped through chemical means.

  Today: Policy makers pay more attention to mental health than previously, and treatment of mental illness is more accessible and patient centered. Although mental illness continues to carry a social stigma, there is progress in educating the public. However, many people still do not receive proper care, either because they live in a community without services or because they cannot afford counseling or medication.

---

but others responded defensively when their land and safety were threatened. A smaller number were more proactive, raiding white settlements to discourage encroachment on their territory.

In the summer of 1864, tensions rose after the murder of a white family near Denver. The territorial governor, John Evans, formed a new

regiment of soldiers led by Colonel John Chivington, who had been a minister and staunch abolitionist before the war and had distinguished himself as a Union officer. The government advised the Native American population to find places of safety, such as federal forts, and sent Chivington and his men to punish those who resisted.

On November 29, 1864, upon returning from Sand Creek, Chivington reported ordering his seven hundred men to attack a Cheyenne village and defeating almost one thousand well-armed young warriors. However, survivors of the attack soon contradicted Chivington's story, as did Captain Silas Soule, who refused to order his men into the fray and later wrote his own detailed account. When the soldiers arrived in the village, many residents waved white flags, and the chief, Black Kettle, raised a US flag. The Cheyenne believed themselves to be under federal protection, but they were gunned down. In an article for *Smithsonian* magazine, Tony Horwitz quotes from Soule's report, in which he describes "hundreds of women and children... coming towards us, and getting on their knees for mercy." Few of the villagers were armed, and most tried to flee. Of the approximately two hundred Cheyenne killed, Soule estimated all but sixty were children and women. Some soldiers scalped the dead and cut off other body parts as trophies.

The federal government condemned the actions of Chivington and his men, but the event was largely forgotten. Modern historians, however, see the massacre at Sand Creek as the end of any hope for peaceful settlement between the Plains Indians and the settlers and government. Chief Black Kettle continued efforts to keep the peace but was killed in a massacre led by Custer in 1868. Many tribes took Sand Creek as clear evidence that promises of protection could not be trusted. More raiding parties harried white settlements, and leaders were less willing to form treaties with government officials they no longer believed to be trustworthy. Rather than easing westward expansion, the massacre at Sand Creek ensured fierce resistance by local tribes and the continuation of hostilities for years to come.

Marcus and Narcissa Whitman

Marcus and Narcissa Whitman traveled across America in 1836 to found a mission to convert the Cayuse in the Walla Walla valley in Oregon. The Whitmans had little success with conversion, mostly because they made no effort to understand the beliefs of the Cayuse themselves. The giving of gifts was essential to Cayuse society, but the Whitmans refused to engage in the practice, thinking it improper to barter for faith. Cayuse religion was deeply tied to day-to-day home life, but the Whitmans refused to hold services in their home when they had put great effort into constructing a church. The Whitmans were more productive in helping other white settlers reach the area and put down roots, but this did little to endear them to the Cayuse, who viewed the increasing number of settlers with suspicion.

A measles epidemic in 1847 decimated the community. Most of the settlers, who had already been exposed to the disease and become immune to it, survived. However, half the Cayuse died, including nearly all the children. The Cayuse blamed the settlers, particularly the Whitmans, for bringing the illness. Several Cayuse, along with their chief, Tiloukaikt, killed fourteen white settlers, including Marcus and Narcissa Whitman, and burned all the buildings of the mission.

Hostilities between the Cayuse and the settlers raged for two years. Finally, Tiloukaikt and some of his followers surrendered in the hope of sparing the rest of the tribe. The Cayuse, however, were hopelessly diminished by the fighting and disease carried by the settlers. The people were absorbed by other local tribes, such as the Yakima and the Nez Perce, ending the existence of the Cayuse as an independent people.

The American Indian Movement

The American Indian Movement, or AIM, is a civil rights organization founded in 1968 with the central purpose of helping Native American people, many of them living in near poverty, who had been forced from their reservations by government policies. As the group grew, its goals grew with it, focusing on many issues important to the Indian community, such as the protection and revitalization of traditional culture and the restoration of tribal lands that had been seized by the government.

AIM was also one of the Native American groups involved with the occupation of the island of Alcatraz in 1969–1971. After the infamous Alcatraz federal prison was closed in 1963, a local group tried to seize control of the island using as justification an 1868 treaty allowing surplus federal land to be appropriated by Native Americans. The small initial effort in 1964 failed, but when a larger group led by the Mohawk college student Richard Oakes tried again to claim the island on November 20, 1969, the protest gradually swelled to more than six hundred people. The occupation lasted

John takes work at a construction site because he read about Mohawk workers building skyscrapers
(© Pavel Ganchev - Paf | Shutterstock.com)

until June 11, 1971, when federal marshals removed the remaining protesters, whose numbers had dwindled to barely over a dozen.

Although the end of the Alcatraz protest was less than spectacular, the awareness brought to Native American concerns was productive and influential. Activists were encouraged and staged other protests at sites like Mount Rushmore and Plymouth Rock. One such protest took place at Wounded Knee, where in 1890 hundreds of Lakota who had peacefully followed US Cavalry orders to vacate their land were slaughtered. In 1973, Native American protesters occupied the historic site to demand civil rights and reform of government policies related to Indian affairs. For seventy-one days, they were surrounded by US military, including jets flying overhead.

Mark Tilsen, an Oglala Lakota man who was at Wounded Knee with his parents in 1973, believed the protest accomplished something important. In a piece for the *Huffington Post*, he writes, "Wounded Knee 1973 did not end the oppression, but it strengthened our will to resist

it." The efforts of AIM and public sympathy generated by the occupations of Alcatraz and Wounded Knee led to changes in federal policy. Legislation began to favor Indian self-determination and self-rule and the return of ancestral lands to Native American tribes.

CRITICAL OVERVIEW

Throughout his career, Alexie has won countless awards and garnered much critical praise. The reaction to *Indian Killer* was also positive overall. A *Publishers Weekly* reviewer praises Alexie's eye for detail and believes the novel "offers abundant evidence of a most promising talent extending its range." According to *Kirkus Reviews*, the "novel rips along at a breathless pace" and is both a splendidly constructed and wonderfully readable thriller—and a haunting, challenging articulation of the plight and the pride of contemporary Native Americans." Several critics single out Alexie's large cast of characters for particular praise. *Kirkus Reviews* lauds the "host of keenly observed and rigorously analyzed characters," and *Publishers Weekly* points out Alexie's "startling control" as he "flips points of view among a wide array of characters without ever seeming to resort to contrivance."

Alexie's signature sense of humor is popular with critics, but it is a strength that *Indian Killer* did not show off to its best advantage. The *Publishers Weekly* reviewer admits that "some readers will miss the lyricism and humor of the author's earlier work." Richard E. Nicholls of the *New York Times* agrees that a bald description of the novel's plot will make it "sound unrelievedly grim." Nicholls notes, however, that "it is leavened repeatedly...by flashes of sardonic wit, the humor that Indians use to assuage pain."

Some critics and readers, Native American and not, were taken aback by the racially charged anger in *Indian Killer*. *Time* magazine (quoted by Duncan Campbell in a 2002 interview with Alexie) cites *Indian Killer* as evidence that Alexie is "septic with his own unappeasable anger." Alexie was amused by the negative reviews. He tells Campbell, "I got a T-shirt with the quote on it. I loved the reaction." Alexie also freely admits that some "Indians didn't like it." In a 2007 interview with Dave Weich, Alexie faulted the book on more literary grounds. He no longer liked the novel's tone, explaining that it "feels to me like a big cartoon," and believed that it would have been a better book if he had completed it as a genre mystery novel rather than attempting something more literary that he came to fear was pretentious. Most interestingly, he disowned the novel because of its anger and tribalism after connecting the violence of such thinking with the September 11, 2001, terrorist attacks.

In spite of some negative press, and Alexie's own criticisms, most critics found much of interest in *Indian Killer*. In his essay "Negotiating Violence and Identity in Sherman Alexie's *Indian Killer*," Giorgio Mariani asserts that

> though the impulse to embrace violence may be deeply unethical and politically self-defeating, it is in a sense at least emotionally justifiable given what Indian peoples have had to endure for centuries. However, to me there can be no doubt that while the final chapter flirts with the notion of violence as a "creative" force, the narrative as a whole moves in an opposite direction by emphasizing the essentially destructive and morally indefensible nature of violence.

CRITICISM

Kristen Sarlin Greenberg

Greenberg is a freelance writer and editor with a background in literature and philosophy. In the following essay, she examines the search for identity in Alexie's Indian Killer.

Indian Killer is a mystery novel but not in the usual sense. Though readers may speculate about the identity of the serial murderer, Alexie poses a far more interesting question: What is a real Indian? The novel's characters provide a broad range of opinions and examples, from homeless Native Americans wandering downtown Seattle through wannabe Indians like Clarence Mather and Jack Wilson to racist whites like Buck Rogers and Bird Lawrence. Throughout the novel, as the characters struggle to define the characteristics of a real Indian, they also work toward defining their own identities.

John Smith, taken away from his birth mother when he is only moments old, is on a literal search for identity. Physically, John looks like many people's textbook example of a real Indian. The first time the writer Jack Wilson sees John, he is "shocked by John's obvious resemblance to his own hero, Aristotle Little Hawk." Aristotle is the protagonist of Wilson's novels: tall, strong, handsome—the ideal Indian. However, John's interior does not match his exterior. He feels completely cut off from his heritage. He does not even know his tribe: "His adopted parents had never told him what kind of Indian he was" because "they did not know." Though John seeks out the company of other Native Americans, he is always uneasy in their company, feeling like an impostor. He is nervous to speak with Marie when they meet, knowing that "Indians quizzed Indians about all the Indian friends, family, lovers, and acquaintances they might have in common." John quickly grows "afraid she would discover that he was an Indian without a tribe."

John constantly wonders how things would be if he were a real Indian. Two entire chapters are devoted to John's imaginings of what his life would have been like if he had never been taken away from his fourteen-year-old birth mother and had grown up on the reservation. His daydreams are idyllic, not in any material way, for his imagined family is poor. They live in a small house crowded with lots of relatives and play Scrabble, though their secondhand set is missing

> THE LACK OF BELONGING IS CENTRAL IN THE
> SEARCH FOR IDENTITY FOR JOHN—INDEED, FOR ALL
> OF THE CHARACTERS. THEY HOPE THAT IF THEY CAN
> DEFINE THEIR OWN SELVES, THEY WILL FIGURE OUT
> WHERE THEY BELONG IN THE WORLD."

all of the *E* tiles. He is sure he would love his mother's cooking, "the best commodity beef stew in Indian history." They struggle to make do, but there is a real feeling of family and community in John's dreams that he never experiences in real life. The lack of belonging is central in the search for identity for John—indeed, for all of the characters. They hope that if they can define their own selves, they will figure out where they belong in the world.

For example, Marie Polatkin seems to be a confident person. She stands up for what she believes and reaches out to help her community. However, Alexie reveals Marie's insecurities. At times, as a little girl, she wanted to be white. She remembers sitting on the front porch scrubbing at "her face with a piece of her dad's sandpaper, trying to get rid of her color. Her skin was raw and bloody when she quit, still Indian." Marie is now

> proud of being Indian, but it wasn't a simple feeling. In the eyes of the white world, any Indian woman was the same as all other Indian women. Only white people got to be individuals.

Perhaps this is why Marie is so angry at wannabe Indians. They can choose to be Indian just by saying so, whether they have one drop of Indian blood or none at all. Marie has no choice. She feels like an outsider because she believes that her Indian appearance and heritage forever exclude her from fully taking part in mainstream society.

Marie also fears that her efforts to achieve success in mainstream society have distanced her from her roots. When she was a teenager, some of her classmates were "more interested in Spokane Indian culture than in a public school education." They were "intelligent and humorous, and never wanted to leave the reservation."

Marie focuses on a mainstream education and excels, but she "both resented and envied them. Because she did not dance or sing traditionally, and because she could not speak Spokane, Marie was often thought of as being less than Indian." The fear that she is somehow less drives her to expose and attack poseurs like Mather. She is "careful to test people, to hear their stories, to ask about their tribes, their people, and their ties to the land from which they originated. The pretend Indians had no answers for these questions." Her own insecurity fuels her need to define herself in relation to others:

> Indians were always placing one another on an identity spectrum, with the more traditional to the left and the less traditional Indians to the right. Marie knew she belonged somewhere in the middle of that spectrum and that her happiness depended on placing more Indians to her right.

Marie's cousin Reggie is also distanced from his Native American heritage, but rather than choosing his path, Reggie is forced away from his roots by his abusive white father, Bird Lawrence. Bird divides all Native American people into good Indians and hostile Indians and condemns the latter completely without taking into consideration the provocation that drove some Native Americans to fight. Bird justifies his worldview with simplistic categories and images, such as the stereotype of a drunken Indian. He angrily demands of Reggie, "You want to be a drunk? You want to be one of those Indians staggering around downtown?" Desperate to satisfy his father, Reggie "pretends to be white" and "buried his Indian identity so successfully that he'd become invisible." When Reggie gets away from the violent atmosphere of his father's house and goes to college, he "immediately felt a strange kinship" with Mather, "the white man who wanted to be so completely Indian." Reggie identifies with the desire to be something one is not, but he is also able for the first time to see his own heritage as something positive.

Mather is a white man who "loved Indians, or perhaps his idea of Indians" and who sees himself as "the official dispenser of 'Indian education' at the University." Mather has an idealized conception of what it means to be Native American—the powerful but gentle warrior in touch with the land—and wants to associate with that image to feel good about himself and connected to that culture. Similarly, Jack Wilson learns selected details about Native American

WHAT DO I READ NEXT?

- Alexie's *The Absolutely True Diary of a Part-Time Indian* (2007) is a partially autobiographical young-adult novel. As Alexie did as a teenager, the fourteen-year-old protagonist, Junior, leaves his home on the Spokane Reservation to enroll in a high school with a mostly white student body. Though he makes it onto the varsity basketball team, Junior struggles to fit in. The book contains illustrations that enhance the humor in the text.

- In his novel *Monster* (1999) the award-winning young-adult author Walter Dean Myers presents the tale of the protagonist, Steve, through unusual formats, such as journal entries and screenplay scenes. Steve is in jail, accused of being an accessory to murder. As the story progresses, Steve learns to cope with his anger and recover his humanity until he is no longer the monster described by the prosecution in his trial. In 2015, Guy A. Sims adapted the story into a graphic novel.

- In *Crossing* (2010), by Andrew Xia Fukuda, a series of disappearances plagues a small town in upstate New York. Suspicion for the crimes falls on Chinese-born Xing Xu, a shy student longing for acceptance.

- *An Indigenous Peoples' History of the United States* (2014), by the activist and historian Roxanne Dunbar-Ortiz, frames the story of America from the perspective of its first inhabitants. Whereas most histories ignore or justify the colonialist policies of the US government in the name of Manifest Destiny, Dunbar-Ortiz exposes these practices, which resulted in the genocide of Native American peoples.

- In addition to publishing fiction, Alexie is an award-winning poet. Although much of his poetry is free verse, in his 2009 collection, *Face*, he experiments with traditional forms such as the villanelle and the sestina.

- Approximately 60 percent of Native Americans live in cities. In *American Indians and the Urban Experience* (2001), the editors Susan Lobo and Kurt Peters gather a broad collection of essays, poetry, fiction, and art—including forms from rap to photography to graffiti—that reflect the struggles and successes of city-dwelling Native Americans.

culture and latches on to them as his own needs dictate. Growing up as an orphan in foster homes, he is delighted to read about the community in Native American villages, where "a child could be loved and disciplined by any adult in the tribe." Because he has no true family, he is comforted by the idea of being parented by an entire village. He buys a traditional dance outfit and "dreamed of being the best traditional dancer in the world. Wilson saw himself inside a bright spotlight in a huge arena while thousands of Indians cheered for him. Real Indians."

In their desperate desire to connect meaningfully in any way to the people around them— to feel that they belong—both Mather and Wilson appropriate Native American identity and culture. However, their ideas about Native American life and culture are not much more accurate than those of Reggie's abusive father. Part of the reason Marie is angered by Mather and Wilson is that they cannot truly understand what it is to be Indian, not when they have come from a background of white, male privilege in American society. Wilson may have struggled through a series of foster homes as a child, but, as Marie points out to Mather, "Indians are just plain hungry. Not for power. Not for money. For food, for breakfast, lunch, and dinner. Wilson doesn't know anything about that. You don't know anything about that."

As anger and fear erupt all over the city, Truck Schulz encourages racial tension on his radio show
(©Billion Photos | Shutterstock.com)

Marie challenges wannabe Indians because for her, "being Indian was mostly about survival, and she'd been fighting so hard for her survival that she didn't know if she could stop." She holds on to even the painful things about the reality of being Native American, like the struggle to survive and the fear of not getting enough to eat, because they make her feel more secure in her identity. John echoes this when he says to Wilson before jumping to his death, "let us have our own pain." The pain of the Native American people as a whole makes John feel more like a real Indian.

Rather than being in the mystery genre, *Indian Killer* is better described as postcolonial literature. It portrays the effects on Native American people of the colonization of their land by Europeans. In addition to being robbed of land and life and security, America's native peoples were robbed of their culture and now struggle to get it back. What does it mean to be a real Indian in a time when more than half of Native Americans live in cities, integrated into mainstream society? Modern Native American

literature is in part an attempt to answer that question.

Source: Kristen Sarlin Greenberg, Critical Essay on *Indian Killer*, in *Novels for Students*, Gale, Cengage Learning, 2017.

Meredith James

In the following excerpt, James characterizes Indian Killer *as a captivity narrative.*

Sherman Alexie's novel *Indian Killer* (1996) has been described as a detective novel and a suspense thriller; however, these classifications are too simplistic. Alexie's novel does not set out to pose and solve a mystery, at least not in the conventional manner of detective novels. There is no sleuth, and the killer's identity is never solved. The novel reveals the injustices forced upon Native people, particularly as they journey through a modern cityscape. The Puritans who landed on the East Coast of North America saw the wilderness as symbolic of evil forces that were to test their souls, and they recorded these trying experiences with the Indigenous peoples

"ONLY ON ANOTHER PLANE OF EXISTENCE OUTSIDE OF THE CONFINES OF THE CITY CAN JOHN ACHIEVE PEACE, WHETHER IN DEATH OR DREAMS. IN THE CITY, THE ONLY PLACE HE FEELS AT HOME IS THE IMAGINARY RESERVATION OF HIS DAYDREAMS."

in captivity narratives. In *Indian Killer*, Alexie plays with the concept of captivity narratives because his Native characters are trapped in an urban wilderness, dealing with the perils of modern, urban life. In one sense, *Indian Killer* is a mystery since all the characters attempt to solve their own mysteries in relation to the particular landscapes of their tribal and urban identities, and John Smith—adopted as an infant by a white family with no knowledge of his tribal heritage—seems the most lost.

John Smith is the focus of the novel, and readers follow his struggle to find his place in the Seattle wilderness. Smith was born on a reservation, and all he knows of his birth is that his mother was fourteen years old when she had him. All other information was concealed from him and his adoptive parents. As the focus of the novel, John's story deviates from the form of a more traditional detective novel. The superficial, sensational story of *Indian Killer* focuses on determining the identity of the serial killer/kidnapper and finding out whether he or she is Native. All of this seems irrelevant in relation to the story of John Smith's captivity. It's especially irrelevant because at the end of the novel, none of the characters are certain about the identity of the killer. Alexie withholds the pleasure of knowing, unequivocally, the satisfying conclusion that results from reading a standard detective novel where a suspect is singled out by a cunning detective and all questions are answered and wrapped up neatly. By the conclusion of *Indian Killer*, the killer is neither apprehended nor identified. Furthermore, John's quest similarly ends without answers.

One of the devices that Alexie employs throughout the novel follows a long tradition in Native American literature (in English), a device that I call the reverse captivity narrative. Since

European settlers began coming to North America, they have written accounts of their encounters with Indigenous populations, and many of them document their captures. Among the most famous are *The Captivity of Mary Rowlandson* and the several travel journals of Captain John Smith. At the turn of the twentieth century, Native writers like Gertrude Simmons Bonnin related their captivity experiences as young children forced into boarding schools and missions. These writers used similar structures to those of the earlier colonial writers. Similarly, Alexie, at the turn of the twenty-first century, is writing about a form of captivity experienced by young Indians adopted before the Indian Child Welfare Act of 1978.

Alexie's story is not about his personal experiences as much as his generation; it is a story about Indians who are raised among whites with little or no understanding of their culture, who often do not even know the name of their tribe. Like some of the white missionaries that Bonnin had to endure, the adoptive parents of John Smith do not intend to harm their child; in fact, Alexie portrays the parents as sympathetic despite their naïveté in raising a nonwhite child and giving him a horribly ironic name. To understand *Indian Killer*, one must first examine the federal policies of Indian reform during the late twentieth century that pushed Indian people into urban environments—the wilderness that Alexie and other Native authors create—as well as the history of the reverse captivity narrative and John Smith's capture and quest for identity. Also, readers must realize why the Indian killer is never identified and defying standard detective novel format and expectations is a symbolic gesture.

The lonely urban landscapes that Alexie depicts are not uncommon to Native people. Diana Meyers Bahr reports, "Although urban Indians constitute more than 50 percent of the North American native population, Indians in the city are often considered the invisible minority." The title of my essay comes from a Carroll Arnett poem, which Alexie refers to in *Reservation Blues*. In this poem, the speaker clearly expresses his feeling about urban identities: "Indians do not live in cities, they only reside there." This is not to suggest that Indians only belong in pristine natural settings, but rather to clarify that the current urban environment is an unwelcoming Euro-American construction. Grappling with issues of urban identity is nothing new to Native authors. Alexie follows in a long line of Native authors critiquing the colonial imposition of termination and relocation projects in the 1950s. These projects—masked as helping Indians become part of mainstream American society—left Indian people disconnected from their tribal lands and struggling in large cities.

The termination and relocation projects began in the 1940s. In 1943 the Senate Interior Committee was ready to do away with the Bureau of Indian Affairs. Committees were formed to find ways to end federal supervision of Indian tribes. By February 1954, Senator Arthur Watkins, head of the Indian Subcommittee of the Senate Interior Committee, pushed to "get rid of as many tribes as possible before the 1956 elections." Termination procedures sought to abolish tribes' power and gain reservation land. Termination "was coupled with the 'Relocation Act,' a statute passed in 1956 and designed to coerce reservation residents to disperse to various urban centers around the country." Along with the termination proceedings, the enactment of Public Law 280 "placed many reservations under the jurisdiction of individual States of the Union, thereby reducing the level of native sovereignty to that held by counties or municipalities." Many Indians moved to large cities because of the promise of economic success, but most did not experience a better life.

Vine Deloria refers to the Relocation Act of 1956 as one of the most "disastrous" policies ever initiated. He writes, "It began as a policy of the Eisenhower administration as a means of getting Indians off the reservation and into the city slums where they could fade away." Many Indians eventually returned to the reservations; however, even today, Native people are forced economically to leave reservations or other rural lands to make a living.

Many Native authors have responded to the urban experience. N. Scott Momaday's protagonist Abel in *House Made of Dawn* finds himself lost in Los Angeles, but he does not reconcile his issues of identity until he is back on his home ground. Greg Sarris's *Grand Avenue* offers a more contemporary view of Indians coping with urbanization in Los Angeles. Most of the characters go there for no other reason than work. Nila northSun writes in her poem "up & out" about her family moving off the reservation to the city to find jobs: "the city had jobs but it also / had high rent / high food high medical /

high entertainment high gas / we made better money but it / got sucked up." At the end of the poem, she writes, "God how I hated living on the reservation / but now / it doesn't look so bad."

This awkward position of Indian people between homeland and the need for jobs to survive is best summed up in Simon Ortiz's poem "Final Solution: Jobs, Leaving," which relates the way Ortiz as a child lamented his father having to leave the Acoma Pueblo for work: "Surrounded by the United States, / We had come to need money." Encroaching ranches, mining enterprises, and other economic ventures forced—and still do—Indians to take places in an ever-expanding marketplace that only seems to destroy their tribal lands and identification with these lands. When they reach the city, they are held captive by bills and other financial obligations, as well as the lifestyle. northSun writes about the way the money gets eaten up by "lunches in cute places / by drinking in quaint bars."

Native authors also refer to the conspicuous invisibility of being an Indian in a city. To echo the words of the earlier Deloria quotation, relocation and termination projects caused Indians to "fade away" in an urban setting. Alexie plays with the concept of urban invisibility and alienation as well. From the beginning of the novel, he clearly establishes imagery that evokes feelings of despair about Seattle's cityscape. John is working on "the last skyscraper in Seattle," and later in the novel, he wonders "what would happen to him after the construction was complete."

The city exacerbates John's agony about his identity and future. As he works on the skyscraper, he fears plummeting to his death despite using the safety precautions his coworkers take: "John was attached to the building by a safety harness, but he knew that white men made the harnesses. It would only save white men" (*IK*). The cityscape itself is unreliable, and any connection to the structures for John—or Indians in general insofar as he represents them—means death. The city is described in terms of destruction and depression. Alexie details Seattle's early settlers' taste in developing land: "The Danes, the Swedes, and Norwegians had missed the monotonously flat landscapes of their own countries, and wanted their new country to remind them of home. Since the first days of their colonization of the Americas, European immigrants had strived to make the New World look exactly like the Old. . . . All John knew was that everything in this country had been changed, mutated" (*IK*).

This city is a place of war, a national monument to colonization. To John cities represent European victory and—like the safety harnesses—are built for whites only. He looks at the city as a waste of space, and he sees the building he works on as being "pointless." Before John jumps off the skyscraper to his death, he thinks that the world around him seems to be busy and alive but the city represents death: "John knew that every building in Seattle contained the bones of fallen workers. Every building was a tomb" (*IK*). He knows that his search for identity in the city is futile because he believes only whites can make sense of themselves in an urban setting.

Only on another plane of existence outside of the confines of the city can John achieve peace, whether in death or dreams. In the city, the only place he feels at home is the imaginary reservation of his daydreams. John's reservation of the mind is a happy place with a loving family, and "it's a good life, not like all the white people believe reservation life to be" (*IK*). The reservation he believes he belongs to is a place of warm memories, memories that John feels have been robbed. His life in the city away from his tribe is a time of captivity. . . .

Source: Meredith James, "'Indians Do Not Live in Cities, They Only Reside There': Captivity and the Urban Wilderness in *Indian Killer*," in *Sherman Alexie: A Collection of Critical Essays*, edited by Jeff Berglund and Jan Roush, University of Utah Press, 2010, pp. 171–76.

Joelle Fraser

In the following interview excerpt, Alexie talks about Native American versus mainstream culture.

. . . *Joelle Fraser: You're called "the future of American fiction" by the* New Yorker.

Sherman Alexie: It's because they needed a brown guy. They had five of us I think. A guy asked me how do you feel about there being so few white men on the (1996) *Granta* list. I said there were eleven out of twenty: how could that be "few"? And sixteen overall were white! I got all sorts of grief for being on the *Granta* list by the way. Like I didn't belong on it—

JF: You only had Reservation Blues *then. What about the response to the* New Yorker *list?*

> THE CREATION OF ART IS STILL AN EVERYDAY PART OF OUR CULTURE, UNLIKE THE DOMINANT CULTURE, WHERE ART IS SORT OF PERIPHERAL. IT'S NOT A BIG LEAP FROM A KID WHO DANCES TO A KID WHO WRITES POEMS. IT'S THE SAME IMPULSE. IT JUST NEEDS A LITTLE PUSH."

SA: Everybody's really happy with it.

JF: You've earned your place?

SA: Yeah, I guess. I'm an important brown guy now. (Laughs.) Being different helps. I'm not going to deny that it helps a lot. I mean the work has to be good, but the fact that I'm different makes it more attractive to magazines.

JF: So you grant that?

SA: Oh, yeah. I'm a firm believer in affirmative action—nobody unqualified ever gets a job through affirmative action. Maybe less qualified, but not unqualified. Certainly I might get on lists or get opportunities because I'm different, because I'm Indian.

JF: And it doesn't bother you?

SA: No! Hell no! Reparation. (Laughs.) Nobody white is getting anything because they're white. It doesn't happen in the literary world, never, never once has a white guy gotten more because he's white. But then you have that cabal of New York writers, young good-looking New York literary boys, and they have their own sense of entitlement. I'm not anywhere near that stuff.

JF: How did people react to your story in the New Yorker*, "The Toughest Indian in the World"?*

SA: When I wrote it, I honestly didn't think about the reaction people would have to it. It's funny—it really brings up the homophobia in people. When a straight guy like me writes about a homoerotic experience in the first person with a narrator who is very similar to me—I could see people dying to ask me if it was autobiographical. They always ask in regard to everything else, but no one's asked me about that story. In the Seattle paper here, the critic called it a "graphic act of homosexuality" and I thought "graphic"? There's nothing graphic about it at all. It was three sentences. He talked about me being a "literary rabble-rouser" again.

JF: Someone else called you a similar name—the young rouser, the young something from Seattle—

SA: Oh, yeah—Larry McMurtry. Rambler. "The Young Rambler from Seattle." Yeah, I liked that one. It made me feel like I was in a bar brawl.

JF: You've said of writers who aren't Indian, like McMurtry, that they shouldn't write about Indians.

SA: Not exactly.

JF: Clarify that.

SA: At the beginning it was probably that but it's changed. People can write whatever they want—people accuse me of censorship when I say these things. But what I really want to say is that we should be talking about these books, written about Indians by non-Indians, honestly and accurately. I mean, they're outsider books. They're colonial books. Barbara Kingsolver's novels are colonial literature. Larry McMurtry's books are colonial literature. These are books by members of the privileged, of the powerful, writing about the culture that has been colonized. This is no different than Nadine Gordimer, who's a colonial writer, and she would call herself that.

So I think this illusion of democracy in the country—it's the best country in the world—but this illusion allows artists to believe that it isn't a colony. When it still is. The United States and South Africa: the only difference is about fifty years, not even that much. And people forget that. So when McMurtry does what he does, he thinks he's being democratic, but he's actually being colonial. I wish we could talk about the literature in those terms, beyond the quality of it, but actually talking about in terms of "hey, this person doesn't know this—it's completely a work of imagination."

JF: How does this compare to, say, occupying the other gender?

SA: (Laughs.) Oh that's the same thing.

JF: You've done that, and written from a white person's view, too.

SA: Well, I know a lot more about being white—because I have to, I live in the white world. A white person doesn't live in the Indian world. I have to be white every day.

JF: What about your female characters?

SA: I'm not a woman. (Laughs.) Never was. I think often my characters, outside of Spokane Indian guys, are often a little bit thin because I have a difficult time getting into them and getting to know them. My white people often end up being sort of "cardboardy"—which is thematically all right—but it isn't necessarily my original purpose. I just get uncomfortable writing about them.

JF: Really. Is that something you're trying to develop and work on?

SA: Yeah, I'm trying to become a better writer. I think in the end I'll get closer to that. And about women's experience—I'm better than most male writers. They see the Madonna-whore—it's incredible: these progressive, liberal, intelligent, highly-educated men are writing complex, diverse, wonderful male characters in the same book where the female characters are like women in a 3 a.m. movie on Showtime.

JF: You've said having come from a matriarchal culture gives you more insight.

SA: I think it helps. And I give my stuff to the women around me. "Does this work?" I spend my whole life around women—I should know something. If I don't know it, I ask. It has to be a conscious effort. It's too easy to fall back on stereotypes and myths, and I think that's what most writers do about Indians and what most men do when they write about women.

JF: So you're conscious of it . . .

SA: I'm conscious of the fact that I mythologize. (Laughs.) I'm still a caveman. I just like to think of myself as a sensitive caveman.

JF: Going back to your growth as a writer, as you develop and gain facility—you're getting better technically, for example—do you fear that you'll lose some of that tension that comes from being a struggling new writer?

SA: My friend Donna, who helps me edit, we talk about this. When I first started, my grammar was atrocious, but she said that often people don't care when so-called "unprivileged people's" grammar is atrocious because it's part of the "voice." And they account for it in that way.

JF: In fact readers might think it's "appropriate."

SA: When in fact it's just bad grammar. It's the result of a poor education. But I'm better now. Most of my sentence fragments now are intentional. (Laughs.)

JF: What did your parents expect you to be?

SA: Oh, God. Alive. In their fondest hopes. I'm the first member of my family—that's extended—who's graduated from college. No one else has since. I was a very bright kid; I was a little prodigy in all sorts of ways. There were friends and family telling me I was going to be a doctor or a lawyer. Nobody predicted I would be doing this, including me.

JF: So you didn't have a sense of yourself as a writer until college?

SA: Right. I wrote and I loved reading, and brown guys—you're supposed to be Jesus, saving the world with law or medicine.

JF: And with writing can you save the world?

SA: You can do more than a doctor or a lawyer can. If I were a doctor nobody would be inviting me to talk to reservations. I'd be a different person. Writers can influence more people.

JF: Can poetry change the direction of society?

SA: I don't know. A lot of people are reading my poems and other people's poems because of me. This fifty-five-year-old white guy at a reading said, "I never got poems, I hated them, and then I read your book and liked them, and now I'm reading all sorts of poems." And that's great. If I can be a doorway . . .

JF: Paula Gunn Allen says of Native Americans, "We are the land." What do you think of that?

SA: I don't buy it. For one thing, environmentalism is a luxury. Just like being a vegetarian is a luxury. When you have to worry about eating—you're not going to be worried about where the food's coming from, or who made your shoes. Poverty, whether planned or not planned, is a way of making environmentalism moot. Even this discussion is a luxury.

JF: This interview.

SA: You and me—doing this. Besides, Indians have no monopoly on environmentalism. That's one of the great myths. But we were subsistence livers. They're two different things. Environmentalism is a conscious choice and subsistence is the absence of choice. We had to use everything to survive. And now that we've been assimilated and colonized and we have luxuries and excesses, we're just as wasteful as other people.

JF: But the myth persists with contemporary Indians.

SA: Part of it is that we had a land-based theology, but all theologies are land-based. Christianity is land-based in its beginnings. I think in some ways Indians embrace it because it's a cultural or racial self-esteem issue. We're trying to find something positive that differentiates us from the dominant culture. And the best way to do that—because the U.S. is so industrial and so wasteful—is to say, "OK, we're environmentalists" and that separates us. When in fact, we're just a part of the U.S. as well, and the wastefulness. The average everyday Indian—he's not an environmentalist—he could give a shit. Just like the average white American. I grew up with my aunts and uncles and cousins throwing their cans out the window.

JF: How does this tie in with literature?

SA: You throw in a couple of birds and four directions and corn pollen and it's Native American literature, when it has nothing to do with the day-to-day lives of Indians. I want my literature to concern the daily lives of Indians. I think most Native American literature is so obsessed with nature that I don't think it has any useful purpose. It has more to do with the lyric tradition of European Americans than it does with indigenous cultures. So when an Indian writes a poem about a tree, I think: "It's already been done!" And those white guys are going to do it better than you. Nobody can write about a tree like a white guy.

JF: Now why is that?

SA: I don't know. They've been doing it longer.

JF: I'd like to see what you'd write about a tree.

SA: I'm not even interested! I'm interested in people. I think most native literature is concerned with place because they tell us to be. That's the myth. I think it's detrimental. I think most Native American literature is unreadable by the vast majority of Native Americans.

JF: It's not reaching the people.

SA: If it's not tribal, if it's not accessible to Indians, then how can it be Native American literature? I think about it all the time. Tonight

I'll look up from the reading and 95 percent of the people in the crowd will be white. There's something wrong with my not reaching Indians.

JF: But there's the ratio of whites to Indians.

SA: Yeah. But I factor that in and realize there still should be more Indians. I always think that. Generally speaking Indians don't read books. It's not a book culture. That's why I'm trying to make movies. Indians go to movies; Indians own VCRs.

JF: And maybe they'll read your books after.

SA: I'm trying to do that—sneak up on them.

JF: This is what your purpose is—to reach Indian people?

SA: It's selfish in the sense that we haven't had our Emily Dickinson or Walt Whitman; we haven't had our Shakespeare or Denis Johnson or James Wright. We haven't written a book that can compare to the best white novel. But they're out there. There's a kid out there, some boy or girl who will be that great writer, and hopefully they'll see what I do and get inspired by that.

JF: There are many celebrated Indian writers—

SA: But we haven't written anything even close to Faulkner or Hemingway or Jane Austen. Not yet. Of course, white people are about thirty, forty generations ahead in terms of writing. It'll happen. I meet young people all the time, email a lot of kids. The percentage of Indian kids doing some sort of artistic work is much higher than in the general population—painting, drawing, dancing, singing. The creation of art is still an everyday part of our culture, unlike the dominant culture, where art is sort of peripheral. It's not a big leap from a kid who dances to a kid who writes poems. It's the same impulse. It just needs a little push . . . .

Source: Joelle Fraser, "An Interview with Sherman Alexie," in *Conversations with Sherman Alexie*, edited by Nancy J. Peterson, University Press of Mississippi, 2009, pp. 83–88.

Daniel Grassian

In the following excerpt, Grassian asserts that the anger captured in Indian Killer *resulted in its mixed critical reception.*

Whereas *Reservation Blues* was in large part gentle in its social criticism, often presenting Indians as resilient survivors and utilizing

> JOHN'S EXCLUSION GRADUALLY DEVELOPS INTO FEELINGS OF INFERIORITY IN CONTRAST TO THE OTHER WHITE STUDENTS, WHOM HE DEEMS TO BE MORE INTELLIGENT AND COMPLEX THAN HIMSELF."

comedy to diffuse anger, pain, and tragedy, Alexie's next novel, *Indian Killer* (1996), is an uncompromising look at rage, anger, and violence both in the Indian community and in the larger world. In *Reservation Blues*, Alexie argues that ethnic hybridity can often be a space of productive creation, but in *Indian Killer* that same hybridity turns violent and destructive. In an interview, Alexie explains the initial genesis of the novel, dating back to when "I was sitting at Washington State [University] with frat guys in the back row who I wanted to kill. And I would fantasize about murder." Alexie further explains how his own anger and dissatisfaction motivated the writing of *Indian Killer*: "It was a response to the literary movement where a lot of non-Indian writers are writing Indian books. Non-Indian authors enjoy a success that is not determined or critiqued by American Indians. So I want to make sure they're aware of an Indian critical response to their work." Indeed, through his criticism of Clarence Mather, a white professor of Native American studies, and other pseudo-Indian fiction writers like Jack Wilson, Alexie does exactly that.

Whereas Alexie's previous works met almost universal praise, reviews of *Indian Killer* were mixed, presumably because of the sometimes graphically violent subject matter. In a review of the book, *Time* magazine called Alexie "septic with his own unappeasable anger." With his characteristic humor, Alexie shrugged off *Time*'s criticism, telling an interviewer that, "I got a T-shirt with the quote on it. I loved the reaction. In some masochistic way, I love the really violent reviews more than the good reviews." Still, Alexie claims that *Indian Killer* "was the hardest to write" of his works to date and that it "troubled" him the most, but it is also the book he "probably cares most about."

More common were mixed reviews from critics such as John Skow, who describes the novel as "sad and eloquently written" but "also ugly," accusing Alexie of further polarizing ethnic groups. However, such a viewpoint simplifies Alexie's novel, which may be pessimistic and vilify white society but also vilifies aspects of Indian culture and attitudes. While it is clear that Alexie's sympathies lie more with Indians, he does not excuse or endorse their actions and attitudes. Indeed, the ambiguity of the novel is apparent in the title, which can be read as an Indian who kills or an individual, presumably nonwhite, who kills Indians. In that, the title manifests a veritable circle of violence, which the novel itself plays out.

The protagonist of *Indian Killer* is John Smith, an Indian who was adopted by a white couple, Daniel and Olivia Smith, themselves incapable of having children. For Alexie, a good deal of the novel's tragedy stems from the adoption. In an interview, he explains: "I've met a lot of people like him [John Smith]—'lost birds'—Indians adopted out by non-Indian families—we call them lost birds. . . . The social problems and dysfunctions of these Indians adopted are tremendous. Their suicide rates are off the chart, their drug and alcohol abuse rates are off the chart." Indeed, the fictional protagonist, John Smith, was adopted at a time (in the 1960s) in which Indians were sometimes coerced into adoption since "until the passage of the Indian Child Welfare Act in 1978, many religious organizations actively recruited Native American parents to give up their children for adoption."

Olivia and Daniel, John's white adoptive parents, represent the well-intentioned ignorance and obliviousness that Alexie perceives in the relationships of certain non-Natives with and toward Indians. Olivia and Daniel are far from malicious; rather, they are more like vapid pawns who subscribe to the ideas of the cultural majority without really thinking anything through. Olivia, a highly attractive white woman, is particularly narcissistic and oblivious, more a blank slate than an individual, who has never had any real ambition other than to be artistically cultured and wealthy. They decide to adopt a baby not because they are altruistic but because they cannot have one of their own and because they feel that at their age, it is socially proper to have a child. Daniel, the well-meaning but ultimately ineffectual father figure, tries his best to interest John in sports and in Indian culture, but Daniel lacks authority; he is unwilling to give up on John as a basketball player even though it turns out that John has no aptitude or even great interest in the sport. Furthermore, when John becomes a teenager and plays loud Native American music, which clearly disturbs Daniel, Daniel cannot confront John about it. In a way, Olivia and Daniel are products of a politically correct culture. Wanting to do the socially accepted right thing by exposing John to Native American culture, they both inundate John with all the information they learn about Indians and take him to Indian functions in order to expose him to "his culture." They even insist that an Indian Jesuit baptize John. However noble their intentions might be, Daniel and Olivia only serve to distance John from the Indian world, which in part excludes him because of his adopted white parents and because John, who does not know anything about his biological parents other than that his mother was fourteen when he was born, cannot claim heritage from any single Indian tribe.

All this leads John to misguided beliefs about Indians and whites. When Daniel and Olivia take John to an all-Indian basketball tournament, John misinterprets and romanticizes the various Indians of different tribes. He interprets their frequent laughter and joking to be evidence of their security and happiness when it is more like a self-defense mechanism to stave off despair. Along similar lines, as John gets older, he further romanticizes reservation and Indian life as well as his own feelings of ostracism. John's perception of Indians as noble savages may be informed by the overdramatic descriptions of Indians and their culture in the books that Daniel and Olivia give him, many of which were probably written by non-Natives without much or any direct knowledge of reservation life. *Indian Killer* begins with a chapter appropriately called "Mythology" in the sense that it is John's overly self-conscious elevation of his adoption into tragedy. John imagines being stolen by white people from his mother at birth, taken by a man in a jumpsuit into a helicopter, who randomly fires on people in the reservation, igniting a mini-war, while John is brought to his adopted white parents. No doubt the actual adoption process was significantly more innocuous than John would like to believe.

In other chapters of *Indian Killer*, Alexie identifies how John idealizes life on the reservation and imagines his biological family to be loving, strong and mutually supportive. In John's vision, everyone in the family eats well and as a unit; the children are taught Indian culture, and there is no conflict whatsoever between anyone. John's wizened grandfather tells stories while John dutifully prepares for college, planning to be a doctor and to later practice on the reservation. Missing from John's portrait, of course, is violence, alcoholism, rage, extreme poverty, and humor, all hallmarks of reservation life as Alexie details it in his previous works.

While it is undeniable that John is somewhat mentally unstable, at the very least, Alexie leaves it unresolved as to how much John's problems are genetically or socially based. That John often has trouble distinguishing between fantasy and reality indicates psychosis. In addition, his consuming paranoia toward virtually everyone and the imaginary voices he hears indicate possible schizophrenia. He even believes that there are several different Olivias and Daniels, all of whom are in some way out to get him. Further evidence of John's instability includes how, at twenty, John believed himself to be pregnant, a psychotic fantasy he takes to the point of buying birthing supplies. While Daniel and Olivia try to treat John's problems by getting him to take pills and threatening institutionalization, they are ultimately too weak as parents, in some ways probably fearing John. Despite evidence to the contrary, Daniel describes John's behavior as merely "little teenage rebellions."

To be fair, John's mental problems may be exacerbated by his social milieu, such as being the only Indian teenager at a private school— which Alexie himself has experienced—leading John to feel ostracized from others. John's exclusion gradually develops into feelings of inferiority in contrast to the other white students, whom he deems to be more intelligent and complex than himself. To some extent, the attitudes of others cause John's feelings of inferiority. When John dates white girls, their parents view John with suspicion and subtly disapprove of their budding relationships. Like Daniel and Olivia, John's teachers are often overwhelmingly acquiescent of his frequently erratic behavior, never realizing that their response to John also makes him feel further isolated. When John gets into a fight, the principal lets John go without even a reprimand because of his ethnicity. To some extent, his teachers have good intentions in that they realize that, being an orphan and an Indian in a predominantly white school, John has a much more difficult time than most, but like Daniel and Olivia, John's teachers' seemingly good intentions actually evince a stereotypical and demeaning attitude toward Indians, whom they dehumanize in their generalized pity. What they don't realize or understand is that John, although adopted, comes from a wealthy family, and that one cause of his social problems are actions like those of his teachers that make him acutely aware of his ethnicity, which, because of his adopted status and his lack of knowledge about his biological parents, he has to deny.

…Some critics take fault with Alexie's uncompromising ending, which they interpret as justifying or glorifying violence against whites. At the end of the novel, an Indian, possibly the killer him- or herself, performs a Ghost Dance. The Ghost Dance, over five hundred years old, was performed in hopes that it would dispel the invading whites and resurrect dead relatives and loved ones, while returning the land to a precolonized state. Earlier in the novel, Marie had castigated Mather for not understanding the full rationale behind the Ghost Dance. Whereas Mather views it as a benevolent, symbolic act, Marie interprets it literally as an expression of anger against the historical oppression of whites to the point of wanting them banished forever from the continent. Mather claims that the Ghost Dance was "about peace and beauty," but Marie claims it is more about retribution and that in the late twentieth century, given the decrepit state of reservations and of Indian life both on and away from the reservation, there is more reason than ever to feel angry at the oppression of whites and to support the Ghost Dance. In the last chapter, during a final vision, when the killer begins to perform the Ghost Dance, other Indians (hundreds) come and dance it along with him. Alexie describes the killer as planning on "dancing forever" and that the surrounding trees grow "heavy with owls." As established earlier, according to traditional Indian folklore, the owl is a sign of evil, sickness, or death. Alexie thus suggests that the killings will continue in the future. This is not to suggest that Alexie encourages an attempted violent revolution, for he surely recognizes that such an attempt would ultimately prove futile, but that the desire for revolt and revenge remains an important, albeit repressed desire for many Indians, a startling revelation for many who believe in the stereotype of Indians as docile, despondent, and nature-loving.

Source: Daniel Grassian, "*Indian Killer*," in *Understanding Sherman Alexie*, University of South Carolina Press, 2005, pp. 104–109, 125–26.

SOURCES

"American Indian Movement," in *Encyclopædia Britannica*, http://www.britannica.com/topic/American-Indian-Movement (accessed May 1, 2016).

Alexie, Sherman, *Indian Killer*, Warner Books, 1996.

Andrews, Evan, "Native American Activists Occupy Alcatraz Island, 45 Years Ago," *History.com*, November 20, 2014, http://www.history.com/news/native-american-activists-occupy-alcatraz-island-45-years-ago (accessed May 1, 2016).

Campbell, Duncan, "Voice of the New Tribes," in *Conversations with Sherman Alexie*, edited by Nancy J. Peterson, University Press of Mississippi, 2009, p. 115–16.

"Census 2010: Service-Based Enumeration (SBE) Operation," National Coalition for the Homeless website, http://www.nationalhomeless.org/factsheets/CensusFactSheet.pdf (accessed May 1, 2016).

"Demographics: Minorities by the Numbers," in *Civil Rights 101*, http://www.civilrights.org/resources/civilrights101/demographics.html?referrer = https://www.google.com (accessed May 1, 2016).

Donovan, Georgie J., "Biography of Sherman Alexie," in *Critical Insights: Sherman Alexie*, edited by Leon Lewis, Salem Press, 2012, pp. 20–29.

Henry, Meghan, Azim Shivji, Tanya de Sousa, and Rebecca Cohen, "Point-in-Time Estimates of Homelessness," in *The 2015 Annual Homeless Assessment Report (AHAR) to Congress*, November 2015, https://www.hudexchange.info/resources/documents/2015-AHAR-Part-1.pdf (accessed April 30, 2016).

Horwitz, Tony, "The Horrific Sand Creek Massacre Will Be Forgotten No More," in *Smithsonian*, December 2014, http://www.smithsonianmag.com/history/horrific-sand-creek-massacre-will-be-forgotten-no-more-180953403/?no-ist (accessed May 1, 2016).

Jaggi, Maya, "All Rage and Heart," in *Guardian*, May 2, 2008, http://www.theguardian.com/books/2008/may/03/featuresreviews.guardianreview13 (accessed April 30, 2016).

Kuiper, Kathleen, "Sherman Alexie," in *Encyclopædia Britannica*, http://www.britannica.com/biography/Sherman-Alexie (accessed April 30, 2016).

"Marcus Whitman (1802–1847) Narcissa Whitman (1808–1847)" in *New Perspectives on the West: People*, http://www.pbs.org/weta/thewest/people/s_z/whitman.htm (accessed May 1, 2016).

Mariani, Giorgio, "Negotiating Violence and Identity in Sherman Alexie's *Indian Killer*," in *Forum for Inter-American Research*, Vol. 4, No. 2, November 2011, http://interamericaonline.org/volume-4-2/mariani (accessed April 30, 2016).

Mechanic, David, "Mental Health Services Then and Now," in *Health Affairs*, http://content.healthaffairs.org/content/26/6/1548.full (accessed May 1, 2016).

Nicholls, Richard E., "Skin Games," in *New York Times*, November 24, 1996, http://wwwnytimes.com/1996/11/24/books/skin-games.html (accessed April 30, 2016).

Review of *Indian Killer*, in *Kirkus Reviews*, August 1, 1996, https://www.kirkusreviews.com/book-reviews/sherman-alexie/indian-killer/ (accessed April 30, 2016).

Review of *Indian Killer*, in *Publishers Weekly*, http://www.publishersweekly.com/978-0-87113-652-7 (accessed April 30, 2016).

"Sherman Alexie," Poetry Foundation website, http://www.poetryfoundation.org/poems-and-poets/poets/detail/sherman-alexie (accessed April 30, 2016).

"1600–1754: Native Americans: Overview," 1997, in *Encyclopedia.com*, http://www.encyclopedia.com/doc/1G2-2536600359.html (accessed May 1, 2016).

"Snapshot of Homelessness," National Alliance to End Homelessness website, http://www.endhomelessness.org/pages/snapshot_of_homelessness (accessed April 30, 2016).

Snipp, C. Matthew, "The Size and Distribution of the American Indian Population: Fertility, Mortality, Migration, and Residence," in *Changing Numbers, Changing Needs: American Indian Demography and Public Health*, National Center for Biotechnology Information website, http://www.ncbi.nlm.nih.gov/books/NBK233098/ (accessed May 1, 2016).

Tilsen, Mark, "1890 and 1973: Do We Really Know What Happened at Wounded Knee?," in *Huffington Post*, November 7, 2014, http://www.huffingtonpost.com/mark-tilsen/wounded-knee_b_6117502.html (accessed May 1, 2016).

Weich, Dave, "Revising Sherman Alexie," in *Conversations with Sherman Alexie*, edited by Nancy J. Peterson, University Press of Mississippi, 2009, p. 174.

Williams, Sarah T., "Man of Many Tribes," in *Star Tribune*, March 23, 2001, http://www.startribune.com/man-of-many-tribes/11435616 (accessed April 30, 2016).

FURTHER READING

Alexie, Sherman, *Ten Little Indians*, Grove Press, 2003.
    In this short-story collection, Alexie uses his trademark humor to explore his most commonly

occurring theme: what it means to be an Indian in the modern world.

Moore, MariJo, ed., *Genocide of the Mind: New Native American Writing*, Nation Books, 2003.

In this essay collection, Moore gathers the work of emerging authors along with that of established writers like Alexie, Leslie Marmon Silko, Paula Gunn Allen, Simon Ortiz, and Maurice Kenny. The essays explore issues of identity for Native Americans in the modern world.

Ortiz, Simon, *Men on the Moon: Collected Short Stories*, University of Arizona Press, 1999.

Though Ortiz is best known for poetry, this collection of short stories was praised by critics for its style. The stories capture elements of the Native American oral tradition and portray an interesting array of characters, both Indian and Anglo.

Scalp Lock, Ruth, with Jim Pritchard, *My Name Is Shield Woman: A Hard Road to Healing, Vision, and Leadership*, DayTimeMoon, 2014.

Scalp Lock's story is representative of that of many in her generation. She was taken from her family as a child to attend boarding school and later faced addiction and abuse. She overcame these obstacles to become a leader in her community and to achieve peace on a personal spiritual level.

SUGGESTED SEARCH TERMS

Sherman Alexie AND Indian Killer

Sherman Alexie AND interview

Sherman Alexie AND tribalism

Sherman Alexie AND criticism

Native American versus Indian

Native American literature

mystery AND literary genre

postcolonial literature

urban Indian

Jane Eyre

2011

Director Cary Fukunaga's adaptation of Char-lotte Brontë's 1847 novel *Jane Eyre*, starring Mia Wasikowska as Jane and Michael Fassbender as Rochester, debuted in US theaters in April 2011 (after a limited release in March). The film, both a coming-of-age tale and a gothic romance, is notable for its more understated depiction of Brontë's tale; earlier adaptations (of which there are many) often focused more on the sensationalist or gothic elements. For a movie of this type—an independent film adapting a nineteenth-century novel—it did well at the box office, grossing more than thirty-four million dollars worldwide. Critical response was predominantly positive as well, though some felt the relatively muted handling of the story lacked energy.

The novel was first published in 1847 as *Jane Eyre: An Autobiography*, under the pseudonym Currer Bell. (Charlotte Brontë's sisters, also novelists, published under similar pseudonyms: Emily as Ellis Bell and Anne as Acton Bell.) Though the novel was not actually an autobiography, many of its elements are taken from Brontë's life. For example, Charlotte and her sisters attended a boarding school with the same harsh conditions of Lowood. There Charlotte's older sisters, Maria and Elizabeth, were both taken ill, Maria with tuberculosis and Elizabeth with typhoid fever. Both died shortly after.

Charlotte Brontë *(©Everett Historical / Shutterstock.com)*

The story follows the title character, an orphan, from her unhappy childhood with her aunt, who resents her presence in the house and treats her with indifference at best, through her miserable early years at Lowood and to her employment as a governess at Thornfield Hall. There she meets the enigmatic and passionate Mr. Rochester, wealthy master of Thornfield. They fall in love, and though it seems that their difference in station is the only impediment to overcome, Mr. Rochester has a secret that, once revealed, may separate them forever.

The novel was notable in its time for its progressive depiction of a strong, independent young woman who insists upon her rights, stands up to men (including her employer), and craves adventure and independence. Though the novel was popular when released, these elements were considered controversial. The book is viewed by many as an early feminist novel. *Jane Eyre* and the later novel *Villette* (1853) are widely considered to be Brontë's finest works.

PLOT SUMMARY

In contrast to the novel, the film opens midway through the story, when Jane is leaving Thornfield. A distressed Jane emerges from a set of dark doors and hurries out onto the open moors. The footage is shot with a handheld, shaky camera, echoing Jane's chaotic state of mind. Day turns to night and a storm arises; Jane staggers through the downpour, weak and ill. She sees a house in the distance, struggles to the door and knocks. Just as she is collapsing, a young man arrives and helps her into the house.

The man (St. John Rivers) and his sisters ask Jane who she is and how she has come there. Faces come in and out of focus and voices echo, illustrating Jane's delirious state. She flashes back to scenes from her childhood. She is being tormented by her cousin John, who strikes her hard across the head with a book; when she fights back, her aunt has the servants lock her up alone overnight in a frightening room. Jane's aunt, Mrs. Reed, contacts Mr. Brocklehurst, schoolmaster at Lowood school. Mrs. Reed tells him that Jane has a spiteful heart and that she is a liar. Jane tells her aunt she hates her and that someday she will be judged for treating her so poorly. Jane is taken then to the gloomy Lowood school, where she is dressed in a uniform. (Throughout the film, Jane has very few dresses; she wears the same ones repeatedly.)

Jane first encounters fellow pupil Helen Burns when she sees her being beaten on the back with a stick as punishment for not paying attention. When young Jane, shocked, drops her slate and breaks it, Mr. Brocklehurst makes her stand on "the pedestal of infamy" all day and tells the other girls to shun her. Helen kindly brings Jane a piece of bread from her meager dinner and later encourages Jane by telling her she is loved by God and an invisible world of spirits, who will guide her. When Helen falls ill, Jane visits, lying next to her and holding her hand. The two girls fall asleep with their foreheads pressed together; shot from above, they look like mirror images of each other. When Jane awakens, Helen is dead.

The film returns to Jane's current life. Jane has told St. John, who is a clergyman, that she wishes to work to support herself. Now St. John tells Jane he has found her a position: Jane is to be schoolmistress of a local village school in the

FILM
TECHNIQUE

- Fukunaga uses bounce lighting, in which light sources (like the candlelight and firelight in *Jane Eyre*) are "bounced," or reflected, toward the actors using reflective boards. Bounce lighting generally produces a softer, more natural feel than direct lighting.

- Handheld camera work is used in several scenes of *Jane Eyre* to reflect Jane's agitation and anxiety. In the first scenes of the film, in which Jane is fleeing Thornfield after her hopes of marrying Rochester are dashed, the handheld camera work is very shaky, reflecting Jane's chaotic state of mind. The handheld camera is used again when Jane is impatiently awaiting Rochester's return, shortly after Mrs. Fairfax warns her that "men of Mr. Rochester's station generally don't marry their governesses." In this scene the camera is steadier, reflecting a milder anxiety.

- Fukunaga also uses jump cuts to add to the chaotic nature of Jane's flight from Thornfield. A jump cut is an edit in which the film "jumps" between two similar shots of the same subject, giving the impression of jumping forward in time.

- High overhead shots of Jane, dwarfed by the open landscape, are used to demonstrate her isolation and vulnerability after she leaves Thornfield. One high overhead shot of Jane shows her literally standing at a crossroads, a metaphor for the crisis she is experiencing. Long shots that depict the Rivers's home as a small structure in the middle of nowhere give the viewer an idea of their isolation as well. Because Jane and the Rivers family are not wealthy, they are all more vulnerable to the forces of nature—Jane nearly dies of exposure while running from Thornfield, and in another scene, St. John arrives at Jane's cottage (also shown from a distant camera angle, isolated in a snowstorm) shivering and covered in snow. By comparison, Thornfield is shown from a low camera angle, looming large, when Jane first arrives. When Jane and Rochester are shown on the grounds together, the weather is rarely harsh, except in one rainy scene where they easily run for the safety of the manor.

- A smash cut is when the scene abruptly cuts to another, usually very different scene for emotional effect. Fukunaga uses a jarring smash cut from a quiet scene in the Rivers's home to Helen Burns being struck on the back with a wooden rod at Lowood, to emphasize the violence and cruelty of the punishments dealt out at Lowood school.

parish. It pays little, but gives her a small cottage and means to live on.

Another flashback shows Jane, now grown and leaving Lowood School for the first time. She is taken in a carriage to Thornfield, a large manor house, and greeted by Mrs. Fairfax, the kindly housekeeper. Mrs. Fairfax tells Jane that the child to whom she will be governess is named Adele and is a ward of Mr. Edward Rochester, master of Thornfield. The next day Jane is introduced to Adele. There is a montage of scenes in which Jane teaches Adele and bonds with her. Adele tells Jane that one of the servants claims there is a ghostly woman who walks the halls of Thornfield at night. Jane dismisses it as nonsense.

One day Jane, feeling restless, goes out for a walk, and encounters a man on a horse. The horse is spooked by Jane's sudden appearance and rears up, unseating its rider and injuring him. The man asks Jane for assistance in getting back on the horse. Wary of the dark stranger, Jane reluctantly helps him. He gallops off into the mist.

When Jane returns to Thornfield, Mrs. Fairfax tells her Mr. Rochester has arrived and is in a bad humor because he was thrown from his horse. Mr. Rochester summons Adele and Jane to sit with him. He is imperious, blunt, and inquisitive, but Jane is undaunted and speaks to him as an equal; close-ups of Jane's face show her meeting his gaze head-on, unflinching. Rochester is intrigued by Jane. He tells her he envies her openness and her "unpolluted mind." When he was her age, he says, fate dealt him a blow, but he does not tell Jane what this blow was. Rochester says that he sees in her "a restless captive" who, if set free, "would soar, cloud high."

Late one evening, Jane is in bed when she hears strange noises. Using a candle to light her way, she follows the noises to Mr. Rochester's bedroom and discovers that it is on fire. She wakens him and together they smother the fire with the bed covers. Rochester instructs Jane to tell no one what has happened. As Jane turns to leave, Rochester stops her, saying she has saved his life, and takes her hand. He leans in close as if to kiss her, but Jane says good night and leaves.

The next day, Mrs. Fairfax tells Jane that Rochester has left on a visit to Blanche Ingram, a "favorite" of his; she speculates that Rochester may intend to propose marriage to her. While Rochester is gone, Jane is pensive and preoccupied. After several weeks, Mrs. Fairfax tells her that he is returning and bringing a party with him, including Miss Ingram.

When the guests arrive, Adele and Jane watch Mr. Rochester escort Blanche Ingram to the house, holding her arm. Mrs. Fairfax later tells Jane that Mr. Rochester wants her to join the party in the drawing room after dinner. Jane sits wordlessly to one side as the elegant party ignores her. The imperious Blanche carelessly dismisses all governesses as "detestable." Jane leaves the room; Rochester follows and asks why she has said nothing to him, after his long absence. As Jane tries to explain, Mrs. Fairfax enters and announces a visitor for Mr. Rochester from Jamaica, a Mr. Richard Mason. Rochester is visibly shaken. Cryptically, he asks Jane what she would do if all the people in the next room condemned and left him. Jane answers that she would stay with him. Then Mason enters, Rochester greets him warmly, and they leave the room.

Later that night, Jane is once again awakened by strange noises. When she goes into the hall, Rochester is there and asks Jane to follow him. He takes her to another room where Mr. Mason is lying across a chair, bleeding from gashes in his arm and neck. Rochester says he must leave to find a doctor and tells Jane to care for Mason. He forbids them to speak to each other. Unsettled and confused, Jane does as Rochester tells her. While he is gone, she hears more strange noises through the wall.

Rochester returns with the doctor. After being examined, Mason is rushed off in a carriage with the doctor in the first light of morning. Jane asks Rochester who has inflicted Mason's wounds, but Rochester says he cannot tell her. He says his existence has been blighted by a "capital error" made in his youth but that recently he had "met a gentle stranger whose society revives [him]." Jane assumes he is speaking of Miss Ingram. (In the novel, Rochester purposely leads her to believe he is going to marry Miss Ingram, to make her jealous and goad her into confessing her love.) Rochester asks what Jane would do to help him be happy. Jane answers, "I would do anything for you, sir."

Some days later, Jane learns that her aunt has had a stroke and goes to visit her on her deathbed. Aunt Reed shows her a letter from Jane's paternal uncle, requesting Jane's address. The uncle, John Eyre, had had some financial success and wished to adopt Jane. The letter is three years old. Aunt Reed confesses that to spite Jane, she told John Eyre that Jane had died. Jane tells her aunt that she forgives her and leaves the room. She writes a letter to her uncle, informing him she is alive and living at Thornfield.

When Jane returns to Thornfield, she learns that Mr. Rochester is soon to marry Miss Ingram. When Jane next sees Mr. Rochester, she congratulates him and says she will be leaving as soon as she can find a new position. Rochester neither confirms nor denies the news. Jane goes for a walk, and Rochester follows her. He tells Jane he will miss her, and she tells him, "It strikes me with anguish to be torn from you." Rochester asks why she must leave, and Jane says, "Because of your wife." Rochester says he has no wife and tells her to stay. Jane, angry, asks if Rochester thinks she is a "machine without feelings." She turns to leave, but Rochester grabs her arm and passionately asks her to become his wife. Jane is incredulous. Rochester says Miss Ingram is the machine without feelings and that he wants only Jane. Jane accepts his proposal, and they kiss. The weather turns stormy, and they run hand in hand back to the manor. Rochester kisses her again and Mrs. Fairfax sees them; she is shocked. Later she warns Jane to be skeptical of Rochester's intentions and keep her distance until they are safely married.

A montage of romantic vignettes follows, as Rochester and Jane enjoy the spring weather together. When the wedding day arrives, Rochester grabs Jane's hand and hurries her along to the church. He seems agitated and preoccupied. As they stand before the minister preparing to exchange vows, a man enters the church and exclaims, "The marriage must not go on!" He asserts that fifteen years earlier, Rochester married a woman named Bertha Antoinetta Mason in Spanish Town, Jamaica. Richard Mason—the man whose wounds Jane cared for—enters and says Bertha is living in Thornfield. Rochester attacks him.

After Rochester is restrained and calms down, he tells the group to follow him to Thornfield to meet his wife. He charges into the manor, throws open the secret inner room (from which Jane had heard the strange noises), and introduces them all to his wife: a thin, unkempt woman with sunken eyes and long, matted hair. She spits at Jane, and after first embracing Rochester she attacks him, clawing at his face. Jane, horrified, runs from the room and returns to her own bedroom. Weeping, she hastily removes her wedding dress. (Jump cuts during the unlacing of the dress accentuate Jane's agitation.)

By the time she emerges, it is dark; Rochester is lying in the hallway outside her room, waiting for her. Jane staggers, and he catches her and carries her to sit by the fireplace. She tells him she must leave him, but he begs her to stay. He explains that his father wished him to wed Bertha for her fortune and that he barely spoke to her before they were married. Then, she gradually descended into madness. Rather than commit Bertha to a madhouse, he confined her at Thornfield and had servants care for her. Jane admits she still loves him but remains firm; she will not stay. "I must respect myself," she tells him, and weeping, she leaves the room.

In the next scene, the flashback catches up to where the movie first began, with a distraught Jane emerging from the dark doors of Thornfield and running onto the moors. An abrupt cut brings the viewer to Jane's humble village schoolhouse, where St. John is visiting to see how she is doing at her new teaching post. Jane

has not told St. John or his sisters about Mr. Rochester or Thornfield, but St. John can tell that her past troubles her. He cautions her about dwelling on the past. He pauses to look at some of the drawings Jane has done, and then leaves.

The scene cuts to a long shot of Jane's tiny cottage in a snowstorm. Inside, Jane is sitting by the fire, wrapped in a blanket, when there is a heavy pounding at the door. Jane rises to answer it, and when she opens the door, Mr. Rochester is there. They fall into each other's arms, kissing passionately. A quick cut, however, reveals that this is only a fantasy in Jane's mind, and the actual visitor is St. John, shivering in the snow. As she lets him in and takes his coat, he addresses her as "Miss Eyre"; Jane has never told him her real name. He has discovered it by looking at a signature she made on one of her drawings. He tells her that he has been contacted by a lawyer named Briggs, who is trying to find her. Her uncle, John Eyre, has passed away and left his entire estate to Jane. She is now a wealthy woman.

Jane is stunned, both at this revelation and because her only remaining relative is now dead. She tells St. John she would like to share the money with him and his sisters and live with them as their sister. In the next scene, she is living at their house, and St. John is reading a prayer. He gives them each a kiss before bed, except Jane. When his sister objects, he and Jane kiss awkwardly. Later St. John speaks to Jane alone, saying that he is leaving for a mission to India in six weeks, and he wants Jane to come along as his wife. Jane says she is not fit for it. St. John insists that he and Jane are fellow souls.

In the next scene, Jane approaches St. John on the moors and tells him she will go with him to India but will not marry him; she thinks of him as a brother. St. John insists that she must marry him to come along. Jane refuses. St. John tells her he knows why and demands that she say Rochester's name. As he shouts at Jane, Jane suddenly hears Rochester's voice in her head, calling her. She says, "I am coming" and runs from St. John.

Jane returns to Thornfield, but when she gets out of the carriage and runs toward the manor, she sees that it is a charred ruin, destroyed by fire. As she walks tearfully through the scorched halls, now open to the bright light of day, she meets Mrs. Fairfax, who tells her the sad tale of the fire: Bertha started it, and Mr. Rochester saved everyone in the house by making sure they all escaped. He tried to save Bertha, but she climbed to the top of the house and jumped to her death. Jane asks Mrs. Fairfax where Rochester is.

In the next scene, Jane is walking through a field, approaching a smaller house. She sees Mr. Rochester, ragged, bearded, and blinded by injuries from the fire, sitting on a bench with his dog by his side. She approaches him, touches his hand and tells him she has come back to him. They embrace. Rochester says he must be dreaming. Jane answers simply, "Awaken, then."

CHARACTERS

Bessie

Bessie is Jane's nurse as a child. In the film she is barely mentioned and appears in few scenes, but in the novel she is the only person in the Reed household who cares for Jane, though she scolds her often.

Mr. Brocklehurst

Mr. Brocklehurst is the manager of the miserable Lowood School, a charity institution for children who have lost one or both parents. In the film, he chastises Jane for being deceitful (based on Mrs. Reed's assessment); when Jane accidentally breaks her slate, he makes her stand on a chair alone and tells the other girls to shun her. In the novel, he is also responsible for the harsh way of life, meager rations, and generally unhealthy conditions at Lowood School; his neglect is eventually revealed to the public, and the school improves in Jane's later years there.

Helen Burns

Helen is Jane's best friend at Lowood. She is very kind to Jane and devout in her faith. She advises Jane not to bear grudges toward those who harm her but instead to follow the example of Jesus and forgive them. Sadly, Helen contracts tuberculosis and dies, with Jane at her side. In deleted scenes from the film, the spirit of Helen appears to Jane in her darkest moments, when she is wandering the moors after leaving Thornfield. In one deleted scene, they lie on the ground beside each other, in the same manner they did on Helen's deathbed. In the novel, Helen is something of a martyr, persecuted by some of the teachers who regularly punish and shame

her. Helen bears it all patiently, while the more passionate Jane becomes furious on her behalf.

Jane Eyre

Jane is a complex character. As a child, no one loves her with the exception of Bessie, her nurse, who appears in the film only as a background character (and even in the novel, Bessie is more often scolding than kind). Her aunt keeps her only to fulfill a promise to her late husband, Jane's maternal uncle, and when she proves too burdensome, she sends Jane away to Lowood with instructions that she is to spend vacations there as well. In the film, Mrs. Reed and Mr. Brocklehurst refer to Jane as "it" when discussing her education.

However, Jane possesses an instinctive sense of her own worth. Unlike Helen, who meekly accepts the criticisms of her teachers, Jane will not agree with Mrs. Reed's poor assessment of her character. In the early portion of the film, when Jane is a child, she has a fiery temper; she attacks her cousin after he hits her with a book and later tells Mrs. Reed exactly how much she dislikes her. (In the novel, she goes even further in her rant, saying, "If any one asks me how I liked you, and how you treated me, I will say the very thought of you makes me sick, and that you treated me with miserable cruelty.") When Jane is older, she is much more self-contained and composed. However, some of her earlier fire comes out when Rochester pushes her too far, asking her to stay with him when she believes he will be married to Miss Ingram. Likewise, when St. John all but orders Jane to marry him, Jane lashes out, telling him, "To marry you would kill me." Jane's independent thought, her fierce will, her strength, and her refusal to bow to any man have all earned her the label of an early feminist heroine. Jane values others for their intellect and their kindness; as she tells Mr. Rochester, "Beauty is of little consequence."

Jane is often described as plain in the novel, and her lack of beauty is alluded to in the film, although the actress who plays her — Mia Wasikowska — is very attractive. Assuming that the character is as plain as she is supposed to be, however, Jane's refusal to submit to the will of men is even more daring, given that her prospects for finding a husband (and in turn, having a family and home of her own) are limited.

Mrs. Fairfax

Mrs. Fairfax is an older woman whose sole purpose in life is to keep Thornfield in constant readiness for the mercurial Mr. Rochester, who gives little notice of his comings and goings. With little company to talk to (there are the other servants, but she tells Jane, "One cannot talk to them on terms of equality"), Mrs. Fairfax grows very fond of Jane and enjoys imparting little tidbits of gossip about Mr. Rochester and Miss Ingram, ignorant of the pain it causes her.

Being elderly, a woman, and unmarried (she is a widow), Mrs. Fairfax is almost more invisible than Jane, except for her position of authority over the household. Mr. Rochester regularly insults her and treats her dismissively.

Blanche Ingram

Elegant, jaded, and haughty, Blanche Ingram is beautiful and stylish, and Jane is led to believe that Mr. Rochester intends to marry her. She is opinionated and domineering. (In one deleted scene, Jane overhears Blanche's mother caution her not to have so many opinions but to make herself a "blank canvas" on which Mr. Rochester can paint.) When the encounter between Bertha and Richard Mason wakes up everyone in the house, Blanche gives Jane a scathing look before she returns to bed; she suspects that there is a connection between them.

Richard Mason

We see little of Richard Mason in the film; his main purpose is to add to the mystery by appearing as a troubling figure from Rochester's past. In the novel, Richard is hailed by the women in the party as "a beautiful man," but Jane finds that despite his handsomeness, she is "repelled." The reader learns that Richard Mason is goodhearted but weak man who fears Rochester; we see a hint of this in the film when he allows the lawyer Briggs to confront Rochester and Jane at the wedding, and cowers behind the lawyer when Rochester advances on him. Therefore, it puzzles Jane that Rochester seems to be afraid of Mason as well. The explanation, of course, is that Richard is Bertha's brother, and Rochester fears that he will reveal his secret: Bertha is alive and living at Thornfield.

John Reed

John Reed is Jane's cousin and Mrs. Reed's son. He has only a brief appearance in the film, at the beginning, when he cruelly strikes Jane across the head with a book. His role is not much bigger in the novel. He leads a dissolute life with bad company, spends time in prison, and eventually commits suicide, which precipitates Aunt Reed's stroke.

Mrs. Reed

Mrs. Reed is Jane's aunt; Jane's mother was her late husband's sister. Mrs. Reed takes in the orphaned Jane only because her husband wished it. As soon as she finds Jane too troublesome, she sends her off to Lowood School. Mrs. Reed is a cold, unfeeling woman, but not without a shred of conscience: on her deathbed, she feels the need to confess to Jane that she told her other uncle, who wished to adopt Jane, that Jane had died of typhus.

Bertha Antoinetta Mason Rochester

Bertha, Mr. Rochester's mentally ill wife, is a figure of some controversy in literature. Bertha is a Creole from Jamaica, and Rochester only married her at his father's request, because she was very wealthy. Then, after her married her, "her vices sprang up," and she descended into madness. In postcolonial British literature, women from exotic locales are often portrayed as hypersexual, wanton, and uncivilized. These stereotypes helped British colonizers justify the oppression of colonial subjects. (Jamaica was a British colony until 1962.)

In the film, Bertha is played by the beautiful actress Valentina Cervi; her hair is unkempt and matted and her clothes ragged, but overall she is still a very attractive woman. Fukunaga's vision of Bertha is a far cry from Brontë's description in the novel:

> What it was, whether beast or human being, one could not, at first sight, tell: it grovelled, seemingly, on all fours; it snatched and growled like some strange wild animal, but it was covered with clothing, and a quantity of dark, grizzled hair, wild as a mane, hid its head and face.

In addition, Brontë writes that Bertha was "a big woman, in stature almost equalling her husband." Casting Cervi as the current Mrs. Rochester makes the viewer more sympathetic toward her plight than if he portrayed her as the hulking monster Brontë describes.

Edward Fairfax Rochester

Mr. Rochester is a mercurial, mysterious character. He is at turns rude, dismissive, poetic, and insightful. Though he is kind at heart, he does his best to hide it. For instance, he often says unkind things about Adele and her mother, but he supports and educates Adele, even though he is not sure if she is his child or not (in one of the deleted scenes, he explains her questionable parentage). Likewise, he keeps Bertha at Thornfield to be cared for by servants, rather than placing her in a madhouse. In the film, Rochester asks Jane if she has ever been in a madhouse; he tells her the inmates are treated so cruelly, he wanted to spare Bertha that horrible fate. This speech does not take place in the novel, although Rochester does tell Jane that only cruelty would check Bertha's vices, and he rejects that cruelty.

In the film, Rochester's character is softened considerably for modern audiences. In the novel, Rochester is much more manipulative of Jane, deliberately leading her to believe he is going to marry Miss Ingram, and he speaks more cruelly of his mad wife, calling her a hag, a monster, and a maniac. However, because modern audiences are more sympathetic to the plight of the mentally ill, these speeches would bias viewers against him. In the novel, Rochester is portrayed as a flawed man, damaged by tragedy, but not a cruel or unfeeling one.

As with the character of Jane, Mr. Rochester is portrayed by an actor far handsomer than his literary description warrants. In the novel, Jane says, "I am sure most people would have thought him an ugly man," before going on to explain why she shares that opinion. Similarly, in the film, when Jane blushes, Rochester tells her, "Though you are not pretty any more than I am handsome, I must say it becomes you." Rochester is played by Michael Fassbender, an actor few would describe as ugly. This is not the first time, however, that Hollywood has made this concession. Rochester has been played by a succession of actors, most of them attractive, including a young Orson Welles, George C. Scott, William Hurt, and Timothy Dalton.

Diana Rivers
Diana is St. John's sister, who becomes like a sister to Jane in her recuperative stay at the Rivers home and even more so later, when Jane goes to live with them.

Mary Rivers
Mary is St. John's other sister. She and Jane become very close while she lives with the Rivers family.

St. John Rivers
St. John is a pastor who lives with his sisters in their late father's home; in the novel he lives at his parish house nearby but spends most of his free time with his sisters. St. John is an intense, unyielding, driven, and ambitious clergyman. Jane is a little intimidated by him, as well as awed. In the novel, he is described as handsome (though Jane also says he is "cold as an iceberg"). Despite his devout belief in God, St. John is not a content or peaceful man. He is restless and tormented, and he is eager to leave for India as a missionary.

In the novel, St. John also wishes to marry Jane and take her on the mission; to that end, he spends hours and hours tutoring her in foreign languages. When Jane refuses his proposals, he continues to pressure her, going so far as to tell her that to deny his offer is to deny God. Jane still refuses.

In the film, Jane tells St. John that she wishes to be his sister, and a sister to Diana and Mary as well. In the novel, it is discovered that Jane is actually related to the Rivers family; her father's sister (Jane's paternal aunt) was their mother, and so they are cousins. That coincidence, however, is omitted from the movie.

Adele Varens
Adele is the daughter of a French woman with whom Mr. Rochester had an affair. She was unfaithful, and he left her. In the novel, Adele's mother abandoned her to run off with one of her lovers, and Mr. Rochester took her in; in the film, Adele says her mother has passed away. Mr. Rochester tells the story to Jane in a deleted scene from the film, but in the finished film it is left unexplained.

Eliminated Characters
Most of the novel's characters eliminated from the film are minor ones, such as additional servants at Gateshead and Thornfield and fellow students at Lowood. However, there were three fairly significant characters in the novel that were either eliminated or drastically minimized in the film. The first is Maria Temple, who does not appear in the film. In the novel, she is the superintendent of Lowood School. Miss Temple has to answer to Mr. Brocklehurst, but where he is hard and merciless, Miss Temple is caring, intelligent, and fair. Early on, she clears Jane of Brocklehurst's accusation of lying, and she

breaks the rules to provide an extra meal for the girls one day when their breakfast is ruined. She has a special bond with Helen, who, despite being persecuted by the Lowood teachers, is extraordinarily bright.

Another character who appears in the film but is barely seen is Grace Poole. In the novel, all the strange noises and maniacal laughter heard in the night are blamed on this odd and reclusive servant. When Rochester's room is set on fire and when Richard Mason is injured, Jane is led to believe that Grace is responsible. Understandably, Jane is puzzled as to why Grace remains employed there, but it is later revealed that Grace's actual job is to care for Bertha. Unfortunately, Grace occasionally drinks too much and nods off, allowing Bertha to escape and threaten the household.

The third significant eliminated character is Rosamond Oliver, a very beautiful young woman with whom St. John Rivers is smitten. Her father is a successful businessman who owns a factory in the town near Jane's village school. Because Rosamond has charitably furnished supplies for the school, she often drops by to observe Jane in her teaching efforts. Though St. John confesses to Jane that he loves Rosamond, he believes she would not make a good wife for a missionary, and so he resists the attraction, feeling that his calling as a missionary is more important.

THEMES

Feminism

Jane Eyre is considered an early feminist novel. In 1847, when the novel was first published, the idea that a woman would put herself on an equal intellectual plane with a man was controversial, even incendiary. Though not such a radical concept in 2011, when the film was released, feminism is still a relevant issue, as women still fight for equal pay and advancement in business and politics. In the novel, Jane states her feminist theme overtly, saying that just like men, women need a "field for their efforts." She declares that "it is narrow-minded in their more privileged fellow-creatures to say that they ought to confine themselves to making puddings and knitting stockings." In the film, Jane's feminism is demonstrated more than openly stated. She refuses to submit to Mr. Rochester, and even though she

loves him, she is not willing to lose herself to keep him. Her own dignity and self-worth are more important to her; as she leaves him, she says, "I must respect myself." Given that Jane has known hardship and would have had a comfortable life as Rochester's mistress, this shows great strength of character. Jane takes pride in her independence and self-sufficiency. In the film, when St. John finds her a job as a teacher, which provides her with a tiny, primitive cottage in which to live, she thanks him heartily, saying, "This is my first home where I'm neither dependent nor subordinate to anyone."

Human Rights

Just before Mr. Rochester proposes to Jane in the novel, she tells him angrily, "Do you think, because I am poor, obscure, plain and little, I am soulless and heartless? You think wrong!— I have as much soul as you,—and full as much heart." She does not say, "because I am a woman"; she advocates for the rights of all human beings. Jane does not admit inferiority to anyone. She tells him that insolence is something that "nothing free-born should ever submit to, even for a salary." In the film, Mr. Rochester is portrayed as a man less conscious of class difference than others (such as Miss Ingram). He is shown helping laborers on his property remove a tree stump from the grounds, and he tells Jane, "I do not wish to treat you as inferior." Though the theme of human rights is not a major one in the film, its inclusion in the novel was controversial. The idea that all people should have equal rights, regardless of class or wealth, was not a universally accepted one in 1847. In the introduction to the Penguin Classics version of *Jane Eyre*, Brontë scholar Stevie Davies quotes an 1848 issue of the *Quarterly Review* that criticized the novel for espousing "a proud and perpetual assertion of the rights of man, for which we find no authority either in God's word or in God's providence." In fact, at the time of the novel's publication, only a small percentage of men (and no women) had the right to vote in England.

Nature

Both Jane and Mr. Rochester share a love of nature, which is reflected in the film. Many of the film's and novel's pivotal scenes take place in nature: Jane's first encounter with Mr. Rochester, his confession of love and proposal of marriage, Jane's flight from Thornfield, and Jane's refusal of

READ.
WATCH.
WRITE.

- The DVD includes several scenes deleted from the film. In one deleted scene, Bertha visits Jane's room late one night before her wedding, puts on Jane's wedding veil, and then violently shreds it. In another, the spirit of Helen Burns appears to Jane when she is wandering the moors. And in one especially eerie deleted scene, Adele appears beside Jane's bed one night, opens her mouth and emits a low, guttural scream. Why do you think the director eliminated these scenes? Do you think their omission improves or diminishes the film? If you were the director, would you restore any of the scenes to the film, and why? Write a letter to director Cary Fukunaga, explaining why you feel he should include the scenes you chose (or why you agree with his choice).

- Watch the movie and pay special attention to mentions of the characters' mental states. Take notes as you watch. Rochester's wife, Bertha, is described as "mad," but other characters sometimes talk of being "driven to madness," and the two main characters are often described as passionate. Can you draw any parallels between the actions of "sane" characters and the actions of Bertha? How do you think Bertha's condition would be handled today? Write an essay on the themes of madness in *Jane Eyre*.

- The screenwriter (Moira Buffini) rearranged the order of the story to begin with Jane's flight from Thornfield. Having read the novel, which order do you prefer? Think of at least two alternate ways to order the events of the film, and write a paper describing how each new order would change the feeling of the film.

- The only major male characters in the film are Mr. Rochester and St. John Rivers. Given Brontë's descriptions of them in the novel, do you think the roles were well cast? Make a list of other film actors—either living or dead—who you think would have fit the role well, according to Brontë. Why do you think these two actors were chosen? Post a blog including your list and thoughts about the chosen actors. Allow your classmates to comment.

- The film received an Oscar nomination for Best Costume Design. Watch the movie and pay special attention to how characters are dressed, especially Jane. How is she dressed differently than other characters? When she changes dresses, does it signify any other change in her life? Make a list of all of Jane's clothes and make note of when she wears them and why.

- Read the young-adult novel *A Breath of Eyre* (2012), by Eva Marie Mont, in which a teen travels back and forth between her modern life and the life of Jane Eyre. Now imagine the situation reversed: What if Jane Eyre were transported into the world of your favorite modern-day novel? What difficulties would she have? Which aspects of modern life do you think she would enjoy most? Write a short story of Jane Eyre's adventures in the modern world.

St. John. In the novel, Mr. Rochester enjoys walks in nature with Jane, and he points out creatures to her; he also often likens her to a fairy or a bird. St. John, by contrast, does not share this affinity. In the novel, Jane says, "Nature was not to him that treasury of delight it was to his sisters. . . . Never did he seem to roam the moors for the sake of their soothing silence." This is consistent with St. John's practice of denying his own nature and emotions, stifling his natural impulses in the service of his all-consuming ambition for God's glory. Likewise, the film depicts the land around St. John's house as harsh and barren, especially compared with the lush greenery of Thornfield.

Some critics praise the natural lighting used in the production instead of dark, Gothic moodiness
(©EVERETT COLLECTION, INC.)

Religion

The theme of religion, more overt in the novel, occurs subtly in the film. Through the characters of Helen Burns and St. John Rivers, a dilemma is presented: should one sacrifice earthly happiness for the promise of heavenly rewards in the afterlife? Helen Burns, perhaps aware of her limited time on earth, suffers persecution from her teachers at Lowood quietly and without complaint, saying that the teacher who hits her does it only to "improve" her. In contrast, Jane tells her that if the teacher hit her, she would "break that birch under her nose." Helen preaches forbearance, and on her deathbed she tells Jane she is happy to go to God. Jane, she says, has a "passion for living," but Helen says that someday Jane will come to the "region of bliss." In scenes deleted from the finished film, the spirit of Helen appears to Jane when she is wandering on the moors after leaving Thornfield. It seems that Jane is deciding between continuing to struggle for survival and joining Helen in her blissful afterlife. She chooses survival.

In the film, St. John Rivers sees self-denial as a path to salvation. In the novel, he sets aside his love for Rosamond because he feels she would not be a good missionary's wife. In the film, he tells Jane, "A year ago, I myself was intensely miserable. I scorned this weakness; I fought against it and won." This exact passage does not occur in the novel, but he does make a similar comment when admitting his passion for Rosamond: "I scorn the weakness. I know it is ignoble: a mere fever of the flesh." St. John sees natural emotions as weakness to be conquered. Likewise, he counsels Jane to set aside her love for Rochester and marry him instead, denying her desire for love. "Crush this lawless passion," he tells her.

STYLE

Color

The colors in the film are muted, consisting mainly of grays, greens, and browns. Colors are not saturated (bright or intense), but rather toned back in value, reducing contrast in color. Jane, in particular, is often dressed in colors that blend with her surroundings. In contrast,

Blanche Ingram is often dressed in more ornate or patterned dresses that stand out, as does her dark hair against her pale complexion. Jane appears to be a part of nature; Rochester often refers to her as an elf or fairy (traditionally creatures of the forest) who has "bewitched" him. Jane's camouflaged appearance also emphasizes her invisibility as an employee and woman of meager means. When Jane tells Mrs. Fairfax she does not have a suitable dress to wear with Mr. Rochester's elegant company, Mrs. Fairfax answers, "Well don't worry, child. Who will notice?"

Flashbacks

One of the biggest differences between Brontë's novel and the 2011 film is the order in which the story's events occur. The novel is told chronologically, from Jane's miserable childhood on forward. In the film, though, the story is rearranged as a nonlinear narrative, beginning in medias res (a Latin term meaning "in the middle of things") with Jane's flight from Thornfield after her wedding is ruined by the revelation of Rochester's previous marriage. Her childhood, her time at Lowood School and friendship with Helen Burns, and her early days at Thornfield are all told as long flashbacks. The flashbacks do not converge with the current story until an hour and thirty-four minutes into the film (the entire film is about two hours long).

Rearranging the narrative in this way increases the suspense and piques the viewer's curiosity: Why is Jane so upset? Why is she alone on the moors, with no money and nowhere to go? How did she come to be so destitute that she collapses on the Rivers's doorstep? It also allows the director to contrast Jane's two very different suitors, St. John in the present-day segments and Mr. Rochester in the flashbacks.

Lighting

The lighting in *Jane Eyre* is largely indirect lighting. Direct lighting refers to light that shines directly on the actors in the scene; it can produce a harsher, less natural feel than indirect lighting, especially indoors. Indoor scenes in *Jane Eyre* are often lit indirectly by candlelight, oil lamps, or a large fire in the fireplace. In an interview with Fukunaga (one of the DVD's bonus features), the director mentions that the frequent use of candles in Rochester's dark and ancient manor creates a "dizzying sense of isolation,"

which adds to the mystery and suspense surrounding the odd occurrences at Thornfield.

Outdoor scenes are mostly illuminated by natural light. Many scenes that take place indoors in the novel occur instead outdoors in the film, to take advantage of the scenic countryside as well as natural light.

Thematically, darkness in the film represents mystery, suppression, and complexity. The Reeds's elegant house, Gateshead, is very light and airy, and none of the scenes at Gateshead take place at night. The Reeds lack depth, and the house holds no mystery (with the possible exception of the Red Room, which is the darkest hued in the home). In contrast, Thornfield is much darker and mysterious, and many of the most dramatic scenes (the fire in Rochester's room, Richard Mason's injury, Rochester's plea for forgiveness) take place at night, lit only by candlelight or fire. After Thornfield and Bertha Mason are destroyed in the fire and Jane walks through the ruined halls, sunlight streams into the charred manor; the mystery is gone.

Mood

The mood of *Jane Eyre* is subdued, muted, and restrained, with an undercurrent of suspense, as though something more violent is being suppressed. This mood reflects the truth of the story: Mr Rochester is suppressing a dark secret, in much the same way that Jane suppresses her passions and her longing for adventure. Mr. Rochester likens her to a caged bird. In most of the film, characters speak quietly and politely, as social conventions dictate. Only Mr. Rochester is accustomed to lashing out verbally at others or raising his voice, and he is acknowledged as being somewhat eccentric. When Jane is upset, the viewer is alerted to it by very subtle expressions or movements. For instance, when Jane is showing Adele locations on a globe shortly after Rochester has left to visit Blanche Ingram, the camera focuses on her hand slightly shaking as she grasps the globe's frame. Adele asks her what is wrong. "Nothing," she replies.

CULTURAL CONTEXT

Mental Illness

In 1847, when *Jane Eyre* was published, there was little real understanding of mental illness, its causes, or its treatment. Compassion for those

Mia Wasikowska plays Jane Eyre, with Michael Fassbender as Mr. Rochester (©*EVERETT COLLECTION, INC.*)

suffering with mental illness was in short supply. Thus, when Mr. Rochester speaks dismissively, even disgustedly of his wife and her behavior, his words probably did not offend the nineteenth-century reading public. In the novel, Rochester calls his wife a "lunatic," "monster," "fearful hag," and "filthy burden." He tells Jane that she also had a brother with mental problems, who he describes as "a complete dumb idiot." None of these descriptions, of course, make it into the 2011 film. Greater understanding and study of mental health issues has made modern audiences more compassionate. In the film, Mr. Rochester asks Jane if she has ever been inside a madhouse. He tells her, "The inmates are caged and baited like beasts. I spared her that, at least." This explanation does not occur in the novel. In fact, the main reason Bertha is concealed is so that no one will know Rochester's shame and he can continue to associate with others in polite society, who would scorn him if they knew the truth.

While what Mr. Rochester says about mental asylums is largely true of public institutions at the time, by the latter half of the century, more luxurious private hospitals began to open up for those with the wealth to afford them. Here the rich could tuck away their mentally ill relations in comfort and secrecy. If *Jane Eyre* had taken place a few decades later, Mr. Rochester would have had this option.

Religion

The novel features discussions of religious topics between Jane and various characters. In 1847, it was a safe assumption that most readers believed in God and were well acquainted with the Bible. In the novel, St. John's mission to go to India and convert its people to Christianity would have been viewed as a noble calling by most readers, and indeed Jane greatly admires his ambition to do so. Though she finds him cold as a suitor, in the novel Jane is in awe of his greatness as a man of God. The last three paragraphs of the novel are devoted to praise of St. John's efforts in India. Jane tells the reader, "His is the ambition of the high master-spirit, which aims to fill a place in the first rank of those who are redeemed from the earth—who stand without fault before the throne of God." In the novel, even Mr. Rochester undergoes a sort of religious transformation when Jane returns to him after he is blinded. He says, "I thank my Maker, that, in the midst of judgment, He has remembered mercy. I humbly entreat my Redeemer to give me strength to lead henceforth a purer life than I have done hitherto!"

Little of this remains in the film. The film ends with Jane and Mr. Rochester's reunion (without Mr. Rochester offering thanks to God) and there is no further mention of St. John's exploits in India. While Jane is grateful to St. John for his assistance, the viewer does not get the sense that she is awestruck by his religious devotion. While the romance and coming-of-age components of the novel are retained, the religious message is largely abandoned. This is not surprising, as far fewer people today consider themselves religious than in Bronte's time, at least in the traditional sense. In 1900, well over 30 percent of the British population were church members. In 2010, the figure was less than 11 percent. Church membership has declined in the United States as well.

CRITICAL OVERVIEW

After dozens of film versions of *Jane Eyre*, reviewers were likely to be a little picky about yet another movie attempting to bring Brontë's classic to life for modern audiences. Considering the close scrutiny the film inevitably received, the reviews were largely positive. Fukunaga's handling of the countryside, the period details, and the lighting were highly praised; Tim Robey, in a review in the *Telegraph*, calls his direction "delicate artistry," and Ann Hornaday of the *Washington Post* writes that "no movie in recent memory has exploited nineteenth-century lighting implements with as much rich, lambent luster."

The point of contention for many reviewers was the performance of Mia Wasikowska as Jane; opinions varied widely. A. O. Scott of the *New York Times* calls her "a perfect Jane," whereas Hornaday finds her performance "elegant but inert." Reviewer Mick LaSalle, in the *San Francisco Chronicle*, agrees with Hornaday when he writes, "There's an extra something, a depth of soul or an understanding that's lacking." But at the other end of the spectrum, *Chicago Reader* reviewer J. R. Jones calls Fukunaga's version of

Jane Eyre "far and away the best I've seen, thanks largely to the skilled young actress Mia Wasikowska," Tim Robey agrees, calling the team of Wasikowska and Fassbender "leaps and bounds better than Orson Welles and Joan Fontaine." Peter Bradshaw of the *Guardian* felt the production lacked energy, but he did not pinpoint the problem on any one particular performance. He writes of the film, "I can't fault it, and yet I can't quite get excited about it either." Bradshaw took more of an issue with the pacing, noting that some pivotal scenes, like the revelation of Bertha, were too rushed.

Still, reviewers found plenty to like in the 2011 film. Hornaday praises Fassbender's performance, writing that his Rochester exhibits "suitable proportions of menace, vulnerability and Byronic melancholy," and Roger Ebert credits Fukunaga's "sure visual sense... expressed in voluptuous visuals and ambitious art direction." Even the reviewers who felt the film lacked passion found little to fault in the look of the film, and several credited Moira Buffini's deft handling of the script. A. O. Scott writes that the film is "a splendid example of how to tackle the daunting duty of turning a beloved work of classic literature into a movie." With such a well-known and widely read work, the odds against creating one definitive version that pleases every fan of the novel are astronomical. This version, most agree, is a praiseworthy and beautiful effort.

CRITICISM

Laura B. Pryor

Pryor has a master's degree in English and over thirty years of experience as a professional writer. In the following essay, she explores how the heroine of Jane Eyre *is repeatedly asked to choose between a life of the spirit and a life of earthly pleasures and how she reconciles these two extremes.*

At one point in Fukunaga's 2011 film version of *Jane Eyre*, Jane stands at a crossroads, literally, trying to decide which way to go. Jane makes many choices throughout the film, but one that recurs throughout is the choice between a life spent looking toward heaven and a life focused more on happiness on the earth. Jane chooses to focus on earthly life, but what is curious is how often others try to persuade her

WHAT DO I SEE NEXT?

- Of the many film adaptations of *Jane Eyre*, the most famous is the 1943 unrated black-and-white version, starring Orson Welles (also an accomplished director) and Joan Fontaine. The film handles Mr. Rochester's mad wife in a far less subtle manner than the Fukunaga film—the viewer hears much more shrieking and maniacal laughter coming from Bertha's secret chamber. Though the film was directed by Robert Stevenson, it is easy to see Welles's influence (Welles was not known for keeping his opinions to himself). This version is much darker and more brooding than Fukunaga's, a function of both the black-and-white medium and the director's lighting choices.

- The 1940 film *Rebecca*, an adaptation of the 1938 Daphne du Maurier novel, has a similar plot line and the same gothic feel as *Jane Eyre*, though the novel was written almost a century later. The plot features very similar elements: an inexperienced young woman falls in love with a mysterious and wealthy man who lives in a mansion and harbors a dark secret. Starring Joan Fontaine (who would later play Jane Eyre in the 1943 film) and Laurence Olivier, the unrated black-and-white film was directed by Alfred Hitchcock and won an Academy Award for Best Picture in 1940.

- The 1993 adaptation of Frances Hodgson Burnett's 1911 novel *The Secret Garden* (rated G) features a recently orphaned girl, Mary, who goes to live in a Victorian mansion with a tragic secret. There she gets to know her ailing cousin and begins unraveling the mysteries of the old home. Kate Maberly plays the role of Mary, and the forbidding housekeeper Mrs. Medlock is played by acclaimed British actress Maggie Smith.

- *Sangdil* is a loose Bollywood interpretation of *Jane Eyre*, released in 1952. Directed by R. C. Talwar, the unrated film tells the story of Kamal (Jane) and Shankar (Mr. Rochester). Unlike Jane and Mr. Rochester, Kamal and Shankar have met before in their youth; when they are reunited later in life, Kamal is wealthy and has a dark secret in his home. Shankar is played by Dilip Kumar, and Kamal is played by Madhubala.

- Like *Jane Eyre*, the Jane Austen classic *Pride and Prejudice* (1813) has been adapted numerous times, both for film and television. Though *Pride and Prejudice* is much lighter in tone, the protagonists are very similar: a spirited young woman who insists on marrying for love and will not be intimidated by the high-born and a brooding, mysterious man who enjoys verbally sparring with her. The PG-rated 2005 film adaptation of *Pride and Prejudice* stars Keira Knightly as Elizabeth Bennet and Matthew Macfadyen as Mr. Darcy and is directed by Joe Wright. Like the 2011 *Jane Eyre*, it is a Focus Features production, and the score is written by the same composer, Dario Marianelli. It also features Judi Dench, the actress who plays Mrs. Fairfax in *Jane Eyre*, as the snobbish Lady Catherine de Bourgh.

- The acclaimed 2005 BBC TV miniseries adaptation of Charles Dickens's *Bleak House* (1853), starring Gillian Anderson and Anna Maxwell Martin, has many of the same plot elements as *Jane Eyre*: a downtrodden orphan girl, a grand estate, and a wealthy character with a secret past (in this case, a woman). The story, in part a murder mystery (though other mysteries are revealed as well), is told across fifteen episodes. The film techniques are unusual for a period piece, with fewer long, sweeping camera shots and more fast-paced editing. The series is unrated.

**JANE IS NOT A GODLESS WOMAN; RATHER,
SHE REJECTS THE BLACK-AND-WHITE, BINARY
OPPOSITION OF SPIRIT AND FLESH."**

otherwise. Helen, Mr. Brocklehurst, and St. John all direct Jane toward heaven, and St. John almost succeeds in persuading Jane to become a martyr. Jane, however, struggles with the choice. As Helen points out, she has a "passion for living," which her passion for God does not equal.

Jane stands at the crossroads, having fled Thornfield after deciding she cannot remain with Mr. Rochester because he is a married man. This decision has already been made ("Mr. Rochester, I must leave you," Jane states plainly), so the crossroads represent a different choice. Scenes deleted from the finished film provide a clue to this dilemma. In these scenes, Jane sees Helen (or Helen's spirit), and lies with her on the ground in almost the same position in which Helen passed away. On the day Helen died, she and Jane both lay in their white nightgowns, mirror images of each other. When Jane awakened, they were taken in opposite directions: Helen dead and covered with a sheet, and Jane being carried away, calling Helen's name. Now the spirit of Helen appears to Jane in the same pose, beckoning her to the "region of bliss" where her heartbreak and privation will be over. Jane struggles up from the ground, however, and continues on. She makes it to the home of St. John Rivers.

Just as Helen rescued Jane at Lowood, befriending her and giving her a crust of bread in her darkest hour, St. John takes her in and nurses her back to health. With a name like St. John (one of the most important Christian saints), it is not surprising that Rivers is, like Helen, more concerned with matters of the spirit than of the flesh. The bread of life, the river of life—these are Christian symbols of salvation. It is not known whether Jane was ever baptized, but if not, now she has been brought to the Rivers, where yet another character will preach to her about the region of bliss and its superiority to life on earth.

However, Jane is not designed for a life of the spirit. When St. John entreats her to become his wife and go on a mission to India, she states, "I'm not fit for it." Whereas Jane sees God in nature, St. John has little affinity for the natural world that Jane delights in. And where Mr. Rochester constantly likens Jane to woodland creatures, magical and nonmagical—fairies, birds, elves—St. John pronounces that "God and nature intended you for a missionary's wife. . . . You are formed for labour, not love." One can scarcely imagine a less romantic proposal of marriage. Jane feels that if she goes to India, she will not survive. She sees the mission as a prison sentence (and when she thinks of it, her mind is a "rayless dungeon"). Still, she volunteers to go with St. John as a platonic companion. She fears his disapproval more than she fears the threat to her survival. Jane is finally given a family (in the novel, we learn that St. John is actually Jane's cousin, though the film does not touch on this), and this tie means more to her than the mission to India. When Jane learns that St. John and his sisters are her relations, she exults, "Glorious discovery to a lonely wretch! This was wealth indeed!" St. John, on the other hand, is amused by her excitement, calling the news "a matter of no moment."

Jane's most passionate ties are to the living: people and nature. In the film, Jane's clothing often blends with nature, especially in the scenes where she is running from Thornfield. When she lies on the moors, weeping, she almost disappears; Jane is one with the earth. This runs counter to her religious teachings, however. At Lowood, when Mr. Brocklehurst disapproves of a girl with curled hair, he is told her hair curls naturally; he replies, "Yes, but we are not to conform to nature."

Brontë's father was a clergyman, and she was no doubt well acquainted with what she was, as a Christian woman, supposed to do and feel, according to scripture. But we can hear her warring with herself throughout the story. Even after she makes her decision to leave Mr. Rochester, she continues to muse on the earthly pleasures of the life she might have had. Long after she has left Rochester behind, when she is ensconced in her tiny cottage, she says to herself, "Meantime, let me ask myself one question— Which is better?—To have surrendered to temptation; listened to passion . . . ." And here Jane loses her train of thought in a rapturous

Cary Fukunaga (© *AF archive* / *Alamy*)

description of what life would have been like as Mr. Rochester's mistress, which continues for a paragraph before she catches herself: "But where am I wandering, and what am I saying, and above all, feeling?" When she concludes that she made the right decision, the language is much flatter and sounds as though it is scripted by St. John: "God directed me to a correct choice: I thank His providence for the guidance!"

In an early scene in the film, Jane is made to stand on a chair in front of the other schoolgirls of Lowood and be shunned. The bright sun beams in upon her like a halo; here, Jane looks like a martyr indeed, raised up like Christ upon the cross while others persecute her. However, in the novel we learn that what gives Jane the strength to endure her ordeal is not inspiration from God, but a fellow student who passes by and lifts her eyes to Jane's. "It was as if a martyr, a hero, had passed a slave or victim, and imparted strength in the transit." Jane assigns the role of martyr to another, not to herself. (Fukunaga communicates the same message in the film when, in the very next scene, Jane is still full of anger, while Helen preaches that "life is

too short to nurse animosity.") Similarly, when Mr. Rochester calls Jane an angel, Jane refuses the label. "I am not an angel," she states, "and I will not be one till I die. Mr. Rochester, you must neither expect nor exact anything celestial of me, for you will not get it." In the film, she tells him, "I'm the same, plain kind of bird as all the rest."

Jane's morality stems more from a desire to be at peace with herself, and to respect herself and others, than to please God or to get into heaven. This pragmatic outlook is demonstrated in one of the film's and novel's earliest scenes, when Mr. Brocklehurst asks Jane how she can avoid being condemned to the pit of fire that is hell. Jane answers, "I must keep in good health, and not die." This clear-eyed, honest view of life is something that Brocklehurst hopes to drill out of Jane at Lowood, and St. John sees as a denial of her duty to God. Mr. Rochester, however, tells Jane in the film, "I envy you . . . your openness, your unpolluted mind."

Jane is not a godless woman; rather, she rejects the black-and-white, binary opposition of spirit and flesh. She finds spiritual inspiration in earthly joys. St. John, in contrast, seems impatient for life to be over so that he can gain admittance into heaven; at the close of the novel, he writes to Jane that God is coming for him. His response is, "And hourly I more eagerly respond, 'Amen, even so come, Lord Jesus!'" Jane, however, tells the reader, "I know what it is to live entirely for and with what I love best on earth. I hold myself supremely blest." She has resisted both the loss of her self-respect (by first leaving Mr. Rochester) and St. John's call to martyrdom and, in following her pragmatic, unpolluted mind, has entered her own personal region of bliss.

Source: Laura B. Pryor, Critical Essay on *Jane Eyre*, in *Novels for Students*, Gale, Cengage Learning, 2017.

Chris Tookey

In the following review, Tookey compares the 2011 adaptation unfavorably with earlier versions.

This is the 27th screen version of Charlotte Bronte's classic novel *Jane Eyre*—and, unlike the book, it lacks passion, romance and suspense.

Here, alas, Jane is rather plain.

The film is decently acted, well photographed and sumptuously costumed—but dry, drab and a little dull.

Rather than follow the novel's linear storyline, screenwriter Moira Buffini (who also adapted Tamara Drewe) makes an ill-judged decision to start late on in the narrative, with Jane Eyre (Mia Wasikowska) running away, weeping and traumatised, from Mr Rochester's great house.

This means that much of the film takes place in emotionally distancing flashback.

It also gives away far too early the fact that Jane's romance with Rochester is not going to have a conventionally happy ending.

That, combined with the relentlessly miserable nature of Jane's early years—being orphaned, victimised first by a vicious aunt (Sally Hawkins, playing against type) and then at school (with the ubiquitous Simon McBurney playing the nasty headmaster eager to place her on his 'pedestal of shame')—makes for a dreary first half-hour.

It's only when Jane becomes a governess and is mothered by Mr Rochester's kindly housekeeper (Judi Dench) that the gloom begins to lift.

But then Mr Rochester appears—and he is no fun either.

Michael Fassbender plays him naturalistically, rather than as a broodingly Byronic, scarily Gothic anti-hero.

He is fatally prosaic, and too grouchy to emanate much sex appeal.

In the novel, Jane comes across as a serious-minded, fiercely independent young woman with a talent for teaching.

Wasikowska, almost as stiff as she was in Tim Burton's *Alice In Wonderland*, plays her as starchy and unappealing.

She makes Holly Hunter in *The Piano* look like a party girl.

Her Jane is not that great a catch, and it's hard to see why the two main men in the film—the tediously pious St John Rivers (Jamie Bell) and the rather more worldly Rochester—fall for her.

I felt the latter would be better off with Jane's rival Blanche Ingram (Imogen Poots).

At least she might cheer him up a bit.

Director Cary Fukunaga, 34, doesn't have a new angle on the old story and fails to exploit the suspense of the spooky elements.

The storytelling is sometimes unclear, and we never find out exactly why one visitor is carried off the premises with his throat cut.

And the fact that Jane is uninterested in gaining an explanation makes her seem dim as well as grim.

The novel wowed readers when it came out because it encapsulated the point of view of a new kind of free-spirited, rebellious heroine.

This remake does have its moments—the proposal scene, in particular, is touching—but it gives few hints of why the story is a romantic classic or a landmark in sexual politics.

You'd be better off seeing the Orson Welles version from 1944, or even the one with William Hurt and Charlotte Gainsbourg in 1996.

Neither is perfect, but both come closer to capturing the novel's Gothic grandeur.

This visually arresting but emotionally low-key effort will impress on TV, but on the big screen it needed to be more gripping, passionate and cinematic.

Source: Chris Tookey, "Jane's Too Plain! It Looks Beautiful, but a Starchy Leading Lady and Clumsy Storytelling Make This *Jane Eyre* Dull," in *Daily Mail*, September 8, 2011.

Kate Ellis and E. Ann Kaplan

In the following excerpt, Ellis and Kaplan examine previous film adaptations of the novel through a feminist lens.

Charlotte Brontë's *Jane Eyre* is the story of a woman who understands instinctively the inequities of patriarchal structures but who cannot, finally, move entirely beyond them. Published in 1847 at the height of the Victorian era, the book won immediate popular acclaim, along with some harsh criticism. But it is the intense ambivalence toward male domination on the part of Brontë and her heroine that speaks so strongly to present day feminists, who have claimed Brontë as one of the "foremothers" of the contemporary women's movement. Jane's strength comes to the reader through the clear, strong voice of the first person narrative as she describes her situations: analyzing them, commenting on them, and giving us her thoughts and reactions at every point. Neither the 1944 nor the 1972 film version is ultimately able to retain the centrality of Jane's point of view, though there is, in Stevenson's 1944 version, a voice-over narration that is a very much watered-down version of Brontë's strong diction. This dilution of Jane's rebellious vision has partly to do with the limitations of film form, but mainly it is a result of a reversion on the part of the two directors, Robert Stevenson and Delbert Mann, to accepted patriarchal structures so that Jane is seen, for the most part, from a male point of view.

In allowing Jane to narrate her own story, Brontë allows her heroine the complexity of a double vision. On the one hand, we see Jane chafe against the constrictions and inequities of the patriarchal spaces within which she is placed: Gateshead, Lowood School, Thornfield Hall, and finally Marsh End. She is "thrilled with

ungovernable excitement" as she declares to her aunt, in words very close to those she will later say to Rochester, "You think I have no feelings, and that I can do without one bit of love or kindness; but I cannot live so" (Chapter 4). This declaration will be, in fact, the motif of Jane's life, drawing her away from the Reeds, away from Lowood, toward and then away from Rochester and the ascetic St. John Rivers, until she finally finds, at Ferndean, a love and kindness that do not patronize her. On the other hand, when she discovers that she might have "some poor, low relations called Eyre," she will not leave Gateshead to go to them.

"Not even if they were kind to you?"
I shook my head. I could not see how poor people had the means of being kind; and then to learn to speak like them, to adopt their manners, to be uneducated, to grow up like one of the poor women I saw sometimes nursing their children or washing their clothes at the cottage doors of the village of Gateshead: no, I was not heroic enough to purchase liberty at the price of caste. (Chapter 3)

Again at Lowood, we see Jane raging against the submissiveness of Helen Burns, but also learning from it. When Miss Scratchard pins the word "Slattern" on Helen, Jane tells us:

I ran to Helen, tore it off, and thrust it into the fire: the fury of which she was incapable had been burning in my soul all day, and tears, hot and large, had continually been scalding my cheek; for the spectacle of her sad resignation gave me an intolerable pain at the heart. (Chapter 8)

At the same time she has her first real experience of love and kindness there from Miss Temple and Helen, and this causes her to declare: "I would not now have exchanged Lowood with all its privations, for Gateshead and its daily luxuries." Therefore she stays on there for two years as a teacher (a post she rejects in both film versions) and leaves only when her "motive" for staying is taken away by the marriage and removal of Miss Temple.

Brontë gives us the same juxtaposition of need and contempt in Jane's view of Thornfield. Explaining why she does not want to leave in the wake of her master's purported marriage to Blanche Ingram she says:

I love Thornfield—I love it because I have lived in it a full and delightful life—momentarily at least. I have not been trampled on. I have not been petrified. I have not been buried with inferior minds, and excluded from every glimpse of communion with what is bright and energetic, and high. I have talked, face to face, with what I reverence; with what I delight in—with an original, a vigorous, an expanded mind. (Chapter 23)

But she sees the necessity of leaving, acknowledges that this place that has given her her first real experience of a home is an appropriate setting for the kind of life Rochester will have with Blanche Ingram. But "I would scorn such a union," she says, "therefore I am better than you—let me go!" When Rochester offers her a form of "union" that in her view is just as debased as this one without love, she does scorn it. Finally, she scorns Rivers's offer of marriage based not on mutual affection but on dedication to a higher cause. Jane extricates herself from this temptation, yet it is only because Rivers insists on marriage that she refuses. While she lives under his roof she notices that "I daily wished more to please him: but to do so, I felt daily more and more that I must disown half my nature" (Chapter 34). She sees that she cannot give her body as well as her soul to him, yet she freely consents to go with him as his fellow missionary. Clear-headedly she reasons: "I should suffer often, no doubt, attached to him only in this capacity: my body would be under a rather stringent yoke, but my heart and mind would be free." Yet she is not immune to the attraction of heroic action. It was she, after all, who in her first months at Thornfield looked out at the skyline and "longed for a power of vision that might overpass that limit; which might reach the busy world, towns, regions full of life I had heard of but never seen" (Chapter 12).

The question is: does she relinquish this restless side of her nature when she gives up her independent life and career to care for a blind, dependent man? In some ways, Brontë is simply following the narrative demands of her genre, which imitate the dominant bourgeois code. She brings the lovers safely back together, the woman firmly back in her place caring for the man. Yet Rochester's blindness suggests a fundamental weakness in men that belies the original harsh, invulnerable, controlling exterior that Rochester presents. Ultimately, he is terribly dependent on Jane, needing her more than she, with her newly inherited income, needs him. She, on the other hand, turns out to be the stronger, thus fulfilling the symbolism of their first meeting where she helps him up after a fall from his horse. Yet this strength of hers is little more than the strength that mothers have in caring for their children: one wonders if this was the only alternative model that Brontë had to the traditional "he for God only, she for God in him" paradigm of male-female relationships. That is to say, Brontë offers only the alternative of women feeling subordinate and vulnerable to men, living with them "as sisters" or without them altogether, or undertaking a nurturing, mothering role that gives them all the control. Here we see Brontë's ambivalence toward the institution (as opposed to the experience, to borrow a distinction from Adrienne Rich) of marriage that becomes increasingly unmistakable in her later work. Then again, perhaps she is simply saying that it takes rather drastic events (blindness on the male side, a large inheritance on the female) to equalize, even in a place as far from "society" as Ferndean, the drastic sexual inequalities with which her age presented her.

What is interesting, from our point of view, about the film versions, is the ways in which Stevenson in 1944 and Mann in 1972 liquidate Brontë's ambivalence toward patriarchy. The Stevenson film was made in the post-World War II period when *film noir* was dominant. Having played active roles in the public sphere during the war, women were now being told to go back into their homes and care for their husbands and children. It is thus not surprising to find Joan Fontaine playing a very meek, docile, and submissive Jane in the second half of the film. Interestingly enough, the first half of the film, prior to Orson Welles's appearance as Rochester, sticks close to the novel in showing Jane's rebelliousness and defiance, first toward the Reed family and then at Lowood. Stevenson uses expressionist, nonrealist cinematic techniques to show the monstrosity of the Reed family and the vulnerability of Jane by using high and low angles. Mrs. Reed and John lower over her menacingly, or we see her small, pathetically cooped up, in the Red Room. But Jane fights back against these looming figures, putting up a brave, if pointless, fight. The camera angles thus express some of the Gothic terror that emerges from Brontë's description.

The use of high contrast in this black and white film also brings out the Gothicism of a book in which the room where a man died is filled with secrets and a mad woman is confined to an attic. In this film, as in the novel, a sadistic Mr. Brocklehurst enjoys piling hardships on his pupils in the name of religion, and has no remorse even when Helen Burns (Elizabeth Taylor) dies as a result of harsh rules carried out by an equally unrelenting Miss Scratchard. The one mitigating female presence in the novel, it is important to note, is replaced by an added character, the kindly Dr. Rivers whose name is taken from the novel's stern St. John Rivers who does not appear in the film. Dr. Rivers tries to circumvent Brocklehurst's insane regulations and to explain their danger for the girls. But even though he is a man confronting another man, he is powerless to effect a change. While he comforts Jane, his role is essentially to teach her her place, to beg her to conform, to submit to the will of God. Like the Rivers of the novel, this essentially virtuous male figure sees no possibility for changing the omnipresence of male domination, and he tries to undermine Jane's independent spirit. In the novel it is Miss Temple who objects strongly to the rules and sometimes breaks them. Her warm, nurturing presence offsets the horror of Lowood for Jane. But even more importantly, she provides a powerful model for both Jane and Helen of a principled and intelligent, if ultimately powerless, woman.

One can only speculate on the reasons for a change like this: balancing the hateful Brocklehurst with the kindly Rivers mitigates an absolute condemnation of male authority that might be implied. Rivers is the good father to Jane canceling out the bad one. Yet Brontë had been more interested in Miss Temple as the good mother balancing out Mrs. Reed, the bad one. The film, in removing one side of this balance, represses the mother who in the novel brought about Jane's growth. Male authority is thereby left supreme.

While Jane's point of view is given prominence in the Lowood section of the film, the tension comes from the way it shows male authority trying to silence it. But once Joan Fontaine replaces Peggy Ann Garner, as Jane arrives at Thornfield Hall, the directing consciousness becomes Rochester's, in a complete reversal of the situation in the novel. This is partly because Orson Welles, who plays Rochester, always dominates whatever scene he is in. But it also has to do with the camera work, about which Welles may possibly have had some say. Cinematically, Jane is placed as Rochester's observer: she yearns for him, waits upon him, watches him from the window, the stairwell, a corner of the room, hiding her tears from him behind closed doors. We retain Jane's point of view, but her gaze is fixed on Rochester as object of desire, an odd reversal of the usual situation in film where the male observes the woman as object of desire in such a way that the audience sees her that way too. Interestingly, the reversal of the look does not give Jane any more power: Rochester comes and goes, commands and manages, orders Jane's presence as he wishes. Jane's look is of a yearning, passive kind as against the more usual controlling male look at the woman.

Jane's subordination and passivity are particularly marked in the scenes where Blanche Ingram and Rochester's other guests come to Thornfield. Jane then skulks around with Adele, shot often behind the guests, in the rear of the room, glimpsed behind a door, or through the richly dressed, loud party. Rochester places her in the impossible position of forcing her to be present, and then ignoring her and relegating her to the status of an observer of his love affair with Blanche. Since her voice-over commentary is silent at this point, we do not get her thoughts and analysis or the contempt for the situation that Jane's point of view in the novel so strongly registers. When the pain is intolerable she does of course ask to leave and, as in the novel, thus precipitates the marriage proposal. But overall we see Jane as passive and long-suffering, putting up with this treatment without complaint.

Jane's passivity is heightened by the naturally subservient and self-effacing style of Fontaine the actress. While this manner may have suited her role in Hitchcock's 1940 film *Rebecca*, it is quite unsuitable for Jane. But reinforcing this is the equally natural bombast of Welles, who dominates his co-star in a way that Olivier did not in *Rebecca*. Yet Welles's baroque sensibility is in many ways suited to the Gothic elements in the original novel, and on this score Stevenson's version does much better than the later Mann one, largely due to Welles's influence. While he sometimes overplays his hand in an embarrassing manner—for instance, by the macho riding-off into the snow-swept landscape, storm blowing, and huge mastiff at his side (Jane meanwhile looking on passively from a window with a diminutive Margaret O'Brien as Adele, one sewing, the other painting)—he *has*, caught the tenor of Brontë's image, the swashbuckling

Byronic overtones of her male character. Anachronistic as is the medieval castle that constitutes the set for the Thornfield section, it again fits Brontë's Gothic imagination. And while the film cannot reproduce the symbolism of Bertha in the novel, where she embodies the repressed parts of Jane, in not letting us see her properly, Stevenson surrounds her with mysterious and sinister elements.

The omission of the St. John Rivers sequence in this film seems to fit in with the subordination of Jane's point of view. In the novel, it is through her experiences away from Rochester that Jane learns to be strong and to function effectively on her own. The delay between the romantic passion and its fulfillment enables her to mature and return to Rochester as an equal. Stevenson deals with the necessity of sending Jane somewhere, after she has left the still-married Rochester, by moving forward the brief return to the Reed household that Jane in the novel makes prior to Rochester's proposal. In the novel Jane comes as a result of this visit to pity her former tormentors, and the freedom from them that she thereby acquires is a necessary prelude to her ability to understand and express her feelings about Thornfield and its owner. But in the film Jane falls into the same passive, observing, subordinate role that she had at Thornfield. Dr. Rivers appears again as the emissary between herself and Rochester, and as a storm swirls around her she hears the voice of Rochester that calls her to his side. It is significant, we think, that they meet in the burned shell of the castle, the charred remnants surrounding them menacingly. Welles limps through the ruins but is hardly the mellowed, chastened Rochester (could Welles ever appear chastened?) of Brontë's closing chapters. Their coming together simply represents the typical lovers' reunion, with male and female traditionally placed. Jane is overjoyed to be back with Rochester and he is relieved at her return to take care of him. One has no sense of real change having taken place in either of them.

Delbert Mann's 1972 made-for-television version of *Jane Eyre* makes an interesting contrast to the 1944 film. The dominance of *film noir* as a film form in the postwar period enabled Stevenson to re-create quite effectively some of the Gothic aspects of the novel: *film noir* looked back to expressionism, which in turn drew on the Gothic revival and romanticism for its themes and styles, so that the line from Brontë's novel to 1940s film aesthetics was reasonably direct. On the other hand, the ideology of the same postwar period in relation to women was partly responsible for the omission of Brontë's feminist leanings. But Mann's version, made in the period when the new wave of feminism was in its most exuberant, optimistic phase, humanizes Rochester and Bertha Mason, and removes much of the conflict from the relationship between Rochester (George C. Scott) and Jane (Susannah York). In doing this the characters become much more human and familiar, or at least familiar as film characters. But by the same token, the theme of personal growth through struggle and hard-won self-knowledge, which makes Brontë's novel an important document for feminists still, is swept away in a tide of rich, sensuous images.

To begin with, the lush, colorful photography is completely at odds with the Gothicism of the original. All is bright, colorful, and unmysterious. Mann has a strong feeling for textures as well as colors, and on this level the film appeals strongly. The inmates in Lowood wear uniforms and nightgowns that could have been designed for the pages of *Vogue*. Thornfield is now an elegant mansion fitted out with magnificent eighteenth-century objects, furniture, and a stunning staircase. George C. Scott's Rochester is a humane, sympathetic character: instead of the charismatic, blustering Welles we have a tired, jaded, and aging man worn out by a life of too much easy pleasure, seeking in Jane the freshness of a young, innocent woman. His grief about Bertha is stressed, and to make this convincing, Mann lets us into Bertha's prison after the aborted wedding, as Stevenson did not. A desperate Rochester insists that the priest, Jane, and Bertha's brother Mason follow him to see the wife now preventing his happiness with Jane. Bertha is beautiful but catatonic, in contrast to the violent, "unchaste" creature described in Brontë's novel and implied in Stevenson's film. Rochester sits wearily down beside her and asks what they should do that night, making it clear that it is her incapacity for companionship that has driven him away in despair. His words thus highlight not only his utter loneliness but also her total isolation. Bertha has a strange kind of magnetism, and Rochester's words to Jane that he loved Bertha once as he now loves her give the relationship a compelling dignity. Similarly the separation between Jane and Rochester after the marriage is realistically and touchingly done. We have a sense of two equal people, each determined to press for what he or she wants and thinks is right.

Having omitted the Reed family at the beginning, Mann includes the Marsh End section of the novel, and this enables him to show a different, more charismatic type of man. Black-haired and starkly handsome, Rivers represents a force that Jane must learn to withstand, and it is when she does so that she hears Rochester's mysterious call. The final reunion is extremely real and touching in this version. Rochester is humbled, not expecting anything, and fully supposing her to be married already. When he realizes she wants to stay with a blind, crippled man, his pleasure is quietly expressed in their embrace. Fittingly, the reunion happens not in the Gothic ruin Thornfield but in the peace and quiet of Ferndean, and here Mann is closer to Brontë than Stevenson was, conveying that sense of peace and transcendence with which Brontë ends.

In humanizing Rochester, Mann comes closer to portraying an equal relationship, but the camera still favors Rochester and shows Jane looking up to or being looked down upon by a male observer. Structurally Rochester is still in command, and it is significant that the equality comes not from Jane's rebellion or his questioning intelligence, but simply from the fact that Rochester's weaknesses are on the surface right from the beginning. While Welles made Rochester's anger at Jane's departure come from a defensive wounded pride, Scott makes us see the utter loneliness and loss that Rochester experiences—a loss that seems equal to Jane's in a way that it does not in either Brontë or the Stevenson film. Mann allows us to see more of Rochester's pain than Jane sees (she is not there when he tries to converse with Bertha, for instance) so that we become sensitive to his view of things, which thereby becomes the dominant point of view in the film.

It is worth dwelling a moment on the significance of the humanizing of Rochester in the Mann version in terms of what it does to the original Gothic pattern. The Gothic is premised on the father's being distant, unknown, unapproachable, commanding. Once he is known, his threat diminishes and the premise for Gothic emotions is removed. Patriarchal structures are premised on the mysterious father's defining woman's place for her. Once he is no longer mysterious, once he enters into the structure as a human entity, his power is lost and the woman has room to interact, to enter the sphere from which she has been excluded. Scott's Rochester is thus (to answer Freud's question) what women want: a vulnerable, open, accessible father who is not afraid to reveal his weakness or the depth of his needs. A daughter may not have the same power in the work that a father has, but if they are equal in their need for one another, and can express this equally, then the differences in age and experience (which are the only ones Rochester insisted on in the novel) are not oppressive. The fantasy of "marrying daddy" comes out from behind its Gothic trappings in Mann's film, but it is there in Brontë too, as well as in the innumerable contemporary "drugstore Gothics" on the market today. Behind this gruff, male exterior, it says, lies true love, unable, for the most part, to express itself, but there nevertheless. He may seem distant, dazzled by charms that are beyond your reach, and bound to another, but in fact it is really you that he has loved all along.

A much more blatant departure from the Brontëan Gothic is the fact that Susannah York's Jane is in no way the plain heroine conceived by an author who, Mrs. Gaskell tells us,

> once told her sisters that they were wrong—even morally wrong—in making their heroines beautiful as a matter of course. They replied that it was impossible to make a heroine interesting on any other terms. Her answer was, "I will prove to you that you are wrong; I will show you a heroine as plain and small as myself, who shall be as interesting as any of yours."

Brontë lived in a society that rewarded pretty women but not plain ones; so do we. Fathers have become more casually accessible to their children since the Stevenson movie was made, and certainly since Brontë wrote. And for a brief time in the late 1960s and early 1970s, feminists were caught up in a belief that the world they wanted was right on the horizon: that the fate of pretty women in this culture could be distributed equally, that men could throw down their burdensome defenses, and that age-old struggles could be done away with through a change of consciousness. Fortunately for us now, Charlotte Brontë knew better . . . .

Source: Kate Ellis and E. Ann Kaplan, "Feminism in Brontë's *Jane Eyre* and Its Film Versions," in *Nineteenth-Century Women at the Movies: Adapting Classic Women's Fiction to Film*, edited by Barbara Tepa Lupack, Bowling Green State University Popular Press, 1999, pp. 192–202.

SOURCES

Bradshaw, Peter, Review of *Jane Eyre*, in *Guardian*, September 8, 2011, http://www.theguardian.com/film/2011/sep/08/jane-eyre-film-review (accessed May 4, 2016).

Brontë, Charlotte, *Jane Eyre*, Penguin Classics, 2006.

Davies, Stevie, Introduction to *Jane Eyre*, Penguin Classics, 2006.

Ebert, Roger, Review of *Jane Eyre*, Roger Ebert website, March 16, 2011, http://www.rogerebert.com/reviews/jane-eyre-2011 (accessed May 4, 2016).

Fukunaga, Cary, *Jane Eyre*, Twentieth Century Fox DVD, 2011.

Holtzman, Ellen, "A Home away from Home," in *American Psychological Association*, March 2012, Vol. 43, No. 3, http://www.apa.org/monitor/2012/03/asylums.aspx (accessed May 6, 2016).

Hornaday, Ann, Review of *Jane Eyre,* in *Washington Post*, March 18, 2011, http://www.washingtonpost.com/gog/movies/jane-eyre,1164774.html (accessed May 4, 2016).

"Introduction: UK Christianity 2005–2015," in *Faith Survey*, http://faithsurvey.co.uk/download/csintro.pdf (accessed May 5, 2016).

"*Jane Eyre* (2011)," IMDb, http://www.imdb.com/title/tt1229822/ (accessed May 5, 2016).

Jones, J. R., Review of *Jane Eyre*, in *Chicago Reader*, March 17, 2011, http://www.chicagoreader.com/chicago/jane-eyre-movie-review/Content?oid=3431608 (accessed May 4, 2016).

LaSalle, Mick, Review of *Jane Eyre*, in *San Francisco Chronicle*, March 18, 2011, http://www.sfgate.com/movies/article/Jane-Eyre-review-Hazy-affair-trumps-loneliness-2389003.php (accessed May 4, 2016).

Robey, Tim, Review of *Jane Eyre*, in *Telegraph*, September 8, 2011, http://www.telegraph.co.uk/culture/film/filmreviews/8750162/Jane-Eyre-review.html (accessed May 4, 2016).

Scott, A. O., Review of *Jane Eyre*, in *New York Times*, March 10, 2011, http://www.nytimes.com/2011/03/11/movies/jane-eyre-starring-mia-wasikowska-review.html?_r=0 (accessed May 4, 2016).

FURTHER READING

Chevalier, Tracy, *Reader, I Married Him: Stories Inspired by "Jane Eyre,"* William Morrow Paperbacks, 2016.
This collection includes short stories by more than twenty different modern women authors. All the stories were inspired by the famous line from Brontë's novel "Reader, I married him." Among the celebrated authors contributing stories are Francine Prose, Jane Gardam, Emma Donoghue, and Tracy Chevalier (who also edited the collection).

Faye, Lindsay, *Jane Steele*, G. P. Putnam's Sons, 2016.
In this dark satire based on *Jane Eyre*, Jane suffers the same childhood of hardship and persecution, but she takes revenge by becoming a serial killer, murdering each of her tormentors. Later she returns to her childhood home, now owned by the Rochester-esque Charles Thornfield, to work as a governess. Faye's thriller *The Gods of Gotham* (2012) was nominated for an Edgar Award in 2012 and won the American Library Association's Reading List Award for Best Mystery.

Harman, Claire, *Charlotte Brontë: A Fiery Heart*, Knopf, 2016.
Award-winning literary biographer Harman wrote this new and revealing biography of *Jane Eyre*'s author. Harman tells Charlotte's story in an engaging, almost novelistic fashion, using the author's correspondence as well as autobiographical portions of her fiction to flesh out a complete portrait of the author.

Rhys, Jean, *Wide Sargasso Sea*, W. W. Norton, 1998.
Originally released in 1966, this novel tells another side of *Jane Eyre*; it is the story of Antoinette Cosway (Bertha Mason), Mr. Rochester's mad wife. Antoinette has an unhappy childhood growing up in the Caribbean. Her parents arrange her marriage to an English gentleman, who changes her name to Bertha, takes her from her home, and moves her to England. Her husband, who has learned of her family history of mental illness, sees Bertha's growing depression and paranoia as proof that she is insane, and he locks her away. Author Jean Rhys, like Bertha, was white Creole (a person of European descent born in the Caribbean).

SUGGESTED SEARCH TERMS

Jane Eyre

Charlotte Brontë

Cary Fukunaga

Mia Wasikowska

Michael Fassbender

Jane Eyre AND Cary Fukunaga

Jane Eyre AND feminism

Jane Eyre AND movies

Jane Eyre AND Mia Wasikowska

Brontë AND films

Libra

DON DELILLO

1988

Libra, published in 1988, is a novel by American author Don DeLillo. It tells the story of Lee Harvey Oswald, the man who assassinated President John F. Kennedy in 1963; its account of his life leading up to his murder after the assassination is interwoven with other characters, who play various roles in the plot. It is DeLillo's tenth novel, written in the wake of *White Noise* (1985), his first major commercial success, and became an international best seller. Here, the Kennedy assassination, which is intended to fail, is arranged by rogue CIA agents in order to rekindle US efforts to eradicate communism in Cuba.

Its major themes are best described by DeLillo himself, who called the assassination

> a story about our uncertain grip on the world—a story exploded into life by a homeless man who himself could not grip things tightly and hold them fast, whose soul-scarred loneliness and rage led him to invent an American moment that echoes down the decades.... We seem from that moment to have entered a world of randomness and ambiguity.

Readers should take note that the novel is liberal in its use of profanity and racial epithets; it also contains sexual scenes and depictions of domestic violence.

Don DeLillo *(©Jeff Morgan 06 | Alamy)*

AUTHOR BIOGRAPHY

DeLillo was born on November 20, 1936, in New York City. He was raised in the Bronx by parents who had immigrated from Italy; his father was an insurance company representative, and his mother was a seamstress. To play football, DeLillo and his neighborhood playmates "used to wrap up a bunch of newspaper with tape and use that." As for the household, "There were eleven of us in a small house, but the close quarters were never a problem. I didn't know things any other way."

Childhood reading consisted solely of comic books, and in high school DeLillo "slept for four years." He only discovered a love for literature when he was eighteen.

> I got a summer job as a playground attendant— a parkie.... And this is where I read Faulkner, *As I Lay Dying* and *Light in August*. And got paid for it. And then James Joyce, and it was through Joyce that I learned to see something in language that carried a radiance.

At Fordham College, however, he "didn't study much of anything. I majored in something called communication arts." Following this he took a job as a copywriter at an ad agency, which he quit after five years at the age of twenty-eight "because I wanted to write novels. One morning I woke up and thought: Today I'm quitting." This was in 1965. DeLillo, living in a "small apartment with no stove and a refrigerator in the bathroom," scraped by on savings and freelance copywriting to write his first novel, *Americana*, which was published in 1971.

From 1972 to 1982 DeLillo published seven more novels, a testament both to his work ethic and the respect his work earned from critics; nonetheless, he remained relatively unknown, even when, after receiving a Guggenheim Fellowship, he published *The Names* (the last of those novels) to positive reviews. His next novel, *White Noise*, a darkly comic cultural critique, won him a National Book Award for Fiction; it was both a critical and commercial success and marked the beginning of DeLillo's career as a well-known and widely respected writer. Subsequent work elevated him to the ranks of great American authors. *Libra*, his next novel, was a finalist for the National Book Award; *Mao II*, published in 1991, earned him a PEN/Faulkner Award and a Pulitzer Prize nomination; and *Underworld*, a novel about the Cold War that appeared in 1997, won seven major literary awards. Since then DeLillo has published the novels *Cosmopolis* and *Zero K*, among others. Other work from across his career includes numerous short stories, stage plays, screenplays, and essays.

PLOT SUMMARY

Chapter 1, or In the Bronx
Lee Harvey Oswald, a seventh-grader, rides the subway across New York, aimlessly and for pleasure. Back in their apartment his mother, Marguerite, recalls her sufferings over the years and quarrels with him about his truancies. Later, at the zoo, two classmates harass him; they are all stopped by a truant officer, and Lee is committed to a juvenile detention center. His mother muses obsessively about both her son and her past miseries. The chapter ends with Oswald's returning to the subway for solace after his release.

Chapter 2, or 17 April

Nicholas Branch, a retired senior analyst for the CIA, has been hired to write the secret history of the assassination of President Kennedy. In his office, crammed with thousands of files, books, photographs, and other documents, he enters a date on his computer: April 17, 1963.

The chapter flashes back to that date and the home of Walter Everett Jr., another CIA officer. Everett helped plan the US invasion of Cuba at the Bay of Pigs two years earlier. The invasion's failure meant his downfall in the agency, and he has been punished with a job teaching at a women's college in Texas. He meets with a former colleague, Laurence Parmenter, who planned the invasion with him, and T-Jay Mackey, a veteran of the invasion itself. Everett proposes an attempt on the life of President Kennedy, to be attributed to Cuba, which will galvanize the United States to act against Cuba once and for all.

Mackey contacts the office of Guy Banister, an ex-FBI agent and current detective in New Orleans; Banister can supply the plotters with the arms they need. David Ferrie, a pilot and pedophile with ties to the anti-Castro movement, answers the phone, but Mackey hangs up. Parmenter mulls over the plot while Everett and his wife settle in for the night.

Chapter 3, or In New Orleans

The story flashes back to Oswald, now a high school student in New Orleans, where he educates himself about communism. At home his strained relationship with his mother continues. He and a classmate, Robert Sproul, argue amiably about his politics; when Oswald makes plans to join the Marines, he and Robert meet with Ferrie to buy a rifle from him. Ferrie's odd behavior unnerves both of them, but Oswald buys the rifle. The chapter ends with another of his mother's litanies of woe while Oswald continues his self-education.

Chapter 4, or 26 April

Everett plans to invent a person on whom the assassination attempt will be blamed. Meanwhile Parmenter meets with George de Mohrenschildt, a Russian expat and freelance intelligence agent. De Mohrenschildt laments the US stance toward Cuba. Someone has recently shot at General Walker, an ultraconservative enemy of Cuba; de Mohrenschildt says he

knows the gunman, a young Marxist, and Parmenter inwardly enjoys the "vast and rhythmic coincidence" of the conspiracy's need for just such a person.

The novel flashes forward to Branch and his secret history as he dwells on suspicious deaths linked to the assassination, among them Ferrie's and de Mohrenschildt's.

The novel flashes back to Mackey, who meets with Banister. They discuss procuring a pilot (Ferrie) and rifles. Ferrie arrives to describe available weapons and piloting details. Later, Mackey remembers landing on shore with guerrillas at the outset of the Bay of Pigs invasion and broods over their subsequent executions by Castro.

Parmenter calls Everett to tell him about Oswald as a potential shooter. Later that night Everett thinks of clues for investigators to find after the assassination attempt.

Chapter 5, or In Atsugi

The story flashes back to Oswald, now a Marine stationed in Japan. A fellow Marine arranges for him to lose his virginity to Mitsuko, a prostitute in Tokyo; through her he meets Konno, a Japanese leftist. The two men discover their mutual interest in communism, and Oswald reveals his knowledge about the newly developed U-2, a reconnaissance aircraft.

Oswald shoots himself in the arm to avoid having to ship out from Japan and claims it was an accident, but his deception is obvious, and he is confined to a military prison. His cellmate, a black Marine named Bobby Dupard, is consistently beaten by guards for his casual misconduct. Oswald, too, is beaten, by a malevolent guard who quizzes him on minute details from rule books.

After his release, Konno introduces Oswald to Dr. Braunfels, a German teacher at Tokyo University who also works for the Soviet Union. He shares his military knowledge with her and says he wants to go to the USSR, but she discourages him.

The chapter ends with a U-2 pilot crash-landing somewhere in the Urals.

Chapter 6, or 20 May

Parmenter and Mackey discuss Oswald and details about the planned assassination attempt. Mackey later meets with Ramon Benitez and

Frank Vásquez, Cuban exiles and Bay of Pigs veterans, and hires them as additional shooters. He does not tell them that the target is Kennedy or that they are supposed to miss. That evening Parmenter reflects on his life and work for the CIA.

Oswald, by another strange coincidence, walks into Banister's office that day looking for work as an undercover detective.

Chapter 7, or In Fort Worth

The story flashes back to Marguerite Oswald, who is thinking about her son as if defending him before a court. Meanwhile, Oswald, who is still in the Marines, plans to travel to the USSR after he leaves active duty.

Chapter 8, or 19 June

Everett discusses Oswald with Parmenter. They marvel at how exactly he matches their needs and at the coincidence of his arrival at Banister's office looking for work. Everett plans the fabrication of news stories and government memos.

Banister drinks at a bar and broods about US failures abroad and civil rights victories at home. Back at the office his secretary complains to him about Oswald, who keeps pro-Cuba flyers in the room he is renting from them.

Wayne Elko, a former soldier of fortune who once trained Cuban guerrillas in preparation for the Bay of Pigs, now homeless and drifting, contacts Mackey looking for work.

In his basement, Everett assembles the details of a false life for Oswald, forging cards, address books, and so forth.

Chapter 9, or In Moscow

The story flashes back to Oswald's arrival in Russia. Stymied by Russian bureaucracy in his attempts to extend his visa, he cuts his wrist and is taken to a hospital. Later he is visited by Alexei Kirilenko, a KGB officer who questions him about his motives and befriends him. He shares with Kirilenko everything he can recall about the U-2 plane and other military details, but Kirilenko knows he is too unstable to work for the USSR as an agent. Oswald is sent to live in Minsk.

Chapter 10, or 2 July

Ferrie meets with underworld billionaire Carmine Latta and his bodyguard, Tony Astorina. The three men discuss Cuba, where Latta hopes

to make use of gambling concessions post-Castro. Astorina hands Ferrie a duffel bag full of cash to finance the conspiracy.

Benitez and Vásquez meet with Elko in Florida and tell him to bide his time until Mackey gets in touch with him. Elko reminisces with them about his work training anti-Castro guerrillas.

Everett, after Mackey searches Oswald's apartment, realizes that Oswald has already done his work for him: he has different aliases, weapons, and leftist literature everywhere.

The story flashes forward to Branch, hopelessly surveying piles of documents. He reflects further on suspicious deaths, including Vásquez's and Banister's.

The story then flashes back to Vásquez and Benitez at a softball game, reminiscing about the Bay of Pigs. Both men originally fought for and not against Castro; Benitez, in particular, cannot forget Castro's betrayal of the revolution.

Chapter 11, or In Minsk

The novel flashes back to Oswald, living in Minsk when the U-2 pilot crash-lands. The pilot is interrogated by the KGB about U-2 technology; Kirilenko summons Oswald to confirm the truth of the pilot's testimony. Oswald is beginning to chafe at his regimented life in the Soviet Union.

His mother, meanwhile, contacts the State Department to tell them that her son is in Russia.

Oswald begins dating a young woman named Marina. Two weeks after the Bay of Pigs invasion, they marry. Oswald's dissatisfaction with life there grows: he suspects he is being spied on, his university application is rejected, and his efforts to write about Russia are hampered by his own ineptitude. He persuades Marina, who is now pregnant, to move to America with him.

Chapter 12, or 15 July

Mackey distrusts everyone in on the conspiracy except Everett and dislikes Everett's plan: he has decided that the assassination should be successful. He meets with Elko in Florida; he doesn't trust Elko either, because of the man's violent temper, but enlists him as a short-range shooter (to kill Oswald after the assassination).

Chapter 13, or In Fort Worth

The novel flashes back to Marina and Oswald, who now live in Dallas. Marguerite visits them, discomfiting Oswald; they quarrel, subsequent visits increase his frustration, and when Marina defends his mother, Oswald strikes her.

The FBI visits him and asks if he will become an informer.

At a dinner with émigrés from the USSR, Oswald meets de Mohrenschildt; the Russian sympathizes with his liberal views but encourages him to visit a CIA agent, Marion Collings.

Back home Oswald beats Marina for confiding to her Russian friends about his rough treatment of her. Meanwhile, working as a house cleaner, Marguerite mentally prepares a defense, long and rambling, of her son.

Oswald finally meets with Collings, who encourages him to apply for a position at a graphic arts firm with ties to the CIA.

Chapter 14, or 12 August

Baby LeGrand, a stripper at a club owned by Jack Ruby, discusses his behavior with another stripper. When Ruby (carrying thousands in cash, a revolver, and stimulants) arrives, she confronts him about unfair pay. Then he receives a visit from mob investment counselor Jack Karlinsky about paying back money he owes to Carmine Latta.

Parmenter and his wife discuss Cuba; she is skeptical of US policy toward the island. Everett calls with concerns about Mackey's whereabouts.

Ruby pursues and beats a man who groped one of his strippers. Then he brings sandwiches to the local police station in appreciation for the officers' service.

Chapter 15, or In Dallas

The story flashes back to a laundromat where Oswald runs into Bobby Dupard, his cellmate in the brig at Atsugi. They catch up on each other's lives, talking until 2 a.m. They meet several more times; after a lengthy discussion on politics, race, and Cuba, they decide to assassinate General Walker, a racist and anti-Cuban conservative. They plan carefully, but things go awry, and when the time comes, Oswald misses.

Marina, meanwhile, is pregnant with their second child, and Oswald has been fired from his job when de Mohrenschildt pays them a visit, attempting to joke about the near miss.

Chapter 16, or 6 September

Elko, Ferrie, Benitez, and Oswald are target practicing at a camp in the bayous. They trade stories about prison; Benitez recalls amusing details about the aftermath of the Bay of Pigs. Vásquez, meanwhile, has been with Alpha 66, an anti-Castro paramilitary group training in the Everglades, and has deduced that they want to kill Kennedy. They want to recruit Mackey for help.

The story flashes forward to Branch, who is receiving still more documents from his superiors: memos about the president's brain, ballistics tests carried out on goat carcasses, and so on. He muses about the various identities adopted by people linked to the assassination.

The story flashes back to Vásquez, who confronts Mackey about Alpha 66's intention to kill Kennedy. Mackey admits that this is his plan as well. Later he thinks about the dangerous number of groups involved now, and the importance of safeguarding the attempt; he decides to tell Everett about Alpha 66.

Chapter 17, or In New Orleans

The story flashes back to Oswald, who has returned to New Orleans with his family. One day he is approached by an FBI agent. The agent wants Oswald to pose as a Castro hater and work at Banister's office, an unofficial headquarters for local anti-Castro groups, so the government can monitor those groups. He is to tell Banister he wants to infiltrate leftist organizations.

At the office he meets Ferrie; the two recognize each other from Oswald's gun purchase seven years earlier. He and Ferrie go out for a drink and meet Clay Shaw, who tells Oswald about his astrological sign, Libra. Ferrie reveals to him that the group has been investigating him and lets Oswald in on the existence, but not the details, of the conspiracy, telling him that he matches an identity the plotters have been struggling to create. After this exchange Ferrie and a woman named Linda Frenchette take Oswald for a ride and smoke hashish with him; Linda and Oswald have a brief sexual encounter in the car.

The novel's two narrative time lines meet as Oswald begins target practice at the remote Louisiana camp with Elko, Ferrie, Benitez, and Mackey. Back in New Orleans Ferrie brings up Kennedy's name in relation to the plot. Oswald begins to suffer extreme anxiety and decides to flee to Mexico and from there to Cuba.

He says goodbye to Marina, but at the bus station Ferrie appears and persuades him to return with him to his apartment. Here, at last, he tells Oswald that he is to kill the president.

Chapter 18, or 25 September
Ferrie attempts to force himself sexually on Oswald; afterward, Oswald tells him of his continued intention to go to Mexico City.

Jack Ruby, taking stimulants off and on throughout the day, struggles to resolve his financial difficulties. Tony Astorina pays him a visit about his loan from Carmine Latta, after which Ruby makes a series of frantic calls to shore up his businesses.

Banister is visited by Ferrie, who tells him Oswald has fled for Mexico but that Mackey can arrange for Cuban officials to deny him entry. Banister tells Ferrie that Mackey is in Miami setting up two camps, one for Alpha 66 and one for his own team, and that there will be multiple shooters on the day of the assassination.

Chapter 19, or In Mexico City
Oswald's efforts to get to Cuba from Mexico City are blocked at every turn. In a restaurant, he spots someone watching him and suspects that it is Mackey. The next day he returns to the United States.

Chapter 20, or 4 October
Everett frets over his wife's health, she worries about their daughter's odd manner, and he is particularly unnerved that the president's tour will take him to Dallas after Miami ("The plot coming to the plotter"). He fantasizes about confessing the conspiracy to the CIA and being forgiven.

Mackey and Benitez have discovered yet another group planning to kill the president; they also discuss Oswald's return to the United States and his expendability, since they have all the paper trails and false leads they need to create "our own model Oswald."

The chapter closes with Everett's daughter, Suzanne, arranging little figurines near her bed for protection "in case the people who called themselves her mother and father were really somebody else."

Chapter 21, or In Dallas
Oswald finds work at the Texas School Book Depository. He has a growing sense that his life is governed by conspiracy and is out of his control; he also receives a third visit from the FBI and learns that the president is coming to Dallas in late November.

The story flashes forward to Branch, uncovering details about the conspiracy. He has found evidence of Oswald lookalikes across Dallas in the days prior to the assassination and thinks of yet more suspicious deaths, including those of Everett and Elko.

The story flashes back to Elko, Benitez, and Vásquez, who are traveling to Dallas. En route, Benitez tells Elko he wants to euthanize his aged dog, who is in the car with them; Elko cuts the dog's throat with a knife.

Ferrie pays Oswald a visit, exclaiming about the strange coincidence that the president's motorcade will pass directly under the window where Oswald works. Mackey meets Oswald not long after, goes over the details of the shooting, and tells him to flee to a movie theater when the deed is done.

In the morning Marina wakes up to find Oswald gone, having left her all of his money.

Chapter 22, or 22 November
The president's motorcade arrives in Dallas. Oswald is in the book depository. When the motorcade appears, he fires and hits the president in the neck; he fires again and wounds Governor Connally, sitting near the president. Meanwhile, Vásquez has driven himself and Benitez to another location, where Benitez has positioned himself with a rifle and witnesses Oswald's errors. He fires and hits the president in the head; Oswald was ready to fire a third time himself, sees the killing shot through his scope, and realizes that he has been duped.

As other passengers in the car react to the shooting, Oswald escapes from the book depository and makes his way toward the movie theater. A police officer stops him, and he kills the officer with a .38 before going on his way.

Elko is waiting for him in the theater with a gun when Oswald arrives; before he can kill him, police officers raid the theater and arrest Oswald. Elko decides to watch the rest of the movie.

In his jail cell, Oswald recognizes the full horror of his position and decides to confess that he was not a lone gunman and that he's been set up.

Chapter 23, or In Dallas

The next day Ruby, vomiting with emotion and obsessing about Oswald, drives across Dallas in a delusional state looking for signs of a conspiracy. Oswald, meanwhile, is visited in jail by his mother and subjected to her complaints. Marina visits him too. After their departure he considers claiming he was, in fact, the lone assassin, for the fame such a claim would bring him.

Ferrie, meanwhile, is in Galveston, driving in circles and panicking. Banister assures him that there is a plan in the works to resolve everything.

Jack Karlinsky visits Ruby, further inflames him with a discussion about anti-Semitism, and tells him that his debt to Latta will be forgiven if he kills Oswald. Oswald, meanwhile, sits in his cell, imagining a life sentence during which he will be free to write and educate himself. The next morning Ruby takes a stimulant, pays one of his strippers, and drives to the jail; as Oswald is being led out, Ruby shoots him in the stomach.

The novel flashes forward to Branch, who, as more and more material arrives from his superiors at the CIA, wonders what the agency might be hiding. He indulges in one last roll call of the dead: Baby LeGrand, Dupard, and Jack Ruby, who goes insane while awaiting retrial for Oswald's murder.

In a flashback, Parmenter's wife watches the news of Oswald's murder and weeps.

Chapter 24, or 25 November

The novel closes with an extended internal monologue on the part of Oswald's mother, which mingles her pain at his life and death with fond remembrances and her characteristic self-pity.

CHARACTERS

Tony Astorina

Astorina is crime boss Carmine Latta's bodyguard.

Guy Banister

Banister, once an FBI agent, operates a private detective agency in New Orleans. He is described as "a tough and somber man in his sixties.... His hatred had a size to it, a physical force." Banister once shipped weapons and funneled money to anti-Castro forces; he keeps extensive files on both left- and right-wing groups in Louisiana, has published a white supremacist magazine, is obsessed with Cuba, and maintains a compound full of firearms. "Everyday lawful pursuits don't meet our special requirements," he says to a CIA operative. His role is to provide weapons and logistical help to the plotters.

Ramon "Raymo" Benitez

Benitez is a Cuban exile who originally fought for Castro, then changed sides. Benitez fired the first shots at the Bay of Pigs invasion; he is animated by a profound sense of personal betrayal at Castro's postrevolution policies and use of repression and torture. He fires the shot that kills President Kennedy.

Nicky Black

Nicky is a schoolmate of Oswald's in New York who bullies him.

Nicholas Branch

Branch, a retired senior analyst at the CIA, appears throughout the novel long after the assassination. He has devoted himself to assembling a library of documents and files related to the assassination, and this library has become almost maze-like in its complexity: endless, self-reflective, full of dead ends and circles. It contains everything from the complete "Warren Report, of course, with its twenty-six accompanying volumes of testimony and exhibits, its millions of words," to a microphotograph of three strands of Oswald's pubic hair.

Dr. Braunfels

Braunfels, a German teaching at Tokyo University, also works for the USSR and recruits Oswald while he is stationed in Japan as a Marine.

Bushnell

Bushnell is a radarman who finds Oswald just after he has shot himself in the arm. He mercilessly mocks and badgers the wounded Oswald for several pages about the futility of making the shooting look like an accident and the legal trouble he will be in as a result.

Marion Collings

Collings is a CIA agent to whom de Mohrenschildt introduces Oswald. He promises Oswald a job at a graphic arts firm that makes maps for the CIA; in return, Oswald must cooperate with the agency and describe the details of his three-year stay in the USSR.

Delphine

Delphine is Banister's secretary.

Bobby Dupard

Oswald's cellmate in military detention, soft-spoken but resentful of his treatment, Dupard is quietly, calmly transgressive and is beaten repeatedly by guards for it. After a chance reunion four years later in Dallas, he and Oswald decide to assassinate General Walker, an ultra-conservative racist who at the time was demanding that communism be eliminated from Cuba by military force.

Wayne Elko

Elko is an out-of-work pool cleaner, former soldier of fortune, criminal, and drifter. He was once a soldier with Interpen, a group that trained anti-Castro guerrillas in Florida and Louisiana. Elko has an instinct for violence and is easily offended. He calls Mackey looking for work and is brought into the conspiracy. Elko's role is to kill Oswald after the assassination attempt so that the plot is never revealed, but police arrest him before Elko can act.

Mary Frances Everett

Mary Frances is Win Everett's wife.

Suzanne Everett

Suzanne is Win and Mary Francis Everett's daughter.

Walter (Win) Everett

Everett, a CIA officer in disgrace with the CIA over the Bay of Pigs, was a chief member of the group responsible for its creation and planning. The agency has punished him for the invasion's failure by forcing him into an undignified post as a teacher of history and economics at Texas Women's University. He loves his wife and his country, but his bitterness, rage, and pride, combined with his background in intelligence, have made him an extremely dangerous man. "The more people who believed as he did, the less pure his anger. The country was noisy with fools who demeaned his anger." Everett is the architect of *Libra*'s assassination plot; he develops the idea of creating a persona, a fictive pro-Castro assassin, who can be blamed for the attempt on Kennedy's life, thereby setting the stage for a US-led end to communist Cuba once and for all. Oswald happens to be exactly the persona he had in mind.

David Ferrie

As a pilot and instructor in the Civil Air Patrol, Ferrie once commanded the very unit Oswald and Robert Sproul are enrolled in as high school students, and he sells the young Oswald a rifle for fifteen dollars, a chance encounter years prior to Oswald's entanglement in the assassination plot. Ferrie's peculiar appearance, demeanor, and pedophilia make him an object of distaste for some, but his piloting skills, general intelligence, and longtime involvement in the anti-Castro movement are of value to the plotters. Ferrie has "studied psychology through the mail with Italian masters" and has "devised a theology based on militant anticommunism. He was a sometime master of hypnotism. He studied languages, studied political theory, knew diseases intimately." He is emblematic of the mix of chaos, coincidence, and deliberation that moves *Libra* forward.

Dale Fitzke

Fitzke is a fellow intern at the CIA-affiliated graphic arts firm where Oswald finds employment.

Linda Frenchette

Frenchette is a "bar girl" enlisted by Ferrie to have a brief sexual encounter with Oswald in the back of Ferrie's car after he urges Oswald to assassinate Kennedy.

Guard at Atsugi

Nameless and menacing, the guard tests Oswald and a fellow Marine on their knowledge of rules and codes of behavior. He beats them when they fail, and he beats them when they succeed.

Jack Karlinsky

Karlinsky, an "investment counselor" with a twenty-room mansion on the Texas coast, works for crime boss Carmine Latta, to whom Jack Ruby owes a substantial amount of money. He acts as an intermediary between the two. After the assassination, Karlinsky tells Ruby that the loan will be forgiven if he kills Oswald.

Alexei Kirilenko

Kirilenko, a KGB officer, is Oswald's sole source of friendship in the USSR. Kirilenko is fond of Oswald but aware of the young man's deficiencies and potential lack of value to Russia.

Konno

Konno is a Japanese leftist whom Oswald meets through Mitsuko, a prostitute, while stationed in Japan as a Marine. He introduces Oswald to Dr. Braunfels.

Carmine Latta

Latta, "frail and spotted, with the drawn and thievish look of a figure in a ducal portrait," is a figure in the Louisiana underworld with connections around the hemisphere. Latta owns slot machines, prostitution, and drug-trafficking rings; a shrimp fleet; motels; banks; tour buses; vending machines; and more. He detests the Kennedys. A billionaire, Latta provides money to the plotters to purchase arms for anti-Castro groups so that he can get gambling concessions in Cuba when Castro falls.

Baby LeGrand

LeGrand is a stripper working for Jack Ruby in Dallas.

T-Jay Mackey

Mackey, a veteran field officer in the CIA who trained Cuban exiles in assault weapons and supervised early phases of the landings at the Bay of Pigs, is venerated by many Cuban members of the failed invasion. He has also trained rebels in Sumatra and elsewhere for the agency. For refusing to sign a letter of reprimand following the failed invasion of the Bay of Pigs, he has been demoted to training new CIA recruits in light weapons. He puts the group in touch with Guy Banister for weapons and with Ramon Benitez as a shooter. He also decides that Everett's plan to deliberately miss Kennedy "lacked the full heat of feeling" and that an actual assassination would be better. He hires Wayne Elko to kill Oswald after the assassination attempt.

Mitsuko

Mitsuko is a prostitute in Tokyo and fan of the game of pachinko.

George de Mohrenschildt

De Mohrenschildt, Russian expat and freelance intelligence agent, meets Oswald and brings him to Parmenter's attention. "It was part of George's attractiveness that he continually emerged from a different past," involving Nazis, Polish and French intelligence, and the Soviets. He knows the Kennedys, is a baron and a petroleum engineer, and commands a bird's-eye view of the world and its inner workings.

Lee Harvey Oswald

Oswald is the main character of the novel, which derives its title from his astrological sign. His life is one long struggle for autonomy and a pursuit of something huge and worthwhile, to erase his embarrassingly humble and anonymous background; all of these efforts fail. Others see him as unpredictable but potentially useful, suited (but not particularly well) to the role of a dupe. A KGB officer perceives him as

> some kind of Chaplinesque figure, skating along the edges of vast and dangerous events. Unknowing, partly knowing, knowing but not saying, the boy had a quality of trailing chaos behind him, causing disasters without seeing them happen, making riddles of his life and possibly fools of us all.

The gulf between his dreams and ambitions on one hand and people's perceptions of him on the other gives his life pathos and ultimately destroys it.

Marguerite Oswald

Oswald's mother has lived a life marked by struggle and disappointment. Her love for Oswald is smothering and further flawed by endless complaint and her sense of victimhood. DeLillo writes interior monologues in her voice, which capture her pettiness, self-pity, and obsessive nature; her final monologue ends the book and gives her a kind of dignity.

Marina Oswald

Oswald's Russian wife emigrates from the USSR to America with him. She was born out of wedlock and is an orphan. Their marriage, initially happy and full of promise, is marked by abuse and unhappiness in America.

Beryl Parmenter

Beryl is Larry Parmenter's charismatic wife.

Laurence Parmenter

Educated and worldly, Parmenter, like Everett, was one of the chief planners of the Bay of Pigs invasion. A longtime CIA operative, he also engineered the downfall of Guatemala's government by creating the illusion of an imminent invasion. Over dinner with de Mohrenschildt, Parmenter learns about Oswald and brings the young man to the attention of his fellow conspirators. He has long since given up any pretenses to genuine certainty about the world:

> He believed that nothing can be finally known that involves human motive and need. There is always another level, another secret, a way in which the heart breeds a deception so mysterious and complex it can only be taken for a deeper kind of truth.

Francis Gary Powers

Powers is a U2 pilot who crash-lands in the USSR. Oswald observes his interrogation by the KGB and is asked afterward to verify the truth or falsehood of Powers's replies.

Donald Reitmeyer

Reitmeyer is a Marine stationed in Tokyo with Oswald; though Reitmeyer is easily provoked by Oswald's atheism and politics, the two men have an easy camaraderie.

Jack Ruby

Temperamental, outraged by communism and Castro, almost pathologically patriotic, and addicted to Preludin (a stimulant), Ruby is a financially struggling owner of strip clubs in Dallas. On his second appearance in *Libra* he and his cohorts beat a man who groped one his strippers; Ruby pursues him for half a block to continue beating him, then brings a dozen sandwiches to a local police station to express his appreciation for the officers' service. He is deeply in debt to underworld billionaire Carmine Latta. Jack Karlinsky tells Ruby at the novel's end that his debts will be forgiven if he kills Oswald; already in a white rage over the assassination, Ruby approaches Oswald the next day and shoots him.

Scalzo

Scalzo is a schoolmate of Oswald's in New York who bullies him.

Clay Shaw

Shaw is visited one day by Ferrie and Oswald and tells the young man about his astrological sign.

Robert Sproul

Sproul, a high school classmate of Oswald's in New Orleans, is the only person the teenage Oswald fraternizes with. Together they visit David Ferrie to purchase a rifle.

Frank Vásquez

Like Benitez, Vásquez is a Cuban exile who originally fought for Castro, then changed sides. He drives his compatriot to the site from which Benitez fires the shot that kills Kennedy.

Ted Walker

Known as General Walker, a retired general and ultraconservative, race-baiter, and anticommunist. Oswald shoots at him but misses.

THEMES

Disempowerment

Among *Libra*'s many themes is disempowerment. Almost everyone in this novel, from the least significant to the ones who seemingly pull all the strings, is fundamentally without power or autonomy.

This theme is most evident in the figure of Oswald himself, whose pathos derives from his desire, eternally frustrated, to have control over his destiny. His other great desire is to play an important role in history, which he can do only as a pawn. Increasingly as the novel moves forward he finds himself blocked at every turn: he winds up in the brig at the mercy of sadistic guards, his life in the USSR is totally regimented, the conspirators stop him from fleeing to Cuba, and so on. His greatest sense of freedom, in a supreme irony, is as a twelve-year-old rider on the New York subway system, going wherever it takes him. The only practical effect of his efforts to exert power in his life is to be consistently fired from one job after another.

His fellow characters are scarcely better off. Everett, Parmenter, and Mackey, adept as they are at manipulating events, still live at the mercy of the CIA, which demotes them for their errors and which they still feel bound to, and much of the conspiracy develops beyond their control anyway. Benitez, Vásquez, Elko, and other lesser conspirators act at the behest of the more powerful or face grinding poverty and homelessness. Ferrie at least faces his own submission to systems of power with good cheer, but only by virtue of being somewhat insane. Of course, as

TOPICS FOR FURTHER STUDY

- The assassination of President John F. Kennedy spawned a vast number of conspiracy theories; there are countless more about other elements of American history. Research the underlying meaning of conspiracy theories—their nature, causes, and importance for contemporary America. Include a PowerPoint presentation of evidence (photographs, film stills, etc.) about the assassination; use this presentation to discuss the strengths and weaknesses of the conspiracy theorists' use of the evidence.

- Write an essay in which you research Cuban American relations and what they have meant for the Cuban community, both in Cuba and in American exile; describe the differences between these two communities. There is a long and complex history between the countries, predating Fidel Castro's revolution, so be sure to include this as well as the latest efforts toward normalization on both sides.

- Write an essay in which you compare and contrast the fictional Oswald of *Libra* with the real-life figure. How well did DeLillo capture his nature and likely motives? Was anything left out, or, conversely, was anything added that doesn't seem to fit?

- Invent your own conspiracy theory about a current event in America, whether political or social. Use the available direct evidence but feel free to use circumstantial evidence as well. Once you have made your argument for a conspiracy in an oral presentation, add a refutation, describing the theory's weak points.

- Read *The Tyrant's Daughter*, by J. C. Carleson (a former undercover CIA officer). In this novel, Laila, the daughter of an assassinated Middle East dictator, has fled with her family to America; there she must strike a delicate balance between school life, her mother's schemes for revenge and a return to power, and contacts with the CIA and rebel factions. Write a paper comparing Laila and Oswald, focusing on the ways they respond to conspiracy in their lives and their struggles for independence.

Branch observes, most of them meet suspiciously untimely ends.

DeLillo saves the most tragic expression of disempowerment for the novel's last lines. Oswald's mother, a veritable mascot of victimhood, has just unleashed a stream-of-consciousness barrage of love and pain over the death of her son:

> No matter what happened, how hard they schemed against her, this was the one thing they could not take away—the true and lasting power of his name. It belonged to her now, and to history.

Oswald's fight for agency is over; in death, he is owned more than ever by others. .

Conspiracy

A twin theme, and a consistent one in DeLillo's fiction, is conspiracy. Born from powerlessness or a desire for power, conspiracies have a tendency to develop beyond the control of the people who design them. "Plots," Everett realizes, "carry their own logic. There is a tendency of plots to move toward death....He had a foreboding that the plot would move to a limit."

Their insidious nature is most clear to those individuals who are thoroughly enmeshed in them. Coincidences begin multiplying in an ominous way: Oswald, back in America after finding his escape to Cuba inexplicably blocked, watches

Branch is given the task of reconstructing the events of the assassination with information in the CIA archive *(©Garsya / Shutterstock.com)*

two movies in a row on TV, both about the assassinations of political leaders. Ferrie remarks on this phenomenon excitedly: "We don't have that kind of reach or power. There's something else that's generating this event. A pattern outside experience."

These patterns, man-made or not, are camouflaged by the randomness of life, most notably in the office where Nicholas Branch struggles to write about the assassination. The documents piling up ever higher seem to contain a sort of "ruined city of trivia" and a "mind-spatter"; at one point "the Curator sends a special FBI report that includes detailed descriptions of the *dreams* of eyewitnesses following the assassination." But Branch discerns enough connections to uncover the existence of the plot; it is suggested that numberless other plots are hidden in the documents as well.

Linked to this theme is the subtheme of deception, employed by virtually every major character and most of the minor ones. Whether used by reflex, in self-defense, or as a weapon, an inherently deceptive nature seems to move people toward or force them to look for conspiracy.

STYLE

Structure

Libra is structured in three distinct layers: a time vaguely in the present, when Nicholas Branch attempts to write his secret history; the year 1963 from April to November, from the hatching of the plot by Everett and his cohorts to Oswald's taking the fall for the assassination; and Oswald's life from 1952 to his death in Dallas. It is a complex structure, with flashes forward and backward within almost every chapter as Oswald's life draws ever closer to the conspiracy, and demands an attentive reading.

Point of View

Much of the novel's force comes from its alternating points of view. The narrative moves from Oswald, forever in the dark, to Everett and the others, whose perspectives are significantly wider, to Branch, who can survey a near infinity of information unavailable to anyone else and barely make sense of any of it. These different perspectives underline *Libra*'s theme of powerlessness and create a narrative tension as the reader, privy to the schemes and intrigues of

COMPARE & CONTRAST

- **1963:** Both the Vietnam War and the Cold War are escalating, the civil rights movement organizes a march on Washington, and President John F. Kennedy is assassinated.

  1988: President Ronald Reagan is near the end of his second term in office; the Cold War winds down, and the Iran-Iraq war draws to a close.

  Today: Syria and other areas in the Middle East are in turmoil, terrorism is a national concern, and President Barack Obama is ending his second term.

- **1963:** The ideologies of the American counterculture (including the hippie movement, socialists and communists, and others) and conservative groups stand in stark contrast.

  1988: The decade is marked by a wholesale popular embrace of consumer culture, American pop music is ever more explicit, and TV features more sexuality and violence.

  Today: The ideological gulf between liberals and conservatives is widening; socially liberal policies trigger a conservative backlash.

- **1963:** Overtures aimed at ending the space race between the United States and the Soviet Union are scuttled by Kennedy's assassination; the "butterfly effect" advances chaos theory.

  1988: Personal computer use is expanding exponentially in the United States, and the first computer virus makes its appearance.

  Today: 3D printing makes tremendous advances, and advances in "5D" data storage mean input could survive for billions of years.

---

one character, moves to the character unknowingly affected by them.

Interior Monologue

Interior monologue is a narrative technique in which characters' thoughts are revealed in a way that appears to be uncontrolled by the author. DeLillo's writing style is economical; he disdains flowery language and keeps his sentences short. Still, he abandons this economy for the painful interior monologues of Oswald's mother, which occupy rambling, monolithic paragraphs.

> I stand here on this brokenhearted earth and I look at the stones of the dead, a rolling field of dead, and the chapel on the hill, and the cedar trees leaning in the wind, and I know a funeral is supposed to console the family with the quality of the ceremony and the setting. But I am not consoled.

Colloquialism

A colloquialism is a word, phrase, or form of pronunciation that is acceptable in casual conversation but not in formal, written communication. DeLillo is a master at capturing the natural cadences of American speech. Examples include "Which anyway the lice jump down on top of me." "Tony, I have plans I'm painting the club."

HISTORICAL CONTEXT

DeLillo took three years to write *Libra*. Those three years, from 1985 to the book's publication in 1988, were marked (as most years are) by global and domestic insecurity, with occasional prospects of stability. Of particular relevance to *Libra*, the decade is notable for a number of assassinations (Indira Gandhi and Anwar Sadat) and attempted ones (Ronald Reagan, Pope John Paul II, Margaret Thatcher). The Cold War between the United States and the Soviet Union was beginning to subside when DeLillo started writing, and during that time Soviet leader Mikhail Gorbachev initiated the

Oswald is portrayed as intelligent and well-read, though his dyslexia makes it difficult for him to read and write (©Gajus | Shutterstock.com)

policy of perestroika, which ultimately led to the USSR's dissolution. The period featured war and economic trouble as well: the Iran-Iraq war was in full swing, ending only the year the novel was published, and the United States bombarded Libya in 1986 in retaliation for its sponsorship of terrorism (terrorism is a frequent concern in DeLillo's work). Peace was further threatened by the debt crises experienced by developing countries globally.

Within the United States, Reagan's second term in office had begun the year before. The soothing slogan used by his reelection campaign, "It's morning again in America," must have been especially jarring to a cultural critic like DeLillo, who would have been well aware of the period's instability. The nationwide AIDS crisis was exacting a toll on American society. New York City, DeLillo's birthplace, was experiencing a spike in crime rates as crack hit the streets; the city's subways in this decade (ridden with pleasure in the early 1950s by *Libra*'s youthful Oswald) had the highest crime rate of any transit system in the world.

Perhaps because of the overall political and social context, the period was a fertile one for postmodern literature. DeLillo, though he resists the label, is often described as a postmodern writer, and others published during these years. The term, a very broad one, is applied to literature that embraces a degree of disorder or fragmentation (in structure, for example, as *Libra* does) and pushes other conventional literary boundaries; paranoia is also a common feature (again as in *Libra*). Among postmodern writers who published during these three years were Paul Auster (*The New York Trilogy*), John Fowles (*A Maggot*), Haruki Murakami (*Hard-Boiled Wonderland and the End of the World*), Nicholson Baker (*The Mezzanine*), and Umberto Eco (*Foucault's Pendulum*).

Of particular note relating to language, the media, and DeLillo's interest in them is a jury verdict in Miami in 1986. E. Howard Hunt, a CIA officer and convicted conspirator in the Watergate scandal, brought a suit against the conservative journal *Spotlight*, which had claimed a role for him in the assassination; the jury ruled against him. The verdict was reached (in accordance with jury instructions) solely because Hunt could not prove that the journal acted with "actual malice." Nevertheless, it was promptly taken as evidence for a conspiracy—one small example of media (in this case, news coverage about the trial) altering perceptions of reality, occurring as DeLillo wrote his conspiracy novel.

CRITICAL OVERVIEW

Libra elicited praise from many critics for its depth of characterization, its themes, and its treatment of the assassination; it was also condemned for some of these same things. Anne Tyler, writing for the *New York Times*, calls it his "richest novel. It is also his most complicated, with a dual slate of characters and a plot line that might be described as herringbone-shaped." She goes on to praise the book's treatment of those passages that illuminate characters rather than move the plot forward:

> It's in those commonplace moments that Mr. DeLillo reveals his genius. . . . He takes the stale facts and weaves them into something altogether new, largely by means of inventing, with what seems uncanny perception, the interior voice that each character might use to describe his own activities.

Richard Eder, in the *Los Angeles Times*, writes that "in the hands of a writer of DeLillo's fierceness and subtlety, the strengths [of the historical fiction genre] are supercharged." Like Tyler, he acknowledges the challenges of its complex structure:

> DeLillo disassembles his plots with the finest of jigsaw cuts, scrambles their order and has us reassemble them. As the assorted characters go about their missions, we discern them more by intuition than by perception. The chronology goes back and forth, disorienting us. We do not so much follow what is going on as infiltrate it.

On the other hand, he perceives a weakness associated with the genre as well, namely, a burdensome obligation to conform the book to its subject: "The characters must schedule themselves to the demands of the real as against the fictional event. It is like touring Paris with so many appointments to keep that the sense of travel is curtailed."

In a review for the *Washington Post*, Jonathan Yardley takes issue with DeLillo's

> THIS IS THE FACTOR THAT FRIGHTENS
> EVERETT. HIS CREATIVE EFFORTS, INTENDED TO
> IMPOSE ORDER AND CONTROL ON CHAOS, ARE
> RUNNING INTO A LARGER PATTERN, ONE THAT
> THREATENS TO TAKE CONTROL OF THE CONSPIRACY
> AWAY FROM HIM; BIZARRE COINCIDENCES BEGIN TO
> TAKE ON SINISTER SIGNIFICANCE."

"ostentatiously gloomy view of American life and culture" and writes that he engaged in "pamphleteering rather than the durable art of fiction." Perhaps the negative review most frequently quoted is George Will's, also in the *Washington Post*, who refers to the novel as "an act of literary vandalism and bad citizenship." He takes DeLillo to task particularly for his cultural stance, writing: "It is well to be reminded by books like this of the virulence of the loathing some intellectuals feel for American society, and of the frivolous thinking that fuels it."

CRITICISM

William Rosencrans

Rosencrans is a writer and copy editor. In the following essay, he examines the conspiracy and other machinations in Libra *as creative acts intended to impose order on a chaotic world.*

"I don't think my books could have been written in the world that existed before the Kennedy assassination," DeLillo has stated. He continued:

> I think that some of the darkness in my work is a direct result of the confusion and psychic chaos and the sense of randomness that ensued from that moment in Dallas. It's conceivable that this made me the writer I am—for better or for worse.

The creative impulse is often described as a reaction to what DeLillo calls psychic chaos. It is worth examining, then, the striking ways in which the conspiracy in *Libra*, as well as Oswald's various small-scale deceits, amount to

WHAT DO I READ NEXT?

- DeLillo's previous novel *White Noise* (1985) is regarded as his most accessible. As its protagonist flees a toxic chemical cloud, the novel explores consumer culture, addiction, fear of death, and the ways in which media and technology distort reality.

- *Dreaming in Cuban* (1992), a novel by Cuban author Cristina García, focuses on three generations of women in Cuba whose lives are disrupted by revolution, in some cases leading to exile in America.

- Norman Mailer's book *Oswald's Tale: An American Mystery* (1995) presents a largely factual, well-researched, and sympathetic biography of Lee Harvey Oswald. Mailer's suppositions about Oswald's inner life take liberties with the genre, but it was generally well received.

- For a different take on the CIA, readers can turn to *Legacy of Ashes* (2007), by Tim Weiner. Exhaustively researched and full of interviews, this nonfiction study was published to high praise. It is deeply critical of the agency's mishandling of covert affairs, including the Bay of Pigs, which led some reviewers to accuse Weiner of a lack of objectivity.

- *The Ministry of Fear* (1943) is a classic thriller about conspiracy and fear, written by British author Graham Greene. Set in London during the Blitz, the novel follows an ordinary man whose life is upended by a Nazi plot.

- For another novel about assassination, readers can turn to *The Feast of the Goat* (2001), by Peruvian author Mario Vargas Llosa. The novel explores the nature of dictatorship in the Dominican Republic and the effect of the murder of President Rafael Trujillo on politics and society.

---

creative acts and the fact that they are efforts to impose order and a sense of control on a seemingly chaotic world.

Everett and Parmenter have devoted themselves to an organization and a country they believe in. For the Bay of Pigs, particularly, they can claim a sense of ownership, since they were involved in the planning and development behind it. Whatever the ethics of the invasion itself, they attribute its failure and bloody aftermath to their superiors: "Good men died because the administration delayed," which was "too unbelievably stupid and cruel." Nevertheless, these men were the ones who took the blame and whose careers and reputations were ruined.

It is clear from the beginning that the conspiracy is at least as much a response to what DeLillo calls "confusion and psychic chaos" as it is an effort to correct government policy. Everett, retreating to his office,

> worked patiently on his bitterness, honing and refining. It was something he returned to periodically as if to some legend of his youth... searching for a grim justice in the very recollection of what they'd done to him.

Parmenter is less obsessively bitter, still ready to work his way back into the CIA's good graces, but as eager to embrace the notion of an attempted assassination.

It is the design of the conspiracy that resembles an artistic reaction, a creative act, almost a literary one, with Everett as the main author and the figure of Oswald as his creation. *Libra* makes this explicit. "We do the whole thing with paper," he tells his co-conspirators.

> Passports, drivers' licenses, address books. Our team of shooters disappears but the police find a trail. Mail-order forms, change-of-address cards, photographs. We script a person or persons out of ordinary pocket litter.

Mackey's job is to "find a model for the character Everett was in the process of creating. They wanted a name, a face, a bodily frame they might use to extend their fiction into the world."

Parmenter may be the lesser artist (his contribution to the Bay of Pigs plagiarized "cryptic messages from spy movies of the forties"), but he has the same instinct. Parmenter recalls with enormous pleasure his creation of a fictitious radio station run by rebels in Guatemala and their false broadcasts. "Rumors, false battle reports, meaningless codes, inflammatory speeches, orders to non-existent rebels. It was like a class project in the structure of reality," and it aroused such anxiety that it toppled the Guatemalan government.

While Everett's prior work is barely mentioned, his labors to create an assassin are described in minute and painstaking detail, from phone numbers jotted down by the fictitious gunman indicating "a number of ordinary stops (florist, supermarket)" to the items in Everett's workshop ("cutting instruments, acetate overlays, glues and pastes, a soft eraser, a travel iron") and the methods for using them to create a Diner's Club card and an address book. "He would show the secret symmetries in a nondescript life."

The "vast and rhythmic coincidence" of the discovery of Lee Harvey Oswald, who so perfectly matches the identity they wish to create, is a source of great amusement for Parmenter; Everett, however, experiences "a sensation of the eeriest panic [at this] glimpse of the fiction he'd been creating, a fiction living prematurely in the world" when Mackey informs him of the wealth of paper trails (letters, false identities, draft cards, passports, and so on) waiting to be used in Oswald's apartment. Later, worried about losing control of his creation, he draws a direct comparison between the conspiracy and a literary work, reflecting that "the idea of death is woven into the nature of every plot. A narrative plot no less than a conspiracy of armed men."

This is the place to reckon with Oswald himself and his role in the plot. Everett, as demonstrated, is an artist of a sort; it is the job of the rest to help build an environment in which Everett's creation can be seen, like set designers for a play. Oswald, eternally frustrated, has pretensions akin to Everett's but no ability. His deceits (about everything from his name to his intentions) are numerous, almost instinctual, but on such a small scale that they never amount to much and are seen through easily by the men who seek to use him; these deceits fail to cohere in any meaningful way.

His ineptitude as a writer showcases how misplaced his desires are. While he is in Minsk he strives to write a "Historic Diary" of his impressions of Soviet life and imagines future readers

> moved by his loneliness and disappointment, even by his wretched spelling, the childish mess of composition. Let them see the struggle and humiliation, the effort he had to exert to write a simple sentence. . . . In every direction he came up against his own incompleteness. Cramped, fumbling, deficient.

Thus his terror, like Everett's, when he discovers his role as someone else's creation. He develops nosebleeds; he loses weight. Ferrie, a malevolent trickster figure, is perfectly honest with him about this. "What were they looking for?" asks Oswald. Ferrie replies,

> Signs that you exist. Evidence that Lee Oswald matches the cardboard cutout they've been shaping all along. You're a quirk of history. You're a coincidence. They devise a plan, you fit it perfectly. They lose you, here you are. There's a pattern in things.

This is the factor that frightens Everett. His creative efforts, intended to impose order and control on chaos, are running into a larger pattern, one that threatens to take control of the conspiracy away from him; bizarre coincidences begin to take on sinister significance. Ferrie and Oswald have actually met years earlier, when Oswald, as a teenager, purchased a rifle from him; de Mohrenschildt happens to meet the adult Oswald and mentions him to Parmenter; interest in him grows, but before they can take advantage of him he disappears, only to turn up at Banister's office looking for a job not long after. "Mackey was supposed to ask Guy Banister to find a substitute for our boy. What happens? The original walks in off the street." This last incident occurs not as pure coincidence but at the behest of an FBI agent, supposedly for unrelated reasons, and is part of a larger pattern influencing the conspiracy Everett has worked so hard to develop.

More strange patterns begin manifesting. Some are clearly attributable to human effort, in particular, an endless doubling of both Kennedy ("You know this Kennedy goes around with ten or fifteen people who look just like him") and Oswald (whose doubles Nicholas Branch identifies all over Dallas before the assassination). Some are not, as, for example, Oswald's going by the name "Leon" for a time, which happens to be the middle name chosen for himself by Jack Ruby, who will later kill him. There is a larger artwork, then, whether man-made or generated by some other source, that Everett has failed to take into account and which frequently looks like the randomness or disorder on which he is struggling to impose his own creation.

Branch, assigned to write a history of the assassination from the virtually infinite quantities of data the mysterious Curator at the CIA sends him, might be faced with a hopeless task. But from his vantage point in the future and with

Lee Harvey Oswald being escorted by police officers *(©Bettmann / Getty Images)*

all the data at his disposal, he is able not only to pick out a few of the details of the conspiracy but also to start seeing its place in the mix of chaos and intention that it springs from. He, unlike Everett or Oswald, is spared the impossible hope of imposing control.

Source: William Rosencrans, Critical Essay on *Libra*, in *Novels for Students*, Gale, Cengage Learning, 2017.

Marco Codebò

In the following excerpt, Codebò characterizes Libra *as an archival novel.*

Early in *Libra*, Don DeLillo's novel that narrates the assassination of President Kennedy, readers come across a character, Nicholas Branch, who retrieves information by entering a date on his computer. As a retired intelligence analyst who is writing the secret story of the assassination, Branch carries out the same operation as DeLillo the novelist. Given this analogy, the first scene with Branch at the keyboard is once again reminiscent of the intention behind the description of the lawyer Derville and his clerks working in his office in Balzac's *Le Colanel Chabert*. In both cases, the novel displays its archival foundation. In *Libra*, this means demonstrating how one should handle data in the messy archive of Late Modernity: by way of databases and search engines, as Branch does. The appearance of the digital database aids in framing the reader's experience of the text, as well as highlights the technological context for arranging records in *Libra*. In a novel that narrates an event of enormous historical significance such as the Kennedy assassination, the digital database speaks of a new epoch in the

history of archivization. *Libra* carries the archival novel into the age in which its epistemic partner, the paper archive, has reached the threshold of its technological obsolescence. Clearly moved by the same concerns as Georges Perec in *La Vie mode d'emploi*, DeLillo strives to create a novel that might combine historical accuracy with a critique of the prevailing methods for keeping those records on which historicity is based. In the history of the archival novel, *Libra* applies the paradigm of challenge to an extreme situation, when what is at stake is not so much a critique of the archive as the very possibility of shaping a truthful narrative within the technological boundaries that delimit archivization in the paper age. Appropriately, DeLillo's novel executes a strategy for surviving the archive's entropy that is the opposite of the one implemented in Balzac's *Comédie humaine*, the text that epitomizes the coincidence between the novel's and the bureaucratic archive's epistemologies. As it emphasizes limitation against totality and chance against determinism, *Libra* outlines a design to replace the archive rather than relying on it. It does so by both foregrounding archivists' inability to arrange their archives and proposing a manner for shaping narratives out of archival documentation that can function even when the archive falls prey to radical disorder.

At the time of the writing of *Libra*, two opposite principles, contingency and conspiracy, informed the extant narratives of the assassination. Theories based on contingency maintained that a lone gunman, Lee Harvey Oswald, was the sole person responsible for the president's death: as a Marxist and a pro-Castro activist, Oswald killed President Kennedy in retaliation for the US government's hostile policy toward Communist Cuba. On a personal level, as a deranged individual who had repeatedly failed in his private life, Oswald hated John Kennedy and everything he represented: success, popularity, and power. Since Oswald's crime originated in a mix of ideological zealotry and personal troubles, it neither followed any rational and predictable plan, nor required an investigation into a possible conspiracy: the assassination began and ended with Lee Harvey Oswald. Narratives based on the hypothesis of a conspiracy followed an opposite pattern. They insisted that the CIA, the White House, and the top brass in the military had joined anti-Castro hard liners and the mob in a plot to kill the president. After the assassination, the conspirators masterminded the institutional cover-up of their plan, the systematic elimination of witnesses, as well as the disruption of all the investigations into their plot. In narratives inspired by the idea of a conspiracy, Lee Oswald was a mere decoy, a scapegoat that the real killers of President Kennedy had offered to public opinion.

Contingency and conspiracy theories found distinct supporters in the cultural and political arena. While the establishment (the United States government, the military, academia, and the mainstream media) endorsed narratives based on contingency, an army of freelance researchers, grassroots organizations, and alternative media supported histories inspired by conspiracy. The report presented by "The President's Commission on the Assassination of President Kennedy" on September 24, 1964, a.k.a. the *Warren Commission Report* from the chairman of the commission, Chief Justice Earl Warren, represented the institutional truth on the assassination. As for the conspiracy theories from the opposite camp, no narrative could achieve a prestige comparable to that of the *Warren Commission Report*. Instead, it was the sheer number of studies critical of the government's version of the assassination published in the span of more than two decades that conveyed the idea of an alternative history of Kennedy's death. Although triggered by different motivations, both the supporters of contingency theories and their opponents shared an equal mistrust in the archive. Those who believed in the institutional accounts of President Kennedy's death were suspicious of any new record that could undermine the official version of the assassination. They would have liked to seal the files on the killing forever, thus shutting out

what they perceived as an unpredictable component of the archive. For the believers in conspiracy theories, instead, government-run repositories were by definition prone to the manipulation and destruction of truthful records. Only investigators independent from the secret powers that rule over society could discover the truth hidden among the files of the Kennedy assassination. Ultimately, in conspiracy theories, it is the authority in charge of the investigation that enjoys the power of turning the archive into either a trustworthy or a deceitful institution.

In the late 1980s, the gargantuan Dallas archive (the collection of police records, intelligence memos, institutional reports, and independent stories written on the assassination) seemed to hit an epistemic wall. While its official constituent continued to produce the same immutable truth, its unauthorized component could generate only unchanging stories of plots against democracy. Only an act of cognitive imagination could enable a writer to shape a meaningful story out of the worn-out documentation on the killing of the president. This is what DeLillo did as he composed *Libra* by keeping his distance from both contingency and conspiracy theories. Without postulating the existence of an almighty power hidden in an obscure area of the government, he imagined a scheme that originated in the mid management of the CIA and counted on accomplices in the administration and in organized crime. In particular, by describing the assassination as the result of a chain of accidents, DeLillo differentiated himself from paranoid readings of recent American history. *Libra* traces an anti-Kennedy plot initially meant to fire shots at the president without hitting or killing him. Chance, however, inexorably derails the plotters' original plans. At the end of the day, hazard—in the form of: an unreliable gunman, Lee Oswald, certain conspirators' personal hatred for the president, the itinerary chosen for Kennedy's visit to Dallas, and good weather—determines the outcome of the conspiracy. Letting things unfold on their own, rather than controlling every detail of the intrigue, is the cipher of the machination that kills JFK in *Libra*. The plot starts when a disgruntled CIA agent, Win Everett, forced out of active service after the Bay of Pigs fiasco, decides to stir up anti-Cuban sentiment in the United States by organizing a failed attempt on President Kennedy's life. By planting evidence that ties the assassins to the Cuban Intelligence Directorate, Everett plans to cause an anti-Castro backlash and gain support for a military strike against Communist Cuba. After recruiting three veterans of the Bay of Pigs invasion, Frank Vásquez, Wayne Elko, and Raymo, Everett and his coconspirators, Larry Parmenter and T. J. Mackey, get in touch with a pro-Castro activist, Lee Harvey Oswald. As a former defector to the USSR, Oswald appears to be a perfect patsy, one who can easily shift the suspects from the real assassins to a communist machination. As T. J. Mackey deliberately omits to tell the hit men to miss their target, the plot inexorably proceeds toward its deadly conclusion. On November 22, 1963, while Oswald just wounds Kennedy, Raymo kills the president by shooting from behind a fence on top of the grassy knoll bordering Elm Street.

As the following "Author's Note" at the end of the novel spells out, a peculiar relationship between the archive and the fictional text underpins DeLillo's narrative of the assassination.

. . . The immediate goal of DeLillo's note is to shield *Libra* from the heated debate on John Kennedy's death, including its possible legal ramifications, by reiterating the novel's fictional status, playing down its ambition to establish the historical truth, and carefully pointing out the imaginary nature of the intelligence officers that it represents. To this purpose, the first two paragraphs of the note places the novel on the sideline of the archive, in a parasitic position where the novelist has simply to cherry-pick the records that best fit his project. This defensive goal achieved, the note assesses the deplorable situation of the Dallas archive and flaunts DeLillo's plan of turning *Libra* into a viable alternative to the extant narratives on the assassination.

Initially, it may appear that replacing the missing links in the record on the assassination as a series of data points, facts, details, and somewhat shadowy clues is the method for emending the documentation on Kennedy's death that *Libra*'s author advocates. The Dallas archive, however, is mired in such chaos (conflicting sets of evidence, official subterfuge, labyrinthine theories) that bridging the gaps in its collections of documents becomes an impossible feat. Indeed, when the archive deteriorates into a messy storeroom where facts are undistinguishable from rumors and suspicion, how can a researcher detect which records are missing?

Blank spaces are evident in well-ordered series, not in chaotic collections in which the relations among records appear misleading and obscure. In this context, a novelist aiming at emending the historical record must first elaborate a strategy for imposing some order on the available archival material and only then can he or she attempt to complete the extant documentation through fictional methods. What sets *Libra* apart from the archival novels of its age is the fact that DeLillo, in his attempt to fix the Dallas archive, by which I mean to repair its inconsistencies and gaps, as well as to stabilize and fasten it into place so that it is no longer a slippery mess of information and suspicions of varying reliability, not only answers the specific questions arising from the Kennedy assassination, but also addresses the larger relationship between the novel and the archive in the epistemic context of postmodernism. In other words, DeLillo manages to write an archival novel that centers and relies on an archive whose integrity is soiled by omissions, contradictions, hypertrophy, and intrusions from powerful external agents. He can succeed in this endeavor by creating a refuge for readers left stranded by the postmodern archive's failure to provide its users with conclusive documentation about a given event. *Libra* answers this need for finality because it is a complete object, a haven from the chaos of external reality. Being such a refuge, a mission that the classic archive routinely performed, is a task that its postmodern counterpart executes with increasing difficulty . . . .

Source: Marco Codebò, "*Libra* by Don DeLillo: The Archival Novel in the Autumn of the Paper Archive," in *Narrating from the Archive: Novels, Records, and Bureaucrats in the Modern Age*, Fairleigh Dickinson University Press, 2010, pp. 137–42.

Paul Civello

In the following excerpt, Civello examines the looping patterns in Libra.

While *End Zone* depicted the collapse of the classical scientific paradigm and its effect on the self, DeLillo's later novel *Libra* focuses on the predicament of that self trapped within the "new" order adumbrated by the new physics and systems theory. The individual must now try to locate himself in and reconcile himself to this new world of nonlinear causality and uncertainty, the comforts of the old order—knowability and the subsequent possibility of control or "mastery"

AS SUCH, THE NOVELIST DOES NOT
PRESUME TO STAND APART FROM HIS MATERIAL,
FOR HE KNOWS HE CANNOT. HE AND HIS FICTION
BECOME A PART OF THE EVENT ITSELF, A PART OF
THE CULTURAL CONSCIOUSNESS THAT IS THE
KENNEDY ASSASSINATION."

over the external world—no longer available to him. "Mystery" replaces "mastery"—or even the illusion of mastery. *Libra* is thus a novel more firmly in the naturalistic vein, for it is a reworking of the naturalistic leitmotiv of the self caught in a universe of force, a universe that defies the reason and with which the self has no moral or spiritual affinity. Yet it is a reworking that effectually "undoes" the naturalism of Zola and Norris, for it plays out this naturalistic leitmotiv within a universe whose conception by definition undermines the basic tenets of classical science—the foundation, as we have seen, of nineteenth-century literary naturalism.

We remember that Zola had compared the novelist to a scientist and argued that, like the scientist, the novelist in writing a novel essentially conducted an experiment. Such a comparison implicitly granted the novelist the same working assumptions of the classical scientist—namely, that the universe was a conglomeration of discrete parts, that these parts interacted according to the laws of linear causality, that by studying these parts and the laws governing their behavior one could comprehend the universe, and most important, that the scientist could stand apart from his experiment and watch it unfold objectively. In *Libra*, we see what amounts to a parody of Zola's "experimental novelist" in the character of Nicholas Branch. While Branch in writing his "history" of the Kennedy assassination is certainly not conducting an experiment, nor—he hopes—is he writing fiction, he nevertheless approaches his material and the task of assembling it into a cohesive narrative with the same assumptions that Zola's novelist had in mind. His interpretive

paradigm, in other words, is the same; however, the world in which he finds himself is far different, the material resisting such a paradigm. We first encounter Branch in a "small room," a metaphor that recurs throughout the novel. On its most fundamental level of meaning, the small room suggests isolation, and in the context of Branch, it initially seems to suggest an objective distance from the assassination that he is trying to piece together. In this way, Branch is akin to the rational man of science, alone in his "book-filled room, the room of documents, the room of theories and dreams." Yet such objectivity is immediately undercut when we learn that he is also in "the room of growing old," his isolation granting him not perspective on the assassination but trapping him within the interpretive paradigm he brings to it. He cannot escape his paradigm, can never see the assassination in itself, and as a result can never construct a cohesive narrative that will render a "true" picture of the event. Branch and his facts, theories, and dreams grow old together. We learn that he has written very little since the CIA hired him to write the secret history of the assassination, that he cannot even reach the "end" of his accumulated data.

It is, of course, his paradigm that is primarily at fault, for it is based on a false conception of reality. Despite his growing frustration and despair, Branch continues to view his intractable data as an assembly of parts that can be linked, given enough rational analysis, into a cohesive pattern. "Everything is here," we are told, in his room of theories and facts:

> Baptismal records, report cards, postcards, divorce petitions, canceled checks, daily timesheets, tax returns, property lists, postoperative x-rays, photos of knotted string, thousands of pages of testimony, of voices droning in hearing rooms in old courthouse buildings, an incredible haul of human utterance.

This is but one list of several that are given in reference to Branch's data, the list itself indicative of the disjunctiveness of the parts as he perceives them. The implication is that while "everything" may be here, nothing is here, for reality is not composed of discrete parts but of those parts *in relation* to one another. As Hayles has commented, in the field concept of reality, "The whole is composed of parts but cannot be reduced to them." Branch wants such reductiveness, such simplicity—the same desire we saw in Harkness and in other characters in *End Zone*.

Yet only after years of study and frustration does Branch begin to see that such simplicity is impossible. He begins to doubt that "the true nature of the event" is contained in the various exhibits that the Curator sends him: "There is nothing to understand," he muses, "no insight to be had from these pictures and statistics." Yet he remains at a loss as to an alternative paradigm.

In the course of the novel we begin to see that the various parts that comprise the Kennedy assassination are all connected in a nonlinear, looping pattern of interconnecting systems. This systems pattern is the "true" relation of parts to one another, and therefore is the more accurate picture of the event itself. Branch, however, like Harkness in *End Zone*, can only see fragments of this pattern due to his inherent limitations as a human being and to his interpretive paradigm that discounts those limitations. The looping pattern thus appears to him to be linear, and his *ex post facto* attempts to connect the parts into a cohesive whole are constrained by his imposition of the laws of linear causality. He wants to analyze the "six point nine seconds of heat and light," as if the linear, chronological unfolding of events must contain the truth of the assassination. He searches in vain for a beginning, for an original cause of the assassination. Likewise, he searches in vain for an end—the linear paradigm, of course, positing a clearly defined beginning and end. In fact, Branch wonders "if he ought to despair of ever getting to the end." "It is impossible," we are told, "to stop assembling data. The stuff keeps coming." The assassination, just as it defied reduction to discrete parts, defies linear causality. Branch cannot bracket the event within a spatial or temporal frame. He cannot discern a linear pattern with a clear beginning and end. The pattern stretches beyond both space (i.e., Dallas) and time (i.e., six point nine seconds). The past is even "changing as he writes."

Thus, rather than the accumulated data leading to greater knowledge, to greater certitude regarding the assassination, it leads to greater uncertainty. The more isolated "facts" Branch knows, the less he knows about the entire picture. "It is essential," he tells himself, "to master the data," but it does him no good. The facts themselves are too ambiguous, their meaning too uncertain; moreover, they point in too many different directions, each direction resisting closure. As a result, Branch has no hope of coming to a definitive end to his investigation. In his frustration, he yearns for certitude, wanting "a thing to be what it is." We are reminded here of Harkness, who wanted to find the "thing unalterably itself," and, like Harkness's, Branch's wish goes unfulfilled. Toward the end of the novel he begins to accept uncertainty, abandoning his search for a linear pattern of cause and effect, and resigning himself to the indeterminate conclusion that "the conspiracy against the President was a rambling affair that succeeded in the short term due mainly to chance."

Of course, of all the assumptions of classical science that Zola granted his experimental novelist, the most fundamental to his methodology was the separation of observing subject from observed object. As Branch's "objective" investigation progresses, we become increasingly aware that such a separation is an illusion. Branch is indeed a "branch" of the event: a part of it, not separate from it. He is part of the same field. In fact, in the same way that Heisenberg's scientist made something happen merely by watching it happen, Branch creates the "reality" of the assassination by writing about it. The event cannot remain isolated and discrete; it becomes something different when it is interpreted, assuming aspects of the interpretive paradigm applied to it. Laurence Parmenter's comment to his secretary—"Every bit and piece and whisper in the world . . . doesn't have a life until someone comes along to collect it"—can be applied to the data that Branch himself imbues with meaning. So too can the narrator's comment regarding Oswald's Historic Diary: "the writing of any history brings a persuasion and form to events." Again, that form is determined by the writer and his paradigm. Heisenberg's statement that "what we observe is not nature in itself but nature exposed to our method of questioning" comes to mind here, and we can see why, on another level, "the past is changing as he [Branch] writes": the act of writing changes it.

Thus Branch's "history" of the Kennedy assassination does not give us an objective picture of the event, but rather a picture of someone taking a picture of the event. Branch is like the second woman at the scene of the assassination: "There was a woman taking a picture and another woman about twenty feet behind her taking the same picture, only with the first woman in it." And like the experience of the first woman who, when she turns to see the other woman taking her picture, feels that that other woman is she and, simultaneously, that she herself is the person whom she had just seen shot in her own viewfinder (in other words, that she is both observing subject and observed object), Branch too is both observer and observed. He is observing himself observing the event. As a result, Branch's "history" inevitably becomes a self-referential fiction. Branch at one point senses this:

> it has taken him all these years to learn that his subject is not politics or violent crime but men in small rooms. Is he one of them now? Frustrated, stuck, self-watching, looking for a means of connection, a way to break out.

Branch *is* "one of them," a man in a small room, watching other men in small rooms such as Oswald, Ruby, the CIA, FBI, Alpha 66—indeed, "self-watching." He has become the subject of his own history.

Nicholas Branch thus comes to represent the impossibility of the objective observer and, by extension, the experimental novelist. He cannot presume to stand apart from events, to watch them unfold objectively. Neither do those events conform to the classical scientific paradigm he would subject them to: they are not discrete and isolatable, nor do they follow the laws of linear causality. Knowledge and certainty, then, the ends of classical science and Zola's experimental novel, are necessarily replaced by uncertainty. All this, of course, raises the question of the novelist's "position" in a postmodern text that reworks the conventions and concerns of literary naturalism. DeLillo, in an interview with Anthony DeCurtis, claimed that the fiction writer tries to "redeem" the despair felt by Branch in the face of his overwhelming data. We find a clue as to the means of this redemption in DeLillo's "Author's Note" at the conclusion of *Libra*:

> In a case in which rumors, facts, suspicions, official subterfuge, conflicting sets of evidence and a dozen labyrinthine theories all mingle, sometimes indistinguishably, it may seem to some that a work of fiction is one more gloom in a chronicle of unknowing.

> But because this book makes no claim to literal truth, because it is only itself, apart and complete, readers may find refuge here—a way of thinking about the assassination without being constrained by half-facts or overwhelmed by possibilities, by the tide of speculation that widens with the years.

DeLillo in effect privileges fiction over history, for fiction provides a new "way of thinking" about reality without being accountable to "facts" or the necessity of historical accuracy. It provides, in other words, a new paradigm, one that we shall see is based on that of the new science. As such, the novelist does not presume to stand apart from his material, for he knows he cannot. He and his fiction become a part of the event itself, a part of the cultural consciousness that is the Kennedy assassination. (Note the reaction to the publication of *Libra*. Many seemed to think, despite DeLillo's disclaimer, that he was promulgating yet another "conspiracy theory." George Will was incensed enough to call DeLillo a "bad citizen." After the publication of *Libra*, the past, indeed, has changed. The assassination, or at least our way of thinking about it, will never be quite the same.) Nor does the novelist make any claim to certainty. After all, even "history" is fiction, and therefore the open acknowledgment of the text as such precludes any pretension to the contrary. Like Oswald's mother, who at the end of the novel claims that "it takes stories to fill out a life," the novelist, too, must tell a story. Significantly enough, the story is not the linear narrative of Zola's experimental novel, complete with clearly discernible causes and effects. Rather, to use Marguerite Oswald's words, "there are stories inside stories." It is a narrative of looping, interconnecting stories. . . .

Source: Paul Civello, "*Libra*: Undoing the Naturalistic Novel," in *American Literary Naturalism and Its Twentieth-Century Transformations: Frank Norris, Ernest Hemingway, Don DeLillo*, University of Georgia Press, 1994, pp. 141–46.

SOURCES

Amend, Christoph, and Georg Diez, "I Don't Know America Anymore," Dum Pendebat website, http://dump endebat.net/static-content/delillo-diezeit-Oct2007.html (accessed March 10, 2016); originally published in *Die Zeit*, October 11, 2007.

Begley, Adam, "The Art of Fiction No. 135: Don DeLillo," in *Paris Review*, No. 128, Fall 1993, http://www.theparis review.org/interviews/1887/the-art-of-fiction-no-135-don-delillo (accessed March 23, 2016).

Cain, William E., "Making Meaningful Words: Self and History in *Libra*," in *Critical Essays on Don DeLillo*, edited by Hugh Ruppersburg and Tim Engles, G. K. Hall, 2000, pp. 58–69.

Civello, Paul, "*Libra*: Undoing the Naturalistic Novel," in *American Literary Naturalism and Its Twentieth-Century Transformations: Frank Norris, Ernest Hemingway, Don DeLillo*, University of Georgia Press, 1994, pp. 141–61.

DeCurtis, Anthony, "'An Outsider in This Society': An Interview with Don DeLillo," in *Introducing Don DeLillo*, edited by Frank Lentricchia, Duke University Press, 1991, pp. 46–57.

DeLillo, Don, *Libra*, Viking Penguin, 1988.

Dewey, Joseph, "Narratives of Redemption," in *Beyond Grief and Nothing: A Reading of Don DeLillo*, University of South Carolina Press, 2006, pp. 92–102.

Eder, Richard, "Imagining the Kennedy Assassination," in *Los Angeles Times*, July 31, 1988, http://articles.latimes.com/1988-07-31/books/bk-10585_1_don-delillo (accessed March 28, 2016).

Hunt v. Marchetti, 824 F.2d 916 (11th Cir. 1987), August 19, 1987, http://law.justia.com/cases/federal/appellate-courts/F2/824/916/122053/ (accessed March 31, 2016).

Keesey, Douglas, "Chapter 10: 'An Aberration in the Heartland of the Real': *Libra*," in *Don DeLillo*, Twayne's United States Author Series, No. 625, Twayne Publishers, 1993, pp. 151–76.

Lentricchia, Frank, "*Libra* as Postmodern Critique," in *Introducing Don DeLillo*, edited by Frank Lentricchia, Duke University Press, 1991, pp. 193–215.

Martucci, Elise A., Conclusion to *The Environmental Unconscious in the Fiction of Don DeLillo*, Routledge, 2007, pp. 154–61.

Passaro, Vince, "Dangerous Don DeLillo," in *New York Times*, May 19, 1991, http://www.nytimes.com/books/97/03/16/lifetimes/del-v-dangerous.html (accessed March 10, 2016).

Sim, Stuart, ed., *The Routledge Companion to Postmodernism*, Routledge, 2005, p. 224.

Tyler, Anne, "Dallas, Echoing Down the Decades," in *New York Times*, July 24, 1988, https://www.nytimes.com/books/97/03/16/lifetimes/del-r-libra.html (accessed March 23, 2016).

Yardley, Jonathan, "Appointment in Dallas," in *Washington Post*, July 31, 1988, https://www.washingtonpost.com/archive/entertainment/books/1988/07/31/appointment-in-dallas/a95c9778-8d21-4636-8b29-d85f9c8b1a56/ (accessed March 26, 2016).

Will, George, "Shallow Look at the Mind of an Assassin," in *Critical Essays on Don DeLillo*, edited by Hugh Ruppersburg and Tim Engles, G. K. Hall, 2000, pp. 56–57.

FURTHER READING

Farber, David, *The Age of Great Dreams: America in the 1960s*, Hill and Wang, 1994.

> This volume is part of the American Century Series. The decade of the 1960s, famous for its political and social turbulence, is presented here in an eminently readable fashion.

Fenster, Mark, *Conspiracy Theories: Secrecy and Power in American Culture*, University of Minnesota Press, 2008.

> Books on conspiracy theories tend either to dismiss or endorse them. Fenster's study carefully does neither, instead focusing on the phenomenon of "conspiracism" itself and examining what its prevalence means for American society.

Lentricchia, Frank, ed., *Introducing Don DeLillo*, Duke University Press, 1991.

> This collection of essays, along with an excerpt from one of his novels and an interview, was the first book-length study of DeLillo. It includes critiques by scholars and others about the author and his work, themes, and language.

Rasenberger, Jim, *The Brilliant Disaster: JFK, Castro, and America's Doomed Invasion of Cuba's Bay of Pigs*, Scribner, 2012.

> Gripping and clear, *Brilliant Disaster* draws on newly released CIA documents and other sources to provide a complete account of the invasion itself and an accompanying analysis of its inception and failure.

Summers, Anthony, *Not in Your Lifetime*, Headline Book Publishing, 2013.

> There are hundreds of books about the Kennedy assassination, many of uneven quality. Summers' account, which includes a balanced reckoning with the event itself and the conspiracy theories that surround it, is generally held to be reliable and well written.

SUGGESTED SEARCH TERMS

Don DeLillo

DeLillo AND cultural critique

Libra AND DeLillo

Libra AND historical figures

Lee Harvey Oswald

assassination AND Kennedy

conspiracy theories

historical fiction

The Lovely Bones

ALICE SEBOLD

2002

Alice Sebold's best-selling novel *The Lovely Bones*, published in 2002, tells the extraordinary story of Susie Salmon, who at the age of fourteen is murdered in a cornfield bordering her quiet neighborhood. From heaven, she watches her family and friends cope with the catastrophic emotional fallout from her death, powerless to intervene as the fibers holding her family together begin to tear. Yet, in the place of old relationships broken by grief, new and unexpected connections form, and Susie's spiritual connection to a girl named Ruth provides a channel through which Susie can effect change on Earth. Celebrating the power of family, whether related by blood or chosen by the heart, Sebold uses her novel's dark foundation to build a home of light and love where Susie's restless spirit can at last find peace. Because of the mature themes in the novel, it is more appropriate for older students.

AUTHOR BIOGRAPHY

Sebold, born in Madison, Wisconsin, on September 6, 1963, was the younger of two children in an academically focused family. Her father was a professor of Spanish and her mother a journalist. Overshadowed by the academic achievements of her older sister, Mary, Sebold grew up envious of her success but with a

Alice Sebold (©ZUMA Press, Inc. | Alamy)

powerful mind of her own. She knew she wanted to be a writer from an early age. After graduating from high school in Paoli, Pennsylvania, Sebold enrolled in Syracuse University in 1980. During her first semester in college, as she was walking to her dorm one night, she was brutally raped and beaten in an underground tunnel leading to an amphitheater on campus. A woman had been raped and murdered in the same tunnel not long before, and a police officer responding to her call told Sebold she was lucky to be alive.

Months after the rape, she saw her attacker walking down a street near the campus. She brought him to court and gave powerful testimony against him. He served a prison sentence and is now free. Sebold stayed at Syracuse, enrolling in the creative writing program. In her senior year, she was named editor of the university's literary magazine, the *Review*. After graduation she moved to New York City, where she became an adjunct professor at Hunter College. After a decade in New York, she moved to California to

join the Dorland Mountain Arts Colony, living in the woods without electricity. She then enrolled in graduate school at the University of California, Irvine. There she met her future husband, the novelist Glen David Gold, before graduating in 1998 with her MFA. Her memoir on the subject of her rape, *Lucky*, was published in 1999. She and Gold were married in 2001.

In 2002, she published *The Lovely Bones*, a novel she had been writing for many years under the working title *Monsters*. The novel became an overnight success, topping the *New York Times* best-seller list for four months after its publication and selling well over a million copies. The novel was such a commercial sensation that *Lucky* rose to the top of the nonfiction best-seller list as well. *The Lovely Bones* was awarded the Bram Stoker Award for First Novel as well as the American Booksellers Association Book of the Year Award for Adult Fiction. Sebold's second novel, *The Almost Moon*, was published in 2007. It, too, reached the top of the best-seller list. In 2009, *The Lovely Bones* was adapted into a film by Peter Jackson. That same year, Sebold served as guest editor for the *Best American Short Stories 2009* anthology. She lives in San Francisco, California.

PLOT SUMMARY

One

The Lovely Bones begins on December 6, 1973. On her walk home from school, Susie Salmon takes a shortcut through the cornfield that separates the junior high school from her neighborhood. George Harvey, a neighbor with whom she has never interacted, stops her to ask if she wants to see something he has built. After hesitating, Susie follows him to an underground room he has dug out, with a bench and a fluorescent lamp for light. At first she is extremely curious about the construction process, but George Harvey begins to make her feel uncomfortable after telling her she is pretty and asking if she has a boyfriend. He rapes her and then murders her.

Two

Susie arrives in heaven, which resembles the high school she dreamt of attending on Earth. She meets Holly, who arrives in heaven at the same time and becomes Susie's best friend and roommate. She also meets Franny, her intake counselor, who helps her understand that in heaven she can have whatever she wants as long as she concentrates on it. However, Susie realizes, "I could not have what I wanted most: Mr. Harvey dead and me living.... But I came to believe that if I watched closely...I might change the lives of those I loved on Earth."

Susie's father, Jack, takes a call from Detective Len Fenerman. A neighborhood dog found a piece of Susie's body. The police begin to search the cornfield for more evidence, while the family continues to hope that Susie is still alive.

Three

When her spirit fled from Earth to heaven, Susie accidentally brushed passed a girl from her school—Ruth Connors. Ruth becomes obsessed with Susie's death. Meanwhile, Susie accidentally breaks through the barrier between heaven and Earth in late December, showing her face to

MEDIA ADAPTATIONS

- *The Lovely Bones*, adapted as a film by Peter Jackson and starring Mark Wahlberg, Rachel Weisz, Susan Sarandon, Stanley Tucci, Michael Imperioli, and Saoirse Ronan, was produced by Dreamworks Pictures, Film4 Productions, and WingNut Films and distributed by Paramount Pictures in 2009.

- Sebold narrates the unabridged audiobook of *The Lovely Bones*, which was released by Hachette Audio in 2007. The running time is approximately eleven hours.

her father in the myriad shards of broken glass after he smashes the ships in bottles they used to build together.

Four

George Harvey locks Susie's bones in a safe and buries the safe in a sinkhole. He begins to build a ceremonial tent in his backyard after reading about such tents used by the Imezzureg tribe in Mali. Susie's father helps him but begins to get a terrible feeling and to see Susie's face everywhere he looks. He comes to the sudden realization that George Harvey is the murderer. He attempts to confront him, but George tells him to go home.

Five

Susie's father tells Len Fenerman about his suspicions. Len questions George but finds nothing remarkable. The family begins to fray, as Susie's mother, Abigail, indulges in secret binge eating; her father becomes obsessed with bringing George Harvey to justice; and her sister, Lindsey, withdraws emotionally. On Christmas Day, Samuel Heckler comes to the door unannounced with a present for Lindsey, breaking the barrier she has tried to create between herself and others. They kiss.

Six–Eight

Two weeks before her death, Susie and Ray Singh cut homeroom together, sitting in the scaffolding above the stage. They overhear Ruth being reprimanded for her anatomically correct drawings by Miss Ryan and Mr. Peterford. After Susie's death, Ruth and Ray begin to meet in the cornfield, reading poetry together and talking about life in Norristown as an outcast. Jack visits Ray's mother, Ruana, to reassure her the family does not see Ray as a potential suspect. He confesses his certainty that George Harvey is the murderer, and Ruana tells him if she were in his shoes she would kill George.

Len comes to the Salmon house to speak to Jack, but Susie's mother tells him he is away. Len waits with her for Jack to get home while Susie's little brother, Buckley, and his friend, Nate, play. He tells her she reminds him of his wife, who died. Buckley tells Nate that he can see Susie, though Susie knows she has never shown herself to him. Meanwhile, George remembers how his father left his mother, forcing her out of the car by the side of the road in the New Mexican desert.

Nine

Grandma Lynn arrives at the house for Susie's funeral. She is extravagant, eccentric, and boisterous. Her loud, playful mood at first strikes the members of the grim household as inappropriate but unexpectedly begins to lift the family's spirits. The funeral is a painful experience for everyone involved. Grandma Lynn subtly points out George Harvey in the crowd for Lindsey, who is curious about the man her father suspects is the murderer. She faints. Ray does not attend, preferring to mourn Susie in private.

Ten

That summer, while Lindsey attends a symposium for gifted students along with Ruth and Samuel, Susie learns from Franny that the heaven she experiences is more like a waiting room between death and the next step. In order to move on, she will have to give up her interest in Earth and the fate of her loved ones.

Eleven

Jack's obsession with George Harvey grows as the case goes cold. Len visits the house in order to ask Jack to stop calling the station. His calls about George's every movement are beginning to become a joke among the force. Jack is devastated, as is Lindsey, who believes the detective is giving up. That night Jack sees a light in the cornfield. Convinced it is George revisiting the scene of the crime, Jack takes his baseball bat and walks out into the darkness. Instead of George he runs into Clarissa, Susie's best friend, startling her. She was waiting in the field for her boyfriend, Brian Nelson, who—believing Clarissa is being attacked—beats Jack with his flashlight.

Twelve

Jack's knee is injured badly in the beating and requires surgery. Lindsey gets a ride to the hospital with Samuel's older brother, Hal. Hal is sitting in the waiting room when Abigail, Susie's mother, greets Len. Hal notices how close they are. Abigail recognizes Hal and asks Len if they can go outside to talk. Once they are alone, Abigail kisses him. They separate, and Abigail goes back inside the hospital in a daze. Hal catches her attention, repeating the phrase that her daughter is inside the room with her husband, in order to focus her on the reality of her situation before she walks inside. Watching from heaven, Susie decides she will not hold a grudge against her mother.

Thirteen

The new school year brings changes for all of Susie's friends. Lindsey is dogged by rumors of her father's insanity on top of the whispers of her sister's death, but she finds comfort in Samuel. Buckley enters kindergarten and grows closer than ever to his father, who walks with a pronounced limp following the surgery. Lindsey and her dad grow closer as well, after they have a conversation about George Harvey's guilt. Lindsey wants to help her father prove he is the murderer. Grandma Lynn arrives for Thanksgiving and instantly sniffs out Abigail's affair. She tries to confront her but finds her daughter is distant and disinterested.

Fourteen

Lindsey breaks into George Harvey's house in search of evidence that will tie him to Susie's murder. In an upstairs room she discovers his sketchbook. As George unlocks the front door, she finds the schematics he drew for the underground room in the cornfield where he murdered Susie. He hears her moving, rushing up the stairs to catch her. She rips the page out of the sketchbook and hurls herself through the window, falling into the bushes below. She delivers the sketch safely to the hands of her father. Her mother, exasperated, withdraws from the conversation. In heaven, Susie meets the other women murdered by George and shares her story.

Fifteen

George remembers how he used to steal things with his mother. They were a team: shoplifting from stores, even robbing graves of their flowers. Watching Lindsey run from his home, he takes a moment to collect himself before calling the police to report a break-in. When Jack calls for Len, he is not in the office. Instead, two officers are dispatched to George's house, and he answers their questions smoothly. However, he knows the police will come back for him after Len sees the notebook page. Susie watches breathlessly from heaven: "I saw the chances of Mr. Harvey's capture diminish as I watched the end of my family as I had known it ignite." Abigail meets Len in the mall, and he takes her into a room deep inside the building's inner workings. As she commits adultery with Len, George leaves his house, never to return.

Sixteen

One year after Susie's murder, Ray and Ruth go to the cornfield to remember her. Hal and Samuel are already there, as well as bouquet of yellow daffodils that was there when they arrived. Mrs. Stead sees the gathering and joins them, along with Grace Tarking, the Gilberts, Ruana, teachers from the junior high school, and many others. Lindsey sees the impromptu vigil from the window and tells her mother, but Abigail does not want to join. Lindsey realizes her mother is going to leave the family soon, but when she asks this out loud her mother denies it. Lindsey, Buckley, and Jack are the last to arrive at the cornfield, after nightfall. There are candles and the crowd sings, led by Mr. O'Dwyer.

Snapshots

Abigail abandons her family, moving to California, where she works in a winery. In her absence, the neighbors begin to leave food on the Salmon family's doorstep. Grandma Lynn comes to live with them, taking Susie's old room. On a visit to the police station, Lindsey discovers her mother's scarf on Len's desk and, with it, the affair. Now seven, Buckley builds a fort in the backyard with Hal's help.

As the years pass, the annual memorial in the cornfield diminishes, populated by students from the high school who had not known Susie personally but who "knew only my name and even that only as a large dark rumor invoked as a warning to any student that might prove too much a loner. Especially girls."

Ray goes away to college, while Ruth moves to New York City. Ruth becomes convinced she can sense and release the spirits of dead women and children from their painful last moments on Earth. One night in heaven, Holiday, the Salmon family dog, arrives, ecstatic, at Susie's side.

Seventeen

Lindsey and Samuel graduate from college. On the ride home, they are caught in a storm and have to pull the bike under the trees for cover. In the woods nearby, they find an abandoned house. Samuel falls in love with it instantly. He says he wants to buy the house, fix it up, and live there with Lindsey. He asks her to marry him. They run home in the rain to tell their worried family the news.

Eighteen

Ruth plans to return home from New York to visit the sinkhole one last time before it is filled. She keeps a list of the places where she has sensed a woman's death: "She was unaware that she was somewhat of a celebrity up in heaven." Susie "told people about her," so "women lined up to know if she had found where they'd been killed." Buckley develops an interest in gardening, but Jack stops him from using Susie's old clothes to tie his tomato stakes. They argue. Suddenly Jack drops to the ground, suffering a heart attack. In the hospital room, Buckley begs Susie not to let their father die.

Nineteen–Twenty

In California, Abigail receives word of Jack's heart attack and begins the long journey home. She finds Lindsey distant and Buckley openly hostile after seven years without her in their lives. Jack, however, is happy to have her back. He has fallen in love with her all over again in her absence. At first, Abigail is determined to leave for California, but she returns to his room. They kiss, beginning the process of reconciliation.

Twenty-one

Susie remembers her first and only kiss, when Ray kissed her by her locker just days before her death. Len arrives at the hospital room to deliver a charm from Susie's bracelet that was found at a gravesite in Connecticut. He lets Jack and Abigail keep it, though it is against police protocol. George Harvey, increasingly unstable, returns to the neighborhood, cruising the streets in search of Lindsey. Ruth and Ray visit the sinkhole together. Ruth thinks this may be the place Susie's body was buried. She speaks to Susie, asking if there is anything she wants that Ruth can give her. Suddenly, Susie falls to Earth.

Twenty-two

Susie wakes up in Ruth's body. Ray rushes to her side, asking if she fainted. Susie tells him she is okay but is overwhelmed by the sensations of being alive. They get back into Ray's car. He senses something strange has happened. She demands to be kissed. They kiss. She directs him to Hal's bike shop, where she uses a hidden key to get inside. While Ruth visits with her fans in heaven, Susie—in Ruth's body—and Ray make love on Earth. He recognizes her as Susie, and they remember the short time they shared together before her death. Afterwards, Susie returns to heaven and Ruth to her body.

Twenty-three

The Salmon family, including Abigail, returns home from the hospital. Grandma Lynn, Hal, and Samuel are there, as well as Ray and Ruana, who stop by unexpectedly and join the toast to his recovery: "These were the lovely bones that had grown around my absence: the connections—sometimes tenuous, sometimes made at great cost, but often magnificent—that happened after I was gone." Samuel mentions the abandoned house he and Lindsey want to buy only to find out from Ray that Ruth's dad owns the property and is looking to sell. Susie, seeing this, celebrates in heaven. She is at peace with the fate of her family on Earth.

Bones

Susie returns to her observations from time to time. Lindsey finds out she is pregnant. A falling icicle kills George. Grandma Lynn passes away. Ruth and Ray remain best friends. Lindsey names her daughter Abigail Suzanne. Susie wishes everyone a long and happy life.

CHARACTERS

Mr. Botte

Mr. Botte is Susie's favorite teacher at her junior high school. He teaches biology. He has a sick child at home, so the students at school treat him with compassion. He is deeply saddened and disturbed by Susie's murder.

Principal Caden

Principal Caden is the principal of Susie and Lindsey's junior high school. He meets with Lindsey after Susie's murder in an attempt to comfort her but finds her too angry to accept his offer of emotional support.

Sophie Cichetti

Sophie Cichetti is one of George Harvey's victims.

Clarissa

Clarissa was Susie's best friend on Earth. She wears blue eye shadow and mini dresses, which Susie's mother finds inappropriate. Abigail resents Clarissa for being alive while her daughter is dead. After Susie's death, Clarissa begins to date Brian Nelson. She is waiting for Brian in the cornfield one night when Jack Salmon stumbles upon her. She cries out, believing he is an attacker, and Brian beats Jack with a flashlight. She and Brian use the incident to establish themselves as cool and dangerous when they enter high school the next year.

Ruth Connors

Ruth Connors is a girl from Susie's school whom Susie brushes past in spirit form on her way to heaven. This action connects the two girls, though they had little interaction on Earth. Ruth is an immensely talented artist but odd compared with the other kids in school. She is intelligent and cynical and loves the mysterious and strange. She forms a friendship with Ray and an obsession with Susie's death. After graduation, she moves to New York City, where she works as a waitress. She comes to believe she can sense the locations of violent deaths of women and keeps a journal of her observations. As a result, she becomes popular in heaven, with a fan club of women who adore her work. When Susie inhabits her body in order to make love to Ray, Ruth spends time in heaven with her fans.

Len Fenerman

Len is the detective assigned to Susie's case. He is dedicated to finding Susie's killer and willing to follow up on Jack's suspicions of George Harvey but fails to capture him. He is distracted from the case by his affair with Abigail. The affair ends not long after Abigail leaves her family. His wife committed suicide, driving Len's ambition to bring those families fearful for their missing children a sense of closure. He carries in his wallet pictures of the missing people from the cases he has worked on, along with a photo of his wife. Len returns a charm from Susie's charm bracelet to her parents after Jack's heart attack.

Len Fenerman's Wife

Len's wife committed suicide. He carries her picture in his wallet. He tells Abigail that she reminds him of his wife.

Leah Fox

Leah Fox is one of George Harvey's victims.

Franny

Franny is Susie's intake counselor in heaven. She explains to Susie how heaven works and offers emotional support as she observes her family's struggles. On Earth, Franny was a social worker, working with homeless and endangered women and children. Susie and Holly realize that Franny is with them because they long for their mothers. Franny loves to serve those in need.

Mr. Gilbert

Mr. Gilbert is one of Susie's elderly neighbors. His dog discovers Susie's remains.

Mrs. Gilbert

Mrs. Gilbert is one of Susie's elderly neighbors.

George Harvey

George Harvey rapes and murders Susie. He is a serial killer with a long list of victims. Jack Salmon becomes convinced he is the murderer after he helps George build a tent in his backyard and senses Susie's distress. George remains in the neighborhood undetected until Lindsey breaks into his house to retrieve the evidence of his guilt—a sketch of the hole he dug in the cornfield where Susie was killed. On the run, George is haunted by the women and children he has murdered until his mental state deteriorates. He returns to the neighborhood seeking revenge on Lindsey but is reported as suspicious and asked to move on by a police officer. He is later killed by a falling icicle.

George Harvey's Father

George Harvey's father built art structures and taught George how to construct different types of dwellings. He left George's mother in the desert in New Mexico, after forcing her out of the car.

George Harvey's Mother

George Harvey's mother taught him how to steal from people, stores, and even the dead. He spent much of his childhood with her, before his father abandoned her on the side of the road.

Hal Heckler

Hal is Samuel's older brother. He is tall and handsome. A motorcycle enthusiast, he owns a bike shop. He is a pillar of strength throughout the Salmon family's trials, adopting them as his own. He reminds Abigail that her family is waiting for her inside the hospital room after she has kissed Len. He forms a powerful alliance with Grandma Lynn, and he acts as an older brother to Buckley.

Samuel Heckler

Samuel Heckler is Lindsey's steady boyfriend from the age of thirteen. He and Lindsey graduate from high school and college together, get married, and have a daughter. Samuel falls in love with an abandoned house he finds on the side of the road during a rainstorm and becomes intent on buying it. He succeeds after learning the house belongs to Ruth's father. He is always there for Lindsey and her family.

Flora Hernandez

Flora Hernandez is one of George Harvey's victims.

Holiday

Holiday is the Salmon family's dog. He provides emotional support in the days following Susie's death. He joins Susie in heaven when he dies.

Holly

Holly is Susie's best friend in heaven. They are the same age, with similar interests: fashion magazines, high school, sweets, suburbia, and a longing for their mothers. Like Susie, Holly spends time looking after the people she left on Earth, and she sometimes disappears into parts of heaven that are private to her and inaccessible to Susie.

Leidia Johnson

Leidia Johnson is one of George Harvey's victims.

Grandma Lynn

Grandma Lynn is Abigail's firebrand mother, whose sharp eye and sharp tongue combine to expose the family's weaknesses. A fashion devotee, she teaches Lindsey how to use makeup. She is eccentric and bombastic but provides the spark that lifts the family from their spiraling depression in the days immediately following Susie's death. She moves in permanently after Abigail deserts the family.

Jackie Meyer

Jackie Meyer is one of George Harvey's victims.

Nate

Nate is Buckley's friend. Buckley stays at Nate's house through the initial investigation of Susie's death.

Brian Nelson

Brian Nelson is Clarissa's boyfriend. He beats Jack Salmon with a flashlight, mistaking him for an attacker in the cornfield.

Stan O'Dwyer

Stan is one of Susie's neighbors. She loved to hear him sing when she was alive. He leads the singing at the memorial a year after her death.

Mr. Peterford

Mr. Peterford is a teacher at Susie's junior high school. He chastises Ruth for her drawings of naked women.

Wendy Richter

Wendy Richter is one of George Harvey's victims.

Miss Ryan

Miss Ryan is a teacher at Susie's junior high school. She and Mr. Peterford confront Ruth about her anatomically correct sketches of nude women.

Abigail Salmon

Abigail is Susie's mother. She is a prim and distant woman, nicknamed "Ocean Eyes" by her husband for the unfathomable depths inside her mind. After Susie's death, she struggles to fulfill her role as mother to Lindsey and Buckley. She begins an affair with Len Fenerman shortly before leaving the family to strike out on her own. She moves to California, where she finds work in a winery. However, she cannot escape her grief. When she receives the news of Jack's heart attack, she returns home to see her family for the first time in seven years. Though her instinct is to run away again, she remains by Jack's side.

Buckley Salmon

Buckley is the youngest child of Jack and Abigail Salmon and their only son. He is four years old when Susie is murdered. He does not comprehend the death, asking his family where Susie is in the first days of her absence. His parents send him to stay with his friend Nate. He receives special treatment from everyone—his teachers, family, and the neighbors—but never fully adjusts to the world as a result of this early trauma. He considers himself his father's keeper, always watching to make sure he is okay. He develops a love of gardening and claims to talk to Susie often, though Susie is not aware of speaking to him. The Susie Buckley speaks to is more of an imaginary friend. He has an argument with his father over who he loves more, his living children or Susie, just before Jack has a heart attack. Wracked with guilt, Buckley begs Susie not to let Jack die. When his mother returns from California, Buckley does not forgive her easily for abandoning them.

Jack Salmon

Jack Salmon is Susie's father. After her death, he is full of restless energy and the need to help the police in some way. He becomes convinced that George Harvey is guilty after helping him build a tent in his backyard. Jack seems to sense Susie calling to him and sees George in a new light. George tells him to go home. Jack shares his suspicions with Ruana, his wife, his mother-in-law, the police department, and Lindsey. He begins to report all of George's suspicious activity to the police, until Len is forced to ask him to stop. That same night, Jack believes he sees George in the cornfield and goes out into the darkness with a baseball bat. Instead, he stumbles upon Clarissa and Brian. Brian beats him with a flashlight, under the impression that he is attacking Clarissa. Jack has surgery and walks with a limp afterward, but Lindsey retrieves evidence from George's house that proves his guilt, giving Jack a new lease on life. After his wife leaves him, Jack becomes closer to his children. He gradually falls back in love with Abigail, looking through old photos of her. He survives a heart attack that brings Abigail back to him from California. They reconcile as a couple.

Lindsey Salmon

Lindsey Salmon is Susie's younger sister. She is thirteen when Susie is murdered. Lindsey is an especially gifted student as well as a talented athlete. She withdraws emotionally following her sister's death but is saved from total isolation by Samuel, who stays by her side through school and asks her to marry him after they have graduated. Lindsey retrieves from his house the notebook page that serves as evidence of George's guilt, breaking in after hearing her father explain why he believes George is guilty. She attempts to be a good daughter to her mother but finds her mother is too distant to notice her efforts. She and her father have a strong connection, and she is a caring sister to Buckley. At the end of the novel, she gives birth to a daughter named Abigail Suzanne, after her mother and sister.

Susie Salmon

Susie Salmon is the novel's narrator. She is raped and murdered by her neighbor, George Harvey, at the age of fourteen, after he lures her into an underground room he has built in a cornfield. She watches the events of the novel from heaven. Her heaven is made of what she wanted most when she was alive: the life of a high school student, an endless supply of fashion magazines, and the simple pleasure of her favorite kind of ice cream. She has a best friend in heaven, Holly, and a helpful intake counselor, Franny. Later the family dog, Holiday, joins her. Though her every whim is satisfied in heaven, she cannot help but watch the lives of her loved ones on Earth. She breaks through the barrier between Earth and heaven in moments of high drama in her family members' lives, showing herself to them in brief glimpses. Through her connection with Ruth, established the night of her death, she is able to briefly return to Earth while Ruth takes her place in heaven. Susie remains fourteen while her family grows older, and she watches Lindsey wistfully as she becomes a woman. As the years pass and a new equilibrium settles between the ones she loves, Susie at last feels at peace with the world she left behind.

Dr. Singh

Dr. Singh is Ray's father and Ruana's husband. A professor, he is more devoted to his work than to his family. He is rarely home.

Ray Singh

Ray Singh is an initial suspect in Susie's case, after the police recover an unread love note he had slipped into Susie's notebook. In reality, Ray is Susie's crush, with whom she had her first and only kiss. He has a sharp mind and a British accent. He is ostracized at school after being named a suspect but makes fast friends with Ruth as fellow outcasts. Their friendship lasts through high school and college. He becomes a successful doctor.

Ruana Singh

Ruana is Ray's mother, a beautiful and intelligent woman who generally gets her way. She encourages Jack in his desire to seek vengeance against George Harvey and shares her cigarettes with Abigail. She is disappointed in her husband's disinterest but takes solace in Ray's brilliance as a student and kindness as a human being.

Mrs. Stead

Mrs. Stead is one of Susie's neighbors as well as a therapist.

Grace Tarking

Grace Tarking is one of Susie's neighbors.

THEMES

Coming of Age

The Lovely Bones is a coming-of-age novel, though the main character is stuck perpetually at the age of fourteen. Susie ages emotionally rather than physically as she watches her friends and family grow older. While Lindsey's coming of age takes place at a normal pace, Susie goes from teenage innocence to celestial omnipotence in a matter of an hour. Though she is blessed with cosmic wisdom, she is still a fourte-year-old girl, as evidence by the form her heaven takes: ice cream shops, fashion magazines, packs of friendly dogs, a high school campus

TOPICS FOR FURTHER STUDY

- Read Jay Asher's young-adult novel *Thirteen Reasons Why* (2007). How does Hannah's narration of her own life through the tape-recorded messages compare to Susie's narration from heaven? What are the major differences between the two novels? How are the main characters similar? Organize your thoughts into an essay.

- Choose a chapter from the novel to explicate in a PowerPoint presentation. Create slides in which you summarize the plot of the chapter, explain its context and importance within the novel as a whole, address any main themes that appears in the chapter, and discuss the character development that occurs. Include relevant quotes from the novel in your presentation.

- Create a blog in which you explore different concepts of heaven across cultures, religions, and times. In a minimum of seven posts (one of which should be devoted to the heaven depicted in *The Lovely Bones*), use quotations, artworks, and any other materials you may find to represent seven versions of heaven. Be sure to include your own descriptions along with your linked sources. After you have made seven posts, explore your classmates' blogs and leave comments on two versions of heaven that are unfamiliar to you. Free blogspace is available at blogger.com.

- In small groups, choose a character in *The Lovely Bones* other than Susie or her immediate family to examine more closely. How does Susie's death affect this character's life directly? In what ways does Susie's death affect this character's life indirectly? What was his or her relationship with Susie while she was alive? How does Susie feel about this character after her death? What are the circumstances of his or her final appearance in the novel? Take notes in preparation for a class discussion on the novel's minor characters.

without classes, lime Kool-Aid, soccer fields, and a caring, matronly figure in the always-helpful Franny.

As Susie matures, her heaven expands with pathways leading to new areas. For example, after she has watched Lindsey escape George Harvey's house with the evidence needed to prove him guilty, Franny gives Susie a map to a lone olive tree (a symbol for peace), where she meets George Harvey's other victims. In sharing her story with them and hearing their stories in return, Susie's spirit grows stronger as she lets go of her pain. While Lindsey completes her journey from childhood to adulthood through pursuing her education, embracing the love she feels for Samuel, and forgiving her mother for her long absence, Susie's journey is to find peace. She achieves this after witnessing the rebirth of her family after their long struggle with her death.

Death

Susie's death drives the plot of the novel. The close-knit Salmon family loses a member not only unexpectedly but also violently, while their peaceful Pennsylvania community must face the dark reality that their children are not safe, even in the suburbs. Susie's death brings some characters closer together: for example, Ray and Ruth forge a friendship in the cornfield, Lindsey finds a support system in Samuel, and Grandma Lynn pivots from family nuisance to family savior. For others, Susie's death causes entropy and dissociation: Abigail walks away from motherhood, Len cannot recover from the mounting losses of his life, Jack's obsession with George Harvey leads him to make poor decisions, and Buckley—whose childhood was shaped by the tragedy—never finds his balance. Death in *The Lovely Bones* takes Susie from her family physically but not spiritually. She must learn to navigate heaven while those left on Earth learn to navigate their lives without her. In this way, Susie's death is not an absolute ending but a catalyst for change.

Family

The Salmons are a suburban family remarkable in their unremarkable normalcy: a mother; father; three happy, healthy children; and a loyal dog. In the beginning of the novel Susie is pretty and generous, Lindsey is smart and athletic, and Buckley is a curious and charming four-year-old. Their father is playful, their

After her marriage to Jack falls apart, Abigail ends up at a California winery (©Pia Benzer | Shutterstock.com)

mother is prim, and their Grandma Lynn is embarrassingly outrageous by comparison. Their family is as forgettable as it is peaceful: a functioning household with petty sibling dramas and everyday triumphs.

After Susie's murder, the family implodes. Susie's death brings Abigail gasping to the surface of the ocean-like depths of her personality. She becomes hyperaware of the mundane hours she spends washing dishes and folding laundry. She seeks immediate escape from her role as suburban mother and wife. Jack becomes, as a result, the sole provider and caretaker for his children—teaching Lindsey how to shave her legs and explaining Susie's death to Buckley. Grandma Lynn fills the vacancy her daughter left in the house with a quick wit and baked goods, while the Heckler brothers adopt the Salmons as their own: Samuel through his love for Lindsey and Hal through his relationship with Buckley.

By the end of the novel, the Salmon family is an amalgamation of neighbors, friends, and relations that bears little resemblance to the untroubled nuclear family to which Susie belonged before her death. This new family, with all the uniqueness of its connections, is as unforgettable as it is atypical.

STYLE

First-Person Omniscient Point of View

The first-person omniscient point of view is an extremely rare point of view in fiction in which the narrator speaks in the first person ("I") but knows the inner thoughts and feelings of the other characters. Susie's first-person omniscient narration is possible because she is watching the events of the novel from heaven after her death. As a result of this perspective, she knows and can express to the reader everything from the contents of George Harvey's dreams, to Samuel's ecstatic proposal to Lindsey inside the abandoned house they find the day of their college graduation, to her own longing for Ray as she watches him sleep. By contrast, in heaven Susie is limited to the first-person point of view: she knows only her thoughts and what the others tell her about themselves. On Earth, however, she can be simultaneously in New York City with Ruth and at home with her father and brother, moving easily from person to person as she watches them live their lives paradoxically with and without her.

Antagonist

An antagonist is a character who acts in direct opposition to the protagonist. In *The Lovely Bones*, the antagonist is George Harvey. He is evil and villainous. His actions are reprehensible, selfish, violent, and unforgivable. He takes Susie's life, as well as many others, and is never brought to justice. If Susie represents youthful innocence, George Harvey represents the dangerous, unknowable adult world. However, from her position in heaven, it is Susie who occupies a space George does not and cannot know. Their roles reverse, and the ghosts of the women he has killed return to haunt him in his final days, driving him to make the rash decisions that ultimately lead to his death by a falling icicle.

HISTORICAL CONTEXT

Elizabeth Smart

The Lovely Bones was published in the midst of a desperate search for a missing fourteen-year-old girl, Elizabeth Smart, who was abducted from her home in Salt Lake City, Utah, on June 5, 2002. Brian David Mitchell, a religious zealot who believed he was a prophet named Immanuel, broke into Smart's home and abducted her at knifepoint, threatening her family if she made a sound. Her sister, Mary Katherine, witnessed Smart's kidnapping. They shared a bedroom, and Mary Katherine, pretending to be asleep, studied Mitchell's face closely in the hope of identifying him. Mitchell took Smart deep into the woods to a campsite where his wife, Wanda Barzee, met them wearing long robes and ordered Smart to undress. Mitchell married Smart in a hasty wedding ceremony before raping her. Afterwards, she was chained to a tree. Starved and beaten, Smart endured nine months of torture at the hands of Mitchell and Barzee. They left the camp in the woods to wander the streets of Salt Lake City for food, with Smart disguised by a wig and veil, and then moved on to California. In California, Mitchell

began to talk of moving to the East Coast. Recognizing her chances of being rescued were growing slim, Smart persuaded Mitchell to return to Utah instead.

Mary Katherine, meanwhile, had recognized the kidnapper as a local handyman who had worked on their home and called himself Immanuel. Authorities confirmed that Immanuel was Brian David Mitchell and aired a sketch on *America's Most Wanted* in February 2003. Mitchell and Barzee were spotted with Smart on the streets of Sandy, Utah, and taken into police custody on March 12, 2003. Smart was returned to her family that day, where she quickly resumed her normal activities, determined to put the horrific ordeal behind her. Mitchell was sentenced to serve life in prison while Barzee was sentenced to fifteen years.

Missing Children in the 1970s

Following the May 25, 1979, disappearance of six-year-old Etan Patz on his first walk alone to his school bus stop, advocacy groups for missing and abducted children began numerous campaigns in order to quickly and effectively spread information about kidnappings and disappearances of minors. Not only citizens but also private companies took up the call, most famously with dairies printing the faces of missing children on the sides of milk cartons. This advocacy led to hundreds of laws passed at the local, state, and national levels and the establishment of a number of national institutions. Missing children cases are part of the FBI's National Crime Information Center database, and the AMBER Alert system and National Center for Missing and Exploited Children function to aid the hunt. Before 1979, however, very few laws were in place to aid the search of missing children.

Parents of missing children in the 1970s were made to wait between one and three days before filing a missing-persons report. Very few police officers were specifically trained to deal with cases of child abduction at the time, and there was no national database available in order to enter or cross-reference information about suspects or victims. In fact, there was little cooperation from state to state or even from city to city in missing-persons cases. Such specialized forces as a missing-persons unit of a police department did not exist, and without the use of the internet, word of a disappearance spread by mouth, telephones, letters, and faxes rather than instantaneously.

Jack has trouble coming to terms with Susie's death and suspects his neighbor *(©wavebreakmedia / Shutterstock.com)*

Susie, abducted and murdered in 1973, explains: "This was before kids of all races and genders started appearing on milk cartons or in the daily mail. It was still back when people believed things like that didn't happen."

CRITICAL OVERVIEW

While critical reception of the *The Lovely Bones* was positive, the novel became a surprise success with readers, leading to the novel's holding the number one position on the *New York Times* best-seller list and quickly selling over a million copies. This is an admirable and rare feat for a debut novel. As Rebecca Mead explains in her review for the *London Review of Books*, the book's "success is a categorical surprise, since literary novels hardly ever reach a mass audience in America; but its subject-matter is so perfectly resonant with the tenor of the times that its appeal is transparent." The novel was awarded the Bram Stoker Award for First Novel in 2002

and the American Booksellers Association Book of the Year Award for Adult Fiction in 2003.

Most reviews are filled with praise for the novel. In the *New York Times*, Katherine Bouton points out Sebold's deft handling of her novel's difficult and dark topics: "The very idea of Sebold's subject matter might make a reader queasy. But there's nothing prurient or exploitative in *The Lovely Bones*. Susie's story, paradoxically, is one of hope, set against grim reality." In "A Perfect Afterlife," for the *Guardian*, Ali Smith is impressed most by the novel's first chapters, in which the description of the violent crime and its immediate aftermath are powerfully juxtaposed against a peaceful suburban setting, explaining that the "opening chapters are shattering and dazzling in their mix of horror and normality." Tasha Robinson finds the narrative effect of Susie's narration from heaven compelling in her review of the novel for the A.V. Club: "Through this perspective, Susie explores...the history of family members, friends, and outsiders whom her death touched. She weaves

COMPARE
&
CONTRAST

- **1973:** The majority of police departments in the United States require a waiting period of between twenty-four and seventy-two hours before the relatives of a missing person can file a missing-persons report.

  2002: Twenty-six states use the AMBER Alert system to alert civilians of missing children. The system, initiated in 1998, is designed to spread information about missing children or child abductions as widely and rapidly as possible to increase the chances of rescue.

  Today: All fifty states utilize the AMBER Alert system. Additionally, the alerts are sent electronically over the Wireless Emergency Alert program and over social media networks.

- **1973:** The first mobile phone is invented, weighing nearly four and half pounds. Cell phone technology is not yet available to the public, and telephone communication is achieved strictly through landlines.

  2002: Compact cell phones capable of calling and texting are widely available. Students begin to carry phones with them as a way of quickly contacting family and friends.

  Today: Smartphones, with Internet capability, GPS tracking, and cameras are carried by a majority of American mobile phone users.

- **1973:** No program exists at the national level of government to organize data concerning missing children. Although police can enter information about stolen objects such as cars or jewelry in a national FBI database, they cannot do the same for missing persons.

  2002: The National Center for Missing and Exploited Children provides resources for the families and friends of missing children, as well as performing twenty-two functions to help protect and recover missing children; resources include the CyberTipline, Child Victim Identification program, and the national hotline 1-800-THE-LOST.

  Today: As of 2015, there are over four hundred thousand entries for missing children in the FBI's National Crime Information Center. In that year alone, the National Center for Missing and Exploited Children provided assistance with over thirteen thousand of these cases.

them all into a conjoined, cinematic tapestry, but maintains an intimate perspective."

For its enormous response from American readers, *The Lovely Bones* is considered by many critics to be the most popular debut novel in the United States since Margaret Mitchell's 1936 classic *Gone with the Wind*. Tony Buchsbaum explains the novel's appeal in "Voice from Beyond," for *January Magazine*: "It's a slight, serious novel that almost comes across like a narrated photo album, with each searing, carefully selected image worth its requisite thousand words."

CRITICISM

Amy L. Miller

Miller is a graduate of the University of Cincinnati, and she currently resides in New Orleans, Louisiana. In the following essay, she examines the Salmon family's collapse and rebirth following Susie's death in Sebold's The Lovely Bones.

In Sebold's *The Lovely Bones*, the concept of family is defined not by shared blood but by the cherished connections that grow from hardships people face together. Susie's death not only disrupts her immediate family's lives but

WHAT DO I READ NEXT?

- Sebold's second novel, *The Almost Moon* (2008), takes place in the twenty-four hours following Helen Knightly's murder of her own mother, a rash and violent deed in the otherwise unremarkable life of a middle-aged divorcee and mother of two. Skipping between flashbacks to her childhood and the tense hours after the crime, the novel explores a mother-daughter relationship gone horribly wrong and the toxic atmosphere that led to Helen's decision.

- In Kiran Desai's *The Inheritance of Loss* (2005), an isolated family living in a dilapidated house in the Himalayas live separate but nevertheless interconnected lives as they fight through the fog of the past in an attempt to grab hold of a brighter future. Sai, a sixteen-year-old orphan, must navigate the dramas of her first love as her crush, the intelligent and impoverished Gyan, joins a local militia that pits him against her adopted family.

- In Jandy Nelson's young-adult novel *The Sky Is Everywhere* (2012), seventeen-year-old Lennie copes with the sudden, cataclysmic death of her younger sister, Bailey, as well as her mother's absence from her life, while navigating her shifting attraction to her boyfriend, Toby, who is also grieving Bailey's death, and a new student, Joe, whose musical genius offers a breath fresh air.

- *A Stolen Life: A Memoir*, by Jaycee Dugard (2012), is the firsthand account of the eighteen years Dugard was held in captivity by her kidnappers, Philip and Nancy Garrido. From 1991 to 2009, Dugard endured unimaginable abuse, recounted in her memoir using pages from the journal she kept while she was held prisoner in a makeshift cell in the couple's backyard.

- *The Collector*, by John Fowles (1997), explores the mind of a violent psychopath as he stalks an unsuspecting art student, Miranda Grey, eventually kidnapping her and holding her captive in his basement. Told through both Miranda and her attacker's perspectives, the novel is as engrossing a psychological thriller as it is terrifying as a glimpse into a disturbed and dangerous mind.

- Harper Lee's *To Kill a Mockingbird* (1960), to which *The Lovely Bones* is frequently compared, is an undisputed classic of American literature. Set in small-town Alabama, the novel portrays dark subject matter—the wrongful arrest and trial of Tom Robinson for the rape of Mayella Ewell—through the innocent eyes of a young girl, Scout Finch.

- Following a tragic school bus crash, the members of the small town in Russell Banks's *Sweet Hereafter* (1992) cope with the loss of fourteen children while searching for someone to blame. Told through four complex and conflicting points of view, the novel emphasizes how grief can shape perception and how perception shapes reality.

- Anna Quindlen's *Black and Blue* (1998) tells the story of Fran Benedetto, who takes on a new identity in order to escape her abusive marriage. Starting over with her son and the help of a relocation agency, Fran cannot shake the fear that one day her husband will come looking for her.

---

also turns the quiet town she lives in on its side, revealing both the good and the bad in neighbors, classmates, teachers, and friends. As the community struggles with the implications of Susie's death—an unspeakably violent murder of a child in their peaceful hamlet—her family members struggle to maintain their equilibrium.

" EACH FAMILY MEMBER'S ROLE IS CALLED INTO QUESTION BY SUSIE'S DEATH, AND EACH OF THEM MUST FIGURE OUT HOW TO LIVE SIDE BY SIDE WITH THEIR SORROW RATHER THAN AT WAR WITH IT."

Abigail asks, in her soul-searching following the death, if she is still capable of being a mother. Jack wonders if catching the murderer himself will make up for the fact that he could not protect his daughter. Lindsey cannot look at herself in mirrors without seeing her sister's face. Buckley is too young to understand the special treatment he receives, though he recognizes that bad news always follows the trip for ice cream or a new toy. Each family member's role is called into question by Susie's death, and each of them must figure out how to live side by side with their sorrow rather than at war with it. The process is a slow one: for Abigail it takes seven years of running away, while Lindsey is pulled from the act of sealing herself forever inside a protective shell by Samuel. Susie, too, must face the fact that her role within the family has changed forever. The Salmons do not have a choice in the matter of Susie's death. Their choices lie instead with what they will do afterwards.

Susie's afterwards is heaven, where she cannot have what she wants most ("Mr. Harvey dead and me living"), but she can have anything else her heart desires. Not surprisingly, her attention is held more by the chaos she left behind on Earth than by the lazy, perfect infinity of heaven: "Horror on Earth is real and it is every day. It is like a flower or like the sun: it cannot be contained." She watches in dismay as Brian Nelson beats her father in the cornfield, as her mother kisses Len at the hospital, and as George Harvey escapes justice. She watches with envy as Lindsey grows up and with bittersweet longing as Ray and Ruth become close. However, despite the injustice and sorrow she helplessly observes, as well as the unfairness of her own situation, her youthful perspective as a clever and confident fourteen-year-old brings light to the weight of her cosmic omniscience.

In the *London Review of Books*, Rebecca Mead describes the novel as "a coming of age story told by a character who isn't of age and never will be. Susie is a bright and ironical observer, even of her own murder." Susie finds humor where others would never dare and forgiveness where it seems undeserved. She does not judge her mother for either her affair or her flight from home, and though she desperately wants to be in Lindsey's shoes as she graduates from college, Susie recognizes her own desire as a strict impossibility—the silly fantasies of an immature schoolgirl. Susie grows in the novel through her gradual acceptance of her fate, which is tied to her family's ability to move forward without her. As they come to terms with her loss and form new connections in place of the old, she finds the peace she needs for her spirit to move on.

Katherine Bouton writes in the *New York Times*, "The bones of *The Lovely Bones* belong not to the victim but to an abstract and quite positive idea—namely, that bones are the structure on which living things are built." Susie's death becomes the foundation on which a new Salmon family is built. The connections between its members are made through generous acts of sympathy, forgiveness, and humor during hard times—all the traits that make Susie special for a girl her age. Ray Singh and his mother, Ruana, become honorary members of the family, as do Ruth, Hal, and Samuel. Many of these characters begin the story as strangers. Susie had spoken to Ruth only once to compliment her art and shared her first kiss with Ray only days before her death. Lindsey's crush on Samuel was similarly new and undeveloped, while Hal and Ruana were especially private members of the community.

However, after Susie's death, these characters begin to spiral closer and closer to the Salmons, until fate finds most of them gathered together in the Salmon house for a celebration of Jack's return from the hospital. Hal has become like a brother to Buckley, Samuel a husband to Lindsey, Ruana a best friend for Abigail, and Ray a lover to Susie. Ruth is the conduit that connects Susie directly to Earth, allowing her a fleeting moment of physical contact with the only boy she ever loved. The selfless acts of the new family members—from Ruana's companionable declaration to Abigail, "This is a weird place we both live," to Ruth's willingness to swap bodies with Susie—comes from a need

When Lindsey and Samuel have a child, they name her in part after Susie (©*Luna Vandoorne | Shutterstock.com*)

within them not just to help a family clearly in need of rescue but to feel a sense of belonging in a town where they never entirely fit in. The Salmons' extraordinary circumstances make the others leave the steady comfort of their quiet lives to help, turning all of them into extraordinary human beings.

In this context, Samuel Heckler arriving on the Salmons' doorstep on Christmas Day with a present for Lindsey is an act of heroism. Lindsey was "was working hard keeping everyone out, everyone," Susie explains, "but she found Samuel Heckler cute. Her heart, like an ingredient in a recipe, was reduced, and regardless of my death she was thirteen." Samuel prevents Lindsey from collapsing in on herself as she had planned. Instead, through Samuel's steady love and support, she is able to stay in contact with her emotions instead of dissociating herself, to interact with others in a healthy, productive way rather than maintaining the stony silence she had adopted after Susie's death, and to see herself instead of Susie in the mirror's reflection. Samuel saves her from sacrificing her identity to the loss of Susie.

For Abigail, however, Susie's death unlocks feelings she had successfully buried in the secret depths of her "Ocean Eyes," feelings deemed inappropriate for a stable, suburban mother of three. In his review "Voice from Beyond," Tony Buchsbaum explains that "Susie's mother finds herself released emotionally by the event, and uses it as a way to escape the prison of her life." Her first step outside the former boundaries of her existence is to pursue her interest in Len. The affair goes unnoticed by her husband, who is consumed by his obsession with bringing George Harvey to justice. In fact, the slight against her husband is twofold, as she unintentionally sabotages Jack's only chance at seeing George imprisoned: Len cannot be found the day Lindsey retrieves the evidence because Abigail, sick of her family's focus on Susie's death, has arranged to meet him at the mall. This coincidental timing leads to Len's downfall as a character and Abigail's abandonment of her family.

Once Abigail has a taste of freedom with Len, she wants more. However, even after seven years alone in California, she thinks of Susie constantly. Though she cannot be a perfect mother, she comes to realize she belongs with her family, loving Susie even though she was gone. For Susie, watching from heaven, her mother's freely given love is the last puzzle piece that leads to her release from earthly concerns. Susie understands that her mother "needed the time to know that this love would not destroy her, and I had . . . given her that time, could give it, for it was what I had in great supply."

Jack's fight against the reality of Susie's death is especially physical. He is determined to help the police whether through aiding in the search or reporting on George Harvey's activities. He ends up in the hospital twice: from the beating he takes in the cornfield and from a heart attack following an argument with Buckley. Both hospitalizations are the result of his inability to let go of Susie, with whom he had a special connection that he cannot replicate with his other children. He finds, instead, that he can connect with Lindsey and Buckley in different ways. His years as a single parent have made his children fond of him, and Buckley especially feels an urge to watch and protect his father from harm. A new love for Abigail springs from his old love for her, making their reunion a happy one despite her misgivings. Jack finds that letting go of Susie does not mean giving up his love for her, but seeing those around him—his wife and children—with clear eyes, unclouded by a tragedy he could not prevent.

With Susie's death, her family dies as well. As Buchsbaum points out, "For Susie's nuclear family the event is a nuclear explosion, breaking the tight cluster of her loved ones apart, tossing them into an emotional tempest they didn't anticipate or dream they would ever experience." However, just as Susie is given new sight in heaven, her family is given the chance to start again. The connections that once held them together as a happy family snap under the strain of their collective grief. However, with the help of their friends and with genuine effort on the part of the Salmons to overcome the urge to lie down and give up, they are able to raise a new home to replace the old, using their love for Susie as their unshakable foundation.

Source: Amy L. Miller, Critical Essay on *The Lovely Bones*, in *Novels for Students*, Gale, Cengage Learning, 2017.

> BUT THIS NEW NOVEL OWES LESS TO HER CHILDHOOD AND MORE TO WATCHING HER MOTHER CARE FOR HER OWN MOTHER. THAT'S AS FAR AS SHE WILL GO."

John Freeman
In the following interview excerpt, Sebold declares she is surprised that some find her novels "bleak."

Eight years after publishing a harrowing memoir about being raped, and half a decade since her debut novel, *The Lovely Bones*, became a worldwide blockbuster, Alice Sebold has discovered she is a more private person than she thought. You can see it in her face as she strides, 15 minutes late, onto the podium of New York's flagship Barnes & Noble store at Union Square, dressed in black and holding a ginger ale. She was out all night and on TV this morning. More bad reviews of her new novel, *The Almost Moon*, are on the way, perhaps explaining the setting of just 300 seats in a room that can squeeze in more than 1,000. Flanking one side of the podium is a wood-cut of Moby Dick, a monster who entranced and eluded Melville's hero in a way the heroine of Sebold's new novel could relate to—except that the monster she confronts is her mother. In the first line, Sebold's heroine kills her dead. "All right," Sebold jokes into the microphone after reading a poem by the Polish Nobel laureate, Wislawa Szymborska, "Who's ready for more of my peppy, happy fiction?"

Five minutes later, the reading is over. Q&As commence, and one begins to appreciate why such appearances might be a little battering for Sebold. "I am curious to know if the story you read has a parallel to your own life?" asks one woman. "Is your mother living and what did she think of *The Almost Moon*?" asks another. "Can you tell us about your background?" asks a man, apparently unaware of *Lucky*. "Did you have siblings, where did you grow up, had you any other ambitions besides writing?" "My weight?" Sebold tries to joke. "It's visible," the man shoots back.

The barrage continues and then dies down, but one presumption remains in the air: that no matter what Alice Sebold writes, there will be a code, a key to it somewhere, buried in her real life or her memoir, if only the public can keep her still long enough to ask about it. And she's not entirely a victim to this assumption. "What did you like to read growing up?" one guest asks, to which Sebold replies, a little too quickly to be fibbing: Sylvia Plath, Robert Lowell, all the confessionalists.

"I knew I made a mistake when I said that," Sebold tells me two days later from San Francisco, where she moved recently with her husband, the novelist Glen David Gould. Her voice has a husky, deadpan pallor—the sound of brutal honest[y]. Then she catches herself and changes to a more controlled timbre. "Those were the perfect poets for me at the time, living in the suburbs where I was growing up, because they had a certain intelligence and spice which told me where I was living and what I was experiencing was not the whole fabric of the world." The world she would eventually encounter almost need not be explained, so familiar is it from *Lucky*: the brutal rape, her quest to put her rapist behind bars, the recovery then non-recovery in 1980s New York, reckless behaviour, drugs, moving to California, a new start at writing, and meeting her husband.

Domestic happiness—where Sebold washed up in her late thirties like a shipwreck—won't be a threat to her production. "I wasn't able to write very well the whole time I was in my darkest mood," she says now. "I had to get to the place where I could write well—I'll try not to get too happy, but you know what that's not really a threat." She's right.

The Almost Moon grew out of this mood and stability, and is even darker yet than *The Lovely Bones*: somewhere between Patricia Highsmith and Stephen King. After all, this novel has a much more complicated, ambiguous sense of victimhood to it, and it begins with one of the most swiftly plotted lines in recent memory. "When all is said and done, killing my mother came easily," says Helen Knightly after smothering to death her 88-year-old mother on the patio behind her home. Mrs Knightly was suffering from dementia.

"It's a shock that I am suddenly being accused of being bleak," Sebold says. But there is something far darker about *The Almost Moon* than *The Lovely Bones*, which told the story of a raped and murdered 14-year-old girl who looks down from heaven as her death remains unsolved.

Helen's is not a freak crime of malicious intent, nor even a loving attempt to put her mother out of a degrading misery. It is a fantasy of revenge, acted out. "Once begun," Helen says, "I did not stop. She struggled, her blue-veined hands, with the rings she feared would be stolen if she ever took them off, grabbed at my arms...I held the towels for a long time, staring right at her, until I felt the tip of her nose snap and saw the muscles of her body go suddenly slack and knew that she had died."

Helen tries to cover up her crime, calling on her ex-husband, who flies out from California, and then her best friend's son, whom she takes to bed in a fury. Neither can help, especially as chips of memory drift back, and a reader discovers that Helen and her troubled father lived their lives in thrall to her mother and the mental illness that incapacitated her. In *Lucky*, Sebold discovered "memory could save, that it had power, that it was often the only resource of the powerless, the oppressed, the brutalized." In *The Almost Moon*, she has written a character who turns to that recourse for solace and is crushed by it.

It's hard not to point out the similarities between Helen and Sebold. In *Lucky*, she described her mother as an ex-alcoholic who took to bed some days, so frail that Sebold's first concern after being raped was to protect her from it. But this new novel owes less to her childhood and more to watching her mother care for her own mother. That's as far as she will go. "If you take all [a writer's] family members, and the dynamics they have, and you put them in a blender, there is a lot of the glue of their work, but not the work itself; the same is true for me. There is this desire—and how could you avoid it?—to find the roots. But I am not Helen, my mother is not Clair."

The Pennsylvania Sebold writes about does remain true to life, only shaded a bit darker, as Katherine Anne Porter did with Texas and Louisiana. "I was talking about Philadelphia with a couple friends who are New Yorkers," Sebold says, "and they were saying the difference between New York and Philly is there is a replacement when something breaks in New York. In Philadelphia they paint over it, put a bright blue coat on top—there's a freshen-it-up kind of feeling, layers of patina, a sepia which is also in my mind creepier, and richer."

I ask if, in some way, Helen is the self she could have been had she never left, as Rabbit Angstrom was the person John Updike could have been had he never left Shillington. She pauses, and says, "I have seen many people who are unable to break that oppressive, destructive, duty-bound bond—not just to a parent who is ill, but a mentally ill parent who can be full of personality and very dominating. They are . . . inherently more interesting—either you break free from that or you don't."

For her, this calls to mind Highsmith, whose work she adores. "A detail about her life which not many people know," Sebold says: "Her mother tried to abort her by her drinking turpentine, and Highsmith wound up taking care of her in her old age. Here was this woman who was known as being a people-hater, taking on this incredible burden of a woman who tried to erase her." In other words, people are not their books, and vice versa.

It's not something Sebold has said just to journalists and reading groups. *Lucky* and *The Lovely Bones* prompted an avalanche of letters, some disturbing, some amusingly disturbing (fan fiction from grandmothers with ideas for how she could have killed off the rapist in her novel), some of it so involved she has had to disengage. "It's only me and my husband," she says.

So now, a week after her US publication, Sebold has already begun to retreat. She was on the road for three years with *The Lovely Bones*, and that part of her life is over. "I think you only learn what kind of personality you have by committing to things." So while she feels grateful for her success, she doesn't feel she owes the world herself in response. In fact, she is being so irresponsible now as to moonlight with poetry, rather than work on the next novel. "I'd like to go back to poetry again," Sebold says, for the first time sounding sheepish. "I really, really revere good poetry. It's been my private discipline." The question remains, though, whether Alice Sebold can have privacy any more . . . .

Source: John Freeman, "Alice Sebold: 'Happiness Is Not a Threat'," in *Independent*, October 25, 2007.

Publishers Weekly

In the following review, the anonymous reviewer praises Sebold's "bold" decision to narrate the story from Susie's perspective from heaven.

Sebold's first novel—after her memoir, *Lucky*—is a small but far from minor miracle. Sebold has taken a grim, media-exploited subject and fashioned from it a story that is both tragic and full of light and grace. The novel begins swiftly. In the second sentence, Sebold's narrator, Susie Salmon, announces, "I was fourteen when I was murdered on December 6, 1973." Susie is taking a shortcut through a cornfield when a neighbor lures her to his hideaway. The description of the crime is chilling, but never vulgar, and Sebold maintains this delicate balance between homely and horrid as she depicts the progress of grief for Susie's family and friends. She captures the odd alliances forged and the relationships ruined: the shattered father who buries his sadness trying to gather evidence, the mother who escapes "her ruined heart, in merciful adultery." At the same time, Sebold brings to life an entire suburban community, from the mortician's son to the handsome biker dropout who quietly helps investigate Susie's murder. Much as this novel is about "the lovely bones" growing around Susie's absence, it is also full of suspense and written in lithe, resilient prose that by itself delights. Sebold's most dazzling stroke, among many bold ones, is to narrate the story from Susie's heaven (a place where wishing is having), providing the warmth of a first-person narration and the freedom of an omniscient one. It might be this that gives Sebold's novel its special flavor, for in Susie's every observation and memory—of the smell of skunk or the touch of spider webs—is the reminder that life is sweet and funny and surprising.

(Review of The Lovely Bones, *in* Publishers Weekly, *July 3, 2002.)*

Ron Charles

In the following review, Charles describes the spirituality in the novel as "ecumenical to a fault."

Still, there are reasons not to open this runaway bestseller. In the first chapter, 14-year-old Susie Salmon describes how she was enticed into a little cave by a neighbor on a snowy day. He stuffs her hat into her mouth. They both hear her mother calling her for dinner. He rapes her, cuts her throat, and then dismembers the body. It's the most terrifying scene I've ever read.

For the next seven years, she describes how her family and friends—and even her murderer—cope with her absence. She's in heaven, so she can see everything from up there. It sounds mawkish, like a ghastly version of *Beloved* for white suburbia, but Alice Sebold has done something miraculous here.

It's no coincidence that the novel has been embraced during a period of high anxiety about child abductions—perhaps the only dread darker than our new fear of terrorism.

With her disarming wit and adolescent candor, Susie drags us behind those stories from Salt Lake City and Stanton, Calif., forcing us to consider the mechanics of rape and murder and grief in a way no news report ever could.

A few days after her death, Susie realizes that all the people she's with now are experiencing their own versions of heaven, reflecting their simplest dreams and aspirations from earth.

"There were no teachers in the school," she tells us about her paradise. "We never had to go inside except for art class for me and jazz for my roommate. Our textbooks were *Seventeen* and *Glamour* and *Vogue*. Our heaven had an ice cream shop where, when you asked for peppermint stick ice cream, no one ever said, 'It's seasonal'; it had a newspaper where our pictures appeared a lot and made us look important."

She also discovers that heaven isn't perfect. What she wants most is "to be allowed to grow up." But that's out.

. . . The power of *Lovely Bones* flows from this voice, a voice at once charmingly adolescent and tragically mature. She cares for her parents and siblings beyond measure, but the cosmic distance between them gives her a perspective that resolves the blur of sentimentality or vengeance even when the pain she's describing makes you wince.

Her father spends his days squirming under the weight of guilt for not being there to save his child. Her mother, who always felt cramped by maternal duties, finds the new burden of grief more than she can bear. And her sister moves through school trapped in the "Walking Dead Syndrome—when other people see the dead person and don't see you."

Her classmates react across a full spectrum, from macabre comedy to obsessive sympathy. Most walk through the usual itinerary of community grief—assembly, funeral, anniversary memorial. But a couple of them find that emotional journey inadequate and follow Susie's

disappearance to a deeper sense of themselves and their responsibility in the world.

Susie also watches the bland neighbor who murdered her. She sees him offer condolences. She sees him check on the carving knife in his bedroom. She sees him sweat. These are catch-your-breath scenes that teeter between the possibility of justice or another murder. But the author is so careful here. Susie's vision of his abusive childhood doesn't absolve or even, ultimately, explain the crimes he commits.

She wishes he were dead, but there's no passion in that wish, only a sharp concern for the safety of her sister as she closes in on the truth. By the end, the retribution he receives is perfectly calibrated—ignominious and anonymous.

Susie watches her family for years, long enough, in fact, to note that "it was no longer a Susie-fest on Earth." They eventually reach that once-impossible-to-imagine future with moments, hours, and then somehow whole days of happiness.

But this is as much a story about the dead as about the living. On her side, Susie must realize that she has progress to make, too, but first she insists on returning for one rite of passage that was denied her. Indeed, if the novel stumbles, it's on a weird scene of sexual fulfillment that runs embarrassingly close to Patrick Swayze's finale in *Ghost*.

Some readers—and certainly most reviewers—are likely to treat the religious elements of the plot merely as literary devices, sweet bits of comfort or wit in a novel about family survival and emotional recovery. But that may be like thinking of John Edward's *Crossing Over* as just a talk show.

It's significant that this wildly successful novel comes with a heavy serving of spiritualism—messages from the dead, ghostly visitations, and bodily possessions. None of the characters finds solace in anything as dusty as prayer or a sacred text. And as pleasant as Susie's heaven is, there's no God there, and certainly no Jesus. This is spirituality for an age that's ecumenical to a fault.

But emotionally, it's faultless. Sebold never slips as she follows this family. The risks she walks are enough to give you vertigo. A victim of rape herself when she was in college, she includes some deadly satire of the shallow advice people offer in the face of great loss. There is no "moving on," and time alone won't bring relief either. That only comes through the hard work of learning to care for the living while cradling the memory of this loved one. As her father eventually realizes, "You live in the face of it."

Source: Ron Charles, Review of *The Lovely Bones*, in *Christian Science Monitor*, July 25, 2002.

Becky Ohlsen

In the following review, Ohlsen calls the premise of The Lovely Bones *"inventive."*

When you kill off your narrator in the first 10 pages of a novel and tell readers who the killer is you'd better have one compelling story up your sleeve. Alice Sebold does.

"I was fourteen when I was murdered on December 6, 1973," Susie Salmon tells us in the second sentence of *The Lovely Bones*. She shows us who did it—a neighbor everyone thinks is weird—and describes the horrible scene, a brutal assault and dismemberment in an underground hideout in a bleak winter cornfield. Sebold's triumph is in making Susie's voice so immediately compelling that we don't want to let her go, even after she's dead. We want to know what happens next. So does Susie.

From up in what she calls "my heaven," Susie watches the repercussions of her death among her friends and family. She sees her broken parents crumble away from each other, her younger sister harden her heart, her classmates cling to each other for comfort. She watches her murderer in the calm aftermath of his awful deed. She longs for the one boy she's ever kissed, knowing she'll never touch him again. She misses her dog. She aches for her parents and siblings, yearning to comfort them but unable to interfere. In her heaven, she's granted all her simplest desires—she has friends and a mother-figure—and she delights in her ability to see everything and everyone in the world. Observing her sister one Christmas, she says, "Lindsey had a cute boy in the kitchen . . . I was suddenly privy to everything. She never would have told me any of this stuff . . . She kissed him; it was glorious. I was almost alive again."

But watching the world without being among the living isn't enough for Susie. She's 14 forever, and the pain of her unfulfilled promise infuses her voice as she watches her younger brother and sister growing into roles she'll never play. Still, Susie's no wispy, thinly drawn ghost;

like nearly every other character in the book, she's a remarkable, complex person who has as much humor and kindness as grief.

In the end, what Sebold has accomplished is to find her own inventive way of expressing the universal alienation and powerlessness we all feel, trapped in our own small worlds apart from each other. More than that, she has convinced us that, through love and hope and generosity, these things can be overcome.

Source: Becky Ohlsen, "*The Lovely Bones*: When a Child Disappears," in *Bookpage*, July 19, 2002.

SOURCES

"Alice Sebold," Barclay Agency website, http://barclay agency.com/site/speaker/alice-sebold# (accessed March 24, 2016).

Bouton, Katherine, "What Remains," in *New York Times*, July 14, 2002, http://www.nytimes.com/2002/07/14/books/what-remains.html (accessed March 24, 2016).

Buchsbaum, Tony, "Voice from Beyond," in *January Magazine*, http://www.januarymagazine.com/fiction/lovelybones.html (accessed March 24, 2016).

Glaug, Natalie C., "Sebold, Alice," Pennsylvania Center for the Book website, http://pabook2.libraries.psu.edu/palitmap/bios/Sebold__Alice.html (accessed March 24, 2016).

Goldstein, Bill, "A Dark First Novel Suddenly Soars to the Top," in *New York Times*, October 21, 2002, http://www.nytimes.com/2002/10/21/business/media-a-dark-first-novel-suddenly-soars-to-the-top.html (accessed March 24, 2016).

Greenblatt, Alan, "The Face That Changed the Search for Missing Kids," NPR website, May 24, 2012, http://www.npr.org/2012/05/24/153623769/the-face-that-changed-the-search-for-missing-kids (accessed March 24, 2016).

Hensher, Philip, "An Eternity of Sweet Nothings," in *Guardian*, August 10, 2002, http://www.theguardian.com/books/2002/aug/11/fiction.features2 (accessed March 24, 2016).

Jarrett, Tracy, "'I Was Broken Beyond Repair': Elizabeth Smart Recalls Kidnapping Ordeal," NBC website, October 5, 2013, http://www.nbcnews.com/news/other/i-was-broken-beyond-repair-elizabeth-smart-recalls-kidnapping-ordeal-f8C11336267 (accessed March 24, 2016).

"*The Lovely Bones* (2009)," in *The Numbers*, http://www.he-numbers.com/movie/Lovely-Bones-The#tab = summary (accessed March 24, 2016).

McCrum, Robert, "Adventures in Disturbia," in *Guardian*, October 14, 2007, http://www.theguardian.com/books/2007/oct/14/fiction.features (accessed March 24, 2016).

Mead, Rebecca, "Immortally Cute," in *London Review of Books*, Vol. 24, No. 20, October 17, 2002, http://www.lrb.co.uk/v24/n20/rebecca-mead/immortally-cute (accessed March 24, 2016).

Miller, Laura, Review of *The Lovely Bones*, in *Salon*, August 1, 2002, http://www.salon.com/2002/08/01/sebold_2/ (accessed March 24, 2016).

"Our History," National Center for Missing and Exploited Children website, http://www.missingkids.org/History (accessed March 24, 2016).

Palmer, Brian, "Why Did Missing Children Start Showing Up on Milk Cartons?," in *Slate*, April 20, 2012, http://www.slate.com/articles/news_and_politics/explainer/2012/04/ etan_patz_case_why_did_dairies_put_missing_children_on_their_milk_cartons_.html (accessed March 24, 2016).

Robinson, Tasha, "Alice Sebold: *The Lovely Bones*," AV Club website, August 19, 2002, http://www.avclub.com/review/alice-sebold-ithe-lovely-bonesi-5894 (accessed March 24, 2016).

Sebold, Alice, *The Lovely Bones*, Back Bay Books, 2002.

Smith, Ali, "A Perfect Afterlife," in *Guardian*, August 16, 2002, http://www.theguardian.com/books/2002/aug/17/fiction.alismith (accessed March 24, 2016).

FURTHER READING

Anderson, Laurie Halse, *Speak*, Farrar, Straus and Giroux, 1999.

> A National Book Award finalist, *Speak* follows the life of Melinda, a high school freshman shunned by her classmates for calling the police on a house party the previous summer. Melinda was raped by a popular upperclassman that night, but in the face of scorn from her peers, she withdraws into silence to protect herself from further abuse. Her only release is in art class, where she begins to find her voice again and prepares to let the truth be known.

Atwood, Margaret, *Negotiating with the Dead*, Anchor, 2003.

> This collection of six essays about the writing process includes Atwood's meditations on the ways in which fiction writing seeks to resurrect the dead, as well as her ideal relationship between reader, author, and book. She shares her experiences as a best-selling novelist as well as her struggles as a young, unknown poet and explores what it means personally and culturally to identify as a writer.

Sebold, Alice, *Lucky*, Charles Scribner's Sons, 1999.

> Sebold's memoir of surviving violent rape as a college freshman focuses in particular on the long-lasting damage the attack caused physically, emotionally, socially, mentally, and in her deteriorating relationship with her family as they struggled to understand what she had endured.

Smart, Elizabeth, *My Story*, St. Martin's Griffin, 2013.

> Elizabeth Smart was kidnapped from her home at the age of fourteen and held captive for nine months by Brian David Mitchell and Wanda Barzee. Her story of capture, abuse, rescue, and the long healing process is an incredible testament to her personal strength. Her kidnapping in the summer of 2002 and rescue in 2003 coincided with the publication of *The Lovely Bones* and its rapid climb to the top of the best-seller list.

SUGGESTED SEARCH TERMS

Alice Sebold

The Lovely Bones

Alice Sebold AND The Lovely Bones

fiction AND dead narrator

fiction AND child abduction

fiction AND families

recovery from trauma AND families

young-adult literature AND trauma

The Narrow Road to the Deep North

RICHARD FLANAGAN

2013

The Narrow Road to the Deep North is a novel by Australian writer Richard Flanagan. It was published in Australia in 2013 and the United States in 2014. Much of the book is set in a Japanese prisoner-of-war camp in 1942–1943, where in appalling conditions a group of Australian POWs are forced to build the infamous Thai–Burma railway. The men suffer beatings at the hands of their cruel guards; severe malnutrition leads to rampant disease; and while their commander, Colonel Dorrigo Evans, a surgeon, does everything he can to protect and save his men, many of them die. The novel is largely told through his eyes and surveys his entire life from childhood to old age. In his later years, he is a war hero who must live with his memories of the POW camp and deal with a very public postwar life that affords his restless spirit little comfort. With its vivid themes of love and war, the novel brings to the fore one of the most harrowing episodes in World War II—and readers should be warned that some of the violence is graphically presented.

AUTHOR BIOGRAPHY

Richard Miller Flanagan was born in 1961 in Longford, Tasmania, Australia. He was the fifth of six children; his father was a former prisoner of war in World War II who survived the building of the Thai–Burma railway. Flanagan left school when he was sixteen but later graduated with a

Richard Flanagan (©WENN Ltd | Alamy)

bachelor of arts degree from the University of Tasmania. In 1984, he attended Worcester College, University of Oxford, in England, on a Rhodes Scholarship. He was awarded a master of letters degree in history.

Flanagan worked as a laborer and river guide but also had a calling to become a writer. His first novel was *Death of a River Guide* (1994), about a river guide who recalls his life as he drowns; this was followed by *The Sound of One Hand Clapping* (1997), which features Slovenian immigrants. The latter was a best seller, and on the strength of his first two novels, Flanagan was established as a major Australian writer. His third novel was *Gould's Book of Fish: A Novel in Twelve Fish* (2001), based on the life of an early nineteenth-century convict. The novel won the Commonwealth Writers' Prize in 2002. In 2006, *The Unknown Terrorist*, Flanagan's fourth novel, was published, followed in 2008 by *Wanting*, which was named a *New Yorker* Book of the Year and won the Queensland Premier's Prize, the Western Australian Premier's Prize, and the Tasmania Book Prize.

Flanagan published *The Narrow Road to the Deep North* in 2013, and it won the prestigious Man Booker Prize, the Queensland Literary Award for Fiction, and the Prime Minister's Literary Award for Fiction in 2014. Flanagan has also written numerous essays and articles on topics such as literature, politics, and the environment for newspapers and magazines in Australia and abroad. *And What Do You Do, Mr Gable?*, a collection of Flanagan's nonfiction, was published in 2011. In addition, Flanagan wrote and directed the 1998 film adaptation of *The Sound of One Hand Clapping*. It was shown at the Berlin Film Festival that year and was nominated for the Golden Bear. As of 2016, Flanagan was living in Hobart, Tasmania, with his wife, Majda, and three daughters.

PLOT SUMMARY

Part I
1-3

In Tasmania in the mid-1920s, Dorrigo Evans is nine years old, living in the hamlet of

MEDIA ADAPTATIONS

- An audio version of *The Narrow Road to the Deep North* is available from Audible and as a CD, as read by David Atlas and produced by Blackstone Audio in 2014. Running time is a minute under fifteen hours.

Cleveland. It is a poor village; his father works on the railways. When he is twelve, Dorrigo attends high school on a scholarship. He is good at football and enjoys the companionship of other boys.

4–5

Dorrigo, a doctor, is now twenty-seven years old and is in a hotel room with his paramour, Amy. World War II is under way, and Dorrigo is about to ship out with the troops.

6–10

Dorrigo is seventy-seven years old. He is in a hotel room with Lynette, one of his mistresses. For decades he has been famous as a war hero and surgeon, although he does not feel he deserves the honors that are bestowed on him as a result of what happened in the Japanese prisoner-of-war camp. He is writing a preface to a book about that experience, which began in 1943, when, as a colonel in the army, he was a POW along with twenty-two thousand other Australians. The POWs were forced to build a railway between Thailand and Burma. Conditions for the POWS were terrible, and one in three died, Dorrigo writes.

11–17

The Australians begin the war with a campaign in Egypt and Syria against Vichy French forces. Dorrigo is second-in-command of a casualty-clearing station. Later, after capture and after the fall of Singapore, they are transported to the jungle, where they begin to clear the forest for the first stage of the railway line the Japanese are determined to build. Conditions are not too bad at first, and in the evenings the men amuse themselves by staging concerts. But then things take a turn for the worse. Rest days are eliminated, work quotas go up, and shifts get longer. Dorrigo is in command of the POWs, and he tries to keep morale up as beatings, starvation, and disease cause increasing numbers of deaths as the men are forced to work on what they call the Line.

18

As he lies in bed with Lynette, Dorrigo tries to recall some of the most terrible incidents that happened on the Line, all those years ago.

Part II

1–3

It is 1940, and Dorrigo is in army training in Adelaide. One day he visits a bookstore, where he gets into a conversation with an attractive woman who wears a flower in her hair. There is an attraction between them, which Dorrigo finds disturbing, perhaps because he already has a girlfriend, named Ella.

4

In the POW camp, Dorrigo negotiates with the Japanese commander, Major Nakamura, to get a day's rest for his men.

5

Dissatisfied, in an unfulfilling marriage, and feeling that he no longer fits in the world, Dorrigo leaves Lynette and drives off somewhat drunk.

6–7

Back in 1940, Dorrigo returns to Melbourne on leave to stay with Ella. His feelings for her have been disrupted by his encounter with the woman in the bookstore. The following weekend, he sets out to visit his uncle Keith Mulvaney, who runs a pub/hotel outside Adelaide. Keith is not there, but Dorrigo meets Keith's wife, Amy, and finds that she is the same woman he met in the bookstore.

8

Major Nakamura is awakened at night by his lieutenant and must find a way of getting a truck freed from a road that has become impassable owing to rain. The truck carries important supplies, and Nakamura orders that twenty prisoners be dispatched to rescue the truck, which is three kilometers away.

9–13

Dorrigo meets Uncle Keith for the first time in his life. Keith has to go away overnight to attend a conference, so Dorrigo is left with Amy. They go to a nightclub, and Dorrigo knows they are on the brink of starting an affair. On his next leave, trying to forget Amy, Dorrigo visits Ella in Melbourne.

14

Colonel Kota arrives at the POW camp and informs Nakamura of new, more arduous requirements for the railway. The deadline for completion has also been brought forward, and Nakamura regards it as impossible. More and more of his workers are dying.

15

Amy reflects on the fact that she feels empty in her marriage to Keith. She also tries to put Dorrigo out of her mind.

16

Colonel Kota tells Nakamura of his experience of beheading a prisoner with a sword. They also talk about traditional Japanese literature, which they both love.

17–27

Dorrigo and Amy begin their affair. Later, Amy tells of how she married Keith because she was pregnant. However, he persuaded her to have an abortion. Although Keith is kind, they are not happily married. Dorrigo spends as much time as he can with Amy. Their romance continues all summer, until Keith tells her that he knows what is going on. Amy tells Dorrigo he should go back to Ella. Dorrigo says that when the war is over, he will come back and marry her. He is then told he is to be shipped out to the Pacific to join the war. Some while later, Keith tells Amy he has heard that Dorrigo, who is known to be a POW, is dead. There is an explosion at Keith's hotel, which kills Keith.

Part III

1–2

In the tent that houses twenty POWs, Darky Gardiner returns in the night after having been sent to rescue the truck. Other men in the tent include Tiny Middleton, Rabbit Hendricks, Chum Fahey, Sheephead Morton, Rooster Mac-Neice, and Jimmy Bigelow. The men are in various stages of ill health, having suffered torture,

beatings, starvation, and unreasonable labor demands.

3–4

In the morning Bigelow plays reveille, and the men rouse themselves. When the guards come to inspect, one of them, known as the Goanna, beats Darky because he folded his blanket in the wrong way.

5–6

Dorrigo tries to keep up prisoner morale and, as a doctor, to save their lives, in impossibly difficult circumstances. For the first time in nearly a year, he receives a letter; it is from Ella. Dorrigo, though, thinks of Amy and how he longs to see her again.

7–8

The men receive their breakfast of watery rice. Darky slips in the mud, spilling his food. Rooster MacNeice gulps his down, but Tiny Middleton, seeing what happened, shares his food with Darky. The men assemble for morning parade; the number of sick men has increased. Nakamura says he needs five hundred men to work, but Dorrigo says he has only 363 men capable of working. They eventually settle on 429.

9–10

The POWs get their tools from the depot and walk to the Line. Darky has a fever. His shoe is broken, and he falls and cannot get up. The men wait. Eventually, Sheephead Morton pulls him up, but he falls again. He tells the men to go on without him.

11–13

Dorrigo goes on his morning rounds of the cholera camp, in which there are nearly fifty sick men. Many die quickly of the disease, and there are daily funerals, at which Bigelow performs as bugler. On this day there is a funeral for a man named Lenny, and also for Rabbit Hendricks and two other men.

14

Darky struggles along but is left far behind. He passes out. When he comes to, he stumbles upon seven POWS who are hiding out, taking a rest day unbeknownst to the Japanese. Darky knows they should be in his gang, and they ask him to cover for them. He does not care to and tells them to go with him, but only one does so.

15–16

Colonel Kota inspects the railway line. He finds Darky lying in the mud and goes to behead him with his sword, but he loses his nerve and walks away. The Goanna, surprisingly, tells Darky he must go to the hospital. Darky crawls off and manages to get there, where a POW named Shugs takes care of him.

17–18

Dorrigo operates on Jack Rainbow, who has a bleeding, infected stump following an earlier operation. Dorrigo tries everything he can but is unable to keep the man alive.

19–27

The Japanese officers discover that some men have been hiding, and they decide to punish the POW sergeant who is responsible for that work gang. The sergeant is Darky, who is severely beaten while the other prisoners are forced to watch. Dorrigo tries in vain to get the beating stopped. Darky dies later that night after falling into the latrine.

Part IV

1–2

In immediate postwar Japan, Nakamura lives in poverty in a squalid, ruined area of Tokyo. He knows he is being hunted by the Americans as a possible war criminal. In a violent incident, he kills a boy and robs a prostitute, using the money to buy false identity papers and travel by train to Kobe.

3

Choi Sang-min, the Korean whom the POWs knew as the Goanna, has been condemned to death as a war criminal by an Australian military court. He sits in his jail cell contemplating his life and his imminent end.

4–6

Several years after the war, survivors of the Line meet in a pub. They drink a lot and laugh at their memories. Then, late at night, they go to a fish shop that Darky Gardiner always spoke about. They throw rocks through the window and take the fish. The following night they go to the owner to apologize.

7

Dorrigo leaves the army in 1948 and returns to Sydney, where he marries Ella, somewhat reluctantly.

8–10

Choi Sang-min is hanged, while gradually Nakamura rebuilds his life, working in a hospital and living with a woman named Ikuko. He forms a friendship with a doctor, Kameya Sato. Later, he marries Ikuko, and they have two children. In 1959, he gets a job with the Japan Blood Bank in Osaka, largely because Kota, the former colonel, also works there.

11–13

Dorrigo visits Jack Rainbow's widow to give her Jack's medals. She is lonely, and he comforts her. After Dorrigo leaves, she puts the medals into the fire.

Part V

1–2

Nakamura gets throat cancer, and his wife cares for him with devotion. In the mid-1960s, he visits his former corporal, Tomokawa.

3–4

Dorrigo has a very public life in Melbourne, attending memorial dinners, fund-raising breakfasts, and the like, and he is a patron of many charities. All this bores him, however, as does Ella, his wife. Ella, however, continues to love him.

5

Nakamura talks with Tomokawa. He remains proud of what he did in the war, helping to get the railway built. He remains devoted to the emperor and convinces himself he has lived a good life. He dies within a few months.

6–9

Dorrigo is lonely, even though he lives a companionable life with Ella. In 1967, he visits his brother Tom, who has had a heart attack. Dorrigo learns that Tom fathered a child by Ruth Macguire, wife of Jackie Macguire. Ruth was an Aborigine, and the child was raised by another family under the name Frank Gardiner—known in the POW camp as Darky. Darky was therefore Dorrigo's nephew. Later that day, in the street in Sydney, Dorrigo sees Amy, but they walk past each other without speaking.

10

Over the years Amy had thought of trying to contact Dorrigo, and she knew it was he when she passed him on the street. But she did not know how she would tell him that she had terminal cancer.

11

Dorrigo drives to a village just outside of Hobart to visit Ella's sister, where Ella and their three children also are staying. But there is a bushfire, and Dorrigo fears Ella may be trapped. He breaks through a roadblock and heads into the fire.

12–13

Ella and the children flee the danger on foot. They take refuge in a fibro shed that will not burn. Dorrigo arrives and rescues them. He then drives desperately through the fire until they reach safety.

14

Jimmy Bigelow lives to old age, and his memories of being a POW soften. Eventually he recalls no acts of violence in the camp, and then, later, he forgets the entire experience.

15–17

Dorrigo is fatally injured in a car crash in a suburb of Sydney. As he lies dying, he recalls an incident in the POW camp, when he had to select one hundred men to march to another camp a hundred miles away. He knew they would all most likely die. Three days after the accident, he dies.

18

The night before the selection of the hundred men, Dorrigo reads a letter from Ella he received earlier that day. Ella says that Keith and Amy Mulvaney have been killed in a hotel fire. At the time, he does not realize that Ella is lying to him. He goes to the latrine, and coming back shines his light on a crimson flower he spots along the trail.

CHARACTERS

Bonox Baker

Bonox Baker is an Australian POW. He is a corporal who works as an orderly in the cholera camp.

Jimmy Bigelow

Jimmy Bigelow is an Australian POW bugler who plays at funerals and also reveille at dawn. He survives the war, but his dreams of becoming a musician do not work out. He works as a storeman at a factory. He has children and grandchildren and lives to the age of ninety.

Dorrigo Evans

Dorrigo Evans grew up in a poor family in Tasmania. His mother died when he was nineteen. A gifted individual, Dorrigo won a scholarship to study medicine at the University of Melbourne, and he became a surgeon. In World War II, he is a colonel in the Australian army and ends up as the officer in charge of the POWs who are forced to build the Thai–Burma railway. Dorrigo does everything he can to ease the suffering of the men, putting their own interests ahead of his own, and they look up to him. After the war, he eventually becomes famous, as both a war hero and a surgeon. He marries Ella, and they have three children, but he is not close to his family and takes many mistresses, even into his late seventies. Dorrigo is not a happy man; he is bored by his celebrity status, and he spends time cogitating on the meaning of his existence and his harrowing experiences in the POW camp, without ever reaching any firm conclusions.

Ella Evans

Ella becomes Dorrigo Evans's wife. She comes from a professional family in Melbourne. Her father is a solicitor, and she is a teacher. She is an attractive woman whom Dorrigo met while doing his surgical training. Eventually, however, he finds her rather dull. She remains faithful to him in spite of his infidelities.

Tom Evans

Tom Evans is Dorrigo's older brother. Dorrigo sees little of him through their early adulthoods, but they meet up again in later life after Tom has a heart attack. Dorrigo learns that Tom fathered a child by the wife of Jackie Maguire, and the child turns out to have been Darky Gardiner.

Chum Fahey

Chum Fahey is an Australian POW. He survives the war and is one of the ex-POWs who meet up in a pub later for a reunion.

Lieutenant Fukuhara

Lieutenant Fukuhara is a Japanese officer at the POW camp. He acts as interpreter for Major Nakamura.

Frank "Darky" Gardiner

"Darky" Gardiner is an Australian POW. His real name is Frank, but he is called Darky because he is of mixed race; his mother was an Aborigine woman, the wife of Jackie Macguire. Darky's father is Tom Evans, but he is unaware of his parentage, since he was raised by a foster family. Darky has a habit of singing on the edge of the camp as the POWs return from their work at night. As a sergeant, Darky is held responsible by the Japanese when some men on his work gang go missing. He is severely beaten and dies shortly afterwards.

Goanna

The Goanna, whose real name is Choi Sang-min, is a brutal Korean guard at the POW camp. After the war he is hanged as a war criminal.

Guy "Rabbit" Hendricks

Rabbit Hendricks is an Australian POW. He is an artist who makes sketches of life in the prison camp. He dies of cholera, but after the war his illustrations are published in a book, with a preface by Dorrigo Evans.

Ikuko

Ikuko is a Japanese woman who marries Nakamura after the war. She nurses him through his final illness.

Colonel Kota

Colonel Kota is a Japanese officer who arrives at the POW camp with orders to speed up the work on the railway. Kota prides himself on his skill at beheading people, but when he intends to behead Darky Gardiner, he loses his nerve and walks away. He shares with Nakamura a love of Japanese poetry. After the war, he works at the Japan Blood Bank in Osaka, and he finds a job for Nakamura there.

Lenny

Lenny is a young Australian POW who dies of cholera.

Jackie Macguire

Jackie Macguire lived in the neighborhood when Dorrigo Evans was growing up in Hobart. Dorrigo overhears Jackie telling his mother, Mrs. Evans, that his wife has deserted him.

Ruth Macguire

Ruth Macguire was the Aborigine wife of Jackie Macguire. She bore a child to Tom Evans but gave it up for adoption. The child grew up as Darky Gardiner.

Rooster MacNeice

Rooster MacNeice is an Australian POW. Every night he memorizes a page from Adolf Hitler's *Mein Kampf*, even though he says he hates the book and Hitler. He hates anyone who is different from himself. For this reason he hates Darky Gardiner, who is of mixed race. He survives the war.

Lynette Maison

Lynette Maison is one of Dorrigo's mistresses when he is an old man. She works as deputy editor of a magazine and is married to one of Dorrigo's colleagues.

Major John Menadue

Major John Menadue is third in command of the camp POWs, but he is a quiet man who prefers to just do what he is told rather than give orders. He dislikes Dorrigo Evans.

Tiny Middleton

Tiny Middleton is an Australian POW. He is a big man who prides himself on his work ethic, even in building the railway for the enemy. He always exceeds work quotas, but that makes things worse for the other men, because the Japanese then raise the quota, expecting everyone to work as hard as Middleton. Eventually, Middleton gets sick and becomes a pitiful shell of his former self. He lingers for a while but then dies.

Sheephead Morton

Sheephead Morton is an Australian POW. His name comes from the fact that when he was growing up in Tasmania, his family was so poor that they could afford only sheep heads for food. He survives the war and takes part in the reunion at a pub some years later.

Amy Mulvaney

Amy Mulvaney is the wife of Keith Mulvaney. She became pregnant by him before they were married, but Keith insisted she have an abortion. After that, they got married. Keith is much older than Amy; she is restless in her marriage and has an affair with Dorrigo before the war, which Keith later discovers. After the war, Dorrigo still thinks of Amy, although he believes that she died in an explosion while he was a POW, since that was what his wife told him in a letter. Amy, in fact, dies of cancer while still quite young.

Keith Mulvaney
Keith Mulvaney is Dorrigo's uncle and the husband of Amy. He owns a pub/hotel near Adelaide. Dorrigo has never met him until he visits him, at Keith's invitation, before the war. Amy is Keith's second wife; his first wife was killed in a car accident. Keith's world revolves around Amy, his hotel, and his work on the local council, where he has a seat as an alderman. Keith treats Amy well, but this does not stop her from having an affair with Dorrigo. Keith is killed in an explosion at the hotel.

Major Tenji Nakamura
Major Nakamura is the Japanese officer in charge of the POW camp. He maintains harsh discipline. After the war he is afraid that he will be charged as a war criminal. He changes his identity, moves from Tokyo to a different city, finds work, and gradually loses his fear of arrest. He does not believe he was guilty of any crime during the war. He marries a woman called Ikuko, and they have two daughters.

Jack Rainbow
Jack Rainbow was a hop farmer before the war, being married with five children. As a POW he fares badly, first going blind and then twice having to have part of his leg amputated. When gangrene sets in, Dorrigo tries to save his life with a third surgery, but Jack does not survive it.

Mrs. Jack Rainbow
Mrs. Jack Rainbow is Jack's widow. Dorrigo visits her after the war to give her Jack's medals.

Colonel Rexroth
Colonel Rexroth is the commanding officer of the Australian POWs in the earliest days of the Line. He is an Australian but identifies strongly with the British Empire. He dies of dysentery.

Choi Sang-min
See Goanna

Kameya Sato
Kameya Sato is a Japanese doctor who becomes a friend of Nakamura's after the war. He tells Nakamura stories about how he witnessed the vivisection of live American servicemen during the war.

Shugs
Shugs is an Australian POW. He is a taciturn man who before the war was a trapper in Tasmania.

Squizzy Taylor
Squizzy Taylor is an Australian POW. Before the war, he was a doctor in Adelaide. He holds the rank of major and assists Dorrigo Evans in the surgery they perform on Jack Rainbow.

Aki Tomokawa
Aki Tomokawa is Nakamura's corporal during the war. After the war, Tomokawa writes to him, and Nakamura visits.

Gallipoli von Kessler
Gallipoli von Kessler is an Australian POW. He used to own an apple orchard and has a habit of greeting everyone with a halfhearted Nazi salute. He is one of the men who go into hiding to avoid a day's work, and the only one who returns to work when ordered to do so by Darky Gardiner.

THEMES

Comradeship
Although conditions in the POW camp are appalling, the prisoners do their best to keep up their spirits: "They tried to hold together with their Australian dryness and their Australian curses, their Australian memories and their Australian mateship," although as conditions get even worse it becomes harder and harder to do so. Nonetheless, there are some striking acts of comradeship and selflessness. When a kitchen hand brings Dorrigo a piece of steak for dinner, Dorrigo refuses it and tells the incredulous man to take the steak to the hospital and share it with the sickest men there. When Darky Gardiner slips in the mud and spills his food, Tiny Middleton picks him up and shares his own rations with him. A little later, Middleton is so sick he can only crawl to the parade ground, and Darky walks beside him, making it clear that he is not going to desert him. When Darky is himself extremely sick, Shugs helps him reach the hospital and washes him. "It's good to be clean, cobs," he says. Shugs is a "foul-mouthed" character but

TOPICS FOR FURTHER STUDY

- Create a time line, consisting of at least fifteen entries, that shows the course of the war in the Asia-Pacific theater in World War II. Be sure to include both major and minor events relating to the construction of the Thai–Burma railway.

- Go to Umapper.com and create a map of the region of the Thai–Burma railway, showing why the route was important.

- Research the war crimes trials that took place in Australia after the war and make a class presentation about them. Include discussion on whether the passages in the novel where the trials are mentioned give an accurate picture of what happened.

- A film of *The Narrow Road to the Deep North* is in the making. Go to Glogster.com and create a poster that would advertise such a film. In doing so, cast the leading roles, and assemble still photos of the relevant actors and actresses to make an appropriate collage.

- Read *Unbroken: An Olympian's Journey from Airman to Castaway to Captive*, published by Laura Hillenbrand in 2014 as an abridged version of her 2010 novel *Unbroken* for young adults. The book is about Louis Zamperini, a former track star whose US Air Force plane was shot down over the Pacific in World War II. He was captured and spent time as a POW in Japan. Write a short essay in which you discuss how his experience as a POW compares to that of the Australians in *The Narrow Road to the Deep North*.

does not lose his sense of decency about how to behave toward a comrade in distress. Then, after the war, Jimmy Bigelow remembers one of the prisoners, a man named Wat Cooney, who would always wait at the cookhouse until the last man arrived, keeping some food for him, just to make sure that everybody had at least something. Human goodness thus manages to survive in hellish circumstances.

Meaning of Life

Dorrigo, a restless, discontented character in spite of his success in life, is given to philosophical and poetic speculation about why life is the way it is and what it all might mean. However, he never manages to figure things out or develop a coherent faith or philosophy. There are simply too many questions and not enough answers.

"There was no point to it," he thinks to himself as he remembers Darky Gardiner's death several decades earlier, and the thought might well apply to his view of life as a whole. Meditating on the railway pegs on the Line, he knows that so much of his experience at that time was "incomprehensible, incommunicable, unintelligible, undivinable, indescribable." But since then, nothing much has changed in terms of his ability to find meaning in life. All he can conclude, as he says more than once, is that "the world is.... It just is"; it is a mystery that cannot be explained.

Love

In Dorrigo's long life, his principal love affair is not with his wife but with Amy Mulvaney, the young wife of his uncle. When Dorrigo and Amy first meet in a bookstore, there is an immediate connection between them:

> She laughed in a way that made him feel that she had found in him all the things most appealing in the world. It was as if her beauty, her eyes, everything that was charming and wonderful about her, now also existed in him.

For a time, Dorrigo later recalls, she was "his entire reason for existence." However, circumstances dictate that their love affair does not last longer than one summer, since Dorrigo is called off to war. But he never forgets her. It is as if he regards her as his one true love. Even after the war, when he has married Ella, he thinks often of Amy, even though for twenty years or so he believes she is dead, since that was what Ella told him in a letter he received in the POW camp. (The reader is only informed of this last fact in the final chapter of the novel.) He struggles to put into words the feelings he

The novel tells the story of the Korean and Japanese guards as well as the prisoners (©Astrelok / Shutterstock.com)

experienced with Amy. What he knew with her, he later thinks, "seemed a power beyond love."

When he sees Amy unexpectedly in a street in Sydney, around the mid-1960s, a quarter of a century after they met, all his old feelings for her rush to the surface, along with his surprise that she is alive. But for some reason that even he does not understand, he walks on past her without a word. Even so, it seems that she is never quite gone from his mind. When in his late seventies he appears distracted in the presence of Lynette, one of his many lovers, she thinks he must be thinking of Amy.

Dorrigo's love for Amy is quite different from his feelings for Ella. Although he acknowledges the valuable connection with her that comes from living a life together, their partnership is loaded up, in his mind, with contradictory, difficult feelings; it consists of "the tormented, hopeless feeling of two people who lived together in a love not yet love, nor yet not; an unshared life shared."

STYLE

Narrative Structure

The narrative structure of the novel is complex, especially in the first two sections; it jumps back and forth in time, sometimes alluding to events that will become clear only later in the narrative. It starts simply enough, with the first three chapters recounting Dorrigo's childhood. Then, in chapter 4, it jumps forward eighteen years, to the time of his affair with Amy Mulvaney, although no explanation is given at this point of who Amy is or why they are together. Chapter 6 is another leap forward, by as much as five decades, to when Dorrigo is in his late seventies, in bed with his mistress Lynette Maison. He looks back and alludes to the death of Darky Gardiner, but again the reader is at this point given no clue as to who Darky was. As this back-and-forth pattern continues, the reader is gradually able to grasp the different stages of Dorrigo's life and how they might fit into the whole. Part III, however, is structured differently, in that all twenty-seven chapters present a chronological sequence of events in the POW camp. Parts IV and V, although they shift frequently from one character's story to another, are also arranged more chronologically, with the exception of chapters 16 and 18.

Poetry

Poetry from both West and East is referenced frequently in the novel. Dorrigo often quotes from Alfred, Lord Tennyson's poem "Ulysses," suggesting that he sees himself in the same light as the ancient Greek hero Odysseus (also known by the Latin name Ulysses), although in Tennyson's poem, Ulysses is a restless figure upon his return to Ithaca after the Trojan War and longs once more for adventure. Dorrigo also quotes Walt Whitman.

The title of the book is a quotation from a collection of writings by seventeenth-century Japanese poet Matsuo Basho, a collection that Colonel Kota alludes to in his discussion about Japanese literature with Major Nakamura. Issa, the Japanese master of haiku, is also mentioned, and Flanagan uses haiku by both Basho and Issa as epigraphs for each part of the novel.

HISTORICAL CONTEXT

The Thai–Burma Railway

The Thai–Burma Railway was begun in October 1942 and completed in October 1943. It stretched for about 258 miles. The Japanese needed the railway as an overland route to supply their forces in Burma, since sea routes were no longer reliable following Japanese naval defeats. Approximately 12,000 Japanese and 800 Korean soldiers worked on the railway as engineers or guards. The actual hard labor of clearing the ground and building the railway across difficult terrain was done by more than 60,000 Allied prisoners of war, including British, Dutch, some 13,000 Australians, and a much smaller number of US troops. The number of Australians was relatively high because during 1942 more than 22,000 Australian soldiers were captured in the Asia-Pacific region, most of them following the fall of Singapore in February and Java in March. The Japanese also used around 200,000 Asian laborers, including Burmese, Malays, and Chinese, to construct the railway.

Because of inadequate food and medicine, overwork, and the brutality of many of the guards, thousands of POWs died. Of some 12,000 Allied prisoners who died during the railway's construction, more than 2,700 were Australians. This was about 20 percent of all Australian deaths in World War II. The greatest killer was disease. More than one-third of deaths were due to dysentery and diarrhea. Other diseases were beriberi and pellagra, which were caused by vitamin deficiencies in the POWs' diet, which consisted mainly of white rice. Cholera was another common disease, accounting for about 12 percent of deaths, followed by malaria, with 12 percent, and tropical ulcers, 2 percent. Death rates were high in part because even when men were extremely sick, they were still forced to work.

As is also apparent from the novel, Japanese soldiers were taught to be unquestioning in their obedience to authority and, if commanded to ill-treat a prisoner, would do so. Soldiers in the Japanese army were themselves subject to beatings from their superiors, so they had no qualms about beating POWs. Also, during World War II, Japan was a highly

Dorrigo Evans is haunted by memories of his time as a prisoner of war and guilt over an affair with his uncle's wife (©Zurijeta | Shutterstock.com)

militarized society in which people believed that the honorable thing to do in war was to fight to the death. If a soldier was facing defeat, he was expected to avoid capture by committing suicide. Since the Allied POWs had not done this, they were not accorded any respect by their Japanese captors. The Thai–Burma Railway & Hellfire Pass website quotes a Korean guard named Cho Mun-San, who said, "One of the instructors at the training camp at Fuzan instructed us that we were to treat POWs like animals; otherwise they would look down on us." This explains the brutality of the guard known as the Goanna in the novel.

After completion, the railway transported food and ammunition to Burma as well as to Japanese troops who were massing for an invasion of India. Although it was bombed by the Allies, the railway continued to function until the end of the war.

COMPARE & CONTRAST

- **1940s:** Australian troops fight against the Japanese in World War II. Thousands are captured and forced to work on the Thai–Burma railway. After the fall of Singapore in 1942, Australians at home fear an invasion by Japanese forces, although this does not take place.

  Today: Australia and Japan maintain cordial relations based on shared values and trading partnerships.

- **1940s:** Australia conducts trials from 1945 to 1951, in which 924 Japanese servicemen are accused of war crimes. Over two-thirds are convicted, and 148 are sentenced to death, although eleven have their sentences commuted. In particular, in 1946 and 1947, 111 Japanese and Korean soldiers are convicted for crimes on the Thai–Burma railway. Thirty-two are executed.

  Today: The memory of what the Australian POWs endured is kept alive at a number of sites in Australia and abroad, especially in the Hellfire Pass Memorial Museum in Thailand, which shows the history of the Thai–Burma railway.

- **1940s:** Some Australian POWs publish their memoirs about their wartime experiences. War correspondent Rohan Rivett publishes *Behind Bamboo* (1946), an eyewitness account.

  Today: Many POW memoirs are available, and in a sense *The Narrow Road to the Deep North* is a tribute to Flanagan's father, Archie Flanagan, who worked on the Thai–Burma railway. Archie Flanagan dies two days after his son completes the novel.

CRITICAL OVERVIEW

As might be expected concerning a novel that won the Booker Prize, many reviewers were full of praise for the novel. Michael Gorra, in the *New York Times Book Review*, for example, admires both the author's use of language, which has "a sinewy incantatory power," and the novel's structure. Flanagan

> manages ... shifts in time and perspective with extraordinary skill. They're never confusing but they are dizzying, and demand the reader's full attention in a way that reminds me of Conrad. I suspect that on rereading, this magnificent novel will seem even more intricate, more carefully and beautifully constructed.

Michael Richardson, in the *Newtown Review of Books*, also expresses a positive view of the novel. He notes that it is about "the trauma of loss and of survival, and its complicated relationship with heroism." He also observes that "there are passages of brutal beauty, where his flair for the sentence that rises from the muck into soaring poetry allows him to connect small moments to the larger forces of life history."

Critical opinion was not unanimous, however. In the *Times Literary Supplement*, Craig Raine took a largely negative view. "It is a novel saturated, not always judiciously, in poetry," he comments, noting also that to the author, "'poetry' means exaggerated imagery, an uncertain, elevated tone, and generous rights of repetition."

CRITICISM

Bryan Aubrey

Aubrey holds a PhD in English. In the following essay, he examines Flanagan's portrayal of the Japanese officers and Korean guard in The Narrow Road to the Deep North.

> AS FOR CHOI SANG-MIN, THE GOANNA, HE IS ONE OF NATURE'S UNFORTUNATES, AS CIRCUMSTANCES CONSPIRE TO GIVE HIM VERY LITTLE CHANCE IN LIFE. HE DIES ON THE GALLOWS WITHOUT ANY WELL-FORMULATED IDEAS ABOUT LIFE."

Evans, the surgeon and leader of the POWs in the Japanese camp, is a man who behaves courageously during the war, revealing strength of character and an unshakeable sense of duty. After the war he has nothing to reproach himself for, but he is nonetheless haunted by his memories and feels undeserving of the high esteem in which he is held in Australian society. He feels it is all a misperception because he is not who people think he is; the label does not fit. In fact, Dorrigo does not seem at all comfortable in his own skin; he is restless and dissatisfied, living as if strangely removed from his own life, watching it as an observer. He takes refuge in the literature he loves, of various different kinds, although not even that can supply him with an explanation of why existence is as it is.

It is a believable and quite moving portrait, but Flanagan is not content simply to get into the mind of his Australian protagonist. He wants also to investigate the enemy, the Japanese soldiers and Korean guards who were responsible for the suffering and death among the POWs. He therefore allows them their say, too, even allocating whole chapters, mostly in the last section of the book, to their point of view. The three characters examined in most detail are Major Nakamura, Colonel Kota, and the Goanna, the brutal Korean guard. What emerges from the stories of the first two is that they have no remorse for what they did; they were part of a military and social system that they admired, and they feel they have nothing to be ashamed of. As for the young Goanna, he was caught up in a situation over which he had no control, and it is ultimately unsurprising that he acted as he did.

Major Nakamura is the officer in charge of the day-to-day running of the camp. In terms of the timetable for completing the railway, he knows that his superiors have given him an impossible task, but there is nothing he can do about it. He regards the building of the railway as a great achievement, and he is proud of it. It is, after all, the desire of the emperor that it be built, and he would never conceive an opinion that was contrary to the wishes of the emperor. As far as the ill treatment of the POWs is concerned, this does not trouble his conscience. Had the POWs had the right spirit, he thinks, they would have killed themselves rather than be captured. "What was a prisoner of war anyway? Less than a man, just material to be used to make the railway, like the teak sleepers and steel rails and dog spikes," he thinks. He believes strongly in the power of the "Japanese spirit"; he cares about "the railway, honour, the Emperor, Japan, and he had a sense of himself as a good and honourable officer." If he sometimes has to be harsh, it is the uncooperative nature of the POWs that makes him that way; they leave him no choice. Nakamura is a man who likes certainty and keeps doubt at bay. Just occasionally he does feel some confusion about the position he is in, but he never tries to explore it further. His mind is limited in that respect.

After the war, Nakamura's views undergo little change. There is no development. He does go through some turbulent times at first, but this is because he fears he will be captured by the Americans and tried as a war criminal, which he knows he is not. Any accusations against him are false, he believes. He regards the war crimes trials, although he does not use the exact term, as "victor's justice." He sticks to his views that a prisoner of war is a despicable, cowardly man and that a beating is of no great account. He reveals that he himself was beaten while ascending the ranks in the army. It was just the way discipline was instilled. As the years go by, his equanimity about his role in the war only increases: "He found he was haunted only by the way he was haunted by so little of it" (a marked contrast to the experience of Dorrigo Evans). He maintains his devotion to the emperor to his dying day. As in the war, however, there is something discordant that lurks on the margins of his consciousness that might, if he ever chose to examine it, result in a painful reassessment of his complacent self-image. But he never manages it. He is a product of the militaristic, totalitarian society in which he grew up and lacks the ability to question its fundamental principles.

WHAT DO I READ NEXT?

- Flanagan's novel *Wanting* (2008) is about the colonization of Tasmania in the mid- to late nineteenth century, and it also hinges on the failed Arctic expedition of British explorer Sir John Franklin.

- *Last Man Out: Surviving the Burma–Thailand Death Railway* (2006) is a memoir by former American Marine H. Robert Charles, who survived the experience of slave labor on the infamous railway.

- *The Men of the Line: Stories of the Thai–Burma Railway Survivors* (2008), by Pattie Wright, is a history of the Thai–Burma railway.

- *A Boy Called H: A Childhood in Wartime Japan* (1999) is a memoir by Kappa Senoh—translated from the Japanese by John Bester—of his childhood in Kobe, Japan, during World War II. In fifty short chapters he gives a vivid portrait of life in a society torn by war.

- *The Pacific War* (1981), by John Costello, is an account of World War II in China, Malaya, Burma, the East Indies, the Philippines, New Guinea, the Solomon Islands, and the Aleutians.

- *World War II* (2013), written by Sean Callery for the Scholastic Discover More series, is packed with information about World War II in an easy-to-grasp, highly visual format suited for young readers.

Such is also true of Colonel Kota, although he is a far more disturbing figure than Nakamura. When he talks with Nakamura in the POW camp, they express nearly identical views. Kota thinks the POWs are lazy; they grumble about trivial things like being slapped, whereas if a Japanese soldier shirks his duty he would expect to receive a beating. The colonel's view is quite simple: the work on the railway has to be completed, even if everyone dies. Colonel Kota is a man who has gotten used to killing. In the army he was shown how to behead prisoners with a sword, and he enjoyed it so much he made a habit of it: if a few weeks passed and he had not beheaded anyone, he would find a prisoner whose neck he took a liking to, make the man dig his own grave, and then lop off his head. Thus he reveals himself as a sadist and a serial killer, whose "gentle voice" Nakamura nonetheless somehow enjoys. So much in the grip of his obsession was the colonel that whenever he met a man, he would size up his neck, assessing whether it would be easy or hard to cut.

After the war, Colonel Kota further reveals his character when it transpires that he was interrogated by Australian prosecutors after the war but was released without being charged, having saved his own skin by blaming Korean and Formosan guards such as the Goanna for having ordered the deaths of prisoners. Long after the war, Kota is regarded by Japanese nationalists as a "distinguished soldier" also known for his published poetic and philosophical reflections on the nature of the Japanese spirit. He dies an old man untroubled by his past.

As for Choi Sang-min, the Goanna, he is one of nature's unfortunates, as circumstances conspire to give him very little chance in life. He dies on the gallows without any well-formulated ideas about life. His main postwar complaint is that since he is still considered a member of the Japanese military, he should be receiving his monthly pay, but he has not received any money for two years. He also knows that the charge on which he has been convicted, of ordering the murder of a prisoner, is false—absurd even—since he had no power to do so. He was the lowest of the low in the Japanese imperial machine, despised alike by his Japanese superiors and the POWs over whom he was given authority as a guard. Choi Sang-min was raised in Japanese-occupied Korea and was only sixteen years old when he was given some brutal military training and sent off to the Line to be a prison guard. After the war, he remains proud of the role he played in getting the railway built and acknowledges to himself that when he was beating a prisoner he felt fully alive for the first time, and this gave him a feeling of freedom. He felt like he was more of a man than his victims.

In prison awaiting execution, Choi Sang-min has thoughts similar to many who have been convicted of war crimes: caught up in the

Japan built the Burma railway to support its troops during World War II (©apiguide | Shutterstock.com)

militaristic system that had conquered his own country, how was he, a person of no significance whatsoever, supposed to disobey the will of the emperor? Adolf Eichmann, one of the architects of the Holocaust in World War II, claimed similarly that he was merely following orders and had no choice in the matter. His defense did not save him though; Eichmann was tried in Israel, convicted, and hanged in 1962. Readers may well feel that, the weakness of the Eichmann defense notwithstanding, the Goanna—in spite of his brutality and rage—is in a sense as much a victim as the POWs, used ruthlessly by the Japanese to further their goals and then scapegoated as the victors enact a flawed system of justice in which Colonel Kota (a war criminal if ever there was one) goes free while those lower on the totem pole are hanged. Choi Sang-min sees this very plainly for himself, when he asks the question why, if the acts of those condemned as war criminals were expressions of the emperor's wishes, was the emperor himself not being prosecuted for war crimes?

The novel shows that justice can never be absolute or perfect, that some of the oppressors were victims too, and that the Japanese officers were products of their society and culture who had their own deeply ingrained ways of believing that they were good men, loyal and true. The POWs on the Line, however, had very different ways of seeing the enemy, and *The Narrow Road to the Deep North*, in the end, and in spite of the author's generosity in allowing the oppressors space to explain themselves, does little to soften the cruelty and inhumanity of the emperor's loyal subjects.

Source: Bryan Aubrey, Critical Essay on *The Narrow Road to the Deep North*, in *Novels for Students*, Gale, Cengage Learning, 2017.

Julie Hale

In the following review, Hale describes the novel as "gripping" and "complex."

Richard Flanagan's *The Narrow Road to the Deep North* is a gripping, complex novel about war, love and loss. Tasmanian physician Dorrigo Evans is 77, an age that's ripe for reflection, and his recollections provide the underpinning for an expansive narrative. Dorrigo's affair with

Amy Mulvaney, his uncle's wife, and his experience as a prisoner in the hands of the Japanese during World War II are the formative experiences of his life. As a POW, he worked on the Thailand-Burma Railway in the Burmese jungle, performing backbreaking labor that takes its toll on him and his fellow prisoners, a varied cast of men that Flanagan brings to memorable life. The narrative moves fluidly through time, shifting backward to Dorrigo's childhood and moving forward again into wartime. Dorrigo's postwar years are filled with memories of Amy and of the comrades who toiled beside him in the jungle. Winner of the Man Booker Prize, this impressive novel has earned Flanagan much-deserved acclaim. He writes with deep compassion about heartbreak, the horrors of war and the difficulties of escaping the past.

Source: Julie Hale, "Memories of a POW," in *Bookpage*, April 2015, p. 9.

Michael Hofmann

In the following review, Hofmann criticizes the relationships in the novel as "implausible."

It's May or June, the Cam is stuffed with expensive punts, which in turn are stuffed with moneyed tourists. A bunch of under-employed post-examinal students are dementedly heaving and levering away at one of the massive ornamental granite balls crowning the parapet of one of the college bridges. They've prised it loose, the entire river—the strollers and dawdlers and smoochers along the Backs, the rest of the shipping—seems to be watching in horror as it's directly threatening a punt-load of Japanese tourists: the looming atrocity is of diplomatic, hemispheric, intercultural dimensions. The tourists abandon their vessel, bitterly going over the side with their smartphones and their wallets and their cameras, and next thing the great orb is sitting on the water, maybe 99 per cent above the surface, you never saw anything bobbing like that. The wicked students piss themselves laughing, the bedraggled victims straggle and angrily bark their way ashore through the rushes. That's how I felt reading the Tasmanian novelist Richard Flanagan's Booker Prize-winning and almost universally adored (some reviewers reached for their Tolstoy; others forbade any comparisons at all) *Narrow Road to the Deep North*: watching tourists hoaxed by polystyrene.

It used to be that a novel would put you among people, tell you a story or stories, give

> THE WAR PASSAGES HAVE A BULLYING AUTOMATISM THAT LEAVES FLANAGAN QUITE AT SEA IN THE REST OF THE BOOK. THE WAR WON'T SETTLE, AND IT DOESN'T HELP. IT EITHER MATTERS OR IT DOESN'T. FLANAGAN TRIES BOTH, AND NEITHER SEEMS RIGHT."

you some sense of what it might be like to see a different cut-out and perspective of the world: as a schoolteacher, an adulteress, the wife of a member of Parliament, an officer, a cockroach. *The Narrow Road to the Deep North* is the novel in an advanced and showy state of dissolution. It is as though the contemporary novel—like film (4-D, coming soon to a cinema near you), like theatre, like so much else—is in competition with itself, falling over itself to offer you more inferiority, more action, more understanding, more vision. But the form, the vessel, is an exploded form; it is basically rubble, fragmentary junk, debris. It's not even leaky anymore; it can hold nothing. The human focus—here, an Australian surgeon, Dorrigo Evans—is neither formed by his experience, nor capable of his actions, which for a novel is pretty disabling. He is one character—or one character's name—irritatingly and implausibly played by five actors: the boy, the Aussie-rules-playing youth, the romantic lead, the suffering hero, the old adulterous geezer who "skulled the last of the last Glenfiddich miniature" before leaving behind his "book of Japanese death poems." More likely, he is a mechanical record of endurance, plus pixels, plus medical destiny. Nothing that won't fit onto a screen.

This novel is truly an entitled thing: it demands both action and high-value misty contemplation or "memory." It is a universal solvent, or claims to be. You want love, it says; I got love! You want death? I got it. All the kinds. Any amount. It is all bite, and no chew. The quantity of expensive set-piece or special effect scenes on offer is astonishing: a sudden deadly explosion in wartime, a hotel fire, a Japanese slave-labour camp in the Burmese jungle with half-starved

Australian POWs in "cock rags," a hanging, an amputation without implements or drugs, a fatal car crash, rescue from a forest fire in a big old American street-cruiser, and I'm sure I've left some out. Oh yes, a romantic reunion on Sydney Harbour Bridge. There are scenes in Tasmania, in two or three cities on the big island, in Syria, Burma, Korea, Japan. And yet this is a book—and a really chi-chi book, one would have to say—that has a memorably awful false beginning with light (opening sentence: "Why at the beginning of things is there always light?"), and an awful false ending with a flower (I wish it had said: "Why at the end of things is there always a flower?"); a book that says trust me, I'm sensitive, that offers you, repeatedly offers you, all the tender and sensitive things: light, and "gas-flame" eyes, and women's hands running down your "withered" thigh. But these things are all quoted, all sampled, they are all well-loved items from a catalogue or anthology, an exploded anthology, just as the title is Basho and the epigraphs are from Issa and Celan, and the Tennyson never stops.

In construction, the book is the half-hearted retrospective of a dying old man (the life flashing before the eyes—think of something like Hermann Broch's *Death of Virgil*) that forsakes its tether for the more leisurely freedom of an impersonal series of chronological flashbacks; only to leave that in turn for an account of other characters in their own personal circumstances, in Australia, in Japan, in Korea, of which Dorrigo Evans can have known little or nothing at all. The final effect is of an unplanned collage, a rather sticky collage. It is the story of Evans, half-submerged in a group biography of fellow survivors and alien torturers; a war story, half-lost in the subsequent peaceful and prosperous career of a national celebrity, a medical man and a ladies' man; a brutal, cartoonish war novella, swallowed in prequel and long finish. The big losers are scale and consequence. There is no map but a streetview; no dolly but a drone-mounted camera. Except for those who die (the designated, audience-approved victims of any Hollywood film), life goes on, mostly better than before. And what matters in the end is anyone's guess: Amy or Ella, love or war, heartbreak or beri-beri, the Japanese poetry aficionado (and war criminal) or the Australian Tennysonian (and hero). It's all sham texture, bossy imagery and compressible or expandable time.

At least two books are at war—fought to a standstill—in *The Narrow Road to the Deep North*. There are the scenes of comradely endurance and hardship and vile death from South Asia: brisk, transactional, matey and visceral, roughed in rudimentary characters, surges of plot and little rat-a-tat-tat pieces of dialogue ("He's looking fucked, said Chum Fahey. His shoe's fucked, said Sheephead Morton. Same thing, said Chum Fahey.") These are all heroically and sometimes rather instructionally held up to our pale neophytes' admiration:

> Dorrigo Evans is not typical of Australia and nor are they, volunteers from the fringes, slums and shadowlands of their vast country: drovers, trappers, wharfies, roo shooters, desk jockeys, dingo trappers and shearers. They are bank clerks and teachers, counter johnnies, piners and short-price runners, susso survivors, chancers, larrikins, yobs, tray men, crims, boofheads and tough bastards blasted out of a depression that had them growing up in shanties and shacks without electricity, with their old men dead or crippled or maddened by the Great War and their old women making do on aspro and hope, on soldier settlements, in sustenance camps, slums and shanty towns, in a 19th-century world that had staggered into the mid-20th century.

The choice slang ("desk jockeys," "aspro," "crims") masks the somewhat indifferent or disingenuous quality of the thought here: because "typical of Australia" is of course exactly what this one-for-the-price-of-two catalogue means to be, and is.

But there are also elements of a much more pointillist, particulate, unsensational—and precious—book. One drawn persistently to light and dust and "moments": what I rather unfeelingly referred to as "pixels" earlier. This is a bid for atmosphere, soft focus and the destruction of subject matter; certainly, it has both creative and destructive designs. Here is Dorrigo, after a year in a labour camp, getting a letter from Ella—the "wrong woman," though she will be and remain his wife: "Two-thirds of the way down the first page, he halted... The letters of Ella's elegant copperplate hand kept scattering and rising off the page as dust motes, more and more dust motes bouncing off one another, and he was having trouble bringing her face to his mind." And then, typically irresolutely, bullyingly and having it all ways: "It seemed too real and entirely unreal at the same time." This is the author as CERN physicist, bashing matter, albeit with a hammer; Ella may have written the letter, but the message is all Flanagan's. The destroying and destroyed dust, as many earlier passages spell out, is Amy's Theme: "He was thinking not of hair or eyes but a feeling as baffling as a million dancing and meaningless dust motes." The linkage is insistent, and a little overt: "For Amy, love was the universe touching, exploding within one human being, and that person exploding into the universe. It was annihilation, the destroyer of worlds."

Ella, meanwhile, is all background—background and metonymy. "Ella's father was a prominent Melbourne solicitor, her mother from a well-known grazing family; her grandfather was an author of the federal constitution." Scantily described herself (just the rather humiliating "she herself was a teacher"), she seems in lieu of personal happiness to confer life membership of an elite Anglo society: "with her came a world . . . of darkwood living rooms and clubs, crystal decanters of sherry and single malt, the cloying, slightly intoxicating, slightly claustrophobic smell of polished must." But this is the author's doing, not Ella's; he is making things far too easy for himself. A marriage contracted in wartime can perfectly well involve huge and catastrophic feelings, for the reader as well, as witness, say, Joseph Roth's *The Emperor's Tomb*. Amy's marriage to the publican Keith is similarly trotted out in material terms, as a cheaper class of cushion-cover: "It felt like the Edwardian horsehair furniture he had refused her requests to replace after their marriage: sagging, comfortable if one nestled in the soft spots and avoided the hard. He was unselfish and he was kind. But he was not Dorrigo." Writing like this, commended by reviewers as "devastating" and "hugely affecting" and "without an ounce of melodrama," requires Oscar Wilde's "heart of stone" to read without laughing. Twenty pages before the end you get this: "Thinking: How empty is the world when you lose the one you love."

The war passages have a bullying automatism that leaves Flanagan quite at sea in the rest of the book. The war won't settle, and it doesn't help. It either matters or it doesn't. Flanagan tries both, and neither seems right. He tries little inserts—subliminal or flashback?—and he tries longer narrative events, for normality or aesthetic dominance? Bigger, hieratic, ordering ideas are so rare as to be conspicous, and when they do occur—"feeling became fashionable" or "the

coming of television and with it the attendant idea of celebrity"—they only make one think wistfully of Les Murray, who handles these things better, with the brilliance and flair of an ironic adman: "the Coffee Revolution" or "the Smallgoods Renaissance." Basically, Flanagan is never happier as an author than when he has a poetry-loving psychopath of a Japanese officer (Colonel Kota) who stares single-mindedly at men's necks because he has nothing in his own head but how to cut off those of others. Or when he can describe the buttocks of the starving Australian POWs as "little more than ropes" or "little more than wretched cables," or "so wasted that the anus protruded obscenely" or "its strange prominence amidst his wasted flesh" or "like a turkshead of filthy rope." The straightforwardness of wartime leaves the characters wriggling and slithering when it's over, and the author straining credulity. The Amy / Ella part refuses to have anything to do with the Burma Railway. Can a narrative strand be rejected? Like a donated organ? This one badly wants not to be in the same book. The character of Dorrigo—or is his name Alwyn?—seems to consist in being anything he is required to be: the poetry-loving doctor adulterer survivor hero. The affair with Amy is handily killed off by two spousal lies: Keith's to Amy (claiming Dorrigo has died in the war), and Ella's to Dorrigo (claiming it was Amy in a convenient gas explosion at home). Dorrigo doesn't get to be Zhivago. But Flanagan isn't ready to give up on his multipurpose protagonist either:

> He was alone in his marriage, he was alone with his children, he was alone in the operating theatre, he was alone on the numerous medical, sporting, charity and veterans' bodies on which he sat, he was alone when addressing a meeting of a thousand POWs. There was around him an exhausted emptiness, an impenetrable void cloaked this most famously collegial man.

This sounds to me suspiciously and wretchedly like the one hand clapping of an author talking up his hero.

> War holds things together—it is the "theatre"—while peace scatters the protagonists and settings, has the author repeatedly stretching and overstretching. Too many of the human ties and turns here seem implausible, unsecured, unbelievable. The vile Orientals age into gentle wisdom. The writing is overstuffed, and leaks sawdust. "Peppermint gums" are "writhing" on one page, and "wildly snaking" on the next. Prisoners are killed "like so many flies"—unless, that is, they are sleeping

"like logs in their swags." Dorrigo finds himself "the subject of biographies, plays and documentaries," and in the next sentence: "The object of veneration, hagiographies, adulation." There is a kind of descriptive cant that is equally strenuous and inefficient:

Even when he was away from her he could see her, smell her musky neck, gaze into her bright eyes, hear her husky laugh, run his finger down her slightly heavy thigh, gaze at the imperfect part in her hair; her arms ever so slightly filled with some mysterious feminine fullness, neither taut nor flabby but for him wondrous.

This lacks the basic dignity of prose, which should not be heard at first reading to be rhyming; it is ingratiating and gassy. The "wondrous" is luckily left where it is (it's about as dead as any word can be), which leaves the "imperfect" to be run with. The following sentence begins: "Her imperfections multiplied every time he looked at her and thrilled him ever more," which doesn't sound like a good idea, and a contrived resolution four lines further on, "more of her perfect imperfections," simply bankrupt. It's hard to believe that the man to whom these responses are credited is not only a reader of Tennyson, but also a doctor on the side.

The Narrow Road to the Deep North has the scope of a big and ambitious novel. It was surely a difficult book to write, covering so much in terms of time, geography, cultures, destinies and outcomes: both an important but difficult piece of Australian history (brave, but also inglorious), and a fictional account, to boot, of the experience of Flanagan's father, who, as one read in the press, died on the very day the book was completed. (It is said there is nothing of which one knows less and that fascinates one more than the period immediately preceding one's birth.) The book was described as having gone through many drafts, with Flanagan using those that didn't make it to "light the barbie." I can't help thinking this wasn't the right one to spare.

Source: Michael Hofmann, "Is His Name Alwyn?," in *London Review of Books*, Vol. 36, No. 24, December 18, 2014.

Amelia Lester

In the following review, Lester points out that the island of Tasmania is like another character in the story.

Richard Flanagan, who yesterday became the third Australian to win the Booker Prize,

> FLANAGAN'S TENDER, DIRECT WAY OF WRITING ABOUT THE BODY IS REMINISCENT OF D. H. LAWRENCE, AND SOME HAVE FOUND THIS SIDE OF HIS WORK A LITTLE EMBARRASSING, EVEN CHEESY, BUT I'M MOVED BY FLANAGAN'S SENTIMENTAL MEN, KNOWN IN THE BEGINNING AS NUMBERS AND BY THE END REVEALED TO POSSESS SECRET WELLS OF SENTIMENT."

for his novel *The Narrow Road to the Deep North*, was born in Tasmania. More than mere biographical detail, this remote island and its troubled, often violent history is one of his obsessions. In a piece for this magazine in 2013, Flanagan described Tasmania, where he still lives, as an "island Wunderkammer, crammed full of the exotic and the strange, the beautiful and the cruel, conducive not to notions of progress but to a sense of unreality."

That sense of unreality pervades *Gould's Book of Fish* (2001), Flanagan's third novel and first masterpiece; it's a work of magical realism, reminiscent of Gabriel García Márquez with its shape-shifting, anthropomorphic characters and time-travelling narrative. *Gould*, which is really a book about how history is told and transmitted, is set predominantly in Tasmania's colonial era and centers on a prisoner referred to by his jailers only as a number. He is William Buelow Gould, a convict-artist who was transported to the prison island in the early nineteenth century and forced by the colony's surgeon to paint local fish as part of a scientific survey. That survey is Flanagan's organizing principle. The sections each begin with one of the fish Gould studied, and they start to resemble, or perhaps become, human characters in his life, the most memorable of whom is the sadistic, syphilitic Commandant, whose "folly was to think you could turn a penal colony into a nation."

What emerges, through the murky depths, is the love story of Gould's affair with Twopenny Sal, an indigenous woman who is held as the mistress of the Commandant. Referring to Tasmania by its original European name, Gould writes in his diary, while imprisoned in isolation, that "in the entire unknown, unmapped western half of Van Diemen's land, only savages roamed & no white settlement was to be found, save for this one gaol for the recalcitrant." Along with the appalling treatment of the convicts themselves, the invasion and subsequent genocide of Tasmania's Aboriginal population by British colonists is never far from the surface.

A love story set amid horrific historic events is also a way to describe *The Narrow Road to the Deep North*. It took Flanagan twelve years to write, and there has been a definite shift in style: here, the brutality comes to the forefront of the narrative, and the strange, almost mythical qualities of *Gould* are replaced by a jarring realism. The central subject is the Thai-Burma railway, built between Bangkok and Rangoon by a quarter of a million forced laborers during the Second World War, to support the Japanese in their Burma campaign. The workers, made up of Asian civilians and Allied prisoners of war, were denied medical attention, starved, and assaulted by the guards. Flanagan's attention to the minute horrors of the prison camps is relentless, as when he describes an Australian surgeon, with no equipment or resources, attending to a dying comrade:

> A severe, untreated ulcer left a thin strip of intact skin down the outer side of the calf, the rest of the leg being a huge ulcer from which poured offensive, greyish pus. Sloughing tendons and fasciae were exposed, the muscles were tunneled and separated by gaping sinuses, between which he could glimpse a raw tibial bone that looked as if a dog had gnawed it. The bone, too, was starting to rot and break off into flakes. He lifted his gaze to see a pale, wasted child.

Although there were nine thousand Australian P.O.W.s who worked on the railroad, a third of whom died while imprisoned, the episode never took hold of the national imagination. Flanagan himself has said that "it's a strange story that isn't readily absorbed into any nation's dreams," quite unlike, say, the landing at Gallipoli by Australian soldiers in the First World War, which has become the country's defining narrative of itself. He is clearly interested in describing events that are often called indescribable, and perhaps that's part of why he chose to tackle the death railroad. Flanagan

knew about the railroad, too, because his father, Archie, was in the prison camps. *Narrow Road* also begins with a prisoner number, but this time it is in the dedication: to his father, who died as Flanagan was finishing the book.

Tasmania is again a major character, a land of "writhing peppermint gums and silver wattle that waved and danced in the heat," that is "hot and hard in summer, and hard, simply hard, in winter." The story begins in a rural part of the island in the years before the war. Dorrigo Evans, who was imprisoned by the Japanese and who worked on the railroad, returns to Tasmania in 1945 an ambivalent hero. Yet, although it frames the story, to call this a war novel would be misleading. Just as in *Gould*, Flanagan is ultimately concerned with love and its redemptive qualities. As a young man completing his final training as an Army doctor, Dorrigo meets Amy at a bookshop. She is wearing a red camellia in her hair, and he is enthralled. Things are, as they tend to be, complicated: she is married to Dorrigo's uncle, and just before he leaves for war Dorrigo marries another woman, Ella. Much of the book is about how single moments come to define lives, and into his old age Dorrigo thinks of Amy. Flanagan's prose in *Narrow Road* has often been described as "unflinching," and there's certainly no shortage of violence in the passages about the prison camp, but he can be unflinching about desire, too. ("He would live in hell, because love is that also.") What strikes me most is the way Flanagan writes about the vivid and terrifying experience of falling in love:

> When he looked back down, Amy's eyes had changed. Her pupils seemed saucer-like, lost—and lost, he realized, in him. He felt the terrible gravity of her desire for him pulling him back to her, in a story that was not his, and now that he had all he had dreamt of in recent days, he wanted to escape it as quickly as possible. What had a moment before aroused him so intensely now seemed charmless and ordinary, and he wished to flee. But instead he closed his eyes.

The book is about the first moment, but it is also about all that follows—startling instances of intimacy contained within a decades-long relationship, described in highly specific, explicitly physical ways, like this: "They lay silently together for a long time. With a finger he swept the hairs that fell across her face behind her ear. The shape of its shell always moved him."

> WHILE THIS NEW NOVEL HAS MUCH
> INSIGHT INTO HEROISM AND THE TRAUMA
> CARRIED BY THE MEN WHO LIVED THROUGH
> THE CAMPS, ITS CRITIQUE OF NATIONAL
> MYTHOLOGIES EXTENDS ONLY TO THE TREATMENT
> AND TRIAL OF THE JAPANESE AFTER THE WAR."

Flanagan's tender, direct way of writing about the body is reminiscent of D. H. Lawrence, and some have found this side of his work a little embarrassing, even cheesy, but I'm moved by Flanagan's sentimental men, known in the beginning as numbers and by the end revealed to possess secret wells of sentiment. In *Narrow Road*, Dorrigo is celebrated for his machismo and for being a paragon of his gender: brave, strong, stoic. Australians traditionally value hyper-masculine men who don't expose their vulnerabilities, and Flanagan is deliberately writing against type. You might even say that he's proposing another way of being, though he would hate the didacticism implied there. And it's perhaps why reading the book ends up an uplifting experience, fundamentally of the material, not the dramatic, world. Flanagan said recently in an interview that "love is the scent of a sleeping back, death a slight draft of bad breath," and, on finishing *Narrow Road*, that seems about right.

Source: Amelia Lester, "Richard Flanagan's Way with Intimacy," in *New Yorker*, October 15, 2014.

Michael Richardson
In the following review, Richardson faults Flanagan's constant literary references.

Inspired by both his father's experiences as a prisoner-of-war and the life of Weary Dunlop, Richard Flanagan's new novel explores trauma and heroism on the Thai-Burma railway.

Beside the funeral pyre of Australian soldiers killed by cholera, Dorrigo Evans, surgeon and leader of a camp of prisoners on the Thai-Burma railway, wants at first to burn the sketchbook of one of the dead men. One of his

assistants in the camp hospital points to watercolours of atrocities, of torture, and of the everyday life of the camp. "Memory is the true justice," he says. Dorrigo disagrees:

> We remember nothing. Maybe for a year or two. Maybe most of a life, if we live. Maybe. But then we will die, and who will ever understand any of this? And maybe we remember nothing most of all when we put our hands on our hearts and carry on about not forgetting.

Richard Flanagan's *The Narrow Road to the Deep North* is an unflinching attempt to stave off that forgetting and, in doing so, to explore heroism, sacrifice, suffering, love, trauma, and memory. This is an ambitious order, and for the most part Flanagan is up to the task. There are passages of brutal beauty, where his flair for the sentence that rises from the muck into soaring poetry allows him to connect small moments to the larger forces of life history. Flanagan's father was a prisoner-of-war in the Japanese camps, and that lived knowledge of the trauma carried by the surviving soldiers gives the novel its solidity.

Dorrigo Evans, loosely modelled on the famous camp doctor Edward "Weary" Dunlop, is the novel's central figure. Divided into five parts, each broken into smaller chapters, the book moves seamlessly back and forth between Dorrigo's youth in Tasmania, his pre-deployment in Adelaide, his time in the camps, and his life and the fame that follow. Dorrigo is the story's lodestone, but not always its focus; other voices take over the narrative for chapters at a time, including those of his lover Amy, the prisoners Darky Gardiner and Jimmy Bigelow, and the Japanese commandant Major Nakamura, among others.

Magnetic and ambitious, with a self-destructive streak, Dorrigo finds in his flaws the means to overcome [and] keep his men alive. In a scene early in the novel, Dorrigo forces himself not to accept a steak he is offered:

> He so desperately wanted to eat it, and the men wanted him to have it, as a tribute of sorts. And yet, much as he knew no one would have begrudged him the meat, he also understood the steak to be a test that demanded witnesses, a test he had to pass, a test that would become a necessary story for them all.

This instinct for the symbolic, the necessity of sacrificing his own desires, separates Dorrigo from the other men. Repeatedly faced with impossible choices—which sick men will work, which will be sent away, which will be allowed to die—his deep self-doubt, his belief that he is always a breath away from eating the steak, paradoxically makes him stronger. Every moment is a test, a challenge. And yet he "hated virtue, hated virtue being admired, hated people who pretended he had virtue or pretended to virtue themselves."

This hidden self-loathing arises from his personal failings. Engaged to the upper-class and patiently loyal Ella before the war—"another thing like completing his medical degree, receiving his commission, another step up, along, onwards"—he had undertaken an affair with Amy, his uncle's much younger wife. During the war, Amy learns of Dorrigo's supposed death and, shortly afterwards, her husband's pub explodes. On his release from the camps, Dorrigo falsely believes Amy to have died in the explosion and so does not seek her out. Instead, he marries Ella, becomes a surgeon and, after a television documentary about his exploits, a national icon. A heavy drinker with a reputation for chasing "the pleasures of the flesh" although "in truth nothing interested him less," Dorrigo feels hidden within him "a great slumbering turbulence that was also a void, the business of unfinished things."

At its core, the novel is about that turbulence, the trauma of loss and of survival, and its complicated relationship with heroism. Its beating heart is the long third part, set in a camp on what the men simply call the Line. Unlike the other parts, this one is set solely within the men's imprisonment and told from the perspective of both Dorrigo and Darky Gardiner, called the Black Prince for his ability to procure all manner of necessities. With boots broken and legs ulcerated, Darky is violently punished for something he didn't do, his decline and death narrated in brutal yet beautiful prose.

Flanagan refuses to shrink from the horrible realities of the camp. Men wear "cock rags" and the sick are "shrivelled husks ... barked skin, mud-toned and black-shadowed, clutching twisted bones." With dysentery and malnutrition rife, men shit themselves, anuses protruding from wasted shanks, and even drown in the camp latrine. Much of the novel's best writing occurs in this middle section. Monotonous and back-breaking, the forced labour of the men is rendered in muscular, uncompromising prose. Set against this tragic horror is mateship:

But he had to help Tiny. No one asked why he did; everyone knew. He was a mate. Darky loathed Tiny, thought him a fool and would do everything to keep him alive. Because courage, survival, love—all these things didn't live in one man. They lived in them all or they died and every man with them; they had come to believe that to abandon one man was to abandon themselves.

For Flanagan, it is these bonds of mateship that bring the survivors through the camps, and endure for years after.

This passage also reveals the layered, recursive style Flanagan employs. Here is another example, from a description of the camp. "The trees began sprouting leaves and the leaves began covering up the sky and the sky turned black and the black swallowed more and more of the world." In this and many other passages, Flanagan builds the visceral, repetitive quality of war and its trauma into the language of the book itself.

This poetic quality is echoed in the novel's references to poetry. It takes its name from a work by the writer Basho that expresses "the genius of the Japanese spirit," as one of their officers puts it. Haikus separate each part of the book and are discussed repeatedly by the Japanese characters. Dorrigo himself, like Weary Dunlop, is obsessed with Tennyson's *Ulysses* and quotes and reflects endlessly upon the poem. This, Flanagan seems to be saying, is no mere historical fiction, but definitively literature.

This literariness extends into the story itself and, I suspect, Flanagan's desire for the novel to be satisfying and widely read. Events are often too neat—late twists tie together too many threads to be entirely convincing. This neatness jars with the messy, fragmentary and uncomfortable quality of trauma—and oddly so, since Flanagan does a fine job conveying trauma itself.

Nor are all elements of the no.vel equally successful. Commendable as it is to offer the other side's view, the sections from the perspective of Major Nakamura, the Japanese commandant, and Choi Sang-min, the harsh Korean guard known as the Goanna, lack the comfortable, known quality Flanagan brings to Dorrigo, Darky and Jimmy Bigelow's stories. Similarly, Amy's chapters can be overly melodramatic.

Yet these complaints are minor. *The Narrow Road to the Deep North* is a welcome return to form from the author of *Death of a River Guide* and *Gould's Book of Fish* after the strange *Wanting* and the politically urgent but flawed *The*

Unknown Terrorist. While this new novel has much insight into heroism and the trauma carried by the men who lived through the camps, its critique of national mythologies extends only to the treatment and trial of the Japanese after the war. Mateship, masculinity, war and their place in Australian identity go largely unquestioned. For many, this will not matter—and perhaps it should not. After all, Flanagan's purpose is to convey the suffering men endured on the Line and the price they paid in later life. It is for his readers—and for Australia—to decide what that means for who we were, who we are, and who we want to be.

Source: Michael Richardson, Review of *The Narrow Road to the Deep North*, in *Newtown Review of Books*, 2013.

SOURCES

Flanagan, Richard, *The Narrow Road to the Deep North*, Alfred A. Knopf, 2014.

Gorra, Michael, "Bridge to Nowhere," in *New York Times Book Review*, August 31, 2014, p. 12.

Hodges, Michael, "Booker Winner Richard Flanagan on His Father's Time on the Death Railway," in *RadioTimes*, July 21, 2015, http://www.radiotimes.com/news/2015-07-21/booker-winner-richard-flanagan-on-his-fathers-time-on-the-death-railway-i-felt-the-weight-of-that-utterly-pointless-crime-against-humanity (accessed April 15, 2016).

Raine, Craig, "He Might Be Falling," in *Times Literary Supplement*, No. 5816, September 19, 2014, p. 20.

Richardson, Michael, Review of *The Narrow Road to the Deep North*, in *Newtown Review of Books* (Sydney, Australia), December 17, 2013.

The Thai–Burma Railway and Hellfire Pass, Department of Veterans' Affairs, Australian Government website, http://hellfire-pass.commemoration.gov.au/ (accessed April 7, 2016).

FURTHER READING

Ambrose, Hugh, *The Pacific*, Canongate, 2010.
    Ambrose's historical text follows five US servicemen in the Asia-Pacific theater in World War II; one of the soldiers recounts his experience in a Japanese POW camp.

Brune, Peter, *Descent into Hell: The Fall of Singapore—Pudu and Changi—the Thai–Burma Railway*, Allen & Unwin, 2014.
    Brune tells a fuller story of the Australian campaign in Southeast Asia in World War II.

Gilbert, Adrian, *POW: Allied Prisoners in Europe, 1939–1945*, Thistle Publishing, 2014.
    This is an account of the experiences of the British and American servicemen who were captured by Germany and Italy in World War II.

Maga, Tim, *Judgment at Tokyo: The Japanese War Crimes Trials*, University Press of Kentucky, 2001.
    This is an account of the war crimes trials of Japanese leaders that took place between 1946 and 1948.

SUGGESTED SEARCH TERMS

Richard Flanagan

The Narrow Road to the Deep North AND Flanagan

Basho

Tennyson AND "Ulysses"

Thai–Burma death railway

World War II AND Australian POWs

fall of Singapore

Australian war crimes trials

Snow in August

PETE HAMILL
1997

Pete Hamill's novel *Snow in August* takes place in Brooklyn in 1947. It begins when Michael Devlin, an eleven-year-old boy who attends Sacred Heart School, is on his way to serve Saturday mass in the middle of a violent snowstorm but is stopped by the rabbi at the door of the local synagogue, asking a favor. The two are intrigued with each other, and over the coming months a friendship blossoms, with Rabbi Hirsch teaching Michael Yiddish and Jewish culture and Michael teaching the rabbi, who left Europe while the Nazi Holocaust was killing everyone he knew, about such American staples as popular music and baseball. Soon, a violent local street gang threatens them both, and Michael has to rely on his friend's worldliness and his knowledge of occult and obscure teachings of Judaism to protect his life and family.

Hamill has written ten novels, but his reputation as a writer is based on his long career as a journalist. He has been a reporter and later editor-in-chief for the *New York Post*; he has written for the *New Yorker, Esquire, Playboy*, and *Rolling Stone*; he has covered conflicts in Vietnam, Nicaragua, Lebanon, and Northern Ireland; and he has won awards for his writing about rock musicians. The postwar Brooklyn that Hamill depicts in the book is the world that he knew when he was a child, and the bond that forms between the rabbi and the young Catholic boy is a reflection of what a seasoned reporter, after decades of reporting urban crime stories, can still see in the heart of every community.

Pete Hamill *(©ZUMA Press, Inc. | Alamy)*

AUTHOR BIOGRAPHY

Like Michael in *Snow in August*, Hamill is the son of Irish immigrants. His father, Billy Hamill, came to America from Belfast in 1924. He lost a leg playing soccer in Brooklyn and worked in a grocery store and factories. His mother Anne's maiden name was Devlin, like the characters in this novel: she came from Belfast in 1929 and worked as a nurse's aide and then as a cashier at a movie theater. Together, they had seven children, of whom Pete was the first.

Hamill was born on June 24, 1935, in Brooklyn, in the section called Park Slope. He attended Holy Name of Jesus grammar school and then went to Regis High School, an influential school in Manhattan, dropping out in 1951 to work in the Brooklyn Navy Yard. Working there by day, he attended night classes at the Cartoonists and Illustrators School, planning to become a comic book artist. In 1952, he enrolled in the navy; after his service, the navy paid his tuition at Mexico City College, where he studied painting. It was there that he decided to become a writer.

In 1960, Hamill began a long and distinguished journalism career with the *New York Post*. He went to Europe for the *Saturday Evening Post* in 1963, splitting his time between Barcelona and Belfast. He covered the 1964 Democratic National Convention in Atlantic

City, and in 1965, he began writing a column, again for the *New York Post*. His columns and articles for newspapers and magazines have continued into the twenty-first century,

His first novel, *A Killing for Christ*, was published in 1968. That was followed by *The Gift* in 1973, which was based on his Brooklyn upbringing, establishing a pattern that he would follow in fiction for years. Other novels include *Loving Women* (1989), *Forever* (2003), and *Tabloid City* (2011).

In addition to novels, Hamill has published numerous books of nonfiction, including his acclaimed 1995 memoir *A Drinking Life*, about his early days as a reporter, and the extended essay *Why Sinatra Matters* from 1999. He has written extensively about jazz and rock music, winning a Grammy for Best Liner Notes for Bob Dylan's album *Blood on the Tracks*. He has also written introductions for and contributed to studies of comic book art.

PLOT SUMMARY

Chapter 1
The first chapter introduces readers to the protagonist of *Snow in August*, Michael Devlin. He is eleven years old, soon to be twelve, and lives in Brooklyn. The story begins in the last week of 1946.

Michael is preparing to go out into a powerful winter snowstorm to serve as an altar boy at Sacred Heart Catholic Church a few blocks from his house. The morning mass will probably not be well attended because of the harsh weather conditions. In the kitchen, his widowed mother, Kate Devlin, has started the coal-burning stove. She knows that he cannot eat breakfast before taking communion, but she makes sure that he leaves the house warmly dressed.

Chapter 2
The wind on the street knocks Michael off his feet. He trudges past a huge tavern sign that has been blown down. A giant elm tree has been uprooted and has smashed a car. In this chaos, Michael hears a voice calling for help. It is a bearded man in black, standing in the doorway of the synagogue. Hesitant and suspicious, Michael approaches. He listens to the rabbi explain his problem: it is Saturday, the Jewish Sabbath, and he is not allowed to turn on the

MEDIA ADAPTATIONS

- In 2001, *Snow in August* was adapted to a film, starring Stephen Rea as Rabbi Hirsch, Peter Tambakis as Michael, and Lolita Davidovich as Kate Devlin. Derrick Reeve played the Golem. Richard Friedenberg wrote the script and directed. This film, made for television, is unrated. It is available from Showtime Entertainment.

- Michael Mitchell read *Snow in August* for the 1997 audiobook transcription. This three-hour version was released on two audio cassettes by Books on Tape and has not been released on compact disc.

lights. Michael steps inside and flips the light switch, and the rabbi sends him off with a nickel.

Chapter 3
Michael serves mass. Father Heaney tells him to pray that his suffering in the blizzard will help the souls in purgatory. Thinking about this tradition of praying for the suffering leads Michael to recall meeting the rabbi in need.

Chapter 4
Michael is home alone that afternoon, his mother having gone off to her job as a nurse. He looks through his comic books. The rabbi reminds him of a wizard who gave Captain Marvel his powers. He is looking through a comic book called *Crime Does Not Pay*, about real-life gangsters and the fates they suffered, when he realizes that the blizzard has stopped.

He goes out to the street to meet his friends, Sonny Montemarano and Jimmy Kabinsky. The snow is greater than any of them has ever seen. Unbeatable Joe, who owns the local saloon, offers them money to shovel the sidewalk in front of his bar, and when they are done he pays them a dollar.

They take their money to Mister G.'s store and buy candy. Before they can leave, local hoodlum Frankie McCarthy comes in and tries to take their snow-shoveling money. When Mister G. tries to defend them, Frankie beats the old shop owner savagely, crushing his head in with his cash register. Sonny and Jimmy leave, but Michael is frozen in place. Before leaving, Frankie threatens Michael, who waits until Frankie leaves and then calls for an ambulance.

Chapter 5

That night Michael tells his mother what he witnessed. His mother tells him that he must not cooperate with the police, that only the worst people do that. They talk about anti-Semitism in the recent war. Michael cannot believe the cruelty that some people focus on the Jews. He has heard from his mother, an Irish immigrant, about the way Irish people were oppressed by the English, and it makes no sense that Irish people would be anti-Semitic. He looks in the encyclopedia and learns about Jewish cultural achievements throughout history.

Chapter 6

A few days later, the local police detectives, who are nicknamed Abbott and Costello, are investigating the assault on Mister G. Michael and his friends agree to not tell what they know. Michael tells Sonny and Jimmy about meeting the rabbi. They say they heard there was treasure hidden in the synagogue, but Michael explains that the rabbi was a poor man. They tell him to befriend the rabbi so he can go in and hunt for the treasure.

Chapter 7

After New Year's Eve mass, Michael asks Father Heaney whether it was true that the Jews killed Jesus. The priest laughs and tells him not to listen to the friends who gave him such a foolish idea. Relieved, Michael stops at the synagogue. Rabbi Hirsch invites him in for tea. He shows Michael his books, which he refers to as his treasures. Listening to the words of Yiddish sprinkled into his language, Michael is fascinated. He offers to help Rabbi Hirsch with his English if he will teach him Yiddish. He agrees to be the synagogue's *Shabbos Goy*, a non-Jew permitted to work the lights and the stove on the Sabbath, which is forbidden to strict Orthodox Jews.

Chapter 8

Michael's friends continue to pressure him to look for the synagogue treasure. He continues his lessons, without any interest in searching the house of worship; he has developed a true interest in Yiddish. His mother quits her nursing job. She and Michael will be the building's janitors, and she will work at the Grandview movie theater. One of Michael's fondest memories of his father is seeing a movie with him at the Grandview. They are hopeful about their new situation.

Chapter 9

The rabbi tells Michael a little bit of his history in Prague. He talks about coming home from school one day to find his mother and all their possessions gone, moved to the city's Jewish quarter by the Nazis. The next week Rabbi Hirsch tells Michael a little bit of the story of the sixteenth century in Prague, when Emperor Rudolf learned about Jewish magic, the Kabbalah, from a Rabbi Loew. He promises to tell him more of the story later.

Chapter 10

The police detectives come to Michael when his mother is away at work. They say they know that he was there when Mister G. was beaten, but Michael refuses to talk. When they ask about a Yiddish phrase book on the shelf, Michael tells them about the lessons he is taking, which makes them even more surprised that he will not help Mister G. His mother comes home and chases the police away, telling Michael he was right to not talk.

Chapter 11

Rabbi Hirsch tells Michael the story of Rabbi Loew, living in Prague in the 1500s. Rabbi Loew was a respected, powerful man in the Jewish quarter. The Emperor Rudolf, interested in magic, would visit him in secret and came to respect him. An evil monk, Brother Thaddeus, tried to turn the people of Prague against the Jews. When Brother Thaddeus stirred up a riot that left dozens of Jews dead, Rabbi Loew, following rituals from the Kabbalah, fashioned a man out of mud, bringing him to life. This was the legendary creature, the Golem.

The Golem could turn invisible and infiltrate Brother Thaddeus's residence. He committed playful pranks. When Brother Thaddeus killed a child and left the body in the synagogue, to incite anger against the Jews, the Golem returned the body to Thaddeus's house. The monk went to prison for the murder and died there. The Golem fell in love with the rabbi's housekeeper, but he frightened her. When he was spurned, the rabbi removed the Golem's life source and returned him to the earth.

Chapter 12

Going home after hearing the story of Rabbi Loew and the Golem, Michael is stopped in the street by Frankie McCarthy, who warns him to not tell the police anything about Mister G.'s beating.

Chapter 13

At one of their lessons, Rabbi Hirsch shows Michael the sanctuary. Nobody comes to this synagogue anymore, he explains. Michael sees the prayer book of Yossel Greenberg—Mister G.—and tells the rabbi about witnessing the beating, explaining why he feels he cannot talk to the police. The rabbi says that keeping quiet about a crime is as bad as committing the crime.

Chapter 14

Feeling guilty, Michael avoids the synagogue for a few days, but when he returns, the rabbi acts as if nothing happened. Their conversation revolves around baseball. The Dodgers are thinking of bringing Jackie Robinson up from the minor leagues. The rabbi is intrigued: Robinson would be the first black person to break Major League Baseball's color barrier, and the rabbi knows how it feels to be excluded from mainstream American society. His interest makes Michael wonder about the racial unfairness.

Chapter 15

Michael's mother buys a new, expensive radio. She allows Michael to give their old transistor radio to Rabbi Hirsch. This is the rabbi's first source of popular entertainment. Together, he and Michael listen to big band music.

On his way home, Michael sees the detectives, Abbott and Costello, arresting Frankie McCarthy. As he is put in the police car, McCarthy's eyes meet Michael's, and Michael knows that he is suspected of telling the police what he witnessed. When he goes home, he is terrified that one of the members of the Falcons, Frankie's street gang, will come for him.

Chapter 16

Talking to Jimmy Kabinsky and Sonny Montemarano, Michael determines that the police arrested Frankie because of information from Jimmy's uncle. The Falcons will not know that and will assume that Michael, Jimmy, and Sonny are the source of information. They know that they are in dire trouble.

Chapter 17

At the synagogue, Michael finds Rabbi Hirsch blowing the ram's horn that is used for Rosh Hashanah holy days. Since receiving the radio, the rabbi has been interested in the popular jazz players and is trying to sound like one of them.

Chapter 18

Michael plays stickball with his friends one Saturday morning. They encourage him to look for the treasure they believe to be hidden in the synagogue. On the way home, they see Frankie McCarthy, out of jail on bail.

Chapter 19

Michael has the same strange, ominous dream for three nights in a row. He consults Mrs. Griffin, a neighbor who studies dream symbols. Using a book called *Madame Zadora's Dream Book*, she correctly identifies his fear of Frankie McCarthy.

Michael and his mother go shopping for a new suit for Easter. The Jewish tailor they consult offers a suit for one price but drops it significantly when Michael speaks Yiddish with him. Michael and his mother end up having tea with the tailor.

Chapter 20

Michael finds the rabbi coming home with the ingredients for a traditional Passover meal, even though there are no more congregants at his synagogue. He explains the Passover tradition to Michael. When Michael asks why God was willing to help the Jews against Pharaoh but not against the Third Reich, the rabbi has no answer.

Chapter 21

Coming home from Easter mass, Michael goes by the synagogue and finds that someone has painted Nazi swastikas all over it in red paint. He runs to the church, where Catholics are gathered for the next mass. Father Heaney listens to Michael's insistence that they must help the rabbi and then leads a group of men to the synagogue. In their Easter suits they clean the vile symbols off of the walls with brushes and turpentine. Across the street, they see members of the Falcons street gang, watching and laughing.

Chapter 22

That night, Michael and his mother go to a movie. When they come home they find a swastika painted on the roof door of their building. His mother goes across the street to the bar to phone the police. The two uniformed policemen who answer the call are not interested in investigating, but Kate Devlin insists that they do their job. They look on the roof and find a can of the same paint that was used to deface the synagogue.

Chapter 23

Weeks pass. Jackie Robinson has been brought up to the Dodgers, but he is not playing well. Michael listens to his friends insult the ballplayer with racial slurs, though he and Rabbi Hirsch pray that Robinson will succeed in breaking the color barrier. They pray for Robinson to break his hitting slump. Michael asks why they cannot use the Kabbalah, and Rabbi Hirsch says that magic is only for when all else fails.

Chapter 24

Robinson begins to hit. The rabbi is happy following baseball and popular music, starting to feel like a real American. One evening in June, Michael is walking home from the synagogue and is jumped by members of the Falcons—Tippy Hudnut, Skids, Ferret, and the Russian. They beat him and break his leg.

Chapter 25

When Michael awakens in the hospital, his mother is at his bedside. She tells him that Father Heaney came to visit, but Sonny and Jimmy did not.

Chapter 26

Michael refuses to tell the police who beat him. He is in the hospital for more than a week, but his friends, including Rabbi Hirsch, do not visit him. When he is released, with a cast on his leg, he hears that the gang members were arrested. He knows that his mother talked to the police, even though she was the one who had warned him that doing so was wrong.

Chapter 27

Rabbi Hirsch comes to visit Michael at home, explaining that the police would not let him into the hospital room. Kate Devlin asks him about his wife, a subject that Michael has been curious about. He says that his wife, Leah, was active in Zionist politics in Prague. As the Nazis rose to power, she asked him to deliver a package to some members of the underground in Paris. He made it unharmed, but when he returned to Prague, Leah was gone, having been taken by the Gestapo. The rabbi went to the old Prague synagogue and then escaped from Romania in disguise. He crossed Europe by foot and eventually ended up in the Dominican Republic.

Chapter 28

Michael lifts weights and studies hard to make his body and mind strong for the struggles to come. From the roof he can see Jimmy and Sonny walking the streets, but they never come to visit him. His mother escorts him to school to take his exams. After the tests, he runs into Sonny Montemarano. Sonny says that he and Jimmy were afraid to be seen with Michael because everyone in the neighborhood thinks Michael talked to the police.

Chapter 29

Rabbi Hirsch takes Michael, on crutches, to Ebbets Field to see Jackie Robinson play. Michael considers it one of the great events of his life. While they are there, some tough characters yell racial slurs at Robinson and anti-Semitic slurs at Rabbi Hirsch. Some men in the crowd stand up to them. A fight ensues, and the loud, obnoxious teens are beaten.

Chapter 30

As they are walking home one night, Michael and his mother are accosted by members of the Falcons. They tear open Kate's blouse and reach up her skirt and hit Michael with his crutches. They are only stopped when a neighbor looking out the window threatens to call the police.

Chapter 31

The next morning, Michael goes out, carrying his stickball bat to use as a cane. He finds a swastika carved into the door of the synagogue. Rabbi Hirsch, beaten to a bloody pulp, lies in the gutter between two cars. In his rage, Michael beats on the cars with his bat.

When he goes home and tells his mother, she assures him that they will be moving out of the neighborhood soon. Michael feels the Falcons must be punished.

Chapter 32

Walking to the hospital the next morning, Michael and his mother see the Falcons who attacked them and are amazed that they are not in jail. Michael has his plaster cast cut off at the hospital, and he finds the rabbi's room, but the rabbi is still in a coma. When they go home, Sonny and Jimmy are waiting. They brought a warning: Frankie has a gun. They heard that Frankie is planning to come for Michael and his mother after a big party that weekend.

Chapter 33

Michael's mother tells him she found a new apartment in the Sunset Park neighborhood. When she is at work that night, he sneaks away to the hospital to see Rabbi Hirsch and ask him the secret name of God, which is the key to bringing the Golem to life.

Chapter 34

Michael makes trip after trip between the park and the synagogue, carrying buckets of mud. He follows instructions from the rabbi for finding the elements at the synagogue that were used centuries before to make the Golem.

Chapter 35

After working with mud at the synagogue, Michael goes home to clean up, dressing in pure white clothes, as the rabbi instructed. He returns to the synagogue that night and completes the ritual of dance and chant. The Golem arises. Michael tells him about Frankie and the Falcons. The Golem blows the traditional ram's horn, and it snows.

They go to the pool room where the Falcons are having a party for Frankie. Michael and the Golem are invisible while they walk there but become visible soon after they arrive. Michael offers mercy to Frankie if he will go to the police, confess to beating Mister G. and the rabbi, and apologize to Kate. However, Frankie is defiant, so the Golem beats up the Falcons. Michael orders them to strip and run home naked in the snow.

Frankie empties his pistol into the Golem and then holds a knife at Michael's throat. Under the Golem's gaze, the knife melts. The Golem beats up Frankie and throws him into the air; he lands on the theater marquee.

Chapter 36

Michael and the Golem go to Rabbi Hirsch's hospital room. He revives and dresses. Back at the synagogue, the Golem restores the teeth the rabbi lost when he was beaten. The rabbi says he tried to raise the Golem when he was being hunted by the Nazis in Prague but that he must have lacked enough faith in God.

In the sanctuary of the synagogue, Michael sees an image of countless Jews who have been persecuted over the centuries. He sees Leah, the rabbi's wife, and Rabbi Hirsch dances with her. Michael leaves them to their private moment and goes out into the once-more hot August night.

CHARACTERS

Abbott

The detective called "Abbott" is the taller and thinner of the two detectives who investigate the beating and robbery of Mister G. The people in Michael's Brooklyn neighborhood have given him his nickname because he resembles William "Bud" Abbott, of the famous Abbott and Costello comedy team.

Costello

The detective called "Costello" is the short, stocky member of the detective duo that the people in the neighborhood refer to as "Abbott and Costello." He is supposed to resemble comedian Lou Costello.

Mary Cunningham

Mary Cunningham is a girl who attends Sacred Heart School with Michael. He has something of a crush on her, though she is only mentioned a few times in the novel and only talks with him on Easter, when he wears his new suit to church: still, he thinks about her now and then.

Kate Devlin

At the start of the story, Michael's mother, Kate, is a nurse at Wesleyan Hospital. She eventually quits that job to work as a ticket taker at the huge Grandview movie theater.

Kate is an immigrant from Belfast, Ireland. Like Rabbi Hirsch, she has known oppression in her life: at the time, Ireland was ruled by England, with violent hostilities between the two countries. She is a tough woman who tells her son that talking to the police, even if it is about something as awful as the beating that he saw Frankie McCarthy give Mister G., is dishonorable. She believes that the police are enemies of ordinary people.

After she is sexually attacked by members of the Falcons, Kate changes her approach. She appears to have talked to the police, though she will not admit as much to Michael. She makes arrangements for them to move to a new apartment in a different section of Brooklyn.

Michael Devlin

Michael is the protagonist of the novel. He is eleven years old at the book's start and twelve at its end, and he grows emotionally throughout the story. Michael lives with his mother in Brooklyn. His father died a few years earlier in World War II. He is a practicing Catholic who knows little about Jewish people except what he has heard from gossip. When Rabbi Hirsch asks for his help in turning on the lights at the synagogue one Saturday, Michael finds himself fascinated by the man and his mysterious lifestyle. Michael arranges to teach the rabbi American culture and slang in exchange for lessons in Yiddish.

Michael gets on the wrong side of local tough Frankie McCarthy when he is witness to a beating that Frankie gives to Mister G., a local Jewish store owner. After that, Michael is in constant danger in his neighborhood, fearful that Frankie will hurt him to keep him quiet. He has his leg broken by Frankie's street gang members, and he and his mother, Kate, are accosted by them.

Michael's interest in comic book heroes, particularly Captain Marvel, leads him to focus on a story the rabbi tells him about the Golem of Prague. The Golem is a clay creature brought to life by a mystical rabbi to protect the Jewish population of the city in the sixteenth century. After Michael, his mother, and his friend Rabbi Hirsch have all been assaulted by the Falcons street gang, and Michael hears that Frankie has a gun and has promised to come and kill him, he finds out from the rabbi how to bring the Golem to life. At the end of the story, he is successful: the magical being stands up for Michael and his loved ones and fights his enemies. Rabbi Hirsch believes that Michael was successful in calling the Golem forth because he truly believed that he could do it.

Tommy Devlin

Tommy Devlin is Michael's dead father. He appears in this story only in a picture that Michael and his mother keep in a prominent place in their apartment and in a flashback that Michael has about a time his father took him to the movies.

Dvorele

Dvorele was the housekeeper for Rabbi Hirsch in Prague in the sixteenth century. The Golem fell in love with her and offered to take her off to the mountains with him, but because he could not talk, she thought he was threatening to take her back to the village she came from. Dvorele panicked and ran away, causing the Golem to run amok in an angry rage.

Ferret

Ferret is a member of the Falcons street gang. He is a follower, not a leader, but when the Golem beats the Falcons and Michael tells them to take off their clothes, Ferret is the first to comply.

Mister G.

Mister G., whose real name Michael eventually finds out is Yossel Greenberg, owns a candy store in the neighborhood. It is the less popular one, but Michael and his friends go there with money they earned from shoveling snow. While they are there, Frankie McCarthy robs and brutally beats Mister G., shouting anti-Semitic insults at him and caving his skull in. The man is taken to the hospital in a coma. His family shows up weeks later to close out the store. Everyone in the neighborhood, including the local detectives, knows that Michael and his friends witnessed the beating, but they refuse to talk about it.

Golem

The Golem is a legendary mythical creature, with roots going back at least to the Book of Psalms. During the course of *Snow in August*, Rabbi Hirsch tells Michael one of the most famous Golem stories of all, the story of the Golem of Prague.

This story took place in the sixteenth century, when the famous Rabbi Loew, a true historical personage, is said to have used Jewish mysticism to bring a man made of clay to life when the Jews needed help from persecution. The Golem of Prague had superhuman strength, could turn himself invisible, and could understand many languages, although he could not speak. He had emotions and was given a human name, Joseph. Having saved Rabbi Loew and the Jewish community, he fell in love with the rabbi's housekeeper. When it became clear that she would not love him back, Rabbi Loew returned him to the clay he came from.

In this novel, Michael is desperate because bullies from the Falcons gang are threatening him, his mother, and his friend Rabbi Hirsch. Using the rabbi's knowledge of the Kabbalah, he brings the Golem to life. The Golem beats the Falcons and also makes it snow. He melts a steel knife with his gaze. He also returns Rabbi Hirsch, who has been badly beaten, back to health with just a touch.

Joseph Golem
See Golem

Yossel Greenberg
See Mister G.

Mrs. Griffin
Mrs. Griffin is the neighbor who helps Michael interpret his dream.

Father Heaney
Father Joe Heaney is a tough, no-nonsense priest who served in the war. He talks to Michael with direct honesty. When the synagogue has been vandalized with swastikas on Easter morning, Michael implores Father Heaney to help. At first, the priest does not see why he should be involved, but the boy's steady insistence eventually works on his conscience. He leads a brigade of parishioners to help clean the synagogue. Near the end of the novel, Father Heaney's intention to depart on a missionary assignment is one of the things that leave Michael feeling vulnerable in the neighborhood.

Rabbi Judah Hirsch
The core of this story is the friendship formed by Michael Devlin, a young Catholic boy, and Rabbi Hirsch. Born in 1908, Rabbi Hirsch is thirty-eight or thirty-nine at the time of this story. He spent the first part of his life in Prague and left as the Nazis took over the country, escaping to the Dominican Republic and eventually coming to Brooklyn. At the time of this story, he is the rabbi at a synagogue that has no followers or attendees for weekly Sabbath.

At first, Rabbi Hirsch seems timid because of his weak command of the language and poor understanding of American social customs. Michael teaches him American slang, the sort of language not found in books. He also gives the rabbi a radio, which helps him connect to such mainstays of American life as baseball and popular music. He develops a particular interest in Jackie Robinson, the first black player in Major League Baseball, whose struggle for acceptance resonates with the rabbi.

In the book, Rabbi Hirsch suffers a crisis of faith. He has seen the persecution of the Jews during the Holocaust. He has lost the love of his life, his wife, Leah, to the Nazis. He tells Michael that he is not sure that he believes in God, which is a position that the boy did not know a religious person could hold.

Eventually, Rabbi Hirsch is disabled by a severe beating by the Falcons, the local, anti-Semitic street gang. He is barely able to talk, having had his teeth knocked out, but he does tell Michael the secrets that enable the boy to bring the Golem to life to overpower the thugs.

Leah Yaretzky Hirsch
When he was a young man in Prague, Rabbi Hirsch fell in love with Leah Yaretzky. She was a political radical, a worker for the Zionist cause, promoting the establishment of a land for Jews in the Middle East that eventually became the nation of Israel. After they were married, she enlisted the rabbi's help in her political cause, sending him to Paris to deliver a package for the underground resistance movement. When he returned to Prague, Leah was gone, taken away by the Gestapo. In the book's last scene, Michael sees Rabbi Hirsch reunited with his wife, dancing.

Tippy Hudnut
Tippy is a member of the Falcons street gang. He is one of the people who accosts Michael outside of a factory fence and breaks his leg. Later, when the gang members are accosting Michael and his mother in an alley, Tippy puts his hand up Kate Devlin's skirt.

Jimmy Kabinsky
Jimmy is one of Michael's two friends, along with Sonny Montemarano. Jimmy is an immigrant from Poland, where his parents were killed in the war. He lives with his uncle, who runs

a junk yard. His uncle is a bad role model: an offensive drunk. Jimmy is never seen in the novel without Sonny. Michael thinks of the three of them as having a tight sense of camaraderie until he is beaten up by the Falcons; after that, Jimmy, like Sonny, avoids Michael, afraid that he will be targeted by the gang, as Michael was.

Rabbi Loew

The Rabbi Loew discussed in this story is an actual historical personage, Judah Loew ben Bezalel, who lived in Prague in the 1500s. His story is a familiar tale in the Jewish tradition. In the novel, Rabbi Hirsch tells Michael that Rabbi Loew was in possession of the secrets of the Kabbalah, which gave him access to magical powers. He was a friend of the ruling monarch, Emperor Rudolph, and would consult with him and give advice that helped the emperor with his troubles. That drew the attention of Brother Thaddeus, who hated the Jews and incited riots against the people of the Jewish quarter. For protection, Rabbi Loew used his mystical powers to conjure up the Golem, a legendary creature made of clay. The Golem helped him defeat Brother Thaddeus and keep the Jewish people of Prague safe.

Frankie McCarthy

Frankie is a dangerous street hoodlum. Violent and mentally unstable, he poses a threat to the novel's protagonist, Michael Devlin. Frankie already has a reputation for unprovoked violence when, early in the book, he robs and beats a local grocer, Mister G. Because Michael was a witness to the beating, Frankie threatens him. Eventually, the police learn that it was Frankie who put Mister G. in a coma, and Frankie assumes that Michael spoke up. While Frankie is in jail, the members of his street gang, the Falcons, try to intimidate Michael. They assault him and break his leg and later sexually assault his mother. When Frankie is out on bail, he obtains a pistol. He has sworn to silence Michael and his mother, but Michael stops him by showing up at the pool hall the Falcons use as a headquarters with the all-powerful Golem.

Sonny Montemarano

Sonny is one of Michael's best friends at the beginning of the book. They have practically the same ideals. However, while Michael changes, through his friendship with the rabbi, Sonny retains the same small-minded view. He believes rumors about hidden treasure in the synagogue and encourages Michael to go there under false pretenses, imagining that they could make a lot of money robbing Rabbi Hirsch. He repeats the racist attitudes that he has heard about Jackie Robinson

After Michael is assumed to have informed the police about Frankie McCarthy and has his leg broken by his gang, Sonny avoids him. He eventually runs into Michael and explains that he is afraid: he knows that Michael did not talk, but he still could not risk people thinking they were associated. Michael sees how superficial their friendship has been.

Emperor Rudolf

The emperor in the story that Rabbi Hirsch tells Michael about Rabbi Loew is based on a real person, Holy Emperor Rudolph II of Hungary. He is known to have had an intense interest in the occult. In the story, he seeks the consul of Rabbi Loew, who can tap into the mysterious magical power of the Kabbalah, a method of Jewish mysticism. The emperor's relationship with Rabbi Loew was opposed by Brother Thaddeus, a Christian cleric who was determined to oppress Prague's Jews.

Russian

"The Russian" is the nickname of a member of the Falcons street gang. He does not speak in the novel, but he is usually present when other Falcons are around.

Skids

Skids is a member of the Falcons street gang. He is present when Michael's leg is broken. When they are harassing Michael and his mother, Skids is the one who tears Kate Devlin's blouse open.

Brother Thaddeus

Brother Thaddeus is the bald, snarling villain in Rabbi Hirsch's story of the Golem of Prague. He is a conniver who tries to incite riots against the city's Jewish population when he can. When he is thwarted by Rabbi Loew, he arranges for the rabbi to be framed for the murder of a Christian child. The rabbi uses the Golem, a legendary creature of stone brought to life, to put evidence of the murder back in Thaddeus's house, and Brother Thaddeus goes to jail for the rest of his life.

Unbeatable Joe

Unbeatable Joe is the owner of a neighborhood tavern. After the terrific blizzard that starts the novel, he pays Michael and his friends Sonny and Jimmy a dollar to shovel the sidewalk in front of his bar.

THEMES

Community

Throughout this book, starting in the first line, author Hamill reminds readers again and again of its setting, Brooklyn. This setting is significant because Brooklyn is a place that has traditionally had much ethnic diversity but has also had small, close-knit pockets of cultures. It is a borough of New York City and as such is a magnet for people from around the world, from places as diverse as Prague and Ireland. However, it is also provincial. The people who surround Michael have a communal view of the world.

To a large extent this sense of community focuses on the positive relationships that bind the people in Michael's world, such a love of their church and baseball. When the sign from Unbeatable Joe's tavern is blown down, the local men pitch in to hang it again. Michael has two close friends, one of Italian descent who grew up in Brooklyn and one of Polish descent who is a war orphan. Michael thinks of them being as close as the Three Musketeers.

On the other hand, this sense of community can be unwelcoming and exclusionary. The Catholics need some persuading to help their Jewish neighbor when the synagogue is defaced. Everyone in the neighborhood is suspicious of Jackie Robinson: as Michael reflects, there are no black people living there, and so there are people who rush to assume the worst when Robinson plays badly for the Dodgers.

In a sense, this book is about how a community expands its identity. The people around Michael learn to trust Rabbi Hirsch. They also learn to reject Frankie McCarthy, an Irishman like them who is a destructive element.

Magical Realism

Young Michael reads comic books and imagines what it would be like to be Billy Batson, the boy who learns a secret word that will turn him into superpowered Captain Marvel. When he learns about Rabbi Loew and the Golem of Prague,

Michael's imagination is engaged: he sees how the Golem is just like the heroes of comic books. As the threat from the Falcons gang mounts, he wonders what it would be like to have a powerful defender like the Golem.

In an ordinary novel, Michael's dream of magical powers would be treated as just that, a dream. Hamill crosses the line, though, presenting magic as reality in the context of the story. He does not have the Golem swoop in from nowhere: Michael has to go through a very logical, realistic process to bring him to life. The novel is realistic in its details, showing how the mud came to the synagogue and having Michael find the scroll that lays out what he has to do. However, the story is also magical in the way that the secret name of God, like Billy Batson's word "Shazam," calls forth a powerful creature.

Anti-Semitism

Hamill presents a thread of small-minded anti-Semitism, or hatred of Jews, throughout the story. The criminals of the Falcons gang are the worst in this respect: they violently beat Mister G. and Rabbi Hirsch, and they deface the synagogue with paint. When the paint is washed off, they carve a swastika, a symbol of the recent Holocaust against the Jews, into its wooden door. Almost as crude are the young thugs at Ebbets Field who shout insults at Rabbi Hirsch, a man they do not even know.

Anti-Semitism shows up in less direct ways, too. The policemen who go to Michael's home are suspicious to find that he has a Yiddish phrase book: they do not know what it means, but they think it is unnatural for a boy to cross the line that separates Catholicism and Judaism. Michael's friends Sonny and Jimmy would not think that they are showing hatred for the rabbi by believing that he has a fortune hidden away, but they are perpetuating a stereotype that has been used for centuries to stir up resentment and justify anti-Semitic violence. The book touches on the Holocaust years and goes into the history of Prague, hundreds of years earlier, showing that Jews have been isolated and abused for a long, long time.

Immigrant Life

Michael's mother, Kate, is an immigrant. One of the things that she was has brought from her native Ireland, a land where the justice system was under the control of England at the time, is a

TOPICS FOR FURTHER STUDY

- Nobel Prize laureate Gabriel García Márquez is considered to be one of the great masters of magical realism. Read Marquez's short story "The Handsomest Drowned Man in the World," about the impact that the body of an immensely huge corpse inspires in the inhabitants of a poor fishing village. Then write an argument for why you think the Golem will or will not inspire the residents of Michael's neighborhood in the same way.

- Is climate change softening the impact of this novel's title? Using the Internet, research how many times it has snowed in New York City since the 1940s, what the odds are that it could snow now, and how much more likely it will be in the coming fifty or one hundred years. Provide climatological charts to support your findings.

- Are all of the social barriers broken? Write a report about a sports figure who is currently an inspiration to her or his own small demographic but who is rejected by the world at large. End your report with your assessment about whether this person will succeed in being a Jackie Robinson figure.

- In this novel, Michael is able to perform duties Rabbi Hirsch is not able to do for himself, functioning as a *Shabbos goy*. Some people think that this is a good way for a devout Jew to avoid breaking the ancient rules. Others find this solution to be a clever way of looking at things, but no more legitimate than if the rabbi were to light his own lights and stove. What do you think of the legitimacy of the *Shabbos goy*? Consult sources that refer to the Torah in making your case for or against this tradition.

- In her young-adult novel *The Clay Messiah*, Karen Rae Levine examines the difficult life of an American soldier involved in liberating the captives at the Nazi concentration camp at Dachau. The Golem-like character in her novel is a friend and protector before the captives are set free, but he becomes a threatening figure after the liberation. Read *The Clay Messiah* and compare its Golem figure to the Golem Michael conjures up at the end of *Snow in August*. Make a chart of characteristics they have in common and places that they are dissimilar. Put your explanations before classmates to have them vote about whether the Golem of Brooklyn would be bound to become dangerous after a while.

- The rabbi is so interested in hearing a fellow Jew, Ziggy Ellman, on the radio that he tries to play Ellman's signature piece "And the Angels Sing" on the shofar, with little success. Listen to a recording of Ellman playing "And the Angels Sing" and translate it into the kind of music that you like to listen to. Play your new arrangement for your class with an explanation about what makes that song special.

- The children in Michael's neighborhood believe that Rabbi Hirsch has a treasure hidden in his synagogue, even though he is obviously poor. Make a list of five ridiculous things that people believe about other religions, either from things you have heard or from the Internet. Research one in depth and explain the historical roots of that belief.

---

suspicion of the police. Because of this, she tells Michael to keep quiet and not testify against Frankie McCarthy. Other than this view of the criminal system, however, Kate seems to have assimilated into American life. She works hard and then takes on two more jobs to move up in the social system. Her husband fought and died for his adopted country in the war.

The story is set in Brooklyn in the years after World War II (©*Christian Mueller | Shutterstock.com*)

Rabbi Hirsch shows the true immigrant experience at its core. Because of his religion, the people in this Catholic neighborhood would treat him as an outsider anyway, but it does not help that he is from another land. It does help him, though, that Michael becomes as interested in learning about the rabbi's native culture as the rabbi is in learning about American culture. It also helps that Rabbi Hirsch's interest in American culture is deep and sincere. Through his identification with baseball outsider Jackie Robinson and Jewish trumpeter Ziggy Elman, he is able to see where he can fit into America.

Justice

In addition to superhero comic books, Michael reads *Crime Does Not Pay*, which illustrates the stories of notorious criminals and how they were brought to justice. He believes that the honest will prevail and the wicked will be punished. As *Snow in August* unfolds, however, he sees the exact opposite occur. Mister G. tries to help him and ends up with his skull fractured, Michael keeps quiet about what he saw and has his leg broken, his mother is assaulted and

almost raped, Rabbi Hirsch is beaten until his teeth are knocked out, and the criminals who perpetrated these crimes are allowed back on the streets after only a day or two in jail.

The Golem is needed to restore a sense of justice to the situation. While this gives the novel a satisfying, happy ending, it does not settle the real-world issues Hamill raises. The social corruption he describes in this novel is real, but he suggests no reasonable way for people who do not have a powerful Golem at their disposal to find justice.

STYLE

Imaginary Participation

This story is told by a third-person narrator who focuses his attention on Michael. Information is given to readers as Michael experiences it, and things that Michael does not experience, such as what happened to Sonny and Jimmy while he was in the hospital, are left to the reader's imagination.

However, Michael has such a vivid imagination himself that he is able to put himself into stories he hears if they capture his interest. Thus, when Rabbi Hirsch tells him about Rabbi Lowe and the Golem, Hamill relates the story as if Michael where there, interacting with the characters who lived hundreds of years before his time. Doing this engages readers in the ancient tale, and it also fills in some information about Michael. It shows how strongly he is moved by the story without explicitly having to tell readers that he is captivated by the rabbi's words.

Dominant Symbol

As with any novel, this one has numerous objects that can be read as symbolizing different things. The fact that the Golem uses Michael's Jackie Robinson pin to hold his cape, for instance, shows that he is a superhero (the cape) fighting for social equality (the pin). The swastika painted on the synagogue obviously represents all of the hatred against Jews the world had recently seen during the Holocaust, and the fact that the Catholics help remove this on Easter, one of the most holy days of the Catholic year, shows that these Brooklynites are more interested in real-world actions than in talking about good behavior at mass.

The book has one major symbol: snow. The novel begins with a tremendous snowstorm unlike anything Michael has ever seen and ends with a snowstorm caused by the Golem's magical powers, which lasts for a short time and covers only a few city blocks. In each case, the story shows awe at superhuman powers. The storm at the end is a strange detail—snow does not help the Golem defeat the Falcons; it seems to be a manifestation of the creature's rage. In the beginning, however, the ferocity of the blizzard begins the story by showing how small and powerless a boy like Michael—and also a man like Rabbi Hirsch—can feel.

HISTORICAL CONTEXT

The Irish in Brooklyn

Brooklyn, one if the five boroughs of New York City, was just a village of about a hundred homes at the time the Declaration of Independence was signed in 1776. It became popular as a place of entry to Manhattan, where people and goods could be ferried across the East River onto the

island, which by the start of the nineteenth century had already developed into one of the most important cities in the country. When the United States Navy opened up the Brooklyn Navy Yard in 1801, for constructing and maintaining military vessels, it provided a source of employment for generations of unskilled immigrant workers.

Around that time began the first great wave of Irish immigration. Political activity in their home country caused many to leave for America. Inspired by the French and American revolutions, the Society of United Irishmen led other organizations in an effort to overthrow the British, who controlled Ireland. Their defeat at Vinegar Hill on June 1, 1798, put hundreds of Irish citizens in prison, while hundreds more, fearing retribution and not hopeful about what the future held in their native country, immigrated to America. Many of them ended up in Brooklyn—a section of Brooklyn, mentioned in *Snow in August*, is named Vinegar Hill after the site of that last battle.

Another wave of Irish immigrants came to America in the middle of the nineteenth century. In Ireland, a blight was destroying the country's main agricultural product, the potato crop, and people were forced to flee the great potato famine just to avoid starvation. They came to settle in places like Brooklyn, where friends and family and people familiar from their culture were already established. The population of Brooklyn doubled between 1840 and 1845, and by 1860 it was the third-largest city in the country. Of that population, half were immigrants, and half of the immigrants were Irish.

For the century that followed, the status quo remained intact. Brooklyn was a working-class town, attracting Europeans as they came through the huge processing center at Ellis Island. A large portion of the Europeans settling in Brooklyn were Irish, living in the section of town informally dubbed "Irishtown."

The Brooklyn Dodgers

It has been nearly sixty years since the Dodgers left Brooklyn for Los Angeles, but the bond between the team and the town is still legendary. For more than half a century, the Dodgers were a significant part of the borough's identity.

The team's roots extended back to 1889 when, as the Brooklyn Bridegrooms (a name chosen because many of its members had married recently), they won the American League

2 3 6

N o v e l s   f o r   S t u d e n t s ,   V o l u m e   5 4

COMPARE
&
CONTRAST

- **1947:** Baseball is known as the national pastime. Children and adults follow the team rosters, their records, and their chances throughout the summer and into the fall World Series.

  Today: Football has eclipsed baseball in popular interest. The 2014 World Series was watched by 13.8 million viewers, while Nielsen's "Year in Sports Media Report" put viewership for the Super Bowl that year at 112.2 million viewers.

- **1947:** Comic books are a popular medium for children: they are produced quickly and inexpensively, telling sensationalistic stories with low-grade production values, from artwork to writing to the inexpensive, pulpy paper they are printed on.

  Today: Characters who have survived since the 1940s, such as Superman and Captain America, are the subjects of the most expensive movies produced. The graphic stories that were once dismissed as "comic books" are discussed in college seminars, reprinted in high-quality collectors' editions, and rewritten again and again in modern settings.

- **1947:** In the aftermath of World War II, people around the world begin to realize what anti-Semitism can lead to when taken as a country's official policy, as it was in Nazi Germany.

  Today: Hostile acts by organizations such as al-Qaeda and Islamic State of Iraq and the Levant have led some American politicians to call for national policies that would give followers of Islam different legal status than other Americans.

- **1947:** Radio is the dominant method of mass communication. Commercial television stations are just beginning the process of building networks, and only a few thousand people in the country have television sets that can capture the broadcasts.

  Today: Broadcast media, requiring their audiences to watch or listen to programs when they are played, are generally a thing of the past. Most television shows and radio broadcasts, as well as almost any song, can be downloaded from the Internet and played at the consumer's leisure.

- **1947:** Jackie Robinson shatters baseball's color barrier by becoming the first black player in the major leagues and proving to be extraordinarily good for his team.

  Today: Color barriers still need to be torn down. Some conspicuous examples of this are how few black Academy Award winners or executives of Fortune 500 companies there are in relation to the racial makeup of the population.

- **1947:** Fingerprinting is available but not always used for small crimes. Without testimony from a witness, a crime like the horrific beating of Mister G. in the novel cannot be prosecuted.

  Today: DNA evidence is routinely used, but most stores, even small ones like Mister G.'s candy shop, have video surveillance that discourages many crimes because the perpetrators know how easily they can be identified.

---

pennant before losing the final contest against the New York Yankees. The following year, the Bridegrooms had switched to the National League; again, they won their division, though a subsequent match against American League leaders from Louisville ended up in a tie.

In the first decade of the twentieth century, the team was known by the name Brooklyn Superbas. In the 1911–1912 season, they used the name Brooklyn Trolly Dodgers, a reference to the busy urban venue where they played. That name was quickly shortened to simply the Dodgers.

In 1902, the team was up for sale: it was almost bought by an investor who hoped to move the organization to Baltimore, but Charlie Ebbets, who worked for the team, raised enough money to buy it. One of his first decisions was that they could no longer play at Washington Park, at Fourth Avenue and Third Street. It took ten years for Ebbets to get financing and arrange for construction of a new ball park; on opening day in 1913, a reporter asked him the new park's name, and when he had no answer, the reporter suggested that he call it "Ebbets Field." That is the name of the famous stadium that Michael and Rabbi Hirsch visit in 1947 in this novel.

The team had a reputation for working hard and never winning. In the post–World War II years, they had seasons in which they won more games than any other team. They were beaten in the World Series in 1947, 1949, 1952, and 1953. In 1955, they finally won the championship.

In the 1950s, team owner Walter O'Malley proposed a new stadium to be paid for with taxpayers' money. He felt that the team's popularity warranted a new venue with expanded seating, but he also reportedly feared that the neighborhood around Ebbets Field, which was changing in demographics, was becoming too identifiably black and that white fans would be afraid to come to games. When the New York Parks Commissioner refused to allocate the money needed for the new stadium, O'Malley followed through on his threat to move his team. In 1957, the Dodgers moved to Los Angeles. Thousands of Dodgers fans, among the most loyal team fans in all of baseball, were stunned, shocked, and dismayed by O'Malley's betrayal. That same year, the New York Giants, who played at the Polo Grounds in Upper Manhattan, moved to San Francisco. The rivalry between the two teams continued on the West Coast, but the days when New Yorkers rode a streetcar to a baseball game were over.

The Holocaust

As indicated by the history of Rabbi Loew that Rabbi Hirsch tells to Michael, there has been a long simmering animosity between Christians and Jews in Europe going back centuries. During the Middle Ages, there were laws against Judaism and open segregation, separating Jews from mainstream culture. For instance, the Anti-Defamation League notes the following among the early institutional marks of anti-Semitism: in the year 399, Jews and Christians were forbidden to marry; in 439, Jews were forbidden to hold government positions; and in 531, Jews could not testify in court against Christians. These laws were not consistent through the years, but they indicate a sense of the tradition in which anti-Semitism has thrived. As late as the nineteenth century, the French population was divided as people watched the government pursue a conviction against a Jewish lieutenant colonel, Alfred Dreyfus, in a celebrated case of espionage. Even after it was clear that Dreyfus was innocent, the government still pushed for a conviction against him, apparently because they wanted a Jew to be prosecuted for the crime. In the early twentieth century, after the Russian Revolution, the Soviet Union carried out a series of pogroms that killed about sixty thousand Jewish people and erased about five hundred Jewish communities in Ukraine.

In Germany between the two world wars, Adolf Hitler rose to power in large part by scapegoating the country's Jewish citizens, blaming them for Germany's problems. Hitler passed laws in 1933 and 1938 that barred Jews from working in certain professions, from teaching to medicine to law. Many German citizens supported these laws out of prejudice, but it did not hurt their popularity that excluding Jews from these professions opened up more job opportunities for non-Jews. Jews were also kept out of government positions with the allegation that they would sympathize with the Communists who controlled the Soviet Union—the same people who had perpetrated the pogroms against the Jews.

Eventually Germany's anti-Semitic policies expanded. With the pretense of guarding their safety, Jews were moved from their homes to ghettos, where thousands of people were forced to live in buildings designed for hundreds. As World War II intensified with the entry of the United States in 1941, the urban ghettos were not considered enough: concentration camps were designed. As Germany did worse in the war and was faced with defeat, the camps that were said to "contain" Jews became equipped for massive extermination. In all, the most reliable estimates are that the Nazi Holocaust killed six million Jews before Hitler's Third Reich was defeated in 1945.

Michael bonds with Rabbi Hirsch over Jewish folktales and baseball (©*Boris Stroujko | Shutterstock.com*)

CRITICAL OVERVIEW

Perhaps because he made his international reputation as a journalist, the literary world has shown limited interest in Hamill's fiction. He has published over a hundred short stories and twelve novels, but he is still, in the public's mind, strongly associated with the newspaper business, where he has been a high-profile reporter, columnist, and editor. This is not to say that reviewers do not appreciate his fiction, only that reviewers tend to put it more into the category of "popular art" than "literature." Overall, reviews of his novels have been positive, particularly those about *Snow in August*, his eighth.

Publisher's Weekly, for instance, included a brief review of the book in its roundup of recent publications when it came out, informing readers that "Hamill, in this beautifully woven tale,

captures perfectly the daily working-class world of postwar Brooklyn." The review's last line emphasizes the book's feel-good qualities: "Sounding religious overtones that will thrill believers and make non-believers pause, he examines with a cool head and a big heart the vulnerabilities and inevitable oneness of humankind." *Library Journal* was just as complimentary, describing the book as "strongly evoking time and place" before recommending it for most public libraries. Robert Lipsyte, writing in the *New York Times*, characterizes the book as "gritty, sentimental and ultimately optimistic" and Hamill's writing style as "blunt," "didactic," and "pleasing."

When the book was released in its paperback edition in 1998, *Entertainment Weekly*, which had given the hardcover edition a grade of "A" the previous year, continued the trend of giving it positive but brief recognition with a one-sentence review that characterized it as "a fable full of snap and humor." A review of the audio-book version by *Publisher's Weekly* continued the trend of mentioning Hamill's journalism credentials (referring to the author as "an icon of New York journalism") and praising his fiction writing almost as an afterthought, noting that, in *Snow in August*, his writing is "surer than ever."

CRITICISM

David Kelly

Kelly is an instructor of creative writing and literature. In the following essay, he describes how the ending of Snow in August *might look unearned if one looked at the book's two Golems separately, whereas looking at them together shows that the magic of the ending is actually earned.*

It would be easy to write off Hamill's novel *Snow in August* as being more of a commercial than a literary accomplishment. The book, about a twelve-year-old Catholic boy in postwar Brooklyn who befriends a local rabbi, is rich in details, from the rosters of the major league ball clubs to the films and books that would have made the strongest impressions on a boy like young Michael to the tunnels under the streets of Prague in the sixteenth century. Stylistically, Hamill has complete control of his writing, knowing how to turn a phrase, bouncing from urban slang to Latin to Hebrew, sometimes all within the same sentence. Readers go through the book feeling that they are clearly in the hands of a master craftsman.

Yet some readers may feel there is a tinge of insincerity about the whole thing. The protagonist, Michael, sees the world's problems as something that his comic book hero, Captain Marvel, can cure. Even at a time when comics dealt with promoting good clean living, when Superman was widely promoted as a defender of "truth, justice, and the American way," did kids really believe in virtue so strongly? One has to question whether this is a case where the author is trying to give his readers a warm, fuzzy feeling by touching on how innocent the world was "back then," in a time that never really was. Michael listens to his friends spout anti-Semitic beliefs they picked up from their elders while he himself draws increasingly closer to Rabbi Hirsch. Michael has no trouble finding their beliefs

> LOOKING AT THE EVENTS TOGETHER LIKE THIS, IT SEEMS ALMOST OBVIOUS THAT THE GOLEM OF BROOKLYN IS JUST A PLOT DEVICE, THERE TO TIE UP LOOSE ENDS. OF COURSE, HE IS NEVER GIVEN A NAME, LIKE THE PRAGUE GOLEM, WHO WAS DUBBED JOSEPH. HE IS NEVER GIVEN A PERSONALITY EITHER."

false: this protagonist is a kid with nothing but goodness in his heart.

Then there is the rabbi, a man who has lived through the Holocaust. He lost his wife just days after they were married; escaped through a long, grueling trip that took him to the strange, exotic Dominican Republic; and finally ended up at a mostly deserted synagogue in a deeply Catholic neighborhood in Brooklyn. That he might accept all this stoically is easily acceptable as a sign of his intellectual nature. However, Hamill, to show the joy that the boy and man bond with as their friendship grows, tends to make Rabbi Hirsch a bit cute, with his "how-do-you-say" struggles with English, his pride about sounding like a famous trumpeter when he can squeak a note out of a candy box, and his enthusiasm about baseball as he comes to understand America's pastime. These touches of boyishness help explain the bond between Michael and Rabbi Hirsch, but they strain credulity.

Finally, there is the novel's happy ending. The magic of the story's conclusion can easily be viewed as coming from out of nowhere. Every reader will have to answer for himself whether this happy ending is earned or unearned: whether it is more an artistic or a commercial choice.

To keep the story's building tension, chapter by chapter, Hamill fills Michael's life with danger. The source of the danger is local psychotic criminal Frankie McCarthy. Michael recalls having once seen Frankie beat a drunk man to a bloody pulp in the street. At the start of the story, Michael stands by in fear while Frankie robs and pummels a local merchant and drops a heavy metal cash register on the man's skull. To keep Michael quiet, Frankie's gang, the Falcons, beat up the boy and break his leg with a bat.

WHAT DO I READ NEXT?

- Hamill returns to postwar Brooklyn for the stories in his 2012 collection *The Christmas Kid and Other Brooklyn Stories*. The stories are short—most of them ran as part of Hamill's "Tales of New York" column in the *New York Post* in the 1980s—and they are certain to ring familiar to readers of *Snow in August*. In the title story, for instance, neighborhood Catholic boys meet the Jewish boy who has just moved into the neighborhood, and they all learn about other cultures from each other.

- Michael Chabon's Pulitzer Prize–winning novel *The Amazing Adventures of Kavalier & Clay* (2000) concerns two Jewish cousins who, at the beginning of the golden era of comic books, invent a new character, similar to the way two young friends came up with Superman. The book begins with a description of one of them, Josef "Joe" Kavalier, escaping from Prague during the war in a coffin designed to enable the famed Golem of Prague escape and follows the two cousins into old age.

- The general setting of Hamill's book is explored with more detail in Colm Tóibín's best-selling novel *Brooklyn* (2009), which tells the story of a girl from a small Irish family who emigrates to New York in the early 1950s. In the melting pot of immigrant cultures, she falls in love with an Italian hardcore Dodgers fan. The film version of this book was nominated for a Best Picture Oscar.

- Chaim Potok's 1967 novel *The Chosen* was a finalist for the National Book Award and has become a classic in the fifty years since it was first published. The story concerns two young friends and their fathers—one family Hassidic Jews and the other Orthodox—who form a friendship in the Williamsburg section of Brooklyn during World War II, and the social forces, particularly the Zionist movement (only touched on in *Snow in August*) that conspire to pull them apart.

- The story of the Golem of Prague has been handed down as legend by generation after generation. In 1983, Elie Wiesel, one of the greatest writers of the twentieth century and a Nobel Peace Prize winner for his work in documenting the Holocaust, wrote and published a collection of many of the legends. The resulting book, *The Golem, as Told by Elie Wiesel*, gives readers more depth and richness than Hamill's considerably well-wrought telling. The book includes illustrations by Mark Podwal.

- Baseball legend Jackie Robinson's daughter, Sharon Robinson, has written several books about her father, including the heart-warming young-adult novel *The Hero Two Doors Down: Based on the True Story of Friendship between a Boy and a Baseball Legend* (2016). As the title implies, this book mirrors Hamill's in the way that it depicts a boy and adult from two different cultures: eight-year-old Steven Satlow does not know how to cope with it when Robinson, the first black man he has ever known, moves into his neighborhood, learning about prejudice and tolerance as Robinson changes the world with his playing.

- Rebecca T. Alpert's study *Out of Left Field: Jews and Black Baseball* (2011) tells the history of the complex relationship between black players, playing in segregated leagues before Jackie Robinson integrated Major League Baseball, and the predominantly Jewish owners of those leagues. The book focuses on how a sense of social responsibility is central to the Jewish tradition and how that arguably helped advance the business of sports and the cause of race relations.

Later, they accost Michael and his mother, tearing her clothes off and pawing under her skirt. They beat Rabbi Hirsch, too, knocking out his teeth, leaving jagged stumps. Jails cannot hold Frankie, and at the end of the story he has a gun and vows to kill Michael. It is a hopeless situation with no resolution until Michael brings a magical, bulletproof, all-powerful Golem to life from clay, and the Golem gives Frankie and his Falcons the beating they so richly deserve.

This, of course, is where readers expecting realism cry foul. They would say that it is one thing to have one character tell a boy an imaginative folktale about a man brought forth from mud, as Rabbi Hirsch does in the middle of the novel. He gives Michael an insider's account of the most famed Golem of all, the Golem of Prague. But it is another thing entirely for the author to tell his readers that things like that can really occur in Brooklyn.

Whether the appearance of the Golem at the end of the book is adequately prepared for or is a *deus ex machina*—a plot twist meant to get the author out of an unsolvable situation—all hinges on what readers can tell of the author's intent. The best way to understand the function of the Brooklyn Golem is in this book is to compare him to the Golem of Prague.

The story of the Golem of Prague is abundant in detail and emotional impact. That Golem has a sense of humor. He pulls pranks. He has the capacity to love and he can feel the sting of rejection. He rages. When Rabbi Hirsch tells his story, it is a fully rounded story. The Jews of Prague feel the stings of persecution in the sixteenth century, so there is a need for the Golem before he even exists; Rabbi Loew, versed in ancient magic, calls him forth with the necessary incantations. The Golem falls in love. The girl he loves, Dvorele, does not understand him, and so she rejects him. He lashes out in anger at the world, going on a destructive rampage with an ax. Rabbi Loew decides that it would be best for all to take back the life he gave to the Golem.

The story of the Golem of Brooklyn, by contrast, is a hundred times more simple. He is brought to life by Michael, who is at his wits' end about how to cope with the maniac Frankie McCarthy. The Golem takes the shofar to the roof and blows it, causing a snowstorm; he sneaks into the lair of Michael's enemies by turning invisible; he beats up Michael's enemies; and

he cures the rabbi's injuries and mends his broken bones.

Looking at the events together like this, it seems almost obvious that the Golem of Brooklyn is just a plot device, there to tie up loose ends. Of course, he is never given a name, like the Prague Golem, who was dubbed Joseph. He is never given a personality either. His single most interesting action is the calling forth of snow, which serves no practical function in the defeat of Frankie and his gang. If it seemed that he did this to show off or, even more simply, because he just enjoyed snow, that would go a long way toward making the Golem of Brooklyn a credible, independently minded being. It is just too possible, though, that he made it snow because Hamill thought that the final battle would play out better if it took place in snow.

The Golems are reflections of the people who call them forth. To this degree, the Golem of Brooklyn serves the book's plot artistically. Of course, Rabbi Loew would be capable of creating a man who is emotionally complex; he is a magician. Also, it is quite clear that Rabbi Hirsch, in the twentieth century, is embellishing on the ancient tale, filling in details that are not part of the traditional story—he is himself a man who has faced institutionalized evil, in all of its complexity, just as his predecessor did. Michael, on the contrary, is just a boy. He knows that he is being bullied, and he would like the strength to respond. It is the vagueness of function with which he was created rather than his short time on the earth that defines the difference of this Golem's personality. The Golem of Prague wears pants and a shirt, like a human. The Golem of Brooklyn wears the breechclout of an action movie hero and the cape of a superhero, because a child's imagination has only a limited number of references to draw from.

The salient aspect of these two Golems, despite their relative emotional capacities, is that each is able to understand language but is unable to talk. Despite their many powers, they are each vulnerable—they can fly, turn invisible, lift tons, change the weather, and so on, but neither one is very good at communicating his thoughts or ideas. For the Golem of Prague, this inability to communicate is a fatal flaw. He cannot make Dvorele understand that he wants only to love her, and she flees from him. He cannot make any other humans understand his heartache, so he expresses his misery with an ax.

Rabbi Hirsch fled from Czechoslovakia during World War II (©*Chris Parypa Photography | Shutterstock.com*)

Maybe he is intelligent enough to get through this, but that is a chance that his maker, Rabbi Loew, cannot count on. He is sent back to the earth he came from before he can act out in frustration anymore.

There is no apparent frustration in the Golem of Brooklyn. He performs his duties even when, in the last chapter, Rabbi Hirsch changes his position from avenging angel to butler, assigning him the task of making tea. He is not a threat to humankind, but he does represent a threat to the book's overall message because this is a story about communication. Michael and Rabbi Hirsch become good friends, but their mutual respect starts with a mutual respect for language. Michael teaches the rabbi English, and the rabbi teaches Michael Yiddish, and they both grow because of it.

Of course, the appearance of the Golem is sudden and abrupt, and it might not be entirely earned in the context of the story. However,

focusing on the Golem and the street gang and who will or will not talk to the police about which crimes is putting one's attention in the wrong place. Eventually, Rabbi Hirsch and Michael would be able to adapt to the violent world around them with communication. To that end, it is entirely fitting that the sinister criminals of this novel should be so quickly dispatched by a character who shows up from nowhere, out of dirt, and who is written away just as quickly. He is a plot device, but he is there to show readers what really is important: that superpowers might show up when needed but that words endure.

Source: David Kelly, Critical Essay on *Snow in August*, in *Novels for Students*, Gale, Cengage Learning, 2017.

Sean Callery

In the following review, Callery asserts that Snow in August *is "immune from criticism."*

> For now, Michael stood quietly in the hot Brooklyn night while clouds tried to become angels and birds talked and stones became roses and white horses galloped over rooftops, and the rabbi, at last, danced with his wife.

So ends *Snow in August*, Pete Hamill's new novel.

For decades, literary critics have referred to Graham Greene's milieu as "Greeneland." Pete Hamill's body of work, both as a journalist and as a novelist, deserves a similar designation. "Hamilland" is the working-class neighborhood in Brooklyn where the author spent his childhood and young adulthood. "Greeneland" is a metaphysical concept easily transportable to anywhere on the map, but "Hamilland" is a fixed location and the author all but identifies armories, churches, hospitals, and other public institutions. He does not go to the trouble to disguise sites convincingly. For instance, Brooklyn's Methodist Hospital is referred to as Wesleyan in the text. The neighborhood is familiar to this reviewer. I grew up just slightly north and a bit east of "Hamilland."

To write disparagingly of *Snow in August* would be akin to telling a child there is no Santa Claus. A strength of this tale is the author's unabashed romanticism. How to judge where romance and fantasy end and reality begins is not always apparent. But this might be of little account in the end. The book is a good read, and such a technicality will not matter to many readers.

The goings on in "Hamilland" are familiar to readers of Hamill, Jimmy Breslin, and a few others. In this novel, its inhabitants include, chiefly, a hard-working widow raising her prea-dolescent son, Michael Devlin. Natives are sharply divided between good guys and bad guys. The bad guys are the Falcons, a rowdy and lethal gang. An assortment of decent folk includes a socially responsible priest. Hamill's attitude toward the clergy in this work is far more friendly than it has been in the past. Is this a symptom of advancing age and the terror we sometimes feel when many things remind us of our own mortality?

The Falcons beat an innocent Jewish mer-chant almost to death. Shortly after this, as Michael is passing a synagogue, he encounters a rabbi. Rabbi Hirsch asks Michael to flick on a switch that will illuminate his home. "A Shabbos goy I need in here," says Rabbi Hirsch. This is the beginning of enlightenment for both the rabbi and Michael. Michael learns something of Jewish history, religion, and mythology, and the rabbi begins to understand both good Eng-lish and slang.

Soon the violent world intrudes. The Fal-cons smear swastikas on the wall of the syna-gogue. Michael is first to see the outrage and tells Father Heaney, for whom he is about to serve as an altar boy. Some good guys are importuned by the priest to accompany him and Michael to the synagogue and wash and scrape away the vicious graffiti.

The Falcons, who are suspected by the police of being the perpetrators, erroneously conclude that Michael has singled them out as the culprits. In the code of honor among such people, cooperating with the police is a mortal sin that must be punished. Now Michael is a target in his own neighborhood, as is his mother, who endures a near-rape from some of the Falcons.

Soon Rabbi Hirsch is beaten savagely, and so is Michael. The rabbi has told Michael of the powers of a *golem*, the creature from Jewish lore who is forceful and intelligent enough to attack successfully persons who threaten a Jew who invokes the mysterious power.

As the severely injured rabbi lies in the hos-pital, Michael enters his room and beseeches him to reveal the secret name for God. This, along with complicated chanting and detailed ritual, will create a *golem*.

Michael enters the dark synagogue by him-self and quickly finds the hidden materials nec-essary for bringing the *golem* to life. The supernatural creature blows three long alarming notes on the *shofar* and . . . well, you can guess what happens. The *golem* then accompanies Michael to the pool hall, which is the Falcon's headquarters. The *golem* and Michael terrify and humiliate the gang. The bad guys are utterly defeated.

Hamill's mixture of reality and fantasy will not yield easily to conventional appraisal. In fact, *Snow in August* is almost immune from criticism.

Source: Sean Callery, "Boy, Rabbi, Golem," in *Common-weal*, Vol. 124, No. 14, August 15, 1997, p. 26.

Publishers Weekly

In the following review, the anonymous reviewer highlights the religious elements in the novel.

It's Christmastime, 1946. A blizzard has hit Brooklyn, but altarboy Michael Devlin, 12, is determined to be on time to serve the eight o'clock mass. On his way, he passes the local synagogue, where he sees old Rabbi Hirsch ges-turing to him. It is the Jewish Sabbath, and the rabbi needs a non-Jew to switch on the light. Michael does, and is rewarded with a nickel. The boy lives with his Belfast-born mother in a tenement—his father was killed during WWI—and dreams winter dreams of Captain Marvel and of the new Dodgers rookie, Jackie Robin-son. But soon neighborhood events will alter Michael's life. He witnesses Frankie McCarthy, a "nasty prick," beat the Jewish owner of the corner candy store into a coma. McCarthy warns Michael to keep quiet, and the frightened boy does. Michael becomes Rabbi Hirsch's Shabbos goy, the gentile who does the needed work on the Sabbath. Soon he is teaching the rabbi, a war refugee, English and baseball. In turn, the rabbi teaches Michael Yiddish and about the golem, a monstrous, animated artifi-cial human being. The idyll is broken as McCar-thy and his gang, the Falcons, continue their reign of terror. They paint swastikas on the syn-agogue. They beat up Michael and sexually har-ass his mother. Then they batter Rabbi Hirsch nearly to death. Vowing "never again," the boy, possessed of the absolute purity of belief, calls into the Talmudic past for help that will forever change his neighborhood. As in his memoir *A Drinking Life*, Hamill, in this beautifully woven tale, captures perfectly the daily working-class world of postwar Brooklyn. Sounding religious overtones that will thrill believers and make non-believers pause, he examines with a cool head and a big heart the vulnerabilities and inevitable oneness of humankind.

(Review of Snow in August, *in* Publishers Weekly, *Vol. 244, No. 11, March 17, 1997, p. 76.)*

Kirkus Reviews

In the following review, the anonymous reviewer calls the novel opening "slow-moving" but praises the "terrific descriptions."

The eighth novel by New York journalist/now New York Post editor Hamill (*Loving Women*, 1989; the memoir *A Drinking Life*, 1994, etc.) finds him as readable as ever. In postwar working-class Brooklyn, Irish Catholic Michael Devlin, 11, is obsessed with comics, worships Captain Marvel, and wonders why shouting SHAZAM! doesn't turn him into a superhero. His naiveté is crucial to the story, it turns out, since this slice-of-life tale metamorphoses at the finish completely and unexpectedly into fantasy. Michael and two friends are in Mr. Greenberg's candy store when psychopathic bully Frankie McCarthy, 17, comes in, beats up friendly "Mister G," and drops the cash register onto the owner's head, putting him into a coma. Although Michael is a witness, the code of the Irish goes against being a squealer. As his widowed mother Kathleen reminds him, Judas was the world's worst informer. Frankie is detained by the police and lets Michael know that he'll get his face carved up if he turns rat. For good measure, Michael is beaten up by Frankie's gang, the Falcons, who break his leg. After he's released from the hospital, he's attacked again, along with Kathleen. She still won't let Michael rat on Frankie, but she plans to move to Bay Ridge. Meantime, Michael has become the goy who works on the Jewish sabbath for a very poor rabbi. While the rabbi teaches him Yiddish in return for Michael's correcting his own English, the two become richly involved in the career of Jackie Robinson, the first black player to crack the majors. The rabbi also tells Michael about Rabbi Loew's golem, the Captain Marvel of the Jews. When Michael hears that Frankie McCarthy has got a pistol and intends to kill him, he decides to summon up a superhero of his own. A slow-moving opening, with Hamill as earnestly humorless as ever, but the time-warp element and terrific descriptions will appeal to many.

(Review of Snow in August, *in* Kirkus Reviews, *May 7, 1997.)*

SOURCES

"Audio Reviews: Snow in August," in *Publisher's Weekly*, October 6, 1997, p. 38.

"Biography," PeteHamill.com, http://www.petehamill.com/biography.html (accessed May 2, 2016).

"A Brief History of Anti-Semitism," Anti-Defamation League, 2013, http://www.adl.org/assets/pdf/education-outreach/Brief-History-on-Anti-Semitism-A.pdf (accessed May 7, 2016).

"Brooklyn Dodgers," Baseball-Reference.com, http://www.baseball-reference.com/bullpen/Brooklyn_Dodgers (accessed May 7, 2016).

"Forecast—Snow in August," in *Publishers Weekly*, March 17, 1997, p, 76.

"History of Brooklyn: From Village to City," Thirteen: Media with an Impact, WNET, 2015, http://www.thirteen.org/brooklyn/history/history3.html (accessed May 7, 2016).

"Irish Rebellion," in *Encyclopædia Britannica*, Britannica.com, http://www.britannica.com/event/Irish-Rebellion-Irish-history-1798 (accessed May 7, 2016).

Lipsyte, Robert, "Shazam!" in *New York Times*, May 4, 1997, https://www.nytimes.com/books/97/05/04/reviews/970504.04lipsytt.html (accessed May 6, 2016).

Mancini, Mark, "Why Did the Dodgers and Giants Leave New York?," in *Mental Floss*, 2016, http://mentalfloss.com/article/55491/why-did-dodgers-and-giants-leave-new-york (accessed May 7, 2016).

McMillan, Dan, "Posing the Question," in *How Can This Happen Here?*, Basic Books, 2014, pp. 1–14.

"New in Paperback," in *Entertainment Weekly*, February 27, 1998, http://www.ew.com/article/1998/02/20/new-paperback-feb-2027-1998 (accessed May 6, 2016).

Payne, Marissa, "NFL Dominated Sports Fans' Televisions in 2014, Beating World Cup, Olympics and Other Coverage, Nielsen Report Says," in *Washington Post*, February 11, 2015, https://www.washingtonpost.com/news/early-lead/wp/2015/02/11/nfl-dominated-sports-fans-televisions-in-2014-beating-world-cup-olympics-and-other-coverage-nielsen-report-says/ (accessed May 7, 2016).

Rungren, Lawrence, Review of *Snow in August*, in *Library Journal*, February 15, 1997, p. 162.

FURTHER READING

Baer, Elizabeth R., *The Golem Redux: From Prague to Post-Holocaust Fiction*, Wayne State University Press, 2012.
    This book, as its title implies, is an overview of ways the Golem has been used in literature over the centuries. It includes a long examination of *Snow in August*.

Bokser, Ben Zion, *From the World of the Cabbalah: The Philosophy of Rabbi Judah Loew of Prague*, Philosophical Library, 1954.

Rabbi Loew is an internationally known figure, but few books have been written about him. This book, though currently out of print, is available from libraries. It explains what likely drove Rabbi Loew to become a political activist.

Davidson, Bruce, *Brooklyn Gang, 1959*, Twin Palms Publisher, 1998.

Davidson was an acclaimed photojournalist who, with the help of a social worker, was able to spend the summer recording the activities of an active gang. Though gang activity had changed significantly throughout the 1950s, which led to a situation not exactly like that of the Falcons in Hamill's novel, the black-and-white pictures of this book are still useful for evoking urban youth in crisis in a time of zip guns and rumbles.

Willensky, Elliot, *When Brooklyn Was the World, 1920–1957*, Harmony Press, 1986.

Written with a sense of nostalgia, this book is valuable for readers of Hamill's novel because it contains photos and background explanations for the relevant time period. Readers can gain a stronger sense of place about the novel's setting, which plays such a strong role in the book.

Zeitz, Joshua M., *White Ethnic New York: Jews, Catholics, and the Shaping of Postwar Politics*, annotated edition, University of North Carolina Press, 2007.

This book covers the two social groups that come together in the novel. While Hamill was writing from experience, Zeitz is a sociologist who studied the changes in relations after the war from a larger perspective, focusing on political involvement and power.

SUGGESTED SEARCH TERMS

Pete Hamill AND Brooklyn

Pete Hamill AND rabbi

Brooklyn AND Jew AND Irish

Pete Hamill AND Dodgers

Brooklyn AND Golem

Pete Hamill AND Brooklyn

Snow in August AND Golem

Pete Hamill AND childhood

Jackie Robinson AND Jewish culture

Brooklyn AND postwar AND street gangs

The Temple of My Familiar

ALICE WALKER

1989

Alice Walker's *The Temple of My Familiar* (1989) is, in her own words, an attempt to write the history of the last 500,000 years. Walker shaped a new feminist and black power mythology that demonstrates how civilization was created by women and blacks and stolen and destroyed by white male oppressors. While this is not literal history—and despite her characterization of the work—Walker clearly does not intend it to be taken as such; like any mythology, it forms meaning in the minds of its audience. Beginning with the intimate stories of families— families that completely break apart the familiar pattern of American society—Walker creates a vision of the world that tries to makes sense of the oppressive environment faced by women and blacks in modern America. She gives the reader a dialectical myth of fall and redemption that offers an account of the reader's suffering, suggests its cause, and offers a way out of it. The novel is political and ideological in its intentions.

AUTHOR BIOGRAPHY

Alice Malsenior Walker was born on February 9, 1944, as the youngest of eight children in a family of sharecroppers in Putnam County, Georgia. Her mother, Minnie, was determined that Alice would break out of poverty through education, insisting she go to grammar school

Alice Walker (©ZUMA Press, Inc. / Alamy)

over the objections of her employer. When Alice was a child, her eye was struck by a BB pellet, and, owing to her family's poverty, she was not able to see a doctor for a week and went blind in that eye. Walker was the valedictorian in her high school and attended Spelman College, where she studied under the activist historian Howard Zinn. She later transferred to Sarah Lawrence College, where she took her degree in 1965.

Walker then worked as a volunteer in the civil rights movement, registering black voters and meeting Martin Luther King Jr. Having published her first book of poetry in 1968, Walker worked as a writer in residence at various schools in the South in the 1970s, meanwhile publishing her first novels, a collection of stories, and more poetry. In 1975 she wrote an article for *Ms.* magazine that helped bring Zora Neale Hurston back to popular consciousness. Walker's own breakthrough to mass popularity came in 1982 with her novel *The Color Purple*. She won the Pulitzer Prize for Fiction, and the book was also made into a Hollywood film. Like

all of her work, the novel deals with themes of feminism and racism. Her later novels *The Temple of My Familiar* (1989) and *Possessing the Secret of Joy* (1992) feature some characters from *The Color Purple*, though they are not formal sequels.

In 2013 Walker published a collection of essays, *The Cushion in the Road: Meditation and Wandering as the Whole World Awakens to Being in Harm's Way*, and another of poems, *The World Will Follow Joy: Turning Madness into Flowers*. Walker cites (in an interview with Rudolph B. Byrd) as major influences on her thought and writing such diverse sources as the psychology of Carl Jung and Buddhism and Sufism, the latter two being gleaned from sources including Jack Kornfield's *Buddhism for Beginners* and Coleman Barks's *The Essential Rumi*.

Walker has continued to devote as much energy to political activism as to writing. On the eve of the Iraq War in 2003, she was arrested for protesting. She has been outspoken in her criticism of atrocities committed by the Israeli government in Gaza and has described Israel as an apartheid state. In 2011 she took part in the Gaza flotilla, in which a number of high-profile activists tried to sail a ship of relief supplies into Gaza, drawing the attention of international journalists to the fact that their ship, like any ship carrying aid to Gaza, would be turned away by the Israeli navy on the excuse that even food and building supplies could be used by terrorists. In protest, Walker has refused to authorize a Hebrew translation of *The Color Purple*. Walker has been subjected to charges of anti-Semitism, but recognition that the rule of the Israeli government in the Occupied Territories brings about human suffering has nothing to do with hatred of Jews. In fact, Walker's ex-husband (the civil rights lawyer Melvyn Leventhal) and daughter (Rebecca Walker, a journalist, activist and novelist) are Jewish.

PLOT SUMMARY

Part One

The Temple of My Familiar begins in a South American village where Zedé's mother plays a role in the ritual life of her people, making headdresses and costumes for the village priests (decidedly not Christian priests) out of peacock feathers. Then the government comes and outlaws the rituals of her village and starts to cut down the forest to make way for factories. Zedé herself received a Western education and is able to teach at a village school, but after six months she is arrested as a Communist. By some means left mysterious in the narrative at this point, she is eventually able to flee her country with her daughter Carlotta and reach the United States. They live in San Francisco, and Zedé at first supports her daughter by working in a dressmaking sweatshop but is eventually able to take up her mother's profession of making feathered costumes, which, in the 1960s, prove to be popular with members of the hippie movement. Zedé makes them, and Carlotta, whose English is better, sells them. The famous rock star Arveyda buys a cape from them and begins an affair with Carlotta. He soon marries her, and they have two children. It is also the case that he and Zedé fall in love, and they have an affair. Not that he ever stops loving Carlotta, he says, but she does not see it that way. She divorces him and takes their children while she finishes graduate school to become an English professor. Zedé takes her daughter's place living with Arveyda.

Perhaps twenty years later, Suwelo is in Baltimore living in the house his uncle (who had been a Pullman porter, generally regarded as the best job a black man could get in the 1930s or 1940s unless he took a professional degree) left him together with enough money to live for about a year. He needs the time to reorganize his life. One of his areas of failure is the search for a woman to be in love with. He is failing badly with two women: Fanny, his ex-wife, and Carlotta, Arveyda's ex-wife, with whom he is in a relationship. One of Suwelo's uncle's neighbors, who had done the yard work at the house, is Hal, an old friend of his uncle's who had known Suwelo as a boy. Giving him coffee after he mows the grass, Suwelo learns from Hal his uncle's life story. The two older men had grown up on the Sea Islands off the coast of South Carolina. They had also grown up with Lissie, the subject of a journal of sorts Suwelo's uncle had kept scribbled in the margins of books or on old magazine covers.

Arveyda and Zedé sail to her unnamed home country on his boat, and she tells him some of the folklore of her people. In the time of creation, she says, human society was matriarchal, that is, dominated by women rather than men.

Suwelo is told a similar story by Lissie, an old lover of both his uncle's and Hal's, who claims to know the whole history of the black race first-hand through the remembrance of her past lives. Blacks originally worshipped a mother goddess, but first their religion was attacked by patriarchal Muslims and Christians, and then their civilization was destroyed and the race enslaved. She tells Suwelo a horrific narrative of the transportation of one of her past selves to America in a slave ship. The story ends with her being beaten to death after running away.

Zedé continues telling Arveyda her life story. Although slavery supposedly does not exist in the modern world, she was nevertheless held as a slave in the prison camp where she was sent as a Communist. There she became pregnant with Carlotta by a member of the mythical Krapokechuan tribe, the last mother goddess–worshipping resisters to oppressive patriarchal religion. Although this man is murdered by their captors, Zedé is eventually helped to escape by his fellow tribesmen, who use their jungle craft to make a raid on the compound and rescue her. Finding herself alone and pregnant in the nearest village, Zedé takes a job as a maid at a peculiar institution, a sort of rest home, and finds herself again essentially enslaved. The home caters to wealthy Americans who have relatives that they wish to be rid of because they are schizophrenic, mentally retarded, or deformed or have leftist political ideas. The rest home will take such relatives and keep them drugged and out of the way. Zedé befriends one of these children, Mary Ann, and writes to her parents to tell them how much worse the conditions there are than even they were led to believe. After Mary Ann's parents come to take her away, she eventually comes back for Zedé and Carlotta and sails them to San Francisco on her yacht, where it sinks in a storm, apparently killing everyone but the two refugees.

Lissie continues to tell Suwelo the stories of her past lives, relating a life from the dawn of human history.

Hal and Suwelo's uncle were drafted into the army during World War I. Lissie insisted that Hal marry her before he left, but he soon came back, his poor eyesight getting him discharged. He had to deliver their first child and, seeing the terrible way Lissie suffered in labor during a breech birth, rejected the idea of ever having sex again. Lissie would go on to have four more children, two of them by Suwelo's uncle and three of whom died in childhood. Suwelo's uncle eventually invited them to move into his house in Baltimore.

Lissie tells Suwelo of a past life in which she was a priestess in a temple and was visited by one of Suwelo's past lives, a white man. Distracted by talking to him, she insulted and drove off her familiar, a supernatural creature with characteristics of a bird and a lizard.

Part Two

The narrative shifts to Suwelo's marriage with Fanny and her life. She was descended from American missionaries working in Africa. Her father had been a revolutionary leader in the country they worked in, and she was born illegitimately to the daughter of a missionary couple. She had wanted to end her marriage to Suwelo to gain freedom. She did not want to stop making love to him or even stop living with him, but she wanted a sense of freedom in her independence that she had never known.

Suwelo eventually sells his uncle's house and returns to San Francisco. He plans to use the money from the sale to support himself while he writes an oral history based on everything Hal and Lissie have told him. When he leaves, Lissie gives him a letter written in invisible ink, which outlines her past lives in an entire alternative history of medieval Europe as a place where goddess-worshipping Africans fled by the millions to escape Islam, only to be murdered by the Christian Inquisition in the greatest genocide in history. All trace of this mass migration and the fact that millions of Africans lived in Europe for centuries was also wiped out, except for the story of Othello, the Moor of Venice. He had to marry the white woman Desdemona because by then all of the black women had been burned. Shakespeare, she hints, dared to tell the story only because he, too, was black.

Part Three

Mary Ann did not drown after rescuing Zedé and Carlotta. Rather, the whole scene was staged so that she could disappear and assume a new identity. She eventually settles in South Africa and becomes a respected playwright, but her first stop is England, where she reads the papers of her great aunt who wrote a number of anthropological works about Africa. Her aunt came from an aristocratic family and had

the title Lady Peacock. She reads her aunt's diary, which describes her youthful slumming in brothels in drag and her visit to a human zoo, a type of display common at the turn of the twentieth century in the United States and Europe in which indigenous people would be moved to St. Louis or London or another large city and displayed living in re-creations of their villages, in a manner comparable to animals displayed in a zoo.

Part Four

Suwelo describes his life in the 1970s to Hal and Lissie. He has divorced Fanny as she wished, but they go on living together in San Francisco. He gets a teaching job and at his new university meets Carlotta and begins an affair with her. Fanny becomes a masseuse and spends much of her time in Africa, where she has relatives. Her letters to Suwelo from Africa demonstrate the Afrocentric doctrine of the unity of ancient Egyptian and modern sub-Saharan African culture.

Part Five

Fanny starts to see a psychiatrist because she is troubled by obsessive fantasies of murdering white people. In her fantasy, she cuts off the head of a white person with a sword, and then, she says,

> I'm down in the gutter grabbing the head and reaching for the body, which is still walking along, by the way, and furiously fastening the head back on. I won't be a racist.... I won't be a murderer. I won't do to them what they've done to black people. I'll die first.

She realizes that not all white people are racists and it is irrational to hate an entire race, hence her need for psychiatric treatment.

Part Six

Miss Lissie dies peacefully of old age, and Hal mails Suwelo some tapes she recorded for him during her last days. She tells of another of her past lives. In this one she was the first white man, born into a matriarchal community of blacks through some sort of genetic mutation, in a time when animals and people lived in complete harmony and when snakes had legs, a reference to the biblical Garden of Eden. In order to cover up his white skin, he began, for the first time in history, to wear clothes made from the skins of animals. This horrified his tribesmen but also inspired them to effect a patriarchal revolution, enslaving the women and driving off their animal familiars, substituting them with dogs, which they had also enslaved.

The two family groups—Arveyda, Zedé, Carlotta, Fanny, and Suwelo—now begin to live together in a kind of matriarchal group marriage.

CHARACTERS

Arveyda

Arveyda is the ideal of a man able to function within a matriarchal context. He loves and makes love to the women who love him, unconcerned by patriarchal structures such as marriage and monogamy. The conventional bar to his relationship with the mother (Zedé) of his wife (Carlotta) does not restrain him because he sees it as alien to the traditional, authentic matriarchal ethos he is still able to live by. While Arveyda can play an electric guitar, as any rock star has to, in his performances he also plays a flute, like a West African griot (a traditional storyteller). His music seems to cast a healing spell over his audience, exorcising them of the modern world. Generally Walker is quite uncompromising on the corrupting power of money; wealth turns its holders into monsters. Most often this is connected with white people, but she does not spare her criticism of rich and powerful blacks, such as Idi Amin. (The dictator of Uganda was a byword for depravity and cruelty in the popular media in the late 1980s.) However, Arveyda, from his profession of a rock star, is undeniably rich, yet unexpectedly he seems uncorrupted by his wealth, a good person in spite of it. This is because his character is not shaped by the pressures of modern, white, racist society, in contrast to the many American and colonized blacks whose lives are ruined by their internalizing the culture imposed upon them by their conquerors and slave masters.

Carlotta

Carlotta is the daughter of Zedé, the wife of Arveyda, and later the lover of Suwelo. She has internalized patriarchal culture to the extent that she cannot conceive of romantic relationships outside of marriage in a matriarchal spirit. Her relationship with Suwelo makes her the connection between the story of Zedé and the story of Lissie, which are the two main discourses of the novel. Much of her story arc in the novel concerns her coming over to matriarchy.

Fanny

Fanny was married for many years to Suwelo before she left him to gain freedom. She is regularly possessed by the ghosts of dead Africans, a fact that Suwelo has difficulty explaining to his analyst. She was the illegitimate daughter of a woman whose parents had been African missionaries. When the family returned to America, Fanny was largely raised by her grandmother, who left her husband to live in a gay relationship with a retired blues singer. Fanny gives up her career as a literature professor to become a masseuse and practices acupuncture. In relation to characters from *The Color Purple*, Fanny is the granddaughter of Miss Celie and the daughter of Olivia.

Mary Ann Haverstock

Mary Ann is an inmate at the institution in South America where Zedé is virtually enslaved as a maid. Mary Ann's family is worth nearly a billion dollars (which would have been one of the largest fortunes in the world in the 1960s, when these events take place). Her parents decided to store her out of the way when she complained about the terrible environmental destruction their industry produces and suggested they deserved to be assassinated. Zedé takes pity on her and writes to her parents, telling them how their daughter is being mistreated beyond what they could have imagined; she is kept pliant by being constantly drugged. (Zedé's employers never suspect her, since they believe she is an illiterate girl from a jungle village.) Shortly after they come to get their daughter, Mary Ann, now free of drugs, returns in a sort of commando raid with mercenaries to rescue Zedé and Carlotta, which even the characters say is more like an event in a television show than real life. She does not feel she can go on with her current life, or else she would become a corrupted capitalist too; once she inherits some money of her own, she sets aside as much as she will need for the rest of her life in secret bank accounts, gives away the rest to charity, and fakes her own death in the yachting accident that brings Zedé and Carlotta to America. She eventually moves to South Africa and, after reading of the matriarchal history of her aunt, becomes a prominent playwright under the name Mary Jane Briden.

Hal Jenkins

Hal is one of the few characters in *The Temple of My Familiar* whose surname is mentioned—and it is only used by white characters. He is the husband of Lissie. Hal, like Suwelo, is damaged by patriarchal society. His father attempted to thwart his natural talents as a painter because he associated art with homosexuality. Hal has a nurturing relationship with Lissie when they are first married, but after he sees the realities of childbirth, which seem alien to his artificial male identity, he is traumatized past the point of ever having sex again. Even so, he remains married to Lissie and is supportive of her in every way other than the physical acts of love. The patriarchy has essentially castrated him. This can be associated with the stories of castrations that frequently accompanied lynchings in the Jim Crow South, of which Hal and Lissie tell Suwelo, and which Lissie diagnoses as a symptom of depraved patriarchal male sexual identity.

Lissie

Suwelo meets Lissie as one of the old neighborhood ladies who hospitably bring him food after he moves into his great-uncle's house. At first, he takes no special notice of her but learns of her role in his uncle's life from Hal. In time, through several chapters, she tells Suwelo not only her past story but the stories of her "earlier lives in Egypt and Atlantis." At one point Lissie ruminates on "how many different women I was." In another novel, this might mean that the character has changed over time according to circumstance, but Lissie means it quite literally. She found a photographer who, each time he photographed her over the years, was "able to photograph the women I was in many of my lifetimes before." Suwelo cannot make out at all that the women in the photos are the same woman, yet at the same time he feels that they have to be. To him, this seems no more miraculous than the periodic return of Halley's comet (a topical reference after its 1986 appearance).

Lissie begins with an explanation of reincarnation and the memory of past lives that she presents as traditional African wisdom. However, reincarnation (*metempsychosis* in Greek) is unknown in Egypt or African culture and is an Indo-European belief, famously expressed in Hindu culture and in the teaching of the ancient Greek philosophers Pythagoras and Plato. Her discussion of *anamnesis* (recollection of past

lives) seems indebted to Plato's *Meno*. In particular, she says that most blacks are prevented from remembering their past lives because of the unhealthy diet (pork-based *soul food*) that was introduced to them in the time of slavery by their masters. She says that her own mother, once she was given vitamin shots by public health workers that restored her to nutritional balance, was able to sober up, as it were, and see her own past lives in dreams. She also cites another Platonic trope, that the invention of writing decreased the human power of memory. In the 1970s Lissie became a griot, or West African storyteller, simply telling the past lives she remembered. She was once approached by a white African studies professor who was troubled by her claim to remember these things and, just to be rid of her, pretended they were things she found out by research. The meaning of this material for the modern reader is connoted when Lissie says that the blacks she remembered working for the slavers, enslaving their own people, she has seen reincarnated in modern Baltimore in the form of black street-corner drug dealers.

Lissie's memories of her past life also impose feminist readings on history. She says that she and her family were worshippers of the mother goddess up until the time her previous incarnation was kidnapped by Muslim and Christian slave traders and that worship of the great mother was particularly hard for the patriarchal religions to wipe out because of the fierce devotion of its adherents. However, the kind of matriarchal mother goddess–worshipping society she (with Zedé) describes never really existed but was created in the work of white European feminist intellectuals like Robert Graves and Maria Gimbutas. Lissie eventually reveals that she was also in a past life the first white man, responsible for the creation of patriarchy. This idea is no doubt meant to reflect on the overall unity of the human race beneath the divisions imposed by ethnic race in much of Walker's account.

Lady Peacock

Lady Peacock was Mary Ann's great-aunt and lived most of her life in Africa, working as an anthropologist. Mary Ann visited her in her nursing home in England, pretending to be an anthropology student, but by then she was in the last stages of Alzheimer's disease. Mary Ann found her personal journal from before World War I in the special collection she had endowed at a university library. The staff there seemed strangely uninterested in it. It chronicles her wild youth.

Suwelo

Suwelo's name was originally Louis, but he decided to change it to an African name. He is the husband of Fanny and the lover of Carlotta as well as the conduit for the stories of Lissie and Hal. He represents a black man corrupted by white patriarchal society. He wants to reform himself to become the partner that women need, but he realizes his efforts so far have resulted in failure; at every turn his intentions are undercut by his desires for power and domination over women and for pornography, which have been instilled in him by patriarchal Western culture. One reason that he does not return to his job teaching American history is that the revelation of Lissie's past lives has convinced him that the standard history he has been trained to teach is a collection of lies.

Zedé

Zedé is the mother of Carlotta and the lover of her son-in-law, Arveyda. She is a living link to the traditional matriarchal culture Walker posits for the entire non-Western world, which persisted in some form in her remote village until the exploitative force of the colonized, Westernized government of her South American country intruded. Her story recapitulates the larger arc of Walker's vision of history as the destruction of primitive matriarchy by modern patriarchy. Zedé says she cannot resist a priest, and her relationships with the two primitive priestly figures—the priest from the even more isolated mountain tribe who fathered Carlotta in the government prison camp and Arveyda—represent the ideal that Walker wishes to restore.

THEMES

Feminism

For Walker, feminism and racial justice are intertwined and almost interchangeable in that they represent movements of resistance to the effort of white, male civilization to suppress the original and authentic goddess religion of African women. Black men are implicated in the problem, too, since they were the first to oppress black women. Suwelo, one of the exemplars of positive masculinity in the novel after considerable development, begins by recognizing the failure of the feminist movement:

> His generation of men had failed women— and themselves—he mused.... For all their activism and political development during the sixties, all their understanding of the pervasiveness of oppression, for most men, the preferred place for women had remained the home.

In *The Temple of My Familiar*, Walker is especially concerned about the double and, as she sees it, original oppression of black women. This is also one of the chief concerns of her life as a political activist, and she coined the term *womanism* to mean a specifically black feminism.

Racism

In *The Temple of My Familiar*, Walker sees racism as closely linked to the oppression of women, both of which she deems expressions of the intrinsically oppressive character of Western culture. On the one hand, she presents racism in America through concrete real-world examples, as shown, for example, in the journal entries Suwelo's uncle scribbled everywhere, such as "Between rock and hard place. Colored voter. Two parties but one race running both. White one." Another entry reads:

> Lissie called me up today. Crying. Some crackers hurt her feelings. Bus was crowded with white people coming home from a game. They made her get off and walk. She was all dressed up in her white lace. Was muddied.

He had kept those mud-covered shoes for decades.

In this realistic vein, Walker ties racism to class oppression: the rich must maintain their position by taking more than their share of the wealth produced by the poor, so oppression is an inherent effect of class stratification. She suggests this in her vituperative descriptions of the rich: "They were not good people—they had too much money to have ever been good people."; Even more directly she says, "In a world like this one,... great wealth immediately makes one think of great crimes." She also points out that other social institutions are used by the exploitative classes to secure their position, conceiving of "Christianity as a religion of conquest and domination inflicted on other peoples." She is not analyzing Christianity as an abstract or

TOPICS FOR FURTHER STUDY

- One way to look at *The Temple of My Familiar* is as a science-fiction story. It begins far back in human prehistory and shows how the current human condition came into existence and how its difficulties can be overcome. Precisely the same description, at that broad level of outline, could be applied to Arthur C. Clarke's novel *2001: A Space Odyssey* (1968), which was developed in tandem with the famous film. Write a paper comparing the two novels at a finer level of detail, highlighting the different choices that the two authors make in their depictions of human history and destiny.

- David Icke has a broad web presence espousing his conspiracy theory–based history of the human race (https://www.davidicke.com/). This is in many ways comparable to the alternate history of human evolution and culture presented by Walker in *The Temple of My Familiar*, which helps account for why Walker has in recent years embraced Icke's ideas. Make a multimedia presentation comparing the two alternate visions of human history.

- David C. Conrad and Sjanka Tassey Conde recorded songs from a family of bards (griots) in West Africa singing about the foundation of the medieval kingdom of Mali. They edited and translated their results into a single corpus, which they published as the book *Sunjata: A West African Epic of the Mande Peoples* in 2004. Write a paper comparing griot poetry, from this or any other available source, and Lissie's narrative of her past lives in *The Temple of My Familiar*.

- *My Jim* (2005), by Nancy Rawles, is a young-adult novel that tells the backstory of the character Jim from Mark Twain's *Huckleberry Finn*. In this telling, Jim is presented as a prophet, and his wife, left behind when he was forced to flee with Huckleberry to avoid being sold away, is punished by her master for practicing witchcraft in connection with Jim's escape. Write a paper comparing this novel to *The Temple of My Familiar*, with which it shares themes of witchcraft, feminine oppression, and slavery.

ideal but has in mind the use made of Christianity by, for example, the southern slaveholder in producing a moral justification for slavery— "making the Bible say whatever was necessary to keep his plantations going, and using it as a tool to degrade women and enslave blacks." Walker is keen to point out that the same kind of exploitation still goes on and has called forth a coded language to conceal itself, as when she says:

> The Africa that we encountered had already been raped of much of its sustenance...for the benefit of foreign invaders. I almost said, as foreigners do, 'investors.' And Africa itself became—was made—in the world imagination, an uninhabited region, except for its population of wild and exotic animals.

On the other hand, Walker also indulges, through the narrative of Lissie's past lives, in a fantastic, mythological narrative of racism whose only connection with reality can be through allegory. She presents stories that are easy to understand and that correspond to the essential points of a less clear reality. The earliest life that Lissie relates seems to come from the dawn of human history—as she has said in interviews, 500,000 years ago, when several hominid species existed side by side. These creatures exist in harmony, until those from the species ancestral to human beings decide that they want the land of another species, to whom they refer as their "cousins," and wage war on them to get it. This is the original sin of Walker's mythology, a primordial act of genocide, as the cousins are

Images of slavery and bondage echo throughout the book (*©Asmus Koefoed / Shutterstock.com*)

wiped out of existence. Moreover, the protohuman males, inspired by the idea of ownership of land, form the idea of owning women and children also, creating patriarchy and slavery (prefiguring the second invention of patriarchy and slavery by the first white man much later). This is reinforced by the genocide of black women that Walker creates as the foundation of European society during the Middle Ages.

Lissie's most ancient self and her husband want no part of this and go off to form their own community. It is implied that they are ancestral, if not to all blacks, to African pygmies (as Walker calls the Mbenga, Mbuti, and other African ethnicities who are of shorter than average height, a word she might not have used if she were writing today). The idea that different human groups descended from different hominids, rather than sharing common ancestry, aside from being false, would play directly into the hands of white supremacists, who in their most malignant form argue that blacks are inferior because they do not share human ancestry. This idea is called polygenism and was a common view before Charles Darwin developed the theory of evolution, which conclusively demonstrates how closely related all so-called races are.

STYLE

Allegory

Allegory is a way of writing or reading a text so that it produces a second meaning, besides the literal one. This is done by assigning consistent symbolic values to the various elements of the surface narrative. The technique of allegorical interpretation was originally developed in ancient Greece as a means of finding deeper meaning within religious texts, but the process was quickly reversed, and texts began to be composed encoding allegorical meaning and challenging the reader to find it. John Bunyan's *The Pilgrim's Progress* (1678) is an example of allegory. Pilgrim seems to be traveling overland and having various encounters or adventures, but really the story is about his moral progress.

In *The Temple of My Familiar*, Zedé tells a myth that she represents as being part of her traditional culture, but really it is an allegorical commentary on modern life. She says that after the gods created human beings, men and women lived apart for many generations. Women ate a vegetarian diet and devoted their time to devising beautiful costumes out of feathers; the only pain they felt was in childbirth, and that fleeting and insignificant. Men lived on the fringes of the community, constantly trying to impress the women but unable to do so; all they could offer them was meat. At last they tried imitating the women's feathered style of dress, and this was the origin of the priesthood. For a long time they did not know how babies were born, but when they discovered the secret, they thought they could gain the same power if they castrated themselves, and this was the origin of the celibate Catholic priesthood. Reading this allegorically, Walker is telling the feminist myth that the power balance between the sexes is out of its natural equilibrium in modern Western culture and that violence towards women is inspired by men's unconscious recognition of their own inferiority to women. It is possible to read much of *The Temple of My Familiar* in this way, but Walker's own statements about the novel and her beliefs create a tension between allegory and literal reading.

Stream of Consciousness

The term *stream of consciousness* refers to two separate but related categories: a style of literary composition and a technique of analytical psychology. The way that the mind behaves in the privacy of a person's thoughts is quite different from, for example, written narrative prose. Each thought seems to provoke another, the next as often as not seemingly unrelated to the first. Writers in the late nineteenth and early twentieth centuries tried to copy the randomness of the stream of consciousness, culminating in many famous passages in James Joyce's *Ulysses* (1922). At the same time, Sigmund Freud developed a practice, free association, in which he would say a list of random words and make his patients immediately respond to each, without thought or deliberation, with whatever word came into their minds. By analyzing the responses he hoped to find some reason why one word was spoken in response instead of another, convinced that where they had no conscious meaning, the selection must be made by the unconscious mind, revealing something that the patient did not consciously know or even something kept secret from himself or repressed. Freud's student Carl Gustav Jung took this much more seriously than Freud did and developed a rigid, scientific form of the technique, using standard lists of words and timing each session with a stopwatch so that statistical information could be kept. This is the form of the procedure often caricatured in popular culture.

In any case, assessing a stream-of-consciousness text as a literary critic, one must look for meanings that will reveal something greater than the mere order of the words or ideas, in the same way the analyst views his patient's stream of consciousness. In the case of *The Temple of My Familiar*, Walker has stated that the composition of the novel began when some friends of hers brought back vanilla beans from a trip to South America and she thought they resembled boats. She began to free associate, and the resultant string of ideas grew into the novel. This is an image that she has embedded many times in the text of the novel, such as when Zedé thinks, "The only boats I'd seen were small boats that my mother used to say looked like the dried pods of vanilla beans."

By looking for unexpected connections, it is possible to see how quite disparate parts of the narrative are bound together. For example, the episode of Mary Ann being freed by Zedé and then freeing her in turn seems to have been suggested by the case of Patty Hearst, an heiress of the Hearst newspaper fortune who was kidnapped in 1974 by a left-wing terrorist organization that called itself the Symbionese Liberation Army (SLA); Walker seems to winkingly refer to this by describing the media reaction to Mary Ann's faked death as *Hearstian*. Hearst soon announced to the media that she had undergone a political awakening with her captors and had freely joined them, and she was filmed robbing a bank while holding a machine gun. But when the police finally captured her, she claimed she had been brainwashed and went to live in seclusion out of the public eye.

Mary Ann's experience in part mirrors Hearst's story, and in part is exactly the opposite (which is still a kind of parallel). The odd name *Symbionese* derives from the word *symbiosis* and was made up by the SLA to signify their belief that all people and the entire natural world were part of a single organism that ought to live in a balanced harmony that has been upset by Western capitalism, which attacks not only human society but also nature itself. This rhetoric is very closely matched by the beliefs of Lissie's "cousins" in her prehistoric past life: "They seemed nearly unable to comprehend separateness; they lived and breathed as a family, then as a clan, then as a forest." These creatures are specially characterized as being both human and animal, bridging culture and nature, and,

COMPARE & CONTRAST

- **1980s:** During the Cold War, the black characters in *The Temple of My Familiar* are concerned that the entire human race will be exterminated in a nuclear war waged between whites.

  Today: The Cold War has ended, lessening the possibility of a general nuclear war.

- **1980s:** Nelson Mandela is imprisoned by the South Africa government, an international scandal signifying the racist ideology of apartheid South Africa.

  Today: The apartheid system collapsed in 1990, and Mandela was released from prison, going on to become president of South Africa.

- **1980s:** A main focus of social protests is the general environmental degradation industrial corporations produce. Examples include dumping pollutants into the Cuyahoga River in Ohio to the point where it caught fire and rendered uninhabitable entire communities such as Times Beach, Missouri, or Love Canal in Niagara Falls, New York.

  Today: A main focus of social protest against industrial corporations is their contributions to the single overriding problem of global warming.

by adopting Lissie, connecting her to the world: "If I hurt myself and cried, they cried with me, as if my pain was magically transposed to their bodies." It is already quite a stretch to put together leftist political ideas and sympathetic magic, but combining all of these elements, the paramilitary gunplay, the kidnapping, early hominids, and so on, makes little conscious sense, so its meaning must be looked for in the unconscious.

HISTORICAL CONTEXT

Pseudo-history

Blacks in America have suffered a long history of oppression, including two and a half centuries of enslavement and a more than century-long struggle for equal political rights and social acceptance that is still ongoing. From their viewpoint, there is something desperately wrong with American society, but for most of that time, and to a shocking degree even today, most white Americans have insisted the opposite. This has resulted in many false versions of history being given great prominence in American culture. White slave owners, for example, claimed that they were actually benefiting their slaves by exposing them to Christian civilization. Looking in high school history textbooks that are not that old, one can read that the Civil War was fought over states' rights, as if the condition of African Americans could never have been the nation's priority. This popular version of history (which actually has very little contact with the academic discipline of history) has all too often created a view of American history that draws attention away from the oppression of blacks in America. Noam Chomsky, writing with Edward S. Herman in *Manufacturing Consent* (1988), has shown, for instance, how popular culture is controlled and reshaped for the benefit of elite classes. The black community is very sensitive to the fact that the standard presentation of American history is not their history. The purpose of establishing Black History Month, for example, was to call attention to the disconnect between common white perceptions and reality.

Another response has been to reject the standard view of history altogether and create a different history that addresses the needs and concerns of the black community. Often this resulted in the substitution of fiction for history in the work of black community leaders during

Miss Lissie has been reincarnated as people of different genders and races, and once even as a lion
(©Johan Swanepoel / Shutterstock.com)

the Jim Crow period. This kind of reaction is represented most famously in *The Autobiography of Malcolm X* (1965). Although Malcolm X realized it was completely false, a recognition that was one cause of his break with the Nation of Islam, he discusses (and implicitly accords some validity to) the view of history developed within that movement. According to this view, civilization began among black people living at Mecca ten thousand or more years ago. They invented philosophy, medicine, and science as well as the arts, but they also carried out a eugenics experiment (mirroring the eugenics policies that blacks were subjected to in the Jim Crow South) that went awry and created a savage and bestial race, white people, who proceeded to enslave their creators and steal civilization from them. While this is in no sense true, the story offers a mythical explanation for the status of American blacks to stand against the equally mythical white supremacist story of black inferiority.

Walker has been adamant that the history she was taught in school (and, oddly, even more the science) is both false and partial, so while she

is not a member of the Nation of Islam, she has turned to the same realm of thought. In *The Temple of My Familiar*, she rejects, through the character of Lissie, academic history, which she sees as popular propaganda; Suwelo eventually comes to believe that the standard academic history he taught was nothing but lies. Lissie says, and thereby seems clearly to be acting as a mouthpiece for Walker, "I do not share their vision of reality, but have, and cherish, my own." The *their* in this statement has a wide range of possible referents, including white people and academic historians, whom Lissie does not or cannot differentiate between. She recalls of an African American black studies professor she once met that "he was a well-educated, smooth-talking zombie, and he had sort of jerky movements, too." *Zombie* is the standard description of white culture in the novel. Walker does give an accurate description of the African slave trade and stresses the roll of Africans and Arabs in it, something often glossed over in black studies, but this is part of Lissie's memories of her past lives, reincarnations she went through in Atlantis, Egypt, and Africa and over many generations of African slaves in America. Her memories reveal how men stole and destroyed the civilization created by women and how Europeans stole and destroyed the civilization created by blacks.

In terms of the novel, it would be easy to view these ideas as allegorical, but Walker is famous for espousing these and even more extreme beliefs in real life. As indicated on her website and in many interviews, in recent years Walker has embraced the belief system of the conspiracy theorist David Icke. According to this, the originators of the human race were aliens brought to earth thousands of years ago to mine gold as slaves of other aliens of a lizard-like appearance. The relationship has not changed but has become covert, enabling a more effective means of social control than raw violence. Icke believes that the wealthy and powerful today are the descendants of the alien lizards whose true appearance is hidden from ordinary human beings by advanced technology. In Walker's particular reading, the descendants of the alien slaves are Africans, and white people are the disguised lizards. These beliefs can be seen as a development of the pseudo-history in *The Temple of My Familiar*.

CRITICAL OVERVIEW

Coming after Walker's best-selling *The Color Purple*, *The Temple of My Familiar* was extensively reviewed, and its feminist, New Age themes have attracted considerable postmodernist critical attention. The Nobel Prize–winning South African novelist J. M. Coetzee was among the initial reviewers of *The Temple of My Familiar*. He asks in the *New York Times Review of Books*, "How seriously can we take Lissie's Europe, whose aboriginal 'dark peoples' have been exterminated by white invaders, or her Africa, which reads like an overlay of South Africa over a vaguely realized Nigeria?" His immediate answer is that this is the wrong way to read the book. It should be taken "as a fable of recovered origins, as an exploration of the inner lives of contemporary black Americans as these are penetrated by fabulous stories." That does not satisfy Coetzee either. He has no doubt that the writing of the history of Africa has been affected by ideological distortion and that a legitimate purpose of literature is to show not how the world is, but how things ought to be or might be. He finally concludes in criticism of Walker, "Whatever new worlds and new histories we invent must carry conviction: they must be possible worlds, possible histories, not untethered fantasies; and they must be born of creative energy, not of dreamy fads."

Gerri Bates, in her critical companion to Walker, notices, "Critics nationally voiced disappointment with this novel. They found it too conversational, too New Age." Bates argues against this perception by trying to substantiate links between Walker's metaphysics and traditional African religion but can get no further than the fact that some African pantheons included goddesses, since there was no henotheistic or monotheistic mother goddess worship in Africa of the type Walker supposes.

Oralia Preble-Niemi, in her "Magical Realism and the Great Goddess in Two Novels by Alejo Carpentier and Alice Walker" (1992), wants to use the concept of magical realism to interpret *The Temple of My Familiar* but considers this a radical step, since she thinks the technique is used only by authors writing in Spanish. She defines magic realism as the appearance of elements of the supernatural in a work of literature in a matter-of-fact way that calls for the suspension of disbelief from the reader rather than for the author to offer a justification for the supernatural (as opposed to the strain of the gothic novel in which all the apparently supernatural events are revealed at the end to be the result of misunderstandings or deceptions). She applies this to Walker's novel, accepting its presentation of the dialectical replacement of matriarchy by patriarchy and its historicized correlates, such as the persecution of witches in the Middle Ages being directed against the millions of black women then living in Europe, as historical realities, approaching history from a postmodern perspective that lets the reader create any reality she wants. Preble-Niemi suggests that Walker does not ask the reader for the suspension of disbelief, but rather for belief.

Nagueyalti Warren and Sally Wolff, writing for the *Southern Literary Journal* in 1998, suggest that for Walker peacock feathers, with their eyes that do not see, are symbols for the blindness of the establishment to real history. They relate this to the fact that Walker is herself blind in one eye and suggest that her *womanism* originates from her resentment against her brother, who shot her with a BB gun; against her father, who, owing to his poverty, was unable to get her timely medical treatment that might have saved her eye; and against her mother, who meekly accepted her husband's decisions on the matter. Evelyn C. White in her biography of Walker reports that Walker traced the origin of *The Temple of My Familiar* to some vanilla bean pods a friend of hers had brought back from South America. She thought they looked like boats, and the resulting string of associations led to the novel, a key to understanding this recurring symbol in the book.

CRITICISM

Rita M. Brown

Brown is an English professor. In the following essay, she examines Walker's metaphysics in The Temple of My Familiar, *presented under an orientalizing veneer of Afrocentrism, in light of their roots in the New Age movement, which in turn traces back to Hellenistic philosophy.*

Orientalism is a tool of critical research that in the modern period, or, one should say, the postmodern period, is associated with the literature professor Edward Said and his 1978 book *Orientalism* and other writings. Said had noticed that Western discourses (which include formal literature, popular conceptions, and any other sets of information) had a peculiar way of representing the peoples and cultures of non-Western societies. He was primarily interested in the Arabic world and India—hence the term *orientalism*—but the idea applies as well to Africa or South America. Rather than giving an accurate assessment of a non-Western culture, an orientalist discourse presents an essentially fabricated picture of that culture, based on the needs of Western culture. The non-Western culture is presented as an *other* in distinction to the West. While the West is presented as progressive, liberal, rational, and modern, the oriental other is despotic, irrational, and backward. The other is also exotic and colorful; the mind of the other is simple and childlike or at best wily and devious. The other is not feminine but feminized, in distinction to the virtuous masculinity of the West. Above all, the West is superior, while the other is inferior. Orientalism developed as the discourse of imperialism, offering a justification for why the superior Western powers had to conquer and administer the cultures of

IT IS THIS KIND OF ANCIENT GREEK MAGIC THAT WALKER VALORIZES IN *THE TEMPLE OF MY FAMILIAR*."

the rest of the world for their own good. Said traced the origin of orientalism back to the Greco-Persian Wars at the beginning of the fifth century BCE, when an Asian power came close to conquering Europe, and its basic outline can be seen in one of the oldest Greek plays, Aeschylus's *The Persians* (in distinction to the older *Iliad*, where the Asiatic Trojans are presented as no different from the Greeks).

Walker's goal in *The Temple of My Familiar* is to deconstruct orientalism and turn its propositions around, presenting oriental culture as superior to a West corrupted by its oppression of racial minorities and women. The point is made explicitly in Walker's celebration of all the foreign communities in San Francisco, whom she calls "other 'exotic' ethnic groups." The quotes around *exotic* show that Walker is well aware she is engaged in eroticizing orientalist discourse, but she wants to invert the narrative and make explicit the Orient's cultural superiority to the West. This is what she means when she says of Carlotta:

> And Balinese men; she could always recognize them because of the expression of horror in their faces as they looked about them at the glass and concrete of the city. They were not seduced, not at all.

A true Easterner, ostensibly, is shocked at how ugly Western civilization is. However, the matter is not as simple as Walker makes out. The modern architecture being described was invented by Le Corbusier and Walter Gropius, self-professed enemies of Western tradition who wanted to tear it down and start over. Walker seems to have no clear grasp of what either Western or oriental culture is, but only of the stereotypical representation of each. She has fallen into the same trap as the elites of the colonized countries described by Said as having internalized orientalism. She mistakes the orientalist mirage for the true picture of non-Western cultures.

WHAT DO I READ NEXT?

- *The Color Purple* (1982) is Walker's best-known work. It was filmed in 1985 by Steven Spielberg. Framed as a collection of letters, the novel demonstrates how a group of African American women in Georgia in the 1930s were oppressed by racism and sexism.

- Jacqueline Woodson's *Brown Girl Dreaming* (2014) is a memoir in the form of a poetry collection, intended for young-adult readers, telling the coming-of-age story of an African American girl in the 1960s and 1970s.

- Since about 2010, the Sahel region of Nigeria has been swept by a fad for novel writing among local Muslim women. The novels can be distributed thanks to recent developments in electronic publishing, and they focus on courting and romance in protest against the prevailing practice of arranged marriage in the region. Balaraba Ramat Yakubu's *Sin Is a Puppy That Follows You Home* (2012) is one of the few that have been translated into English, in this case by Aliyu Kamal.

- In 1993, Walker collaborated with filmmaker Pratibha Parmar to write a book and make a film both titled *Warrior Marks: Female Genital Mutilation and the Sexual Blinding of Women*. The shared project is an indictment of traditional African culture with regard to the practice described in the title.

- Charles Johnson's *Middle Passage* (1990), set in the 1830s, is the story of a freed slave who signs on as a crewman on the first ship he can in order to avoid his creditors. He discovers it is a slave ship leaving New Orleans to pick up human cargo in Africa. He finds that the "savage" captives are from a fictional tribe possessed of a seemingly superhuman wisdom, far superior to the supposed civilization of their captors.

- During the nineteenth and twentieth centuries, many black Freemasons and other intellectuals in the English-speaking world responded to the racist mythology created by white supremacists with their own mythology, trying to turn the tables, as they saw it, on oppressive white culture. Between 1987 and 2006, Martin Bernal, a white expert in Chinese literature, tried to make as careful and as full a case as possible for this tradition in his three-volume set *Black Athena: The Afroasiatic Roots of Classical Civilization* (a title Walker obliquely refers to in *The Temple of My Familiar*). Based on his analysis of the linguistic and historical evidence, Bernal criticized the profession of classics (the study of Greek and Roman literature) as being blinded by inherited institutional racism from the eighteenth and nineteenth centuries and as covering up or ignoring the Greek debt to the Near East. However, he deemphasized the degree to which that debt is in fact acknowledged by classicists (the tremendous growth of Greek culture in the eighth century BCE, for example, being generally called the Orientalizing Revolution precisely because the influence of Near Eastern culture is so obvious) and relied on rather forced, if not dubious, philological evidence and the interpretation of myth as literal history. *Black Athena Revisited* (1996), edited by Mary R. Lefkowitz and Guy MacLean Rogers in response to Bernal's first volume, is a collection of papers by experts in the various necessary fields that examine and criticize each of his arguments in turn.

To see how, it is useful to look at the orientalizing fantasies of the Greeks, since those ancient tropes are what she has inherited. For instance, the religious practices of the Persians were carried out by a priestly tribe called *magoi*, and the Greeks called their rites *magic*. In fact, the main *magian* rite was tending perpetual fires on altars in their temples, but the Greeks attributed to them all sorts of bizarre practices. In one, when rough water prevented the Persian army from crossing the Bosporus Strait on a pontoon bridge, they beat the waves with whips as if they were trying to control unruly slaves. The Greeks used "magic," the religion of their enemies, to stand for the irrational and superstitious, the un-Greek. More particularly, the Greeks had their own rituals that were carried out in temples in the heart of every Greek city by the population as a whole. To the Greeks, this was the proper exercise of religion.

There were also other traditional religious rituals in Greek culture that had nothing to do with cities. Prophets, priests, and healers would remove curses, wash away the effects of sin, cure disease, and tell the future for private individuals. Although these practices were authentically Greek, Greek public intellectuals began calling them "magic"—the name for Persian religion—and in some cases even pretended the relevant rituals had been taught to Greek peasants by *magoi* at the time of the invasion. Indeed, it was these very Greek practices that mainly had the name of *magic* and which were later routinely ascribed to the foreign other.

It is this kind of ancient Greek magic that Walker valorizes in *The Temple of My Familiar*. Arveyda is Walker's prototype of the magician. He is a champion of traditional wisdom in the face of hegemonic Western culture, but his wisdom is non-Western only within the context of the orientalist discourse. The magic of music and diet that he propagates are Western ideas that the West itself tries to reject as foreign. Because Walker participates in (rather than deconstructs) the orientalist discourse, she accepts its characterizations. She wants to valorize the non-Western but instead celebrates the discredited part of Western culture, mistaking it, as orientalism intends, for the non-Western. Although Arveyda is American, his mixed African and Native American heritage signals that he is an *other* to Western culture. He is a rock musician, which was viewed in the 1960s, when his career began, as something counter to American culture. Decisively, he meets Zedé and Carlotta when he buys a priestly feathered cape from them to wear during his performances. He continues the traditions of Zedé's village priests on center stage, as it were, in America.

In a related thread, when Arveyda begins to see Carlotta, he introduces her to the same vegetarian diet that he eats. It is true that many people in Western culture eat more meat than is healthy, resulting in obesity and heart disease. Early humans were all hunter-gatherers, and they evolved to eat a mixed diet but often preferred meat since it contained the protein and fat that are necessary, in the right amounts, for health. But meat was hard to come by, so evolution favored those individuals who could go to some trouble to obtain it. Now the abundance of meat in Western culture makes it too easy to obtain. The same is true of fruit. Foods that are high in sugar are even more damaging to the Western diet, but they are the most in demand because the body reacts to them with positive signals, as it would to concentrated fruit, so it is again a matter of getting too much of what in moderation is good. Walker is well aware of this. She says of Carlotta: "Left to herself, she ate nothing but sweet cakes—chocolate cream puffs or Twinkies.... She thought she hated fruit." The effects of diet have only been discovered by modern Western medicine. Traditional cultures did not, of course, have any scientific knowledge about diet. Physicians do not generally recommend a vegetarian diet because even today it is too difficult to ingest sufficient fat and protein without meat (though it is possible with much diligence). Yet vegetarianism is part of ancient Greek culture. The Greek philosopher Pythagoras advised a vegetarian diet for his followers, not on grounds of health but because he believed that human beings were liable to be reincarnated as animals in many cases, so eating meat was a form of cannibalism. Walker makes Arveyda a vegetarian because she sees it as something *other* to Western culture, because she views it through the lens of her own internalized orientalism. In fact, vegetarianism is part of the Western tradition.

Arveyda is principally a musician, but Walker says, "Arveyda and his music were medicine, and, seeing or hearing him, people knew it. They flocked to him as once they might have to priests." His music is, in fact, a prayer. Walker is contrasting this with the rock music made by white musicians, which she says turns its hearers into zombies. (Interestingly, the zombie in this sense is an orientalist reading of authentic Haitian ritual practices.) Walker is positioning Arveyda's non-Western music as a healing power, a form of prayer that comes close to

Fanny dreams of a rich feast where only white people are seated at the table *(©Petinov Sergey Mihilovich /*
Shutterstock.com)

casting a spell on his audience. This kind of use
for music, as a means of healing, of exorcism,
and of entering a trance, was among the practices of the traditional healers and shamans of
ancient Greece, the ones marginalized by intellectuals like Plato as magicians, represented in
myth by the lyre player Orpheus. The philosopher Heraclitus referred to them as "night-wan-
derers, mages, bacchants, Lenaeans [i.e.,
followers of Orpheus], mystery initiates . . . for
they are initiated into men's customary mysteries
in unhallowed fashion." They traced their practices back to the mythical hero Orpheus, whose
music had the power to tame wild animals, make
streams run backward, and raise the dead. So
again, Walker is herself orientalizing, reading
rejected fragments of Western culture as if they
had non-Western origins. She makes Arveyda
into a modern-day Orpheus while asserting that
the Greek Orpheus is something from outside
the West.

The examples of Walker's reuse of ancient
tropes of Greek philosophy and mysteries are
too numerous to catalog exhaustively. Another
example comes when Zedé tells Arveyda that the
women of her village purified themselves in a
waterfall at the time of their menstrual cycle,
which, she says, was controlled by the phases of
the moon. This, too, is the ancient Greek conception, explained in the natural history of Pliny
the Elder and the medical writings of the Hippo-
cratic corpus. Perhaps the most telling example
of orientalizing comes at the very beginning of
the novel. Zedé's mother is said to be an expert in
preparing the traditional decorative priestly costumes of her tribe, which are largely composed
of peacock feathers. Whether or not it was
Walker's decision, the peacock theme dominates
the artwork used on the cover and as ornaments
in the first edition of *The Temple of My Familiar*.
However, the peacock is native to India and
Iran, not South America. While peafowl have
been introduced into South America and formed
wild populations long after the Spanish discovery of the continent, since they are not native,
they play little role in the practice of traditional
South American religion. Moreover, while some
shamans in South America do wear feather

headdresses, the feathers used are those of macaws and toucans, not peacocks. Also, the practice is largely limited to the Amazon watershed, in Brazil and Guyana, away from the Spanish-speaking areas of South America where Zedé's tribe lived. Walker is relying not on real knowledge about the indigenous cultures of South America, but on a Western stereotype, albeit one turned around so that the stereotype is meant to represent something beautiful and authentic rather than primitive.

What Walker attributes to African spirituality seems rather to largely belong to the New Age movement. The various flavors of New Age spirituality take the mélange of magic, philosophy, and religion that existed in the Roman world, was revived during the Renaissance, and was rejected by the Enlightenment and dress it in a number of exotic garbs: Native American, Indian, Tibetan, or African. Walker stated, in her political pamphlet *Sent by Earth* (2001), that her knowledge of "traditional, pre-colonial and perhaps pre-patriarchal, Ancient African life-ways" derived most recently from Malidoma Patrice Somé's *The Healing Wisdom of Africa* (1998). Somé's book has little to do with traditional African culture and is explicitly written for Westerners who feel alienated and want to heal themselves by getting in touch with primitive spirituality; it is a compilation of rituals that are admittedly of Somé's own invention. In other words, it is a book of New Age spirituality that recombines odd bits of ancient Western religious and philosophical belief and uses an oriental flavor to give them an air of non-Western authority—a work of pure orientalizing. Walker follows her sources closely.

Source: Rita M. Brown, Critical Essay on *The Temple of My Familiar*, in *Novels for Students*, Gale, Cengage Learning, 2017.

SOURCES

Bates, Gerri, *Alice Walker: A Critical Companion*, Greenwood Press, 2005, pp. 103–14.

Coetzee, J. M., "The Beginnings of (Wo)man in Africa," in *New York Times Book Review*, April 30, 1989, https://www.nytimes.com/books/98/10/04/specials/walker-temple.html (accessed March 31, 2016).

Fryer, Roland G., and Steven D. Levitt, "The Causes and Consequences of Distinctively Black Names," National Bureau of Economic Research Working Paper No. 9938, September 2003, http://www.nber.org/papers/w9938 (accessed March 25, 2016).

Hammer, Olav, "New Age Movement," in *Dictionary of Gnosis & Western Esotericism*, edited by Wouter J. Hanegraaff, Antoine Faivre, Roelof van den Broek, and Jean-Pierre Brock, Brill, 2006, pp. 855–61.

Hanegraaff, Wouter J., *Esotericism and the Academy: Rejected Knowledge in Western Culture*, Cambridge University Press, 2012, pp. 7–11.

———, *New Age Religion and Western Culture: Esotericism in the Mirror of Secular Thought*, SUNY Press, 1998, pp. 262–75.

Heraclitus, Fragment 14, translated in *Magic, Witchcraft, and Ghosts in the Greek and Roman Worlds: A Sourcebook*, by Daniel Ogden, Oxford University Press, 2002, p. 16.

Herman, Edward S., and Noam Chomsky, *Manufacturing Consent: The Political Economy of the Mass Media*, Pantheon Books, 2002, pp. 1–36.

Lefkowtiz, Mary, *Not Out of Africa: How Afrocentrism Became an Excuse to Teach Myth as History*, rev. ed., Basic Books, 1997, pp. 134–54.

Preble-Niemi, Oralia, "Magical Realism and the Great Goddess in Two Novels by Alejo Carpentier and Alice Walker," in *Comparatist*, Vol. 16, May 1992, pp. 101–14.

Said, Edward, *Orientalism*, Vintage, 1979, pp. 1–112.

Somé, Malidoma Patrice, *The Healing Wisdom of Africa: Finding Life Purpose through Nature, Ritual, and Community*, Jeremy P. Tarcher/Putnam, 1998, pp. 275–314.

"South American Feather Headdresses," Pitt Rivers Museum website, https://www.prm.ox.ac.uk/feathers.html (accessed March 31, 2016).

Walker, Alice, "Commentary: Human Race Get Off Your Knees," Alice Walker website, February 2013, http://alicewalkersgarden.com/2013/02/human-race-get-off-your-knees-i-couldnt-have-put-it-better-myself/ (accessed April 5, 2016).

———, "David Icke: The People's Voice," Alice Walker website, http://alicewalkersgarden.com/2013/07/david-icke-we-are-change/ (accessed April 5, 2016).

———, "On Raising Chickens: A Conversation with Rudolph P. Byrd," in *The World Has Changed: Conversations with Alice Walker*, edited by Rudolph P. Byrd, New Press, 2010, pp. 311–22.

———, *Sent by Earth: A Message from the Grandmother Spirit after the Attacks on the World Trade Center and Pentagon*, Seven Stories Press, 2001, p. 10.

———, *The Temple of My Familiar*, Harcourt Brace Jovanovich, 1989.

Warren, Nagueyalti, and Sally Wolff, "'Like the Pupil of an Eye': Sexual Blinding of Women in Alice Walker's Works," in *Southern Literary Journal*, Vol. 31, No. 1, Fall 1998, pp. 1–16.

White, Evelyn C., *Alice Walker: A Life*, W. W. Norton, 2005, pp. 445–66.

X, Malcolm, with Alex Haley, *The Autobiography of Malcolm X*, Grove Press, 1965, pp. 167–88.

FURTHER READING

Hanegraaff, Wouter J., *Western Esotericism: A Guide for the Perplexed*, Bloomsbury Academic, 2013.
In this volume Hanegraaff, the leading historian of the New Age movement, gives a general account of its doctrines and historical development in as popularizing a fashion as the difficulty and obscurity of the subject matter permit.

Naipaul, V. S., *The Middle Passage*, Macmillan, 1962.
Naipaul, already a prominent writer in England, was commissioned in the 1960s by the government of his native Trinidad to write a travel book about the country to coincide with its independence from Great Britain. In an essentially novelistic narrative, Naipaul is surprised by the degree to which the Trinidadians, as well as the inhabitants of several other nearby Islands in the same circumstance, along with French Guyana on the mainland, pride themselves on a rather ridiculous imitation of the norms of the colonial society they were supposedly being freed from.

Rumi, *Mystical Poems of Rumi*, translated by A. J. Arberry, edited by Ehsan Yarshater and Hasan Javadi, University of Chicago Press, 2009.

Rumi was a thirteenth-century Persian Sufi poet and is cited as a major influence by Walker. Arberry produced the standard scholarly translation of a selection of Rumi's verse (a complete translation is an urgent need for Islamic studies) in the 1970s, and this edition includes a large body of explanatory notes by the editors.

Zinn, Howard, *A People's History of the United States*, Harper & Row, 1980.
Zinn, purposefully reacting against the standard presentation of American history in popular culture and mass education, tells the history of the country from the point of view of its oppressed and exploited classes. Zinn was a teacher of Walker's.

SUGGESTED SEARCH TERMS

Alice Walker

The Temple of My Familiar AND Walker

Black Arts movement

orientalism

New Age

radical feminism OR third wave feminism

magic realism

Afrocentrism

Their Eyes Were Watching God

2005 *Their Eyes Were Watching God* (2005) is a made-for-TV adaptation of Zora Neale Hurston's classic 1937 novel, starring Halle Berry as the irrepressible Janie Crawford: a woman determined to find a true love who will lift her spirit up rather than tying her down. Produced by the American Broadcasting Company, Do We Inc., and Oprah Winfrey's Harpo Films; directed by Darnell Martin; and written by a trio led by Pulitzer Prize–winning playwright Suzan-Lori Parks, *Their Eyes Were Watching God* premiered on March 6, 2005, to positive reviews. Critics were especially enamored of Berry's charming performance as well as the vivid depiction of the novel's settings—from Logan Killicks's muddy farm to the vast, green Everglades in all their wild beauty.

Hurston's novel is considered among the greatest works of American literature, a celebration of one woman's journey from obedient wife to unapologetic rebel. Set in the 1920s in rural Florida and written in the vernacular of the Gulf South, Hurston's novel challenges the idea that a woman can be defined, categorized, or controlled by anyone but herself. Janie refuses to live by the standards set for her against her will by the people of Eatonville, who see her only as the mayor's elegant wife. Instead, she chooses to follow her own path, paying no mind to the scandalized gossip she inspires. The love between Janie and Tea Cake is as pure as it is untamed, sweeping them off their feet with the force of a hurricane.

Michael Ealy plays Tea Cake (©AF archive / Alamy)

PLOT SUMMARY

Their Eyes Were Watching God begins with a close-up of Janie Crawford's dirty, bare feet as she limps down the road. Her overalls are ragged and streaked with mud, and her long hair is tangled. A voice-over from Janie tells us she has just returned from burying the dead. She walks slowly into Eatonville, which a road sign declares is the first incorporated African American township in the United States.

Townsfolk sitting on the porch of the general store cannot believe what they are seeing. They say Tea Cake must have run off with Janie's money. Pearl Stone tells Janie the town has been worried sick about her, but Janie scoffs under her breath at this and walks through her front gate into the house after picking a red rose from her garden. Inside, she pulls down a sheet covering the piano and plays a simpler version of the movie's sultry theme music.

She overhears her neighbors, who have gathered on the porch next door, gossiping about Tea Cake. As she washes the mud off her feet, her friend, Pheoby, brings a plate of food to her. Pheoby tells Janie that she knows Tea Cake took advantage of her fragile emotional state after her husband's death and stole her money before abandoning her. Janie denies this, saying she and Tea Cake were in love. She says the town only ever saw her as a fine, proper lady at the mayor's side, but that was not the truth.

The scene at Janie's house fades away to a flashback to Janie's childhood, accompanied by Janie's voice-over. Janie never knew her parents. Her grandmother, Nanny, raised her. She felt connected to nature from an early age. In a long white dress, she approaches a blossoming pear tree in her yard to the sounds of a heartbeat, strange whispers, and bees buzzing. There is an extreme close-up of Janie's reverent face and a shot of a bee approaching a blossom. Janie sees Johnny Taylor, a young man with a fishing pole, walking by. She calls out his name and runs to him. His reaction, a slow smile, is shown in an extreme close-up as well. They start to kiss.

Nanny catches them and screams Janie's name. Janie runs back to the house, where

FILM
TECHNIQUE

- In an extreme close-up, an actor's face completely fills the screen. There are several extreme close-ups used in the film: for example, the bee as it approaches the pear tree blossom, Johnny Taylor's face as he watches Janie running toward him, Janie's eyes and forehead as she lets a caterpillar crawl on her face on Logan Killicks's farm, and Janie's lips as Tea Cake smears them with lemon juice. Such close-ups enhance the intimacy felt between the viewer and the movie's characters.

- In shaky cam shots, the camera is held by hand and jostled freely with the cameraperson's movements, as opposed to being fixed on a dolly for a smooth shot. The shaky cam that follows Janie through the energetic chaos of the migrant worker camp in the Everglades is an example of this style of camera work, which makes the viewer feel more like part of the action, as if immersed in the crowd along with Janie.

- When the camera is at a high angle, it records from far above what is being filmed. The high angle is used in *Their Eyes Are Watching God* to show Tea Cake and Janie stranded on a roof in the flooded water after the hurricane. This bird's-eye view, shot from a helicopter, emphasizes the vulnerability of the couple as they cling together in the midst of a disaster.

Nanny tells her how foolish she is, how she clearly wants to run wild like her mother, and that she must be married off to a decent man right away. Logan Killicks is interested in marrying Janie, Nanny tells her. Janie hates this idea. Nanny tells her that Logan has sixty acres and is a good man. Janie runs from the house, diving into a nearby stream. As she floats on her back, the camera shows her perspective from a low angle: the trees and blue sky above. When Nanny asks what Janie is doing, she says she is watching God.

Logan and Janie are married off-screen and begin their life together on his farm. Janie works hard, stooping over to plant potatoes behind the plow. Sitting on the porch, she picks up a caterpillar and lets it crawl onto her forehead in an extreme close-up. Logan tells Janie he is going into town to buy a second plow. He lists the chores he wants done by the time he gets home, including the slaughtering of the runt piglet. Janie falls into the mud trying to catch the piglet, but eventually succeeds. Instead of slaughtering it, she sets all the pigs free, driving them down the road.

A well-dressed man, misunderstanding the situation, catches a pig for her, but Janie hits him with her hat, telling him to let it go. She walks back toward the farm. He follows her, and they flirt on either side of the fence. He is Joe Starks, from Georgia, who has come to invest in an all-black town called Eatonville. He invites her to come see it with him. When she says no, he tells her he will wait for her the next morning on the road, if she changes her mind.

That night she asks Logan what he would do if she were to leave him. He says she does not appreciate him. When he dies, she will inherit everything he owns. She asks the question again. He says for her to do what she has to and falls asleep. She leaves with Joe the next morning.

They arrive in Eatonville as newlyweds. Janie is wearing a brand new dress, a hat, and lace gloves and is holding a parasol. The town is underwhelming but only one year old. Amos Hicks, a resident of Eatonville, mistakes Janie for Joe's daughter, making his interest in her clear. Joe corrects him. He tells the people of Eatonville that he intends to buy more land from Captain Eaton, who donated the land they have and owns the sawmill where the men work. The purchase is successful, and the people of Eatonville name Joe their mayor. He starts transforming Eatonville into a real town, building roads, selling lots to new families, and opening a general store. Janie stands in the doorway of the store, declaring herself happy. She kisses Joe, but he is too distracted looking out over his town to respond to her.

Joe buys a street lamp and plans a lighting ceremony. The women make calico dresses for each other, but Joe insists that Janie wear a dress he has purchased instead—a corseted, blood-red and black silk dress he ordered from Orlando. She likes the calico dress more, but he tells her she should dress better than the other women. At the ceremony that night, Janie cannot breathe in the uncomfortable dress, pacing the porch of the general store. She overhears the women gossiping that she must think herself too good to help them set out the food.

Joe makes a speech before the lighting of the street lamp, announcing the town's incorporation. Amos calls for Mrs. Starks to say a few words, but Joe says that Janie cannot make speeches. He lights the street lamp while the town sings "This Little Light of Mine." Janie holds back tears. That night Joe asks Janie if she likes being Mrs. Mayor. She says she cannot wait for it to be over. Joe tells her he is just getting started. He plans on being a big man and making a big woman of Janie.

The next scene begins with Janie talking and laughing with the porch-sitters at the general store, teasing the men over their game of checkers. Joe, sitting inside the store, sees Amos reach out to stroke Janie's hair without her knowing. He calls Janie inside harshly, telling her she should work instead of playing. Janie says some people like to have fun, unlike Joe. He insists that she wrap her hair up in a scarf to hide it from view. She is the mayor's wife—she must act dignified. She throws the scarf on the ground, runs home, and begins to pack a suitcase. Joe follows, grabbing her roughly as she tries to leave to tell her that no one else will want to marry her. Defeated, she ties up her hair. Every day after that she brings him breakfast, lunch, and dinner at the store without stopping to socialize with the townspeople. This routine continues for twenty years.

One day, Joe's shaky hands cause him to drop a glass jar as he is taking inventory. He blames Hezekiah, a young man who helps out at the store. When Joe goes to cut a piece of tobacco for a customer, Janie steps in so as to not let Joe embarrass himself. But she makes a bad cut, and Joe berates her for being old and ugly. She stands up for herself, embarrassing him in front of the gathered porch-sitters. He slaps her. Pheoby comes to her side, helping her move into the shed rather than share a home with Joe. Later, on his deathbed, Joe tells her he hopes she dies of thunder and lightning just before he passes away.

The town mourns Joe at his funeral, but Janie feels free. She unwraps her hair and admires herself in the mirror. She goes swimming in the stream, smiling in contentment. While she lies in the grass, Pheoby tells her that if she doe not mourn Joe properly people will talk. Janie does not care. Joe has been dead for a year, and Janie believes that mourning should not last longer than the grief.

One day, when Janie is working alone at the store, a man walks in who catches her eye. Everyone else in town is at a baseball game, so he asks Janie to play checkers with him. She is not sure of the rules, but he offers to teach her. His name is Tea Cake, and after they spend the day flirting, he walks her home. Meanwhile, Amos is convinced that he will marry Janie. The other porch-sitters at the general store tease him. Tea Cake arrives, introducing himself to the gathering, then calls Janie over from her own porch to play checkers. Janie comes right over, shocking the crowd. That night, Tea Cake walks Janie home again, and they spend the night fishing, frying their catch, dancing, and laughing. The camera pans from the serving tray Janie used to deliver Joe's meals for twenty years to where Tea Cake and Janie lie on the floor of the porch, eating from the skillet with their bare hands. Tea Cake teaches her to play a song on the piano (the same melody from the opening scene). They kiss. Janie asks if he is popular with other women, then becomes insecure. She asks him to leave. Tea Cake tells her he is at her mercy. She counters that she is almost twelve years his senior. Tea Cake tells her he loves her. Janie dismisses this as his nighttime thoughts. He leaves.

The next morning he arrives early with fresh strawberries—a symbol of his daytime thoughts. She is delighted and asks him to come in for breakfast, but he has to rush to work. They begin to see each other often, scandalizing the town. Tea Cake takes her on picnics, teaches her how to shoot a gun, tickles her bare feet with roses from her garden, and takes her to the movies. Pheoby warns Janie about running off with Tea Cake, reminding her of Annie Tyler, a widow who left town with a younger man and returned in rags after he stole everything from her. Confident in her love, Janie leaves town wearing a stylish dress. Pearl Stone predicts she will be back soon.

Tea Cake and Janie dance together all night in a juke joint, but the next day Tea Cake disappears with Janie's money. She spends the day anxiously waiting in her room. Tea Cake returns early the morning after. He lost her money gambling. She threatens to leave him. He says he wanted to hide his commonness from her, then reveals he has been stabbed. He tells her they will go to the Everglades to work. Instead of living off of her bank account, they will live off of what they can earn together. They arrive at Lake Okeechobee, which fascinates Janie. The migrant workers' camp is full of music, color, and members of many cultures. Janie and Tea Cake are relaxed and happy. She dons a pair of overalls and joins him in the fields to pick cucumbers. At night they dance and play, finally free of Eatonville's judgmental gaze.

The Seminole Indians leave the Everglades, predicting a hurricane, but an old man on the dike reassures Tea Cake and Janie that no storm is coming. The boss man dismisses the Seminoles' fear as well, but the workers, too, begin to leave in droves. As the storm approaches, snakes begin to cross the road in broad daylight, and the crows fly away, but Tea Cake and Janie decide to stay. She watches the sky, telling Tea Cake she is watching God. The hurricane hits. The catastrophic scenes outside their shack are lit only by lightning strikes: brief glimpses of destruction and rapidly rising water. Tea Cake asks Janie if she wishes she were somewhere else, but Janie says she is content. Tea Cake asks how she would feel if they died. She says she would die happy having met him. They kiss, the flooding room lit only by candlelight and flashes of lightning, until a loud rumbling sound interrupts them. The dike holding the rising water of the lake bursts, smashing into their shack and sending them both into the water. Janie loses sight of Tea Cake beneath the waves.

Janie clings to a rooftop sticking out from the floodwaters, only to be attacked by a rabid,

vicious dog. Tea Cake stabs the dog, but it bites his arm. They fall into the water together. Tea Cake emerges and Janie pulls him onto the roof. At dawn, the camera, swooping from a high angle over the calm floodwaters, finds Tea Cake and Janie holding each other on the rooftop.

In a voice-over, Janie says that after a week of flooding, the workers return to camp to help rebuild. But Tea Cake is sick. He cannot drink water without choking. Dr. Gordon comes to see him, telling Janie privately that Tea Cake needs be hospitalized. He has rabies and could spread the disease. Dr. Gordon promises to do his best to personally get him the medicine he needs, though he thinks it is too late. Tea Cake tells Janie that she could make a man forget to grow old and die and that she is lovelier than roses in bloom. That night, Janie finds a gun beneath his pillow. The next day, she unloads the gun of the first three of its six bullets before Tea Cake comes back from the outhouse.

Tea Cake, suspecting Janie of wanting to leave him, starts going mad with jealousy. He throws her down onto the bed and fires the gun, but the chamber is empty. He fires again. Janie grabs the rifle she has hidden by her bedside and aims it at him, begging him to fight the sickness. He fires again. Now only the three bullets are left in the gun. The camera shows Tea Cake's perspective: blurred and shifting visuals with distorted, echoing sound. Janie says she knows Tea Cake loves her. He lifts the gun to aim. The next moment is shown from outside the shack. There is the simultaneous report of two gunshots, then Janie's screams. Inside the shack, she holds Tea Cake's body.

The scene returns to the present time. Pheoby cries for Tea Cake. Janie says he will always be alive in her thoughts. Pheoby says she is going fishing with her husband now. Janie takes Tea Cake's jean jacket and runs laughing to the stream. She jumps in and floats on her back, looking up at the sky. She hears Tea Cake's voice asking what she is doing. Janie answers that she is watching God.

CHARACTERS

Alva

Alva works at the juke joint and offers Janie breakfast when she comes out of her room looking for Tea Cake.

Boss Man

The boss man tells Tea Cake that if the Indians knew anything they would still own the land. Since they do not, he does not believe there is a storm coming.

Daisy Blunt

Daisy Blunt is a pretty young woman who lives in Eatonville. In the novel, the men on the porch playact their desperate love for her as entertainment for all those gathered.

Janie Crawford

Janie is the film's heroine, a beautiful orphan raised by her Nanny with a free and loving spirit. She marries three times. First she is married to Logan Killicks, after Nanny catches her kissing Johnny Taylor and rushes to see her settled down with a decent man. After Logan tries to work her hard and gives her no love in return, Janie runs away to join Joe Starks on his mission to create a real town out of Eatonville. Her life with Joe begins well, but soon he tightens his fist around her—discouraging her from befriending the other women in town and making her cover up her long hair. Once he starts to ridicule her appearance and intelligence in public, she lashes out. His pride never recovers. After his death, Janie lets down her hair and rediscovers her joyful spirit. She meets Tea Cake, a younger man with a similar attitude. They run off together. She and Tea Cake are truly in love, and for the first time Janie feels like herself, living among the migrant workers in the Everglades. They do not choose to evacuate for an approaching hurricane, despite the warnings of their friends. After the dike bursts, a rabid dog bites Tea Cake. He loses his mind to the disease, and Janie is forced to shoot him after he fires a gun at her. Janie returns, barefoot and dirty, to Eatonville, where the townsfolk assume Tea Cake left her just as they had predicted. She tells her story to her best friend, Pheoby.

In the novel, Janie is born as the result of a white schoolteacher, raping her mother. Growing up with white playmates, she believes she is white until the age of six. After she shoots Tea Cake, she is put on trial for murder, but her testimony convinces the all-white jury of her innocence.

Captain Eaton

Captain Eaton donated the land for Eatonville and is well respected by the residents. He owns the sawmill where many of the men in town work. He sells Joe Starks additional acres.

Dr. Gordon

Dr. Gordon is the doctor who diagnoses Tea Cake with rabies. He rushes to West Palm Beach for the medicine Tea Cake needs, but fears it is too late to help him. He warns Janie that Tea Cake could spread the disease to her, so she should not share a bed with him. In the novel, the doctor who treats Tea Cake is named Dr. Simmons, and he testifies on Janie's behalf after she has shot and killed Tea Cake in self-defense.

Hezekiah

Hezekiah is a young man who works at the general store in Eatonville. He spreads the latest news of Janie and Tea Cake's courtship to the customers.

Amos Hicks

Amos Hicks is a resident of Eatonville and a regular fixture on the porch of the general store. He mistakes Janie for Joe Starks's daughter when they first arrive in town, making his interest in her clear. After Joe sees Amos secretly touching Janie's hair on the porch of the general store, he makes her tie it up under a scarf. After Joe's death, Amos believes he is next in line to marry Janie.

Logan Killicks

Logan Killicks is Janie's first husband, a much older man who owns sixty acres of farmland. Janie does not love Logan and finds him physically repulsive. He believes she should work the land alongside him. He goes to town to buy a second plow (in the novel, a second mule) for Janie to use. While he is gone, Janie meets Joe Starks. When Janie asks Logan what he would do if she were to leave him, he tells her that she is too young to understand what she would be giving up. When he dies, all of his land would pass to her. She is not satisfied with his answer, but he refuses to discuss it further. The next day, she leaves him. In the novel, their confrontation continues into the following morning before Janie decides to leave. In addition, the novel does not include the scene in which Janie sets the pigs free.

Motor Boat

Motor Boat is a friend of Janie's and Tea Cake's in the Everglades. Janie sends him to fetch Dr. Gordon as Tea Cake succumbs to rabies. Tea Cake, in his madness, believes that Janie wants to run off with Motor Boat and attempts to shoot her. In the novel, Motor Boat runs from the rising waters of the hurricane along with Janie and Tea Cake. He takes shelter in an empty house that Janie and Tea Cake believe is at risk of being destroyed. However, he remains safe throughout the storm.

Lige Moss

Lige Moss is a resident of Eatonville. He can often be found sitting on the porch of the general store, talking with Walter Stone and Amos Hicks. He is married to Lula Moss. In the novel, he and Amos tease Matt Bonner about his mule.

Lula Moss

Lula Moss is Lige Moss's wife. She lives in Eatonville and enjoys gossiping with the other women.

Nanny

Nanny is Janie's maternal grandmother, who raises her. She is protective of Janie, always wary of signs she will turn out like her mother. After Nanny catches Janie kissing Johnny Taylor, she becomes determined to marry her to a decent man. She arranges Janie's marriage to Logan Killicks. In the novel, Nanny tells Janie that she was born as a result of her mother's rape by a white schoolteacher. Janie's mother, too, was of mixed race. Her father was the owner of the plantation where Nanny was a slave.

Nunkie

Nunkie is a woman to whom Janie introduces herself in the migrant worker camp. In the novel, Nunkie and Tea Cake flirt with each other, making Janie extremely jealous.

Old Man

The old man sitting on the dike tells Tea Cake and Janie that he has been in the Everglades for years. In his opinion, there is no storm coming.

Seminole Indians

The Seminole Indians are the first to leave the Everglades in advance of the hurricane, after they notice that the saw grass has bloomed.

This is a warning sign that they take seriously, but the other workers dismiss their caution as superstition.

Sop-de-Bottom

Sop-de-Bottom is a friend of Tea Cake's and Janie's who works alongside them in the Everglades. In the novel, he appears in court to speak out against Janie but apologizes afterward for acting irrationally in his grief.

Joe Starks

Joe Starks is Janie's second husband, a wealthy Georgian who has traveled to Florida to invest in Eatonville. With his help, the town prospers. The townsfolk name him mayor and show him respect. Joe believes that Janie should act like a sophisticated woman and not socialize with the men and women on the porch. He is especially jealous of others admiring her long hair, which he insists she wear hidden under a scarf. Joe begins to verbally abuse Janie as a way of hiding his own failing health. Finally, Janie snaps and insults him in front of the town. Joe slaps her, and the two never reconcile afterward. He dies cursing Janie. In the novel, the townspeople respect Joe to his face but resent him behind his back.

Pearl Stone

Pearl Stone is a resident of Eatonville and Walter Stone's wife. She spots Janie stumbling back into town in the first scene of the film. She tells Janie they have all been worried sick over her, but Janie does not stop to talk. Pearl gossips with the other women about Janie's running off with Tea Cake.

Walter Stone

Walter Stone lives in Eatonville and is married to Pearl Stone. He sits on the porch of the general store with Lige and Amos, playing checkers and telling stories.

Johnny Taylor

Johnny Taylor passes by Nanny's house with a fishing pole and bucket one day while Janie is admiring the blossoming pear tree in the yard. Janie calls out to him, running to where he has stopped on the road. They start to kiss. Nanny catches them, outraged. She tells Janie that he was wiping his feet on her, which she denies. It is because of this incident that Nanny makes Janie marry Logan Killicks. In the novel Janie leans over the gatepost to kiss Johnny, but there is no gate separating them in the film.

Tea Cake

Tea Cake comes to the general store while the rest of the town is at a baseball game. He and Janie spend the day together, playing checkers. They become fast friends, sharing a playful spirit and a reckless attitude. As they grow closer, the townspeople begin to object—warning Janie that Tea Cake only wants her money. However, Janie believes that Tea Cake loves her, and she returns his feelings. They go to Jacksonville and are married. Tea Cake attempts to hide his love of gambling from Janie, but she quickly finds out after he arrives home bleeding from a stab wound. He now swears that they will not touch her fortune but will instead live off of whatever he can make. They move to the Everglades together to bring in the harvest. Although they are warned many times of an approaching hurricane, they choose to stay. The hurricane destroys their home, and as they struggle to find high ground, Tea Cake kills a dog that is threatening to bite Janie. The dog bites Tea Cake instead, and though he survives the hurricane, he succumbs to rabies. The disease makes him violent and unpredictable. He begins to sleep with a gun beneath his pillow, his paranoia growing each day. He fires the gun at Janie in a fit of blind rage, unable to distinguish reality from the disease, but she has emptied the chamber of three of its bullets, leaving three behind. He continues to fire despite her begging him to remember her, until Janie is forced to shoot him in self-defense. In the novel, Janie is put on trial for Tea Cake's murder and found innocent. She spares no expense for his funeral.

Annie Tyler

Annie Tyler was an Eatonville widow left with a fortune, much like Janie. A younger man seduced her and persuaded her to start spending her money on fine things for herself. They left town together to get married, but Annie Tyler returned alone. Her lover had stolen her money and run off, leaving her to limp back into town in disgrace. Pheoby reminds Janie of her story before she runs off, as Annie's circumstances seem to mirror Janie's whirlwind affair with Tea Cake.

Annie Tyler's Young Man

Annie Tyler's young man sweeps her off her feet and takes her out of Eatonville in style. Rather than marry her as he had promised, however, he cons her out of her money and disappears.

Pheoby Watson

Pheoby Watson is Janie's best friend in Eatonville. She is supportive, kind, and nonjudgmental. When Janie returns to town without Tea Cake, Pheoby brings her supper and tells her Tea Cake will be chased from Eatonville if he ever shows his face again. She assumes, like the rest of the town, that Tea Cake has stolen Janie's money. However, after hearing Janie's story, Pheoby is deeply moved by their love for each other. She tells Janie that she is going to go home and tell her husband Sam to take her fishing right away, inspired by the spontaneity of Tea Cake and Janie's passion. Unlike the other women in town, Pheoby does not see Janie as conceited. Instead, she feels sympathy for her after noticing how Joe Starks keeps Janie under his thumb. This is exemplified in the streetlamp-lighting ceremony scene, in which Joe does not let Janie give a speech: while Janie holds back tears, Pheoby smiles at her reassuringly from the crowd.

Sam Watson

Sam Watson is Pheoby's husband. He is seen most often sitting on the porch, gossiping with the other townsfolk. Like Pheoby, Sam is partial to Janie and willing to defend her against the judgment of the others. In the novel, Sam leads the teasing of Matt Bonner and his mean, skinny mule.

THEMES

Love

Janie's search for true love propels her through her three marriages. After her first kiss with Johnny Taylor, the year of her sexual awakening, she is forced to marry Logan Killicks. Quickly realizing that she does not love Logan, she runs away with Joe Starks. While her marriage with Joe begins passionately, his thirst for power soon overtakes his love for her. As the mayor's wife, he expects her to behave according to her station, rather than acting like herself. Janie despises this treatment, as it goes against

READ.
WATCH.
WRITE.

- Read Nikki Grimes's young-adult novel *Jazmin's Notebook* (1998). What do Jazmin and Janie have in common? How are they different? What role does setting play in each of their stories? If you were the director of a movie adaptation of this novel, who would you cast as Jazmin and why? Organize your answers into an essay.

- In small groups, compose and perform a short skit based on the film, in which two or more of the characters appear. For example, you could do an episode of *The Dating Game*, with Janie choosing between Logan, Amos, Joe, and Tea Cake, or a public service announcement about rabies safety featuring Tea Cake and Dr. Gordon. One member of your group will be the director, in charge of filming the skit. Edit the footage to form a finished product to share with your class. Free video-editing tools are available at EDpuzzle.com.

- Compare and contrast the hurricane in the novel and in the film. What details from Janie and Tea Cake's struggle to survive the hurricane does the film omit or alter?

Why do you think these changes to the scene were made? What aspects of the hurricane are unchanged from novel to film? What techniques does Hurston use to create tension during the crisis? What techniques are used in the film to do the same? How do you feel personally about the film's adaptation of the hurricane? Does it do the novel justice or fall short? Organize your answers into an essay.

- Choose Logan Killicks, Joe Starks, or Tea Cake to examine more thoroughly. Watch their scenes closely and take notes on the following: their costume design, their speech and body language, the musical accompaniment to their scenes, the lighting, and any special camera techniques (zoom, pan, angles, close-ups, etc.) used when they are on-screen. How do these aspects of the cinematography work to bring Hurston's characters to life? What do they add to the story and, in particular, to the theme of love? Take notes in preparation for a group discussion.

---

her playful nature. After his death, Janie at last discovers true love with Tea Cake. He is as passionate, wild, and free as she has always wanted to be, but she was prevented by Nanny's, Logan's, and Joe's expectations of her. Tea Cake treats her as an equal, unlike her treatment in previous relationships.

As important as romantic love is to both novel and film, self-love is a crucial aspect of Janie's journey. Once she is free from Joe's control, Janie embraces her own identity. She has little concern for what others think of her or how she is expected to behave by the residents of Eatonville, well before Tea Cake walks into her store. By loving herself and trusting in her instincts, she is able to recognize true love when

it comes for her, although those in Eatonville try to convince her that what she feels is wrong. In the film love is indisputably the central theme, while in the novel love shares a thematic spotlight with issues of African American womanhood and racial identity, especially as it relates to complexion. These issues were deemphasized in the film, and the focus on Janie's search for true love was accentuated.

Identity

Janie is determined to be herself, rather than live up to the standards that others impose on her. Nanny, Logan Killicks, Joe Starks, and the people of Eatonville try to tame Janie's spirit. Nanny does not want her to be free with her

Acclaimed actress Halle Berry plays Janie (©AF archive | Alamy)

love, insisting that she marry a proper man. Logan Killicks wants her to work hard by his side as a farmwife in a loveless marriage. Joe Starks wants Janie to fit his image of the perfect mayor's wife, while the people of Eatonville see Janie as a high-class and respectable woman and expect her to live up to their vision of her. In reality, Janie is none of these things. She wants desperately to be herself, in the same way that the blossoming pear tree she admires is nothing but itself: beautiful, boisterous, and natural. This is, however, unacceptable in a society that seeks to control women and keep them in their place. Janie's beauty is particularly threatening to those most concerned with controlling her; for example, Joe Starks demands that she keep her long hair hidden from view.

After Joe's death, Janie becomes younger in spirit. Freed from the weight of his oppression, she begins to embrace her identity. She lets her hair down and gazes at her reflection in the mirror, learning her features again. Tea Cake encourages her in her daring exploration of her impulses and desires. His wish is not to control

Janie but to watch her come into her own self-hood. Janie is left alone at the end of the novel, robbed of Tea Cake but armed with self-assurance. Although she began her journey as an easily malleable seventeen-year-old, Janie becomes an immovable rock in the face of the gossip of the town. She gives no value to gossip or the expectations of others, having found her true self working and playing in the Everglades with the man she loved.

The novel's focus on identity deals especially with racial identity. As a mixed-race woman, Janie's light complexion leads to her preferential treatment by Mrs. Turner, a self-hating African American whom Janie meets in the Everglades. Mrs. Turner not only puts Janie on a pedestal because of the lightness of her skin but also despises Tea Cake for his dark complexion. Janie is mystified by Mrs. Turner's obsession with skin color and desperately wants to be rid of her, as Mrs. Turner attempts with each visit to drive a wedge between Janie and Tea Cake. The film's focus on identity is on Janie's womanhood and self-awareness rather than her experience of race.

STYLE

Flashback

The majority of the film's action takes place in an extended flashback, as Janie tells the story of her life to Pheoby after she returns home from burying Tea Cake. This plot structure is loyally adapted from the novel. The scene at Janie's home fades out as she is speaking to Pheoby, and then fades into a scene from her girlhood days, as she admires the blossoming pear tree. In addition to this transition marked by the film editing, Janie's voice-over clues the viewer into the change. She narrates the action throughout the flashback, until the film's eventual return to the present through a similarly edited fade-out/fade-in sequence.

Vernacular

Vernacular refers to the dialect of the people of a specific region. In the case of *Their Eyes Were Watching God*, the rural Floridian vernacular dominates both novel and film. The film is dedicated to re-creating the 1920s dialect of the book, which is notoriously difficult for readers to parse. Consider, for example, the townspeople's scandalized mutterings upon seeing Janie return to Eatonville after running off with Tea Cake: "What dat ole forty year ole 'oman doin' wid her hair swingin' down her back lak some young gal?—Where she left dat young lad of a boy she went off here wid?" The film eases the difficulty of understanding the novel's vernacular dialogue through the added context of visual and auditory clues: the speaker's body language and tone of voice and the reactions from other characters make the dialect simple to understand.

CULTURAL CONTEXT

Eatonville, Florida

Founded on August 15, 1886, Eatonville, Florida, became the first incorporated African American township in the United States. Eatonville began as an enclave of twenty-seven African American families who preferred to live independently of the more established white community of Maitland in the years following the Civil War. Joseph C. Clarke, on whom the character of Joe Starks was based, purchased one hundred and twelve acres from the mayor of Maitland, Josiah C. Eaton, in 1882, which he then sold as lots to African Americans looking to settle in the town. The town was named after Eaton in gratitude of his contribution, and Clarke served as the first mayor. Today the town is one of the few surviving communities of its kind founded during Reconstruction. In Damien Cave's *New York Times* article "In a Town Apart, the Pride and Trials of Black Life," he writes: "Hidden in the theme park sprawl of greater Orlando ... lies a quiet town where the pride and complications of the African-American experience come to life."

Both novel and film illustrate the founding of Eatonville, from its humble origins to its incorporation and beyond. The film utilizes a montage that includes the clearing of roads, selling of lots, building of homes, arrival of new families, and opening of the general store. There is an enormous visual contrast between the first scene in Eatonville, as Janie makes her way barefoot and muddy into a gorgeous, vibrant town, and the next scene set in Eatonville, which shows in flashback Janie's arrival to town in a horse and buggy, wearing beautiful clothes and holding a parasol, while the town is only a few shacks in the woods, and the people are dirty and poverty stricken. Missing from the film is Matt Bonner's mule, a skinny beast with a foul temper that Joe Starks purchases from Matt and sets loose after overhearing Janie pity the creature's lot in life. The mule roams the town freely until its death, which is both widely and irreverently mourned by the residents. The mule is a representation of the heritage of the African American residents: once forced to work for a cruel and demanding master against its will, the mule is freed to live its life how it chooses. Its absence from the film is one way in which the thematic focus is narrowed from the wider racial issues of the novel to Janie's search for love.

1928 Okeechobee Hurricane

The second-deadliest hurricane in US history, the 1928 Okeechobee hurricane claimed the lives of over 2,500 people, 75 percent of whom were migrant workers caught in the storm without sufficient warning or means of escape. A category 4 hurricane with winds of 150 miles per hour, the storm passed directly over Lake Okeechobee on September 16, 1928. The dikes were insufficient to hold back the storm surge, allowing a ten-foot-tall tidal wave to crash over the top and flood the low-lying land below. At their strongest, the floodwaters rose one inch per minute to a height of seven feet, and the flooded area stretched over seventy-five miles. After the storm, as depicted in the novel, white victims were buried in coffins, while black victims were either buried in mass graves or else burned in pyres. In addition, traumatized survivors were made to find and bury the bodies of the victims. In the novel, Tea Cake is forced to join one of these unlucky search parties by a man carrying a rifle: "Tea Cake found that he was part of a small army that had been pressed into service to clear the wreckage in public places and bury the dead." The film leaves out the immediate aftermath of the hurricane, focusing instead on Tea Cake's slow fight with rabies.

CRITICAL OVERVIEW

The film debuted to generally positive reviews and received an 81 percent audience-approval rating at RottenTomatoes.com. Twenty-five million viewers watched the premier. Michael Ealy won Best Actor in the Television category from the Black Reel Awards for his portrayal of Tea Cake, while Terrence Howard earned the Breakthrough Artist Award from the Austin Film Critics Association for his role as Amos Hicks.

Halle Berry received universal critical praise in her role as Janie Crawford. Alynda Wheat writes in her review for *Entertainment Weekly*: "She's never looked better—perfectly cast as a woman whose beauty is so overpowering, it's almost a liability."

John Leonard finds much to admire in his review of the film for *New York* magazine, from the smallest supporting role to the natural disaster that brings Janie, a force of nature herself, to her knees: "Ruby Dee is the grandmother anyone would want. Suzan-Lori Parks seems ideally suited to turn the novel into a screenplay. And the hurricane is terrific."

Ronda Racha Penrice, too, found the natural setting of the film particularly impressive. She writes in her review for *Alternet*: "The film is visually stunning. It looks lush, Southern and rural." The oppressively humid heat of the Gulf South is a character itself in the film, one Janie flees just as she flees the oppression of society: by jumping into the clear, cool water for a swim.

Virginia Heffernan writes of the unique challenge of adapting a classic work of American literature to the small screen in her review, "A Woman on a Quest, via Hurston and Oprah," for the *New York Times*: "Pushing through the novel's 1920's dialect and plot gaps takes stamina. Hurston's novel, frankly, is homework—and Ms. Winfrey has always had an uncanny way of getting people to do their homework. And like it."

CRITICISM

Amy L. Miller

Miller is a graduate of the University of Cincinnati, and she currently resides in New Orleans. In the following essay, she explores Janie's relationship to the natural world in the 2005 film adaptation of Zora Neale Hurston's novel Their Eyes Were Watching God.

In the televised film *Their Eyes Were Watching God*, Janie Crawford's love of the natural world is reflected in the love she has for herself. The moments in the film in which Janie is most attuned to her natural surroundings act simultaneously as the moments in which she is most separated from the restrictions of the society that she struggles against. In this way, Janie seeks out nature in order to seek out the truth of her own soul. This movement of Janie away from society and closer to her true self is exemplified in the film in her repeated self-baptisms in the waters. Janie's God does not live in a church, but in nature. Thus, floating on her back admiring the sky is simultaneously an act of worship and an act of self-love. Janie, God, and nature are united as one in these moments of pure, exalted freedom.

Janie's awakening occurs beneath the pear tree. As she admires its blossoms, voices can be heard calling in hypnotic whispers, and the sound of bees buzzing fills the air. The camera zooms close on Janie and then even closer until her wondering face fills the frame. Janie's heart beats very slowly amidst the other hallucinatory sounds. In fact, everything slows nearly to a halt: a bee hangs in the air above a flower just before Janie spots Johnny Taylor through the branches. These shots, the first of the extended flashbacks that will take the story up to the film's opening scene, establish Janie's sensitivity to nature. Janie is not only sensitive to nature, in that she

THE MOMENTS IN THE FILM IN WHICH JANIE IS MOST ATTUNED TO HER NATURAL SURROUNDINGS ACT SIMULTANEOUSLY AS THE MOMENTS IN WHICH SHE IS MOST SEPARATED FROM THE RESTRICTIONS OF THE SOCIETY THAT SHE STRUGGLES AGAINST."

is compassionate toward helpless animals and encourages seeds to find soft ground, but sensual as well. Sensory experiences tied to the natural world—from a caterpillar crawling on her face to the feel of grass on her skin—are shown in the film as moments of ecstasy for Janie, returning her in memory to the pear tree. In those first moments of her self-realization, kissing Johnny Taylor before her Nanny spots her, Janie acts solely on her natural impulses, outside the realm of right or wrong. Nanny is the first of many who will tell a bewildered Janie that she is wrong. As a first offender, her punishment at Nanny's hands is a swift and passionless marriage to a decent man. This inspires Janie's first dive into the stream.

When she first goes under the water, the sound of her heartbeat returns—but this time it is pounding. The longer she stays under, however, the slower it becomes. The water calms her almost instantaneously. Although the heartbeat effect is not repeated on later dives into the stream, the knowledge that the water is a place of healing and tranquillity for Janie is apparent through her contented expression, the relaxed strokes of her arms and legs, and her declaration, upon being questioned by Nanny, that she is watching God. Janie communes with God on somewhat equal footing as she drifts weightless, immune from gravity, from the pull toward earthly concerns that other mortals feel. The artful cinematography renders her, with her drifting white clothes and wild hair shot from a high angle, as celestial a being as any angel or goddess previously known to man.

Leonard writes that "Halle Berry was a fine—maybe even an inevitable—choice to play the part of Janie Crawford." Janie's almost supernatural beauty, an aspect of the novel brought stunningly to life in the casting of

Halle Berry, is tied directly to nature in the film. When she is laced tightly into the finery of high society at Joe's insistence for the street-lamp-lighting ceremony, her face hidden beneath an oversized hat, Janie resembles a frightened animal more than a woman of high class. Janie's beauty is tied directly to her self-confidence, and her self-confidence is in constant conversation with her connection to nature. When her hair is tied up by a scarf, her tongue is tied down out of fear of Joe's edict against having fun, and her life consists of ferrying her husband's meals between the house and the store, twenty years pass by in a minute, and no one comes to save her. Yet when Joe first found her, freeing pigs from Logan's farm and caked in mud from head to toe, she stopped him in his tracks with her beauty and rebelliousness, and he waited an extra day on his way to Eatonville in the sole hope that she might choose to join him.

Joe, like Logan before him, makes the mistake of seeing through Janie. When at last their town is built, and Janie leans in for a kiss, Joe is too busy surveying his empire to notice her. The soundtrack swells with an anticipatory tension, as if to mimic the strange, hypnotic sounds of Janie's awakening at the pear tree, but when Joe proves unresponsive to her kisses, the swelling note resolves into a bland melody that sounds like the auditory equivalent of settling for less. In his notes on the film for the New York State Writers Institute, Kevin Hagopian describes Janie as "the fictional protagonist of the African American female experience." One of the greatest trials of African American women throughout history has been that of erasure. Hurston herself was a victim of the erasure of African American women's voices from the national consciousness for decades, until Alice Walker personally revived her literary legacy. Janie experiences the erasure of her identity in Eatonville, as her husband uses physical force to mold her into the wife-object he believes fits the image of Mrs. Mayor.

After Joe's death, the town believes that Janie will continue to play her role. More than that, they expect her to continue to validate their feelings of sophistication and importance. As a symbol of Joe's power, she became a symbol of the town's as well. When she does not conform to their ideas of how she should behave, they feel personally hurt and resentful. The contentious relationship between Janie and Joe at the end of

WHAT DO I SEE NEXT?

- *Beloved* (1998), based on the novel by Toni Morrison and produced by Harpo Films, Clinica Estetico, and Touchstone Pictures, tells the story of Sethe, a former slave living in Cincinnati, Ohio, who is haunted by the ghost of the child she murdered in order to save her from a life in chains. The film stars Oprah Winfrey and Danny Glover and is rated R.

- Adapted from the classic novel by Alice Walker, *The Color Purple* (1985) stars Whoopi Goldberg as the long-suffering Celie and Danny Glover as the abusive Mister Albert and was produced by Amblin Entertainment, the Guber-Peters Company, and Warner Bros. Its rating is PG-13.

- *The Women of Brewster Place* (1989) is a television miniseries based on the 1982 novel by Gloria Naylor and produced by Harpo Production and King Phoenix Entertainment. The series explores the lives of a group of women struggling to make ends meet in a run-down tenement building. The series is unrated.

- In *Why Do Fools Fall in Love* (1998), rock-and-roll singer Frankie Lymon's meteoric rise and painful fall from fame is told through the memories of three women competing for the legal rights to his estate following his untimely death. The film, produced by Rhino Films and Warner Bros., is rated R.

- *Lackawanna Blues* (2005) is a TV movie produced by HBO Films and Good Shepherd Entertainment. The movie is an adaptation of a play by Ruben Santiago-Hudson, the actor who plays Joe Starks in *Their Eyes Were Watching God*. The film, rated PG-13, focuses on the relationship between young Ruben and his sole caregiver, Nanny, after his parents have abandoned him.

- *For Colored Girls* (2010), based on the 1976 play *For Colored Girls Who Have Considered Suicide/When the Rainbow is Enuf*, by Ntozake Shange, follows nine African American women whose lives are connected in unexpected ways. The film was produced by Lionsgate, Tyler Perry Studios, 34th Street Films, and FCG Productions and is rated R.

- In *The Help* (2011), an aspiring young journalist in Jackson, Mississippi, writes the story of the daily lives of two African American maids at the height of the civil rights movement. The film, rated PG-13, was produced by DreamWorks, Reliance Entertainment, Participant Media, Imagenation Abu Dhabi FZ, 1492 Pictures, and Harbinger Pictures and is based on the 2009 novel of the same name, by Kathryn Stockett.

- *Eve's Bayou* (1997), produced by Trimark Pictures, ChubbCo Film, and Addis Wechsler Pictures, tells the story of a young girl's discovery of her Louisiana family's darkest secrets. Starring Samuel L. Jackson as the family's adulterous patriarch, the film, rated R, explores themes of family and betrayal.

- *Alex Haley's Queen* (1993) is a three-part TV miniseries produced by Elliot Friedgen, Warner Bros. Television, and the Wolper Organization. Based on Alex Haley and David Steven's 1993 novel *Queen: The Story of an American Family*, the series centers on the struggles of a mixed-race slave (portrayed by Halle Berry) coming of age during the Civil War. This series is unrated.

- In *Cadillac Records* (2008), produced by Light-Wave Entertainment, Parkwood Pictures, and Sony Music Film, Leonard Chess—a Polish immigrant living in Chicago—founds a record label that welcomes African American musicians. The film, rated R, is based on the true story of Chess Records, which launched the musical careers of legends such as Chuck Berry, Muddy Waters, Willie Dixon, Howlin' Wolf, Etta James, and many more in the 1950s and 1960s.

their marriage repeats itself in the relationship between Janie and the town, but the town is weaker without its leader and cannot force Janie down. Dressed in her new freedom, she erupts. Heffernan writes: "Brazen self-love becomes her religion, and her primary eccentricity." In her black mourning dress, she wades into the water, and she smiles as if reunited with an old friend. The touch of nature restores the years she lost as Joe's obedient wife, returning her to a giggling girl. By the next scene the mourning black is gone, as Janie lies in the tall green grass in a matching green dress, basking in the feeling of the earth beneath her as she laughs at Pheoby's concern for her improper behavior.

Tea Cake inspires Janie's passion for nature and shares her spontaneity. Like Johnny Taylor with his fishing pole, Tea Cake is considered by those closest to Janie to be an unfit match. Yet when Tea Cake grabs a fishing pole from Janie's shed and takes off toward the stream, she follows eagerly. He, too, understands the sensory pleasures of the natural world, available for free to anyone who has the time to stop and notice. He presses a lemon to Janie's lips to taste in an extreme close-up that calls to mind the caterpillar on Logan's farm and the bee and pear blossom at Nanny's house. He introduces her to the Everglades, a place of such overwhelming natural beauty that Janie feels she has arrived on the doorstep of her destiny. Later, with her eyes on the approaching storm, Janie tells Tea Cake that she is watching God. She speaks reverently, just as she did in the stream at Nanny's house, but her position has changed. She stands in the field dwarfed by the sky rather than floating on her back as if one with it. More than a blizzard (too cold), or a tornado (too fast), the hurricane is Janie's match. Warm, overwhelming, complex, and devastating, the hurricane floods the earth and forces Janie and Tea Cake into its waters. In a way, Janie chose this, just as she chose to dive into the water for her other baptisms—by staying in the Everglades while the other workers fled, she and Tea Cake made the clear choice to face nature's might. As a result, Tea Cake is lost to rabies, while Janie survives.

The film's final shot shows Janie drifting contentedly in the stream back in Eatonville, watching God. Shot from a high angle, it mirrors previous shots of Janie in the stream, as well as the high-angle shot of Janie and Tea Cake stranded in the high water on top of a roof.

Whereas then they were helpless against nature's power, this final entry in the motif of Janie's submersion in water shows her at peace. Once again, she seeks out the water to heal her pain. Her connection to nature has not been severed by the storm, as it was by her years with Joe, but remains a source of Janie's spiritual strength to be used to stand apart, on her own in a world that would have her conform.

Source: Amy L. Miller, Critical Essay on *Their Eyes Were Watching God*, in *Novels for Students*, Gale, Cengage Learning, 2017.

Alynda Wheat

In the following review, Wheat finds the adaptation disappointing in comparison with the original novel.

We should be so lucky as Oprah. She's richer than Croesus, beloved by people of all hues, and seems to have most of Hollywood on speed dial. We hear she's even got her own book club— which is why it's surprising that her latest print-to-TV adaptation gets lost in translation.

Winfrey exec-produced *Their Eyes Were Watching God* (based on Zora Neale Hurston's novel of the same name), starring Halle Berry as Janie, a woman-child of milky complexion and glorious hair (so long! so pretty!). That hair should get its own billing, so effectively is it used as a metaphor for sex—tightly bound and controlled with spouse Joe (*Lackawanna Blues*' Ruben Santiago-Hudson), free and wild during her scandalous affair with true love Tea Cake (*Barbershop*'s Michael Ealy). It's at Tea Cake's introduction that the movie gets hot—tongue-flicking, shock-the-town hot—as Berry and Ealy show off their college-level chemistry (fitting, given they're rumored to be a real-life item). Call it a romance, pure and simple.

Except that Hurston's novel is about impurity at its most complex. Janie is the inevitable mélange of sex and slavery: a child so racially confused she believes she's white until almost age 6. Pages are devoted to the strain her ethnic ambiguity puts on her relationships—nearly a whole chapter given over to a black friend's vicious rant against darker African Americans. It's the inheritance of slavery's color-coded caste system, a shameful chapter in African-American history.

One that, for some reason, Winfrey and the film's talented black crew—including TV director Darnell Martin and writer Suzan-Lori Parks, who won a Pulitzer Prize for *Topdog/Underdog*—manage to avoid entirely. Winfrey (Oscar nominee for *The Color Purple*, a film with its own racial complications) and Berry (exec producer of *Lackawanna Blues*) are usually so true to their self-imposed responsibility to tell the stories of African Americans that this literary cop-out is as confusing as it is disappointing. They owe Hurston more.

The result: *Eyes* is reduced to toothless entertainment. The all-star cast—among them Terrence Howard, Lorraine Toussaint, and Ruby Dee as Janie's grandma—is solid, as is Berry, who appears to relish her proto-flower child role. And frankly, she's never looked better—perfectly cast as a woman whose beauty is so overpowering, it's almost a liability. And that hair: So long! So pretty!

Source: Alynda Wheat, Review of *Their Eyes Were Watching God*, in *Entertainment Weekly*, March 2, 2005.

Justin Chang

In the following review, Chang asserts that fans of the original novel will find the film a less-than-faithful adaptation.

A meditation on love, independence and the evolution of Halle Berry's hairstyle, ABC's latest *Oprah WinfreyPresents* telepic takes Zora Neale Hurston's classic 1937 novel *Their Eyes Were Watching God* and boils it down to a simple-minded Harlequin hash. With Berry starring as the willful, impulsive, passionately outdoorsy Janie Crawford, this late-'20s Southern romance cleaves to its source material in broad strokes, but crucially lacks the tough lyricism and cohesive vision of Hurston's prose. Result purports to celebrate individualism and free thinking while displaying precious little of its own.

Story opens with Janie returning home to Eatonville, Fla., some months after having run away with a younger man. Sweaty and caked with mud, Berry is convincingly deglammed if never exactly dowdy. Events flash back several years, and Janie is restored to a carefree, fresh-faced girl of 17—a beauty with a lust for life, and particularly the great outdoors.

Fearing for her future, Janie's stern but loving grandmother (a fine Ruby Dee) makes her marry an old farmer, whom she promptly dumps after being swept off her feet by dashing, wealthy entrepreneur Joe Starks (Ruben Santiago-Hudson). The two wed and move to Eatonville, the first incorporated all-black town in America, which prospers with Joe's investments.

He eventually becomes mayor, and the position proves good for his ego and fatal to the marriage. By the time Joe dies, some 20 years of bitter tyranny later, Janie is ready for freedom once again. She finds it in the arms of Tea Cake (Michael Ealy), broodingly handsome and 12 years her junior. Their courtship—they play checkers, have midday picnics and discover the erotic properties of fruit—raises eyebrows all over the town, which has always envied and loathed Janie's beauty and her station as the mayor's wife.

At its heart, *Their Eyes Were Watching God* means to teach a lesson on the conformity and hypocrisy bred by community life—even in an African-American community whose citizens are putatively united in trying to establish a better life for themselves—and the need to seek one's personal identity.

Yet missing from the teleplay by Suzan-Lori Parks, Misan Sagay and Bobby Smith Jr. is Hurston's instinctive sense of rhythm (it takes exactly one scene change for the Starks' perfect marriage to fall apart). More confounding, the racial complications behind Janie's identity crisis have been expunged entirely. In the novel, Janie is the product of her mother's rape by a white man—a galling omission here that reduces the proceedings to colorless, subtext-free melodrama.

Leading a solid ensemble that includes Santiago-Hudson, Terrence Howard and Nicki Micheaux, Berry strives valiantly as Janie, delivering a fierce, spirited and moving portrait of womanhood stifled and liberated. Few actresses could pull off the narrative's 20-year chronological leap—pic certainly never recovers—yet Berry is capable of looking every one of her 38 years and at the same time vibrantly, astonishingly youthful.

But even Berry is roundly upstaged by her own hair—long, lush, radiant tresses (no *Monster's Ball* crewcut for her) that become a tightly coiled metaphor for repressed sexuality after Joe jealously forces Janie to cover her head in public.

Even more literal-minded are pic's attempts to show its heroine in communion with nature. It is Janie's frequent wont to run barefoot through the grass, put caterpillars on her face or—when she really feels trapped—dive into a river fully clothed, turn over on her back and stare at the sun. "I'm watching God," she says. Fans of the novel, however, might be better off watching something else.

Source: Justin Chang, Review of *Their Eyes Were Watching God*, in *Variety*, March 3, 2005.

SOURCES

Cave, Damien, "In a Town Apart, the Pride and Trials of Black Life," in *New York Times*, September 28, 2008, http://www.nytimes.com/2008/09/29/us/29florida.html?_r=0 (accessed April 27, 2016).

Chang, Justin, Review of *Their Eyes Were Watching God*, in *Variety*, March 3, 2005, http://variety.com/2005/scene/markets-festivals/oprah-winfrey-presents-their-eyes-were-watching-god-1200527479/ (accessed April 27, 2016).

"Florida in the 1920's: The Great Florida Land Boom," Florida History Internet Center, http://floridahistory.org/landboom.htm (accessed April 30, 2016).

Hagopian, Kevin, "*Their Eyes Were Watching God*," New York State Writers Institute website, http://www.albany.edu/writers-inst/webpages4/filmnotes/fns07n9.html (accessed April 27, 2016).

Heffernan, Virginia, "A Woman on a Quest, via Hurston and Oprah," in *New York Times*, March 4, 2005, http://www.nytimes.com/2005/03/04/arts/television/a-woman-on-a-quest-via-hurston-and-oprah.html?_r=0 (accessed April 27, 2016).

Hurston, Zora Neale, *Their Eyes Were Watching God*, Perennial Classics, 1998, pp. 2, 170.

Leonard, John, Review of *Their Eyes Were Watching God*, in *New York*, http://nymag.com/nymetro/arts/tv/reviews/11237/ (accessed April 27, 2016).

"1928—Okeechobee Hurricane," Hurricanes: Science and Society, http://www.hurricanescience.org/history/storms/1920s/Okeechobee/ (accessed April 30, 2016).

"Oprah Winfrey Presents: *Their Eyes Were Watching God* (2005)," Rotten Tomatoes, http://www.rottentomatoes.com/m/oprah_winfrey_presents_their_eyes_were_watching_god_2005/ (accessed April 27, 2016).

Penrice, Ronda Racha, "Their Eyes Were Watching Oprah," *Alternet*, March 3, 2005, http://www.alternet.org/story/21403/their_eyes_were_watching_oprah (accessed April 27, 2016).

Sharman, G. K., "Florida's Black History," Absolutely Florida, http://www.abfla.com/1tocf/people/blackhistory3.html (accessed April 30, 2016).

Their Eyes Were Watching God, directed by Darnell Martin, Buena Vista Home Entertainment, 2005, DVD.

"*Their Eyes Were Watching God* (2005)," IMDb, http://www.imdb.com/title/tt0406265/ (accessed April 27, 2016).

"Town of Eatonville: Beginning History," Town of Eatonville website, http://www.townofeatonville.org/about/ (accessed April 30, 2016).

Wheat, Alynda, "Oprah Winfrey Presents: *Their Eyes Were Watching God*," in *Entertainment Weekly*, March 2, 2005, http://www.ew.com/article/2005/03/02/oprah-winfrey-presents-their-eyes-were-watching-god (accessed April 27, 2016).

Wilchek, Deborah, "Made for TV: *Their Eyes Were Watching God*," College Board website, http://apcentral.collegeboard.com/apc/members/courses/teachers_corner/45855.html (accessed April 27, 2016).

FURTHER READING

Hurston, Zora Neale, *Dust Tracks on a Road: An Autobiography*, Harper Perennial Modern Classics, 2006.

First published in 1942, Hurston's autobiography is charming, witty, and full of heart, covering her childhood in Florida, her career as a novelist and anthropologist, and her rise as a bright star of the Harlem Renaissance.

——, *Mules and Men*, Indiana University Press, 1986.

This collection of over one hundred folktales, gathered by Hurston from her hometown of Eatonville, Florida, and first published in 1935, includes notes on context and personal anecdotes. The legends, tall tales, songs, and superstitions—all recorded loyally by Hurston without alterations to the storytellers' vernacular—paint an unforgettable portrait of black life in the Gulf South.

Mask, Mia, ed., *Contemporary Black American Cinema: Race, Gender and Sexuality at the Movies*, Routledge, 2012.

Contemporary Black American Cinema includes essays on the representation of gender, comedic tropes, avant-garde experimentation, the role of politics, and the history of black cinema in the United States, along with much more.

Winfrey, Oprah, *What I Know for Sure*, Flatiron Books, 2014.

Recipient of the Presidential Medal of Freedom and ranked as the only African American billionaire in the United States, Winfrey is considered one of the most influential women in the world. This collection gathers fourteen years of her "What I Know for Sure" inspirational columns, first published in her magazine, *O, the Oprah Magazine*.

SUGGESTED SEARCH TERMS

Their Eyes Were Watching God

Zora Neale Hurston

Their Eyes Were Watching God AND Zora Neale Hurston

Zora Neale Hurston AND Oprah Winfrey

Their Eyes Were Watching God AND film

Oprah Winfrey Presents: Their Eyes Were Watching God

Their Eyes Were Watching God AND Halle Berry

Janie Crawford AND Halle Berry

Janie Crawford AND love

The Tree Bride

BHARATI MUKHERJEE

2004

The Tree Bride is the second book in a trilogy
written by Bharati Mukherjee. It follows the
events of *Desirable Daughters*. Published in
2004, the four-part work of historical fiction is
woven together with the personal narrative of
the main character, Tara Chatterjee, who discovers that the events of her present are clearly
linked to the past. From Victorian England to
the movement for an independent India to modern-day California, every story connects to the
ancestral home of Tara's family. Like many of
the author's works, *The Tree Bride* addresses the
themes of identity as different characters find
themselves caught between two separate cultures. The concepts of family, duty, and assimilation also feature heavily in the novel as
individuals navigate between Indian and Western society.

AUTHOR BIOGRAPHY

Born on July 27, 1940, in Calcutta (now Kolkata),
India, Mukherjee began her life while India was
still a British colony. Her wealthy Brahmin family, part of the highest Hindu caste, originated in
Bengal but relocated to Calcutta when Bengal
became part of Pakistan. The exodus of educated
Brahmin families from Bengal is reflected in the
story of Tara's family in *The Tree Bride*. Mukherjee's parents, particularly her father, influenced

Bharati Mukherjee (©*Keith Beaty | Getty Images*)

her academic career. As Fakrul Alam points out in *Bharati Mukherjee*, "Their three daughters received the best education possible," which meant Catholic school. The family moved to London in 1947, the same year of Indian independence. They returned to Calcutta in 1951, and Mukherjee earned her BA in 1959 from the University of Calcutta. In 1961, she received her MA in ancient Indian culture and English.

Her decision to attend the Writers' Workshop at the University of Iowa in 1961 changed the course of her life. According to Erin Soderberg's "Bharati Mukherjee": "She planned to study there to earn her Master's of Fine Arts, then return to India to marry a bridegroom of her father's choosing in her class and caste." Instead, she met Canadian Clarke Blaise while she was in Iowa and married him in 1963. She earned her PhD from Iowa in 1969. The couple lived in Canada until 1980, and she became a Canadian citizen in 1972. She experienced discrimination during her time in Canada but still managed to publish her first novel, *The Tiger's Daughter*, in 1971 and then *Wife* in 1975.

In 1980, Mukherjee moved to New York with Blaise and their two sons, and they have remained in the United States since. She taught at various colleges, among them, Columbia University, Queens College, and Emory University. In 1985, her first collection of short stories, *Darkness*, was published. In 1986, she became a permanent resident of the United States and earned a National Endowment for the Arts grant. She won the National Book Critics Circle Award for her 1988 collection *The Middleman and Other Stories* and continued to teach. She accepted a position at University of California, Berkeley in 1989, the same year that *Jasmin* was published, and became a US citizen. Over the years, she continued to teach and write fiction and nonfiction. *Desirable Daughters* appeared in 2002 and began a trilogy. *The Tree Bride* followed in 2004, and the trilogy was completed in 2010 with *New Miss India*. As of the 2010s, Mukherjee lived in San Francisco with her husband and taught at the University of California, Berkeley.

PLOT SUMMARY

The Tree Bride is a four-part novel that blends historical fiction with the present. The point of view shifts between the first and third person as the main character searches the stories of the past so she can better understand her world.

Part One

PROLOGUE

Tara Chatterjee recalls the bombing of her home, which occurred in *Desirable Daughters*. A man named Abbas Sattar Hai was responsible for the explosion in her home that severely injured her ex-husband, Bish. She received only minor injuries, and her fifteen-year-old son, Rabi, escaped unscathed. Tara was pregnant at the time but did not know it. Now she is concerned about the safety of her family.

She recalls her grandmother's stories of Kashi, known by the secular name Varanasi, which is the only place "spared during cosmic dissolution" or the end of the world because it is sacred to Shiva. Tara wanted her grandmother taken to Kashi when she died.

1

Tara chooses an obstetrician with an Indian last name. She is surprised to meet a blonde woman with the name Victoria Treadwell Khanna. Dr. Khanna is knowledgeable about India. Before Tara leaves the office, Dr. Khanna asks her if she believes in fate.

2

When Tara returns to the rental home she shares with Bish, he is in his wheelchair working. She remembers how he played sports when they were first married, before he became wealthy and famous creating the communication technology CHATTY. Tara knows that the divorce, bombing, and drop in CHATTY's value have taken a toll on him. Even though she takes care of him and is pregnant with his baby, they are not married. Tara remembers that after her first twenty years in the United States, she returned to India and Mishtigunj, the home of the Tree Bride and Tara's ancestral family home.

3

At her third appointment, Dr. Khanna informs Tara that her husband, Yash, taught Bish at Stanford. Victoria asks if her maiden name is familiar, but Tara does not recall hearing it before. Victoria then tells Tara that her grandfather Virgil ("Vertie") Treadwell was the district commissioner in Mishtigunj from the 1930s through independence, while Tara Lata Gangooly was there. Victoria gives Tara a box of Vertie's papers to research.

4

Victoria shares her family history with Tara. Tara tells it using the third person. Victoria received the journals and letters from her father after Vertie's widow sent them. Victoria's father was illegitimate, and his mother sent him to an orphanage in London after he was born. After being poisoned by gas in World War I, he moved to Canada for his health and never returned to England.

Vertie had a wife named Iris, who took their daughter, Irene, to New Zealand. He married his second wife, Thelma, shortly before his death. Tara concludes that Vertie and Tara Lata were the same age and could have known each other.

Tara returns home with the box and tells Bish that Victoria is the wife of Yash and how Victoria gave her the papers. Bish informs her that there are no coincidences, and Tara decides

that it is her dharma (duty) to tell the world about Tara Lata. Tara had always been drawn to the Tree Bride's story. To save herself from being a widow, Tara Lata married a proxy husband at age five after the death of her groom. She was then free to educate herself, and she educated others.

A year earlier, Tara's mother mentioned "Tara Lata, and the English writer." She tells Tara to go to Mishtigunj. Tara had already been to Mishtigunj three times.

5

Tara explains her view of Indian history. She informs readers that the British targeted Bengali Brahmins in their colonization. In 1833, Thomas Babington Macaulay proposed education in India. The English education created an aristocracy of the Brahmins in the hope of making them allies. Although Tara's family had Western educations, they remained devout Hindus.

6

Tara finds a receipt for Redd Sahib dated 1822. She theorizes about the life he had in the Bay of Bengal, whether he died or created a new life for himself. Tara notes that men could create new lives for themselves in India in the nineteenth century.

7

On her second visit to Mishtigunj, Tara encounters Hajji Gul Mohammed Chowdhury. Chowdhury is a title bestowed by the British on the family, and Hajji indicates that he has traveled to Mecca. He tells her that Tara Lata told him to dig up her dowry so she could give it to Gandhi. He points out where John Mist and Rafeek Hai were hanged. Over tea, he shows her his translation of *Mist-nama* and sells it to her in exchange for five thousand dollars for the school.

Tara remembers finding a crate with the Tree Bride's writings and how Tara Lata described seeing the death of John Mist and Rafeek Hai and how she played with the cook's daughter, Sameena.

Part Two

1

Tara writes the story of John Mist in the third person, occasionally interjecting with her first-person point of view.

An infant is taken to the Orphans and Foundlings Betterment Trust in 1820 and named Jack Snow. He is put to work shoveling the streets and gutters at the age of six. Jack never speaks until he finds an injured man when he is eight and screams for help. The man Jack found is Tom Crabbe. He is an old sailor who dazzles Jack with stories of his travels. Tara points out that Jack and Crabbe were nothing alike, but Crabbe became his mentor, and Jack was eager to please.

2

When they take positions on the *Malabar Queen*, Tom tells Jack that sailing is changing with the onset of modern vessels and the inclusion of women and children on voyages. Jack is twelve when he becomes the assistant to Captain Diligence Partridge, an educated man who passes on his knowledge to Jack. He walks the deck with Partridge and the female passenger, Olivia Todd, which damages his relationship with Crabbe and the other crew members.

Olivia Todd is traveling to meet her future husband, Humphrey Todd-Nugent, in Calcutta. She likes Jack and promises to hire him when they arrive. Partridge develops a crush on Olivia and tells her only good things about Calcutta. Jack knows that his description of Calcutta is not completely honest.

In December of 1831, a mist develops on the voyage. Partridge says that the Mascarene pirates used to hide in the mists before attacking ships but assures Jack and Olivia that they are safe. Soon after, pirates attack.

3

The first newspaper reports of the attack state that the captain and first mate were killed by Danish brigands and Ms. Todd was carried away. Humphrey Todd-Nugent, however, claims that the ship's crew mutinied and killed the officers.

Olivia had hidden Jack in her trunk when Captain Moans attacked the ship. Moans and his men looted the ship after the murder of the officers. They carried Olivia away, but Crabbe persuaded Moans to leave the crew the ship. After the attack, Jack stops speaking. The crew calls him Jack O' the Mists because Crabbe forces him to work the riggings; he eventually chooses the name John Mist. They believe that they will be rewarded for saving the ship, but they are arrested days after arriving.

4

Mr. Todd-Nugent felt that the news about saving the *Malabar Queen* overshadowed the loss of Olivia, which is why he has pressed for an inquiry. Tara notes that a reporter who investigated the crew of the ship connected living in squalor with the depravity. The crew's defender, David Llewellyn Owens, brings his assistant, Mr. Rafeek Hai, to the courtroom.

David Llewellyn Owens lives like a native of India. He has adopted the local dress and has several wives and many children, whom he formally recognized. Owens uses Mist as his chief witness. Mist testifies that Olivia was killed protecting him. He also praises Tom Crabbe's quick thinking in saving the ship and crew.

Thanks to John's testimony, the crew is found innocent of mutiny, but they are held responsible for the financial loss. They are sentenced to ten years of labor, which is the equivalent of a death sentence. John Mist is sent to an orphanage, which Todd-Nugent opposes. In the orphanage, John works as a delivery boy, carting hemp for weaving. Many of the girls who weave die of consumption.

Different women claim to be Olivia Todd, and John Mist is the only one who can identify her. Donny brings Mist to identify one woman and informs John that Todd-Nugent is eager for the woman to be declared a fraud. He wants to remain unmarried and live with his mistress, or bibi. Although John recognizes Olivia, he pushes her away when she reaches for him. Mist hates Donny and vows never to speak again.

5

Feeling guilty about Olivia, John attempts to hang himself. He wishes that he had identified Olivia, even though he knows that Todd-Nugent would kill them both. The rope is too long, and Mist slips to the ground. A few days later, David Llewellyn Owens and Rafeek Hai visit him. They say that Crabbe has an appeal, but twenty other crew members have died. They also say that he is free to leave with them, and Todd-Nugent has a job waiting for him. When Mist does not speak, Hai asks if he forgot English, and John decides that speaking in Bengali would not break his vow of silence. They converse in Bengali, and Owens reveals that Todd-Nugent will arrange Mist's death to keep him silent about Victoria. They plan to send John to Hai's family, who will then tell people that bandits, or goondahs, killed him.

John Mist goes to Todd-Nugent's home to sign papers about Olivia Todd. Donny brings a letter of passage to Mist, and Mist stabs him before killing Todd-Nugent. Mr. Hai picks up Mist in a carriage, and John Mist changes out of his suit, vowing never to wear Western clothing again.

6

Tara wishes that she had purchased the original *Mist-nama*, written in Persian. On her third visit to Mishtigunj, Tara finds that Hajji Gul Mohammed Chowdhury is dead and his son is living in the house. His son has no idea where the *Mist-nama* is. She wonders if Hajji Gul Mohammed Chowdhury is the grandfather of the man who tried to kill her.

The next thirty years of John Mist's life remain a mystery. He is often mistaken for an Indian and makes a fortune in hemp and timber. He then begins plans for his utopian society, which is to include Muslims and Hindus. Mist, however, did refuse Christians access to Mishtigunj.

Part Three

1

At her six-month appointment, Tara remembers her pregnancy with Rabi. Her first doctor made assumptions about her culture and refused to help with her morning sickness because Indian women handle pregnancy well. Tara's mother had enjoyed pregnancies because people doted on her, hoping she would have a son; she had three daughters.

Tara goes to the Khannas' home in Sausalito with Victoria while Bish and Yash work at Tara's table. Tara and Victoria discuss India and their families. They consider the effect that the British Raj had on both Indian and English society and how it helped form Vertie Treadwell. When Tara returns, the sight of Bish and Yash reminds her of the days when Bish was working on CHATTY. The difference is that they are now older and wiser.

2

EAST ANGLIA, 1948

Vertie Treadwell stops to watch boys playing cricket at St. Albans. He has returned to England from India and recalls playing cricket as a boy in 1882. He remembers his teacher, Octavius Rutledge, and his Greek and Latin studies. Vertie used to put Greek and Latin in

his reports, hoping for a promotion. The mist reminds Vertie of India and hunting tigers. Vertie loves India but not Indians. He is unhappy about the loss of India as a colony.

A boy interrupts his thoughts when he asks Vertie to hand him the cricket ball at Vertie's feet. The boy is Indian, which enrages Vertie, and he throws the ball toward the street. He trips, falling on his face and breaking his nose. He swears at the boy when the boy tries to help him. A police officer stops by and offers Vertie a ride to the pub the Painted Lion, which Vertie refuses.

The day that Vertie trips is the day of his death. The boy reminds Vertie of Tara Lata. His mind wanders after the fall. He remembers killing over one hundred tigers because he thought them noble. His friends take him to the hospital when he stops responding to them.

Vertie recalls a boarding house in India and getting Agnes pregnant.

3

Vertie sees Tara Lata in his hospital room. He then addresses Winston Churchill and the king about India. Churchill reveals that the uncles who raised Vertie were in a romantic relationship. Vertie tells Churchill about John Mist and Tara Lata. He is eventually alone with Tara Lata. She tells him to confess his sins, but he refuses, blaming everything on Dominick Mackenzie, even the rice that he burned when people were starving. He informs Tara Lata that Coughlin reported on her to him, and she reveals that Coughlin secretly worked toward independence.

Vertie recalls his attraction toward Tara Lata and sneaking into her house at night, but he was beaten when her servants protected her.

4

Yash and Bish are at Tara's dining table when she goes to Sausalito with Victoria. They discuss Vertie. Victoria points out that killing the tigers he identified may have been a way for him to destroy himself symbolically. Tara believes that Vertie hated England and his family more than India. Victoria talks about contacting her New Zealand relatives. Irene's half-brother told her that Irene married, and her husband murdered her. In another letter, he reveals that his mother hired an Anglo-Indian named Agnes to be their nurse. He believes that the woman hated his family. Tara assumes that she is Victoria's grandmother, making Victoria part Indian.

Tara sees Abbas Sattar Hai on a boat below them. She calls Jack Sidhu, the detective working her case, and he tells her to remain inside. She realizes there is a bomb and drags Victoria outside. An officer meets them, and Jack says that Hai left his phone. Another officer turns it on, and the house explodes. Victoria is hit with debris and dies on the way to the hospital.

At the hospital, Yash asks Tara about giving Victoria a Hindu cremation. Jack blames himself, but Yash says it was not his fault. He and Tara also convince Jack that she has always been Hai's target. She thinks it goes back to Mishtigunj.

Part Four

1

Tara returns to Tara Lata's story. As a child, she played with Sameena, the cook's daughter, but after she married, Sameena became her servant. Additionally, Jai Krishna Gangooly transformed into a devout Hindu, and he moved the Muslim cook from his kitchen to follow caste rules.

When Tara Lata is fifty-four, she decides to meet with Nigel Coughlin. He reminds her of John Mist. He dresses in typical, Indian style and has an excellent knowledge of India and its culture. She tells Coughlin that she witnessed the death of Rafeek Hai and John Mist. John Mist said, "Chalo. Kajey hat lagao" before his death, which means "Let's get on with it." The families were not permitted to bury the bodies. Coughlin informs her that he supports independence, and someone is betraying her because her name has appeared in papers on his desk. He leaves her some files and the names of people to call if she or others are arrested,

2

Tara reads Coughlin's papers and research. She learns that Mist paid to support Olivia Todd through Owens. Sameena married Shafiq Mohammed Hai, Rafeek Hai's son. Shafiq traveled to Mecca after his son was born, and Vertie gave him the title Chowdhury after writing the *Mist-nama*. Tara believes that Sameena betrayed Tara Lata because of her father's lost position. Additionally, the couple plotted to take Tara Lata's home as Sameena's dowry. They are the ancestors of the man who wants to kill her.

3

The ghost of Tara Lata asks Tara to free her spirit by performing funeral rites. She says Mackenzie strangled her and left her body in a ditch, so her soul is trapped. The next morning Bish tells Tara that they can go to Kashi, but he reminds her that she cannot fly when she is eight months pregnant. His only condition for going is that she marry him. They are married one week before Victoria Kallie is born.

Epilogue

Tara's parents, Rabi, and Bish are with her in Kashi, waiting to go to perform the ritual for the Tree Bride. Victoria Kallie is eight weeks old and also accompanies them. As they make their way, a young man attempts to educate Tara about the city. He tells her the story of a king tested by a sage. The sage dresses as a Brahmin beggar and demands the kingdom, which the king gives. The sage demands more money, and the king sells his family and works the cremation grounds at Kashi to pay him. The sage then has a snake kill the king's son. The king refuses to cremate his son when his wife cannot pay. She gives him her ring and sari to fulfill the requirements. The sage then restores everything to the king, including his son, because of the king's virtue.

The family has a proxy body made of raffi. As Tara Lata's only male relative, Rabi lights the head of the body. Tara can hear the Hindu chant, Ram! Ram! Ram! as the body burns.

CHARACTERS

Agnes

The landlady's daughter who became pregnant when Vertie stayed with her family, she is Anglo-Indian and Victoria's grandmother. Agnes worked for Iris and plotted against Vertie's legitimate family.

Bish Chatterjee

Bish is Tara's ex-husband and the father of Rabi and the baby Tara expects. He invented CHATTY, giving him wealth and fame. He is severely injured after the bombing of Tara's home.

Tara Chatterjee

Tara is named after her ancestor, Tara Lata—the Tree Bride. She is in a relationship with her former husband, Bish, and they live in California. After discovering she is pregnant, she finds Dr. Victoria Khanna. Victoria gives her a box of family papers that relate to the Tree Bride. Tara researches the connection between her family, Victoria's family, and the man who bombed her home, Abbas Sattar Hai. Tara hears the ghost of Tara Lata asking her to perform the rites to free her soul. Tara, Bish, and her son, Rabi, travel to India to complete the funeral rite.

Rabi Chatterjee

Rabi is the teenage son of Tara and Bish. He is interested in film and photography and records the family's trip to Kashi. He also performs the funeral rite for Tara Lata.

Victoria Kallie Chatterjee

The infant daughter of Bish and Tara, Victoria is born at the end of the book and named for Victoria Khanna.

Hajji Gul Mohammed Chowdhury

The son of Dr. Shafiq Mohammed Hai, he sells his translation of *Mist-nama* to Tara when she goes to Mishtigunj. He is the grandfather of Abbas Sattar Hai and dug up Tara Lata's dowry for Tara to donate to Gandhi.

Winston Churchill

A ghost or hallucination, the British politician speaks with Vertie on the day he dies.

Nigel Coughlin

A British ICS officer, Coughlin loves India and supports its independence. He assimilates into Indian culture and offers to help Tara Lata in her fight for freedom. He becomes a citizen of India after independence comes.

Tom Crabbe

Discovered by Jack Snow after being beaten, Tom became the boy's mentor. He is a seasoned sailor whose stories of travel intrigue Snow. Tom saves the remaining crew of the Malabar Queen and brings the ship to port. He is sent to hard labor and is one of the few from the ship to survive.

Donny

Donny works for Todd-Nugent. He brings Mist to identify Olivia, and he makes it clear that the identification will affect the futures of John and Olivia. Mist kills him in Todd-Nugent's home.

Jai Krishna Gangooly

The father of Tara Lata, he is a Hindu lawyer who lived in Mishtigunj as part of John Mist's utopia. He became devout and moved the Muslim cook and Sameena's father from the kitchen.

Tara Lata Gangooly

Tara Lata was married to a tree as a proxy husband when she was five years old after the death of her intended groom. She lived in Mishtigunj and left the house only to watch the execution of John Mist and Rafeek Hai when she was six and when she was arrested. She devoted her life to educating and protecting the people of Mishtigunj. Tara Lata worked toward the goal of independence and cataloged and reported British crimes against Indians. She was killed after her arrest.

Abbas Sattar Hai

A descendant of Rafeek Hai, Abbas inserted himself in Tara's life in *Desirable Daughters*. He killed her nephew and put a bomb in her home. Still targeting Tara, he puts a bomb in Victoria and Yash's home.

Rafeek Hai

The assistant of David Llewellyn Owens, Rafeek Hai also assisted John Mist in his escape from the East India Company. When Mist creates Mishtigunj, he invites Rafeek Hai to join him in the new community. Hai is hanged with John Mist.

Sameena Hai

Sameena played with Tara Lata as a child and became her servant after the Tree Bride married. Her father was the cook Jai Krishna Gangooly, who was demoted to adhere to caste order. She married Shafiq Mohammed Hai and was the mother of Hajji Gul Mohammed Chowdhury. Sameena betrayed Tara Lata and plotted to inherit her home.

Shafiq Mohammed Hai

The father of Hajji Gul Mohammed Chowdhury and husband of Sameena, Shafiq is a doctor. He was given the title Hajji when he traveled to Mecca and Chowdhury for completing the Mist-nama.

Rafeek Hai

The assistant of David Llewellyn Owens, Rafeek Hai also assisted John Mist in his escape from the East India Company. When Mist creates

Mishtigunj, he invites Rafeek Hai to join him in the new community. Hai is hanged with John Mist.

Mogens Jespersen
See Captain Moans.

Dr. Victoria Treadwell Khanna
Victoria is Tara's doctor, and the two become friends. She is the granddaughter of Vertie Treadwell, and she gives Vertie's papers to Tara to research. Victoria is married to Yash Khanna and loves India. She discovers that she may be part Indian before dying in the explosion of her home, arranged by Abbas Sattar Hai.

Yash Khanna
Yash was once Bish's teacher. He is married to Victoria, and he works with Bish while Tara and Victoria spend time together.

King
The virtuous king is tested by a sage, and the king works at Kashi to fulfill his duty.

King's Son
The son of the king is killed by a snake to test the king's virtue.

King's Wife
The wife of the king is sold into slavery and brings her son to Kashi after he is bitten by a snake.

Dominick Mackenzie
Dominick Mackenzie was the police contingent in Mishtigunj. He was responsible for many atrocities, including strangling Tara Lata.

John Mist
Originally named Jack Snow, Mist is an orphan who joined the crew of the Malabar Queen at the age of twelve. He is mentored by Crabbe and feels a sense of loyalty to Olivia Todd. Mist assimilates into Indian life and culture after killing Donny and Todd-Nugent. He founds Mishtigunj, but he is executed with Rafeek Hai by the British.

Captain Moans
The leader of the pirates that attacked the *Malabar Queen*, Moans is also known by the name Mogens Jespersen.

David Llewellyn Owens
Owens is the defender for John Mist and the crew of the *Malabar Queen*. Although he is Welsh, he is assimilated into Indian culture. He helps John Mist escape Todd-Nugent.

Captain Diligence Partridge
Captain of the *Malabar Queen*, Partridge is educated and teaches Snow modern sailing techniques. He is young and enamored of Olivia, but he is killed when the ship is attacked by Captain Moans.

Octavius Rutledge
Vertie Treadwell's teacher is Octavius Rutledge.

Sage
The sage tests the king in the story Tara hears at Kashi.

Redd Sahib
A man mentioned in a receipt dated 1822.

Jack Sidhu
Jack is the officer investigating Abbas Sattar Hai and the bombing of Tara's home. He tries to prevent the explosion at Victoria's but is too late.

Jack Snow
See John Mist.

Olivia Todd
A governess and the fiancé of Humphrey Todd-Nugent, Olivia travels to India to marry a man she never met. She is fond of Jack Snow and hides him in her trunk when the ship is attacked. Olivia is carried away by the pirates. When she appears in India to claim her identity, John Mist does not identify her.

Humphrey Todd-Nugent
The fiancé of Olivia Todd, Humphrey Todd-Nugent is with the East India Company. He demands that the crew of *Malabar Queen* be tried for mutiny and works to ensure that Olivia Todd will never be identified. He plots to have John Mist killed, but John kills him instead.

Irene Treadwell
Daughter of Vertie and Iris, Irene grew up in New Zealand and was murdered by her husband.

Iris Treadwell
Vertie's first wife, Iris left him and took Irene to New Zealand, where she remarried and had a son.

Thelma Treadwell
Vertie's second wife, Thelma sends Vertie's papers to Victoria's father.

Vertie Treadwell
Vertie was the district commissioner of Mishtigunj when Tara Lata lived there. He loved India and resented losing his home with its independence. He was attracted to the Tree Bride and was beaten when he sneaked into her home. Vertie also covered up the murder of Tara Lata.

Vertie is Victoria's grandfather. He was married to Iris, who took their daughter, Irene, to New Zealand. He returned to England after the country gained independence and married Thelma. He died after a fall in London.

Virgil Treadwell
See Vertie.

Tree Bride
See Tara Lata Gangooly.

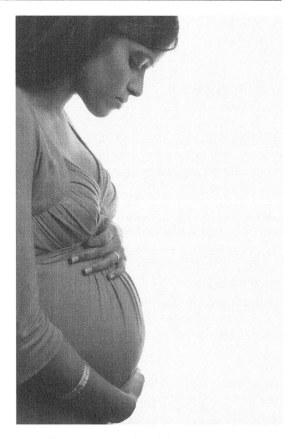

Heavily pregnant and with her marriage in trouble, Tara struggles to find her place in the world (©Philippe Put / Shutterstock.com)

THEMES

Identity
Several characters of *The Tree Bride* struggle with their identities over the course of the story. Tara, for example, has struggled with her identity since moving to the United States. She states, "Wife-of-Bish-Chatterjee was my full identity." She walks away from custom to find herself in a divorce. Still, however, she remains loyal to the faith and traditions. She explains, "I come from a highly religious, orthodox Hindu Brahmin family, but to know me in California, you'd never guess." This contrast of tradition and modernity allows Tara to live independently while still hearing the ghost of her ancestor. The more that Tara discovers about herself as an American, the more she is drawn back to her roots.

In addition to being torn between two cultures, Tara also faces the changes in her life following the bombing of her house. Both she and Bish lost their celebrity identities, which came with the success of his invention. Bish struggles with his physical weakness, and Tara sees that the experience has aged her. Bish finds himself again while working with Yash.

Another character who struggles with identity is Victoria. She feels a connection to India and is married to an Indian man. Her family heritage, however, is English. In fact, all that she knows of her family is that her grandfather was a cruel man who served in India. Over the course of the novel, Victoria learns that she is part Indian. She is delighted to have a biological connection to the land and culture that she loves. Finding the missing piece of her identity makes her complete.

Duty
Dharma is mentioned throughout Mukherjee's book. According to the *Encyclopaedia Britannica*, in Hinduism,

> in addition to the dharma that applies to everyone (*sadharana dharma*)—consisting of truthfulness, non-injury, and generosity, among

TOPICS FOR FURTHER STUDY

- Read *The House on Mango Street*, by Sandra Cisneros. This young-adult novel tells the coming of age story of Esperanza. As she grows up on Mango Street, she faces struggles to find her own identity. Work with a partner; one of you will create a blog for Esperanza, and the other will create a blog for Tara or another character from *The Tree Bride*. The characters will respond to each other's blog posts. What would they say to each other? What advice and experiences can they share?

- Research India under colonial rule and the movement for independence. Create a web page that provides an overview of the history. Be sure to include a link to the East India Company and the events of World War II.

- Research the Indian diasporas and how they have affected the country. Create a multimedia presentation that explains the causes and effects of diaspora. Be sure to include the population shifts after World War II.

- Read the young-adult novel *Keeping Corner*, by Kashmira Sheth. In this story, set in colonial India, child bride Leela is widowed at the age of thirteen. She suffers the fate Tara Lata's father prevented. Create a one-act play where Leela and Tara Lata meet with a small group. Record yourselves acting out the play and upload it using EDpuzzle.

- Research the Hindu religion, including art, culture, and expression. Choose a specific topic, such as funeral rites, and write a short paper explaining the topic. Additionally, create a visual representation of the subject using any artistic medium you prefer—drawing, painting, computer graphics, or sculpture.

---

other virtues—there is also a specific dharma (*svadharma*) to be followed according to one's class, status, and station in life.

In the novel, dharma is closely linked with duty. A character who follows her established path in life is Tara Lata. She never seeks to escape the role of wife to a tree, even though it means she will never marry and have a family. She embraces her role and takes advantage of her status. She becomes educated, and in turn she teaches others. Although she lives a life of seclusion, Tara Lata is beloved in her community as she guides and protects the people of Mishtigunj. The Tree Bride is firm in her resolve; as Tara says, "nothing distracted her from an independent India."

By performing her duty, the Tree Bride inspires Tara to perform hers. Tara takes on the role of a dutiful wife after Bish is injured in the explosion. She takes on the role even though they are divorced, caring for him as he rehabilitates. Additionally, Tara chooses to act on behalf of Tara Lata and makes sure the final rites are performed at Kashi to set her spirit free.

Assimilation

Throughout *The Tree Bride*, cultures collide, and people assimilate. Although Tara faces her own assimilation in the United States, the story addresses more than the assimilation into Western society. Several of the British characters assimilate into Indian culture. One assimilated character is David Llewellyn Owens. Tara describes him as one of the "last of the old 'British Hindoos.'" Mr. Owens dresses in Indian clothing and has four Hindu wives, which does not sit well with the British. He legally defends John Mist and helps the boy establish his own life in India. Owens is the type of man that Vertie Treadwell despised.

John Mist becomes fully assimilated into Indian culture. He refuses to speak English or wear Western clothing. As an orphan from England, Mist saw and suffered from the cruelty and hypocrisy of British colonialism. He was able to transform himself in India, which became his home. Mist attempted to create a utopian city, uniting Hindus and Muslims in a community. His rejection of Western culture remains up to his death, when he utters his final words in Bengali.

Tara Lata compares Coughlin to John Mist. He wears Indian clothing and follows Hindu tradition even though caste laws prevent him from becoming Hindu. He supports Indian independence while working for the British government, placing him in a dangerous position. His love for India is not an infatuation. He becomes a citizen after independence is gained.

STYLE

Symbolism

Symbols appear throughout *The Tree Bride*. One symbol that frequently appears is egg spoons. According to M. H. Abrams in *A Glossary of Literary Terms*, "The term 'symbol' is applied only to a word or a phrase that signifies an object or event." After Tom Crabbe tells Jack Snow that an egg spoon was used to take out his eye, the boy thinks of egg spoons when he senses danger from seemingly harmless sources. For example, he thinks of egg spoons when Partridge talks to Olivia about India. When Donny tells Mist that he should misidentify Olivia, he again thinks of egg spoons. This time, however, he desires to kill Donny when he understands the threat behind the instruction.

Magic Realism

According to William Harmon in *A Handbook to Literature*, magic realism occurs when the "frame or surface of the work may be conventionally realistic, but contrasting elements—such as the supernatural, myth, dream, fantasy—invade the realism and change the whole basis of the art." Magic realism is woven throughout *The Tree Bride*. For example, Tara hears the spirit of Tara Lata in her rental home in California. She asks Tara to release her soul by performing the funeral rites.

Another example of magic realism is Vertie Treadwell's death. He talks with Churchill, and his final word is "Winston." Vertie also speaks with the spirit of Tara Lata, who confronts him about his crimes in India. There is no explanation for these conversations. They could be hallucinations brought on by his own conscience, or they may be ghosts. The knowledge that Tara Lata has indicates a mind separate from Vertie. For instance, she knows the truth about John Mist, which Vertie distorted, blending Mist with Crabbe in his mind.

HISTORICAL CONTEXT

Indian Diaspora

The emigration of Indian people to other nations is not new. In fact, Gijsbert Oonk identifies four diasporas. The first was the diaspora along "coastal communities" of those seeking to trade with Africa and Asia. The second diaspora came when Indians were taken to plantations as indentured servants when legal slavery ended with a sequence of legislative acts. After World War II, at the time of Indian Partition, Muslims traveled to the newly created Pakistan, and Hindus moved from Pakistan to India. Other people left to take on professional work in the West, many of them having Western educations. The fourth diaspora comprised people who had already left India and were living elsewhere who then traveled to Canada and the United Kingdom.

Technology and Indian diaspora are also closely linked, which is reflected in the success Bish found in *The Tree Bride*. Early American immigration laws limited the number of immigrants from India, but these laws loosened in the 1960s. As a result, many Indians entered the country looking for work, often in technology. The IT industry began to develop in India in the 1970s, according to Amba Pande. Pande notes that "by the 1990s, many of the highly skilled Indians in the USA had become high-level executives, venture capitalists, entrepreneurs and Chief Executive Officers (CEOs)." These individuals, according to Pande, outsourced work to India, boosting the economy of their ancestral home. This global development of technology helped to create a "US $100 billion industry" in India.

Indian Colonialism and Independence

Much of *The Tree Bride* takes place when India was a colony of Great Britain. Tara Lata and other characters fight for the independence of India after centuries of British rule. The East India Company was originally a trading company with a charter dating back to 1600. According to George P. Landow, the company developed a military and methods of administration, making it a political power. He writes: "Before Parliament created a government-controlled policy-making body with the Regulating Act of 1773 and the India Act eleven years later, shareholders' meetings made decisions about Britain *de facto* colonies in the East." In 1834, the company was officially an agency of the British government. The East India Company ruled India when John Mist sailed to the country. India was placed under the control of the British government in 1858 with the Government of India Act after the 1857 Sepoy Rebellion.

COMPARE
&
CONTRAST

- **1830s:** The East India Company is a British-based trading company that has a powerful influence in India, acting as a colonizing body. This corporation serves as an agent of the British government.

  1940s: Great Britain has officially ruled over India since the 1858 Government of India Act. Mahatma Gandhi and other members of the Indian National Congress are actively fighting for freedom, which is achieved in 1947.

  2000s: The development of an open market in the 1990s improved India's economy. The middle class begins to expand with the economy.

  Today: India is a growing international power with a stable economy. Much of the nation's wealth is due to its influence on technology, and the number of outsourced positions brought to the country.

- **1830s:** The end of the British slave trade created a labor gap. The British begin to rely on indentured servants from India and China to work on plantations throughout the British Empire, creating a diaspora.

  1940s: Many Indians leave their homes as tensions rise between Muslims and Hindus and the country is partitioned into India and Pakistan. Other Indian people move to other countries looking for employment.

2000s: The diaspora has a complex influence on India's economy. While many have left the country for work, they often bring business back into India.

Today: The Indian government is addressing the needs created by the diaspora, which it estimates to be over thirty million people who have left the country. They have contributed to the country's growing economic status, and the Indian government has programs to keep those in the diaspora connected to the ancestral homeland.

- **1830s:** English education for Indians is proposed in 1833 by Thomas Babington Macaulay. Most of the educated are from the Brahmin caste, such as Tara, which places a greater emphasis on education.

  1940s: Indian custom and culture are dominated by caste. Gandhi and other reformers work to end the injustice lower castes and Untouchables face.

  2000s: K. R. Narayanan is the first Dalit (Untouchable) president. Discrimination based on caste is not legally protected.

  Today: Caste and family heritage still influence society in India. There are, however, legal protections against discrimination.

In 1885, the Indian National Congress was formed. The organization worked toward the goal of national independence. In the 1920s, Mahatma Gandhi led the congress, advocating nonviolent noncooperation. During World War II, the British relied on the support of India against Japan. Sir Stafford Cripps went to India in 1942, promising independence after the war in exchange for support with the war effort. Dissatisfied with the offer, the Quit India movement—a movement of civil disobedience demanding the end of British rule—began. The movement is linked to a speech made by Gandhi, who was part of the All India Congress Committee, on August 8, 1942. He and other leaders were quickly arrested. More extreme leaders, such as Subhas Chandra Bose, supported Japan in the war effort.

The tension between the British and Indians escalated after the arrest of respected leaders. Unfortunately, the Indian people were divided over religion. Patrick French points out in *India:*

The modern-day Tara finds her life disrupted when her home is firebombed (©ChicagoDave | Shutterstock.com)

A Portrait that "many felt that for all the talk of inclusiveness, the Congress leadership was made up largely of Hindus from the higher end of the caste system." Many Muslims feared that they would not be granted equal rights, and they desired their own state. After independence had been achieved in 1947, conflict over the division between India and Pakistan led to the deaths of thousands of people.

CRITICAL OVERVIEW

Mukherjee's work has been both praised and disparaged throughout her career. Her first novel, *The Tiger's Daughter*, was published in 1971 and did not earn high praise. The reviewer for the *Times Literary Supplement* says, "Her novel is charming and intelligent and curiously unmoving." Mukherjee's style developed over time, and she earned a National Book Critics Circle Award for Fiction with the short-story collection *The Middleman and Other Stories* in 1988. Indian and Indian American critics are

particularly critical of her work. Erin Soderberg notes that Mukherjee has "been criticized for a tendency to overlook unavoidable barriers of caste, education, gender, race and history in her tales of survivors."

Critics who did not entirely approve of her work typically noted her skill with words. Uma Parameswaran says in her *World Literature Today* review of the famous 1989 novel *Jasmine*, "Mukherjee shows admirable mastery over voice and vocabulary here." She concludes, however, that "when reading *Jasmine*, one feels only disappointment that potentially powerful experiences have been reduced to superficialities couched in prose that is always readable but never poignant or powerful." Over the course of time reviewers remained critical and divided.

The precursor to The *Tree Bride, Desirable Daughters*, published in 2002, was praised by some and rejected by others. The *Publishers Weekly* review says that "only a writer with mature vision, a sense of history and a long-nurtured observation of the Indo-American community could have created this absorbing tale of two rapidly changing cultures and the flash points where they intersect." Ramlal Agarwal says in his *World Literature Today* review that the characters "fail to impress the reader." The critical views of *The Tree Bride* were a little more flattering. Jyna Scheeren describes the novel in her *Library Journal* review as "dry in spots, compelling in others, packed with Indo-British history, and touching on issues of caste and race" and declares that "this novel is expertly written in often dreamy and silky prose." The 2011 conclusion to the trilogy, *Miss New India*, was judged for its lack of authenticity. Kishwar Desai calls the book entertaining but notes that "it fails to capture India's zeitgeist, or authentically voice the emerging small-town girl."

As the author of short stories, novels, and nonfiction, Mukherjee remained an important figure in American literature despite the voices of her harsher critics. As Fakrul Alam says, "We can conclude that Mukherjee has created original and valuable fiction about the immigrant experience in North America."

CRITICISM

April Paris

Paris is a freelance writer with a degree in classical literature and a background in academic writing. In the following essay, she looks at how Mukherjee examines immigration from a British perspective in The Tree Bride.

Like many of Mukherjee's novels, *The Tree Bride* addresses the theme of immigration and assimilation. It is unique in comparison, however, because the immigrants in this novel are not members of the Indian diaspora. They are the British men who live in India despite their heritage. Like all immigrant stories, some face alienation and unbreakable ties with their past, whereas others are unable to see the true nature of the place where they live. The displaced characters of this novel explore their identities as they search for their home. John Mist, Vertie Treadwell, and Nigel Coughlin are all devoted to India in their own ways, and they do what they can to remain in India.

Vertie Treadwell loved the India of the British Raj, which means he desired to live on the land but had no respect for the native people. Vertie loved his vision of India instead of its

> THE IMMIGRANTS TO INDIA THAT MUKHERJEE DESCRIBES ALL HAVE COMPLEX RELATIONSHIPS WITH THE LAND THAT THEY LOVE. THEIR RESPONSE TO INDIA VARIES ACCORDING TO THEIR IDENTITIES AND CHOICES."

reality. Rather than assimilating to the cultures in India, Vertie attempts to make Indians conform to British culture. In this way, he appears to be the stereotypical British officer. In reality, however, his relationship with India is more complex than that of a bitter demagogue who resents living in an uncivilized land.

Although Vertie embraces the idea of British superiority, much of his behavior is motivated by his own shame. In the absence of his parents, he was raised by his uncles. The brothers had a romantic relationship of which Vertie was aware. Being a child in the late nineteenth century, the boy knew that he had to keep the relationship a secret, and he feared the personal consequences if the truth should come to light. The weight of the secret manifests itself in a deep-seated homophobia that colors Vertie's worldview. For example, he tries to "introduce manly virtues—healthy competition, respect for rules, modesty in victory, dignity in defeat—in the form of cricket, always with predictable results." Any failing of his plans is due to a lack of manliness in the Indian people in his mind. He refuses to see any other point of view. By forcing people to assimilate to his culture and values, he successfully alienates himself from the land that he loves.

Vertie despises assimilation and fears becoming assimilated because of the homophobia that drives him and forces him to turn his back on what he enjoys. For example, he believes that the art and culture are too feminine, even though he appreciates them. Rather than embracing the art and beauty of the land he loves, he turns his back on it because "too much involvement in the feminine side sent an improper message." By remaining separate, Vertie believes that he is the true Indian and explains: "Fully ninety percent of my life has

WHAT DO I READ NEXT?

- *Bharati Mukherjee: A Study in Immigrant Sensibility*, by Stanley M. Stephen, is a critical study of immigration in Mukherjee's work. Published in 2010, the text focuses on the author's view of diaspora.

- *India: A History*, by John Keay, was published in 2011. Keay provides an overview of India and its history and diverse cultures. This nonfiction book is a useful introduction for any reader interested in learning more about the country.

- *Luka and the Fire of Life* (2010), by Salman Rushdie, is a young-adult novel with a magical setting where Luka and his animal friends search for the fire of life. Rushdie is a contemporary of Mukherjee and also emigrated from India.

- Published in 2000, *Esperanza Rising*, by Pam Muñoz Ryan, is a young-adult novel that examines immigration in the United States, along with assimilation. The story of migrant farmworkers reflects many of Mukherjee's ideas and themes.

- In the 2013 nonfiction book *A History of Prejudice: Race, Caste, and Difference in India and the United States*, Gyanendra Pandey examines the history of Indian Untouchables and compares it with the history of African Americans. The text shows how prejudice exists in both countries.

- Mukherjee's novel *Desirable Daughters*, published in 2002, begins the story of Tara Chatterjee and her family. The novel provides greater insight into the characters and events of *The Tree Bride*.

---

been spent in India. I have probably spent a greater percentage of my life in India than Mr. Nehru."

In many ways, Vertie is petty and weak. He withholds food from people for years because a gun failed to fire in the salute recognizing his status as district commissioner. Secretly, however, he is ashamed of his actions and unable to confess them to Tara Lata at his death, blaming everything on Mackenzie. Knowing the damage that he did to India creates a self-loathing and bitterness in him. Victoria points out that in his slaughter of tigers "he was trying to kill Vertie Treadwell. Or something in himself. Given his identification with tigers." In his isolation and anger, Vertie is prevented from finding a home in India.

By 1948, Vertie is living unhappily in England as an exile. India was the home of his heart, even if it was an illusion. His parents were buried in India, and his children were born there. The India he thought he knew, however, is gone. No longer does a British man enforce his views and morality simply by virtue of his ethnicity. In his rejection of England and desire for an India that never existed, Vertie expresses "the recognition of the inauthenticity or the created aura of all homes," according to Rosemary George in Katherine Miller's "Mobility and Identity Construction in Bharati Mukherjee's *Desirable Daughters*: 'The Tree Wife and Her Rootless Namesake.'" Vertie is a man without a home. He could not remain in India, but he is equally out of place in England because, as Tara explains, he hated it. "He'd joined the colonial service because in his family Indian administration was expected; but in his case he always claimed the strongest of motives to get away from England and never return." Vertie's attempt to force Britishness upon India destroys any hope of every connecting with the land or people. He lives his life forever in exile. Other migrants to India, however, would become much more successful in finding contentment and new lives as they embrace their roles in their new communities. One such man is John Mist.

As an orphan in London, John Mist had little reason to love the land of his birth. He was beaten and forced to work hard labor as a child. His loyalties are further tested when he and the crew of the *Malabar Queen* are tried for mutiny simply because acknowledging the attack would be bad for business and Todd-Nugent was unhappy with the attention the sailors received. Given his past, John Mist embraces life in India and finds it easy to assimilate into the culture and society of his new home. In his desire to free himself from the corruption he associates with Great Britain, he refuses to speak English. He also gives up Western clothing after he kills Todd-Nugent, the man who represented everything that he hated about British culture.

Over the decades that he lived in his adopted homeland, Mist "was taken for Indian wherever he went." Mist's assimilation is complete, which allows him to become part of a community. As Katherine Miller says, "Home and community are ideological determinants of identity." In his mind, Mist is Indian, and his Indian identity is fully accepted in the community of Mishtigunj.

After wandering for more than three decades, Mist creates a community of his own, which indicates that he failed to find a real home throughout his travels, spurring the need to build one himself. Despite his assimilation, he may still have a sense of isolation, which is so common with immigrants. Mist's utopian vision included Hindus and Muslims working in cooperation with access to education, health, and justice. He successfully persuades different professionals to join him in Mishtigunj, including Tara Lata's father, the lawyer Jai Krishna Gangooly, and Rafeek Hai, the man who helped Mist begin his new life in India.

The utopian community, however, does not last forever. John Mist is discovered and executed because of the one British connection he refused to sever. Mist paid Owens money for Olivia as "a debt of honour." Tara recognizes that "if that money to Olivia Pereira was traced back to him," it could have been the cause of his destruction. John's guilt over his betrayal of Olivia remains part of his identity before and after he is assimilated into Indian culture. The connection to his past, however, proves to be his undoing.

Another character who successfully embraces Indian culture and assimilation is Nigel Coughlin. The British officer with communist sensibilities finds himself torn between his political position and a desire to see a free India. Despite his job as an ICS officer, Coughlin surprises Tara Lata by dressing in Indian clothing and refusing to travel by car. In many ways, he resembles John Mist. Coughlin promises to use his influence to help Tara Lata and India. Circumstances force him to play both sides, however, which is why she refers to him as a "tragic" character. He is obliged to wait before he can display how far he has assimilated into Indian culture.

The original Tara is betrothed to a tree–a symbolic union designed to save her from a life of shame as an "unlucky" widow (©Alexander Mazurkevich/Shutterstock.com)

According to Chetana Pokhriyal, "The process of survival of the diasporic individual/community in between the 'home of origin' and the 'world of adoption' is the voyage undertaken in the whole process from 'alienation' to final 'assimilation.'" Coughlin's assimilation becomes complete after India gains independence and he becomes a citizen of his adopted home. He is no longer an alien in India. Unfortunately, however, he can never fully participate in the Hindu faith in the same way as those with Indian ancestry. When Coughlin first meets Tara Lata, he describes himself as a spurned Hindu owing to his lack of caste. "He lay outside the pale of brahminical civilization, a *mleccha*, not even an untouchable." Although he is legally and culturally Indian, there are still limits on the depth of his participation.

The immigrants to India that Mukherjee describes all have complex relationships with the land that they love. Their response to India varies according to their identities and choices. Vertie Treadwell rejects the opportunities of India and finds himself forever isolated. Mist and Coughlin, on the other hand, allow India to shape their identities as they embrace their home and assimilate into its culture and history.

Source: April Paris, Critical Essay on *The Tree Bride*, in *Novels for Students*, Gale, Cengage Learning, 2017.

Angela Elam

In the following excerpt, Mukherjee talks about the themes of identity and assimilation in her work.

> " THERE ARE NO COINCIDENCES BUT CONVERGENCES THAT ARE MATHEMATICALLY PROVABLE IF YOU CAN FIGURE OUT THE RIGHT EQUATION. ALL EVENTS ARE COMPUTATIONS AND PERMUTATIONS, AND SO IF YOU'RE MATHEMATICALLY CORRECT, YOU'LL BE ABLE TO FIGURE OUT ALL YOU'RE GIVEN, BISH WOULD SAY."

. . . New Letters: I heard a story about how you ended up going to the University of Iowa, because at the time, it was the only writing workshop that offered a creative-writing M.F.A.

Mukherjee: No one in my family had been to the United States for graduate studies. We all looked to England or Germany or France for the graduate degree. America was not on our radar at all. A group of UCLA students and a drama professor came into India and passed through our town in 1960 as part of an experiment in international living; that group came to our house for dinner, and my father, in a small-talk and expansive way said, "This daughter wants to be a writer. Where should I send her for the two years?" One guy pulled the Iowa University program out of the hat. If he had said, "Send her to Arkansas," I probably would be speaking with an Arkansas accent and would have been married to a Southerner and would have had a different life, with a totally different kind of fiction. Or, if that man hadn't come through, I would have married the decent and accomplished nuclear physicist whom my father had picked for me. If I'd have married that man in an arranged way, I probably would have had just as happy a life, but totally, totally different. My fiction, again, would have been more Jane Austen-ey and in an Indian setting.

NL: Would you have been writing in English, even?

Mukherjee: Yes, I would have been writing in English. This is part of the colonial legacy, and I found myself introspecting through that as I was writing *The Tree Bride*. What if there hadn't been the English, not only coming over but imposing educational policy through people such as Thomas Macaulay, saying we want English-speaking little clerks among the natives? Let the education system be sure that they are proficient in English and that they have the desire to buy consumer goods from Lancashire or Yorkshire, but we don't want them to think like Englishmen and have Gladstonian ideas. That language and educational policy meant that large sections of middle-class urban people are English speaking. The fancy girls' school run by Irish nuns that I was sent to because I was so-and-so's daughter and I couldn't go to a less fancy school, had accent inspectors come from London every year to check the British Broadcasting Corporationness of our accents, so that we wouldn't be accused of a Peter Sellers sing-song kind of parody of Indian English. In my girls' school in Calcutta, run by these Irish nuns, elocution was the most important subject. Forget science and math and all that. Elocution. Next was table manners. I realize now, I mean, thinking back on it as a mature adult, that those were colonial hangovers. If you spoke English with an Indian accent, that meant you were not quite right. Or if you didn't hold your knife and fork the way you were supposed to in London society, then again, you were not quite right. That's a colonial legacy.

My high school certificate does not say Calcutta University but Overseas Cambridge University, and the curriculum, therefore, was geared to Cambridge University demands. I had to take, as my mother tongue, Alternate English, Extra English, and not my real biological, inherited mother tongue, Bengali.

NL: All I can think about is the character Bish, in The Tree Bride, *saying, "There are no coincidences." In some ways,* The Tree Bride *goes off on this metaphysical search about that and the relations of things.*

Mukherjee:The Tree Bride has turned out to be the prequel in what I now think of as a projected trilogy. *Desirable Daughters* was the first book I wrote in this trilogy when I didn't know that there'd be anything more than one book. The narrator for both *Desirable Daughters* and *The Tree Bride* is a thirty-six-year-old woman called Tara; she is educated and from a self-confident reasonably affluent family and is one of three sisters, the only sister who submits to having her marriage arranged by her patriarchal father. She becomes the bride of an immigrant Bengali engineer, who goes to

Stanford University and becomes the Indian Bill Gates of the Indo-American community in the Silicon Valley.

NL: In the book, he gets all these names people put on him. The Guru, the Mogul. Mogul was so wrong for him, but Americans group these Asian titles in one area.

Mukherjee: Tara is caught between ideas she has inherited about how time operates or how destiny operates, and her gradual Americanization and her exercising of free will. But, for her, the world is full of magical coincidences. She thinks, "All right, if I'm to find the clue to mysteries in my life when I'm psychologically, emotionally, psychically ready, the clue will come and I'll be able to recognize it." But Bish, her husband—whom she in one of her misadventures and self-searches decides to divorce and then try to get back together with—is an engineer, is logical, is rational, and that's the other aspect of Hinduism and thinking about destiny: There are no coincidences but convergences that are mathematically provable if you can figure out the right equation. All events are computations and permutations, and so if you're mathematically correct, you'll be able to figure out all you're given, Bish would say. Facts. As an information designer, he wants to put together all this messy pile of facts until it makes sense. So, information design is a way of explaining what appears to us as chaos.

NL: So my sixth-grade math teacher was right: Math will bring you closer to God.

Mukherjee: Yes, and you know, Hindu thought and religion are really a process of metaphorizing, of making up stories or making visual, geophysical cosmic theories. We know all about the discovery of new galaxies and constellations. Chaos theory is close to the Hindu explanation of how the world works. Quantum physics is really what our creation, destruction, re-creation is all about.

NL: That's threaded throughout The Tree Bride *and into, as you say, the prequel,* Desirable Daughters. *Even going back to your book of short stories,* The Middleman and Other Stories. *Speaking of that book, it's the first time somebody from India had won the National Book Critics Circle Award, is that right?*

Mukherjee: I was the first naturalized American to have won that award.

NL: Those are stories about people straddling two worlds.

Mukherjee: Straddling two worlds, yes: These people are the traditional heirs to the American dream, but suddenly America has changed on them; and people like me, who have come from nontraditional countries to America, are having to make accommodations or reject some of the old, while they graft on some of the new. For me, *The Middleman* was a breakthrough, because I realized that my material is about the two-way transformation that America was going through in the eighties, and more so today. It's not simply the immigrant coming and saying, "All right, I've got to Americanize." Melting pot was that old theory that the newcomer will have to become an American. Whereas in real life, more and more nonwhite immigrants are coming in, documented and undocumented, and Americans—traditional Americans—also are having to adjust to that fact.

NL: What's interesting about The Tree Bride, *though, is that this character has dealt with her assimilation into the American way of life and is now looking back and trying to figure out her roots and who she is as a person. That was a fascinating shift for you as a writer, because most of the people in your earlier works are looking forward and how to make it in that new world. This story looks back to see how those two worlds are braided together.*

Mukherjee: You're absolutely right, Angela. What I realized, when I finished *Desirable Daughters*, was that for Tara, her adventures in *Desirable Daughters* were about personal pursuit of happiness. I don't like that; I want to test myself. The moment I finished that final scene in which Tara has this vision of her namesake and female ancestor from the nineteenth century—the tree bride, Taralata, who was married off to a tree in 1879 because of peculiar circumstances, and who became a freedom fighter—I realized that there had to be a roots search. I found myself embarking in an urgent way in an American-roots search, except that the Hindu vision of roots is different from the normal American roots novel, where you track an individual family, find the Italian village or the African village from which the great-grandfather or great-great-grandfather started. For us, colonial forces—the encounter between the imperialistic white man, good and bad, and the language imposed, the sense of right and wrong, democracy or feudalism imposed—has gone into the very shaping of what language I write in. The opposite directions I feel culturally become intensified through tracking an individual family, how one encounter, let's say, with an Englishman by the tree bride in the nineteenth century and early twentieth century, has enormous and continuing repercussions in Sausalito or San Francisco for this very modern Indo-American family. Nothing is ever lost. How you deal with that perception, again, decides what your next circumstance, incident, will be.

NL: Early in your novel Jasmine, *too, that's how Jasmine deals with the world, although she's not as self-aware as Tara in* The Tree Bride.

Mukherjee: Yes. I think Tara grows in self-awareness even from *Desirable Daughters* to *The Tree Bride,* because she's undergone firebombing; and her ex-husband, with whom she wants to get back together, has been so badly injured, crippled, burnt, in trying to rescue her from this firebombed house that she's had to deal with much bigger issues than simply who she is and what she thinks of this personal happiness.

NL: I found it interesting that you had yet another man crippled by an accident: In the novel Jasmine, *Bud, the husband to Jasmine, was—I don't know how much I should reveal—*

Mukherjee: Go ahead.

NL: Anyway, one of the joys of reading your work is how you circle around something. We know that he's crippled, but we don't know how; we're wondering how, and you hold it off for a certain amount of time. You don't just tell the story in a linear fashion.

Mukherjee: Absolutely. I think of my aesthetics as the art of indirection, and more important, the art of compression. I want to be able to squeeze many facts into a single paragraph and then pick up a little thread and unravel it some more, thirty pages down, instead of telling a linear, direct story. I love strong character, and I love plot.

NL: How do you actually make plot work, structurally?

Mukherjee: I do a lot of research for every novel. A lot of interviews, if necessary. In *Jasmine,* I was writing at a time in Iowa when there was a farm crisis, in the mid-to-late eighties; and among my friends was a forty-two-year-old banker who was shot to death in his office, just a few miles from where I lived, because another

forty-two-year-old Iowa farmer who'd gone to school with the banker, thought he was being foreclosed upon. There was great violence out of misunderstanding and the economic circumstances. I didn't want my character to die, but I knew that there had to be sufficient violent damage in order for me to dramatize the confrontations and the miscommunications, so that's why we have Bud Ripplemeyer, the Lutheran blue-eyed blonde, much-older lover of this undocumented Jasmine, in the novel. When I had finished what I thought was my final draft, the final scene had Jasmine just go off with her Columbia University professor/love from another phase of her life, and an adopted Vietnamese orphan boy, with Jasmine pregnant with Bud's child. Then I thought, Oh, poor Bud in his wheelchair.

I then realized that there was a character hanging in the background, Bud's ex-wife, so I made sure that she didn't go off and get remarried. In *The Tree Bride,* I discuss the violence of gangs that want to destroy the economy—there's a reference to "the villains," the suspected villain, the firebomber, being part of a named gang, a real gang. I knew I liked Bish Chatterjee, the husband, and I could see that Tara toward the end of *Desirable Daughters* was saying, "Maybe I misjudged him; maybe he wasn't such a patriarch after all, such a controlling husband after all." So I needed that metaphor for people having gone through extreme trauma that brings them together and makes them reassess their relationships.

Source: Angela Elam, "The True Heirs: An Interview with Bharati Mukherjee," in *Conversations with Bharati Mukherjee,* edited by Bradley C. Edwards, University Press of Mississippi, 2009, pp. 130–35.

Fakrul Alam

In the following excerpt, Alam explains that Mukherjee wants to be seen as an American writer rather than pigeonholed as an Asian American writer.

...Mukherjee's work thus makes her a writer of the Indian diaspora and links her to novelists who are as different from each other as Naipaul or Rushdie or, for that matter, Markandaya. But as an Indian writer who has settled first in Canada and then the United States, Mukherjee can be categorized somewhat more specifically as an Indian-American writer. This is how Craig Tapping locates her in his thoughtful essay "South Asia/North America: New Dwellings

BUT IF LITERARY AMERICA HAS BEEN, ON THE WHOLE, GENEROUS IN WELCOMING MUKHERJEE TO ITS MIDST, IT IS NECESSARY TO NOTE THAT MUKHERJEE'S WORK HAS, ON OCCASIONS, BEEN CRITICIZED AND HER PERSPECTIVE ON IMMIGRATION TO AMERICA HAS EVEN BEEN DENOUNCED, ESPECIALLY BY SOME INDIAN CRITICS."

and the Past." Tapping associates Mukherjee with writers such as Ved Mehta, Rohinton Mistry, Suniti Namjoshi, Michael Ondaatje, Vikram Seth, and Sara Suleri, for, like her, they have distinguished themselves by their work in North America and have tried to "construct alternative identities and communities" in their adopted countries. Comparing Mukherjee to the Sri Lankan-Canadian Michael Ondaatje, Tapping notes how "exuberantly polyphonic" their works can become as they use their diasporic, postcolonial backgrounds in North America. What Tapping deduces about Sara Suleri from *Meatless Days* (1989)—that she can never cut herself off in her writing from the country of her birth, Pakistan, despite her decision to sever her ties to it and become an American—applies in some measure to Mukherjee. Mukherjee, too, cannot but bring India into her works, even though she has announced her intention to loosen her ties to it as far back as *Days and Nights in Calcutta*.

Mukherjee is thus one of a handful of writers who represent the emerging tradition of Indo-American writing. But she can also be placed in the much broader and older tradition of Asian-American literature. Certainly, by focusing attention in some of her *Middleman* stories on characters from the Philippines (Blanquita in "Fighting for the Rebound"), Afghanistan (Roshan of "Orbiting"), Iraq (Alfie Judah of "The Middleman"), and Vietnam (Eng of "Fathering"), and by connecting Jasmine's fate to her adopted Vietnamese son Du's at the end of the third novel, Mukherjee is making the point that she is representing all Asian immigrant lives in America in her fiction and not just South Asian ones. In this respect Mukherjee can be

affiliated with writers such as Maxine Hong Kingston and Amy Tan, who are inspired by the sagas of Asian immigrants and committed to the Asian-American woman's struggle for self-realization and her freedom from oppressive traditions. Like these writers, Mukherjee has produced fiction where her Asian heritage is tied to her American circumstance. Mukherjee's recent fiction resembles the work of Kingston in its self-consciousness, its movement away from realism, and its blend of myth, history, and personal experience. Shirley Geok-lin Lim's comments about Kingston in "Twelve Asian American Writers: In Search of Self-Definition" will also do for a novel such as *The Holder of the World*: "Kingston's works are largely self-referential, appealing not to external historical and sociological validations but to insights that come from the confrontations of invented, historical, and biographical selves."

In another essay, "Assaying the Gold; or, Contesting the Ground of Asian American Literature," Geok-lin Lim has noted how under the impact of theory and the gains made by feminism, cultural studies, and oppositional criticism in general, Asian-American writing has flowered in recent times. She notes, moreover, the impetus given to Asian-American writing by the massive increase in immigration to the United States from Asia since the revision of immigration laws in 1965. Writers such as Bharati Mukherjee, it is clear from the figures presented by Lim about the explosion of Asian immigration to America in the 1970s and the 1980s, have not only been able to draw their material from the increasingly visible Asian presence but have also gained in confidence because of it. While Lim insists that it is no longer possible to treat Asian-American culture as "a fairly homogenous system of values and common ideologies," her essay does allow us to see some of the ways in which Mukherjee's work resembles that of other Asian-American writers. For example, "the three stages of identity in relation to ethnicity" of Asian Americans that Lim deduces by analyzing the autobiography of the Filipino-American writer Carlos Bulosan's *America in the Heart* (1991)— "the pre-ethnic or Asian-national" stage, where the immigrant ruminates on his life in his native country; the "national ethnic identity" stage, where he affiliates himself with other immigrants from his country who have experienced racism in the New World; and the "post-ethnic" stage, where he identifies with a wider, transnational grouping of immigrants—are approximated in the three phases of Mukherjee's fiction (Lim, 152). As we have seen, Mukherjee began by writing about India as someone who had exiled herself from it, moved on to depict the Indian expatriate's vulnerability to racism and sense of alienation in North America, and finally made herself the spokesperson of all immigrants in America regardless of their nationality. That Mukherjee's work can be placed in a broader category linking her to the major practitioners of Asian-American writing is a point made by Lim elsewhere in this essay when she describes how "writers such as Kingston, [David] Hwang, Mukherjee, and [Cynthia] Kadohata have moved beyond the conventional dichotomous, binary constructions of white and Asian-national to a positioning of ethnic identity as interrogative, shifting, unstable, and heuristic" (Lim, 160).

It is important to keep in mind, however, that while Mukherjee has not hesitated to affiliate herself explicitly to writers of the Indian diaspora or implicitly to Asian-American writing, she has gone out of her way time and again in recent years to declare herself to be first and foremost an American writer and to denounce hyphenization. We recall the polemical Preface to *Darkness*, where she had identified herself as an "Ellis Island" writer; the Whitmanesque overtones of "Immigrant Writing: Give Us Your Maximalists!" ("I'm one of you now"); and her unequivocal assertion in "A Four-Hundred-Year-Old Woman" that "I am an American writer, in the American mainstream trying to extend it...not an Indian writer, not an exile, not an expatriate" but an "immigrant" whose "investment is in the American reality, not the Indian" ("Woman").

As this book has indicated, Mukherjee has striven to place her work in one tradition or another of American fiction ever since *Wife*, which resembles the writing of Nathanael West and Flannery O'Connor and could be described as South Asian-American Gothic; *Darkness*, of course, declared itself to be "immigrant" fiction pace Malamud and Henry Roth; the *Middleman* is a language experiment in that it depends on the idioms of America and so carries forward a tradition in American fiction inaugurated by Melville in *Moby-Dick*'s "Call me Ishmael"; *Jasmine* ends as does *Huck Finn*, with the protagonist lighting out, so to speak, for the territory

ahead; and *The Holder of the World* places itself brazenly with *The Scarlet Letter* and the tradition of American romance.

Not content with clearing a space for herself in American letters that will bring her recognition as an "American writer, in the American mainstream, trying to extend it" ("Woman"), Mukherjee seems at times to have ambitions to redirect the flow of contemporary American fiction. She has been open about her dissatisfaction with such recent trends as minimalism and appeared to have her own future achievement in mind when, in a panel discussion on American fiction in 1981, she praised Ruth Prawer Jhabvala for "making for herself a place in American literature and subverting the very notion of what the American novel is and of what American culture is." She has explained that her quarrel with the work of Raymond Carver or Ann Beattie stems from their decision to abandon "an oceanic or social view" and their intent to concentrate on "fiction about personal relationships" or on "small disappointments" (1990 interview, 29). What she and other hybrid, postcolonial writers were bringing to American fiction, on the other hand, was "a social and political vision [which] is an integral part of writing a novel, of being a novelist" (1990 interview, 29).

To their credit, North American writers have welcomed Mukherjee to their fold and have acknowledged her claim to a place in the mainstream of American fiction. Even Canada, which she left in anger and which she has displayed as a hostile and cold country, has shown its appreciation of her work by shortlisting *Wife* for a major award and by giving her a prize for her bitter attack on Canadian immigration policies in "An Invisible Woman." And though *Darkness* did not find a publisher in the United States and had to be first printed in Canada, it was heralded in the *New York Times Book Review*. *The Middleman*, of course, received the National Book Critics Circle Award, and *Jasmine* was chosen as one of the best books of 1989 by the *New York Times Book Review*. When *The Holder of the World* appeared, K. Anthony Appiah supported its claim to kinship with *The Scarlet Letter* by observing that the novel had earned its connection to that great work and that "Nathaniel Hawthorne *is* a relative of hers, and, like Hannah Easton, she [Mukherjee] has every right to claim her kinship across the centuries" (Appiah, 7).

But if literary America has been, on the whole, generous in welcoming Mukherjee to its midst, it is necessary to note that Mukherjee's work has, on occasions, been criticized and her perspective on immigration to America has even been denounced, especially by some Indian critics. In an essay published in *Bharati Mukherjee: Critical Perspectives*, for instance, Alpana Sharma Knippling has questioned Mukherjee's project to radicalize American fiction by bringing to it the story of people who have been hitherto unrepresented in it. As far as Knippling is concerned, Mukherjee's professed elitism—she has herself proclaimed her "top family, top caste, top city" ("Maximalists") status in Indian—very nearly disqualifies her from representing the ordinary South Asian's immigrant experience in North America. In Knippling's view, the manner in which Mukherjee elides the difficulty of the process through which a Punjabi peasant girl like Jasmine becomes the confident "self-willing subject of the West" is indicative of the facile nature of Mukherjee's bid to represent the Other (Knippling, 150). Moreover, Knippling finds in Mukherjee's fiction a tendency to gloss over the cultural specifics of different ethnic groups and a readiness to equate the experience of a Punjabi peasant girl such as Jasmine with her adopted Vietnamese son, Du, or the Trinidadian Jasmine of the *Middleman* story. As Knippling puts it, "To thus homogenize the other (Jasmine = Du; Trinidad Jasmine = Indian Jasmine) is to discount heterogeneity as a viable condition of ethnic minorities in the United States" (Knippling, 154)....

Source: Fakrul Alam, "Conclusion," in *Bharati Mukherjee*, Twayne Publishers, 1996, pp. 141–45.

SOURCES

Abrams, M. H., "Symbol," in *A Glossary of Literary Terms,* seventh edition, Cornell University Press, 1999, p. 311.

Agarwal, Ramlal, Review of *Desirable Daughters*, in *World Literature Today*, Vol. 77, Nos. 3–4, October–December 2003, pp. 86–87.

Alam, Fakrul, *Bharati Mukherjee*, Twayne Publishers, 1996, pp. 1, 147.

"Bharati Mukherjee," in *Encyclopædia Britannica*, http://www.britannica.com/biography/Bharati-Mukherjee (accessed on May 1, 2016).

Desai, Kishwar, "Miss Old India," in *India Today*, May 6, 2011, http://indiatoday.intoday.in/story/kishwar-desai-reviews-bharati-mukherjee-book-title-miss-new-india/1/137300.html (accessed April 28, 2016).

"Dharma," in *Encyclopædia Britannica*, http://www.britannica.com/topic/dharma-religious-concept (accessed on April 28, 2016).

French, Patrick, *India: A Portrait*, Random House, 2011, p. 7.

Harmon, William, "Magic Realism," in *A Handbook to Literature*, ninth edition, Prentice Hall, 2003, p. 297.

"Indian Independence: World War II," British Library, http://www.bl.uk/reshelp/findhelpregion/asia/india/indianindependence/ww2/ (accessed on April 29, 2016).

Landow, George P., "The British East India Company: The Company That Owned a Nation (or Two)," in *Victorian Web*, http://www.victorianweb.org/history/empire/india/eic.html (accessed on April 29, 2016).

Miller, Katherine, "Mobility and Identity Construction in Bharati Mukherjee's *Desirable Daughters*: 'The Tree Wife and Her Rootless Namesake'," in *Studies in Canadian Literature—Études en Litterature Canadienne*, Vol. 29, No. 1, 2004, pp. 63–73.

Mukherjee, Bharati, *The Tree Bride*, Hyperion, 2004.

"Oh, Calcutta!," in *Bharati Mukherjee's Fiction: A Perspective*, Sushma Tandon, Sarup & Sons, 2004, pp. 40–41; originally published in *Times Literary Supplement*, June 29, 1973, p. 736.

Oonk, Gijsbert, "Global Indian Diasporas: Exploring Trajectories of Migration and Theory," in *Global Indian Diasporas: Exploring Trajectories of Migration and Theory*, edited by Gijsbert Oonk, Amsterdam University Press, 2007, p. 11.

Pande, Amba, "The Role of Indian Diaspora in the Development of the Indian IT Industry," in *Diaspora Studies*, Vol. 7, No. 2, 2014, pp. 121–29.

Parameswaran, Uma, Review of *Jasmine*, in *World Literature Today*, Vol. 64, No. 4, 1990, p. 698.

Pokhriyal, Chetana, "The Theme of 'Alienation' and 'Assimilation' in the Novels of Bharati Mukherjee: A Socio-Literary Perspective," http://www.inter-disciplinary.net/wp-content/uploads/2009/08/chetanapaper.pdf (accessed on May 1, 2016).

Review of *Desirable Daughters*, in *Publishers Weekly*, March, 25, 2002, http://www.publishersweekly.com/978-0-7868-6598-7 (accessed May 1, 2016).

Scheeren, Jyna, Review of *The Tree Bride*, in *Library Journal*, August 2004, p. 69.

Soderberg, Erin, "Bharati Mukherjee," in *Voices from the Gaps*, http://voices.cla.umn.edu/artistpages/mukherjee_bharati.php (accessed May 1, 2016).

FURTHER READING

Dascalu, Cristina Emanuela, *Imaginary Homelands of Writers in Exile: Salman Rushdie, Bharati Mukherjee, and V. S. Naipaul*, Cambria Press, 2007.

> The three authors Dascalu examines in this text are exiles from their place of birth. The critic identifies ideas of diaspora, migration, and exile in Mukherjee and compares them with those of her literary contemporaries.

Edwards, Bradley C., ed., *Conversations with Bharati Mukherjee*, University Press of Mississippi, 2009.

> This collection of interviews spans decades and includes translated interviews from India. The volume provides valuable insight into the author's life and work.

Henderson, Carol, *Culture and Customs of India*, Greenwood, 2002.

> This textbook gives a basic overview of India's history and cultures. Henderson's work offers helpful information about the different customs for anyone who has a desire to learn more about India.

Wilson, Jon, *The Chaos of Empire: The British Raj and the Conquest of India*, PublicAffairs, 2016.

> Wilson focuses on the history of the East India Company in India and its effects on the nation.

He examines the history from the perspectives of British and Indian individuals.

Zoon, Atia Anwer, *Bharati Mukherjee's Female Protagonists: A Search for Female Identity*, Lambert Academic Publishing, 2012.

> Like many critics, Zoon notes the influence of immigration and multiculturalism in Mukherjee's work. In this text, she concentrates on the effects of immigration on female characters.

SUGGESTED SEARCH TERMS

Bharati Mukherjee

Bharati Mukherjee AND biography

Bharati Mukherjee AND The Tree Bride

Bharati Mukherjee AND diaspora

immigrant literature

Bharati Mukherjee AND criticism

India AND British colonialism

Indian independence

East India Company

India and diaspora

The Woman in White

The Woman in White is a novel written by British author Wilkie Collins. The novel first appeared in forty weekly parts in *All the Year Round*, a literary magazine founded and edited by Charles Dickens, from November 1859 to August 1860. In the United States, it appeared concurrently in *Harper's Weekly*. The novel was first published in book form in a three-volume ("triple decker") edition in 1860. A one-volume edition appeared in 1861.

The Woman in White is generally regarded as the first "sensation" novel of the Victorian period. These were novels that rely heavily on some combination of melodrama, suspense, plot twists, insanity, tangled legal disputes, prostitution, coincidences, mistaken identity, and long-buried secrets, often involving bigamy, adultery, and the unacknowledged children that result. Victorian readers craved this kind of excitement, which *The Woman in White* provided while quickly becoming what today is called a "blockbuster." Readers eagerly awaited the next installment of the novel; when it was published in book form, long lines formed at the publisher, and it quickly sold out. Many people named their children Walter after the novel's hero, and Fosco, the novel's villain, became a popular name for pet cats. Men swooned over Marian Halcombe, the novel's heroine, while others placed wagers on the nature of the devastating secret that would be revealed at the end. *The Woman in White* also sparked a merchandising craze, with

WILKIE COLLINS

1859

1860

Wilkie Collins (©Time Life Pictures / Getty Images)

all manner of consumer goods—perfume, cloaks, bonnets—given "Woman in White" themes. Dickens, Collins's close friend, collaborator, and mentor, was delighted because the novel boosted the circulation of *All the Year Round*. *The Woman in White* launched a decade, the 1860s, during which Collins rivaled Dickens as England's most popular novelist.

AUTHOR BIOGRAPHY

William Wilkie Collins was born in London on January 8, 1824, to William Collins, a somewhat prominent artist with the Royal Academy, and Helen Geddes. After concluding his formal education in 1840, he was apprenticed to a tea merchant, but he had no interest in commerce, so he tried law as a career. He was admitted as a student at Lincoln's Inn in 1846 and was called to the bar in 1851. The law did not suit him (although legal matters figure prominently in his fiction), so after the death of his father in

1847, he tried his hand as a painter and actually exhibited a painting at the Royal Academy's summer exhibition in 1849. Although he had written fiction prior to this, his efforts failed to find a publisher. His first publication, in 1848, was a memoir of his father. In 1850 his first published novel, *Antonina*, appeared, and at this point it was clear that Collins was determined to be a writer.

A major event in Collins's life was his introduction to Charles Dickens in 1851, when the two took part in an amateur theater production. In the years that followed, until Dickens's death in 1870, the two remained friends, and Dickens acted as a mentor to the younger writer. They collaborated on stage plays, among them *The Frozen Deep*, and Collins published his first short stories in Dickens's periodical, *Household Words*. Novels during this period include *Basil* (1852), a lurid melodrama; *Hide and Seek* (1854), which critics regard as his first mature work; *A Rogue's Life* (1856, the same year he joined the staff of *Household Words*); and *The Dead Secret* (1857), which incorporated some of the "sensation" elements that would figure prominently in *The Woman in White*. Serialization of that novel began in 1859 in the successor magazine to *Household Words*, *All the Year Round*. Meanwhile, he began taking laudanum, an opiate, to relieve the pain from various disorders (possibly gout or neuralgia), and in his later years he struggled with addiction to the drug.

Collins's domestic life was highly unconventional, especially by Victorian standards. In 1859 he began living with a widow, Mrs. Caroline Graves, and her daughter, Harriet, whom he treated as his own. He reputedly met Caroline under circumstances similar to those in which Walter Hartright meets Anne Catherick in *The Woman in White*, although this is uncertain. Except for a two-year period after Caroline married another man in 1868, he lived with her for the rest of his life. Further complicating his domestic life was his liaison with Martha Rudd, whom he met in 1868. Collins installed Martha in a home near his in London, and she would bear him three children. During the time that he spent with Martha, he adopted the name William Dawson, with Martha referring to herself as Mrs. Dawson.

During the 1860s and beyond, Collins continued to write and publish prolifically. *No Name* appeared in 1862 and *Armadale* in 1864.

In 1868 he published *The Moonstone*, generally regarded as his other major work and the novel that is often thought of as the first modern detective story. In 1870 Collins produced a stage version of *The Woman in White*. Later novels include *Man and Wife* (1870), *Poor Miss Finch* (1872), *The Law and the Lady* (1875), and others. Critics agree that much of Collins's later work fails to live up to the high standards he set in *The Woman in White* and *The Moonstone*. Much of this later work is disguised commentary on social issues, particularly the treatment of women and legal issues surrounding marriage and the property rights of women.

In his final years, Collins was losing his eyesight and finding it difficult to write. He spent much of his time mentoring younger writers and helping other writers protect their publication rights. He died in London on September 23, 1889, of a stroke.

PLOT SUMMARY

The Woman in White is divided into three "Epochs," each corresponding to one of the novel's three volumes in book form. It is further divided into sections, each narrated by a different participant in the novel's events. Some of the sections are quite brief, but those of any appreciable length are divided into numbered chapters. Marian Halcombe's diary entries are identified by date. The use of quotation marks around Laura's name indicates that the person in question was not Laura but Anne Catherick.

First Epoch

THE STORY BEGUN BY WALTER HARTRIGHT, OF CLEMENT'S INN, TEACHER OF DRAWING

Walter Hartright is a young drawing master who lives in London. So, too, do his mother and his sole surviving sister, Sarah. One evening in July he visits his mother at her cottage, where he finds that Professor Pesca, an Italian refugee, is also paying a visit. Pesca feels himself under obligation to Walter, for the latter once saved his life. As a form of repayment, Pesca has recommended Walter for a job as a drawing master to two young women living with their uncle at Limmeridge House in Cumberland. As Walter is returning to his rooms, he encounters a mysterious woman who is dressed entirely in white. The woman seems to be fleeing, but the source of

her fears is unclear. Walter comes to her aid, but before he places her in a cab, he learns that she has a past association with Limmeridge House. As Walter continues on his way home, he encounters two men who are searching for the woman in white. He learns from them that she has escaped from a lunatic asylum.

Walter travels to Cumberland, where he will remain for several months as a drawing teacher for Laura Fairlie, a gentle, innocent young woman, and her older half-sister, Marian Halcombe, whose widowed mother married Philip Fairlie and later gave birth to Laura. Both parents have died, so the two women live with their selfish, fretful uncle, Frederick Fairlie, and Mrs. Vesey, an elderly woman who used to be Laura's governess. Walter ultimately learns that the woman in white is Anne Catherick, who, roughly a decade earlier, attended school in the village of Limmeridge under the care of Mrs. Fairlie. She remained deeply grateful to Mrs. Fairlie for her kindness, and to honor her memory, she agreed to always dress in white. Further, Walter sees that Laura bears a marked similarity in appearance to the woman in white.

As the weeks go by, Walter falls in love with Laura and she with him, but their widely different social status renders them unable to express their love or act on it. Further, he learns that some two years earlier Laura promised her beloved father that she would marry Sir Percival Glyde, to whom she is engaged. Walter, heartbroken, resolves to leave Limmeridge. Before he does, however, an anonymous letter arrives denouncing Sir Percival as a monster. Walter and Marian set about investigating the source of the letter, which partially confirms Marian's apprehensions about her sister and the impending marriage. Walter's investigation takes him to a local churchyard, where he comes across the woman in white visiting the grave of Mrs. Fairlie. She confirms to him that she escaped from an asylum; she also informs him that she never knew her father. The woman in white, Anne Catherick, wrote the anonymous letter, for she loves Laura for Mrs. Fairlie's sake and wants to protect her from Sir Percival; Walter is convinced that Sir Percival was responsible for having Anne committed to the asylum, but his motives are unclear.

Vincent Gilmore, the family lawyer, arrives at Limmeridge House. His purpose is to arrange the marriage settlements. He thinks highly of Sir

MEDIA ADAPTATIONS

- A film version of *The Woman in White* was released by Warner Brothers in 1948 and is available on DVD. The film was directed by Peter Godfrey and starred Alexis Smith, Eleanor Parker, and Sydney Greenstreet. Running time is one hour and forty-nine minutes.

- In 1971 German television produced the novel as *Die Frau in Weiß*. The novel was adapted by Herber Asmodi. The series was directed by Wilhelm Semmelroth and starred Christoph Bantzer as Walter Hartright and Heidelinde Weis as both Laura Fairlie and Anne Catherick. Running time is four hours and twenty minutes.

- BBC aired a miniseries of *The Woman in White* in 1982. The novel was adapted by Ray Jenkins, and the series starred Daniel Gerroll as Walter Hartright, Diana Quick as Marian Halcombe, and Jenny Seagrove as Laura. The production consists of five episodes of fifty-five minutes each.

- In 1982 the Soviet Union released a film version of the novel under the title *Zhenshchina v belom*. The film was directed by Vadim Derbenyov and starred Aleksandr Abdulov as Walter Hartright and Grazina Baikstyte as both Laura Fairlie and Anne Catherick. Running time is two hours and twenty-eight minutes.

- BBC aired a loose adaptation of the novel in 1997. The novel was adapted by David Pirie and starred Andrew Lincoln as Walter Hartright, Justine Waddell as Laura Fairlie, and Tara FitzGerald as Marian Halcombe; the production was aired on PBS television the following year. Running time is two hours and five minutes.

- *The Woman in White* has frequently been dramatized; a stage script written by Adrian Flynn was published by Nelson Thornes in 1999.

- In 2004, Andrew Lloyd Webber staged a musical adaptation of *The Woman in White* in London's West End. In 2005 the musical opened on Broadway. The musical was noteworthy for its use of projections rather than traditional physical sets. A cast recording was released by EMI records in 2005 and is available on audio CD or as an MP3 download. Running time is two hours and twenty-four minutes.

- Freeze Tag Games released a video game titled "Victorian Mysteries: Woman in White" in 2010. It can be downloaded at http://itunes.apple.com/us/app/victorian-mysteries-woman/id520775702?mt=8.

Percival, who is expected to arrive in a few days to arrange with Laura a date for their wedding. Walter takes his departure from Laura.

THE STORY CONTINUED BY VINCENT GILMORE, OF CHANCERY LANE, SOLICITOR

Gilmore arrived at Limmeridge House on a Friday in November. Monday marks the arrival of Sir Percival, who has seen a copy of the anonymous letter. In conversation with Gilmore and Marian, he gives his version of events surrounding the commitment of Anne Catherick to the asylum, claiming that Anne suffered from a mental affliction and that he had her committed with the approval of her mother, Jane Anne Catherick. Marian agrees to write and post a note to Mrs. Catherick, who is known to Percival purportedly because of past services to him and his family, asking her to confirm Percival's statement. In her terse and formal reply, Mrs. Catherick confirms Percival's account, but Marian still has misgivings, and Percival claims that he is willing to release Laura from the engagement if she desires him to do so.

Gilmore takes up the issue of the marriage settlements, in particular, the question of what happens to Laura's property when she comes of age. She has a life interest in real property, and on the death of her uncle she would have £3,000 from the estate, which Percival would continue to get if she were to predecease him. A further sum of money would go to her aunt, Eleanor, on her death. The chief question, however, is what would happen to the £20,000 she owns outright, an inheritance from her father. Gilmore wants that money to pass to Laura's children on her death; if there are no children, to others she would name, including Marian. In other words, his position is that the money should belong entirely to her. Percival, through his attorney, Mr. Merriman, wants the money to pass to him on her death. To the extreme annoyance and dismay of Gilmore, Laura's uncle washes his hands of the matter and will not support Gilmore's position, forcing Gilmore to draw up a settlement that he finds dangerous and untenable. Meanwhile, Gilmore bumps into Walter, who informs him that he hopes to find a change of scene in a distant country.

THE STORY CONTINUED BY MARIAN HALCOMBE, IN EXTRACTS FROM HER DIARY

The diary entries commence on November 8, 1849. Percival has continued his stay at Limmeridge House. Laura, in love with Walter, would like to end her engagement, but because she promised her father that she would marry him, she will consent to the marriage if that is Percival's wish. In a conversation with him, attended by Marian, she states that she will marry him but that she will never be able to give him her love. She further states that if Percival breaks off the engagement, she will remain unmarried. Percival claims that her noble offer makes him love her more and declines her offer to end the engagement.

Marian is troubled on two counts. One is that Laura seems languid and depressed. The other is that she remains suspicious of Percival and is frustrated that he continues to get his way. Further, she is worried about Walter, whom she has helped secure a position in an expedition to Honduras. In letters, Walter tells her of his suspicion that he is being followed and watched. Finally, the marriage is fixed for December 22, and Marian is saddened to learn that Percival plans a lengthy wedding tour (that is, honeymoon) in Rome. Marian learns that in Rome, Laura will be introduced to Percival's intimate friend, Count Fosco. His wife, Madame Fosco,

is Laura's aunt Eleanor, who has been estranged from the family since her brother, Philip Fairlie, cut her out of his will because he disapproved of her marriage. She also learns that Percival agrees that Marian should continue to live with her sister after the marriage.

Second Epoch

THE STORY CONTINUED BY MARIAN HALCOMBE

While Laura and Percival are on their wedding trip in Italy, Marian takes up residence at Blackwater Park, Percival's home in Hampshire. Mr. Gilmore has fallen ill and will no longer be tending to the legal affairs of the Fairlies. Reading between the lines of Laura's letters, Marian is convinced that she is unhappy in her married life. Mrs. Catherick, who lives at Welmingham, has been seen lurking about the neighborhood. The Glydes return from their wedding trip, and Marian is confirmed in her belief that Laura is unhappy. Percival learns that a stranger has been inquiring about him during his absence and later learns about the appearance of Mrs. Catherick. Marian meets Count Fosco and Madame Fosco (Eleanor) for the first time, describing the count, whom she vaguely distrusts, as immensely fat but having a magnetic and forceful personality. His wife is entirely under his control. Merriman, Percival's attorney, arrives, and it becomes clear that Percival is involved in some sort of legal or financial difficulty. Percival tries to force Laura to sign a document without allowing her to read it. Percival discovers that the man Laura loves is Walter Hartright. William Kyrle, Gilmore's partner, advises Laura by letter not to sign anything without reading it.

One evening, Laura and Marian are followed through the grounds of the park. Laura later encounters Anne Catherick and learns that it was she who followed them. She says that she has to make atonement to Laura for allowing the latter's marriage to proceed, and she indicates that she is privy to a secret surrounding Sir Percival. Later, Percival peremptorily dismisses Laura's maid, Fanny. Anne Catherick gets a note to Laura, but Percival finds it and is convinced that his wife, as well as Anne, knows his secret, and he is determined to get her to confess as much. Through Fanny, now staying in the nearby village, Marian manages to get letters out, one to the lawyer Kyrle, the other to Frederick Fairlie. Marian eavesdrops on a conversation between Percival and Fosco, learning that both are in dire need of money. Percival, jealous of Walter, had him followed after he left Cumberland. Marian falls ill, and Fosco reads her journal.

THE STORY CONTINUED BY FREDERICK FAIRLIE, ESQ., OF LIMMERIDGE HOUSE

Fanny delivers her letter from Marian to Fairlie, who is immensely annoyed at having to take any trouble in the matter. It appears that Fanny had been drugged by the countess, who then read the letters that Fanny had hidden on her person and replaced the letter to Kyrle with a blank sheet of paper. Marian's letter urges Fairlie to open his home to Laura. Fosco arrives at Limmeridge House and informs Fairlie that Marian is ill. He, too, urges Fairlie to take Laura in, but his motives for doing so are unclear.

THE STORY CONTINUED BY ELIZA MICHELSON, HOUSEKEEPER AT BLACKWATER PARK

Eliza is initially placed in charge of caring for Marian, who is seriously ill, while Percival continues his search for Anne. Eliza, a pious woman, witnesses the conflicts between the doctor and Fosco over the best course of treatment for Marian and over the question of whether she has typhus. The countess brings from London Mrs. Rubelle, purportedly a trained nurse but a suspect character because she is a foreigner. Another doctor arrives from London and confirms a diagnosis of typhus. Percival, claiming the need for economy, instructs Eliza to dismiss most of the servants. He then sends her to Torquay in a fruitless effort to find a house to rent where Marian and Laura, whose health also appears to be failing, can recuperate. The count and countess depart for the home they have taken in a London neighborhood, claiming that they are taking Marian with them and thus leaving Blackwater Park nearly vacant except for Percival and Laura. Laura departs Blackwater Park for London, hoping to catch up with Marian. Mrs. Rubelle appears and reveals to Eliza that Marian has not gone to London but has been secreted in another wing of Blackwater Park.

THE STORY CONTINUED IN SEVERAL NARRATIVES

1. THE NARRATIVE OF HESTER PINHORN, COOK IN THE SERVICE OF COUNT FOSCO

The Foscos have taken up residence in St. John's Wood, a London neighborhood. Hester is their cook. She is present at the apparent death of "Laura" after the latter suffers an aneurysm.

2. THE NARRATIVE OF THE DOCTOR

The doctor, Alfred Goodricke, attests to the death of "Laura" at the home of the Foscos.

3. THE NARRATIVE OF JANE GOULD

Jane is called in to prepare "Laura's" body for burial.

4. THE NARRATIVE OF THE TOMBSTONE

The inscription on "Laura's" tombstone is reproduced, with, of course, the date of her death.

5. THE NARRATIVE OF WALTER HARTRIGHT

Walter has returned from Central America. He visits the cemetery in Cumberland, and as he is reading the inscription on the tombstone, two women appear. He looks up to discover Marian and Laura standing before him.

Third Epoch

THE STORY CONTINUED BY WALTER HARTRIGHT

Walter, Marian, and Laura live in poverty in London under assumed names; the pretense is that the women are Walter's sisters. Walter's connections all believe that Laura is dead and that Walter is being duped by Anne Catherick. The narrative then backtracks and takes up events as they affected Marian from the time Eliza Michelson and Marian arrive in London. Marian investigates Fosco, Percival, and Mrs. Rubelle. She visits the asylum that had housed the "woman in white" and discovers that Laura has been held there under the name of Anne Catherick. She conspires with a nurse to effect Laura's escape. The narrative then takes up events as they affected Laura and her commitment to the asylum. Marian accompanies Laura to Limmeridge House, where Frederick refuses to recognize Laura.

Walter begins an investigation that, he hopes, will establish Laura's identity. He gathers the documents that have already been presented and elicits statements from, for example, Hester Pinhorn. He visits the lawyer, William Kyrle, who tells him that he has no case. In their discussion, it is made clear that the key piece of evidence that would support Walter's position has to do with dates and the discrepancy between the date of the doctor's death certificate and the date of Laura's journey to London. When he leaves the lawyer's office, Walter is followed. He arrives home to discover that Marian has received a vaguely threatening letter from

Fosco, urging her to leave matters alone. Walter concludes that the only way to unravel the mystery is to determine the nature of the secret surrounding Percival that was hinted at by Anne. He travels to Blackwater Park in an effort to find information. Once again, he is followed. He meets with Mrs. Clements, Anne Catherick's friend and companion, who tells him that Count Fosco, with the help of the countess, essentially kidnapped Anne. Thus, Laura was committed to the asylum, while Anne was taken to the count's house to die as "Lady Glyde," allowing Percival to inherit her money.

Walter is determined to discover Percival's secret. To that end, he visits Mrs. Catherick, who finally tells him to go to the church in Welmingham and examine the marriage records held there. Walter goes to the church, where, with the help of a clerk and a local attorney who kept a duplicate registry, he learns that the entry recording the marriage of Percival's parents is a forgery. His parents never legally married, so therefore Percival is not a baronet and is not the rightful owner of Blackwater Park. Knowing that he is in danger of exposure (and possibly imprisonment or even hanging for forgery), he goes to the church and tries to destroy the page with the forgery. In the process, he accidentally sets fire to the church vestry and dies while trapped inside, despite the efforts of Walter to save him. An inquest is held, and Percival's death is ruled an accident.

THE STORY CONTINUED BY MRS. CATHERICK

Mrs. Catherick sends Walter a letter in which she explains the physical resemblance of Laura and Anne: They are half-sisters, sharing the same father. Percival used the physical resemblance of the women to switch them and pass off Anne's death as Laura's. Mrs. Catherick also tells Walter that, in exchange for expensive gifts, she colluded with Percival to forge the marriage registry in the church. Thus, she knew Percival's secret, and Percival was convinced that Anne, too, must have known his secret. Percival had her committed to the asylum because of some chance words she uttered to him, suggesting that she knew his secret; in fact, she knew only that there was a secret but did not know the details of it.

THE STORY CONTINUED BY WALTER HARTRIGHT

Walter returns to London, where he tells Marian the entire story. They tell Laura about her husband's death, and several months later, Laura and Walter marry. They return to Limmeridge House, where Walter explains to Laura what has happened. Walter concludes that Fosco is indeed a foreign spy and is determined to hold him responsible for his role in the conspiracy. For help, he enlists the aid of Professor Pesca. Walter learns that Fosco is planning to attend the performance of an opera. Wanting to keep tabs on Fosco, he attends the opera himself, taking Pesca with him. At one point, Fosco recognizes Pesca, blanches with fear, and hastily leaves. Later, Pesca reluctantly and fearfully confesses to Walter that he is a member of the revolutionary Italian Brotherhood that never hesitates to assassinate members who are disloyal to it.

THE COUNT'S NARRATIVE

Count Fosco's narrative confirms that he is a spy and that Mrs. Rubelle is in league with him. It further elucidates his role at every step in the conspiracy and clarifies the issue of critical dates, noting that Laura did not arrive in London until after the date on Anne Catherick's death certificate. He provides Walter with a note from Percival confirming the date on which Laura left for London.

THE STORY CONCLUDED BY WALTER HARTRIGHT

With Percival's note, a memorandum from the owner of the livery stable from which Fosco ordered a carriage to pick up Laura from the train station on the key date, and Fosco's statement, Walter now has legal proof of Laura's identity. Accompanied by the lawyer Kyrle, Walter returns to Limmeridge with Marian and Laura, where he forces Frederick Fairlie to recognize Laura as his niece and presents all of his evidence that Laura is living to the people who attended "Laura's" interment in the cemetery.

Walter travels to Paris on a project related to his work as an illustrator. While there he learns that Fosco betrayed the cause of the Italian Brotherhood and had a price on his head. Before Fosco can flee Paris, he is assassinated, which Walter confirms by seeing the body at the morgue.

Walter and Laura have a son. Walter returns to London from Ireland after another work-related trip to find that Laura and Marian have left for Limmeridge House and have summoned him to follow them. When he arrives, he discovers that Frederick Fairlie has died. The couple's son is now the heir of Limmeridge House.

CHARACTERS

Anne Catherick

Anne is the mysterious "woman in white." She is the illegitimate daughter of Laura's father. She wears white to fulfill a promise to do so that she made to Laura's mother, whom she loved and who cared for her. She dies at Fosco's London home and is buried as "Laura."

Jane Anne Catherick

Jane is Anne Catherick's mother. A viciously unlikable woman whose greed and vanity were fed by Sir Percival, she conspired with him in having her daughter, Anne, committed to an asylum to preserve the secret surrounding Percival's identity and to continue receiving financial support from Percival.

Mrs. Clements

Mrs. Clements (referred to as "Lizzie" by her husband) is Anne Catherick's friend and companion.

Frederick Fairlie

Frederick is Laura's uncle and the current owner of Limmeridge House, their home in Cumberland. He is a selfish, egocentric hypochondriac who hides behind a persona of mock politeness. He does not want to be troubled by anything and initially refuses to recognize Laura as living when Walter returns to Limmeridge House with her.

Laura Fairlie

Laura is a young, beautiful, innocent, and gentle heiress who falls in love with Walter Hartright but feels obligated to honor her promise to her father to marry Sir Percival Glyde; after the marriage she is often referred to as Lady Glyde. She appears to have died and been buried, but in fact she lived to marry Walter Hartright and inherit the estate after the death of her uncle Frederick.

Fanny

Fanny is Laura's maid. She is peremptorily dismissed by Sir Percival but serves as a conduit that allows Marian to get letters out of Blackwater Park.

Count Fosco

Isidor Ottavio Baldassare Fosco, an Italian count with a shadowy past, is Sir Percival's closest friend. He is obese and given to playing with his pet mice and birds. He is polite and sophisticated, but at the same time vaguely threatening. He has great admiration for Marian. He reveals the truth about the conspiracy surrounding Anne and Laura after Walter threatens to betray him to the Italian Brotherhood, which he had betrayed during Italy's quest for independence.

Countess Fosco

The countess is Laura's aunt Eleanor. Formerly frivolous and flighty, she is now quiet and subservient to her husband, the count. She stands to inherit money from Laura should the latter predecease her, thus providing her husband with financial gain on Laura's death.

Vincent Gilmore

Gilmore is the Fairlie family lawyer. He initially admires Sir Percival but comes to distrust him. He is later incapacitated, and his duties are taken over by his partner, William Kyrle.

Sir Percival Glyde

Percival, whose home is Blackwater Park, is Laura's fiancé, then husband. He can seem charming and polite, but in reality he is cunning, brutal, and mean. He tries to wrest control of Laura's money from her, and to that end he conspires with Count Fosco to pass Anne's death off as the death of Laura. He conspired with Anne Catherick's mother to have young Anne committed to an asylum because he believed that Anne knew his secret. The reader ultimately learns that the secret referred to throughout the novel is that his parents never married, meaning that he could not inherit the title of baronet or the estate. He forged a record of his parents' nonexistent marriage in a church registry, and he dies trying to destroy that record.

Alfred Goodricke

Alfred is the doctor who attends "Laura" at the time of her death, not knowing that his patient is in reality Anne Catherick.

Jane Gould

Jane Gould is called in to care for the remains of "Laura" at the Fosco home in London.

Marian Halcombe

Marian is Laura Fairlie's half-sister, the daughter of Laura's mother by a previous marriage. She is firm, steady, intelligent, and resourceful but not beautiful. She functions as Laura's companion and chaperone, as well as Walter's confidante and adviser.

Sarah Hartright

Sarah is Walter Hartright's sole surviving sister.

Walter Hartright

Walter is a young drawing teacher who has a mysterious encounter with a "woman in white" in London. He takes a job as a teacher in the home of Marian Halcombe and Laura Fairlie. He falls in love with Laura, but her engagement to Sir Percival Glyde leaves her unavailable. Brokenhearted, he leaves the country on an expedition to Honduras. After he returns, he doggedly investigates the conspiracy surrounding the fate of the woman in white and the efforts of Percival and Fosco to gain control of Laura's fortune. Ultimately, he uncovers the secret surrounding Sir Percival. He restores Laura's identity and marries her.

William Kyrle

Kyrle is Vincent Gilmore's partner. He becomes Laura's legal adviser after Gilmore becomes incapacitated.

Mr. Merriman

Merriman is Sir Percival's attorney.

Eliza Michelson

Eliza is the housekeeper at Sir Percival's estate, Blackwater Park. Her chief role is to nurse Marian through her illness. She admires both Percival and Fosco and seems oblivious to their plots and intrigues.

Professor Pesca

Pesca is a teacher of Italian and Walter's friend. He feels obligated to Walter, who once saved his life, so in recompense, he recommends him to the Fairlie family as a drawing teacher. He turns out unexpectedly to be Fosco's antagonist, for he is a member of an Italian revolutionary organization that Fosco fears.

Hester Pinhorn

Hester is the cook employed by the Foscos at their London home. She is a witness to "Laura's" death.

Mrs. Rubelle

Mrs. Rubelle, a "foreigner," is brought from London to nurse Marian during her illness. Walter surmises that she is in league with Count Fosco, which Fosco later confirms.

Mrs. Vesey

Mrs. Vesey is an elderly, sedate woman who formerly was Laura's governess.

THEMES

Women in Literature

A key theme in *The Woman in White* is the position of women in mid-Victorian society. The novel's first sentence—"This is the story of what a Woman's patience can endure, and what a Man's resolution can achieve"—suggests that the role of men and women will figure prominently in the novel. In a sense, the asylum to which Anne Catherick, then Laura, is committed becomes a symbol of the absolute control that men had over women, and it becomes an institution from which women had to escape, in some cases like marriage itself. Marian is depicted as a woman who is resolute, determined, and resourceful, but she is also described as unattractive. Despite her willingness to take matters into her own hands—her success in liberating Laura from the asylum and her exertions in overhearing a crucial conversation between Percival and Fosco are perhaps the best examples—even she acknowledges the shackles that Victorian society places on her. As she looks forward to Laura's return to Limmeridge House after her wedding trip, she offers this somewhat ironic lament:

> The bare anticipation of seeing that dear face and hearing that well-known voice tomorrow, keeps me in a perpetual fever of excitement. If I only had the privileges of a man, I would order out Sir Percival's best horse instantly, and tear away on a night-gallop, eastward, to meet the rising sun—a long, hard, heavy, ceaseless gallop of hours and hours, like the famous highwayman's ride to York. Being, however, nothing but a woman, condemned to patience, propriety, and petticoats for life, I must respect the housekeeper's opinions, and try to compose myself in some feeble and feminine way.

TOPICS FOR FURTHER STUDY

- Diagram a family tree for the extended Fairlie family. Post the diagram on your social networking site (alternatively, make a hardcopy version of your diagram) and share it with your classmates.

- Create a time line or chronology for the events of *The Woman in White*, including events that happened before the time during which the action of the novel takes place. Post it on your social networking site or distribute it as a hard copy to your classmates. Invite them to make any adjustments to the time line based on their reading of the novel. Be prepared to answer questions about points in the novel where the chronology becomes crucial.

- With a willing classmate, write a script for the scene in which Walter first encounters the "woman in white" (or another scene from the novel that you find interesting and dramatic). Perform the scene for your classmates.

- Read Charlotte Bronte's novel *Jane Eyre* (1847), about a young woman who takes a position as a governess at mysterious Thornfield Hall, where she falls in love with her employer, Mr. Rochester. Write a report in which you examine one or more themes that the novel shares with *The Woman in White*.

- *We Were Liars*, by E. Lockhart, is a young-adult novel that, like *The Woman in White*, involves family drama, greed, mystery, secrets, and a young woman with psychological problems, particularly amnesia. Read the novel, then prepare an oral report in which you comment on themes it has in common with Collins's novel.

- *Wordsin the Dust* is a young-adult novel by Trent Reedy. Set in Afghanistan, it deals with issues surrounding the position of girls and young women, who have value only because of their marriage prospects. Set alongside *The Woman in White*, the two novels examine similar issues in differing social and cultural contexts. Write a review of the Reedy novel as you imagine Collins might have responded to it. Share your review with your classmates and invite them to comment.

- Imagine that you are Marian Halcombe—and that Twitter existed at the time. Send one or more tweets to your classmates or exchange tweets with a classmate as the events of the novel unfold—tweets that convey the anxiety and suspense surrounding the events.

The issue of the position of women and their subservience to men at the time arises in connection with Sir Percival's efforts to persuade Laura to sign a document that will give him control of her money. He folds the document in such a way that she cannot see what she would be signing, then reveals himself as the bully he is as Laura resists his entreaties:

> "I have no time to explain," he answered. "The dog-cart is at the door, and I must go directly. Besides, if I had time, you wouldn't understand. It is a purely formal document, full of legal technicalities, and all that sort of thing.

> Come! come! sign your name, and let us have done as soon as possible."

> "I ought surely to know what I am signing, Sir Percival, before I write my name?"

> "Nonsense! What have women to do with business? I tell you again, you can't understand it."

> "At any rate, let me try to understand it. Whenever Mr Gilmore had any business for me to do, he always explained it, first; and I always understood him."

> "I dare say he did. He was your servant, and was obliged to explain. I am your husband, and am *not* obliged."

Later in the dispute, Laura pleads for some measure of autonomy: "'I will sign with pleasure,' she said, 'if you will only treat me as a responsible being.'"

At one point, Madame Fosco makes a remark bearing on this theme. In a conversation about crime, Fosco asks his wife her opinion: "'I wait to be instructed,' replied the Countess, in tones of freezing reproof, intended for Laura and me, 'before I venture on giving my opinion in the presence of well-informed men.'" Marian then comments: "Do you, indeed?... I remember the time, Countess, when you advocated the Rights of Women, and freedom of female opinion was one of them." Perhaps the most trenchant expression of the view that women are inferior comes from Count Fosco, who says that women are "nothing but children grown up."

Legal System

Collins frequently made use of his legal training in his novels. Legal issues added a layer of complexity and mystery to many of his novels, including *The Woman in White*. One of the major legal issues involves Laura's property and the disposition of that property should she die. She has what was called a "life interest" in her uncle's estate, meaning that, after the death of her uncle, she could derive income from that estate during her lifetime but could not inherit the estate. Percival, as her husband, would continue to receive that income should Laura predecease him, but ultimately the estate would pass to a distant relative. Additionally, Laura has £20,000 that she inherited from her father—money that Percival, with the connivance of Count Fosco, wants to get his hands on to extricate himself from heavy debt. It has been pointed out, however, that under the common law legal doctrine of couverture (or coverture), man and wife became one person, and thus Percival would not have needed Laura's consent to gain control of her money. In his preface to the novel, Collins insisted that he submitted the question to a competent attorney and that his treatment of the matter was sound, although he did not provide a detailed explanation.

After Walter returns from Central America, he launches an investigation into the actions of Percival, Fosco, and others with a view to establishing Laura's identity. He speaks with the family attorney, William Kyrle, and after he summarizes events from his point of view—based in part on what he has learned from

Walter Hartright helps a mysterious woman in white, only to learn later that she has escaped from an asylum (©ShutterstockCaptblack76 | Shutterstock.com)

Laura and from Marian's diary—the attorney responds by telling Walter that he has no case. He imagines a legal hearing before a jury and in very methodical fashion deploys the arguments that an opposing attorney would use to "prove" that Laura is dead and buried in the Limmeridge churchyard. He concludes: "I ask you, if this case were to go now into a court of law—to go before a jury, bound to take facts as they reasonably appear—where are your proofs?" Much of the interest of the novel depends on the emergence of proofs resulting from Walter's investigation.

Legal concepts also play a role in the structure of the novel. In the short prefatory chapter at the beginning of the novel, Collins writes:

> As the Judge might once have heard it, so the Reader shall hear it now. No circumstance of importance, from the beginning to the end of the disclosure, shall be related on hearsay evidence.... Thus, the story here presented will be told by more than one pen, as the story of an offence against the laws is told in Court by

more than one witness—with the same object, in both cases, to present the truth always in its most direct and most intelligible aspect.

Thus, the pretense of the novel is that the various accounts given are documents that Walter Hartright has gathered from the participants and assembled into a kind of "closing argument."

STYLE

Point of View

Under normal circumstances, the author of a work of fiction will select a narrative point of view and sustain that point of view throughout the entire work. Thus, for example, J. D. Salinger, in his novel *The Catcher in the Rye*, tells the story from Holden Caulfield's first-person perspective. Other authors will adopt a third-person point of view, narrating the story from an omniscient perspective or from the perspective of a single character. *The Woman in White* differs from these modes by having the story told from multiple perspectives, with each of several characters taking a turn narrating events from his or her point of view so that each section forms a piece of the puzzle. In effect, the structure resembles the epistolary novels, or novels in letters, that were popular in the eighteenth century.

Thus, for example, the novel starts with a lengthy section narrated by Walter Hartright; Walter provides the foundation of the story by introducing the reader to the title character, the Fairlie family, Marian Halcombe, and other participants. He also exposes the first entanglements of the mystery of the story, and later he resumes the narration to describe his investigation of the intrigues of Percival and Fosco. After Walter leaves Limmeridge House, the narration is turned over to Gilmore, the family lawyer, who comments on Laura's legal position. His narration is followed by entries from the diary of Marian Halcombe. Later sections, some of them quite brief, include the narration of the housekeeper who nurses Marian through her illness, Count Fosco's cook, Count Fosco himself, and others. In this way, the novel in a sense turns into something akin to the presentation of a legal case, a notion that Collins himself suggests in the brief prologue at the beginning of the novel. Just as an attorney will call witnesses to the stand and question each about his or her role in the case

being tried, so *The Woman in White* requires the reader to function as a jury, not to pronounce guilt or innocence but to weave the various accounts into a coherent whole.

Foreshadowing

Foreshadowing is a literary device by which an author hints at events that will take place later, usually to arouse suspense. *The Woman in White* relies heavily on foreshadowing that raises questions about the future fate of the characters. This foreshadowing, and the suspense it creates, would have induced readers of the serialized version of the novel to continue to buy the magazine in which it appeared. Numerous examples could be cited. In the first section, narrated by Walter Hartright, Marian tells Walter, who has fallen in love with Laura, that Laura is engaged to be married to Sir Percival. As he reflects on the matter, he says:

> I could only feel that what had passed between Miss Halcombe and myself, on our way from the summer-house, had affected me very strangely. The foreboding of some undiscoverable danger lying hid from us all in the darkness of the future, was strong on me. The doubt whether I was not linked already to a chain of events which even my approaching departure from Cumberland would be powerless to snap asunder—the doubt whether we any of us saw the end as the end would really be—gathered more and more darkly over my mind.

As matters turn out, Walter is correct in his foreboding of a danger. The images of darkness in his thoughts further add to the suspense.

HISTORICAL CONTEXT

The Woman in White makes glancing reference to historical events in the late 1840s, just prior to the months when the main action of the novel takes place. These years marked the end of the first phase to the Risorgimento, or the movement toward Italian unification; before its unification, what is now known as the nation of Italy consisted of a number of independent kingdoms. Events in the 1840s gathered momentum. In 1848 an uprising took place in Sicily. That year, too, the prime minister of the Papal States was assassinated, and an uprising in Rome forced Pope Pius IX to flee for safety. In 1849 a new Roman republic was proclaimed, spearheaded by revolutionary leader Giuseppe

COMPARE
&
CONTRAST

- **1850s:** Many novels are first published in serial form in literary magazines such as *Harper's Weekly* in the United States and *All the Year Round* in England; Mudie's Circulating Libraries are a primary purchaser of novels in book form in England.

  Today: Amazon.com is the largest book retailer in North America, with book sales in 2013 of nearly $11 billion; in the United Kingdom as of 2013, Amazon.com accounted for 70 percent of online book sales. In 2014 vendors such as Apple, Samsung, and Amazon.com ship a total of 229 million tablets—for many consumers, a preferred way to access and read books.

- **1850s:** Under the legal doctrine of couverture, in most common law countries a woman forfeits her property to her husband on her marriage.

  Today: After the passage of the Married Women's Property Acts of 1870 and 1882 (which, with amendments, is still in force in the United Kingdom), the property rights of women are coequal with those of men.

- **1850s:** So-called tabloid journalism begins to expand in England in large part because of the steep drop in the price of newsprint and therefore of newspapers. Some newspapers emphasize crime stories, gossip, and other sensational news, the details of which often find their way into sensation novels.

  Today: Some mainstream newspapers in Britain adopt a tabloid format but try to promote the term *compact* to describe their format to avoid the stigma of sensationalism and gossip; meanwhile, sensationalistic tabloid papers enjoy large circulations.

Mazzini. To defend the new republic against the French, revolutionist Giuseppe Garibaldi returned from exile in South America. The pope was able to return to Rome, but only because of protection provided by French troops. These and other events created a chaotic international situation that would have made Count Fosco, an Italian, a suspect and sinister figure to English readers, who already tended to think of Italy as a place of decadence and duplicity, of intrigue and cunning. Further, readers would have remembered the Crystal Palace Exhibition (sometimes called the Great Exhibition) in Hyde Park in 1851. The exhibition, a kind of world's fair, attracted large numbers of foreigners, and many Britons feared that many of these foreigners were spies or otherwise bent on causing mayhem. In the novel's final chapter, it is revealed that Fosco is a member of an Italian Brotherhood, whose goal was to liberate Italy from foreign control; historically, the effort specifically was to liberate the Lombardo-Venetian Kingdom from Austrian control.

Other relevant historical events have to do with changes in the publishing industry that contributed to the rise of the sensation novel at the hands of such British writers as Collins, Charles Reade, Mrs. Henry Wood, Mary Elizabeth Braddon, and others. In 1855, for example, England abolished the duty (tax) on newsprint, allowing newspapers to publish more frequently and to sell copies at a lower price. This, in combination with the expansion of public education, had the further effect of increasing the number of readers in Victorian England. The expansion of Mudie's Circulating Libraries, a subscription service, along with the growth of free public libraries, added to the size of the market for fiction. At the same time, the prevalence of serial publication in such literary magazines as *Household Words* and *All the Year Round*, both of which were launched and edited by Charles Dickens, led to fiction that emphasized suspense, plot twists, cliffhangers, and surprise revelations, thus ensuring that the public would continue to buy the magazine week after week. In

When Anne dies, she is buried as Laura, who is drugged and taken to the asylum as Anne

(©Steve Heap | Shutterstock.com)

some instances, novels were published in discrete monthly parts printed in a booklet-like format that somewhat resembles that of a modern comic book in size.

The attention of the Victorian reading public was caught and held by sensational events, which were reported by tabloid newspapers—whose circulation, again, was increased by the repeal of the duty on newsprint, lowering their price. One example was the notorious trial of William Palmer, known as the Rugeley Poisoner and as the Prince of Poisoners, who was hanged for murder (the number of his victims was at least thirteen) in 1856 before thirty-five thousand spectators; the complex legal case was so sensationalized that the hangman used extra rope and was able to sell off pieces of it to spectators for a guinea (roughly a pound) apiece. Further, in 1857, the Matrimonial Causes Act established divorce courts, placing divorce, along with bigamy, adultery, and spousal abuse (such as that suffered by Laura Fairlie) at the

forefront of public consciousness. In this environment, readers were unable to ignore the sensational trial of the Hon. William Charles Yelverton, an army officer, for bigamy. The investigation and trial provided readers with three years' worth of drama, intrigue, and juicy gossip, and various writers of sensation novels used details from the trial in their books.

Finally, it should be noted that *The Woman in White* deals with the issue of inheritance and the property rights of women. This was an issue that deeply interested Collins, who would take it up in such later novels as *No Name* (1862), *Man and Wife* (1870), and *The Law and the Lady* (1875). At the time of the events of *The Woman in White*, the legal doctrine of "couverture" said that on her marriage, a woman forfeited all of her property to her husband; in effect, the woman ceased to be a legal person on her marriage. The 1870 Married Women's Property Act began to make significant changes in this doctrine, allowing women to retain as their own any property that they inherited or earned. Novels such as *The Woman in White* exposed the injustice of the earlier doctrine and undoubtedly contributed to public sentiment for changes in the law.

CRITICAL OVERVIEW

The term *sensation novel* was first used in a review in *Sixpenny Magazine* in 1861, where the reviewer calls *The Woman in White* "the greatest success in sensation writing." The term was also used in the *Spectator* that year in a review of another novel: "We are threatened with a new variety of the sensation novel, a host of cleverly complicated stories.... But there is not the slightest probability that the swarm of imitators will construct plots nearly so good" as that of Collins's *The Woman in White*.

Contemporary critics in general praised the intricacy of the plot of *The Woman in White*. The reviewer for the *Morning Advertiser* comments that "the plot is wrought out with great ability," adding that the novel is, "by common consent, Mr. Collins's best work." The reviewer for the *Guardian* agrees, remarking that "Mr. Collins has constructed an original plot of rare intricacy, and has unwound the skein which he had knotted up with a lightness of touch and a patient industry, of which the modern novel furnishes us with very few examples."

The reviewer for *Critic* also agrees that "the plot is in point of intricacy a masterpiece" but objected that "we were more struck by the general tendency of the book to sacrifice everything to intensity of excitement." The reviewer for *Saturday Review* calls Collins "an admirable story-teller" but adds that "he is not a great novelist. His plots are framed with artistic ingenuity—he unfolds them bit by bit, clearly, and with great care." The reviewer, however, goes on to explain his reservations:

> Men and women he draws, not for the sake of illustrating human nature and life's varied phases, or exercising his own powers of creation, but simply and solely with reference to the part it is necessary they should play in tangling or disentangling his argument.

With regard to the novel's characters, he faults Collins by maintaining: "They have characteristics, but not character. They might all be summed up in as many sentences as there are personages."

The reviewer for *Spectator* sharply disagrees, writing: "The vivid and manifold emotions with which we read her [Laura's?] story are still fresh in our memory, and we retain a lively sense of the personality of every actor in it from Marian and Laura down to the old parish clerk." The reviewer for the *Guardian* refers to earlier agreed with this assessment, commenting about the characters: "Each one is very clearly and distinctly, almost visibly, drawn." In contrast, the reviewer for the *Observer* is dismissive of the novel, writing: "The author has so overlaid his story with minute details, which are wholly irrelevant to the issue, that the reader ceases to feel any interest in that result before the work is half concluded."

Among modern critics, William H. Marshall, in *Wilkie Collins*, focuses on the issue of dramatic irony. Referring to various of the novel's characters, he writes:

> The quality most apparent in the brief parts played by these and a number of other minor characters...is dramatic irony. A literary device which developed with rapidity during the nineteenth century, dramatic irony particularly marks Collins' characterizations in a number of his novels; it is attained in great measure through the structural method associated with him by which each person tells his story as it appears to him.

In a book also titled *Wilkie Collins*, Lillian Nayder examines *The Woman in White* from a feminist perspective:

Calling attention to the coercive and violent means by which women's subordination is achieved, Collins undermines ideas of their innate incapacity and dependence. Eroding the distinction between masculine and feminine traits, he undermines the justification for coverture.

Nayder adds:

> At his most subversive moments, Collins disappoints the conventional expectations raised by his opening sentence ["This is the story of what a Woman's patience can endure, and of what a Man's resolution can achieve"] and suggests that the differences between resolute men and patient women are merely constructions of an inequitable legal system. In so doing, he undermines the grounds on which men justified their protection of women.

Nayder cites numerous instances in the novel when women who are under the control of men act in a resolute and determined fashion, while men act with a lack of steadfastness and resolution.

In a 150th anniversary retrospective on the publication of the novel, Jon Michael Varese comments on the continuing appeal of *The Woman in White* in the *Guardian*:

> Collins's storytelling talents were utterly mesmerising for Victorian readers—and they are no less captivating for readers today. He was the master of the "cliff-hanger", and given the 40 or so of them that strategically punctuate *The Woman in White*, it's not difficult to see why this Victorian novel continues to thrill us.... The apparitions that Collins conjures are the ghosts that ensured not just his success but his longevity. They are what have kept readers going back for more during the last 150 years, and they bear testament to the value of Collins's self-professed, "old-fashioned" opinion that "the primary object of a work of fiction should be to tell a story."

Of interest perhaps primarily to bibliophiles is a mistake that appeared in the early versions of the novel. A reviewer for the *Times*, in the context of a discussion of the entanglements of the plot, pointed out an error in the chronology, noting that Laura could not have departed from Blackwater Park before the ninth or tenth of August, a date that would have been consistent with the last entry in Marian's diary and that was crucial. In effect, the chronology was impossible, but the plot depends heavily on that date because it had to be shown that she left Blackwater Park for London *after* the date of her purported death. Collins recognized that the reviewer was correct and tried altered dates in later printings of the novel.

CRITICISM

Michael J. O'Neal

O'Neal holds a PhD in English. In the following essay, he examines Collins's use of dramatic irony in The Woman in White.

Dramatic irony is a literary term that refers to discrepancy between what the reader knows and what a character in a novel (or play or movie) knows. Dramatic irony is often crucial in creating suspense, for it causes readers to anticipate what is going to happen in the future, when the truth emerges. This anticipation is often referred to as *ironic tension*, and it is bounded at one end by a moment of revelation, when the audience becomes aware of information denied to the character, and at the other by a moment of recognition, when the character learns what the audience already knows. Put differently, dramatic irony refers to the relationship between the limited grasp that a character has of his or her situation at a given moment and the audience's fuller grasp of that situation.

Dramatic irony takes place at a moment in time and is dependent on two things: the character's limited understanding of matters up to that point and readers' simultaneous consciousness of a broader perspective. It should be pointed out that the word *dramatic* does not necessarily refer to anything spectacular or extraordinary, as the word is used in such expressions as "a dramatic rescue at sea" or "a dramatic ninth-inning home run." In fact, dramatic irony can refer not only to something thrilling and intense but also to something more ordinary and subtle.

Moviegoers are familiar with dramatic irony, for producers of horror movies and psychological thrillers rely heavily on dramatic irony to foster suspense, anticipation, and fear. A typical situation in a horror movie might involve a group of teens being terrorized by a crazed murderer who is skulking about in the woods surrounding the cabin in the forest where the teens are hanging out. One of the teens does not know that the murderer is lurking behind a closed door, knife or ax raised in menace, but the audience does. Anticipation mounts as the teen reaches out to open the door, but the audience is teased as the teen hesitates. As the teen reaches again for the door, it is common for members of the audience to want to scream (and sometimes they do scream), "Don't open that door! Run!" Other techniques used by

BY PARCELING OUT PIECES OF THE NARRATIVE TO DIFFERENT NARRATORS, COLLINS UNDERSCORES THE NOTION THAT TRUTH IS PROVISIONAL AND NECESSARILY FRAGMENTARY."

filmmakers include the use of shadows, knives, low-key lighting, and confined spaces, all of which create a sense of menace and dread. The viewer sees, for example, a shadow and knows (or suspects) who is producing it as it enters the frame, but the character does not. In written fiction, the sound of footsteps might serve a similar purpose. In *The Woman in White*, Laura and Marian are menaced by the sound of footsteps as they walk from the boathouse at Blackwater Park to the house itself; suspense is intensified, for the audience suspects who is following the women, while the women seem to have no idea. Mysterious and menacing footsteps often pursue Walter as well.

Dramatic irony became prevalent in the fiction of the nineteenth century and beyond as a result of a fundamental evolution in the way people achieved an understanding of truth and value. During the Middle Ages, the prevailing belief was that truth could be arrived at through a single, governing, consistent point of view. This belief gave rise to epics and romances celebrating the exploits of heroes who personified and sustained the fixed values of the community, values embodied in the voice of the poet. During the Enlightenment, the prevailing belief was that truth and value were the products of reason and empirical investigation; the assumption was that a fixed, unalterable, unassailable truth existed and could be identified through human inquiry. By the middle of the nineteenth century, however, England and much of the rest of the world had undergone immense changes. Technology and industrialization were transforming the landscape. New scientific discoveries were undermining old truths. Faith was shaken, and religious views seemed to be under assault. The vagaries of the human mind were being explored by the infant discipline of psychology, and artists were beginning to believe that truth and value, if

WHAT DO I READ NEXT?

- Collins's other major novel is *The Moonstone* (1868), a mystery story about a stolen Indian jewel and the effort to recover it. Like *The Woman in White*, the novel is narrated by several characters in turn.

- *Lady Audley's Secret*, by Mary Elizabeth Braddon, a major best-seller when it was published in 1862, is a tangled tale of bigamy, intrigue, murder, impersonation, and blackmail and a prime example of a sensation novel that rode the coattails of Collins's success in the 1860s.

- Judith Flanders's *The Invention of Murder: How the Victorians Revelled in Death and Detection and Created Modern Crime* (2014) details the Victorians' obsession with sensational crimes.

- Readers interested in how the characters in *The Woman in White* might have looked and dressed will find Alison Gernsheim's richly illustrated *Victorian and Edwardian Fashion: A Photographic Survey* (1982) to be a good introduction.

- Readers who want to know more about the day-to-day lives of the Victorians, from dress to grooming to schooling and more, will enjoy *How to Be a Victorian: A Dawn-to-Dusk Guide to Victorian Life* (2014), by Ruth Goodman.

- *Married Women and the Law: Coverture in England and the Common Law World* (2013), edited by Tim Stretton and Krista J. Kesselring, is a collection of essays that examine the history of the legal doctrine of coverture (or couverture) as it affected women and their legal rights.

- *The Victorian Era* (2013), by John F. Wokovits, an entry in Lucent Books' World History Series for young adults, is an examination of the history and culture of the Victorian era.

- Michael Dorris, the first chair of the Native American Studies program at Dartmouth, is the author of *A Yellow Raft in Blue Water* (1987), a young-adult novel that tells the stories of three generations of Native American women and the secrets that dominate their family. Like *The Woman in White*, the novel is written in parts, with each part narrated by a separate character.

at all attainable, were a function of an individual's limited and sometimes distorted point of view. The notion was that *my* version of what is true and of value will differ from *your* version because I look at experience from a different angle, seeing different things and responding to them in a different way; consider, for example, the contrast between the nobility of Walter, the sometimes hypocritical piety of Eliza Michelson, and the repugnant self-justifications of Mrs. Catherick. In this intellectual climate, fictional point of view began to take on more power as a means of arriving at a version of truth.

The Woman in White carries this concept further. By parceling out pieces of the narrative to different narrators, Collins underscores the notion that truth is provisional and necessarily fragmentary. Each character knows and understands events that fall within his or her purview. No one character has access to all the knowledge and all the facts that, put together, establish truth. The exception is Walter Hartright, who assembles the relevant documents—Marian's diary, the statements of Frederick Fairlie, Count Fosco, Hester Pinhorn, Eliza Michelson, and others, as well as relevant letters, such as the one he receives from Mrs. Catherick. But in the process of assembling the various testimonies, the reader becomes an active participant, for the reader is invited, if not forced, to put snippets of information together in order to make sense of the narrative. This would in large measure

At the close of the novel, Laura and Walter are married, and their son inherits Limmeridge
(©Wedding pictures / Shutterstock.com)

account for the extreme popularity of the novel, for readers, once hooked, felt compelled to follow the maze to the end and arrive at a vision of truth.

Dramatic irony plays a key role in this process, for over and over again, one of the narrators acts or makes a statement in ignorance of a fact that is known to the reader. It would be only a slight exaggeration to say that one could almost open the novel at random and find an instance of dramatic irony, for with each successive account, the interlocking pieces of the jigsaw puzzle become more apparent. A single example will suffice. In the narrative of Vincent Gilmore, the Fairlie family attorney, he reproduces a conversation he has with Mr. Merriman, Percival's attorney. At one point, Merriman asks Gilmore, "Your clients in Cumberland have not heard anything more of the woman who wrote the anonymous letter, have they?"

> "Nothing more," I answered. "Have you found no trace of her?"
>
> "Not yet," said my legal friend. "But we don't despair. Sir Percival has his suspicions that

Somebody is keeping her in hiding; and we are having that Somebody watched."

"You meant the old woman who was with her Cumberland," I said.

"Quite another party, sir. . . . Our Somebody is a man. We have got him close under our eye here in London: and we strongly suspect he had something to do with helping her in the first instance to escape from the Asylum."

Several pages later, Marian records these words in her diary:

> After mentioning that he has neither seen nor heard anything of Anne Catherick, he suddenly breaks off, and hints in the most abrupt, mysterious manner, that he has been perpetually watched and followed by strange men ever since he returned to London. . . . This has frightened me, because it looks as if his one fixed idea about Laura was becoming too much for his mind.

Notice that not one of the characters has the complete picture. Marian believes that Walter has become unhinged. Walter senses he is being followed but does not know by whom or why. The lawyer possesses vague information about

Percival's efforts to locate Anne Catherick and equally vague information that a man has come to her aid, but no one knows who he is, and at this point Percival does not know about Walter and the romantic attachment of Walter and Laura. The reader, on the other hand, sees the bigger picture—or, at the very least, strongly suspects what is true. The "old woman" is Mrs. Clements. The "Somebody" is Walter. Walter is, in fact, being followed, although he is not certain, nor is he certain about why he is being followed and through whose agency, and Marian is reluctant to admit the validity of his apprehensions. This is classic dramatic irony.

Collins makes pervasive and effective use of dramatic irony to comment on the limitations of human understanding. The novel demonstrates the cost that the resulting misunderstandings exact on the characters. His effective use of dramatic irony in conjunction with his use of multiple narrators, each holding a piece of the puzzle, contributed to the unprecedented success of the novel at the time it was written and to its enduring popularity a century and a half later.

Source: Michael J. O'Neal, Critical Essay on *Woman in White*, in *Novels for Students*, Gale, Cengage Learning, 2017.

Lillian Nayder

In the following excerpt, Nayder interprets The Woman in White *as a critique of British marriage law.*

...Writing a novel about an Englishwoman's loss of identity and property in marriage, Collins begins his analysis of marriage law by addressing, more generally, the issues of gender relations and sexual difference. Ostensibly, Collins intends the opening encounter between Walter Hartwright and Anne Catherick to leave us wondering about Anne's identity and her plight. Yet he uses their encounter to raise a larger question central to this work: what right, if any, do men have to control women?

Anne approaches Walter because she is a helpless woman who needs aid in reaching London, knowing nothing of its geography or its ways: "I have only been in London once before," she tells him, "and I know nothing about that side of it, yonder. Can I get a fly, or a carriage of any kind? Is it too late? I don't know." Despite her helplessness, however, what Anne really desires from Walter is autonomy—freedom from interference. "If you will only promise not

> AT HIS MOST SUBVERSIVE MOMENTS, COLLINS DISAPPOINTS THE CONVENTIONAL EXPECTATIONS RAISED BY HIS OPENING SENTENCE AND SUGGESTS THAT THE DIFFERENCES BETWEEN RESOLUTE MEN AND PATIENT WOMEN ARE MERELY CONSTRUCTIONS OF AN INEQUITABLE LEGAL SYSTEM. IN SO DOING, HE UNDERMINES THE GROUNDS ON WHICH MEN JUSTIFIED THEIR PROTECTION OF WOMEN."

to interfere with me," she repeatedly implores him: "Only say you will let me leave you when and how I please—only say you won't interfere with me. Will you promise?" Although Walter promises, he does so begrudgingly, troubled by "self-distrust" and "something like self-reproach," "distressed by an uneasy sense of having done wrong": "What could I do? Here was a stranger utterly and helplessly at my mercy—and that stranger a forlorn woman. No house was near; no one was passing whom I could consult; and no earthly right existed on my part to give me a power of control over her, even if I had known how to exercise it. I trace these lines, self-distrustfully, with the shadows of after-events darkening the very paper I write on; and still I say, what could I do?"

While Walter characterizes as "ill-considered" his "promise to leave [Anne] free to act as she pleased," his regret does not stem, simply, from his knowledge that she has escaped from a lunatic asylum. Indeed, he finds her "quiet and self-controlled," and immediately suspects that she may be "the victim of the most horrible of all false imprisonments." Rather, his "self-distrust" stems from his sense that, in promising not to interfere with her, he has failed in his duty as a man. In declining to exercise his control over a helpless woman, Walter has, in effect, violated the gender norms of his day. According to these norms, as Collins satirically describes them, it is the job of men to confine women in the domestic sphere and to thwart their desires—to "say nay" to their wishes, as Anne's foster mother, Mrs. Clements, puts it. Instead of treating Anne as a special case, and representing her incarceration as necessary if unpleasant, Collins connects her to the other, healthy women in his novel, and he conflates the lunatic asylum from which she escapes with the imprisoning "asylum" of the home. Like Anne Catherick, Marian Halcombe desires independence, complaining that, as a woman, she has been "condemned to patience, propriety, and petticoats, for life," and she praises Walter for "giving [Anne] her liberty": "she seems to have done nothing . . . to show herself unfit to enjoy it." Subjected to her husband's control, Lady Glyde later echoes Anne's plea for autonomy: "I will sign with pleasure . . . if you will only treat me as a responsible being."

Despite such pleas, the men in Collins's novel persistently exercise their right to control the members of the female sex, a right they base on the "natural unfitness" of women to make decisions and act as adults. "Women . . . are nothing but children grown up," Count Fosco asserts, while Percival tells Laura that "others"—that is, her husband—must do her thinking for her. "I wait to be instructed . . . before I venture on giving my opinion in the presence of well-informed men," Countess Fosco tells Laura and Marian, after her advocacy of "the Rights of Women" is beaten out of her by her husband.

Calling attention to the coercive and violent means by which women's subordination is achieved, Collins undermines ideas of their innate incapacity and dependence. Eroding the distinction between masculine and feminine traits, he undermines the justification for coverture. Indeed, virtually all of Collins's characters are sexual hybrids of a sort—either effeminate men or masculine women—and Walter's conventional beliefs about natural sexual difference continually prove inadequate to explain his experiences in the novel. Despite her helplessness, for example, Anne Catherick is "unwomanly" in Walter's view—unaccountably forward and aggressive in her behavior. She touches Walter's arm rather than calling to him and doesn't seem vulnerable or tearful enough to suit his tastes. When Anne thanks Walter for his help, and acknowledges his kindness, he describes "the first touch of womanly tenderness that [he] had heard from her," yet remains disappointed that she hasn't shed any tears.

Similarly, Walter finds Marian Halcombe an unwomanly woman, whose tears, like Anne's, "do not flow so easily as they ought." Struck by "the rare beauty of her form"— "perfection in the eyes of a man"—he registers his surprise at her masculine features, which "flatly contradict" the "old conventional maxim, that Nature cannot err": "The lady's complexion was almost swarthy, and the dark down on her upper lip was almost a moustache. She had a large, firm, masculine mouth and jaw; prominent, piercing, resolute brown eyes; and thick, coal-black hair, growing unusually low down on her forehead. Her expression—bright, frank, and intelligent—appeared, while she was silent, to be altogether wanting in those feminine attractions of gentleness and pliability, without which the beauty of the handsomest woman alive is beauty incomplete." Initially repelled by Marian's appearance, Walter attributes the "masculine form and masculine look of [her] features" to an error of nature. Yet Collins himself does not, since all of his characters appear both male and female, Walter included. While Walter views Marian as manly, Marian views Walter as womanly, and she repeatedly urges him to act "like a man." In explaining that he can "sigh over [his] mournful confession [of love] with the tenderest woman who reads it and pities [him]" and "laugh at it as bitterly as the hardest man who tosses it from him in contempt," Walter calls these very distinctions into question.

So, too, do the other male characters in the novel, all of whom possess feminine traits. With small feet and hands, dressed with "womanish" accessories, Laura's uncle Frederick has "a frail, languidly-fretful, over-refined look," which Walter finds "singularly and unpleasantly delicate in its association with a man." More importantly, Frederick suffers from "nerves," a disorder that Victorians found particularly troubling because it undermined sexual distinctions and brought its male victims "perilously close to the feminine condition." "I am nothing but a bundle of nerves dressed up to look like a man," Frederick confesses. Like Laura's uncle, Walter repeatedly complains of his "nerves," and Sir Percival seems "almost as nervous and fluttered, every now and then, as his lady herself." Even Count Fosco, who prides himself on his ability to tame the female characters in the novel, is a sexually hybrid figure, "nervously sensitive" despite "his look of unmistakable mental firmness and power." "As noiseless in a room as any of us women," he "has all the fondness of an old maid for his cockatoo," and his "nerves are so finely strung that he starts at chance noises." Marian repeatedly remarks on the count's "effeminate tastes and amusements" and describes him as "a fat St. Cecilia masquerading in male attire."

Collins begins *The Woman in White* by claiming that the story of Laura and Walter will illustrate the sharp distinction between women and men: "This is the story of what a Woman's patience can endure, and of what a Man's resolution can achieve." Having drawn this distinction, however, Collins proceeds to break it down, dramatizing the resolute behavior of his female characters. Despite her "womanly" sweetness and delicacy, Laura speaks both "patiently and resolutely" to her first husband and the count, and when patience fails her, she becomes "resolute." While Marian "tr[ies] to be patient," she finds it easier to act "resolutely," and Count Fosco berates Sir Percival for failing to see that "Miss Halcombe . . . has the foresight and the resolution of a man." While Collins's female characters demonstrate their resolve, his hero exhibits the virtues of manly patience: "I am not rash enough to measure myself against such a man as the Count before I am well prepared for him," Walter explains. "I have learnt patience; I can wait my time."

At his most subversive moments, Collins disappoints the conventional expectations raised by his opening sentence and suggests that the differences between resolute men and patient women are merely constructions of an inequitable legal system. In so doing, he undermines the grounds on which men justified their protection of women. Developing his critique, he directs our attention to the two principal forms in which such protection was offered to Victorian wives—that of the marriage settlement, and of coverture itself—legal practices that work against each other, and thus discredit the authority and logic of the law.

For women of the middle and upper classes, the injustice of marriage law was mitigated by the practice of settling separate property on daughters, a costly expedient based on the law of equity. Drawn up by a lawyer, a woman's marriage settlement limited the common-law rights of her husband by stipulating that certain properties were to remain her own, under the management of a trustee. The separate property placed in trust for a married woman could include real or personal property of any kind and was overseen by the Court of Chancery.

In *The Woman in White*, Collins focuses considerable attention on the negotiations involved in drawing up Laura's marriage settlement, and he highlights the crucial importance of a wife's separate property to her future well-being. Twenty years old at the outset of the novel, Laura will inherit from her father's estate a trust worth £20,000 on her next birthday, in addition to a life interest in an additional £10,000, a sum that is to go to her aunt Eleanor, Count Fosco's wife, should Laura die first. She is also the heiress to the family property, with its annual income of £3,000. In negotiating Laura's marriage settlement, her lawyer, Vincent Gilmour, stipulates that her fortune is to be settled upon her, and the income from her personal and real property left at her disposal; that her husband is to inherit her income in the case of her death, and the principal to be left to their children, or to the parties she names in her will. "This was the clause," he explains, "and no one who reads it, can fail, I think, to agree with me that it meted out equal justice to all parties."

Yet "equal justice" proves elusive for Laura Fairlie. Despite the fairness of Mr. Gilmour's stipulations, they are rejected by Sir Percival, who insists, through his lawyer, that Laura's fortune must go to him in the event of her death. To Gilmour, this "audacious proposal" reveals Sir Percival's "mercenary motive" in marrying the heiress. Nonetheless, when Gilmour appeals to Laura's legal guardian, her uncle Frederick, telling him that "Glyde has no shadow of a claim to expect more than the income of the money" and that "the money itself . . . ought to be under her control," Frederick refuses to argue the point with Sir Percival. Laura's uncle forces the lawyer to sacrifice "the just rights of [his] niece, and of all who belong to her," although "it is against all rule to abandon the lady's money entirely to the man she marries." Ironically, Laura's marriage settlement leaves her even more vulnerable than she would have been without it. Although the contract requires Sir Percival to obtain "his wife's permission" to use her income, it also gives him "an interest of twenty thousand pounds in [her] death."

Rather than protecting Laura, her marriage settlement inspires the conspiracy against her, encouraging Sir Percival and the count to substitute the dead Anne Catherick for the living

> WHEN ALL IS SAID, IT IS AS A STORY THAT *THE WOMAN IN WHITE* HAS MOST INTEREST. IT WAS THE STORY-TELLERS—SCOTT AND COOPER AND DUMAS—THAT COLLINS CARED FOR MOST AMONG NOVELISTS; AND HE USUALLY CHOSE TO WRITE IN AN UNADORNED STYLE, RELISHING MOST SUCH PROSE AS THAT OF BYRON'S LETTERS."

Lady Glyde in order to inherit her fortune. Blocking what Victorians generally considered a married woman's escape route from the inequities of common law, Collins highlights Laura's vulnerability and emphasizes the need for legal reform. At the same time, he criticizes the wife's protected status as a *feme covert* by staging the fictitious death of Lady Glyde. In robbing his wife of her identity, Sir Percival commits a crime that is punishable by law. Yet thefts similar to his, Collins astutely suggests, are legally sanctioned by coverture, and committed daily, every time an Englishwoman marries....

Source: Lillian Nayder, "Sensation Fiction and Marriage Law Reform: Wives and Property in *The Woman in White, No Name,* and *Man and Wife*," in *Wilkie Collins,* Twayne Publishers, 1997, pp. 77–82.

Clyde K. Hyder

In the following excerpt, Hyder speculates that Collins drew inspiration from true crime stories.

...It is no secret that Collins was fond of reading records of criminal cases, especially those written in French, and more than one commentator has mentioned casually that Collins derived from such a source suggestions for *The Woman in White.* The exact source, which seemingly has not been pointed out, was the celebrated case of Madame de Douhault, which Collins found discussed fully in Maurice Méjan's *Recueil des Causes Célèbres...* (second edition, Paris, 1808, etc.), a book in his own library.

The relevant parts of this famous case may be briefly outlined: Adéläide-Marie-Rogres-Lusignan de Champignelles (1741–1817) was married in 1764 to the Marquis de Douhault,

and became a widow in 1787. Her father died in 1784. Madame de Douhault's brother, M. de Champignelles, obtained as much of his father's estate as he could, including some of the inheritance rightfully belonging to his mother and his sister. Of the mother's hardships under altered circumstances, another sister, abbess of Montargis, had some knowledge, and urged her sister Madame de Douhault to recover for their mother some share of the paternal bequest. Madame de Douhault thereupon planned a trip to Paris and announced her plan both to her sister and to Madame de Polignac, a correspondent. During a visit to some friends she expressed misgivings about the proposed journey, but her friends succeeded in calming her temporarily. Near the end of December, 1787, she left Chazelet, accompanied by a coachman, a chambermaid, and a servant. She stopped at Orléans, where she usually lodged at the house of M. Dulude (or du Lude), a nephew and an heir. On this occasion Dulude refused to receive her and induced her to go to the house of M. de la Roncière, a relative, whose mother had died suddenly eight days before at her son's house, about four leagues distant from Orléans. On January 15, 1788, on the eve of departing for Paris, Madame de la Roncière invited Madame de Douhault to go for a drive along the banks of the Loire. Soon after taking a pinch of snuff given her by Madame de la Roncière, Madame de Douhault suffered a violent headache which obliged her to return. Directly she fell into a deep slumber and was put to bed.

Madame de Douhault remembered all these events clearly, but what happened subsequently at Orléans was as indistinct as the events in an evil dream. She believed that she slept for several days; she woke to find herself in the Salpêtrière, under the name of Blainville. The supposed Madame de Douhault being dead, her estate was liquidated by M. de Champignelles and her heirs.

The correspondence of Madame de Douhault was for a time intercepted, but in June, 1789, by means of a woman whose favor she had won she succeeded in sending a letter to Madame de Polignac, and through Madame de Polignac's agency regained her liberty.

> Une surveillante reçut l'ordre de lui remettre ses habits, dont l'indication était écrite sur un papier, et Madame de Douhault reprit son déshabillé blanc, le linge et les poches qu'elle avait en entrant à la Salpêtrière.

Madame de Polignac and her friends recognized Madame de Douhault; in fact, nobody at Versailles questioned her identity. When she went to the château at Champignelles, she was recognized by her own former domestics as well as by other people. The elaborate system of intrigue and defamation and the ingenious machinations by which Madame de Douhault's brother sought to discredit her attempt to regain her rightful status need not be reviewed here. The case dragged on for years. To her cause the son of a former member of her household, an advocate named Delorme, with whom Madame de Douhault lived for a time, in vain devoted his talent and his fortune.

Obviously Collins took from the story of Madame de Douhault the idea for Count Fosco's plot, to rob Laura of her property by destroying her identity. Fosco and Sir Percival carry out the plan by burying Anne Catherick, Laura's half-sister, as Laura, and substituting Laura for Anne at the asylum from which Anne had escaped—details which Collins added to make his narrative more logical. Laura's instinctive dread of spending a night at her aunt's house in London, on her journey towards Cumberland, may correspond to Madame de Douhault's misgivings, though a novelist's foreshadowing needs no such explanation. Laura's imperfect memory of the events which preceded her trip to the asylum is possibly a bit more reminiscent of the French case. Finally, one wonders whether Madame de Douhault's "déshabillé blanc" did not suggest the detail from which the novel derives its title, in spite of Millais's story. To be sure, women in white are strangers neither to fiction nor to legend.

The use of a legal case may have influenced the form of the narrative. In the first chapter of *The Woman in White* Collins explains: "The story here presented will be told by more than one pen, as the story of an offence against the laws is told in Court by more than one person . . . ." Thus a section of the story is related by the character whose testimony seems most pertinent; at the same time this character, like the speakers in *The Ring and the Book*, reveals a good deal of himself. An early reviewer pointed out that since each witness tells only what he knows, his ignorance piques the reader's curiosity.

In his introductory remarks to *Basil* Collins called the novel and the play "twin-sisters in the family of Fiction," the one "a drama narrated" and the other "a drama acted." In a dramatic novel like *The Woman in White* every incident is necessarily planned with care. One inconsistency of time in the first edition, subsequently corrected, did escape the author. In a dramatic novel, too, fatalism is often prominent. Dreams, a favorite subject with an author himself susceptible to weird dreams, foreshadow important events: The letter warning Laura against marriage with Sir Percival (Chapter XI of the first part) contains an account of an ominous dream. Before departing on the journey that ended at the asylum, Laura has bad dreams. More important is the dream of Marian Halcombe (Chapter VI in the second epoch) in which she sees Walter Hartright escaping pestilence, shipwreck, and other perils; the dream ends with the prophetic vision of Hartright at a tomb—as events are to prove, the tomb of Anne Catherick. And Anne Catherick herself enters the story like a figure in a vision:

> There, in the middle of the broad, bright highroad—there, as if it had that moment sprung out of the earth or dropped from the heaven—stood the figure of a solitary Woman, dressed from head to foot in white garments, her face bent in grave inquiry on mine, her hand pointing to the dark cloud over London, as I faced her.

And thus she disappears:

> So the ghostly figure which has haunted these pages, as it haunted my life, goes down into the impenetrable gloom. Like a shadow she first came to me in the loneliness of the night. Like a shadow she passes away in the loneliness of the dead.

The plot having been conceived, certain characters were essential. As Collins once explained, a victim can hardly exist without a villain, and because the crime was too ingenious for an English villain, the author chose a foreigner. Since Collins had visited Italy in his boyhood, his choice of an Italian was natural. Moreover, Italy was the home of such organizations as "The Brotherhood." Fosco's tool, Sir Percival, was necessarily a "weak shabby villain."

To Count Fosco, justly regarded as Collins's greatest achievement in characterization, Collins gave a Falstaffian physique, because, he said, of the popular notion that a fat man could hardly be villainous. He accounted for Fosco's pets thus: "I knew a man who loved canaries, and I had known boys who loved white mice, and I thought the mice running about Fosco while he meditated on his schemes would have a fine effect." Fosco's devotion to his pets, like Long John Silver's fondness for his parrot, is a humanizing touch. To be sure, there are harsher qualities behind the Count's kindness: "The Count lit a cigarette, went back to the flowers in the window, and puffed little jets of smoke at the leaves, in a state of the deepest anxiety about killing the insects." Collins attributed to Fosco some of his own tastes and interests—for example, knowledge of the arts, fondness for Italian opera and good cooking, cosmopolitanism, criticism of English ways. His kind of humor is an apt vehicle for Fosco's egoistic gusto and self-assertive banter. Collins's admiration for Napoleon led him to attribute to Fosco the physical appearance of that dramatic character. There is something grandiose, too, in Fosco's *savoir-faire*, his skill in intrigue, his virtuosity in deception, his knowledge of human nature. So convincing is the portrait that one foreigner considered himself the pattern for Fosco, as Collins relates:

> He naturally insisted on receiving satisfaction for this insult, leaving the choice of swords or pistols to me as the challenged person. Information, on which he could rely, had assured him that I meditated a journey to Paris early in the ensuing week. A hostile meeting might, under such circumstances, be easily arranged. His letter ended with these terrible words: "J'attendrai Monsieur Vilkie [*sic*] avec deux temoins à la gare." Arriving at Paris, I looked for my honorable opponent. But one formidable person presented himself whom I could have wounded with pleasure—the despot who insisted on examining my luggage.

Marian Halcombe writes of Fosco: "The one weak point in that man's iron character is the horrible admiration he feels for *me*." Fosco says of Marian:

> With that woman for my friend I would snap these fingers of mine at the world.... This grand creature—I drink her health in my sugar-and-water—this grand creature, who stands in the strength of her love and her courage, firm as a rock, between us two and that poor, flimsy, pretty blonde wife of yours—this magnificent woman, whom I admire with all my soul....

Readers have always shared Fosco's admiration. *The Woman in White* inspired several letters from bachelors who expressed their wish to marry the original of Marian. Next to Fosco she is Collins's most memorable character.

In comparison with Fosco and Marian, Laura and Walter do seem rather colorless—virtuous enough but less interesting than some minor figures: Professor Pesca, Italian teacher of languages, as eccentric as Gabriele Rossetti (at one time perhaps the best-known teacher of Italian in London; and, by the way, a member of the *Carbonari* in his youth, as Pesca was of "The Brotherhood"), important at the beginning and towards the end of the novel; Mr. Gilmore, whose professional and individual oddities are well sketched; Philip Fairlie, a delightfully self-centered hypochondriac (doubtless partly inspired by the author's occasional irritations and drawn *con amore*)—"nothing but a bundle of nerves dressed up to look like a man." Nor can one forget Mrs. Catherick, atoning for an unconventional past by a respectability which rejoices at the clergyman's bow. The Dickensian touch, slight in most of these characters, is more marked in one or two of the servants.

When all is said, it is as a story that *The Woman in White* has most interest. It was the story-tellers—Scott and Cooper and Dumas—that Collins cared for most among novelists; and he usually chose to write in an unadorned style, relishing most such prose as that of Byron's letters. Since Collins himself belongs among the great story-tellers rather than among the great novelists, *The Woman in White* well opens with this thrilling sentence: "This is the *story* of what a Woman's patience can endure, and what a Man's resolution can achieve."

Source: Clyde K. Hyder, "Wilkie Collins and *The Woman in White*," in *Victorian Literature: Modern Essays in Criticism*, edited by Austin Wright, Oxford University Press, 1961, pp. 129–34.

SOURCES

Ablow, Rachel, "'One Flesh,' One Person, and the 1870 Married Women's Property Act," BRANCH: Britain, Representation and Nineteenth-Century History website, http://www.branchcollective.org/?ps_articles = rachel-ablow-one-flesh-one-person-and-the-1870-married-womens-property-act (accessed March 30, 2016).

Allingham, Philip V., "The Victorian Sensation Novel, 1860–1880," in *Victorian Web*, 2013, http://www.victorianweb.org/genre/sensation.html (accessed March 30, 2016).

"Book Sales Statistics," Foner Books website, 2016, http://www.fonerbooks.com/booksale.htm (accessed March 31, 2016).

Collins, Wilkie, *The Woman in White*, Oxford University Press, 1996.

"Corporate Watch: Amazon," Ethical Consumer website, http://www.ethicalconsumer.org/commentanalysis/

corporatewatch/isittimetoboycottamazon.aspx (accessed April 2, 2016).

Dallas, E. S., unsigned review of *The Woman in White*, in *Wilkie Collins: The Critical Heritage*, edited by Norman Page, Routledge & Kegan Paul, 1974, pp. 95–103; originally published in the *Times*, October 30, 1860, p. 6.

Hall, Emma, "Circulation Soars as U.K. Broadsheets Go Tabloid," in *Advertising Age*, January 3, 2006, http://adage.com/article/media/circulation-soars-u-k-broadsheets-tab loid/47926/ (accessed March 31, 2016).

Kiehna, Lauren Harmsen, "Sensation and the Fourth Estate: The *Times* and the Yelverton Bigamy Trials," in *Victorian Periodicals Review*, Vol. 47, No. 1, Spring 2014.

Landow, George P., "Mudie's Select Library and the Form of Victorian Fiction," in *Victorian Web*, 2001, http://www.victorianweb.org/economics/mudie.html (accessed March 30, 2016).

Lindsay, Rowena, "Amazon's Kindle E-Reader Sales Are Down, but So Are Most Tablets," in *Christian Science Monitor*, February 3, 2015, http://www.csmonitor.com/Business/2015/0203/Amazon-s-Kindle-e-reader-sales-are-down-but-so-are-most-tablets (accessed March 31, 2016).

"Local Heroes: William Palmer," BBC Stoke and Staffordshire website, November 13, 2014, http://www.bbc.co.uk/stoke/content/articles/2006/04/11/local_heroes_doctor_william_palmer_feature.shtml (accessed March 30, 2016).

Marshall, William H., *Wilkie Collins*, Twayne Publishers, 1970, p. 59.

Nayder, Lillian, *Wilkie Collins*, Twayne Publishers, 1997, pp. 78–79, 80.

Review of *The Castleford Case* by Frances Browne, in *Wilkie Collins: The Critical Heritage*, edited by Norman Page, Routledge & Kegan Paul, 1974, p. 109; originally published in *Spectator*, December 28, 1861, p. 1428.

Review of *The Woman in White*, in *Wilkie Collins: The Critical Heritage*, edited by Norman Page, Routledge & Kegan Paul, 1974, p. 82; originally published in *Critic*, August 25, 1860, pp. 233–34.

Review of *The Woman in White*, in *Wilkie Collins: The Critical Heritage*, edited by Norman Page, Routledge & Kegan Paul, 1974, p. 91; originally published in *Guardian*, August 29, 1860, pp. 780–81.

Review of *The Woman in White*, in *Wilkie Collins: The Critical Heritage*, edited by Norman Page, Routledge & Kegan Paul, 1974, p. 81; originally published in *Morning Advertiser*, August 20, 1860, p. 3.

Review of *The Woman in White*, in *Wilkie Collins: The Critical Heritage*, edited by Norman Page, Routledge & Kegan Paul, 1974, p. 88; originally published in *Observer*, August 27, 1860, p. 7.

Review of *The Woman in White*, in *Wilkie Collins: The Critical Heritage*, edited by Norman Page, Routledge & Kegan Paul, 1974, pp. 83, 85; originally published in *Saturday Review*, August 25, 1860, pp. 249–50.

Review of *The Woman in White*, in *Wilkie Collins: The Critical Heritage*, edited by Norman Page, Routledge & Kegan Paul, 1974, pp. 108–109; originally published in *Sixpenny*, September 1861, pp. 366–67.

Review of *The Woman in White*, in *Wilkie Collins: The Critical Heritage*, edited by Norman Page, Routledge & Kegan Paul, 1974, p. 93; originally published in *Spectator*, September 8, 1860, p. 864.

Sutherland, John, Introduction to *The Woman in White*, Oxford University Press, 1996, pp. vii–xxiii.

"30 June 1855: Newspaper Stamp Duty Abolished," in *Guardian*, May 10, 2011, http://www.theguardian.com/theguardian/from-the-archive-blog/2011/may/10/guardian190-newspaper-duty-cut (accessed March 31, 2015).

"Timeline: 19th Century," in *Oxford Reference*, http://www.oxfordreference.com/view/10.1093/acref/9780191735622.timeline.0001 (accessed March 30, 2016).

Varese, Jon Michael, "*The Woman in White*'s 150 Years of Sensation," in *Guardian*, November 26, 2009, http://www.theguardian.com/books/booksblog/2009/nov/26/woman-in-white-150-years-sensation (accessed April 3, 2016).

FURTHER READING

Ackroyd, Peter, *Wilkie Collins: A Brief Life*, Nan A. Talese, 2015.

> Readers interested in a relatively compact biography of Collins would do well to examine this book. The biography is part of Ackroyd's Brief Lives series and written by an award-winning biographer.

Gasson, Andrew, *Wilkie Collins: An Illustrated Guide*, Oxford University Press, 1998.

> This volume is an alphabetical reference work. It contains entries about Collins's major novels, short stories, and plays; his family and associates; and the people and places that played a role in his career as a novelist. Numerous illustrations enhance the volume.

Mangham, Andrew, ed., *The Cambridge Companion to Sensation Fiction*, Cambridge University Press, 2013.

> This volume contains fifteen essays about sensation literature, including discussion of the works of Collins. It examines such topics as illustrated sensation novels, sensation literature on the stage, the depiction of women in sensation fiction, and the relationship between sensation literature and both gothic literature and contemporary science.

Pikett, Lyn, *The Nineteenth-Century Sensation Novel*, 2nd edition, Northcote House Publishers, 2011.

> First published in 1994, this volume looks at the sensation novels of the 1860s, bookended

by Collins's two major works, *The Woman in White* and *The Moonstone*. The work studies the phenomenon in the context of the heated critical and moral debates that surrounded sensation literature.

Mill, John Stuart, *The Subjection of Women*, Dover Publications, 1997.

This influential essay by one of the leading thinkers of the Victorian period, published in 1869 but written in 1860–1861, argues on utilitarian grounds that the happiness of society would be increased if men and women enjoyed equal legal, political, social, and economic rights. The essay endures as a milestone document in the history of human rights.

Shanley, Mary Lyndon, *Feminism, Marriage, and the Law in Victorian England, 1850–1895*, Princeton University Press, 1993.

This examination of reforms in marriage laws during the Victorian period takes into account both history and political theory. The book demonstrates that Victorian feminists called for fundamental changes in the marriage

relationship, the kinds of changes Collins would likely have supported and that he advocated in his later fiction.

SUGGESTED SEARCH TERMS

Wilkie Collins AND The Moonstone

Wilkie Collins AND The Woman in White

couverture

Dickens AND All the Year Round

dramatic irony

legal rights of women the nineteenth century

sensation fiction

Victorian novel

Wilkie Collins

Wilkie Collins AND Charles Dickens

Glossary of Literary Terms

A

Abstract: As an adjective applied to writing or literary works, abstract refers to words or phrases that name things not knowable through the five senses.

Aestheticism: A literary and artistic movement of the nineteenth century. Followers of the movement believed that art should not be mixed with social, political, or moral teaching. The statement "art for art's sake" is a good summary of aestheticism. The movement had its roots in France, but it gained widespread importance in England in the last half of the nineteenth century, where it helped change the Victorian practice of including moral lessons in literature.

Allegory: A narrative technique in which characters representing things or abstract ideas are used to convey a message or teach a lesson. Allegory is typically used to teach moral, ethical, or religious lessons but is sometimes used for satiric or political purposes.

Allusion: A reference to a familiar literary or historical person or event, used to make an idea more easily understood.

Analogy: A comparison of two things made to explain something unfamiliar through its similarities to something familiar, or to prove one point based on the acceptedness of another. Similes and metaphors are types of analogies.

Antagonist: The major character in a narrative or drama who works against the hero or protagonist.

Anthropomorphism: The presentation of animals or objects in human shape or with human characteristics. The term is derived from the Greek word for "human form."

Anti-hero: A central character in a work of literature who lacks traditional heroic qualities such as courage, physical prowess, and fortitude. Anti-heroes typically distrust conventional values and are unable to commit themselves to any ideals. They generally feel helpless in a world over which they have no control. Anti-heroes usually accept, and often celebrate, their positions as social outcasts.

Apprenticeship Novel: See *Bildungsroman*

Archetype: The word archetype is commonly used to describe an original pattern or model from which all other things of the same kind are made. This term was introduced to literary criticism from the psychology of Carl Jung. It expresses Jung's theory that behind every person's "unconscious," or repressed memories of the past, lies the "collective unconscious" of the human race: memories of the countless typical experiences of our ancestors. These memories are said to prompt illogical associations that trigger powerful emotions in the reader. Often, the emotional process is primitive, even primordial. Archetypes are the literary images that grow out of the "collective unconscious." They appear in literature as incidents and plots that repeat basic patterns of life. They may also appear as stereotyped characters.

Avant-garde: French term meaning "vanguard." It is used in literary criticism to describe new writing that rejects traditional approaches to literature in favor of innovations in style or content.

B

Beat Movement: A period featuring a group of American poets and novelists of the 1950s and 1960s—including Jack Kerouac, Allen Ginsberg, Gregory Corso, William S. Burroughs, and Lawrence Ferlinghetti—who rejected established social and literary values. Using such techniques as stream of consciousness writing and jazz-influenced free verse and focusing on unusual or abnormal states of mind—generated by religious ecstasy or the use of drugs—the Beat writers aimed to create works that were unconventional in both form and subject matter.

Bildungsroman: A German word meaning "novel of development." The *bildungsroman* is a study of the maturation of a youthful character, typically brought about through a series of social or sexual encounters that lead to self-awareness. *Bildungsroman* is used interchangeably with *erziehungsroman,* a novel of initiation and education. When a *bildungsroman* is concerned with the development of an artist (as in James Joyce's *A Portrait of the Artist as a Young Man*), it is often termed a *kunstlerroman.*

Black Aesthetic Movement: A period of artistic and literary development among African Americans in the 1960s and early 1970s. This was the first major African-American artistic movement since the Harlem Renaissance and was closely paralleled by the civil rights and black power movements. The black aesthetic writers attempted to produce works of art that would be meaningful to the black masses. Key figures in black aesthetics included one of its founders, poet and playwright Amiri Baraka, formerly known as LeRoi Jones; poet and essayist Haki R. Madhubuti, formerly Don L. Lee; poet and playwright Sonia Sanchez; and dramatist Ed Bullins.

Black Humor: Writing that places grotesque elements side by side with humorous ones in an attempt to shock the reader, forcing him or her to laugh at the horrifying reality of a disordered world.

Burlesque: Any literary work that uses exaggeration to make its subject appear ridiculous, either by treating a trivial subject with profound seriousness or by treating a dignified subject frivolously. The word "burlesque" may also be used as an adjective, as in "burlesque show," to mean "striptease act."

C

Character: Broadly speaking, a person in a literary work. The actions of characters are what constitute the plot of a story, novel, or poem. There are numerous types of characters, ranging from simple, stereotypical figures to intricate, multifaceted ones. In the techniques of anthropomorphism and personification, animals—and even places or things—can assume aspects of character. "Characterization" is the process by which an author creates vivid, believable characters in a work of art. This may be done in a variety of ways, including (1) direct description of the character by the narrator; (2) the direct presentation of the speech, thoughts, or actions of the character; and (3) the responses of other characters to the character. The term "character" also refers to a form originated by the ancient Greek writer Theophrastus that later became popular in the seventeenth and eighteenth centuries. It is a short essay or sketch of a person who prominently displays a specific attribute or quality, such as miserliness or ambition.

Climax: The turning point in a narrative, the moment when the conflict is at its most intense. Typically, the structure of stories, novels, and plays is one of rising action, in which tension builds to the climax, followed by falling action, in which tension lessens as the story moves to its conclusion.

Colloquialism: A word, phrase, or form of pronunciation that is acceptable in casual conversation but not in formal, written communication. It is considered more acceptable than slang.

Coming of Age Novel: See *Bildungsroman*

Concrete: Concrete is the opposite of abstract, and refers to a thing that actually exists or a description that allows the reader to experience an object or concept with the senses.

Connotation: The impression that a word gives beyond its defined meaning. Connotations may be universally understood or may be significant only to a certain group.

Convention: Any widely accepted literary device, style, or form.

D

Denotation: The definition of a word, apart from the impressions or feelings it creates (connotations) in the reader.

Denouement: A French word meaning "the unknotting." In literary criticism, it denotes the resolution of conflict in fiction or drama. The *denouement* follows the climax and provides an outcome to the primary plot situation as well as an explanation of secondary plot complications. The *denouement* often involves a character's recognition of his or her state of mind or moral condition.

Description: Descriptive writing is intended to allow a reader to picture the scene or setting in which the action of a story takes place. The form this description takes often evokes an intended emotional response—a dark, spooky graveyard will evoke fear, and a peaceful, sunny meadow will evoke calmness.

Dialogue: In its widest sense, dialogue is simply conversation between people in a literary work; in its most restricted sense, it refers specifically to the speech of characters in a drama. As a specific literary genre, a "dialogue" is a composition in which characters debate an issue or idea.

Diction: The selection and arrangement of words in a literary work. Either or both may vary depending on the desired effect. There are four general types of diction: "formal," used in scholarly or lofty writing; "informal," used in relaxed but educated conversation; "colloquial," used in everyday speech; and "slang," containing newly coined words and other terms not accepted in formal usage.

Didactic: A term used to describe works of literature that aim to teach some moral, religious, political, or practical lesson. Although didactic elements are often found in artistically pleasing works, the term "didactic" usually refers to literature in which the message is more important than the form. The term may also be used to criticize a work that the critic finds "overly didactic," that is, heavy-handed in its delivery of a lesson.

Doppelganger: A literary technique by which a character is duplicated (usually in the form of an alter ego, though sometimes as a ghostly counterpart) or divided into two distinct, usually opposite personalities. The use of this character device is widespread in nineteenth- and twentieth-century literature, and indicates a growing awareness among authors that the "self" is really a composite of many "selves."

Double Entendre: A corruption of a French phrase meaning "double meaning." The term is used to indicate a word or phrase that is deliberately ambiguous, especially when one of the meanings is risqué or improper.

Dramatic Irony: Occurs when the audience of a play or the reader of a work of literature knows something that a character in the work itself does not know. The irony is in the contrast between the intended meaning of the statements or actions of a character and the additional information understood by the audience.

Dystopia: An imaginary place in a work of fiction where the characters lead dehumanized, fearful lives.

E

Edwardian: Describes cultural conventions identified with the period of the reign of Edward VII of England (1901-1910). Writers of the Edwardian Age typically displayed a strong reaction against the propriety and conservatism of the Victorian Age. Their work often exhibits distrust of authority in religion, politics, and art and expresses strong doubts about the soundness of conventional values.

Empathy: A sense of shared experience, including emotional and physical feelings, with someone or something other than oneself. Empathy is often used to describe the response of a reader to a literary character.

Enlightenment, The: An eighteenth-century philosophical movement. It began in France but had a wide impact throughout Europe and America. Thinkers of the Enlightenment valued reason and believed that both the individual and society could achieve a state of perfection. Corresponding to this essentially humanist vision was a resistance to religious authority.

Epigram: A saying that makes the speaker's point quickly and concisely. Often used to preface a novel.

Epilogue: A concluding statement or section of a literary work. In dramas, particularly those of the seventeenth and eighteenth centuries, the epilogue is a closing speech, often in verse, delivered by an actor at the end of a play and spoken directly to the audience.

Epiphany: A sudden revelation of truth inspired by a seemingly trivial incident.

Episode: An incident that forms part of a story and is significantly related to it. Episodes may be either self-contained narratives or events that depend on a larger context for their sense and importance.

Epistolary Novel: A novel in the form of letters. The form was particularly popular in the eighteenth century.

Epithet: A word or phrase, often disparaging or abusive, that expresses a character trait of someone or something.

Existentialism: A predominantly twentieth-century philosophy concerned with the nature and perception of human existence. There are two major strains of existentialist thought: atheistic and Christian. Followers of atheistic existentialism believe that the individual is alone in a godless universe and that the basic human condition is one of suffering and loneliness. Nevertheless, because there are no fixed values, individuals can create their own characters—indeed, they can shape themselves—through the exercise of free will. The atheistic strain culminates in and is popularly associated with the works of Jean-Paul Sartre. The Christian existentialists, on the other hand, believe that only in God may people find freedom from life's anguish. The two strains hold certain beliefs in common: that existence cannot be fully understood or described through empirical effort; that anguish is a universal element of life; that individuals must bear responsibility for their actions; and that there is no common standard of behavior or perception for religious and ethical matters.

Expatriates: See *Expatriatism*

Expatriatism: The practice of leaving one's country to live for an extended period in another country.

Exposition: Writing intended to explain the nature of an idea, thing, or theme. Expository writing is often combined with description, narration, or argument. In dramatic writing, the exposition is the introductory material which presents the characters, setting, and tone of the play.

Expressionism: An indistinct literary term, originally used to describe an early twentieth-century school of German painting. The term applies to almost any mode of unconventional, highly subjective writing that distorts reality in some way.

F

Fable: A prose or verse narrative intended to convey a moral. Animals or inanimate objects with human characteristics often serve as characters in fables.

Falling Action: See *Denouement*

Fantasy: A literary form related to mythology and folklore. Fantasy literature is typically set in non-existent realms and features supernatural beings.

Farce: A type of comedy characterized by broad humor, outlandish incidents, and often vulgar subject matter.

Femme fatale: A French phrase with the literal translation "fatal woman." A *femme fatale* is a sensuous, alluring woman who often leads men into danger or trouble.

Fiction: Any story that is the product of imagination rather than a documentation of fact. Characters and events in such narratives may be based in real life but their ultimate form and configuration is a creation of the author.

Figurative Language: A technique in writing in which the author temporarily interrupts the order, construction, or meaning of the writing for a particular effect. This interruption takes the form of one or more figures of speech such as hyperbole, irony, or simile. Figurative language is the opposite of literal language, in which every word is truthful, accurate, and free of exaggeration or embellishment.

Figures of Speech: Writing that differs from customary conventions for construction, meaning, order, or significance for the purpose of a special meaning or effect. There are two major types of figures of speech: rhetorical figures, which do not make changes in the meaning of the words, and tropes, which do.

Fin de siecle: A French term meaning "end of the century." The term is used to denote the last decade of the nineteenth century, a transition period when writers and other artists abandoned old conventions and looked for new techniques and objectives.

First Person: See *Point of View*

Flashback: A device used in literature to present action that occurred before the beginning of the story. Flashbacks are often introduced as the dreams or recollections of one or more characters.

Foil: A character in a work of literature whose physical or psychological qualities contrast strongly with, and therefore highlight, the corresponding qualities of another character.

Folklore: Traditions and myths preserved in a culture or group of people. Typically, these are passed on by word of mouth in various forms—such as legends, songs, and proverbs—or preserved in customs and ceremonies. This term was first used by W. J. Thoms in 1846.

Folktale: A story originating in oral tradition. Folktales fall into a variety of categories, including legends, ghost stories, fairy tales, fables, and anecdotes based on historical figures and events.

Foreshadowing: A device used in literature to create expectation or to set up an explanation of later developments.

Form: The pattern or construction of a work which identifies its genre and distinguishes it from other genres.

G

Genre: A category of literary work. In critical theory, genre may refer to both the content of a given work—tragedy, comedy, pastoral—and to its form, such as poetry, novel, or drama.

Gilded Age: A period in American history during the 1870s characterized by political corruption and materialism. A number of important novels of social and political criticism were written during this time.

Gothicism: In literary criticism, works characterized by a taste for the medieval or morbidly attractive. A gothic novel prominently features elements of horror, the supernatural, gloom, and violence: clanking chains, terror, charnel houses, ghosts, medieval castles, and mysteriously slamming doors. The term "gothic novel" is also applied to novels that lack elements of the traditional Gothic setting but that create a similar atmosphere of terror or dread.

Grotesque: In literary criticism, the subject matter of a work or a style of expression characterized by exaggeration, deformity, freakishness, and disorder. The grotesque often includes an element of comic absurdity.

H

Harlem Renaissance: The Harlem Renaissance of the 1920s is generally considered the first significant movement of black writers and artists in the United States. During this period, new and established black writers published more fiction and poetry than ever before, the first influential black literary journals were established, and black authors and artists received their first widespread recognition and serious critical appraisal. Among the major writers associated with this period are Claude McKay, Jean Toomer, Countee Cullen, Langston Hughes, Arna Bontemps, Nella Larsen, and Zora Neale Hurston.

Hero/Heroine: The principal sympathetic character (male or female) in a literary work. Heroes and heroines typically exhibit admirable traits: idealism, courage, and integrity, for example.

Holocaust Literature: Literature influenced by or written about the Holocaust of World War II. Such literature includes true stories of survival in concentration camps, escape, and life after the war, as well as fictional works and poetry.

Humanism: A philosophy that places faith in the dignity of humankind and rejects the medieval perception of the individual as a weak, fallen creature. "Humanists" typically believe in the perfectibility of human nature and view reason and education as the means to that end.

Hyperbole: In literary criticism, deliberate exaggeration used to achieve an effect.

I

Idiom: A word construction or verbal expression closely associated with a given language.

Image: A concrete representation of an object or sensory experience. Typically, such a representation helps evoke the feelings associated with the object or experience itself. Images are either "literal" or "figurative." Literal images are especially concrete and involve little or no extension of the obvious meaning of the words used to express them. Figurative images do not follow the literal meaning of the words exactly. Images in literature are usually visual, but the term "image" can also refer to the representation of any sensory experience.

Imagery: The array of images in a literary work. Also, figurative language.

In medias res: A Latin term meaning "in the middle of things." It refers to the technique of beginning a story at its midpoint and then using various flashback devices to reveal previous action.

Interior Monologue: A narrative technique in which characters' thoughts are revealed in a way that appears to be uncontrolled by the author. The interior monologue typically aims to reveal the inner self of a character. It portrays emotional experiences as they occur at both a conscious and unconscious level. images are often used to represent sensations or emotions.

Irony: In literary criticism, the effect of language in which the intended meaning is the opposite of what is stated.

J

Jargon: Language that is used or understood only by a select group of people. Jargon may refer to terminology used in a certain profession, such as computer jargon, or it may refer to any nonsensical language that is not understood by most people.

L

Leitmotiv: See *Motif*

Literal Language: An author uses literal language when he or she writes without exaggerating or embellishing the subject matter and without any tools of figurative language.

Lost Generation: A term first used by Gertrude Stein to describe the post-World War I generation of American writers: men and women haunted by a sense of betrayal and emptiness brought about by the destructiveness of the war.

M

Mannerism: Exaggerated, artificial adherence to a literary manner or style. Also, a popular style of the visual arts of late sixteenth-century Europe that was marked by elongation of the human form and by intentional spatial distortion. Literary works that are self-consciously high-toned and artistic are often said to be "mannered."

Metaphor: A figure of speech that expresses an idea through the image of another object. Metaphors suggest the essence of the first object by identifying it with certain qualities of the second object.

Modernism: Modern literary practices. Also, the principles of a literary school that lasted from roughly the beginning of the twentieth century until the end of World War II. Modernism is defined by its rejection of the literary conventions of the nineteenth century and by its opposition to conventional morality, taste, traditions, and economic values.

Mood: The prevailing emotions of a work or of the author in his or her creation of the work. The mood of a work is not always what might be expected based on its subject matter.

Motif: A theme, character type, image, metaphor, or other verbal element that recurs throughout a single work of literature or occurs in a number of different works over a period of time.

Myth: An anonymous tale emerging from the traditional beliefs of a culture or social unit. Myths use supernatural explanations for natural phenomena. They may also explain cosmic issues like creation and death. Collections of myths, known as mythologies, are common to all cultures and nations, but the best-known myths belong to the Norse, Roman, and Greek mythologies.

N

Narration: The telling of a series of events, real or invented. A narration may be either a simple narrative, in which the events are recounted chronologically, or a narrative with a plot, in which the account is given in a style reflecting the author's artistic concept of the story. Narration is sometimes used as a synonym for "storyline."

Narrative: A verse or prose accounting of an event or sequence of events, real or invented. The term is also used as an adjective in the sense "method of narration." For example, in literary criticism, the expression "narrative technique" usually refers to the way the author structures and presents his or her story.

Narrator: The teller of a story. The narrator may be the author or a character in the story through whom the author speaks.

Naturalism: A literary movement of the late nineteenth and early twentieth centuries. The movement's major theorist, French novelist Emile Zola, envisioned a type of fiction that would examine human life with the objectivity of scientific inquiry. The Naturalists typically viewed human beings as either the products of "biological determinism," ruled by hereditary instincts and engaged in an endless struggle for survival, or as the products of "socioeconomic determinism," ruled by social and economic forces beyond their control. In their works, the Naturalists generally ignored the highest levels of society and focused on degradation: poverty, alcoholism, prostitution, insanity, and disease.

Noble Savage: The idea that primitive man is noble and good but becomes evil and corrupted as he becomes civilized. The concept of the noble savage originated in the Renaissance period but is more closely identified with such later writers as Jean-Jacques Rousseau and Aphra Behn.

Novel: A long fictional narrative written in prose, which developed from the novella and other early forms of narrative. A novel is usually organized under a plot or theme with a focus on character development and action.

Novel of Ideas: A novel in which the examination of intellectual issues and concepts takes precedence over characterization or a traditional storyline.

Novel of Manners: A novel that examines the customs and mores of a cultural group.

Novella: An Italian term meaning "story." This term has been especially used to describe fourteenth-century Italian tales, but it also refers to modern short novels.

O

Objective Correlative: An outward set of objects, a situation, or a chain of events corresponding to an inward experience and evoking this experience in the reader. The term frequently appears in modern criticism in discussions of authors' intended effects on the emotional responses of readers.

Objectivity: A quality in writing characterized by the absence of the author's opinion or feeling about the subject matter. Objectivity is an important factor in criticism.

Oedipus Complex: A son's amorous obsession with his mother. The phrase is derived from the story of the ancient Theban hero Oedipus, who unknowingly killed his father and married his mother.

Omniscience: See *Point of View*

Onomatopoeia: The use of words whose sounds express or suggest their meaning. In its simplest sense, onomatopoeia may be represented by words that mimic the sounds they denote such as "hiss" or "meow." At a more subtle level, the pattern and rhythm of sounds and rhymes of a line or poem may be onomatopoeic.

Oxymoron: A phrase combining two contradictory terms. Oxymorons may be intentional or unintentional.

P

Parable: A story intended to teach a moral lesson or answer an ethical question.

Paradox: A statement that appears illogical or contradictory at first, but may actually point to an underlying truth.

Parallelism: A method of comparison of two ideas in which each is developed in the same grammatical structure.

Parody: In literary criticism, this term refers to an imitation of a serious literary work or the signature style of a particular author in a ridiculous manner. A typical parody adopts the style of the original and applies it to an inappropriate subject for humorous effect. Parody is a form of satire and could be considered the literary equivalent of a caricature or cartoon.

Pastoral: A term derived from the Latin word "pastor," meaning shepherd. A pastoral is a literary composition on a rural theme. The conventions of the pastoral were originated by the third-century Greek poet Theocritus, who wrote about the experiences, love affairs, and pastimes of Sicilian shepherds. In a pastoral, characters and language of a courtly nature are often placed in a simple setting. The term pastoral is also used to classify dramas, elegies, and lyrics that exhibit the use of country settings and shepherd characters.

Pen Name: See *Pseudonym*

Persona: A Latin term meaning "mask." *Personae* are the characters in a fictional work of literature. The *persona* generally functions as a mask through which the author tells a story in a voice other than his or her own. A *persona* is usually either a character in a story who acts as a narrator or an "implied author," a voice created by the author to act as the narrator for himself or herself.

Personification: A figure of speech that gives human qualities to abstract ideas, animals, and inanimate objects.

Picaresque Novel: Episodic fiction depicting the adventures of a roguish central character ("picaro" is Spanish for "rogue"). The picaresque hero is commonly a low-born but clever individual who wanders into and out of various affairs of love, danger, and farcical intrigue. These involvements may take place at all social levels and typically present a humorous and wide-ranging satire of a given society.

Plagiarism: Claiming another person's written material as one's own. Plagiarism can take the form of direct, word-for-word copying or the theft of the substance or idea of the work.

Plot: In literary criticism, this term refers to the pattern of events in a narrative or drama. In its simplest sense, the plot guides the author in composing the work and helps the reader follow the work. Typically, plots exhibit causality and unity and have a beginning, a middle, and an end. Sometimes, however, a plot may consist of a series of disconnected events, in which case it is known as an "episodic plot."

Poetic Justice: An outcome in a literary work, not necessarily a poem, in which the good are rewarded and the evil are punished, especially in ways that particularly fit their virtues or crimes.

Poetic License: Distortions of fact and literary convention made by a writer—not always a poet—for the sake of the effect gained. Poetic license is closely related to the concept of "artistic freedom."

Poetics: This term has two closely related meanings. It denotes (1) an aesthetic theory in literary criticism about the essence of poetry or (2) rules prescribing the proper methods, content, style, or diction of poetry. The term poetics may also refer to theories about literature in general, not just poetry.

Point of View: The narrative perspective from which a literary work is presented to the reader. There are four traditional points of view. The "third person omniscient" gives the reader a "godlike" perspective, unrestricted by time or place, from which to see actions and look into the minds of characters. This allows the author to comment openly on characters and events in the work. The "third person" point of view presents the events of the story from outside of any single character's perception, much like the omniscient point of view, but the reader must understand the action as it takes place and without any special insight into characters' minds or motivations. The "first person" or "personal" point of view relates events as they are perceived by a single character. The main character "tells" the story and may offer opinions about the action and characters which differ from those of the author. Much less common than omniscient, third person, and first person is the "second person" point of view, wherein the author tells the story as if it is happening to the reader.

Polemic: A work in which the author takes a stand on a controversial subject, such as abortion or religion. Such works are often extremely argumentative or provocative.

Pornography: Writing intended to provoke feelings of lust in the reader. Such works are often condemned by critics and teachers, but those which can be shown to have literary value are viewed less harshly.

Post-Aesthetic Movement: An artistic response made by African Americans to the black aesthetic movement of the 1960s and early '70s. Writers since that time have adopted a somewhat different tone in their work, with less emphasis placed on the disparity between black and white in the United States. In the words of post-aesthetic authors such as Toni Morrison, John Edgar Wideman, and Kristin Hunter, African Americans are portrayed as looking inward for answers to their own questions, rather than always looking to the outside world.

Postmodernism: Writing from the 1960s forward characterized by experimentation and continuing to apply some of the fundamentals of modernism, which included existentialism and alienation. Postmodernists have gone a step further in the rejection of tradition begun with the modernists by also rejecting traditional forms, preferring the anti-novel over the novel and the anti-hero over the hero.

Primitivism: The belief that primitive peoples were nobler and less flawed than civilized peoples because they had not been subjected to the tainting influence of society.

Prologue: An introductory section of a literary work. It often contains information establishing the situation of the characters or presents information about the setting, time period, or action. In drama, the prologue is spoken by a chorus or by one of the principal characters.

Prose: A literary medium that attempts to mirror the language of everyday speech. It is distinguished from poetry by its use of unmetered, unrhymed language consisting of logically related sentences. Prose is usually grouped into paragraphs that form a cohesive whole such as an essay or a novel.

Prosopopoeia: See *Personification*

Protagonist: The central character of a story who serves as a focus for its themes and incidents and as the principal rationale for its development. The protagonist is some-

times referred to in discussions of modern literature as the hero or anti-hero.

Protest Fiction: Protest fiction has as its primary purpose the protesting of some social injustice, such as racism or discrimination.

Proverb: A brief, sage saying that expresses a truth about life in a striking manner.

Pseudonym: A name assumed by a writer, most often intended to prevent his or her identification as the author of a work. Two or more authors may work together under one pseudonym, or an author may use a different name for each genre he or she publishes in. Some publishing companies maintain "house pseudonyms," under which any number of authors may write installations in a series. Some authors also choose a pseudonym over their real names the way an actor may use a stage name.

Pun: A play on words that have similar sounds but different meanings.

R

Realism: A nineteenth-century European literary movement that sought to portray familiar characters, situations, and settings in a realistic manner. This was done primarily by using an objective narrative point of view and through the buildup of accurate detail. The standard for success of any realistic work depends on how faithfully it transfers common experience into fictional forms. The realistic method may be altered or extended, as in stream of consciousness writing, to record highly subjective experience.

Repartee: Conversation featuring snappy retorts and witticisms.

Resolution: The portion of a story following the climax, in which the conflict is resolved.

Rhetoric: In literary criticism, this term denotes the art of ethical persuasion. In its strictest sense, rhetoric adheres to various principles developed since classical times for arranging facts and ideas in a clear, persuasive, appealing manner. The term is also used to refer to effective prose in general and theories of or methods for composing effective prose.

Rhetorical Question: A question intended to provoke thought, but not an expressed answer, in the reader. It is most commonly used in oratory and other persuasive genres.

Rising Action: The part of a drama where the plot becomes increasingly complicated. Rising action leads up to the climax, or turning point, of a drama.

Roman à clef: A French phrase meaning "novel with a key." It refers to a narrative in which real persons are portrayed under fictitious names.

Romance: A broad term, usually denoting a narrative with exotic, exaggerated, often idealized characters, scenes, and themes.

Romanticism: This term has two widely accepted meanings. In historical criticism, it refers to a European intellectual and artistic movement of the late eighteenth and early nineteenth centuries that sought greater freedom of personal expression than that allowed by the strict rules of literary form and logic of the eighteenth-century neoclassicists. The Romantics preferred emotional and imaginative expression to rational analysis. They considered the individual to be at the center of all experience and so placed him or her at the center of their art. The Romantics believed that the creative imagination reveals nobler truths—unique feelings and attitudes—than those that could be discovered by logic or by scientific examination. Both the natural world and the state of childhood were important sources for revelations of "eternal truths." "Romanticism" is also used as a general term to refer to a type of sensibility found in all periods of literary history and usually considered to be in opposition to the principles of classicism. In this sense, Romanticism signifies any work or philosophy in which the exotic or dreamlike figure strongly, or that is devoted to individualistic expression, self-analysis, or a pursuit of a higher realm of knowledge than can be discovered by human reason.

Romantics: See *Romanticism*

S

Satire: A work that uses ridicule, humor, and wit to criticize and provoke change in human nature and institutions. There are two major types of satire: "formal" or "direct" satire speaks directly to the reader or to a character in the work; "indirect" satire relies upon the ridiculous behavior of its characters to make its point. Formal satire is further divided into two manners: the "Horatian," which ridicules gently, and the "Juvenalian," which derides its subjects harshly and bitterly.

Science Fiction: A type of narrative about or based upon real or imagined scientific theories and technology. Science fiction is often peopled with alien creatures and set on other planets or in different dimensions.

Second Person: See *Point of View*

Setting: The time, place, and culture in which the action of a narrative takes place. The elements of setting may include geographic location, characters' physical and mental environments, prevailing cultural attitudes, or the historical time in which the action takes place.

Simile: A comparison, usually using "like" or "as," of two essentially dissimilar things, as in "coffee as cold as ice" or "He sounded like a broken record."

Slang: A type of informal verbal communication that is generally unacceptable for formal writing. Slang words and phrases are often colorful exaggerations used to emphasize the speaker's point; they may also be shortened versions of an often-used word or phrase.

Slave Narrative: Autobiographical accounts of American slave life as told by escaped slaves. These works first appeared during the abolition movement of the 1830s through the 1850s.

Socialist Realism: The Socialist Realism school of literary theory was proposed by Maxim Gorky and established as a dogma by the first Soviet Congress of Writers. It demanded adherence to a communist worldview in works of literature. Its doctrines required an objective viewpoint comprehensible to the working classes and themes of social struggle featuring strong proletarian heroes.

Stereotype: A stereotype was originally the name for a duplication made during the printing process; this led to its modern definition as a person or thing that is (or is assumed to be) the same as all others of its type.

Stream of Consciousness: A narrative technique for rendering the inward experience of a character. This technique is designed to give the impression of an ever-changing series of thoughts, emotions, images, and memories in the spontaneous and seemingly illogical order that they occur in life.

Structure: The form taken by a piece of literature. The structure may be made obvious for ease of understanding, as in nonfiction works, or may obscured for artistic purposes, as in some poetry or seemingly "unstructured" prose.

Sturm und Drang: A German term meaning "storm and stress." It refers to a German literary movement of the 1770s and 1780s that reacted against the order and rationalism of the enlightenment, focusing instead on the intense experience of extraordinary individuals.

Style: A writer's distinctive manner of arranging words to suit his or her ideas and purpose in writing. The unique imprint of the author's personality upon his or her writing, style is the product of an author's way of arranging ideas and his or her use of diction, different sentence structures, rhythm, figures of speech, rhetorical principles, and other elements of composition.

Subjectivity: Writing that expresses the author's personal feelings about his subject, and which may or may not include factual information about the subject.

Subplot: A secondary story in a narrative. A subplot may serve as a motivating or complicating force for the main plot of the work, or it may provide emphasis for, or relief from, the main plot.

Surrealism: A term introduced to criticism by Guillaume Apollinaire and later adopted by Andre Breton. It refers to a French literary and artistic movement founded in the 1920s. The Surrealists sought to express unconscious thoughts and feelings in their works. The best-known technique used for achieving this aim was automatic writing—transcriptions of spontaneous outpourings from the unconscious. The Surrealists proposed to unify the contrary levels of conscious and unconscious, dream and reality, objectivity and subjectivity into a new level of "super-realism."

Suspense: A literary device in which the author maintains the audience's attention through the buildup of events, the outcome of which will soon be revealed.

Symbol: Something that suggests or stands for something else without losing its original identity. In literature, symbols combine their literal meaning with the suggestion of an abstract concept. Literary symbols are of two types: those that carry complex associations of meaning no matter what their contexts, and those that derive their suggestive meaning from their functions in specific literary works.

Symbolism: This term has two widely accepted meanings. In historical criticism, it denotes an early modernist literary movement initiated in France during the nineteenth century that reacted against the prevailing standards of realism. Writers in this movement aimed to evoke, indirectly and symbolically, an order of being beyond the material world of the five senses. Poetic expression of personal emotion figured strongly in the movement, typically by means of a private set of symbols uniquely identifiable with the individual poet. The principal aim of the Symbolists was to express in words the highly complex feelings that grew out of everyday contact with the world. In a broader sense, the term "symbolism" refers to the use of one object to represent another.

T

Tall Tale: A humorous tale told in a straightforward, credible tone but relating absolutely impossible events or feats of the characters. Such tales were commonly told of frontier adventures during the settlement of the west in the United States.

Theme: The main point of a work of literature. The term is used interchangeably with thesis.

Thesis: A thesis is both an essay and the point argued in the essay. Thesis novels and thesis plays share the quality of containing a thesis which is supported through the action of the story.

Third Person: See *Point of View*

Tone: The author's attitude toward his or her audience may be deduced from the tone of the work. A formal tone may create distance or convey politeness, while an informal tone may encourage a friendly, intimate, or intrusive feeling in the reader. The author's attitude toward his or her subject matter may also be deduced from the tone of the words he or she uses in discussing it.

Transcendentalism: An American philosophical and religious movement, based in New England from around 1835 until the Civil War. Transcendentalism was a form of American romanticism that had its roots abroad in the works of Thomas Carlyle, Samuel Coleridge, and Johann Wolfgang von Goethe. The Transcendentalists stressed the importance of intuition and subjective experience in communication with God. They rejected religious dogma and texts in favor of mysticism and scientific naturalism. They pursued truths that lie beyond the "colorless" realms perceived by reason and the senses and were active social reformers in public education, women's rights, and the abolition of slavery.

U

Urban Realism: A branch of realist writing that attempts to accurately reflect the often harsh facts of modern urban existence.

Utopia: A fictional perfect place, such as "paradise" or "heaven."

V

Verisimilitude: Literally, the appearance of truth. In literary criticism, the term refers to aspects of a work of literature that seem true to the reader.

Victorian: Refers broadly to the reign of Queen Victoria of England (1837-1901) and to anything with qualities typical of that era. For example, the qualities of smug narrow-mindedness, bourgeois materialism, faith in social progress, and priggish morality are often considered Victorian. This stereotype is contradicted by such dramatic intellectual developments as the theories of Charles Darwin, Karl Marx, and Sigmund Freud (which stirred strong debates in England) and the critical attitudes of serious Victorian writers like Charles Dickens and George Eliot. In literature, the Victorian Period was the great age of the English novel, and the latter part of the era saw the rise of movements such as decadence and symbolism.

W

Weltanschauung: A German term referring to a person's worldview or philosophy.

Weltschmerz: A German term meaning "world pain." It describes a sense of anguish about the nature of existence, usually associated with a melancholy, pessimistic attitude.

Z

Zeitgeist: A German term meaning "spirit of the time." It refers to the moral and intellectual trends of a given era.

Cumulative Author/Title Index

Numerical

1984 (Orwell): V7

A

The A.B.C. Murders (Christie): V30
Abani, Chris
    GraceLand: V35
Abbey, Edward
    The Monkey Wrench Gang: V43
Abbott, Edwin Abbott
    Flatland: A Romance of Many
        Dimensions: V47
Abe, Kobo
    The Woman in the Dunes: V22
Absalom, Absalom! (Faulkner): V13
The Accidental Tourist (Tyler): V7
Abu-Jaber, Diana
    Crescent: V51
Achebe, Chinua
    No Longer at Ease: V33
    Things Fall Apart: V2
The Absolutely True Diary of a Part-
    Time Indian (Alexie): V38
Adam Bede (Eliot): V34
Adams, Douglas
    The Hitchhiker's Guide to the
        Galaxy: V7
Adams, Richard
    Watership Down: V11
Adichie, Chimamanda Ngozi
    Americanah: V54
    Half of a Yellow Sun: V48
The Adventures of Augie March
    (Bellow): V33
The Adventures of Huckleberry Finn
    (Twain): V1

The Adventures of Tom Sawyer
    (Twain): V6
The Age of Innocence (Wharton):
    V11
The Age of Innocence (Motion
    picture): V37
Age of Iron (Coetzee): V51
Agee, James
    A Death in the Family: V22
Alas, Babylon (Frank): V29
The Alchemist (Coelho): V29
Alcott, Louisa May
    Little Women: V12
    Little Women (Motion picture):
        V53
Alexie, Sherman
    The Absolutely True Diary of a
        Part-Time Indian: V38
    Indian Killer: V54
    The Lone Ranger and Tonto
        Fistfight in Heaven: V17
    Reservation Blues: V31
Alias Grace (Atwood): V19
Alice's Adventures in Wonderland
    (Carroll): V7
All the Pretty Horses (McCarthy):
    V36
All Quiet on the Western Front
    (Remarque): V4
All Quiet on the Western Front
    (Motion picture): V36
All the King's Men (Warren): V13
Allende, Isabel
    Daughter of Fortune: V18
    Eva Luna: V29
    The House of the Spirits: V6
    Zorro: V44

Allison, Dorothy
    Bastard Out of Carolina: V11
Alvarez, Julia
    Before We Were Free: V53
    How the Garcia Girls Lost Their
        Accents: V5
    In the Time of the Butterflies: V9
    Return to Sender: V42
Always Coming Home (Le Guin): V9
The Amazing Adventures of Kavalier
    & Clay (Chabon): V25
The Ambassadors (James): V12
The American (James): V44
Americanah (Adichie): V54
American Born Chinese (Yang): V39
American Pastoral (Roth): V25
Amis, Martin
    Time's Arrow; or, The Nature of
        the Offence: V47
Among the Hidden (Haddix): V47
An American Tragedy (Dreiser): V17
Anaya, Rudolfo
    Bless Me, Ultima: V12
    Heart of Aztlan: V49
And the Mountains Echoed
    (Hosseini): V52
Anderson, Laurie Halse
    Catalyst: V49
    Fever 1793: V35
    Speak: V31
Anderson, M. T.
    Feed: V41
Anderson, Sherwood
    Winesburg, Ohio: V4
Angelou, Maya
    I Know Why the Caged Bird Sings:
        V2

Animal Dreams (Kingsolver): V12
Animal Farm (Orwell): V3
Anna Karenina (Tolstoy): V28
Annie John (Kincaid): V3
The Antelope Wife (Erdrich): V44
Anthem (Rand): V29
Anything but Typical (Baskin): V43
Appointment in Samarra (O'Hara):
    V11
April Morning (Fast): V35
Around the World in Eighty Days
    (Verne): V30
The Arrival (Tan): V42
Arrowsmith (Lewis): V34
As I Lay Dying (Faulkner): V8
Asher, Jay
    Thirteen Reasons Why: V51
Asimov, Isaac
    I, Robot: V29
The Assault: (Mulisch) V52
The Assistant: (Malamud) V27
Atlas Shrugged (Rand): V10
Atonement (McEwan): V32
Atonement (Motion picture): V49
Atwood, Margaret
    Alias Grace: V19
    The Blind Assassin: V53
    Cat's Eye: V14
    The Handmaid's Tale: V4
    Oryx and Crake: V39
    Surfacing: V13
Auel, Jean
    The Clan of the Cave Bear: V11
Austen, Jane
    Clueless (Motion picture): V40
    Emma: V21
    Emma (Motion picture): V46
    Mansfield Park: V29
    Northanger Abbey: V28
    Persuasion: V14
    Pride and Prejudice: V1
    Sense and Sensibility: V18
    Sense and Sensibility (Motion
        picture): V33
*The Autobiography of an Ex-
    Coloured Man* (Johnson): V22
*The Autobiography of Miss Jane
    Pittman* (Gaines): V5
Avi
    *Nothing But the Truth: A
        Documentary Novel:* V34
The Awakening (Chopin): V3

B

Bâ, Mariama
    So Long a Letter: V46
Babbitt (Lewis): V19
Baker, Russell
    Growing Up: V48
Baldwin, James
    Go Tell It on the Mountain: V4

Ballard, J. G.
    Empire of the Sun: V8
    Empire of the Sun (Motion
        picture): V42
*Balzac and the Little Chinese
    Seamstress* (Sijie): V39
Balzac, Honoré de
    Le Père Goriot: V33
Bambara, Toni Cade
    The Salt Eaters: V44
Banks, Russell
    The Sweet Hereafter: V13
Banner in the Sky (Ullman): V45
Barchester Towers (Trollope): V42
Bastard Out of Carolina (Allison):
    V11
Barrows, Annie
    *The Guernsey Literary and Potato
        Peel Society:* V43
Baskin, Nora Raleigh
    Anything but Typical: V43
Bauer, Joan
    Hope Was Here: V54
Baum, L. Frank
    The Wizard of Oz (Motion
        picture): V43
    The Wonderful Wizard of Oz: V13
The Bean Trees (Kingsolver): V5
The Beautiful and Damned
    (Fitzgerald): V49
*Beauty: A Retelling of the Story of
    Beauty and the Beast*
    (McKinley): V33
The Beet Queen (Erdrich): V37
Before We Were Free (Alvarez): V53
Behn, Aphra
    *Oroonoko; or, The Royal Slave:
        A True History:* V35
Bel Canto (Patchett): V30
A Bell for Adano (Hersey): V41
The Bell Jar (Plath): V1
Bellamy, Edward
    Looking Backward: 2000–1887:
        V15
Bellow, Saul
    The Adventures of Augie March:
        V33
    Herzog: V14
    Humboldt's Gift: V26
    Mr. Sammler's Planet: V53
    Seize the Day: V4
Beloved (Morrison): V6
A Bend in the River (Naipaul): V37
Benitez, Sandra
    *A Place Where the Sea
        Remembers:* V32
Benito Cereno (Melville): V41
Betsey Brown (Shange): V11
Between Shades of Gray (Sepetys):
    V51
The Big Sleep (Chandler): V17
The Big Sleep (Motion picture): V48

*Billy Budd, Sailor: An Inside
    Narrative* (Melville): V9
The Bingo Palace (Erdrich): V40
Black Beauty (Sewell): V22
Black Boy (Wright): V1
Blair, Eric Arthur
    Animal Farm: V3
Bleak House (Dickens): V30
Bless Me, Ultima (Anaya): V12
Bless the Beasts and Children
    (Swarthout): V29
The Blind Assassin (Atwood): V53
Blindness: V27
Bloor, Edward
    Tangerine: V33
The Bluest Eye (Morrison): V1
Blume, Judy
    Forever...: V24
Body and Soul (Conroy): V11
Bone (Ng): V37
The Bone People (Hulme): V24
The Bonesetter's Daughter (Tan):
    V31
The Book of Laughter and Forgetting
    (Kundera): V27
The Book Thief (Zusak): V44
Borland, Hal
    When the Legends Die: V18
The Bostonians (James): V37
Boulle, Pierre
    The Bridge over the River Kwai:
        V32
Bowen, Elizabeth Dorothea Cole
    The Death of the Heart: V13
Bowles, Paul
    The Sheltering Sky: V50
Boyle, T. C.
    The Tortilla Curtain: V41
Bradbury, Ray
    Dandelion Wine: V22
    Fahrenheit 451: V1
    The Martian Chronicles: V42
    *Something Wicked This Way
        Comes:* V29
Bradley, Marion Zimmer
    The Mists of Avalon: V40
Braithwaite, E. R.
    To Sir, With Love: V30
Brave New World (Huxley): V6
Bread Givers (Yezierska): V29
Breath, Eyes, Memory (Danticat):
    V37
A Breath of Fresh Air (Malladi):
    V53
Breathing Lessons (Tyler): V10
Briar Rose (Yolen): V30
Bridal, Tessa
    The Tree of Red Stars: V17
The Bride Price (Emecheta): V12
Brideshead Revisited (Waugh): V13
The Bridge of San Luis Rey (Wilder):
    V24

The Bridge over the River Kwai
(Boulle): V32
*The Brief Wondrous Life of Oscar
Wao* (Díaz): V36
Brontë, Anne
The Tenant of Wildfell Hall: V26
Brontë, Charlotte
Jane Eyre: V4
Jane Eyre (Motion picture): V54
Villette: V36
Brontë, Emily
Wuthering Heights: V2
Wuthering Heights (Motion
picture): V45
Brookner, Anita
Hotel du Lac: V23
Brooks, Geraldine
March: V26
The Brothers Karamazov
(Dostoevsky): V8
Brown Girl Dreaming (Woodson):
V52
Brown, Rita Mae
Rubyfruit Jungle: V9
Buck, Pearl S.
The Good Earth: V25
The Buddha in the Attic (Otsuka): V54
Bulgakov, Mikhail
The Master and Margarita: V8
Bunyan, John

The Pilgrim's Progress: V32
Burdick, Eugene, and William J.
Lederer
The Ugly American: V23
Burger's Daughter (Gordimer): V50
Burgess, Anthony
A Clockwork Orange: V15
Burney, Fanny
Evelina: V16
Burns, Olive Ann
Cold Sassy Tree: V31
Butler, Octavia
Kindred: V8
Parable of the Sower: V21
Patternmaster: V34
Butler, Samuel
The Way of All Flesh: V44

C

*The Caine Mutiny: A Novel of World
War II* (Wouk): V7
Caldwell, Erskine
Tobacco Road: V49
Call It Sleep (Roth): V47
The Call of the Wild (London): V8
A Canticle for Leibowitz (Miller):
V44
Camus, Albert
The Plague: V16
The Stranger: V6

Candide (Voltaire): V7
Cane (Toomer): V11
Cannery Row (Steinbeck): V28
Caramelo, or, Puro cuento
(Cisneros): V47
Card, Orson Scott
Ender's Game: V5
Carroll, Lewis
Alice's Adventures in Wonderland:
V7
Through the Looking-Glass: V27
Cashore, Kristin
Graceling: V53
The Castle (Kafka): V34
Catalyst (Anderson): V49
Catch-22 (Heller): V1
The Catcher in the Rye (Salinger): V1
Cather, Willa
Death Comes for the Archbishop:
V19
A Lost Lady: V33
My Ántonia: V2
O Pioneers!: V47
One of Ours: V52
The Song of the Lark: V41
Cat's Cradle (Vonnegut): V28
Cat's Eye (Atwood): V14
Ceremony (Silko): V4
Chabon, Michael
*The Amazing Adventures of
Kavalier & Clay:* V25
Chandler, Raymond
The Big Sleep: V17
The Big Sleep (Motion picture):
V48
Charming Billy (McDermott): V23
Chbosky, Stephen
The Perks of Being a Wallflower:
V47
Chesnutt, Charles W.
The House behind the Cedars V45
Chevalier, Tracy
Girl with a Pearl Earring: V45
Chin, Frank
Donald Duk: V41
The Chocolate War (Cormier): V2
Choi, Sook Nyul
Year of Impossible Goodbyes: V29
Chopin, Kate
The Awakening: V3
The Chosen (Potok): V4
Christ in Concrete (Di Donato): V51
Christie, Agatha
The A.B.C. Murders: V30
Murder on the Orient Express: V33
Ten Little Indians: V8
A Christmas Carol (Dickens): V10
Chronicle of a Death Foretold
(García Márquez): V10
Cimarron (Ferber): V45
Cisneros, Sandra
Caramelo, or, Puro cuento: V47
The House on Mango Street: V2

The Clan of the Cave Bear (Auel): V11
Clark, Walter Van Tilburg
The Ox-Bow Incident: V40
Clavell, James du Maresq
Shogun: A Novel of Japan: V10
Cleage, Pearl
*What Looks Like Crazy on an
Ordinary Day:* V17
Clear Light of Day (Desai): V44
Clemens, Samuel Langhorne
*The Adventures of Huckleberry
Finn:* V1
The Adventures of Tom Sawyer: V6
A Clockwork Orange (Burgess): V15
Clueless (Motion picture): V40
Code Name Verity (Wein): V50
Coelho, Paulo
The Alchemist: V29
Coen, Joel and Ethan
O Brother Where Art Thou?
(Motion picture): V50
Coetzee, J. M.
Age of Iron: V51
Dusklands: V21
Cold Mountain (Frazier): V25
Cold Sassy Tree (Burns): V31
The Color Purple (Walker): V5
The Color Purple (Motion picture):
V40
Collier, Christopher
My Brother Sam is Dead V38
Collier, James Lincoln
My Brother Sam is Dead V38
Collins, Wilkie
The Moonstone: V39
The Woman in White: V54
Conan Doyle, Arthur, Sir
The Hound of the Baskervilles: V28
*A Connecticut Yankee in King
Arthur's Court* (Twain): V20
Conrad, Joseph
Heart of Darkness: V2
Lord Jim: V16
Conroy, Frank
Body and Soul: V11
The Contender (Lipsyte): V35
Cooper, James Fenimore
The Deerslayer: V25
The Last of the Mohicans: V9
The Last of the Mohicans (Motion
picture): V32
*The Pathfinder; or, The Inland
Sea:* V38
Cormier, Robert
The Chocolate War: V2
I Am the Cheese: V18
The Corrections (Franzen): V40
The Count of Monte Cristo (Dumas):
V19
The Country of the Pointed Firs
(Jewett): V15
Courtenay, Bryce
The Power of One: V32

Crane, Stephen
  Maggie: A Girl of the Streets: V20
  The Red Badge of Courage: V4
The Crazy Horse Electric Game
  (Crutcher): V11
Crescent (Abu-Jaber): V51
Crichton, Michael
  The Great Train Robbery: V34
Crime and Punishment
  (Dostoyevsky): V3
The Cruel Sea (Monsarrat): V39
Crutcher, Chris
  The Crazy Horse Electric Game:
    V11
  Staying Fat for Sarah Byrnes: V32
Cry, the Beloved Country (Paton): V3
The Crying of Lot 49 (Pynchon): V36
Cunningham, Michael
  The Hours: V23
  The Hours (Motion picture): V48
Curran, Mary Doyle
  The Parish and the Hill: V53

D

The Damnation of Theron Ware
  (Frederic): V22
Dandelion Wine (Bradbury): V22
Dangarembga, Tsitsi
  Nervous Conditions: V28
Danticat, Edwidge
  Breath, Eyes, Memory: V37
  The Dew Breaker: V28
Darkness at Noon (Koestler): V19
Daughter of Fortune (Allende): V18
David Copperfield (Dickens): V25
Davis, Rebecca Harding
  *Margret Howth: A Story of To-
    Day:* V14
Davita's Harp (Potok): V34
A Day No Pigs Would Die (Peck):
  V29
The Day of the Locust (West): V16
De Rosnay, Tatiana
  Sarah's Key: V51
de Cervantes Saavedra, Miguel
  Don Quixote: V8
The Dead of the House (Green): V10
Death Comes for the Archbishop
  (Cather): V19
A Death in the Family (Agee): V22
Death in Venice (Mann): V17
The Death of the Heart (Bowen): V13
The Deerslayer (Cooper): V25
Defoe, Daniel
  A Journal of the Plague Year: V30
  Moll Flanders: V13
  Robinson Crusoe: V9
DeLillo, Don
  Libra: V54
  Underworld: V47
  White Noise: V28

Deliverance (Dickey): V9
Demian (Hesse): V15
Democracy (Didion): V3
Desai, Anita
  Clear Light of Day: V44
Desai, Kiran
  Hullabaloo in the Guava Orchard:
    V28
  The Inheritance of Loss: V49
Desirable Daughters (Mukherjee):
  V45
Dessen, Sarah
  Someone Like You: V50
The Dew Breaker (Danticat): V28
Di Donato, Pietro
  Christ in Concrete: V51
Díaz, Junot
  *The Brief Wondrous Life of Oscar
    Wao:* V36
Diamant, Anita
  The Red Tent: V36
Dick, Philip K.
  *Do Androids Dream of Electric
    Sheep?:* V5
  Martian Time-Slip: V26
Dickens, Charles
  Bleak House: V30
  A Christmas Carol: V10
  David Copperfield: V25
  Great Expectations: V4
  Great Expectations (Motion
    picture): V42
  Hard Times: V20
  Nicholas Nickleby: V33
  Oliver Twist: V14
  The Pickwick Papers: V41
  A Tale of Two Cities: V5
Dickey, James
  Deliverance: V9
Didion, Joan
  Democracy: V3
Digging to America (Tyler): V38
Dinesen, Isak
  Out of Africa: V9
Dinner at the Homesick Restaurant
  (Tyler): V2
The Dispossessed (Le Guin): V52
Divakaruni, Chitra Banerjee
  Sister of My Heart: V38
The Dive from Clausen's Pier
  (Packer): V47
*Do Androids Dream of Electric
  Sheep?* (Dick): V5
Doctor Zhivago (Pasternak): V26
Doctor Zhivago (Motion picture):
  V41
Doctorow, E. L.
  Ragtime: V6
  Ragtime (Motion picture): V44
Don Quixote (de Cervantes
  Saavedra): V8
Donald Duk (Chin): V41

Dorris, Michael
  A Yellow Raft in Blue Water: V3
Dos Passos, John
  Manhattan Transfer: V53
  U.S.A.: V14
Dostoyevsky, Fyodor
  The Brothers Karamazov: V8
  Crime and Punishment: V3
  The Idiot: V40
  Notes from Underground: V28
Doyle, Arthur Conan, Sir
  The Hound of the Baskervilles: V28
Dr. Jekyll and Mr. Hyde (Stevenson):
  V11
Dracula (Stoker): V18
Dracula (Motion picture): V41
Draper, Sharon M.
  Tears of a Tiger: V42
Dreaming in Cuban (García): V38
*Dred: A Tale of the Great Dismal
  Swamp* (Stowe): V47
Dreiser, Theodore
  An American Tragedy: V17
  Sister Carrie: V8
du Maurier, Daphne
  Rebecca: V12
  Rebecca (Motion picture): V50
Dumas, Alexandre
  The Count of Monte Cristo: V19
  The Man in the Iron Mask: V41
  The Three Musketeers: V14
Dune (Herbert): V31
Duong Thu Huong
  Paradise of the Blind: V23
Dusklands (Coetzee): V21

E

East of Eden (Steinbeck): V19
East of Eden (Motion picture): V34
Eco, Umberto
  The Name of the Rose: V22
The Edible Woman (Atwood): V12
Einstein's Dreams (Lightman): V29
Eliot, George
  Adam Bede: V34
  Middlemarch: V23
  The Mill on the Floss: V17
  Silas Marner: V20
Ellen Foster (Gibbons): V3
Ellis, Bret Easton
  Less Than Zero: V11
Ellison, Ralph
  Invisible Man: V2
  Juneteenth: V21
Elmer Gantry (Lewis): V22
Elmer Gantry (Motion picture): V47
Emecheta, Buchi
  The Bride Price: V12
  The Joys of Motherhood: V41
  The Wrestling Match: V14
Emma (Austen): V21

Emma (Motion picture): V46
Empire Falls (Russo): V25
Empire of the Sun (Ballard): V8
Empire of the Sun (Motion picture): V42
The End of the Affair (Greene): V16
Ender's Game (Card): V5
Enger, Leif
    Peace Like a River: V42
The English Patient (Ondaatje): V23
Erdrich, Louise
    The Antelope Wife: V44
    The Beet Queen: V37
    The Bingo Palace: V40
    Love Medicine: V5
    The Round House: V48
Esquivel, Laura
    Like Water for Chocolate: V5
Ethan Frome (Wharton): V5
Eugenides, Jeffrey
    Middlesex: V24
Eva Luna (Allende): V29
Evelina (Burney): V16
Everything I Never Told You (Ng): V52
Everything Is Illuminated (Foer): V52
Extremely Loud & Incredibly Close (Foer): V36

F

Fahrenheit 451 (Bradbury): V1
Fallen Angels (Myers): V30
The Family Moskat (Singer): V53
Far from the Madding Crowd (Hardy): V19
Farewell My Concubine (Lee): V19
A Farewell to Arms (Hemingway): V1
Farmer, Nancy
    The House of the Scorpion: V43
Fast, Howard
    April Morning: V35
Fathers and Sons (Turgenev): V16
Faulkner, William
    Absalom, Absalom!: V13
    As I Lay Dying: V8
    Intruder in the Dust: V33
    Light in August: V24
    The Sound and the Fury: V4
    The Unvanquished: V38
Feed (Anderson): V41
Ferber, Edna
    Cimarron: V45
Fever 1793 (Anderson): V35
Fielding, Henry
    Joseph Andrews: V32
    Tom Jones: V18
The Fifth Child (Lessing): V38
A Fine Balance (Mistry): V43
Fitzgerald, F. Scott
    The Beautiful and Damned: V49
    The Great Gatsby: V2

This Side of Paradise: V20
    Tender Is the Night: V19
The Fixer (Malamud): V9
Flagg, Fannie
    Fried Green Tomatoes at the Whistle Stop Café: V7
Flanagan, Richard
    The Narrow Road to the Deep North: V54
Flatland: A Romance of Many Dimensions (Abbott): V47
Flaubert, Gustave
    Madame Bovary: V14
Flowers for Algernon (Keyes): V2
Foden, Giles
Fools Crow (Welch): V53
    The Last King of Scotland: V15
For Whom the Bell Tolls (Hemingway): V14
Foer, Jonathan Safran
    Everything Is Illuminated: V52
    Extremely Loud & Incredibly Close: V36
Forbes, Kathryn
    Mama's Bank Account: V47
Ford, Ford Madox
    The Good Soldier: V28
Ford, Richard
    Independence Day: V25
Foreign Affairs (Lurie): V24
Forever... (Blume): V24
Forster, E. M.
    Howards End: V10
    A Passage to India: V3
    A Room with a View: V11
    A Room with a View (Motion picture): V47
Fountain and Tomb (Mahfouz): V42
The Fountainhead (Rand): V16
Fowles, John
    The French Lieutenant's Woman: V21
Fox, Paula
    The Slave Dancer: V12
Frank, Pat
    Alas, Babylon: V29
Frankenstein (Shelley): V1
Frankenstein (Motion picture): V37
Franny and Zooey (Salinger): V30
Franzen, Jonathan
    The Corrections: V40
Frazier, Charles
    Cold Mountain: V25
Frederic, Harold
    The Damnation of Theron Ware: V22
The French Lieutenant's Woman (Fowles): V21
Fried Green Tomatoes at the Whistle Stop Café (Flagg): V7
Fuentes, Carlos
    The Old Gringo: V8

G

Gaiman, Neil.
    The Ocean at the End of the Lane: V51
Gaines, Ernest J.
    The Autobiography of Miss Jane Pittman: V5
    A Gathering of Old Men: V16
    A Lesson Before Dying: V7
García, Cristina
    Dreaming in Cuban: V38
García Márquez, Gabriel
    Chronicle of a Death Foretold: V10
    Love in the Time of Cholera: V1
    One Hundred Years of Solitude: V5
A Garden of Earthly Delights (Oates): V54
Gardner, John
    Grendel: V3
A Gathering of Old Men (Gaines): V16
Giants in the Earth (Rölvaag): V5
Gibbons, Kaye
    Ellen Foster: V3
Gibson, William
    Neuromancer: V38
Gide, André
    The Immoralist: V21
Gilead (Robinson): V24
Gilman, Charlotte Perkins
    Herland: V36
Girl with a Pearl Earring (Chevalier): V45
The Giver (Lowry): V3
Glass, Julia
    Three Junes: V34
The Glory Field (Myers): V33
Go Tell It on the Mountain (Baldwin): V4
The God of Small Things (Roy): V22
The Godfather (Puzo): V16
Golden, Arthur
    Memoirs of a Geisha: V19
The Golden Notebook (Lessing): V27
Golding, William
    Lord of the Flies: V2
    Lord of the Flies (Motion picture) V36
Goldman, William
    The Princess Bride: V31
    The Princess Bride (Motion picture): V53
Going after Cacciato (O'Brien): V37
Gone with the Wind (Mitchell): V9
Gone with the Wind (Motion picture): V38
The Good Earth (Buck): V25
The Good Soldier (Ford): V28
Gordon, Sheila
    Waiting for the Rain: V40

Gordimer, Nadine
   Burger's Daugher: V50
   July's People: V4
The Gospel according to Larry
   (Tashjian): V46
GraceLand (Abani): V35
Graceling (Cashore): V53
Grahame, Kenneth
   The Wind in the Willows: V20
A Grain of Wheat (Ngũgĩ Wa
   Thiong'o): V49
The Grapes of Wrath (Steinbeck): V7
The Grapes of Wrath (Motion
   picture): V39
The Grass Dancer (Power): V11
Grau, Shirley Ann
   The Keepers of the House: V52
Graves, Robert
   I, Claudius: V21
Gravity's Rainbow (Pynchon): V23
Great Expectations (Dickens): V4
Great Expectations (Motion picture):
   V42
The Great Gatsby (Fitzgerald): V2
The Great Train Robbery (Crichton):
   V34
Green, Hannah
   The Dead of the House: V10
Green, John
   Looking for Alaska: V48
Green Mansions (Hudson): V46
Greenberg, Joanne
   *I Never Promised You a Rose
     Garden:* V23
Greene, Bette
   Summer of My German Soldier: V10
Greene, Graham
   The End of the Affair: V16
   The Heart of the Matter: V45
   The Power and the Glory: V31
   The Third Man: V36
Grendel (Gardner): V3
Grossman, Lev
   The Magicians: V50
Growing Up (Baker): V48
*The Guernsey Literary and Potato
   Peel Society* (Shaffer and
   Barrows): V43
Guest, Judith
   Ordinary People: V1
   Ordinary People (Motion picture):
     V33
The Guide (Narayan): V50
Gulliver's Travels (Swift): V6
Guterson, David
   Snow Falling on Cedars: V13

H

Haddix, Margaret Peterson
   Among the Hidden: V47
Haggard, H. Rider
   King Solomon's Mines: V40

Haley, Alex
   *Roots: The Story of an American
     Family:* V9
   Roots (Motion picture): V46
Half a Life (Naipaul): V39
Half of a Yellow Sun (Adichie): V48
Hamill, Pete
   Snow in August: V54
Hamilton, Jane
   A Map of the World: V45
Hammett, Dashiell
   The Maltese Falcon: V21
   The Maltese Falcon (Motion
     picture): V49
A Handful of Dust (Waugh): V34
The Handmaid's Tale (Atwood): V4
Hard Times (Dickens): V20
Hardy, Thomas
   Far from the Madding Crowd: V19
   Jude the Obscure: V30
   The Mayor of Casterbridge: V15
   The Return of the Native: V11
   Tess of the d'Urbervilles: V3
Haroun and the Sea of Stories
   (Rushdie): V41
Harper, Frances E. W.
   Iola Leroy; or, Shadows Uplifted:
     V53
Harris, Marilyn
   Hatter Fox: V14
Hatter Fox (Harris): V14
The Haunting of Hill House
   (Jackson): V37
Hawthorne, Nathaniel
   The House of the Seven Gables:
     V20
   The Scarlet Letter: V1
Head, Bessie
   When Rain Clouds Gather: V31
The Heart Is a Lonely Hunter
   (McCullers): V6
Heart of Aztlan (Anaya): V49
Heart of Darkness (Conrad): V2
The Heart of the Matter (Greene):
   V45
Hegi, Ursula
   Stones from the River: V25
Heinlein, Robert A.
   Stranger in a Strange Land: V40
Heinlein, Robert A.
   Stranger in a Strange Land: V40
Heir to the Glimmering World
   (Ozick): V46
Heller, Joseph
   Catch-22: V1
The Help (Stockett): V39
The Help (Motion picture): V52
Hemingway, Ernest
   A Farewell to Arms: V1
   For Whom the Bell Tolls: V14
   A Moveable Feast: V48
   The Old Man and the Sea: V6
   The Sun Also Rises: V5

Herbert, Frank
   Dune: V31
   Soul Catcher: V17
Herland (Gilman): V36
Hersey, John
   A Bell for Adano: V41
Herzog (Bellow): V14
Hesse, Hermann
   Demian: V15
   Siddhartha: V6
   Steppenwolf: V24
Hickam, Homer, Jr.
   Rocket Boys: A Memoir: V48
Highsmith, Patricia
   The Talented Mr. Ripley: V27
Hijuelos, Oscar
   *The Mambo Kings Play Songs of
     Love:* V17
Hinton, S. E.
   The Outsiders: V5
   The Outsiders (Motion picture):
     V35
   Rumble Fish: V15
   Tex: V9
   That Was Then, This Is Now: V16
The Hitchhiker's Guide to the Galaxy
   (Adams): V7
The Hobbit (Tolkien): V8
Høeg, Peter
   Smilla's Sense of Snow: V17
Holes (Sachar): V37
The Home and the World (Tagore):
   V48
Homeless Bird (Whelan): V49
Hope Was Here (Bauer): V54
Hosseini, Khaled
   And the Mountains Echoed: V52
Hotel du Lac (Brookner): V23
The Hound of the Baskervilles
   (Conan Doyle): V28
The Hours (Cunningham): V23
The Hours (Motion picture): V48
The House behind the Cedars
   (Chesnutt): V45
House Made of Dawn (Momaday):
   V10
The House of Mirth (Wharton): V15
The House of the Scorpion (Farmer):
   V43
The House of the Seven Gables
   (Hawthorne): V20
The House of the Spirits (Allende):
   V6
The House on Mango Street
   (Cisneros): V2
Housekeeping (Robinson): V39
How Green Was My Valley
   (Llewellyn): V30
*How the García Girls Lost Their
   Accents* (Alvarez): V5
Howards End (Forster): V10
Howells, William Dean
   The Rise of Silas Lapham: V43

Hudson, Jan
    Sweetgrass: V28
Hudson, William Henry
    Green Mansions: V46
Hughes, Langston
    Tambourines to Glory: V21
Hugo, Victor
    The Hunchback of Notre Dame:
        V20
    Les Misérables: V5
Hullabaloo in the Guava Orchard
    (Desai): V28
Hulme, Keri
    The Bone People: V24
The Human Comedy (Saroyan): V39
Humboldt's Gift (Bellow): V26
The Hunchback of Notre Dame
    (Hugo): V20
The Hundred Secret Senses (Tan):
    V44
Hurston, Zora Neale
    Their Eyes Were Watching God:
        V3
    Their Eyes Were Watching God
        (Motion picture): V54
Huxley, Aldous
    Brave New World: V6

I

I Am the Cheese (Cormier): V18
I, Claudius (Graves): V21
I Know Why the Caged Bird Sings
    (Angelou): V2
I Never Promised You a Rose Garden
    (Greenberg): V23
Ida (Stein): V27
The Idiot (Dostoyevsky): V40
If You Come Softly (Woodson): V46
The Immoralist (Gide): V21
In Babylon (Möring): V25
In Country (Mason): V4
In the Castle of My Skin (Lamming):
    V15
In the Shadow of the Banyan
    (Ratner): V48
In the Time of the Butterflies
    (Alvarez): V9
Independence Day (Ford): V25
Indian Killer (Alexie): V54
The Inheritance of Loss (Desai): V49
Intruder in the Dust (Faulkner): V33
Invisible Man (Ellison): V2
Iola Leroy; or, Shadows Uplifted
    (Harper): V53
I, Robot (Asimov): V29
Irving, John
    A Prayer for Owen Meany: V14
    The World According to Garp: V12
Ishiguro, Kazuo
    Never Let Me Go: V35
    Never Let Me Go (Motion
        picture): V45

The Remains of the Day: V13
The Remains of the Day (Motion
    picture): V39
The Island of Dr. Moreau (Wells): V36
It's Kind of a Funny Story (Vizzini):
    V52
Ivanhoe (Scott): V31

J

Jackson, Shirley
    The Haunting of Hill House: V37
James, Henry
    The Ambassadors: V12
    The American: V44
    The Bostonians: V37
    The Portrait of a Lady: V19
    The Turn of the Screw: V16
    The Wings of the Dove: V32
Jane Eyre (Brontë): V4
Jane Eyre (Motion picture): V54
Japrisot, Sébastien
    A Very Long Engagement: V18
Jasmine (Mukherjee): V37
Jazz (Morrison): V40
Jen, Gish
    Typical American: V30
Jewett, Sarah Orne
    The Country of the Pointed Firs: V15
Jiménez, Juan Ramón
    Platero and I: V36
Jin, Ha
    Waiting: V25
Johnny Got His Gun (Trumbo): V44
Johnson, Charles
    Middle Passage: V43
Johnson, James Weldon
    *The Autobiography of an Ex-
        Coloured Man:* V22
Jones, Edward P.
    The Known World: V26
Joseph Andrews (Fielding): V32
A Journal of the Plague Year (Defoe):
    V30
Journey to the Center of the Earth
    (Verne): V34
The Joy Luck Club (Tan): V1
The Joy Luck Club (Motion picture):
    V35
The Joys of Motherhood (Emecheta):
    V41
Joyce, James
    *A Portrait of the Artist as a Young
        Man:* V7
    Ulysses: V26
Jude the Obscure (Hardy): V30
July's People (Gordimer): V4
Juneteenth (Ellison): V21
The Jungle (Sinclair): V6

K

Kaddish for a Child Not Born
    (Kertész): V23

Kafka, Franz
    The Castle: V34
    The Trial: V7
Kawabata, Yasunari
    Snow Country: V42
The Keepers of the House (Grau): V52
Keneally, Thomas
    Schindler's List: V17
    Schindler's List (Motion picture):
        V38
Kerouac, Jack
    On the Road: V8
Kertész, Imre
    Kaddish for a Child Not Born: V23
Kesey, Ken
    One Flew Over the Cuckoo's Nest:
        V2
    One Flew Over the Cuckoo's Nest
        (Motion picture): V44
Keyes, Daniel
    Flowers for Algernon: V2
Kidd, Sue Monk
    The Secret Life of Bees: V27
Kidnapped (Stevenson): V33
The Killer Angels (Shaara): V26
Kim (Kipling): V21
Kincaid, Jamaica
    Annie John: V3
    Lucy: V51
Kindred (Butler): V8
King Solomon's Mines (Haggard): V40
Kingsolver, Barbara
    Animal Dreams: V12
    The Bean Trees: V5
    Pigs in Heaven: V10
    Poisonwood Bible: V24
Kingston, Maxine Hong
    The Woman Warrior: V6
Kinsella, W. P.
    Shoeless Joe: V15
Kipling, Rudyard
    Kim: V21
Kitchen (Yoshimoto): V7
The Kitchen God's Wife (Tan): V13
Knowles, John
    A Separate Peace: V2
The Known World (Jones): V26
Koestler, Arthur
    Darkness at Noon: V19
Kogawa, Joy
    Obasan: V3
Kosinski, Jerzy
    The Painted Bird: V12
Kundera, Milan
    *The Book of Laughter and
        Forgetting:* V27
    *The Unbearable Lightness of
        Being:* V18

L

Lahiri, Jhumpa
    The Lowland: V52
    The Namesake: V31

Laird, Elizabeth
    A Little Piece of Ground: V46
Lamming, George
    In the Castle of My Skin: V15
Lampedusa, Giuseppe Tomasi di
    The Leopard: V44
Lao She
    Rickshaw Boy: V50
Larsen, Nella
    Quicksand: V48
The Last King of Scotland (Foden): V15
The Last of the Mohicans (Cooper):
    V9
The Last of the Mohicans (Motion
    picture): V32
The Last Picture Show (McMurtry):
    V51
Laurence, Margaret
    The Stone Angel: V11
Lawrence, D. H.
    The Rainbow: V26
    Sons and Lovers: V45
Le Guin, Ursula K.
    Always Coming Home: V9
    The Dispossessed: V52
    The Left Hand of Darkness: V6
The Learning Tree (Parks): V32
Lederer, William J., and Eugene
    Burdick
    The Ugly American: V23
Lee, Chang-rae
    Native Speaker: V42
Lee, Harper
    To Kill a Mockingbird: V2
    To Kill a Mockingbird (Motion
        picture): V32
Lee, Lilian
    Farewell My Concubine: V19
The Left Hand of Darkness (Le
    Guin): V6
L'Engle, Madeleine
    A Wrinkle in Time: V32
The Leopard (Lampedusa): V44
Leroux, Gaston
    The Phantom of the Opera: V20
    The Phantom of the Opera
        (Motion Picture): V52
Les Misérables (Hugo): V5
Less Than Zero (Ellis): V11
Lessing, Doris
    The Fifth Child: V38
    The Golden Notebook: V27
A Lesson Before Dying (Gaines): V7
Lewis, C. S.
    *The Lion, the Witch and the
        Wardrobe:* V24
Lewis, Matthew
    The Monk: V52
Lewis, Sinclair
    Arrowsmith: V34
    Babbitt: V19
    Elmer Gantry: V22

Elmer Gantry (Motion picture):
    V47
Main Street: V15
Libra (DeLillo): V54
Lie Down in Darkness (Styron): V50
Life of Pi (Martel): V27
Life of Pi (Motion picture): V51
Light in August (Faulkner): V24
The Light in the Forest (Richter): V43
Lightman, Alan
    Einstein's Dreams: V29
Like Water for Chocolate (Esquivel):
    V5
Linden Hills (Naylor): V49
*The Lion, the Witch and the
    Wardrobe* (Lewis): V24
Lipsyte, Robert
    The Contender: V35
A Little Piece of Ground (Laird): V46
The Little Prince (de Saint-Exupéry):
    V30
Little Women (Alcott): V12
Little Women (Motion picture): V53
Lives of Girls and Women (Munro):
    V27
Llewellyn, Richard
    How Green Was My Valley: V30
Lolita (Nabokov): V9
London, Jack
    The Call of the Wild: V8
    The Sea-Wolf: V35
    White Fang: V19
*The Lone Ranger and Tonto Fistfight
    in Heaven* (Alexie): V17
A Long and Happy Life (Price): V18
Look Homeward, Angel (Wolfe): V18
Looking Backward: 2000–1887
    (Bellamy): V15
Looking for Alaska (Green): V48
Lord Jim (Conrad): V16
Lord of the Flies (Golding): V2
Lord of the Flies (Motion picture): V36
The Lord of the Rings (Tolkien): V26
Losing Battles (Welty): V15
A Lost Lady (Cather): V33
Love (Morrison): V46
Love in the Time of Cholera (García
    Márquez): V1
Love Medicine (Erdrich): V5
The Loved One (Waugh): V50
The Lovely Bones (Sebold): V54
The Lowland (Lahiri): V52
Lowry, Lois
    The Giver: V3
    Number the Stars: V39
Lucy (Kincaid): V51
Lurie, Alison
    Foreign Affairs: V24

M

Machiavelli, Niccolo
    The Prince: V9
Madame Bovary (Flaubert): V14

Maggie: A Girl of the Streets
    (Crane): V20
The Magic Mountain (Mann): V29
The Magicians (Grossman): V50
The Magnificent Ambersons
    (Tarkington): V34
Magona, Sindiwe
    Mother to Mother: V43
Maguire, Gregory
    *Wicked: The Life and Times of the
        Wicked Witch of the West:* V35
Mahfouz, Naguib
    Fountain and Tomb: V42
Mailer, Norman
    The Naked and the Dead: V10
Main Street (Lewis): V15
Make Lemonade (Wolff): V35
Malamud, Bernard
    The Assistant: V27
    The Fixer: V9
    The Natural: V4
    The Natural (Motion picture): V34
Malladi, Amulya
    A Breath of Fresh Air: V53
The Maltese Falcon (Hammett): V21
The Maltese Falcon (Motion
    picture): V49
Mama Day (Naylor): V7
Mama's Bank Account (Forbes): V47
*The Mambo Kings Play Songs of
    Love* (Hijuelos): V17
The Man in the Iron Mask (Dumas):
    V41
The Man Who Loved Children
    (Stead): V27
Manhattan Transfer (Dos Passos):
    V53
Mann, Thomas
    Death in Venice: V17
    The Magic Mountain: V29
Mansfield Park (Austen): V29
A Map of the World (Hamilton): V45
March (Brooks): V26
Margret Howth: A Story of To-Day
    (Davis): V14
Markandaya, Kamala
    Nectar in a Sieve: V13
Marshall, Paule
    Praisesong for the Widow: V36
Martel, Yann
    Life of Pi: V27
    Life of Pi (Motion picture): V51
The Martian Chronicles (Bradbury):
    V42
Martian Time-Slip (Dick): V26
*Martin Dressler: The Tale of an
    American Dreamer*
    (Millhauser): V48
Mason, Bobbie Ann
    In Country: V4
The Master and Margarita
    (Bulgakov): V8

Maugham, W. Somerset
  Of Human Bondage: V35
  The Razor's Edge: V23
Maus: A Survivor's Tale
  (Spiegelman): V35
The Mayor of Casterbridge (Hardy):
  V15
McBride, James
  Song Yet Sung: V49
McCarthy, Cormac
  All the Pretty Horses: V36
  The Road: V40
McCrumb, Sharyn
  St. Dale: V46
McCullers, Carson
  The Heart Is a Lonely Hunter: V6
  The Member of the Wedding: V13
McDermott, Alice
  Charming Billy: V23
McDonald, Joyce
  Swallowing Stones: V45
McEwan, Ian
  Atonement: V32
  Atonement (Motion picture): V49
McKinley, Robin
  *Beauty: A Retelling of the Story of
  Beauty and the Beast:* V33
McMurtry, Larry
  The Last Picture Show: V51
Melville, Herman
  Benito Cereno: V41
  *Billy Budd, Sailor: An Inside
  Narrative:* V9
  Moby-Dick: V7
  Moby-Dick (Motion picture): V43
  Typee: V32
The Member of the Wedding
  (McCullers): V13
Memoirs of a Geisha (Golden): V19
Méndez, Miguel
  Pilgrims in Aztlán: V12
Middle Passage (Johnson): V43
Middlemarch (Eliot): V23
Middlesex (Eugenides): V24
Midnight's Children (Rushdie): V23
The Mill on the Floss (Eliot): V17
Miller, Walter M., Jr.
  A Canticle for Leibowitz: V44
Millhauser, Steven
  *Martin Dressler: The Tale of an
  American Dreamer:* V48
Mishima, Yukio
  The Sound of Waves: V43
Mistry, Rohinton
  A Fine Balance: V43
The Mists of Avalon (Bradley): V40
Mitchell, Margaret
  Gone with the Wind: V9
  Gone with the Wind (Motion
  picture): V38
Moby-Dick (Melville): V7
Moby-Dick (Motion picture): V43
Moll Flanders (Defoe): V13

Momaday, N. Scott
  House Made of Dawn: V10
  The Way to Rainy Mountain:
  V45
The Monk (Lewis): V52
The Monkey Wrench Gang (Abbey):
  V43
The Moon is Down (Steinbeck): V37
Monsarrat, Nicholas
  The Cruel Sea: V39
Monster (Myers): V40
Monster (Peretti): V46
Montana 1948 (Watson): V39
The Moonstone (Collins): V39
More, Thomas
  Utopia: V29
Mori, Kyoko
  Shizuko's Daughter: V15
Möring, Marcel
  In Babylon: V25
Morpurgo, Michael
  War Horse: V47
Morrison, Toni
  Beloved: V6
  The Bluest Eye: V1
  Jazz: V40
  Love: V46
  Sula: V14
  Song of Solomon: V8
  Tar Baby: V37
Mother to Mother (Magona): V43
A Moveable Feast (Hemingway):
  V48
The Moviegoer (Percy): V51
Mr. Sammler's Planet (Bellow): V53
Mrs. Dalloway (Woolf): V12
Mukherjee, Bharati
  Desirable Daughters: V45
  Jasmine: V37
  The Tree Bride: V54
Mulisch, Harry
  The Assault: V52
Munro, Alice
  Lives of Girls and Women: V27
Murder on the Orient Express
  (Christie): V33
Murdoch, Iris
  Under the Net: V18
My Ántonia (Cather): V2
My Brother Sam is Dead (Collier): V38
My Jim (Rawles): V43
Myers, Walter Dean
  Fallen Angels: V30
  The Glory Field: V33
  Monster: V40
  Sunrise over Fallujah: V45
My Name is Asher Lev (Potok): V38
My Name is Red (Pamuk): V27
My Year of Meats (Ozeki): V49

N

Nabokov, Vladimir
  Lolita: V9

Naipaul, V. S.
  A Bend in the River: V37
  Half a Life: V39
The Naked and the Dead (Mailer):
  V10
The Name of the Rose (Eco): V22
The Namesake (Lahiri): V31
Narayan, R. K.
  The Guide: V50
  The Ramayana: V41
The Narrow Road to the Deep North
  (Flanagan): V54
Native Son (Wright): V7
Native Speaker (Lee): V42
The Natural (Malamud): V4
The Natural (Motion picture): V34
Nausea (Sartre): V21
Naylor, Gloria
  Linden Hills: V49
  Mama Day: V7
  The Women of Brewster Place: V4
Nectar in a Sieve (Markandaya): V13
Nervous Conditions (Dangarembga):
  V28
Neuromancer (Gibson): V38
Never Let Me Go (Ishiguro): V35
Never Let Me Go (Motion picture):
  V45
Nexø, Martin Anderson
  Pelle the Conqueror: V34
Ng, Celeste
  Everything I Never Told You: V52
Ng, Fae Myenne
  Bone: V37
Ngũgĩ Wa Thiong'o
  A Grain of Wheat: V49
Nicholas Nickleby (Dickens): V33
Night (Wiesel): V4
Nineteen Minutes (Picoult): V49
No-No Boy (Okada): V25
No Longer at Ease (Achebe): V33
Norris, Frank
  The Octopus: V12
Northanger Abbey (Austen): V28
Notes from Underground
  (Dostoyevsky): V28
*Nothing But the Truth: A
  Documentary Novel* (Avi): V34
Number the Stars (Lowry): V39

O

O Brother, Where Art Thou? (Motion
  picture): V50
O Pioneers! (Cather): V47
Oates, Joyce Carol
  A Garden of Earthly Delight: V54
  them: V8
  We Were the Mulvaneys: V24
Obasan (Kogawa): V3
O'Brien, Tim
  Going after Cacciato: V37

The Ocean at the End of the Lane
(Gaiman): V51
O'Connor, Flannery
The Violent Bear It Away: V21
Wise Blood: V3
The Octopus (Norris): V12
Of Human Bondage (Maugham):
V35
Of Mice and Men (Steinbeck): V1
O'Hara, John
Appointment in Samarra: V11
Okada, John
No-No Boy: V25
The Old Gringo (Fuentes): V8
The Old Man and the Sea
(Hemingway): V6
Olive Kitteridge (Strout): V39
Oliver Twist (Dickens): V14
Olsen, Tillie
Yonnondio: From the Thirties: V50
On the Beach (Shute): V9
On the Road (Kerouac): V8
The Once and Future King (White):
V30
Ondaatje, Michael
The English Patient: V23
One Day in the Life of Ivan
Denisovich (Solzhenitsyn): V6
One Flew Over the Cuckoo's Nest
(Kesey): V2
One Flew Over the Cuckoo's Nest
(Motion picture): V44
One Hundred Years of Solitude
(García Márquez): V5
One of Ours (Cather): V52
The Optimist's Daughter (Welty):
V13
Orczy, Emmuska
The Scarlet Pimpernel: V31
Ordinary People (Guest): V1
Ordinary People (Motion picture):
V33
Orlando: A Biography (Woolf): V42
Oroonoko; or, The Royal Slave: A
True History (Behn): V35
Orwell, George
Animal Farm: V3
1984: V7
Oryx and Crake (Atwood): V39
Otsuka, Julie
The Buddha in the Attic: V54
When the Emperor Was Divine: V41
Out of Africa (Dinesen): V9
The Outsider (Wright): V53
The Outsiders (Hinton): V5
The Outsiders (Motion picture): V35
The Ox-Bow Incident (Clark): V40
Ozeki, Ruth
My Year of Meats: V49
Ozick, Cynthia
Heir to the Glimmering World:
V46

P

Packer, Ann
The Dive from Clausen's Pier: V47
The Painted Bird (Kosinski): V12
Pamuk, Orhan
My Name is Red: V27
Parable of the Sower (Butler): V21
Paradise of the Blind (Duong): V23
The Parish and the Hill (Curran):
V53
Parks, Gordon
The Learning Tree: V32
A Passage to India (Forster): V3
Pasternak, Boris
Doctor Zhivago: V26
Doctor Zhivago (Motion picture):
V41
Patchett, Ann
Bel Canto: V30
The Pathfinder; or, The Inland Sea
(Cooper): V38
Patneaude, David
Thin Wood Walls: V46
Paton, Alan
Cry, the Beloved Country: V3
Too Late the Phalarope: V12
Patternmaster (Butler): V34
Peace Like a River (Enger): V42
The Pearl (Steinbeck): V5
Peck, Robert Newton
A Day No Pigs Would Die: V29
Pelle the Conqueror (Nexø): V34
Percy, Walker
The Moviegoer: V51
Le Père Goriot (Balzac): V33
Peretti, Frank
Monster: V46
The Perks of Being a Wallflower
(Chbosky): V47
Persuasion (Austen): V14
Petry, Ann Lane
The Street: V33
The Phantom of the Opera (Leroux):
V20
The Phantom of the Opera (Motion
picture): V52
The Pickwick Papers (Dickens): V41
Picoult, Jodi
Nineteen Minutes: V49
Picture Bride (Uchida): V26
The Picture of Dorian Gray (Wilde):
V20
The Pigman (Zindel): V14
Pigs in Heaven (Kingsolver): V10
Pilgrims in Aztlán (Méndez): V12
The Pilgrim's Progress (Bunyan):
V32
Pirsig, Robert
Zen and the Art of Motorcycle
Maintenance: V31
A Place Where the Sea Remembers
(Benitez): V32

The Plague (Camus): V16
Platero and I (Jiménez): V36
Plath, Sylvia
The Bell Jar: V1
Poisonwood Bible (Kingsolver): V24
The Ponder Heart (Welty): V42
Porter, Katherine Anne
Ship of Fools: V14
The Portrait of a Lady (James): V19
A Portrait of the Artist as a Young
Man (Joyce): V7
Potok, Chaim
The Chosen: V4
Davita's Harp: V34
My Name is Asher Lev: V38
Power, Susan
The Grass Dancer: V11
The Power and the Glory (Greene):
V31
The Power of One (Courtenay):
V32
Praisesong for the Widow (Marshall):
V36
A Prayer for Owen Meany (Irving):
V14
Price, Reynolds
A Long and Happy Life: V18
Pride and Prejudice (Austen): V1
The Prime of Miss Jean Brodie
(Spark): V22
The Prime of Miss Jean Brodie
(Motion picture): V51
The Prince (Machiavelli): V9
The Prince and the Pauper (Twain):
V31
The Princess Bride (Goldman): V31
The Princess Bride (Motion picture):
V53
Proulx, Annie
The Shipping News: V38
Pudd'nhead Wilson (Twain): V37
Puzo, Mario
The Godfather: V16
Pynchon, Thomas
The Crying of Lot 49: V36
Gravity's Rainbow: V23

Q

Quicksand (Larsen): V48

R

Rabbit, Run (Updike): V12
Ragtime (Doctorow): V6
Ragtime (Motion picture): V44
The Rainbow (Lawrence): V26
The Ramayana (Narayan): V41
Rand, Ayn
Anthem: V29
Atlas Shrugged: V10
The Fountainhead: V16
Rankin, Ian
Watchman: V46

Ratner, Vaddey
  In the Shadow of the Banyan: V48
Rawles, Nancy
  My Jim V43
The Razor's Edge (Maugham): V23
Rebecca (du Maurier): V12
Rebecca (Motion picture): V50
The Red Badge of Courage (Crane): V4
The Red Pony (Steinbeck): V17
The Red Tent (Diamant): V36
The Remains of the Day (Ishiguro): V13
The Remains of the Day (Motion picture): V39
Remarque, Erich Maria
  All Quiet on the Western Front: V4
  All Quiet on the Western Front (Motion picture): V36
Reservation Blues (Alexie): V31
The Return of the Native (Hardy): V11
The Return of the Soldier (West): V51
Return to Sender (Alvarez): V42
Rhys, Jean
  Wide Sargasso Sea: V19
Richter, Conrad
  The Light in the Forest: V43
Rickshaw Boy (Lao She): V50
The Rise of Silas Lapham (Howells): V43
The Road (McCarthy): V40
Robinson Crusoe (Defoe): V9
Robinson, Marilynne
  Gilead: V24
  Housekeeping: V39
Rocket Boys: A Memoir (Hickam): V48
Rölvaag, O. E.
  Giants in the Earth: V5
A Room with a View (Forster): V11
A Room with a View (Motion picture): V47
Roots: The Story of an American Family (Haley): V9
Roots (Motion picture): V46
Roth, Henry
  Call It Sleep: V47
Roth, Philip
  American Pastoral: V25
The Round House (Erdrich): V48
Roy, Arundhati
  The God of Small Things: V22
Rubyfruit Jungle (Brown): V9
Rumble Fish (Hinton): V15
Rushdie, Salman
  Haroun and the Sea of Stories: V41
  Midnight's Children: V23
  The Satanic Verses: V22
  Shame: V52
Russell, Karen
  Swamplandia!: V48

Russo, Richard
  Empire Falls: V25

S

Sachar, Louis
  Holes: V37
Saint-Exupéry, Antoine de
  The Little Prince: V30
Salinger, J. D.
  The Catcher in the Rye: V1
  Franny and Zooey: V30
The Salt Eaters (Bambara): V44
The Samarai's Garden (Tsukiyama): V43
Sarah's Key (De Rosnay): V51
Saramago, José
  Blindness: V27
Saroyan, William
  The Human Comedy: V39
Sartre, Jean-Paul
  Nausea: V21
The Satanic Verses (Rushdie): V22
The Scarlet Letter (Hawthorne): V1
The Scarlet Pimpernel (Orczy): V31
Schaefer, Jack Warner
  Shane: V36
Schindler's List (Keneally): V17
Schindler's List (Motion picture): V38
Scoop (Waugh): V17
Scott, Walter
  Ivanhoe: V31
The Sea-Wolf (London): V35
Sebold, Alice
  The Lovely Bones: V54
The Secret History (Tartt): V50
The Secret Life of Bees (Kidd): V27
Seize the Day (Bellow): V4
Sense and Sensibility (Austen): V18
Sense and Sensibility (Motion picture): V33
A Separate Peace (Knowles): V2
Sepetys, Ruta
  Between Shades of Gray: V51
Sewell, Anna
  Black Beauty: V22
Shaara, Michael
  The Killer Angels: V26
Shabanu: Daughter of the Wind (Staples): V35
Shaffer, Mary Ann
  The Guernsey Literary and Potato Peel Society: V43
Shame (Rushdie): V52
Shane (Schaefer): V36
Shange, Ntozake
  Betsey Brown: V11
Shelley, Mary
  Frankenstein: V1
  Frankenstein (Motion picture): V37

The Sheltering Sky (Bowles): V50
Shields, Carol
  The Stone Diaries: V23
  Unless: V50
Ship of Fools (Porter): V14
The Shipping News (Proulx): V38
Shizuko's Daughter (Mori): V15
Sister of My Heart (Divakaruni): V38
Shoeless Joe (Kinsella): V15
Shogun: A Novel of Japan (Clavell): V10
Shute, Nevil
  On the Beach: V9
  A Town Like Alice: V38
Siddhartha (Hesse): V6
Silas Marner (Eliot): V20
Sijie, Dai
  Balzac and the Little Chinese Seamstress: V39
Silko, Leslie Marmon
  Ceremony: V4
Sinclair, Upton
  The Jungle: V6
Singer, Isaac Bashevis
  The Family Moskat: V53
Sister Carrie (Dreiser): V8
Slaughterhouse-Five (Vonnegut): V3
The Slave Dancer (Fox): V12
Smiley, Jane
  A Thousand Acres: V32
Smilla's Sense of Snow (Høeg): V17
Smith, Betty
  A Tree Grows in Brooklyn: V31
Smith, Zadie
  White Teeth: V40
Snow Country (Kawabata): V42
Snow Falling on Cedars (Guterson): V13
Snow in August (Hamill): V54
So Far from the Bamboo Grove (Watkins): V28
So Long a Letter (Bâ): V46
Solzhenitsyn, Aleksandr
  One Day in the Life of Ivan Denisovich: V6
Someone Like You (Dessen): V50
Something Wicked This Way Comes (Bradbury): V29
Song of the Lark (Cather): V41
Song of Solomon (Morrison): V8
Song Yet Sung (McBride): V49
Sons and Lovers (Lawrence): V45
Sophie's Choice (Styron): V22
Soul Catcher (Herbert): V17
The Sound and the Fury (Faulkner): V4
The Sound of Waves (Mishima): V43
Spark, Muriel
  The Prime of Miss Jean Brodie: V22

The Prime of Miss Jean Brodie
  (Motion picture): V51
Speak (Anderson): V31
Spiegelman, Art
  Maus: A Survivor's Tale: V35
Spinelli, Jerry
  Stargirl: V45
St. Dale (McCrumb): V46
Staples, Suzanne Fisher
  Shabanu: Daughter of the Wind:
    V35
Stargirl (Spinelli): V45
Staying Fat for Sarah Byrnes
  (Crutcher): V32
Stead, Christina
  The Man Who Loved Children: V27
Stein, Gertrude
  Ida: V27
Steinbeck, John
  Cannery Row: V28
  East of Eden: V19
  East of Eden (Motion picture): V34
  The Grapes of Wrath: V7
  The Grapes of Wrath (Motion
    picture): V39
  Of Mice and Men: V1
  The Moon is Down: V37
  The Pearl: V5
  The Red Pony: V17
  Tortilla Flat: V46
  The Winter of Our Discontent: V53
Steppenwolf (Hesse): V24
Stevenson, Robert Louis
  Dr. Jekyll and Mr. Hyde: V11
  Kidnapped: V33
  Treasure Island: V20
Stockett, Kathryn
  The Help: V39
  The Help (Motion picture): V52
Stoker, Bram
  Dracula: V18
  Dracula (Motion picture): V41
The Stone Angel (Laurence): V11
The Stone Diaries (Shields): V23
Stones from the River (Hegi): V25
The Storyteller (Vargas Llosa): V49
Stowe, Harriet Beecher
  *Dred: A Tale of the Great Dismal
    Swamp:* V47
  Uncle Tom's Cabin: V6
*The Strange Case of Dr. Jekyll and
  Mr. Hyde* (Stevenson): see *Dr.
  Jekyll and Mr. Hyde*
The Stranger (Camus): V6
Stranger in a Strange Land
  (Heinlein): V40
The Street (Petry): V33
Strout, Elizabeth
  Olive Kitteridge: V39
Styron, William
  Lie Down in Darkness: V50
  Sophie's Choice: V22

Sula (Morrison): V14
Summer (Wharton): V20
Summer of My German Soldier
  (Greene): V10
The Sun Also Rises (Hemingway): V5
Sunrise over Fallujah (Myers): V45
Surfacing (Atwood): V13
Swallowing Stones (McDonald): V45
Swamplandia! (Russell): V48
Swarthout, Glendon
  Bless the Beasts and Children: V29
The Sweet Hereafter (Banks): V13
Sweetgrass (Hudson): V28
Swift, Graham
  Waterland: V18
Swift, Jonathan
  Gulliver's Travels: V6

T

Tagore, Rabindranath
  The Home and the World: V48
A Tale of Two Cities (Dickens): V5
The Talented Mr. Ripley
  (Highsmith): V27
Tambourines to Glory (Hughes): V21
Tan, Amy
  The Bonesetter's Daughter: V31
  The Joy Luck Club: V1
  The Joy Luck Club (Motion
    picture): V35
  The Kitchen God's Wife: V13
  The Hundred Secret Senses: V44
Tan, Shaun
  The Arrival: V42
Tangerine (Bloor): V33
Tar Baby (Morrison): V37
Tarkington, Booth
  The Magnificent Ambersons: V34
Tartt, Donna
  The Secret History: V50
Tashjian, Janet
  The Gospel according to Larry: V46
Tears of a Tiger (Draper): V42
The Temple of My Familiar
  (Walker): V54
Ten Little Indians (Christie): V8
The Tenant of Wildfell Hall (Brontë):
  V26
Tender Is the Night (Fitzgerald): V19
Tess of the d'Urbervilles (Hardy): V3
Tex (Hinton): V9
Thackeray, William Makepeace
  Vanity Fair: V13
That Was Then, This Is Now
  (Hinton): V16
Their Eyes Were Watching God
  (Hurston): V3
Their Eyes Were Watching God
  (Motion picture): V54
them (Oates): V8
Thin Wood Walls (Patneaude): V46

Things Fall Apart (Achebe): V2
The Third Life of Grange Copeland
  (Walker): V44
The Third Man (Greene): V36
The Thirteen Reasons Why (Asher):
  V51
This Side of Paradise (Fitzgerald):
  V20
A Thousand Acres (Smiley): V32
Three Junes (Glass): V34
The Three Musketeers (Dumas):
  V14
Through the Looking-Glass: V27
The Time Machine (Wells): V17
*Time's Arrow; or, The Nature of the
  Offence* (Amis): V47
To Kill a Mockingbird (Lee): V2
To Kill a Mockingbird (Motion
  picture): V32
To the Lighthouse (Woolf): V8
A Town Like Alice (Shute): V38
Tolkien, J. R. R.
  The Hobbit: V8
  The Lord of the Rings: V26
Tolstoy, Leo
  Anna Karenina: V28
  War and Peace: V10
Tom Jones (Fielding): V18
Too Late the Phalarope (Paton):
  V12
Toomer, Jean
  Cane: V11
To Sir, With Love (Braithwaite):
  V30
Tobacco Road (Caldwell): V49
The Tortilla Curtain (Boyle): V41
Tortilla Flat (Steinbeck): V46
Toward the End of Time (Updike):
  V24
Treasure Island (Stevenson): V20
The Tree Bride (Mukherjee): V54
A Tree Grows in Brooklyn (Smith):
  V31
The Tree of Red Stars (Bridal): V17
The Trial (Kafka): V7
Trollope, Anthony
  Barchester Towers: V42
Trumbo, Dalton
  Johnny Got His Gun: V44
Tsukiyama, Gail
  The Samurai's Garden: V43
Turgenev, Ivan
  Fathers and Sons: V16
The Turn of the Screw (James):
  V16
Twain, Mark
  *The Adventures of Huckleberry
    Finn:* V1
  The Adventures of Tom Sawyer:
    V6
  *A Connecticut Yankee in King
    Arthur's Court:* V20

The Prince and the Pauper: V31
Pudd'nhead Wilson: V37
Tyler, Anne
　The Accidental Tourist: V7
　Breathing Lessons: V10
　Digging to America: V38
　*Dinner at the Homesick
　　Restaurant:* V2
Typee (Melville): V32
Typical American (Jen): V30

U

U.S.A. (Dos Passos): V14
Uchida, Yoshiko
　Picture Bride: V26
The Ugly American (Burdick and
　Lederer): V23
Ullman, James Ramsey
　Banner in the Sky: V45
Ulysses (Joyce): V26
The Unbearable Lightness of Being
　(Kundera): V18
Uncle Tom's Cabin (Stowe): V6
Under the Feet of Jesus (Viramontes):
　V51
Under the Net (Murdoch): V18
Underworld (Delillo): V47
Unless (Shields): V50
The Unvanquished (Faulkner): V38
Updike, John
　Rabbit, Run: V12
　Toward the End of Time: V24
Uriza Holthe, Tess
　When the Elephants Dance: V42
Utopia (More): V29

V

Vanity Fair (Thackeray): V13
Vargas Llosa, Mario
　The Storyteller: V49
Verne, Jules
　Around the World in Eighty Days:
　　V30
　Journey to the Center of the Earth:
　　V34
A Very Long Engagement (Japrisot):
　V18
Villette (Brontë): V36
Vizzini, Ned
　It's Kind of a Funny Story: V52
The Violent Bear It Away
　(O'Connor): V21
Viramontes, Helena María
　Under the Feet of Jesus: V51
Voltaire
　Candide: V7
Vonnegut, Kurt, Jr.
　Cat's Cradle: V28
　Slaughterhouse-Five: V3

W

Waiting (Jin): V25
Waiting for the Rain (Gordon):
　V40
Walker, Alice
　The Color Purple: V5
　The Color Purple (Motion
　　picture): V40
　The Temple of My Familiar: V54
　*The Third Life of Grange
　　Copeland:* V44
War Horse (Morpurgo): V47
War and Peace (Tolstoy): V10
The War of the Worlds (Wells): V20
Warren, Robert Penn
　All the King's Men: V13
Watchman (Rankin): V46
Waterland (Swift): V18
Watership Down (Adams): V11
Watkins, Yoko Kawashima
　So Far from the Bamboo Grove:
　　V28
Watson, Larry
　Montana 1948: V39
Waugh, Evelyn Arthur St. John
　Brideshead Revisited: V13
　A Handful of Dust: V34
　The Loved One: V50
　Scoop: V17
The Waves (Woolf): V28
The Way of All Flesh (Butler): V44
The Way to Rainy Mountain
　(Momaday): V45
Wein, Elizabeth
　Code Name Verity: V50
We Were the Mulvaneys (Oates):
　V24
Welch, James
　Fools Crow: V53
　Winter in the Blood: V23
Wells, H. G.
　The Island of Dr. Moreau: V36
　The Time Machine: V17
　The War of the Worlds: V20
Welty, Eudora
　Losing Battles: V15
　The Optimist's Daughter: V13
　The Ponder Heart: V42
West, Nathanael
　The Day of the Locust: V16
West, Rebecca
　The Return of the Soldier: V51
Wharton, Edith
　The Age of Innocence: V11
　The Age of Innocence (Motion
　　picture): V37
　Ethan Frome: V5
　The House of Mirth: V15
　Summer: V20
*What Looks Like Crazy on an
　Ordinary Day* (Cleage): V17

Whelan, Gloria
　Homeless Bird: V49
When Rain Clouds Gather (Head):
　V31
When the Elephants Dance (Uriza
　Holthe): V42
When the Emperor Was Divine
　(Otsuka): V41
When the Legends Die (Borland):
　V18
White Fang (London): V19
White Noise (DeLillo): V28
White Teeth (Smith): V40
White, T. H.
　The Once and Future King:
　　V30
*Wicked: The Life and Times of the
　Wicked Witch of the West*
　　(Maguire): V35
Wide Sargasso Sea (Rhys): V19
Wiesel, Eliezer
　Night: V4
Wilde, Oscar
　The Picture of Dorian Gray:
　　V20
Wilder, Thornton
　The Bridge of San Luis Rey:
　　V24
The Wind in the Willows (Grahame):
　V20
Winesburg, Ohio (Anderson): V4
The Wings of the Dove (James):
　V32
Winter in the Blood (Welch):
　V23
The Winter of Our Discontent
　(Steinbeck): V53
Winter's Bone (Woodrell): V48
Wise Blood (O'Connor): V3
The Wizard of Oz (Motion picture):
　V43
Wolfe, Thomas
　Look Homeward, Angel:
　　V18
Wolff, Virginia Euwer
　Make Lemonade: V35
The Woman in the Dunes (Abe):
　V22
The Woman Warrior (Kingston):
　V6
The Woman in White (Collins):
　V54
The Women of Brewster Place
　(Naylor): V4
The Wonderful Wizard of Oz (Baum):
　V13
Woodrell, Daniel
　Winter's Bone: V48
Woodson, Jacqueline
　Brown Girl Dreaming:
　　V52
　If You Come Softly: V46

Woolf, Virginia
   Mrs. Dalloway: V12
   To the Lighthouse: V8
   Orlando: A Biography: V42
   The Waves: V28
The World According to Garp
   (Irving): V12
Wouk, Herman
   The Caine Mutiny: A Novel of
      World War II: V7
The Wrestling Match (Emecheta):
   V14
Wright, Richard
   Black Boy: V1
   Native Son: V7
   The Outsider: V53

A Wrinkle in Time (L'Engle):
   V32
Wuthering Heights (Brontë): V2
Wuthering Heights (Motion picture):
   V45

Y

Yang, Gene Luen
   American Born Chinese: V39
Year of Impossible Goodbyes (Choi):
   V29
A Yellow Raft in Blue Water
   (Dorris): V3
Yezierska, Anzia
   Bread Givers: V29

Yolen, Jane
   Briar Rose: V30
Yonnondio: From the Thirties
   (Olsen): V50
Yoshimoto, Banana
   Kitchen: V7

Z

Zen and the Art of Motorcycle
   Maintenance (Pirsig): V31
Zindel, Paul
   The Pigman: V14
Zorro (Allende): V44
Zusak, Markus
   The Book Thief: V44

Cumulative Nationality/Ethnicity Index

Afghan

Hosseini, Khaled
  And the Mountains Echoed:
    V52

African American

Angelou, Maya
  I Know Why the Caged Bird Sings:
    V2
Baldwin, James
  Go Tell It on the Mountain: V4
Bambara, Toni Cade
  The Salt Eaters: V44
Butler, Octavia
  Kindred: V8
  Parable of the Sower: V21
  Patternmaster: V34
Chesnutt, Charles Waddell
  The House behind the Cedars:
    V45
Cleage, Pearl
  *What Looks Like Crazy on an
    Ordinary Day:* V17
Danticat, Edwidge
  Breath, Eyes, Memory: V37
  The Dew Breaker: V28
Draper, Sharon
  Tears of a Tiger: V42
Ellison, Ralph
  Invisible Man: V2
  Juneteenth: V21
Gaines, Ernest J.
  *The Autobiography of Miss Jane
    Pittman:* V5
  A Gathering of Old Men: V16
  A Lesson before Dying: V7

Haley, Alex
  *Roots: The Story of an American
    Family:* V9
  Roots (Motion picture): V46
Harper, Frances E. W.
  Iola Leroy; or, Shadows Uplifted:
    V53
Hughes, Langston
  Tambourines to Glory: V21
Hurston, Zora Neale
  Their Eyes Were Watching God: V3
  Their Eyes Were Watching God
    (Motion picture): V54
Johnson, Charles
  Middle Passage: V43
Johnson, James Weldon
  *The Autobiography of an
    Ex-Coloured Man:* V22
Kincaid, Jamaica
  Annie John: V3
  Lucy: V51
Larsen, Nella
  Quicksand: V48
Marshall, Paule
  Praisesong for the Widow: V36
McBride, James
  Song Yet Sung: V49
Morrison, Toni
  Beloved: V6
  The Bluest Eye: V1
  Jazz: V40
  Love: V46
  Song of Solomom: V8
  Sula: V14
  Tar Baby: V37
Myers, Walter Dean
  Fallen Angels: V30

  The Glory Field: V33
  Monster: V40
  Sunrise over Fallujah: V45
Naylor, Gloria
  Linden Hills: V49
  Mama Day: V7
  The Women of Brewster Place: V4
Parks, Gordon
  The Learning Tree: V32
Petry, Ann Lane
  The Street V33
Rawles, Nancy
  My Jim V43
Shange, Ntozake
  Betsey Brown: V11
Toomer, Jean
  Cane: V11
Walker, Alice
  The Color Purple: V5
  The Color Purple (Motion
    picture): V40
  The Temple of My Familiar: V54
  *The Third Life of Grange
    Copeland:* V44
Woodson, Jacqueline
  Brown Girl Dreaming: V52
  If You Come Softly: V46
Wright, Richard
  Black Boy: V1
  Native Son: V7
  The Outsider: V53

Algerian

Camus, Albert
  The Plague: V16
  The Stranger: V6

American

Abbey, Edward
  The Monkey Wrench Gang:
    V43
Abu-Jaber, Diana
  Crescent: V51
Agee, James
  A Death in the Family: V22
Alcott, Louisa May
  Little Women: V12
  Little Women (Motion picture):
    V53
Alexie, Sherman
  *The Absolutely True Diary of a
    Part-Time Indian:* V38
  Indian Killer: V54
  *The Lone Ranger and Tonto
    Fistfight in Heaven:* V17
  Reservation Blues: V31
Allende, Isabel
  Daughter of Fortune: V18
  Eva Luna: V29
  The House of the Spirits: V6
  Zorro: V44
Allison, Dorothy
  Bastard Out of Carolina: V11
Alvarez, Julia
  Before We Were Free: V53
  *How the García Girls Lost Their
    Accents:* V5
  In the Time of Butterflies: V9
  Return to Sender: V42
Anaya, Rudolfo
  Bless Me, Ultima: V12
  Heart of Aztlan: V49
Anderson, Laurie Halse
  Catalyst: V49
  Fever 1793: V35
  Speak: V31
Anderson, M. T.
  Feed: V41
Anderson, Sherwood
  Winesburg, Ohio: V4
Angelou, Maya
  I Know Why the Caged Bird Sings:
    V2
Asher, Jay
  Thirteen Reasons Why: V51
Asimov, Isaac
  I, Robot: V29
Auel, Jean
  The Clan of the Cave Bear: V11
Avi
  *Nothing But the Truth: A
    Documentary Novel:* V34
Baker, Russell
  Growing Up: V48
Bambara, Toni Cade
  The Salt Eaters: V44
Banks, Russell
  The Sweet Hereafter: V13

Barrows, Annie
  *The Guernsey Literary and Potato
    Peel Society:* V43
Baskin, Nora Raleigh
  Anything but Typical: V43
Bauer, Joan
  Hope Was Here: V54
Baum, L. Frank
  The Wizard of Oz (Motion
    picture): V43
  The Wonderful Wizard of Oz: V13
Bellamy, Edward
  Looking Backward: 2000–1887:
    V15
Bellow, Saul
  The Adventures of Augie March:
    V33
  Herzog: V14
  Humboldt's Gift: V26
  Mr. Sammler's Planet: V53
  Seize the Day: V4
Benitez, Sandra
  *A Place Where the Sea
    Remembers:* V32
Bloor, Edward
  Tangerine: V33
Blume, Judy
  Forever...: V24
Borland, Hal
  When the Legends Die: V18
Bowles, Paul
  The Sheltering Sky: V50
Boyle, T. C.
  The Tortilla Curtain: V41
Bradbury, Ray
  Dandelion Wine: V22
  Fahrenheit 451: V1
  The Martian Chronicles: V42
  *Something Wicked This Way
    Comes:* V29
Bradley, Marion Zimmer
  The Mists of Avalon: V40
Bridal, Tessa
  The Tree of Red Stars: V17
Brown, Rita Mae
  Rubyfruit Jungle: V9
Buck, Pearl S.
  The Good Earth: V25
Burdick, Eugene J.
  The Ugly American: V23
Burns, Olive Ann
  Cold Sassy Tree: V31
Butler, Octavia
  Kindred: V8
  Parable of the Sower: V21
  Patternmaster: V34
Caldwell, Erskine
  Tobacco Road: V49
Card, Orson Scott
  Ender's Game: V5
Cashore, Kristin
  Graceling: V53

Cather, Willa
  Death Comes for the Archbishop:
    V19
  A Lost Lady: V33
  My Ántonia: V2
  O Pioneers!: V47
  One of Ours: V52
  The Song of the Lark: V41
Chabon, Michael
  *The Amazing Adventures of
    Kavalier & Clay:* V25
Chandler, Raymond
  The Big Sleep: V17
  The Big Sleep (Motion picture):
    V48
Chbosky, Stephen
  The Perks of Being a Wallflower:
    V47
Chesnutt, Charles Waddell
  The House behind the Cedars: V45
Chevalier, Tracy
  Girl with a Pearl Earring: V45
Chin, Frank
  Donald Duk: V41
Choi, Sook Nyul
  Year of Impossible Goodbyes: V29
Chopin, Kate
  The Awakening: V3
Cisneros, Sandra
  Caramelo, or, Puro cuento: V47
  The House on Mango Street: V2
Clark, Walter Van Tilburg
  The Ox-Bow Incident: V40
Clavell, James du Maresq
  Shogun: A Novel of Japan: V10
Cleage, Pearl
  *What Looks Like Crazy on an
    Ordinary Day:* V17
Clemens, Samuel Langhorne
  *The Adventures of Huckleberry
    Finn:* V1
  The Adventures of Tom Sawyer:
    V6
  *A Connecticut Yankee in King
    Arthur's Court:* V20
  The Prince and the Pauper: V31
Coen, Joel and Ethan
  O Brother Where Art Thou?
    (Motion picture): V50
Collier, Christopher
  My Brother Sam is Dead: V38
Collier, James Lincoln
  My Brother Sam is Dead: V38
Conroy, Frank
  Body and Soul: V11
Cooper, James Fenimore
  The Deerslayer: V25
  The Last of the Mohicans: V9
  The Last of the Mohicans (Motion
    picture): V32
  *The Pathfinder; or, The Inland
    Sea:* V38

Cormier, Robert
   The Chocolate War: V2
   I Am the Cheese: V18
Crane, Stephen
   The Red Badge of Courage: V4
   Maggie: A Girl of the Streets: V20
Crichton, Michael
   The Great Train Robbery: V34
Crutcher, Chris
   The Crazy Horse Electric Game:
     V11
   Staying Fat for Sarah Byrnes: V32
Cunningham, Michael
   The Hours: V23
   The Hours (Motion picture): V48
Curran, Mary Doyle
   The Parish and the Hill: V53
Danticat, Edwidge
   Breath, Eyes, Memory: V37
   The Dew Breaker: V28
Davis, Rebecca Harding
   Margret Howth: A Story of
     To-Day: V14
DeLillo, Don
   Libra: V54
   Underworld: V47
   White Noise: V28
Desai, Kiran
   Hullabaloo in the Guava Orchard:
     V28
   The Inheritance of Loss: V49
Dessen, Sarah
   Someone Like You: V50
Di Donato, Pietro
   Christ in Concrete: V51
Diamant, Anita
   The Red Tent: V36
Dick, Philip K.
   Do Androids Dream of Electric
     Sheep?: V5
   Martian Time-Slip: V26
Dickey, James
   Deliverance: V9
Didion, Joan
   Democracy: V3
Doctorow, E. L.
   Ragtime: V6
   Ragtime (Motion picture): V44
Dorris, Michael
   A Yellow Raft in Blue Water: V3
Dos Passos, John
   Manhattan Transfer: V53
   U.S.A.: V14
Draper, Sharon
   Tears of a Tiger: V42
Dreiser, Theodore
   An American Tragedy: V17
   Sister Carrie: V8
Ellis, Bret Easton
   Less Than Zero: V11
Ellison, Ralph
   Invisible Man: V2
   Juneteenth: V21

Enger, Leif
   Peace Like a River: V42
Erdrich, Louise
   The Antelope Wife: V44
   The Beet Queen: V37
   The Bingo Palace: V40
   Love Medicine: V5
   The Round House: V48
Eugenides, Jeffrey
   Middlesex: V24
Farmer, Nancy
   The House of the Scorpion: V43
Fast, Howard
   April Morning: V35
Faulkner, William
   Absalom, Absalom!: V13
   As I Lay Dying: V8
   Intruder in the Dust: V33
   Light in August: V24
   The Sound and the Fury: V4
   The Unvanquished: V38
Ferber, Edna
   Cimarron: V45
Fitzgerald, F. Scott
   The Beautiful and Damned: V49
   The Great Gatsby: V2
   Tender Is the Night: V19
   This Side of Paradise: V20
Flagg, Fannie
   Fried Green Tomatoes at the
     Whistle Stop Café: V7
Foer, Jonathan Safran
   Everything Is Illuminated: V52
   Extremely Loud & Incredibly
     Close: V36
Forbes, Kathryn
   Mama's Bank Account: V47
Ford, Richard
   Independence Day: V25
Fox, Paula
   The Slave Dancer: V12
Frank, Pat
   Alas, Babylon: V29
Franzen, Jonathan
   The Corrections: V40
Frazier, Charles
   Cold Mountain: V25
Frederic, Harold
   The Damnation of Theron Ware:
     V22
Gaines, Ernest J.
   The Autobiography of Miss Jane
     Pittman: V5
   A Gathering of Old Men: V16
   A Lesson Before Dying: V7
García, Cristina
   Dreaming in Cuban: V38
Gardner, John
   Grendel: V3
Gibbons, Kaye
   Ellen Foster: V3
Gilman, Charlotte Perkins
   Herland: V36

Glass, Julia
   Three Junes: V34
Golden, Arthur
   Memoirs of a Geisha: V19
Goldman, William
   The Princess Bride: V31
   The Princess Bride (Motion
     picture): V53
Grau, Shirley Ann
   The Keepers of the House: V52
Green, Hannah
   The Dead of the House: V10
Green, John
   Looking for Alaska: V48
Greenberg, Joanne
   I Never Promised You a Rose
     Garden: V23
Greene, Bette
   Summer of My German Soldier:
     V10
Grossman, Lev
   The Magicians: V50
Guest, Judith
   Ordinary People: V1
   Ordinary People (Motion picture):
     V33
Guterson, David
   Snow Falling on Cedars: V13
Haddix, Margaret Peterson
   Among the Hidden: V47
Hamill, Pete
   Snow in August: V54
Hamilton, Jane
   A Map of the World: V45
Hammett, Dashiell
   The Maltese Falcon: V21
   The Maltese Falcon (Motion
     picture): V49
Harper, Frances E. W.
   Iola Leroy; or, Shadows Uplifted:
     V53
Harris, Marilyn
   Hatter Fox: V14
Hawthorne, Nathaniel
   The House of the Seven Gables:
     V20
   The Scarlet Letter: V1
Heinlein, Robert A.
   Stranger in a Strange Land: V40
Heller, Joseph
   Catch-22: V1
Hemingway, Ernest
   A Farewell to Arms: V1
   For Whom the Bell Tolls: V14
   A Moveable Feast: V48
   The Old Man and the Sea: V6
   The Sun Also Rises: V5
Herbert, Frank
   Dune: V31
   Soul Catcher: V17
Hersey, John
   A Bell for Adano: V41

Hickam, Homer, Jr.
  Rocket Boys: A Memoir: V48
Highsmith, Patricia
  The Talented Mr. Ripley: V27
Hijuelos, Oscar
  *The Mambo Kings Play Songs of
    Love:* V17
Hinton, S. E.
  The Outsiders: V5
  The Outsiders (Motion picture):
    V35
  Rumble Fish: V15
  Tex: V9
  That Was Then, This Is Now: V16
Hosseini, Khaled
  And the Mountains Echoed: V52
Howells, William Dean
  The Rise of Silas Lapham: V43
Hughes, Langston
  Tambourines to Glory: V21
Hurston, Zora Neale
  Their Eyes Were Watching God:
    V3
  Their Eyes Were Watching God
    (Motion picture): V54
Irving, John
  A Prayer for Owen Meany: V14
  The World According to Garp: V12
Jackson, Shirley
  The Haunting of Hill House: V37
James, Henry
  The Ambassadors: V12
  The American: V44
  The Bostonians: V37
  The Portrait of a Lady: V19
  The Turn of the Screw: V16
  The Wings of the Dove: V32
Jen, Gish
  Typical American: V30
Jewett, Sarah Orne
  The Country of the Pointed Firs:
    V15
Johnson, Charles
  Middle Passage: V43
Johnson, James Weldon
  *The Autobiography of an Ex-
    Coloured Man:* V22
Jones, Edward P.
  The Known World: V26
Kerouac, Jack
  On the Road: V8
Kesey, Ken
  One Flew Over the Cuckoo's Nest:
    V2
  One Flew Over the Cuckoo's Nest
    (Motion picture): V44
Keyes, Daniel
  Flowers for Algernon: V2
Kidd, Sue Monk
  The Secret Life of Bees: V27
Kincaid, Jamaica
  Annie John: V3
  Lucy: V51

Kingsolver, Barbara
  Animal Dreams: V12
  The Bean Trees: V5
  Pigs in Heaven: V10
  Poisonwood Bible: V24
Kingston, Maxine Hong
  The Woman Warrior: V6
Knowles, John
  A Separate Peace: V2
Lahiri, Jhumpa
  The Lowland: V52
  The Namesake: V31
Larsen, Nella
  Quicksand: V48
Le Guin, Ursula K.
  Always Coming Home: V9
  The Dispossessed: V52
  The Left Hand of Darkness: V6
Lederer, William J.
  The Ugly American: V23
Lee, Chang-rae
  Native Speaker: V42
Lee, Harper
  To Kill a Mockingbird: V2
  To Kill a Mockingbird (Motion
    picture): V32
L'Engle, Madeleine
  A Wrinkle in Time: V32
Lewis, Harry Sinclair
  Arrowsmith: V34
  Babbitt: V19
  Elmer Gantry: V22
  Elmer Gantry (Motion picture):
    V47
  Main Street: V15
Lightman, Alan
  Einstein's Dreams: V29
Lipsyte, Robert
  The Contender: V35
London, Jack
  The Call of the Wild: V8
  The Sea-Wolf: V35
  White Fang: V19
Lowry, Lois
  The Giver: V3
  Number the Stars: V39
Lurie, Alison
  Foreign Affairs: V24
Mailer, Norman
  The Naked and the Dead: V10
Malamud, Bernard
  The Assistant: V27
  The Fixer: V9
  The Natural: V4
  The Natural (Motion picture): V34
Maguire, Gregory
  *Wicked: The Life and Times of the
    Wicked Witch of the West:* V35
Marshall, Paule
  Praisesong for the Widow: V36
Mason, Bobbie Ann
  In Country: V4

McBride, James
  Song Yet Sung: V49
McCarthy, Cormac
  All the Pretty Horses: V36
  The Road: V40
McCrumb, Sharyn
  St. Dale: V46
McCullers, Carson
  The Heart Is a Lonely Hunter: V6
  The Member of the Wedding: V13
McDermott, Alice
  Charming Billy: V23
McDonald, Joyce
  Swallowing Stones: V45
McKinley, Robin
  *Beauty: A Retelling of the Story of
    Beauty and the Beast:* V33
McMurtry, Larry
  The Last Picture Show: V51
Melville, Herman
  Benito Cereno: V41
  Billy Budd: V9
  Moby-Dick: V7
  Moby-Dick (Motion picture): V43
  Typee: V32
Méndez, Miguel
  Pilgrims in Aztlán: V12
Miller, Walter M., Jr.
  A Canticle for Leibowitz: V44
Millhauser, Steven
  *Martin Dressler: The Tale of an
    American Dreamer:* V48
Mitchell, Margaret
  Gone with the Wind: V9
  Gone with the Wind (Motion
    picture): V38
Momaday, N. Scott
  House Made of Dawn: V10
  The Way to Rainy Mountain: V45
Mori, Kyoko
  Shizuko's Daughter: V15
Morrison, Toni
  Beloved: V6
  The Bluest Eye: V1
  Jazz: V40
  Love: V46
  Song of Solomon: V8
  Sula: V14
  Tar Baby: V37
Mukherjee, Bharati
  Desirable Daughters: V45
  Jasmine: V37
  The Tree Bride: V54
Myers, Walter Dean
  Fallen Angels: V30
  The Glory Field: V33
  Monster: V40
  Sunrise over Fallujah: V45
Naylor, Gloria
  Linden Hills: V49
  Mama Day: V7
  The Women of Brewster Place: V4

Ng, Celeste
  Everything I Never Told You: V52
Ng, Fae Myenne
  Bone: V37
Norris, Frank
  The Octopus: V12
Oates, Joyce Carol
  A Garden of Earthly Delight: V54
  them: V8
  We Were the Mulvaneys: V24
O'Brien, Tim
  Going after Cacciato: V37
O'Connor, Flannery
  The Violent Bear It Away: V21
  Wise Blood: V3
O'Hara, John
  Appointment in Samarra: V11
Okada, John
  No-No Boy: V25
Olsen, Tillie
  Yonnondio: From the Thirties: V50
Otsuka, Julie
  The Buddha in the Attic: V54
  When the Emperor Was Divine: V41
Ozeki, Ruth
  My Year of Meats: V49
Ozick, Cynthia
  Heir to the Glimmering World: V46
Packer, Ann
  The Dive from Clausen's Pier: V47
Parks, Gordon
  The Learning Tree: V32
Patchett, Ann
  Bel Canto: V30
Patneaude, David
  Thin Wood Walls: V46
Peck, Robert Newton
  A Day No Pigs Would Die: V29
Percy, Walker
  The Moviegoer: V51
Peretti, Frank
  Monster: V46
Petry, Ann Lane
  The Street: V33
Picoult, Jodi
  Nineteen Minutes: V49
Pirsig, Robert
  Zen and the Art of Motorcycle Maintenance: V31
Plath, Sylvia
  The Bell Jar: V1
Porter, Katherine Anne
  Ship of Fools: V14
Potok, Chaim
  The Chosen: V4
  Davita's Harp: V34
Power, Susan
  The Grass Dancer: V11
Price, Reynolds
  A Long and Happy Life: V18

Proulx, Annie
  The Shipping News: V38
Puzo, Mario
  The Godfather: V16
Pynchon, Thomas
  The Crying of Lot 49: V36
  Gravity's Rainbow: V23
Rand, Ayn
  Anthem: V29
  Atlas Shrugged: V10
  The Fountainhead: V16
Rawles, Nancy
  My Jim V43
Richter, Conrad
  The Light in the Forest: V43
Robinson, Marilynne
  Gilead: V24
  Housekeeping: V39
Rölvaag, O. E.
  Giants in the Earth: V5
Roth, Henry
  Call It Sleep: V47
Roth, Philip
  American Pastoral: V25
Russell, Karen
  Swamplandia!: V48
Russo, Richard
  Empire Falls: V25
Sachar, Louis
  Holes: V37
Salinger, J. D.
  The Catcher in the Rye: V1
  Franny and Zooey: V30
Saroyan, William
  The Human Comedy: V39
Schaefer, Jack Warner
  Shane: V36
Sebold, Alice
  The Lovely Bones: V54
Sepetys, Ruta
  Between Shades of Gray: V51
Shaara, Michael
  The Killer Angels: V26
Shaffer, Mary Ann
  The Guernsey Literary and Potato Peel Society: V43
Shange, Ntozake
  Betsey Brown: V11
Silko, Leslie Marmon
  Ceremony: V4
Sinclair, Upton
  The Jungle: V6
Singer, Isaac Bashevis
  The Family Moskat: V53
Smiley, Jane
  A Thousand Acres: V32
Smith, Betty
  A Tree Grows in Brooklyn: V31
Spiegelman, Art
  Maus: A Survivor's Tale: V35
Spinelli, Jerry
  Stargirl: V45

Staples, Suzanne Fisher
  Shabanu: Daughter of the Wind: V35
Stein, Gertrude
  Ida: V27
Steinbeck, John
  Cannery Row: V28
  East of Eden: V19
  East of Eden (Motion picture): V34
  The Grapes of Wrath: V7
  The Grapes of Wrath (Motion picture): V39
  The Moon Is Down: V37
  Of Mice and Men: V1
  The Pearl: V5
  The Red Pony: V17
  Tortilla Flat: V46
  The Winter of Our Discontent: V53
Stockett, Kathryn
  The Help: V39
  The Help (Motion picture): V52
Stowe, Harriet Beecher
  Dred: A Tale of the Great Dismal Swamp: V47
  Uncle Tom's Cabin: V6
Strout, Elizabeth
  Olive Kitteridge: V39
Styron, William
  Lie Down in Darkness: V50
  Sophie's Choice: V22
Swarthout, Glendon
  Bless the Beasts and Children: V29
Tan, Amy
  The Bonesetter's Daughter: V31
  The Hundred Secret Senses: V44
  Joy Luck Club: V1
  Joy Luck Club (Motion picture): V35
  The Kitchen God's Wife: V13
Tartt, Donna
  The Secret History: V50
Tarkington, Booth
  The Magnificent Ambersons: V34
Tashjian, Janet
  The Gospel according to Larry: V46
Toomer, Jean
  Cane: V11
Trumbo, Dalton
  Johnny Got His Gun: V44
Tsukiyama, Gail
  The Samurai's Garden: V43
Twain, Mark
  The Adventures of Huckleberry Finn: V1
  The Adventures of Tom Sawyer: V6
  A Connecticut Yankee in King Arthur's Court: V20
  The Prince and the Pauper: V31
  Pudd'nhead Wilson: V37

Tyler, Anne
   The Accidental Tourist: V7
   Breathing Lessons: V10
   Digging to America: V38
   *Dinner at the Homesick
     Restaurant:* V2
Uchida, Yoshiko
   Picture Bride: V26
Ullman, James Ramsey
   Banner in the Sky: V45
Updike, John
   Rabbit, Run: V12
   Toward the End of Time: V24
Uriza Holthe, Tess
   When the Elephants Dance: V42
Viramontes, Helena María
   Under the Feet of Jesus: V51
Vizzini, Ned
   It's Kind of a Funny Story: V52
Vonnegut, Kurt, Jr.
   Cat's Cradle: V28
   Slaughterhouse-Five: V3
Walker, Alice
   The Color Purple: V5
   The Color Purple (Motion
     picture): V40
   The Temple of My Familiar: V54
   *The Third Life of Grange
     Copeland:* V44
Warren, Robert Penn
   All the King's Men: V13
Watkins, Yoko Kawashima
   So Far from the Bamboo Grove:
     V28
Watson, Larry
   Montana 1948: V39
Wein, Elizabeth
   Code Name Verity: V50
Welch, James
   Fools Crow: V53
   Winter in the Blood: V23
Welty, Eudora
   Losing Battles: V15
   The Optimist's Daughter: V13
   The Ponder Heart: V42
West, Nathanael
   The Day of the Locust: V16
Wharton, Edith
   The Age of Innocence: V11
   The Age of Innocence (Motion
     picture) V37
   Ethan Frome: V5
   House of Mirth: V15
   Summer: V20
Whelan, Gloria
   Homeless Bird: V49
Wilder, Thornton
   The Bridge of San Luis Rey: V24
Wolfe, Thomas
   Look Homeward, Angel: V18
Wolff, Virginia Euwer
   Make Lemonade: V35

Woodrell, Daniel
   Winter's Bone: V48
Woodson, Jacqueline
   Brown Girl Dreaming: V52
   If You Come Softly: V46
Wouk, Herman
   The Caine Mutiny: V7
Wright, Richard
   Black Boy: V1
   Native Son: V7
   The Outsider: V53
Yang, Gene Luen
   American Born Chinese: V39
Yezierska, Anzia
   Bread Givers: V29
Yolen, Jane
   Briar Rose: V30
Zindel, Paul
   The Pigman: V14

Arab American

Abu-Jaber, Diana
   Crescent: V51

Argentinian

Hudson, William Henry
   Green Mansions: V46

Armenian

Saroyan, William
   The Human Comedy: V39

Asian American

Chin, Frank
   Donald Duk: V41
Jen, Gish
   Typical American: V30
Kingston, Maxine Hong
   The Woman Warrior: V6
Lahiri, Jhumpa
   The Lowland: V52
   The Namesake: V31
Lee, Chang-rae
   Native Speaker: V42
Mukherjee, Bharati
   Desirable Daughters: V45
   Jasmine: V37
   The Tree Bride: V54
Ng, Celeste
   Everything I Never Told You: V52
Ng, Fae Myenne
   Bone: V37
Okada, John
   No-No Boy: V25
Otsuka, Julie
   The Buddha in the Attic: V54
   When the Emperor Was Divine:
     V41
Ozeki, Ruth
   My Year of Meats: V49

Tan, Amy
   The Bonesetter's Daughter: V31
   The Hundred Secret Senses: V44
   The Joy Luck Club: V1
   The Joy Luck Club (Motion
     picture): V35
   The Kitchen God's Wife: V13
Tsukiyama, Gail
   The Samurai's Garden: V43
Uchida, Yoshiko
   Picture Bride: V26
Uriza Holthe, Tess
   When the Elephants Dance: V42
Watkins, Yoko Kawashima
   So Far from the Bamboo Grove:
     V28
Yang, Gene Luen
   American Born Chinese: V39

Asian Canadian

Kogawa, Joy
   Obasan: V3

Australian

Brooks, Geraldine
   March: V26
Clavell, James du Maresq
   Shogun: A Novel of Japan: V10
Flanagan, Richard
   *The Narrow Road to the Deep
     North:* V54
Keneally, Thomas
   Schindler's List: V17
   Schindler's List (Motion picture):
     V38
Stead, Christina
   The Man Who Loved Children:
     V27
Tan, Shaun
   The Arrival: V42
Zusak, Mark
   The Book Thief: V44

Barbadian

Lamming, George
   In the Castle of My Skin: V15

Brazilian

Coelho, Paulo
   The Alchemist: V29

Cambodian

Ratner, Vaddey
   In the Shadow of the Banyan: V48

Canadian

Atwood, Margaret
   Alias Grace: V19
   The Blind Assassin: V53

Cat's Eye: V14
The Edible Woman: V12
The Handmaid's Tale: V4
Oryx and Crake: V39
Surfacing: V13
Bellow, Saul
  The Adventures of Augie March:
    V33
  Herzog: V14
  Humboldt's Gift: V26
  Mr. Sammler's Planet: V53
  Seize the Day: V4
Hudson, Jan
  Sweetgrass: V28
Kinsella, W. P.
  Shoeless Joe: V15
Kogawa, Joy
  Obasan: V3
Laurence, Margaret
  The Stone Angel: V11
Martel, Yann
  Life of Pi: V27
  Life of Pi (Motion picture): V51
Mistry, Rohinton
  A Fine Balance: V43
Munro, Alice
  Lives of Girls and Women: V27
Ondaatje, Michael
  The English Patient: V23
Peretti, Frank
  Monster: V46
Shields, Carol
  The Stone Diaries: V23
  Unless: V50

Chilean
Allende, Isabel
  Daughter of Fortune: V18
  Eva Luna: V29
  The House of the Spirits: V6
  Zorro: V44

Chinese
Jin, Ha
  Waiting: V25
Lao She
  Rickshaw Boy: V50
Lee, Lilian
  Farewell My Concubine: V19
Sijie, Dai
  *Balzac and the Little Chinese
    Seamstress:* V39

Colombian
García Márquez, Gabriel
  Chronicle of a Death Foretold:
    V10
  Love in the Time of Cholera: V1
  One Hundred Years of Solitude:
    V5

Czechoslovakian
Kundera, Milan
  *The Book of Laughter and
    Forgetting:* V27
  *The Unbearable Lightness of
    Being:* V18

Danish
Dinesen, Isak
  Out of Africa: V9
Høeg, Peter
  Smilla's Sense of Snow: V17
Nexø, Martin Anderson
  Pelle the Conqueror: V34

Dominican
Alvarez, Julia
  Before We Were Free: V53
  *How the García Girls Lost Their
    Accents:* V5
  In the Time of Butterflies: V9
  Return to Sender: V42
Díaz, Junot
  *The Brief Wondrous Life of Oscar
    Wao:* V36
Rhys, Jean
  Wide Sargasso Sea: V19

Dutch
Möring, Marcel
  In Babylon: V25
Mulisch, Harry
  The Assault: V52

Egyptian
Mahfouz, Naguib
  Fountain and Tomb: V42

English
Abbott, Edwin Abbott
  *Flatland: A Romance of Many
    Dimensions:* V47
Adams, Douglas
  *The Hitchhiker's Guide to the
    Galaxy:* V7
Adams, Richard
  Watership Down: V11
Amis, Martin
  *Time's Arrow; or, The Nature of
    the Offence:* V47
Austen, Jane
  Clueless (Motion picture):
    V40
  Emma: V21
  Emma (Motion picture): V46
  Mansfield Park: V29
  Northanger Abbey: V28
  Persuasion: V14
  Pride and Prejudice: V1

Sense and Sensibility: V18
Sense and Sensibility (Motion
  picture): V33
Ballard, J. G.
  Empire of the Sun: V8
  Empire of the Sun (Motion
    picture): V42
Behn, Aphra
  *Oroonoko; or, The Royal Slave:
    A True History:* V35
Blair, Eric Arthur
  Animal Farm: V3
Bowen, Elizabeth Dorothea Cole
  The Death of the Heart: V13
Braithwaite, E. R.
  To Sir, With Love: V30
Brontë, Anne
  The Tenant of Wildfell Hall: V26
Brontë, Charlotte
  Jane Eyre: V4
  Jane Eyre (Motion picture): V54
  Villette: V36
Brontë, Emily
  Wuthering Heights: V2
  Wuthering Heights: (Motion
    picture): V45
Brookner, Anita
  Hotel du Lac: V23
Bunyan, John
  The Pilgrim's Progress: V32
Burgess, Anthony
  A Clockwork Orange: V15
Burney, Fanny
  Evelina: V16
Butler, Samuel
  The Way of All Flesh: V44
Carroll, Lewis
  *Alice's Adventurers in
    Wonderland:* V7
  Through the Looking-Glass: V27
Christie, Agatha
  The A.B.C. Murders: V30
  Murder on the Orient Express: V33
  Ten Little Indians: V8
Collins, Wilkie
  The Moonstone: V39
  The Woman in White: V54
Conan Doyle, Arthur, Sir
  The Hound of the Baskervilles: V28
Conrad, Joseph
  Heart of Darkness: V2
  Lord Jim: V16
Defoe, Daniel
  A Journal of the Plague Year:
    V30
  Moll Flanders: V13
  Robinson Crusoe: V9
Dickens, Charles
  Bleak House: V30
  A Christmas Carol: V10
  David Copperfield: V25
  Great Expectations: V4

Great Expectations (Motion
    picture): V42
Hard Times: V20
Nicholas Nickleby: V33
Oliver Twist: V14
The Pickwick Papers: V41
A Tale of Two Cities: V5
Doyle, Arthur Conan, Sir
    The Hound of the Baskervilles:
        V28
du Maurier, Daphne
    Rebecca: V12
    Rebecca (Motion picture): V50
Eliot, George
    Adam Bede: V34
    Middlemarch: V23
    The Mill on the Floss: V17
    Silas Marner: V20
Fielding, Henry
    Joseph Andrews: V32
    Tom Jones: V18
Foden, Giles
    The Last King of Scotland: V15
Ford, Ford Madox
    The Good Soldier: V28
Forster, E. M.
    A Passage to India: V3
    Howards End: V10
    A Room with a View: V11
    A Room with a View (Motion
        picture): V47
Fowles, John
    The French Lieutenant's Woman:
        V21
Gaiman, Neil.
    The Ocean at the End of the Lane:
        V51
Golding, William
    Lord of the Flies: V2
    Lord of the Flies (Motion picture):
        V36
Graves, Robert
    I, Claudius: V21
Greene, Graham
    The End of the Affair: V16
    The Heart of the Matter: V45
    The Power and the Glory: V31
    The Third Man: V36
Haggard, H. Rider
    King Solomon's Mines: V40
Hardy, Thomas
    Far from the Madding Crowd: V19
    Jude the Obscure: V30
    The Mayor of Casterbridge: V15
    The Return of the Native: V11
    Tess of the d'Urbervilles: V3
Hudson, William Henry
    Green Mansions: V46
Huxley, Aldous
    Brave New World: V6
Ishiguro, Kazuo
    Never Let Me Go: V35

Never Let Me Go: (Motion
    picture): V45
The Remains of the Day: V13
The Remains of the Day (Motion
    picture): V39
James, Henry
    The Ambassadors: V12
    The American: V44
    The Bostonians: V37
    The Portrait of a Lady: V19
    The Turn of the Screw: V16
Kipling, Rudyard
    Kim: V21
Koestler, Arthur
    Darkness at Noon: V19
Laird, Elizabeth
    A Little Piece of Ground: V46
Lawrence, D. H.
    The Rainbow: V26
    Sons and Lovers: V45
Lessing, Doris
    The Fifth Child: V38
    The Golden Notebook: V27
Lewis, C. S.
    *The Lion, the Witch and the
        Wardrobe:* V24
Lewis, Matthew
    The Monk: V52
Llewellyn, Richard
    How Green Was My Valley: V30
Maugham, W. Somerset
    Of Human Bondage: V35
    The Razor's Edge: V23
McEwan, Ian
    Atonement: V32
    Atonement (Motion picture): V49
Monsarrat, Nicholas
    The Cruel Sea: V39
More, Thomas
    Utopia: V29
Morpurgo, Michael
    War Horse: V47
Orwell, George
    Animal Farm: V3
    1984: V7
Rhys, Jean
    Wide Sargasso Sea: V19
Rushdie, Salman
    Haroun and the Sea of Stories: V41
    Midnight's Children: V23
    The Satanic Verses: V22
Sewell, Anna
    Black Beauty: V22
Shelley, Mary
    Frankenstein: V1
    Frankenstein (Motion picture):
        V37
Shute, Nevil
    On the Beach: V9
    A Town Like Alice: V38
Smith, Zadie
    White Teeth: V40

Spark, Muriel
    The Prime of Miss Jean Brodie:
        V22
    The Prime of Miss Jean Brodie
        (Motion picture): V51
Stevenson, Robert Louis
    Dr. Jekyll and Mr. Hyde: V11
    Kidnapped: V33
Swift, Graham
    Waterland: V18
Swift, Jonathan
    Gulliver's Travels: V6
Thackeray, William Makepeace
    Vanity Fair: V13
Tolkien, J. R. R.
    The Hobbit: V8
    The Lord of the Rings: V26
Trollope, Anthony
    Barchester Towers: V42
Waugh, Evelyn
    Brideshead Revisited: V13
    A Handful of Dust: V34
    The Loved One: V50
    Scoop: V17
Wells, H. G.
    The Island of Dr. Moreau: V36
    The Time Machine: V17
    The War of the Worlds: V20
West, Rebecca
    The Return of the Soldier: V51
White, T. H.
    The Once and Future King: V30
Woolf, Virginia
    Mrs. Dalloway: V12
    Orlando: A Biography: V42
    To the Lighthouse: V8
    The Waves: V28

European American

Hemingway, Ernest
    A Farewell to Arms: V1
    For Whom the Bell Tolls: V14
    A Moveable Feast: V48
    The Old Man and the Sea: V6
    The Sun Also Rises: V5
Stowe, Harriet Beecher
    *Dred: A Tale of the Great Dismal
        Swamp:* V47
    Uncle Tom's Cabin: V6

French

Balzac, Honoré de
    Le Père Goriot: V33
Boulle, Pierre
    The Bridge over the River Kwai:
        V32
Camus, Albert
    The Plague: V16
    The Stranger: V6
De Rosnay, Tatiana
    Sarah's Key: V51

Dumas, Alexandre
   The Count of Monte Cristo: V19
   The Man in the Iron Mask: V41
   The Three Musketeers: V14
Flaubert, Gustave
   Madame Bovary: V14
Gide, André
   The Immoralist: V21
Hugo, Victor
   The Hunchback of Notre Dame: V20
   Les Misérables: V5
Japrisot, Sébastien
   A Very Long Engagement: V18
Leroux, Gaston
   The Phantom of the Opera: V20
   The Phantom of the Opera
     (Motion Picture): V52
Maugham, W. Somerset
   Of Human Bondage: V35
   The Razor's Edge: V23
Saint-Exupéry, Antoine de
   The Little Prince: V30
Sartre, Jean-Paul
   Nausea: V21
Verne, Jules
   Around the World in Eighty Days:
     V30
   Journey to the Center of the Earth:
     V34
Voltaire
   Candide: V7

German

Hegi, Ursula
   Stones from the River: V25
Hesse, Hermann
   Demian: V15
   Siddhartha: V6
   Steppenwolf: V24
Mann, Thomas
   Death in Venice: V17
   The Magic Mountain: V29
Remarque, Erich Maria
   All Quiet on the Western Front: V4
   All Quiet on the Western Front
     (Motion picture): V36

Guyanese

Braithwaite, E. R.
   To Sir, With Love: V30

Haitian

Danticat, Edwidge
   Breath, Eyes, Memory: V37
   The Dew Breaker: V28

Hispanic American

Allende, Isabel
   Daughter of Fortune: V18
   Eva Luna: V29

   The House of the Spirits: V6
   Zorro: V44
Anaya, Rudolfo
   Bless Me, Ultima: V12
   Heart of Aztlan: V49
Benitez, Sandra
   A Place Where the Sea
     Remembers: V32
Cisneros, Sandra
   Caramelo, or, Puro cuento: V47
   The House on Mango Street: V2
García, Cristina
   Dreaming in Cuban: V38
Hijuclos, Oscar
   The Mambo Kings Play Songs of
     Love: V17

Hungarian

Koestler, Arthur
   Darkness at Noon: V19
Orczy, Emmuska
   The Scarlet Pimpernel: V31
Viramontes, Helena María
   Under the Feet of Jesus: V51

Indian

Desai, Anita
   Clear Light of Day: V44
Desai, Kiran
   Hullabaloo in the Guava Orchard:
     V28
   The Inheritance of Loss: V49
Divakaruni, Chitra Banerjee
   Sister of My Heart: V38
Malladi, Amulya
   A Breath of Fresh Air: V53
Markandaya, Kamala
   Nectar in a Sieve: V13
Mistry, Rohinton
   A Fine Balance: V43
Mukherjee, Bharati
   Desirable Daughters: V45
   Jasmine: V37
   The Tree Bride: V54
Naipaul, V. S.
   A Bend in the River: V37
   Half a Life: V39
Narayan, R. K.
   The Guide: V50
   The Ramayana: V41
Roy, Arundhati
   The God of Small Things: V22
Rushdie, Salman
   Haroun and the Sea of Stories:
     V41
   Midnight's Children: V23
   The Satanic Verses: V22
   Shame: V52
Tagore, Rabindranath
   The Home and the World: V48

Irish

Bowen, Elizabeth Dorothea Cole
   The Death of the Heart: V13
Joyce, James
   A Portrait of the Artist as a Young
     Man: V7
   Ulysses: V26
Murdoch, Iris
   Under the Net: V18
Stoker, Bram
   Dracula: V18
   Dracula (Motion picture): V41
Wilde, Oscar
   The Picture of Dorian Gray: V20

Italian

Eco, Umberto
   The Name of the Rose: V22
Lampedusa, Giuseppe Tomasi di
   The Leopard: V44
Machiavelli, Niccolo
   The Prince: V9

Japanese

Abe, Kobo
   The Woman in the Dunes: V22
Ishiguro, Kazuo
   Never Let Me Go: V35
   Never Let Me Go: (Motion
     picture): V45
   The Remains of the Day: V13
   The Remains of the Day (Motion
     picture): V39
Kawabata, Yasunari
   Snow Country: V42
Mishima, Yukio
   The Sound of Waves: V43
Mori, Kyoko
   Shizuko's Daughter: V15
Watkins, Yoko Kawashima
   So Far from the Bamboo Grove:
     V28
Yoshimoto, Banana
   Kitchen: V7

Jewish

Asimov, Isaac
   I, Robot: V29
Bellow, Saul
   The Adventures of Augie March:
     V33
   Herzog: V14
   Humboldt's Gift: V26
   Mr. Sammler's Planet: V53
   Seize the Day: V4
Ferber, Edna
   Cimarron: V45
Foer, Jonathan Safran
   Everything Is Illuminated: V52
   Extremely Loud & Incredibly
     Close: V36

Cumulative Nationality/Ethnicity Index

Kafka, Franz
  The Castle: V34
  The Trial: V7
Kertész, Imre
  Kaddish for a Child Not Born: V23
Malamud, Bernard
  The Assistant: V27
  The Fixer: V9
  The Natural: V4
  The Natural (Motion picture): V34
Olsen, Tillie
  Yonnondio: From the Thirties: V50
Ozick, Cynthia
  Heir to the Glimmering World:
    V46
Potok, Chaim
  The Chosen: V4
  Davita's Harp: V34
Roth, Henry
  Call It Sleep: V47
Roth, Philip
  American Pastoral: V25
Salinger, J. D.
  The Catcher in the Rye: V1
  Franny and Zooey: V30
Singer, Isaac Bashevis
  The Family Moskat: V53
Spiegelman, Art
  Maus: A Survivor's Tale: V35
West, Nathanael
  The Day of the Locust: V16
Wiesel, Eliezer
  Night: V4
Yezierska, Anzia
  Bread Givers: V29
Yolen, Jane
  Briar Rose: V30

Kenyan

Ngũgĩ Wa Thiong'o
  A Grain of Wheat: V49

Korean

Choi, Sook Nyul
  Year of Impossible Goodbyes: V29

Mexican

Esquivel, Laura
  Like Water for Chocolate: V5
Fuentes, Carlos
  The Old Gringo: V8

Native American

Alexie, Sherman
  The Absolutely True Diary of a
    Part-Time Indian: V38
  Indian Killer: V54
  The Lone Ranger and Tonto
    Fistfight in Heaven: V17
  Reservation Blues: V31

Dorris, Michael
  A Yellow Raft in Blue Water: V3
Erdrich, Louise
  The Antelope Wife: V44
  The Beet Queen: V37
  The Bingo Palace: V40
  Love Medicine: V5
  The Round House: V48
Momaday, N. Scott
  House Made of Dawn: V10
  The Way to Rainy Mountain: V45
Silko, Leslie Marmon
  Ceremony: V4
Welch, James
  Fools Crow: V53
  Winter in the Blood: V23

New Zealander

Hulme, Keri
  The Bone People: V24

Nigerian

Abani, Chris
  GraceLand: V35
Achebe, Chinua
  No Longer at Ease: V33
  Things Fall Apart: V3
Adichie, Chimamanda Ngozi
  Americanah: V54
  Half of a Yellow Sun: V48
Emecheta, Buchi
  The Bride Price: V12
  The Joys of Motherhood: V41
  The Wrestling Match: V14

Norwegian

Rölvaag, O. E.
  Giants in the Earth: V5

Peruvian

Vargas Llosa, Mario
  The Storyteller: V49

Polish

Conrad, Joseph
  Heart of Darkness: V2
  Lord Jim: V16
Kosinski, Jerzy
  The Painted Bird: V12
Singer, Isaac Bashevis
  The Family Moskat: V53

Portuguese

Saramago, José
  Blindness: V27

Romanian

Wiesel, Eliezer
  Night: V4

Russian

Asimov, Isaac
  I, Robot: V29
Bulgakov, Mikhail
  The Master and Margarita:
    V8
Dostoyevsky, Fyodor
  The Brothers Karamazov: V8
  Crime and Punishment: V3
  The Idiot: V40
  Notes from Underground:
    V28
Nabokov, Vladimir
  Lolita: V9
Pasternak, Boris
  Doctor Zhivago: V26
  Doctor Zhivago (Motion picture):
    V41
Rand, Ayn
  Anthem: V29
  Atlas Shrugged: V10
  The Fountainhead: V16
Solzhenitsyn, Aleksandr
  One Day in the Life of Ivan
    Denisovich: V6
Tolstoy, Leo
  Anna Karenina: V28
  War and Peace: V10
Turgenev, Ivan
  Fathers and Sons: V16
Yezierska, Anzia
  Bread Givers: V29

Scottish

Grahame, Kenneth
  The Wind in the Willows:
    V20
Laird, Elizabeth
  A Little Piece of Ground: V46
Rankin, Ian
  Watchman: V46
Scott, Walter
  Ivanhoe: V31
Spark, Muriel
  The Prime of Miss Jean Brodie:
    V22
  The Prime of Miss Jean Brodie
    (Motion picture): V51
Stevenson, Robert Louis
  Kidnapped: V33
  Treasure Island: V20

Senegalese

Bâ, Mariama
  So Long a Letter: V46

South African

Coetzee, J. M.
  Age of Iron: V51
  Dusklands: V21

Courtenay, Bryce
  The Power of One: V32
Gordimer, Nadine
  Burger's Daughter: V50
  July's People: V4
Gordon, Sheila
  Waiting for the Rain: V40
Head, Bessie
  When Rain Clouds Gather:
    V31
Magona, Sindiwe
  Mother to Mother: V43
Paton, Alan
  Cry, the Beloved Country:
    V3
  Too Late the Phalarope:
    V12

Spanish

de Cervantes Saavedra, Miguel
  Don Quixote: V8
Jiménez, Juan Ramón
  Platero and I: V36

Sri Lankan

Ondaatje, Michael
  The English Patient: V23

Swedish

Spiegelman, Art
  Maus: A Survivor's Tale: V35

Swiss

Hesse, Hermann
  Demian: V15
  Siddhartha: V6
  Steppenwolf: V24

Trinidad and Tobagoan

Naipaul, V. S.
  A Bend in the River: V37
  Half a Life: V39

Turkish

Pamuk, Orhan
  My Name is Red: V27

Ukrainian

Roth, Henry
  Call It Sleep: V47

Uruguayan

Bridal, Tessa
  The Tree of Red Stars:
    V17

Vietnamese

Duong Thu Huong
  Paradise of the Blind:
    V23

West Indian

Kincaid, Jamaica
  Annie John: V3
  Lucy: V51

Zimbabwean

Dangarembga, Tsitsi
  Nervous Conditions: V28

Subject/Theme Index

A

Abandonment
   The Lovely Bones: 184, 193
Abduction
   The Lovely Bones: 188–189, 197
Acceptance
   The Lovely Bones: 192
Adolescence
   Hope Was Here: 87, 91
Adoption
   Indian Killer: 81, 82, 101, 107, 108, 115, 119, 125
Adultery
   The Narrow Road to the Deep North: 205, 214–215
   The Woman in White: 307
Adversity
   Hope Was Here: 72, 82, 85
African culture
   Americanah: 24–27
   The Temple of My Familiar: 264
African history
   Americanah: 18–19
Afterlife
   Jane Eyre: 142
Alienation
   Americanah: 14
   A Garden of Earthly Delight: 53–54, 69
   The Lovely Bones: 198
   The Tree Bride: 297
Allegories
   A Garden of Earthly Delight: 66
   The Temple of My Familiar: 254, 255–256, 259
Allusions
   Americanah: 21

Ambiguity
   Indian Killer: 124
   Libra: 153
Ambivalence
   Jane Eyre: 148
American culture
   The Buddha in the Attic: 31, 34, 40
   A Garden of Earthly Delight: 67–69
   Indian Killer: 124
   Libra: 167
   Snow in August: 223, 227, 228, 231, 235
   The Temple of My Familiar: 257
American dream
   A Garden of Earthly Delight: 67
Anger
   The Buddha in the Attic: 41, 44
   Hope Was Here: 79, 91
   Indian Killer: 99–101, 104, 107–111, 115, 116, 124
   Jane Eyre: 145
   Libra: 153, 160
Antisemitism
   Snow in August: 226, 228, 233, 238, 244
Anxiety
   A Garden of Earthly Delight: 47
Appearance *vs.* reality
   Americanah: 23
Arrogance
   Indian Killer: 108
Assassination. *See* Murder
Assimilation
   Americanah: 1, 4, 6
   The Buddha in the Attic: 34, 35–36, 41

   The Tree Bride: 284, 290, 293, 297–299, 301
Authority
   Jane Eyre: 149
Autobiographical fiction
   A Garden of Earthly Delight: 61–64

B

Beauty
   The Narrow Road to the Deep North: 218
   Their Eyes Were Watching God: 280
Belonging
   Hope Was Here: 94
   The Lovely Bones: 193
Betrayal
   The Buddha in the Attic: 36, 45
   Hope Was Here: 79
   The Tree Bride: 299
Bitterness
   Hope Was Here: 74
   Indian Killer: 100, 107
   Libra: 160
   The Tree Bride: 298
Black history
   The Temple of My Familiar: 258–259
Black power
   The Temple of My Familiar: 247
Black womanhood
   Their Eyes Were Watching God: 278
British colonialism
   Americanah: 18
   Jane Eyre: 135

The Tree Bride: 293, 294–296, 300, 301–302
British culture
The Tree Bride: 297, 299, 300
Brutality
The Narrow Road to the Deep North: 203, 206, 212, 213, 216, 219, 220
Bullying
Hope Was Here: 75, 76, 81, 82
Indian Killer: 102, 106
The Narrow Road to the Deep North: 216, 217
Snow in August: 216, 217, 242, 245
The Woman in White: 316

C

Cancer. *see* Disease
Capitalism
A Garden of Earthly Delight: 66, 68
Challenges. *See* Adversity
Chance
Libra: 170, 171
Change (Philosophy)
The Lovely Bones: 177, 186
Chaos
The Buddha in the Attic: 40
Libra: 167–170
The Lovely Bones: 192
Characterization
Americanah: 17
The Buddha in the Attic: 44
A Garden of Earthly Delight: 61–64
Hope Was Here: 88–89
Indian Killer: 114–115
Jane Eyre: 146
Libra: 167
The Lovely Bones: 198
The Narrow Road to the Deep North: 215, 216
The Tree Bride: 302
The Woman in White: 321, 326–327, 329–330
Child abuse
Americanah: 25
Indian Killer: 101, 106
The Lovely Bones: 197
Childhood
The Buddha in the Attic: 31
Choice (Psychology)
Jane Eyre: 142, 144
Christianity
Jane Eyre: 141
The Temple of My Familiar: 253–254
Civil rights
Americanah: 27
Coincidence
The Woman in White: 307

Colonialism
Indian Killer: 122
Colors
Jane Eyre: 139–140
Comfort
The Lovely Bones: 198
Coming of age
Hope Was Here: 85
The Lovely Bones: 185–186, 192
Communication
Snow in August: 243
Communism
Libra: 153, 155, 156, 160, 162, 172
Community
The Buddha in the Attic: 29, 44
Hope Was Here: 72, 81, 82–84, 87
The Lovely Bones: 191
Snow in August: 233
Comradeship
The Narrow Road to the Deep North: 205, 207–208, 215, 216, 219, 221, 222
Conflict
Americanah: 17
A Garden of Earthly Delight: 68
Hope Was Here: 91
Conformity
Jane Eyre: 149
Their Eyes Were Watching God: 281
Confusion
Indian Killer: 107
Libra: 167
The Narrow Road to the Deep North: 212
Conspiracies
Libra: 155–160, 162, 163–164, 167–172
The Woman in White: 313, 314, 327–328
Consumerism
The Woman in White: 307–308
Contempt
Jane Eyre: 147
Contrast
The Woman in White: 323
Control (Psychology)
Jane Eyre: 148
Libra: 162, 170, 171
Their Eyes Were Watching God: 275
The Woman in White: 315, 321, 325–326
Corruption
Americanah: 12, 15–17, 20, 22, 25
Hope Was Here: 72, 75, 78, *93*
Courage
The Narrow Road to the Deep North: 212
Crime
Libra: 170
The Lovely Bones: 196

The Narrow Road to the Deep North: 213–214
The Woman in White: 328–329
Cruelty
Americanah: 25
Jane Eyre: 134, 136
Cuban history
Libra: 153, 171–172
Cultural conflict
Americanah: 1
The Buddha in the Attic: 32, 36
The Tree Bride: 284, 292, 297
Cultural identity
Americanah: 5, 14
The Buddha in the Attic: 32, 33
Indian Killer: 117, 118, 125
The Tree Bride: 292
Culture
The Temple of My Familiar: 260

D

Daily living
Hope Was Here: 85
Danger
The Woman in White: 318
Death
Hope Was Here: 79
Indian Killer: 99
Libra: 163
The Lovely Bones: 184–187, 190–192, 198
The Narrow Road to the Deep North: 203–206, 212, 216
Their Eyes Were Watching God: 269, 270
The Woman in White: 312, 313
Deception
The Buddha in the Attic: 45
Libra: 164, 167
Defeat
A Garden of Earthly Delight: 67, 68–69
Dependence
Jane Eyre: 148
Description (Literature)
Snow in August: 245
Desire
Americanah: 9–10
The Narrow Road to the Deep North: 219
Despair
Indian Killer: 125
Libra: 173
Destiny
The Tree Bride: 301
Destruction
A Garden of Earthly Delight: 68
Details
The Buddha in the Attic: 29
Determinism
Libra: 170

Didacticism
    Americanah: 17–18, 21, 24
Difference
    Americanah: 19
Dignity
    The Buddha in the Attic: 36
    Jane Eyre: 137, 150
    Libra: 161
Disappointment
    The Buddha in the Attic: 29, 35, 45
    Hope Was Here: 77
    Libra: 161
Disapproval
    A Garden of Earthly Delight: 50
Discontent
    Americanah: 3, 23
Disease
    Hope Was Here: 72, 75–77
    *The Narrow Road to the Deep
       North:* 203
Dishonesty
    Americanah: 23
Dissatisfaction
    *The Narrow Road to the Deep
       North:* 212
Domestic violence
    Libra: 157, 161
Domesticity
    The Buddha in the Attic: 34–35,
       39–40
Dreams
    The Buddha in the Attic: 34, 35,
       40, 45
    Indian Killer: 115–116
    Snow in August: 227
Duty
    *The Narrow Road to the Deep
       North:* 212
    The Tree Bride: 284, 292–293
Dysfunctional families
    Hope Was Here: 89, 91

E

Education
    The Tree Bride: 300
Emotions
    The Buddha in the Attic: 44–45
    A Garden of Earthly Delight: 47
    Jane Eyre: 139
    The Lovely Bones: 193, 197
Endurance
    *The Narrow Road to the Deep
       North:* 216, 222
Environmentalism
    Indian Killer: 123
Equality
    Jane Eyre: 150–151
Escape
    The Lovely Bones: 196
Ethnic identity
    Indian Killer: 126
    The Tree Bride: 303–305

Exile
    The Tree Bride: 29
Expectations
    The Buddha in the Attic: 34

F

Failure (Psychology)
    A Garden of Earthly Delight: 53
Faith
    Americanah: 22
    Hope Was Here: 93
    Snow in August: 244
Familial love
    The Lovely Bones: 194
Family
    A Garden of Earthly Delight: 61,
       70
    Hope Was Here: 82, 85, 91
    Indian Killer: 116
    The Lovely Bones: 177, 182, 185,
       186–187, 190–194, 196–198
    The Tree Bride: 284
Family relationships
    The Lovely Bones: 179, 187, 192,
       194, 195, 198
Fantasy fiction
    Snow in August: 244, 245
Fate
    The Buddha in the Attic: 43
    A Garden of Earthly Delight: 52,
       53, 55, 61, 68
    The Lovely Bones: 192
Father-child relationships
    A Garden of Earthly Delight: 54
    Hope Was Here: 79, 81, 82, 85
    Jane Eyre: 151
    The Lovely Bones: 184, 194
Fear
    The Buddha in the Attic: 40, 44
    A Garden of Earthly Delight: 58
Female identity
    A Garden of Earthly Delight: 68
    Their Eyes Were Watching God:
       266
    The Woman in White: 325–327
Female-male relations
    Americanah: 22
    Jane Eyre: 148–151
    The Temple of My Familiar:
       255–256
    The Woman in White: 315–317,
       321, 325–327
Femininity
    The Woman in White: 326–327
Feminism
    Americanah: 25
    A Garden of Earthly Delight: 66
    Jane Eyre: 134, 137, 147–151
    The Temple of My Familiar: 247,
       252, 253
    The Woman in White: 321

Flashbacks
    Americanah: 18
    Jane Eyre: 131, 140, 146
    Libra: 156
    Their Eyes Were Watching God:
       267, 276
Food
    Hope Was Here: 85
    The Temple of My Familiar: 262
Foreboding
    The Woman in White: 318
Foreshadowing
    A Garden of Earthly Delight: 53
    The Woman in White: 318
Forgiveness
    The Lovely Bones: 186, 192
Free will
    A Garden of Earthly Delight: 61
Freedom
    The Lovely Bones: 193
    *The Narrow Road to the Deep
       North:* 213
    The Temple of My Familiar: 250
    The Woman in White: 325
Friendship
    Hope Was Here: 91
    Jane Eyre: 130, 134, 144, 145
    The Lovely Bones: 182, 185, 196
    Snow in August: 223, 240, 243
    Their Eyes Were Watching God:
       273
Frustration
    A Garden of Earthly Delight: 68
    Indian Killer: 107
    Libra: 173, 174

G

Generosity
    The Lovely Bones: 198
Genocide
    Indian Killer: 99, 109
    The Temple of My Familiar:
       254–255
Good and evil
    Snow in August: 244
Goodness
    Snow in August: 240
Gossip
    Their Eyes Were Watching God:
       267
Gothicism
    Jane Eyre: 129, 146, 148, 150, 151
Great Depression
    A Garden of Earthly Delight: 47,
       49, 58–59, 62, 66, 69, 70
Greed
    A Garden of Earthly Delight: 67,
       70
Greek culture
    The Temple of My Familiar:
       261–263

Grief
  Hope Was Here: 79
  The Lovely Bones: 177, 180, 186, 196–198
Guilt (Psychology)
  A Garden of Earthly Delight: 55
  The Lovely Bones: 197
  Snow in August: 227
  The Tree Bride: 299

H

Happiness
  Jane Eyre: 142
  The Lovely Bones: 197
Hatred
  Indian Killer: 109
  Libra: 170
Healing
  Hope Was Here: 97
  Their Eyes Were Watching God: 278
Heaven
  Jane Eyre: 142, 144, 146
  The Lovely Bones: 179, 181, 183, 192, 196–197
Heritage
  The Buddha in the Attic: 38, 43
  Indian Killer: 108
Heroes
  The Narrow Road to the Deep North: 202, 217–218
Heroines
  The Lovely Bones: 194
Heroism
  The Lovely Bones: 193
  The Narrow Road to the Deep North: 211, 222
Hinduism
  The Tree Bride: 301
Historical fiction
  Libra: 162, 164, 167, 169–171, 173, 174
  The Tree Bride: 285
History
  A Garden of Earthly Delight: 62
  Libra: 173
  The Temple of My Familiar: 247, 249, 252–254, 257–259
Holocaust
  Snow in August: 233, 238, 240
Home
  The Tree Bride: 297–299
Homosexuality
  The Temple of My Familiar: 251, 252
Honesty
  Hope Was Here: 79, 93
Honor
  A Garden of Earthly Delight: 49
  The Narrow Road to the Deep North: 212

Hope
  The Buddha in the Attic: 45
  Hope Was Here: 72, 81, 82, 91, *93*
  The Lovely Bones: 189, 198
Horror
  The Lovely Bones: 189
Human rights
  Americanah: 24
  Jane Eyre: 137
Humanity
  Americanah: 25
Humor
  Hope Was Here: 84, 89, 91, *93–97*
  The Lovely Bones: 192, 198
Husband-wife relationships
  The Buddha in the Attic: 40
  The Lovely Bones: 185
  Their Eyes Were Watching God: 278–279
Hypocrisy
  Their Eyes Were Watching God: 281
  The Woman in White: 323

I

Identity
  Americanah: 19
  A Garden of Earthly Delight: 69
  Indian Killer: 107, 119
  The Narrow Road to the Deep North: 222
  Their Eyes Were Watching God: 274–275, 281
  The Tree Bride: 284, 292, 297, 299, 303–305
  The Woman in White: 315, 325, 328, 329
Illegitimacy
  The Woman in White: 314
Imagination
  Snow in August: 235–236, 242
Immigrant life
  The Buddha in the Attic: 30–31, 35–36, 38, 41
  Snow in August: 233–236
  The Tree Bride: 297–299, 301, 303–305
Imperialism
  A Garden of Earthly Delight: 70
Impotence
  Indian Killer: 109
  Libra: 162–164, 172–173
  The Lovely Bones: 177, 198
Imprisonment
  The Narrow Road to the Deep North: 200, 202, 203, 205, 206, 210, 212, 213, 215, 218, 219, 221, 222
  The Woman in White: 326
Independence
  Jane Eyre: 137
  Their Eyes Were Watching God: 281

Indian culture
  The Tree Bride: 284, 289, 291, 293, 299
Indian history
  The Tree Bride: 286, 294–296
Inequality
  The Woman in White: 327–328
Infidelity
  Americanah: 10, 12
  The Narrow Road to the Deep North: 205
Inheritance
  A Garden of Earthly Delight 51, 52, 58
  Jayne Eyre: 148
  The Temple of My Familiar 251
  Their Eyes Were Watching God: 268
  The Woman in White: 311, 313, 314, 317, 320, 327–328
Insecurity
  Americanah: 11
  Indian Killer: 116
Interior monologue
  Libra: 161, 165
Intimidation
  Americanah: 25
Irony
  Americanah: 16
  A Garden of Earthly Delight: 70
  Indian Killer: 107
  Libra: 163
  The Woman in White: 315, 321, 322–325
Isolation
  The Buddha in the Attic: 40, 41
  A Garden of Earthly Delight: 70
  Jane Eyre: 140
  The Tree Bride: 299
Italian history
  The Woman in White: 318–319

J

Japanese-American internment
  The Buddha in the Attic: 32–38, 40–43
Japanese culture
  The Buddha in the Attic: 32, 36, 43, 44
  The Narrow Road to the Deep North: 214
Japanese history
  The Buddha in the Attic: 36–37
  The Narrow Road to the Deep North: 210
Jealousy
  Their Eyes Were Watching God: 270, 272
Jewish culture
  Snow in August: 223, 226
Judaism
  Snow in August: 223, 233, 238

Justice
   *The Narrow Road to the Deep
      North:* 214
   Snow in August: 235
   The Woman in White: 327–328

K

Kabbalah
   Snow in August: 228
Kindness
   Americanah: 13, 25
   A Garden of Earthly Delight: 54
   Jane Eyre: 134, 147
   The Lovely Bones: 198

L

Language and languages
   The Buddha in the Attic: 45
   Libra: 165
   *The Narrow Road to the Deep
      North:* 211
   Their Eyes Were Watching God:
      276
Legacy
   Hope Was Here: 81
Legal system
   The Woman in White: 317–318,
      320, 326, 327–328
Light and darkness
   Jane Eyre: 140
Loneliness
   Americanah: 19
   Jane Eyre: 151
   Libra: 153
Loss
   The Buddha in the Attic: 29,
      32–33, 43
   The Lovely Bones: 197
   *The Narrow Road to the Deep
      North:* 221
Love
   Americanah: 1, 3, 7, 10, 11, 19
   A Garden of Earthly Delight: 53
   Hope Was Here: 83
   Jane Eyre: 139, 147, 149
   Libra: 163
   The Lovely Bones: 177, 184, 185,
      193, 194, 198
   *The Narrow Road to the Deep
      North:* 200, 208–209, 217–220
   The Temple of My Familiar: 251
   Their Eyes Were Watching God:
      266, 269–271, 273–274, 281
   The Woman in White: 309

M

Madness
   Jane Eyre: 135, 148–149
Magic
   Snow in August: 228, *230–321,*
      233, 240, 242
   The Temple of My Familiar: 262

Magical realism
   Snow in August: 233
   The Temple of My Familiar: 259
   The Tree Bride: 294
Male identity
   The Woman in White: 325–327
Marriage
   Americanah: 11, 12–13
   The Buddha in the Attic: 31, 36–37,
      39, 40
   Jane Eyre: 147–148, 150
   Libra: 161
   *The Narrow Road to the Deep
      North:* 203–206, 217
   Their Eyes Were Watching God:
      268, 271, 272, 275
   The Woman in White: 311, 317,
      320, 325–329
Martyrdom
   Jane Eyre: 144–146
Masculinity
   A Garden of Earthly Delight: 52,
      68
   *The Narrow Road to the Deep
      North:* 222
   The Tree Bride: 297
   The Woman in White: 326–327
Matriarchy
   The Temple of My Familiar: 249,
      251, 253
Meaning of life
   *The Narrow Road to the Deep
      North:* 205, 208
Meaninglessness
   A Garden of Earthly Delight: 55
Melodrama
   The Woman in White: 307
Memorialization
   The Lovely Bones: 181
Memory
   A Garden of Earthly Delight: 62,
      63–66
   Libra: 159
   *The Narrow Road to the Deep
      North:* 204, 205, 212, 215, 216,
      220
   The Temple of My Familiar: 252
Mental disorders
   A Garden of Earthly Delight: 68
   Indian Killer: 105, 107, 108, 126
   Jane Eyre: 140–141
   The Lovely Bones: 196
Metaphors
   A Garden of Earthly Delight: 53,
      69
   Hope Was Here: 85, *94*
   Their Eyes Were Watching God:
      280, 281
   The Tree Bride: 301
Metaphysics
   The Temple of My Familiar:
      262–264

Midwestern United States
   Hope Was Here: 85–87
Military life
   *The Narrow Road to the Deep
      North:* 212–214
Minimalism
   The Buddha in the Attic: 36, 38
Misery
   A Garden of Earthly Delight: 69
Misunderstanding
   The Woman in White: 325
Modern life
   The Temple of My Familiar: 255
   The Tree Bride: 292
Mood
   Jane Eyre: 140
Morality
   Jane Eyre: 145
Mother-child relationships
   The Buddha in the Attic: 31–32, 45
   Libra: 154, 161, 163
   The Lovely Bones: 194
Murder
   Indian Killer: 99, 100, 102, 104
   Libra: 155–156, 170–172, 174
   The Lovely Bones: 177, 179, 183,
      185, 189, 196, 198
   *The Narrow Road to the Deep
      North:* 204
Mystery
   Indian Killer: 110–111, 115, 119
   Jane Eyre: 140
   The Woman in White: 313
Mysticism
   Indian Killer: 111
   Snow in August: 230–321
Mythology
   The Temple of My Familiar: 247

N

Naiveté
   Snow in August: 245
Naming
   A Garden of Earthly Delight: 69
Narrators
   The Buddha in the Attic: 36, 38–41,
      44–45
   A Garden of Earthly Delight: 49
   Indian Killer: 111
   The Lovely Bones: 187–188, 196
   The Woman in White: 318,
      323–325
Native American culture
   Indian Killer: 106, 109, 116–119,
      121–124, 126
Native American history
   Indian Killer: 111–114, 119–120
Native American mythology
   Indian Killer: 126
Naturalism (Literature)
   A Garden of Earthly Delight: 61

Nature
  Jane Eyre: 137–138, 144
  Their Eyes Were Watching God:
    277–279, 281
Nigerian culture
  Americanah: 18–19
Nihilism
  A Garden of Earthly Delight: 69, 70
Nobility
  The Woman in White: 323
Nonconformity
  Their Eyes Were Watching God:
    278
Nostalgia
  A Garden of Earthly Delight: 53, 55

O

Objectivity
  Libra: 175
Observation
  Libra: 175
  The Lovely Bones: 192
Obsession
  The Lovely Bones: 179, 180, 193
Omniscience
  The Lovely Bones: 185, 192, 196,
    198
Oppression
  A Garden of Earthly Delight: 58
  The Temple of My Familiar: 247,
    253
Optimism
  Americanah: 17
Order
  Libra: 168
  The Tree Bride: 301
Orientalism
  The Temple of My Familiar: 260
Ostracism
  Indian Killer: 125
Outsiders
  Indian Killer: 107

P

Pain
  The Buddha in the Attic: 29
  Libra: 159, 163
  The Lovely Bones: 198
Paranoia
  Indian Killer: 126
Parent-child relationships
  Indian Killer: 125
Passion
  Jane Eyre: 144, 150
Passivity
  Jane Eyre: 149
Pathos
  Hope Was Here: 89
  Libra: 162
Patriarchy
  Americanah: 27

Jane Eyre: 147, 149, 151
The Temple of My Familiar:
  250–252, 255
Patronage
  Americanah: 15, 20, 22
Peace
  The Lovely Bones: 186
Persecution
  Jane Eyre: 139
Philosophy
  Hope Was Here: 93
Plots
  The Woman in White: 320–321
Poetry
  *The Narrow Road to the Deep
    North:* 209, 211, 221
Point of view (Literature)
  The Buddha in the Attic: 38–41,
    44–45
  A Garden of Earthly Delight: 49, 50
  Jane Eyre: 147, 149
  Libra: 164–165
  The Lovely Bones: 187–188, 196
  The Woman in White: 318
Politics
  Americanah: 20–24, 26, 27
  Hope Was Here: 93
  Libra: 155, 157–159
Popular culture
  Snow in August: 223, 228
Postmodernism
  Libra: 172
Poverty
  A Garden of Earthly Delight:
    53–58, 66–68
  Indian Killer: 123
Power (Philosophy)
  Americanah: 22
  A Garden of Earthly Delight: 67, 68
  Jane Eyre: 149, 151
  Libra: 162–163, 172–173
  Their Eyes Were Watching God: 273
Powerlessness. *See* Impotence
Prejudice
  Americanah: 17
  The Buddha in the Attic: 36, 44
  Indian Killer: 107, 108–110
Pride
  The Buddha in the Attic: 36
  Libra: 160
Privilege
  Americanah: 5, 23
  A Garden of Earthly Delight: 53
Prophecy
  A Garden of Earthly Delight: 52
Protest
  Indian Killer: 113–114
Psychoanalysis
  The Temple of My Familiar: 256
Public *vs.* private spheres
  Americanah: 25, 27
Punishment
  A Garden of Earthly Delight: 52

Q

Quakerism
  Hope Was Here: 87, *93*
Questing
  Hope Was Here: 73, 85
  Indian Killer: 119

R

Race relations
  Americanah: 4, 16–17, 19
  The Buddha in the Attic: 31, 32, 34,
    41
  Indian Killer: 125, 126
  The Temple of My Familiar: 250
Racial identity
  Indian Killer: 115, 117, 118
  Their Eyes Were Watching God:
    275, 280, 281
Racism
  Americanah: 1, 4, 5, 7, 11
  The Buddha in the Attic: 41, 43
  Indian Killer: 99, 106, 107, 126
  The Temple of My Familiar: 250,
    253–255, 258
Randomness
  Libra: 153, 167
Reality
  The Lovely Bones: 189
  *The Narrow Road to the Deep
    North:* 221
Rebellion
  Americanah: 3
  Hope Was Here: 88
  Their Eyes Were Watching God:
    266
Reconciliation
  The Lovely Bones: 181
Redemption
  The Temple of My Familiar: 247
Reincarnation
  The Temple of My Familiar: 252,
    258–259
Rejection
  A Garden of Earthly Delight: 53
Religion
  Americanah: 21–22
  A Garden of Earthly Delight: 53
  Jane Eyre: 139, 141–142, 144–146
  The Lovely Bones: 197
  Snow in August: 244–245
Repetition
  The Buddha in the Attic: 45
Resentment
  Their Eyes Were Watching God:
    272, 278
Resilience
  A Garden of Earthly Delight: 68
Resistance
  Americanah: 26
Respect
  A Garden of Earthly Delight: 54

Restlessness
 Jane Eyre: 148
 The Lovely Bones: 184
 *The Narrow Road to the Deep
  North:* 212
Revenge
 Indian Killer: 99, 127
Rhythm
 The Buddha in the Attic: 45
Rites of passage
 Hope Was Here: 72
 The Lovely Bones: 197
Roman Catholicism
 Snow in August: 233, 236
Romantic love
 Americanah: 1, 17
 A Garden of Earthly Delight: 50,
  51–52, 54
 Jane Eyre: 129, 132–133, 150
 *The Narrow Road to the Deep
  North:* 203, 219
 Their Eyes Were Watching God:
  274
Romanticism
 Snow in August: 243
Rural life
 Their Eyes Were Watching God:
  277

S

Sacrifice
 Americanah: 17
 Jane Eyre: 139
 *The Narrow Road to the Deep
  North:* 220
Sadism
 Jane Eyre: 149
 *The Narrow Road to the Deep
  North:* 213
Sadness
 The Lovely Bones: 196
Satire
 The Woman in White: 325
Science
 A Garden of Earthly Delight: 53
 Libra: 173–175
Secrecy
 Jane Eyre: 140, 148
 The Woman in White: 307,
  313–315
Seduction
 A Garden of Earthly Delight: 50, 52
Self awareness. *See* Self knowledge
Self deception
 A Garden of Earthly Delight: 67
Self hatred
 *The Narrow Road to the Deep
  North:* 221
 The Tree Bride: 298
Self identity
 Indian Killer: 116, 125

Self image
 *The Narrow Road to the Deep
  North:* 212
Self knowledge
 Americanah: 12
 Hope Was Here: 94
 Their Eyes Were Watching God:
  275
 The Tree Bride: 302
Self love
 Their Eyes Were Watching God:
  274, 277
Self-pity
 Libra: 159, 161
Self preservation
 Indian Killer: 125
Self realization
 Their Eyes Were Watching God:
  275
Self-sufficiency
 A Garden of Earthly Delight: 69
 Jane Eyre: 137
Self worth
 Americanah: 5
 Jane Eyre: 134, 137
Sentimentality
 *The Narrow Road to the Deep
  North:* 220
Setting (Literature)
 *The Narrow Road to the Deep
  North:* 218–220
Sexuality
 Their Eyes Were Watching God:
  280, 281
Shame
 The Tree Bride: 297, 298
Sin
 A Garden of Earthly Delight: 52
Slavery
 The Temple of My Familiar: 249,
  254, 255
Social class
 Americanah: 1, 4, 5
 A Garden of Earthly Delight: 54,
  57–58
 The Temple of My Familiar: 253
Social commentary
 The Temple of My Familiar: 255
Social conventions
 Their Eyes Were Watching God:
  273, 275
Social realism
 Hope Was Here: 89
Southern United States
 Their Eyes Were Watching God:
  266, 276–277
Spirituality
 The Lovely Bones: 196–198
 The Temple of My Familiar: 264
Spontaneity
 Their Eyes Were Watching God:
  273, 280

Sports
 Snow in August: 223, 227, 228,
  231, 233, 235–238, 240
Stereotypes
 Hope Was Here: 89, 94
 Jane Eyre: 135
Stoicism
 Snow in August: 240
Strangeness
 *The Narrow Road to the Deep
  North:* 218
Stream of consciousness
 Libra: 163
 The Temple of My Familiar: 256–257
Strength
 A Garden of Earthly Delight: 68
 Hope Was Here: 77, 93, 94
 Jane Eyre: 147, 148
 *The Narrow Road to the Deep
  North:* 212
 Their Eyes Were Watching God:
  280
Structure (Literature)
 Libra: 164, 167
 *The Narrow Road to the Deep
  North:* 209
Struggle
 The Buddha in the Attic: 29
 A Garden of Earthly Delight: 68
 Jane Eyre: 139
 Libra: 161
Submission
 The Buddha in the Attic: 40
 Jane Eyre: 147
Subservience
 Jane Eyre: 149
 The Woman in White: 315–316,
  321, 325–326
Suburban life
 The Lovely Bones: 189
Suffering
 Americanah: 18, 24
 The Buddha in the Attic: 33, 36
 Jane Eyre: 149
 *The Narrow Road to the Deep
  North:* 205, 212, 220, 222
 The Temple of My Familiar: 247
Suicide
 A Garden of Earthly Delight: 68, 69
Supernatural
 A Garden of Earthly Delight: 53
 The Temple of My Familiar: 259
Survival
 A Garden of Earthly Delight: 66, 68
 Indian Killer: 118
 Jane Eyre: 139
 *The Narrow Road to the Deep
  North:* 221
Suspense
 Jane Eyre: 140
 The Lovely Bones: 196
 The Woman in White: 307, 318, 322

Suspicion
    The Buddha in the Attic: 41
    The Lovely Bones: 184
Symbolism
    A Garden of Earthly Delight: 55
    Hope Was Here: 81, 85, *93*
    Indian Killer: 99
    Jane Eyre: 140, 148, 150
    Snow in August: 236
    The Temple of My Familiar: 259,
       260
    Their Eyes Were Watching God:
       269, 276
    The Tree Bride: 294
    The Woman in White: 315
Sympathy
    The Lovely Bones: 192

T

Tension
    Libra: 164–165
    Snow in August: 240
    The Woman in White: 322
Terror
    Jane Eyre: 148
Tone (Literature)
    A Garden of Earthly Delight: 67
Tradition
    A Garden of Earthly Delight: 53
    The Tree Bride: 292
Tragedy (Calamities)
    A Garden of Earthly Delight: 67
    Indian Killer: 124
Tranquility
    Their Eyes Were Watching God: 278
Trauma
    Americanah: 26
    *The Narrow Road to the Deep
       North:* 220–222
Tribalism
    Indian Killer: 99, 115
Triumph
    Hope Was Here: 85
Truth
    Hope Was Here: 81
    The Woman in White: 322–323

U

Uncertainty
    Libra: 172
Unconscious
    The Temple of My Familiar:
       256–257

Unhappiness
    Libra: 161
    The Tree Bride: 298
    The Woman in White: 311
Urban life
    Indian Killer: 119–121
    Snow in August: 236
Utopia
    The Tree Bride: 299

V

Values (Philosophy)
    The Woman in White: 322–323
Vengeance. *See* Revenge
Victimization
    Americanah: 26–27
    A Garden of Earthly Delight: 55
    Indian Killer: 108
    Libra: 163
    *The Narrow Road to the Deep
       North:* 214
Victorian period literature, 1832-
    1901
    The Woman in White: 307,
       315–317, 319–321
Victorian values
    Jane Eyre: 147
Violence
    Americanah: 25, 26
    A Garden of Earthly Delight: 52,
       66, 68
    Hope Was Here: 77–78
    Indian Killer: 99, 100, 104, 107,
       115, 124, 126
    The Lovely Bones: 191
    *The Narrow Road to the Deep
       North:* 200, 204, 219
    Snow in August: 224, 228, 229,
       232, 242–245
    The Woman in White: 326
Voice (Literature)
    The Buddha in the Attic: 44–45
    The Lovely Bones: 197, 198
Vulnerability
    *The Narrow Road to the Deep
       North:* 220

W

Wars
    *The Narrow Road to the Deep
       North:* 200, 202, 215–217, 222

Weakness
    Jane Eyre: 151
    The Tree Bride: 298
Wealth
    Americanah: 16
    A Garden of Earthly Delight: 51,
       53, 70
    Jane Eyre: 133
Western culture
    The Temple of My Familiar: 260,
       262
    The Tree Bride: 284
Western United States
    Indian Killer: 111–113
Wisdom
    Hope Was Here: 79, 91, 94
    The Lovely Bones: 185
    The Temple of My Familiar:
       262
Wit
    Indian Killer: 99
    The Lovely Bones: 197
Womanism
    The Temple of My Familiar:
       259–260
Women in literature
    The Woman in White: 315–317
Women's rights
    Americanah: 25
    Jane Eyre: 137
    The Woman in White: 317–318,
       327–328
Work
    Americanah: 17
    Hope Was Here: 87–88, 94
Workers
    The Buddha in the Attic: 31, 35,
       41
    A Garden of Earthly Delight: 66,
       67
World War II, 1939-1945
    A Garden of Earthly Delight: 47,
       58–60, 62, 66, 69, 70
    *The Narrow Road to the Deep
       North:* 202, 210, 212–214
    Snow in August: 238

X

Xenophobia
    The Buddha in the Attic: 41, 43